Other Books in the Jossey-Bass Nonprofit & Public Management Series:

Handbook of
Government Budgeting

Roy T. Meyers
Editor

Jossey-Bass Publishers
San Francisco

Jossey-Bass books and products are available through most bookstores. To contact Jossey-Bass directly, call (888) 378-2537, fax to (800) 605-2665, or visit our website at www.josseybass.com.

Substantial discounts on bulk quantities of Jossey-Bass books are available to corporations, professional associations, and other organizations. For details and discount information, contact the special sales department at Jossey-Bass.

Manufactured in the United States of America.

Library of Congress Cataloging-in-Publication Data

Handbook of government budgeting / Roy T. Meyers, editor.—1st ed.
     p.   cm.—(The Jossey-Bass nonprofit & public management series)
    Includes bibliographical references and indexes.
    ISBN 0-7879-4292-8
    1. Budget—United States—Handbooks, manuals, etc. 2. Fiscal policy—United States—Handbooks, manuals, etc. I. Meyers, Roy T. II. Series: Jossey-Bass nonprofit and public management series.
    HJ2051.H338   1999
    352.4'8'0973—dc21   98-40393
FIRST EDITION
HB printing 10 9 8 6 7 8 5 4 3 2 1

The Jossey-Bass
Nonprofit & Public Management Series

CONTENTS

LIST OF FIGURES, TABLES & EXHIBITS

FIGURES

TABLES

EXHIBITS

PREFACE

The *Handbook of Government Budgeting* addresses two broad and interrelated questions. The first is descriptive: How do governments acquire and spend money? The second is normative: How should governments acquire and spend money?

These are not simple questions, and readers will find no simplistic answers here. Instead, this handbook contains much sophisticated guidance from thirty-six expert contributors. Their impressive backgrounds illustrate the broad range of the budgeting field. They are trained in political science, economics, accounting, and management. They have extensive experience in working in governments as executives, managers, and analysts; in serving governments as consultants; and in studying governments as academics. Many have played all three roles and have done so for both small cities and large federal departments.

Each chapter was written especially for this book. The contributors summarize the state of existing knowledge; with the balance depending on the topic and the contributor's background, they outline important theories, report on research findings, and convey expert knowledge. Many of them make good practice recommendations, supporting these with examples of successful innovations by governments. Some offer opinions, not all of which are conventional wisdom, but they are well argued and likely to stimulate thought.

Readers who know little about budgeting except its importance—such as students, novice managers, and budding policy analysts—will find that this handbook provides a comprehensive introduction to the state of the art. But those who have already prepared or reviewed budgets, and have inevitably learned a lot on the job, should find the book valuable as well, because the unavoidable fact is that nobody knows everything about budgeting. (As I tell my students, budgeting is so complicated that asking questions is usually a sign of intelligence rather than inexcusable ignorance.) A handbook written by a wide variety of experts offers more knowledge than any single textbook author can provide.

Budgeting is complicated enough—loaded with jargon, accounting arcana, and convoluted procedures—for bad writing to get in the way. The material we cover is relatively complex, but we hope that because of the ways we present it, reading this book will not be unnecessarily laborious. Yet unlike many textbooks in other fields, this handbook lacks full-color pictures, and there are very few jokes. Perhaps "budget humor" is an oxymoron, but if readers can suggest some thigh-slappers for a second edition, credit is guaranteed!

There are some other (and, I believe, similarly minor) limitations to the book. The constraints of timing and book length prevented my including chapters on all of the topics I wanted to cover. Editing is not unlike budgeting in its tendency to confront a decision maker with unpleasant trade-offs (consumer reluctance to purchase a thousand-page, $100 book is just as worrisome as the potential voter reaction to a large tax increase). Another editorial choice was the decision to emphasize government budgeting in the United States rather than in all developed countries or in the whole world. There were strong reasons for doing so—the difficulty of making comparisons to the American style of government, a paucity of accessible research on selected topics, and my fears about reader disinterest. I am hopeful that budgetary research and knowledge will become more comparative in the coming years.

Readers will also find that this handbook is not a cookbook. It is not a step-by-step, how-to guide for the routine tasks of budgeting (for example, breaking spending plans into objects-of-expense). Chapter references do point, however, to sources on such skills, which are best learned by practicing, whether on the job or in the classroom.

I encourage those who teach budgeting to access my *Handbook* Web page (http://research.umbc.edu/ ~ meyers/handbook.html) or the Jossey-Bass Web page (http://www.josseybass.com) for a supplement that suggests how the handbook can be used in the classroom. This supplement suggests cases and exercises that fit well with each chapter.

OVERVIEW OF THE CONTENTS

The book is organized into eight sections. With the exception of the concluding section, which includes only one chapter, each section presents multiple chapters offering different perspectives on related budgetary topics. Readers may follow my logic of organization by starting at Chapter One and proceeding straight through to Chapter Twenty-Nine, or they may jump around. Using either method, readers may wish to return to chapters they have already covered, for there are numerous linkages between chapters in different sections.

Part One of the book provides an overview of government budgeting. Jerry McCaffery begins by describing, in Chapter One, the essentials of the budgetary process, with emphasis on the stages of budget preparation and enactment. Irene S. Rubin follows with Chapter Two, on how budgetary conflict is inevitable and desirable, but only in moderation. Then, in Chapter Three, L. R. Jones and Jerry McCaffery review financial management reforms in the federal government. Although this book emphasizes how spending plans are prepared and enacted in the context of resource limits, an understanding of the breadth of the financial management perspective is essential for understanding the context of budgeting. The first section concludes with Chapter Four, by A. Premchand, which compares budgeting in the United States to that in New Zealand, Australia, and the United Kingdom. These countries have attempted such ambitious reforms that even though the reforms might not fully transfer to the United States, readers can learn much from the comparisons.

Part Two covers macrobudgetary constraints and goals: credit markets, the economy, and budget balancing. It begins with a state and local perspective. John H. Engstrom explains in Chapter Five how to understand and use government financial reports, which play especially important roles in the credit markets. In Chapter Six, Merl Hackbart and James R. Ramsey cover the changing intricacies of state and local debt finance. The section then turns to the interaction of economic conditions with budgetary policy. In Chapter Seven, Michael Wolkoff covers how state and local governments can cope with their great sensitivity to the ups and downs of the business cycle. In Chapter Eight, Van Doorn Ooms, Ronald S. Boster, and Robert L. Fleegler discuss how federal budgetary policies can affect the economy. Whether governments should balance their budgets, and what that means in practice, is the topic of Chapter Nine by Naomi Caiden, the concluding chapter of this section.

Part Three covers taxation in budgeting. Chapter Ten, by Jane G. Gravelle, describes the complexities of the major tax bases. Bruce F. Davie, in Chapter Eleven, does the same for exceptions to these bases, or so-called tax expenditures. Stuart Bretschneider and Wilpen L. Gorr suggest in Chapter Twelve how governments can best project revenues. Finally, in Chapter Thirteen, Sheldon Pollack explains major theories of tax politics and applies them to federal income tax policies.

Part Four covers three challenges associated with government accounting, which is the informational foundation of budgeting. In Chapter Fourteen, James L. Chan describes the various meanings of accrual accounting and explains how accruals can be used for budgeting and reporting at the different levels of government. In Chapter Fifteen, Fred Thompson covers the complicated field of managerial accounting, which is finally being recognized as an essential tool for budget preparation and management. In Chapter Sixteen, Rowan Miranda addresses another important topic that can no longer be neglected in government—how to design modern information systems to support budgeting and other financial management tasks.

Part Five is on how institutions budget. The first two chapters are by highly respected practitioners. Jacqueline H. Rogers and Marita B. Brown describe in Chapter Seventeen how agency directors should prepare budgets, and they explain why interpersonal dynamics play such an important role in the process. Chapter Eighteen, by Barry White, illustrates how budget examiners can best perform the most challenging role in the budgetary process. In Chapter Nineteen, I describe why it is difficult for legislatures to budget, and why they attempt to do so anyway, with particular emphasis on the U.S. Congress. Phillip J. Cooper then makes a strong argument, in Chapter Twenty, about how the budgetary world should and can pay more attention to the often-neglected but important role of the courts in budgeting.

Part Six is on politics, management, and analysis in budgeting. In Chapter Twenty-One, James D. Savage and Herman M. Schwartz cover cutback budgeting, a topic of great importance in this era of government downsizing. In Chapter Twenty-Two, I give political advice to spending advocates who wish to compete for scarce budgetary resources. Chapter Twenty-Three, by Rebecca Hendrick and John P. Forrester, describes how budget implementation is changing with the conversion of management control from input-based to outcome-based systems. Philip G. Joyce then analyzes, in Chapter Twenty-Four, how performance information can be collected and used in budgeting and, just as important, how budgeting might be designed to improve performance. Finally, in Chapter Twenty-Five, Marvin B. Mandell describes a variety of analytical and evaluation techniques that are potentially useful for different budgetary tasks.

Part Seven contains three chapters that deal with the problem of how to budget when time is a significant variable. The convention in state and local budgeting is to worry most about how to budget for capital assets, which is the topic of the Chapter Twenty-Six by Robert L. Bland and Wes Clarke. Chapter Twenty-Seven, by Joseph White, discusses a problem that currently confounds the political system—how to budget for entitlements. Chapter Twenty-Eight, by Marvin Phaup and David F. Torregrosa, explores budgeting for contingent liabilities.

Finally, in Chapter Twenty-Nine, in the Conclusion, I discuss the future of government budgeting: whether it will retain its current importance, how practitioners and academics can create and acquire budgetary knowledge, and how government budgeting might best be reformed.

ACKNOWLEDGMENTS

I thank the following people for their assistance in preparing this book:

- The contributors, for their willingness to write relatively short chapters on big topics and for their cooperation in putting together the book
- Allen Schick, who as the coeditor in its early stages helped design the book and recruit chapter authors and who has informed many of the chapters with his decades of research
- Irene Rubin and Philip Joyce, for useful advice on this project and for helpful comments on several chapters
- Two anonymous reviewers for Jossey-Bass, who improved many chapters with their suggestions
- Art Johnson and Emma Sellers of the University of Maryland, Baltimore County's Political Science Department, for, respectively, supporting my efforts and providing secretarial assistance
- Alan Shrader, Jennifer Morley, Mary Garrett, and Alice Rowan at Jossey-Bass, for their trust in me as the editor and for their professionalism in producing the book
- My wife, Harriet, for her love, companionship, and humor
- My kids, Perry, Keith, and Jonah, for properly distracting me from my work, and for not asking if I'm going to work on a "footbook" next

Columbia, Maryland   Roy T. Meyers
August 1998

THE EDITOR

ROY T. MEYERS is associate professor of political science at the University of Maryland, Baltimore County. He received his B.A. degree from Colby College and his M.A. and Ph.D. degrees from the University of Michigan. His dissertation won the L. D. White Award from the American Political Science Association.

Meyers was an analyst at the Congressional Budget Office from 1981 to 1990. He has written numerous reports and articles on budgetary topics, and his book *Strategic Budgeting* received the Louis Brownlow Award from the National Academy of Public Administration. He is presently working on a book about the interactions between policy design, administrative capacity, and politics, with a concentration in environmental and public health policies.

Meyers is on the editorial board of *Public Administration Review*, and he lectures and consults on budgeting.

THE CONTRIBUTORS

ROBERT L. (BOB) BLAND is professor and chair of the Department of Public Administration at the University of North Texas (UNT), where he teaches graduate courses in public finance, governmental accounting, and budgeting. He has been on the faculty at UNT since 1982. He is the author of *A Revenue Guide for Local Government* (1989) and coauthor with Irene Rubin of *Budgeting: A Guide for Local Governments* (1997), both published by the International City/County Management Association. He has also written articles on the municipal bond market, property taxation, and municipal budgeting. On two occasions he conducted workshops in Poland on revenue sources for local governments. Bland received his B.S. degree from Seaver College at Pepperdine University, his M.P.A. and M.B.A. degrees from the University of Tennessee, and his Ph.D. degree from the Graduate School of Public and International Affairs at the University of Pittsburgh.

RONALD S. BOSTER was vice president and director of business and government policy at the Committee for Economic Development (CED) at the time he wrote his chapter. His is now a consultant and adjunct professor at Virginia Tech's Center for Public Administration and Policy. He has been senior staff economist, deputy staff economist, and executive staff director of the Committee on the Budget, U.S. House of Representatives. He received his B.A. and M.S. degrees from Ohio State University and his Ph.D. degree from the University of Arizona, where he also taught. Boster is the author of numerous academic articles and chapters, the editor of several volumes and books, and an internationally known lecturer on U.S. fiscal policy and the federal budgetary process. At CED his work has included research and writing on economic growth and opportunity and on tax policy.

STUART BRETSCHNEIDER is professor of public administration at the Maxwell School of Citizenship and Public Affairs at Syracuse University. He received his Ph.D. degree from Ohio State University. He is director of Syracuse University's Center for Technology and Information Policy. His current research interests include public management information systems, decision making in public organizations, and applied statistics. He has published more than twenty-five articles in journals such as *Management Science, Information Systems Review, Public Administration Review, International Journal of Forecasting,* and *Evaluation Review.* He is managing editor of the *Journal of Public Administration, Research, and Theory* and has been a consultant for the U.S. General Accounting Office and for the states of New York, Ohio, and Kentucky.

MARITA B. BROWN has more than twenty years of public sector budget and management experience at all levels of government. She was budget director for Anne Arundel County, Maryland; the director of the Office of Management and Budget for Prince George's County, Maryland; and the secretary of budget and fiscal planning for the state of Maryland. She has also served as a visiting scholar at the U.S. Congressional Budget Office and is on the adjunct faculty of the University of Maryland School of Public Affairs, where she teaches state and local government budgeting. Brown has been a member of numerous county and statewide committees and task forces focusing on spending affordability, debt management, pension management, procurement, information technology, and personnel reform. She also serves as a commissioner of the Washington Suburban Sanitary Commission. She holds a B.A. degree from Marymount Manhattan College and an M.A. degree from the University of Maryland, College Park, and she completed Harvard University's John F. Kennedy School of Government's Program for Senior Executives in State and Local Government.

NAOMI CAIDEN is professor of public administration in the Department of Political Science at California State University, Los Angeles. She has written extensively on comparative and historical aspects of public budgeting. Between 1988 and 1994 she was editor of *Public Budgeting and Finance.* Her publications include *Planning and Budgeting in Poor Countries* with Aaron Wildavsky, *Public Budgeting and Financial Administration in Developing Countries* (editor), *Budgeting, Policy, Politics: An Appreciation of Aaron Wildavsky* (editor with Joseph White), and the revised third edition of Wildavsky's *New Politics of the Bud-*

getary Process. Caiden has also consulted with such organizations as the World Bank, the United Nations, the United States Agency for International development, and the U.S. General Accounting Office. In 1993 she was the first recipient of the Aaron Wildavsky Award for Lifetime Scholarly Achievement in Public Budgeting.

JAMES L. CHAN is professor of accounting at the University of Illinois at Chicago and Emmett Dedmon Visiting Professor in Public Policy at the University of Chicago. His research focuses on the interactions between accounting and budgeting policies and processes and their social and institutional contexts. He has published extensively on these issues and, as the founding editor of *Research in Governmental and Nonprofit Accounting* from 1983 to 1996, edited nine volumes of papers. He has advised numerous governmental and nonprofit organizations on financial management and governance issues. Chan is a member of the Research and Educational Advisory Panel of the U.S. Comptroller General and has chaired the American Accounting Association's Government and Nonprofit Section. He received his B.S. degree (1971), Master of Accounting Science degree (1973), and Ph.D. (1976) degree in accountancy with minors in economic theory and public administration from the University of Illinois at Urbana-Champaign.

WES CLARKE is assistant professor in the Department of Public Administration at the University of North Texas, where he teaches graduate courses in government budgeting, statistics, and administrative law, and a number of undergraduate courses. Clarke's research on state budgeting and municipal debt has appeared in *Political Research Quarterly, Legislative Studies Quarterly,* and *Public Budgeting and Finance.* Recently he completed a revision of the study materials and examinations for the Certified Government Finance Officer program of the Government Finance Officers Association of Texas. Clarke received his B.S. degree in political science from West Georgia College, his M.P.A. degree from the University of Georgia, and his Ph.D. degree from the Martin School of Pubic Policy and Administration at the University of Kentucky.

PHILLIP J. COOPER is Gund Professor of Liberal Arts at the University of Vermont. He received his B.A. degree (1975) in government from California State University, Sacramento, and his M.A. (1977) and Ph.D. (1978) degrees in political science form the Maxwell School of Citizenship and Public Affairs at Syracuse University. Until 1995, Cooper was chair of the Department of Public Administration at the University of Kansas. He has been a consultant to state and federal agencies, the U.S. Congress, the White House, and the United Nations. He is the author of numerous books and articles on public administration, administrative law, constitutional law, law and public policy, and sustainable development.

BRUCE F. DAVIE is currently a financial economist in the Treasury Department's Office of Tax Analysis. His special areas of responsibility include excise taxes, tax-exempt bonds, and housing. He is also a professorial lecturer in the economics department at Georgetown University, where he teaches undergraduate and graduate courses in economic history. His prior government service includes senior economist with responsibility for tax policy at the Office of Management and Budget (1973 to 1978) and chief tax economist, Committee on Ways and Means (1978 to 1989). Before returning to government service in 1992 he was a principal in Arthur Andersen's Office of Federal Tax Services. From 1963 to 1973 Davie was a full-time member of Georgetown University's economics department. He holds a B.A. degree from Pomona College and a Ph.D. degree from Harvard University.

JOHN H. ENGSTROM is KMPG Peat Marwick Professor of Accountancy at Northern Illinois University. He is a member of the Governmental Accounting Standards Board Advisory Council, the American Institute of Certified Public Accountants, and the Government Finance Officers Association's Certification of Excellence in Financial Reporting Review Committee. He has written numerous articles on government accounting and recently coauthored *Essentials of Accounting for Governmental and Not-for-Profit Organizations* and *Essentials of Government Accounting for Public Administrators,* both with Leon Hay.

ROBERT L. FLEEGLER is research associate at the Committee for Economic Development, where he has worked on labor market, workforce development, and education reform issues. He received his B.A. degree with distinction from Swarthmore College in 1995.

JOHN P. FORRESTER is an associate professor in the Department of Public Administration at the University of Missouri-Columbia, where he has worked since 1987. He received his D.P.A. degree in 1988 from the University of Georgia, with emphasis in budgeting, finance, and policy analysis. His current research interests are budgeting theory, financial management, and the state of the public administration profession. Forrester is the author of *Research in Public Administration: Issues on Public Budgeting Theory,* has contributed to *The International Encyclopedia of Public Policy and Administration* and *Budgeting: Formulation and Execution,* and has published in such journals as *Administration and Society, Public Administration Quarterly,* and *Public Administration Review.* He also serves on the editorial board of the *American Review of Public Administration.*

WILPEN L. GORR is professor of public policy and management information systems at the H. John Heinz School of Public Policy and Management, Carnegie-Mellon University. He is also editor of the *International Journal of Forecasting* and director of the Heinz School Geographic Information Systems Laboratory. Gorr's research is in the areas of forecasting, geographic information systems, and decision support systems. He has published in the *International Journal of Forecasting, Management Science, Geographical Analysis,* and other journals.

JANE G. GRAVELLE is a senior specialist in economic policy at the Congressional Research Service (CRS), Library of Congress. She holds B.A. and M.A. degrees in political science from the University of Georgia and a Ph.D. in economics from George Washington University. She has also served at the Labor Department and at the Treasury Department's Office of Tax Analysis and has taught at Boston University. At CRS she specializes in taxation, particularly the effects of tax policies on economic growth and resource allocation. Recent papers have addressed consumption taxes, dynamic revenue estimating, investment subsidies, capital gains taxes, individual retirement accounts, enterprise zones, and corporate tax revisions. She has published numerous articles in the academic journals and is the author of *The Economic Effects of Taxing Capital Income.* She currently serves on the editorial board of the *National Tax Journal.* She was winner of the 1981 award for outstanding doctoral dissertation in public finance from the National Tax Association–Tax Institute of America.

MERL HACKBART is professor of finance and public administration at the University of Kentucky. He previously served as budget director of the state of Kentucky, director of the Martin School of Public Administration at the University of Kentucky, and associate dean of the College of Business and Economics at the University of Kentucky. Hackbart is also an appointed member of the Kentucky Council of Postsecondary Education. His research has focused on public financial management and public budgeting.

REBECCA HENDRICK is associate professor of public administration in the College of Urban Planning and Public Affairs at the University of Illinois at Chicago. She received her B.S. degree (1977) in social sciences and her M.A. (1978) and Ph.D. (1985) degrees in political science from Michigan State University. She was previously an associate professor of political science and director of the Master of Public Administration Program at the University of Wisconsin-Milwaukee. Her teaching interests and work focus on budgeting and financial management in local government, program evaluation, policy analysis, organizational theory, and decision making. Her articles have appeared in *Journal of Politics; Journal of Public Administration Research, and Theory; Public Administration Review; Western Political Quarterly; Social Science Quarterly; Publius; Public Productivity and Management Review; Policy Studies Review; American Review of Public Administration;* and *Public Budgeting and Financial Management.*

L. R. JONES is professor of financial management in the Department of Systems Management, Naval Postgraduate School, Monterey, California. He earned his B.A. degree from Stanford University and his M.A. and Ph.D. degrees from the University of California, Berkeley. He has published more than seventy articles and book chapters and eight books on topics ranging from public financial management to regulatory and environmental policy. His recent works include *International Perspectives on the New Public Management* (1997), *Reinventing the Pentagon* (1994), *Corporate Environmental Policy and Government Regulation* (1994), *Mission Financing to Realign National Defense* (1992), and *Government Response to Financial Constraints* (1989). He continues to conduct research on federal financial management reform.

PHILIP G. JOYCE is assistant professor of public administration at the Maxwell School of Citizenship and Public Affairs, Syracuse University, and a senior associate in the Alan K. Campbell Public Affairs Institute at the Maxwell School. He teaches courses in public budgeting, intergovernmental relations, and the political environment of public administration. He holds a Ph.D. degree from the Maxwell School and has also taught at the University of Kentucky and the American University. He has twelve years of public sector work experience, including four years with the Illinois Bureau of the Budget and five years with the Congressional Budget Office. Joyce's articles on budget procedures, executive-legislative relations, intergovernmental fiscal policies, and government performance have appeared in *Public Administration Review, Public Budgeting and Finance, Administration and Society,* and the *Harvard Journal of Legislation.*

MARVIN B. MANDELL is professor of policy sciences at the University of Maryland, Baltimore County. He holds B.S. and B.A. degrees in civil engineering and sociology, respectively, from the State University of New York, Buffalo, and a Ph.D. degree from Northwestern University. He has published articles on public sector applications of operations research, evaluation research, and the utilization of policymaking in such journals as *Journal of Policy Analysis and Management, Management Science, Evaluation Review,* and *Knowledge.*

JERRY McCAFFERY is professor of public budgeting in the Department of Systems Management at the Naval Postgraduate School in Monterey, California. He earned his B.A., M.A., and Ph.D. degrees from the University of Wisconsin, Madison. He has worked for the Wisconsin Department of Revenue as a budget analyst; taught at the University of Georgia, Willamette University, and Indiana University; and served as chair of the American Society for Public Administration's section on budgeting and financial management. McCaffery has published extensively in the areas of budget process and budget reform at all levels of government and is currently interested in federal financial management reform.

ROWAN MIRANDA is director of research for the Government Finance Officers Association. He holds a Ph.D. degree from the University of Chicago's Harris Graduate School of Public Policy Studies. Miranda was formerly on the faculty of the University of Pittsburgh, Carnegie-Mellon University, and the University of Illinois. He recently completed terms as budget director for the city of Pittsburgh and as chief financial officer for Allegheny County, Pennsylvania. He has served as project manager and consultant for integrated financial systems selection projects for several large cities and counties.

VAN DOORN OOMS is senior vice president and director of research of the Committee for Economic Development. He was executive director for policy and chief economist of the Committee on the Budget, U.S. House of Representatives, from 1989 to 1990 and was the budget committee's chief economist from 1981 to 1988. Previously he was assistant director for economic policy (chief economist) at the Office of Management and Budget (1978 to 1981), chief economist of the Committee on the Budget, U.S. Senate (1977 to 1978), and a professor of economics at Yale University and Swarthmore College (1965 to 1976). Ooms's primary specialties are in macroeconomics and fiscal policy, with special emphasis on the political economy of the U.S. federal budget. He also has an extensive research and applied policy background in international economics, education, and labor markets.

MARVIN PHAUP is deputy assistant director, special studies, U.S. Congressional Budget Office (CBO). He is the author of numerous articles and CBO reports dealing with the budgetary treatment of complex financial transactions, including federal direct loans and guarantees, deposit insurance, pension insurance, structured loan sales, and government-sponsored enterprises. He was previously a senior economist at the Federal Reserve Bank of Cleveland. In 1995 he received the National Distinguished Service Award from the American Association for Budget and Program Analysis. He holds a B.A. degree (1962) from Roanoke College and M.A. (1964) and Ph.D. (1966) degrees in economics from the University of Virginia.

SHELDON POLLACK is assistant professor in the Department of Accounting in the College of Business and Economics at the University of Delaware. He earned a B.A. degree (1974) from the University of Rochester, a Ph.D. degree (1980) from Cornell University, and a J.D. degree (1986) from the University of Pennsylvania Law School. He has a joint appointment in the Department of Political Science and is a member of the executive committee of the Legal Studies Program at the University of Delaware. During the summer of 1995, Pollack was a guest scholar at the Brookings Institution in Washington, D.C. Previously he taught political science at the University of Pennsylvania and Cornell University and practiced tax law with the Philadelphia law firm of Ballard Spahr

Andrews & Ingersoll. Pollack is the author of *The Failure of U.S. Tax Policy: Revenue and Politics* (1966) and numerous articles on income taxation, public policy, and American politics.

A. PREMCHAND is assistant director of the Fiscal Affairs Department at the International Monetary Fund in Washington, D.C. Prior to joining the fund in 1970, he served as assistant professor, faculty of economics, Andhra University, Waltair, India; worked with the Union government in New Delhi; and was a consultant for the Ford Foundation (India). He has published extensively on government finances and financial management. His books include *Control of Public Expenditure in India* (1963), *Government Budgeting and Expenditure Controls* (1983), *Public Expenditure Management* (1990), and *Effective Government Accounting* (1995). His writings have been translated into Arabic, Chinese, Russian, and Spanish. He edited *Comparative International Budgeting and Finance* (1984) with Jesse Burkhead, and a symposium he edited on comparative budgeting is scheduled to appear in the *Journal of Public Budgeting, Accounting and Financial Management* in 1998. Premchand has provided technical assistance in the area of public financial management to more than forty countries.

JAMES R. RAMSEY is professor of economics at Western Kentucky University and budget director for the state of Kentucky. He has served as vice-president for finance at Western Kentucky University and as director of the Office of Financial Management and Economic Analysis. Other previous responsibilities include chief economist for the state of Kentucky and member of the Consensus Revenue Forecasting Group. Ramsey's publications and research have focused on debt and portfolio management and state budgeting processes.

JACQUELINE H. ROGERS is senior fellow at the School of Public Affairs, University of Maryland, College Park. She teaches courses on housing, community development, and finance. From 1987 through 1995 she served as secretary of the Maryland Department of Housing and Community Development under Governor William D. Schaefer. She directed the Montgomery County Office of Management and Budget from 1980 to 1987 and earlier served as an environmental planner and director of the county's Department of Housing and Community Development. She has served on numerous state commissions and at the National Academy of Public Administration (NAPA), reviewing the internal operations of the Department of Housing and Urban Development. She is a fellow of NAPA and holds a Ph.D. degree from Yale University.

IRENE S. RUBIN is professor in the public administration department of Northern Illinois University. She earned her B.A. degree from Barnard College, her M.A. degree from Harvard University, and her Ph.D. degree from the University of

Chicago. She is currently editor of *Public Administration Review* and former editor of *Public Budgeting and Finance*. Recent books include *Budgeting: A Guide for Local Governments* (1997), with Bob Bland, and *The Politics of Public Budgeting* (1998). A forthcoming book is *Class, Tax, and Power: Municipal Budgeting in the United States.*

JAMES D. SAVAGE is associate professor of government and foreign affairs at the University of Virginia. He holds an M.P.P. degree in public policy, an M.A. degree in economics, and a Ph.D. degree in political science from the University of California at Berkeley. He is the author of *Balanced Budgets and American Politics* (1988) and numerous articles, is a member of the editorial board of *Public Budgeting and Finance,* and has recently completed a book manuscript on the pork-barreling of university research funding in the federal budget.

HERMAN M. SCHWARTZ is associate professor of government and foreign affairs at the University of Virginia. He earned a B.A. degree with distinction (1980) from Swarthmore College and M.A. (1983) and Ph.D. (1987) degrees in international relations from Cornell University. He is author of *In the Dominions of Debt* (1989) and *States vs. Markets* (1994) and seven journal articles and is currently working on a book comparing public sector reorganization in Australia, Canada, Denmark, New Zealand, and Sweden in the 1980s and 1990s.

FRED THOMPSON is Grace and Elmer Goudy Professor of Public Management and Policy at the George H. Atkinson Graduate School of Management, Willamette University. He is a recipient of the Willamette University Trustees' Teaching Award, the Gold Medal of the American Society of Military Controllers, *Public Administration Review*'s William E. Mosher and Frederick C. Mosher Award, and the Academy of Management's Outstanding Public Management Paper Award. He was a finalist for the Koopman Prize of the Operations Research Society of America. He is currently a member of the Oregon Government Standards and Practices Commission and chair of the Association for Budgeting and Financial Management. His B.A. degree is from Pomona College, and his Ph.D. degree is from the Center for Politics and Economics, Claremont Graduate University.

DAVID F. TORREGROSA is an analyst in the Special Studies Division of the Congressional Budget Office. He was previously an assistant professor of economics at the College of William & Mary. He holds a B.A. degree (1978) from William & Mary, an M.A. degree (1981) in government from the University of North Carolina at Chapel Hill, and an M.A. degree (1982) in economics from the University of Virginia.

BARRY WHITE is deputy associate director for education, income, maintenance, labor, U.S. Office of Management and Budget (OMB), Executive Office of the

President. He is the OMB career senior executive, with responsibility for presidential budgets and policies for the Departments of Education and Labor, the Social Security Administration, the welfare and children's programs of the Department of Health and Human Service, the food stamp and child nutrition programs of the Department of Agriculture, and related independent agencies. He has been in the federal service since 1968, holding positions in three cabinet departments as well as in OMB, where he has served as budget examiner for training and employment programs (1972 to 1980), education branch chief (1982 to 1995), and deputy associate director (1995 to the present). He is a recipient of both of the Presidential Rank Awards for members of the Senior Executive Service: Meritorious Executive, 1989, and Distinguished Executive, 1995. He is a graduate of Columbia College, New York.

JOSEPH WHITE is a specialist in budgeting and entitlement policy. He currently directs a project for the Twentieth Century Fund Foundation on social security and Medicare. He has been a research associate and senior fellow at the Brookings Institution and has taught at Johns Hopkins University, Carleton College, and Georgetown University. White wrote *The Deficit and the Public Interest* with Aaron Wildavsky; other works include the entry on appropriations for the *Encyclopedia of the United States Congress* and book chapters on defense and foreign aid appropriations. He has written extensively on health care policy, including *Competing Solutions: American Health Care Proposals and International Experience*. His Ph.D. degree is from the University of California at Berkeley.

MICHAEL J. WOLKOFF is deputy chairman of the Department of Economics at the University of Rochester and a member of the faculty in the Public Policy Analysis Program. He received his B.A. degree (1974) from Columbia University, his M.P.A. degree (1976) from the Maxwell School at Syracuse University, and his Ph.D. degree (1981) from the Institute of Public Policy at the University of Michigan. He has published numerous articles in the fields of state and local public finance and economic development and has consulted with a variety of public and private agencies.

Handbook of Government Budgeting

PART ONE

AN OVERVIEW OF GOVERNMENT BUDGETING

CHAPTER ONE

Features of the Budgetary Process

Jerry McCaffery

This chapter reviews the budgetary process and describes the basic stages of budgeting (Keith and Davis, 1991; Berner and Daggett, 1993). The primary focus is on the federal process, but state and local practices are also discussed when they differ greatly from federal patterns.

Aaron Wildavsky (1964) has observed that a budget is a series of goals with price tags attached. He suggests that a budget may be a plan, a contract to accomplish certain ends, a means of control, and even a precedent, because what has been enacted in the current year is likely to be reenacted in the following year. Wildavsky concludes that the purposes of budgets are as varied as the purposes of human beings (pp. 1–4). As might be expected, the multiplicity of purposes for budgets leads to varied budgetary processes. Nonetheless, these processes share some basic features.

STAGES AND SCHEDULES

The budgetary process may be divided into four stages: executive preparation, legislative review, execution, and audit. Although it is easy to erect a linear model of the budget cycle from preparation through execution, in reality these budget cycles overlap in annual budget systems. For example, at the federal level, in the spring a budget officer will be executing the current year's budget, preparing to testify on the budget just submitted to Congress, and beginning to construct the budget for the following year. He also could be responding to audits and reviews of past budgets from congressional and executive branch sources. To discharge their legal responsibilities and to be effective players in the budgetary process, participants have to know where they are in that process and what is expected of them.

The budget cycle allows for a fixed and regular review of policy and program. Budget cycles are based on a fiscal year calendar. The federal budget fiscal year runs from October 1 of each year through September 30 of the following year and is referred to by the date of the year in which it ends. Thus a fiscal year beginning in October 1998 and ending in September 1999 would be called FY99. Until passage of the Congressional Budget Act of 1974, the federal government operated on a July 1 to June 30 fiscal year, as do all states except four (Alabama, Michigan, New York, and Texas).

Although many jurisdictions in the United States use an annual fiscal year, nineteen states use a biennial budgetary process. Annual budgetary processes are designed to lead to review and enactment of a budget each year. Biennial processes lead to a new budget every two years and have a definite on-and-off cycle: executive branch preparation and legislative review occur every other year, whereas in an annual cycle the executive is always building a budget and the legislature is always reviewing a budget.

States are not entirely consistent in the way they implement biennial processes. Some states adopt two one-year budgets; others adopt a single budget for the two-year period. In the former case, any agency surplus would be returned to the general fund at the end of the fiscal year; in the latter case, the surplus could be used in the next fiscal year. As a practical matter, the routines of budget execution (such as apportionments, allotments, and quarterly and annual reconciliation of accounts) make execution of biennial budgets substantially similar to execution of annual budgets. There is a substantial difference, however, in the preparation cycle, because the second year of the biennium is a full year further into the future than it would be in an annual budget system. This means that it is more difficult for administrators and legislators to predict changes that might occur in the second year of the biennium. Greater uncertainty forces biennial systems to have procedures for coping with emergency situations. These procedures range from calling special sessions of the legislature to empowering a legislative committee to meet in the off-year to react to changing financial conditions and perhaps provide agencies with extra funds to meet unanticipated events, to granting power to the governor to manage state spending in order to cope with economic changes.

Because annual budget systems are seen as more flexible than biennial systems, the major trend in the twentieth century has been for states to adopt annual budget systems. In 1940, forty-four of the forty-eight states had biennial budget systems; only four had annual legislative sessions and consequently annual budgets (New Jersey, New York, Rhode Island, and South Carolina). Paula Kearns (1994) found that annual and biennial formats each have proponents among state budget officials. Some prefer the biennial pattern because they believe that budget preparation costs and budget expenditures are lower in such systems and that more opportunity exists for long-range planning, legislative deliberation, and program evaluation and oversight. Others favor the annual pattern, citing increased time for legislative consideration of the budget, increased accuracy of revenue estimates, reduced power of the executive branch (because the legislature remained in session and could continue its routine oversight responsibilities or react to emergencies), and elimination of many special sessions and supplemental appropriations. Kearns suggests that some part of the move toward annual budgets results from the desire of state officials to be able to respond more quickly to federal policy adjustments in order to be eligible for more federal funds.

Recent discussion about a biennial budget for the federal government has centered on the improvement in congressional oversight that would result under a biennial pattern when Congress used the off year to review and consider how well the programs it had legislated were working. Proponents also believe that biennial budgeting would decrease the tremendous annual effort now devoted to developing and implementing the annual budget in both the executive and legislative branches of government. For example, Senator Pete Domenici has commented that each year the Army Corps of Engineers prepares and submits to the Appropriations Committees an eight-volume budget justification amounting to more than two thousand pages for an appropriation equal to two-tenths of 1 percent of the federal budget. Domenici notes that the Senate debates and votes on the same issue three or four times a year, voting on the budget resolution, again on the authorization bill, on a few amendments on the floor, and again on the appropriations bill. He also argues that Congress does not spend enough time reviewing federal government operations, and that oversight within the annual framework is not as good as it should be nor as good as it could be in a biennial cycle (Domenici, 1996, p. 22; see also Meyers, 1988).

Although the federal budget runs on an annual cycle, it is complicated by the use of "out-years" and multiple-year estimates. Both Congress and the executive branch use multiple-year budget estimates in internal documents during budget preparation, during testimony before appropriators, and as required by statutes governing the budgetary process. The Budget Resolution established by the Congressional Budget Act of 1974 requires a display of revenue and spending levels for a multiple-year period; this has usually meant five years, although Congress is free to choose the period to agree with policy goals. For example, the FY96 Budget Resolution used a seven-year forecast to illustrate how a balanced budget would be achieved by 2002. The Senate Armed Services Committee has required a biennial budget presentation by the Department of

Defense since 1987, although the department itself uses a five- to six-year financial planning horizon in its internal budgetary process and a five- to ten-year horizon in its planning processes. Thus budget makers must know not only what step in the process they are dealing with, but also what fiscal year. Years beyond the immediate budget request year are called out-years, and although their numbers are as accurate as estimators can make them, they are commonly acknowledged to be not as accurate as the numbers in the budget year. Figures in these years are said to be "not of budget quality." This is substantially different from biennial budgets, in which detailed appropriations are enacted for all accounts for the second year of the biennium. In biennial systems, the numbers for both budget years are necessarily of budget quality.

Executive Preparation

At the federal level, the process of formulating the executive budget begins in the spring of each year, at least nine months before the budget is transmitted to Congress and at least eighteen months before the fiscal year begins. The executive process begins with the setting of presidential priorities and the transmission of those priorities to the agencies. Although some of this is done verbally, there is an instructional circular to be followed (OMB A-11) that usually includes a letter from the director of the Office of Management and Budget (OMB) indicating any special issues or procedures for the upcoming budgetary process. OMB also holds a spring preview with agencies to identify issues and get initial agreement on budget directions. This preview usually occurs near the middle of the agency budgetary process. Although agency processes differ as a result of the size and complexity of the agency, agencies usually build budgets from the late winter (March) through the summer. In late July or early August, OMB does a midsummer budget review that focuses mainly on the state of the economy and on the impact that changes in economic conditions have on the budget under consideration in Congress and on the agency budgets being constructed. Agency budgets are submitted to OMB for review in the fall, a dialogue ensues, and decisions are made and incorporated into the final draft of the budget document. The process concludes with fine-tuning in December and January and the assembling, printing, and transmission of the presidential budget document to Congress on the first Monday in February. Subsequently, the president may also submit budget amendments to Congress. President Carter submitted two comprehensive budget amendments in 1980 due to quickly changing economic conditions; President Clinton submitted a substantial amendment to his budget in 1995 to match congressional pursuit of a balanced budget by 2002. The first year of a new presidency is also likely to see substantial budget amendments sent to Congress. Once an appropriations bill has been passed, the president may still seek to amend it through a supplemental appropriations bill, basically adjusting the appropriation during the execution phase. Supplemental bills are also used for emergencies such as disaster relief.

Prior to the start of the budgetary process, the president establishes general budget and fiscal policy guidelines. These may result from conversations with close advisors, such as the director of the OMB, the secretary of the Treasury, the chairman of the Council of Economic Advisers, and key cabinet officials from important agencies in which the president has taken a strong substantive interest, such as defense or health. Recent elections also influence priorities; a newly elected president may have made promises he wishes to implement, or an off-year election result may lead him to modify his program. These guidelines are transmitted to the agencies by the OMB. During the budget preparation process, OMB works with agencies to convert the president's general policies into specific policy directions and planning levels, both for the budget year and for the following four years. Specific instructions and forms are circulated to the agencies as part of the general budget circular that controls budget preparation. In general, presidents seem to be most active in budget making in the first years of their terms; in later years they pay less attention to solving problems through the budgetary process, to some extent because so much of the budget is "fixed" or mandated by law and made up of entitlements supported by powerful clientele groups.

Once general guidelines have been set, agencies begin their internal budgeting process. Taking cues from the president's priorities, agency heads set priorities for their own agencies. Agencies concern themselves with personnel staffing levels and supporting expenses. They may ask about the number and type of personnel required, labor-saving efficiencies, program intensity levels, and clientele demands. Budget change requests are then built in terms of additions or reductions to ongoing staffing levels and supporting expenses. Agencies with a responsibility to distribute money directly to citizens through pensions, health care payments, subsidies, contracts, insurance programs, grants, loans, and credit programs will often ask the same kinds of questions, but the focus will be on efficient processing of checks and vouchers and on auditing to ensure that those who are eligible receive what is due them and that those who attempt to defraud the system are thwarted. In these cases the administrative budget to disburse funds may be only a small percentage of the total funds disbursed or collected. In the agency process, budget makers are heavily dependent upon calculations and numerical relationships that have worked in the past. Tax collection agencies carefully monitor their cost to collect a dollar of taxes; welfare agencies tend to focus on number of clients served and fraudulent claims; libraries focus on circulation figures; and police and fire protection agencies may keep response times as key budget indicators. Reviewers tend to monitor the same vital indicators, both within the agencies and in the legislature. Recent trends in performance measurement at all levels of government have enhanced this trend as decision makers try to assess which indicators will enable them to understand how to get the most for what is spent (Gore, 1995, p. 5).

Agency budgetary processes usually combine *centralized* and *decentralized* elements. The budgetary process proceeds on a top-down basis for some decisions and on a bottom-up basis for others. For some decisions, a high degree of centralization may be necessary, particularly in large procurement programs that are unique or experimental. Top-down processes usually dominate jurisdictions under fiscal stress, where the chief executive and the budget bureau will issue guidance about how much agencies can ask for, how much budgets might have to be reduced, or what kinds of programs might have a higher priority. For other decisions, input from field-level commands and district and regional offices is more appropriate; these might include decisions on local maintenance items or local service or clientele needs. Philosophically, the argument is sometimes made that decentralizing the budgetary process spreads the organization's goals and objectives throughout the organization and helps train future managers by making them sensitive to cost trade-offs and forcing a more general view of organizational goals. However, decentralization generally makes for a more complicated and lengthy agency budgetary process; consequently, most agencies use a mix of centralized and decentralized patterns. The basic questions that need to be answered remain focused on what needs to be done, by whom and for how much. These questions should be addressed to the level of organization that can best answer them.

Agencies have their own budgetary process calendar, generally beginning with the guidelines of the chief executive and proceeding through a series of steps culminating in the agency budget. In the federal government this process takes place from spring through early fall, when the budget is presented to OMB. In major agencies, the internal budgetary process may involve a series of hearings, budget presentations, reviews, and appeals at several levels before the final agency budget is ready to be transmitted to OMB.

While budgeting is taking place deep within the agency on matters so mundane as the need for one additional worker or the correct ratio of office supplies to workers, there is also a continuous exchange of information, evaluation, and policy decisions at the highest level of government, among the president, the director of OMB, White House staff, agency heads and secretaries of departments. These decisions result from how the previous budget was treated by Congress, from debate over the budget currently in Congress, and from projections about the economic outlook that are prepared jointly by the Council of Economic Advisers, OMB, and the Treasury Department.

In the fall, agencies submit their budget requests to OMB, where they are reviewed by budget analysts. OMB's review is first done at the staff level, where issue papers are prepared in consultation with the agency and recommendations are made. A director's review is held to discuss major issues with the agencies and to allow the OMB analysts to defend their recommendations. The OMB director then makes his decisions and the numbers are passed back to the agencies. If agencies disagree with these numbers, they can appeal to the director and, if not satisfied, to the president. Large agencies may be reviewed by teams of OMB budget analysts responsible for different functional areas. In smaller governments, one analyst may handle several agencies.

Usually budget analysts are in close touch with their agency and its programs throughout the year on matters of budget execution as well as budget preparation. A large part of their job entails understanding the agency program and its budget needs. The analyst tries to help shape the agency budget before it gets to OMB, to enhance programs the president desires or that the analyst thinks are in line with presidential priorities. Both in execution and in preparation, the budget analyst is a communicator of policy during the year. This ongoing dialogue is beneficial to both parties because it allows the agency to inform the OMB analyst of problem areas early in the process and because it enables both sides to work to shape the areas of disagreement and agreement.

Many issues are solved at the analyst level in concert with the budget office in the agency. Other issues are not so easily solved and may go to higher levels of the OMB and the agency. Unresolved issues of major significance may require the involvement of the president and White House officials as well as the director of OMB and the relevant department secretary. At these later stages, the large agencies are expected to solve their own problems. They usually have a short list of items they can appeal, and when they appeal they usually are required to have a solution within their own agency budget. Usually they cannot look to anyone to suddenly find extra money in another agency to solve a problem for them. When an agency gets less than it wants at this stage in the process, it does not mean that the issue is closed. Most agencies have strong linkages to Congress, to their authorizing and appropriating committees, and may be willing to allow the president's people to make cuts they estimate may be restored by Congress. Moreover, the perspective of the department secretary is not necessarily the same as that of the lower-level program administrator, who may have firm believers in his program on the appropriation committees.

As the process begins to move into its final stages in December and January, it is not unusual to have budget proposals leaked to the press as trial balloons. Most of these trial balloons are quickly exploded, as opponents in Congress speak out directly against them and lobbyists orchestrate letter-writing and faxing campaigns to illustrate the disruption that would occur in a program if the hypothetical solution proposed in the leaked communiqué were adopted as policy. Although it is wise not to put too much credence in these early December budget gambits, a large part of budgeting does involve consensus solutions, and such agreement is gained only by justifying early and often what is about to happen. Later in January, leaks should be taken more seriously as "anonymous sources" representing administration officials, congressional aides, and lobbyists speak to the media "on the condition of anonymity" and with the understanding that "some details are still being fine-tuned." Congressional leaders may also speak directly to presidential suggestions, giving signals about what might or might not be acceptable. For example, in January 1997, a story quoted anonymous sources as saying that President Clinton wanted to restore about $16 billion to welfare programs that had been changed in the summer of 1996. Senate Majority Leader Trent Lott was quoted in the same story as saying it "was too soon to start fiddling with welfare" (Associated Press, 1997, p. 5). Such comments may or may not dissuade the president from including a modified proposal in the budget. They do, however, indicate the outlines of the coming budget struggle.

Once the policy decisions have been made, the numbers have to be calculated and totaled and the actual budget story has to be written for the budget documents. Although much of this part of the process is automated and only needs updating, it is still time-consuming and must be accomplished in a brief period. Cynics observe that the real end of this process occurs only when the Government Printing Office has copy to print the final version of the budget that will be presented to Congress. This usually happens late in January and marks the close of the executive budgetary process for the agencies and the OMB. Roy Meyers (1994) remarks that budget participants want to be seen as meeting the budgetary process deadlines and may accept some accounting gimmicks in order to do so. Meyers describes an OMB political appointee who remarked that the spring preview was a time for serious analytic work with "no gimmicks there," but the December stage was pure gimmicks: "We'd always do net outlay gimmicks, and we'd boost the income tax receipts and slow down the Military's miscellaneous procurement accounts" (p. 54).

The late December time frame gives decision makers one last chance to examine the state of the economy and consider the effects of such economic and technical factors as interest rates, economic growth rates, the rate of inflation, unemployment levels, and the size of beneficiary populations. As the federal budget has become dominated by mandatory payments to people who are entitled to claim benefits, and as continuing deficits have increased the national debt and the amount of interest paid on it, seemingly small percentage changes related to the health of the economy can mean large dollar changes in revenue and spending.

Schick (1990, pp. 164–169) has argued, for example, that the change from a predominance of discretionary spending to mandatory spending in the federal budget has made a substantial difference to OMB and to what budget analysts do. Schick feels that the old routines of budgeting that focus on justifying new personnel or a new capital equipment item are not as important as the factors that drive the economy and changes in budget categories related to the economy. Furthermore, although OMB could deny a personnel increase request and tell the agency to absorb the workload or find a laborsaving device, it is far more difficult for OMB to make an unfavorable trend in the economy vanish. Traditionally, budget analysis was dominated by calculations about what was actually spent and by relationships between personnel and supporting expenses in which historically derived ratios would be applied to the new budget request. With the growth in entitlement programs, such as social security and Medicare and other inflation-adjusted programs, the art of budget analysis has become the craft of forecasting what will happen in the economy over the next three to five years. Past costs are not as relevant as future estimates. Unfortunately, forecasting is imprecise and different forecasters can come to slightly different numbers which, while differing only slightly in absolute terms, can lead to substantial dollar differences when applied to the economy and to the budget and to multiple-year baselines. In general, OMB has been accused of being more optimistic in its economic projections than the Congressional Budget Office (CBO). In a study of deficit estimates, CBO was found to be more correct than OMB in sixteen out of twenty deficit estimates from 1993 to 1996, although OMB tended to be more correct in estimating income shares (U.S. Senate Budget Committee, 1997, pp. 1–2). OMB has suggested that the reason its estimates are more optimistic than those of the CBO is that OMB assumes a fiscal dividend derived from the timely adoption of the president's recommendations for the economy as provided by his budget message. Unfortunately, Congress rarely adopts these recommendations precisely as submitted, and the very makeup of the bicameral legislative system, which emphasizes committee work and deliberation and discussion, precludes maximizing timeliness. In any case, the point is that small changes in these assumptions can affect budget estimates by billions of dollars. Recognizing the importance of these economic factors, each year the budget document explains in great detail its economic assumptions (U.S. Office of Management and Budget, 1995).

If forecasting for one year is difficult, multiyear estimates are even more complex. These forecasts are called *baselines*. They are projections of future spending, assuming existing policy remains unchanged, with spending changing as a result of inflation and workload adjustments. The Congressional Budget Act of 1974 required OMB to prepare five-year forecasts of a continuation of the existing level of governmental services. These forecasts estimate the receipts, outlays, and deficits that would result from continuing current law through the period covered by the budget. OMB provided its first projections in 1974 and CBO in 1976. The two agencies differed in their treatment of inflation. CBO assumed that all appropriations would keep pace with inflation; OMB, however, did not always adjust discretionary appropriations for inflation. In

1985, OMB's approach became law in the Balanced Budget and Emergency Deficit Control Act (known as the Gramm-Rudman-Hollings Act, or GRH), only to be quickly reversed with the amendment to GRH in 1987 to allow baseline calculations for discretionary appropriations to be adjusted to keep pace with inflation (Van De Water, 1997). Subsequently, other adjustments have been made to refine the inflation adjustment. After 1990, personal services were adjusted by the employment cost index and nonpersonnel spending by the gross national product fixed-weight price index (U.S. Office of Management and Budget, 1995).

Baseline forecasts are useful for several reasons. They warn of future problems for individual tax-and-spending programs or for government fiscal policy as a whole. They provide a starting point for formulating and evaluating the president's budget. A baseline may be used as a "policy-neutral" benchmark against which the president's budget and alternative proposals can be compared and the magnitude of proposed changes assessed.

In dealing with programs that are related to an index such as the cost of living, as are many benefit programs, different estimators may make different predictions about the rate of change. Notwithstanding the official baselines, different players in the budgetary process may make their own baseline estimates in order to argue for more or less money for a program. These are tactical positionings for the annual budget struggle. For example, using a baseline that will lead to a higher total in the out-years may make a program seem generously funded, thus supporting a cut in the out-years and perhaps in the present year. Then, too, a reduction in the current year that results in a cut from an inflation-indexed baseline may give a program more than it had the previous year, but less than a full inflation-adjusted increase. Allen Schick (1990, pp. 95–101) has called this phenomenon "baseline alchemy." Irrespective of the confusion that different baselines may cause, baselines do indicate where a program is headed and how much it will cost without any policy change; this is particularly valuable information for policymakers in a system such as the U.S. federal government, where almost 70 percent of the outlays are mandated and most are indexed to inflation as well as affected by demographically driven increases in caseload and medical costs.

The transmittal of the president's budget to Congress is scheduled in law for the first Monday in February. For FY97, President Clinton's budget comprised six volumes and more than 2,100 pages—"a complex and daunting array of tables and charts which provided both summary overviews and detailed break-outs of federal revenues and spending for the budget year" (Curro and Yocom, 1996, p. 1). Amendments to it may also be sent to Congress at any time, until almost the end of the summer, while OMB carefully tracks the progress of appropriation legislation through Congress in order to make the president's preferences known on key issues in each chamber and at various committee hearings and debates.

Although the budget preparation process in some states resembles the federal government process of budget preparation, the pattern is not universal. Edward Clynch and Thomas Lauth (1991, pp. 2–4) suggest that some states may be classified as executive dominant systems, such as those in California, Illinois, and Ohio. In these states the process resembles the federal process: governors prepare a unified budget to serve as the legislative budget agenda, they deny the legislature access to original agency requests, and they possess strong vetoes. In other states, however (including Florida, Mississippi, Texas, and Utah), legislative leaders or key committees develop a unified budget that serves as the legislature's budget agenda. In these states, the executive budget proposal plays a marginal role. A third group of states mixes the two patterns, with the governor preparing the budget and holding a strong budget power but allowing the legislature access to agency budget requests.

There is almost no sensible way to encompass the budget practices of the tens of thousands of local governments and special districts (fire, flood, irrigation, recreation), other than to say that they all have a budgetary process. In the main, local governments have an annual budgetary process embedded within the laws of the state within which they exist, because local governments are creatures of the state and how they operate is fixed in the constitution and organic laws of their state. Historically, many local governments relied on property taxes and balanced operating budgets; as they grew, the demands for service growth were funded by the appreciation of property. This led to a neat equation in which growth in spending had to be balanced by growth in resources. Without the ability to go into debt on the operating budget, spending discipline was tight, balanced budgets were presented, and steps were taken during execution to attempt to avoid overspending if revenues did not come in as predicted (for example, hiring, travel, and procurement freezes). Many jurisdictions also maintained "rainy day funds."

The neatness of this system has declined under the demand for more and different services (for example, the move toward more welfare and social services and away from property protection and development functions) and the increase in intergovernmental revenue flows. Now local governments receive a substantial portion of their revenues from federal and state governments. This has complicated both the budgetary process and execution for recipient governments. First, they must anticipate what the granting government is going to give and when the funds will arrive. Secondly, some grants are given in the expectation that the subordinate government will gradually assume more of the costs of the program. Ultimately this may impose on the recipient government a burden that is greater than it anticipated, a burden supported by a vocal clientele opposed to seeing the program cut. Moreover, it is not unknown for federal and state governments to simply impose mandates on local units and let them worry about funding the mandates. The intercession of courts to provide certain remedies (for example, in handicapped access guarantees or restrictions on the number of prisoners per cell) has also complicated state and local government budgeting.

In general, the smaller units of government—towns, townships, rural counties, and independent school districts—tend to have a legislatively dominated process in which program administrators present budgets to elected boards. The budget may be voted on in an annual meeting. Metropolitan counties and cities may have an executive budgetary process that resembles that of the federal government, including budget instructions, budget guidance, strategic planning, agency procedures and hearings, executive review, and a budget office charged with assembling the budget document and presenting it to the governing board for approval. Then there is a wide range of situations in the middle, in which even very small localities can hire managers to give professional guidance to the budgetary process and even relatively large localities under professional management may make imprudent or inappropriately aggressive decisions.

Legislative Review

Congress is an important player in the budgetary process. It considers the president's budget proposals and can approve, modify, or reject them. It can change funding levels, add programs not requested by the president, and eliminate presidential favorites. It can make changes in taxes and other receipts that fund government. In the U.S. system of shared powers and checks and balances, Congress should be seen as a powerful player in the budgetary process, with rights and responsibilities of its own, focused on protecting the power of the purse. Fundamentally, the power of the purse is given to Congress by Article I of the Constitution. Section 8 provides that Congress shall have the power to provide for common defense and general welfare, and Section 9 adds that no money shall be drawn from the Treasury but in consequence of appropriations. Until the passage of the Budget and Accounting Act of 1921, which created the Bureau of the Budget and an organized executive budgetary process, and the General Accounting Office, Congress tended to deal directly with the agencies. It could be argued that Congress was more important in the budgetary process than the president. From 1921 to 1974 the executive budget power was clearly ascendant, but the Congressional Budget Act of 1974 increased the strength of Congress by organizing its efforts and improving its information resources. The outcome is that the two branches clearly share the budget power. This division of power makes for a complicated budgetary process, and in times when party control is divided in Congress and between Congress and the White House, the orderliness of the budgetary process appears to suffer as neither party nor branch of government can force a conclusion entirely favorable to its side and on a timely basis. Another way of looking at this problem is that the rich diversity of the country sometimes manifests itself in an inability to produce budgets on time and to find clear lines of public policy to which all parties can agree. Reformers who focus simply on the construction of a linear and clean budgetary process must be cautioned that the process must serve the country it reflects; where there is no clear consensus on policy, it is not useful to expect a clean and simple budgetary process.

The legislative budgetary process has a definite beginning, middle, and end. The beginning of the process starts with the receipt of the president's budget by Congress in early February and concludes with the passage of a concurrent resolution on the budget in mid-April. The middle of the process is the period, usually from April through mid-September, when committees review and mark up appropriations bills and the House and Senate debate and amend the appropriations bills and pass them. The end of the process occurs when these bills are passed in each chamber, usually in the form of a vote on a joint conference committee report, and sent to the president and signed. The rules of the Congressional Budget Act of 1974 indicate that this should occur before October 1 of each year, but in most years most appropriations bills are passed late. Thus the endgame usually lasts from mid-September to mid-November while participants seek to resolve issues in controversial bills. During this endgame, those agencies for which the president has not signed an appropriations bill receive their funding through a temporary, stop-gap measure called a Continuing Resolution Appropriation (CR), which enables the work of government to continue. CRs include all appropriations not yet signed and are usually set at the current year's funding level, although Congress has discretion about what level to choose. CRs may last a day, a week, or a month; there may be only one CR, or as negotiations over budget issues are prolonged, several CRs might need to be passed. Because most legislators recognize the futility of government shutdowns as an action-forcing mechanism, CRs are usually not controversial, although the president has vetoed CRs and some nonemergency functions of the federal government have been shut down for short periods of time when the president and Congress were unable to agree on appropriations bills and CRs.

Upon receiving the president's budget, the first task of Congress is to write a budget resolution as required by the Congressional Budget Act of 1974. This budget resolution is a congressional rule and does not go to the president for approval. All standing committees of the House and the Senate are required to recommend spending levels and to report legislative plans within their jurisdiction to their budget committees in "views and estimates" letters. The House and Senate budget committees hold hearings, usually beginning with the director of OMB, the secretary of the Treasury, and the chairman of the Council of Economic

Advisors, and continuing with other experts both in and out of government. The committees draft separate versions of the budget resolution and bring them to their chambers for debate, discussion, and passage. Differences between the versions passed by each chamber are ironed out in a conference committee and then the consolidated final version is passed by both chambers. The concurrent resolution is supposed to be passed by April 15, but it is often late. Between 1976 and 1996, Congress was on time with the budget resolution three times (Domenici, 1996, p. 22). In 1985 the budget resolution was 139 days late (Schick, 1990, p. 174), and in 1990 Congress could not agree on a budget resolution and each chamber passed a "deeming" resolution, which was deemed the budget resolution and allowed the budgetary process to go forward. The actual concurrent resolution passed the House on October 8 and the Senate on October 9—179 days late. Schick (1995, p. 13) notes that the budget committees have a hard time attracting support, and that budget resolutions typically squeak through on party-line votes, in contrast to appropriations bills, which are normally supported by majorities of both parties and often approved by lopsided majorities.

The budget resolution becomes Congress's spending plan. Actual appropriations must still be provided in separate appropriations bills. Tax law and entitlement changes assumed by the budget resolution must also be passed in separate vehicles. This is most often done by one or more reconciliation bills, constructed pursuant to reconciliation instructions developed by the budget committees and included within the conference report on the budget resolution. The FY98 budget resolution set total targets for federal revenues for the years 1998 through 2002, new budget authority (some budget authority is provided by permanent authority), budget outlays, deficits, public debt, direct loan obligations, and primary loan guarantee commitments. The budget resolution also set targets for social security revenues and outlays. The levels on new budget authority, budget outlays, new direct loan obligations, and loan guarantee commitments are then subdivided into twenty major functional areas, ranging from national defense, agriculture, energy, natural resources, health, and income security to net interest, allowances, and undistributed offsetting receipts. The 1998 Budget Resolution Conference Agreement also displays these areas in terms of discretionary and mandatory totals (U.S. House Budget Committee, 1997, pp. 58–59); for FY98 about 33 percent of total spending was classified as discretionary.

As required by sections 302 (1974) and 602 (1990) of the Congressional Budget Act of 1974, the Joint Statement of the Managers of the Budget Resolution includes a statement of the levels of total budget authority, total budget outlays, and for the House only, total entitlement authority, allocated to each committee. These allocations are divided between mandatory and discretionary totals.

For the House, the allocations are broken down by budget function. Most committees have budget authority and outlays in several functional areas; for example, the House Agriculture Committee draws from nine functional areas, and the House Appropriations Committee draws from eighteen of the functional areas and has almost all of the discretionary new budget authority (98.5 percent). Section 602 requires the House and Senate Appropriations Committees to allocate their totals among their thirteen subcommittees, thus creating a control mechanism that links budget totals to specific spending measures (Schick, 1995, p. 88). The appropriations bills built by the subcommittees may not exceed the subtotals allocated to them (602b allocations); the amounts the full committee distributes to its subcommittees may not exceed the total given to the full committees (602a allocations); and the amounts allocated to all of the committees cannot exceed the budget authority and outlay totals in the budget resolution. House and Senate procedures differ slightly and the Senate is generally recognized as having a tougher set of enforcement rules (Schick, 1995, p. 88). Schick compares the 602b allocations for subcommittees to a bank account: the allocation endows the account. Whenever a subcommittee produces spending legislation, it is charged against that account. The subcommittee is not permitted to overspend its account; when its account reaches zero, it is out of business for that year (Schick, 1995, p. 91).

Subcommittees of the House and Senate appropriation committees write the appropriations bills within the dollar allocations they have been given by their appropriations committee. These 602b allocation numbers (subcommittee allocations) are used by participants in the budgetary process for scorekeeping. At any time in the floor discussion of an appropriations bill, a member of Congress may raise a point of order (formally complain to the presiding officer) that a bill has exceeded its allocation amount. If the point of order is held to be well founded, the bill will have to be modified. In this way the budget resolution passes responsibility to the committees, which are its experts in substantive areas, to build appropriations bills and then holds them accountable by dollar totals for what they have developed. The House and Senate budget committees are the principal scorekeepers; they issue reports as the passage of legislation dictates, assisted by the CBO, which provides cost estimates for legislation reported out of committee for floor action. The scorekeeping reports help in sustaining or rejecting points of order against bills that might appear to break the budget resolution discipline. Since 1990, mechanisms in addition to scorekeeping and points of order have been created to control the budgetary process in Congress, including spending caps for discretionary appropriations, which give a dollar ceiling to defense and nondefense discretionary expenditures, beyond which they are not supposed to be able to go, and the reconciliation process and pay-as-you-go provisions for mandatory expenditures in the Senate.

Pay-as-you-go provisions force Congress to find "billpayers" for tax or entitlement changes so that new provisions are paid for by the elimination of old provisions or by the creation of a new revenue source. This is a way to keep the effect on the deficit neutral. Setting specific targets for the discretionary expenditures has capped their growth rates and also serves to retard the growth of the deficit.

In the 1980s Congress had to solve the dilemma of integrating annual appropriations, spending authority carried by permanent law, tax policy, and the level of deficit. It did this by using the reconciliation provision of the Congressional Budget Act of 1974. By adding reconciliation instructions to a budget resolution, Congress instructs specified committees with jurisdiction over entitlement laws to restructure their programs so that the rate of spending will be reduced. Thus most of the budget resolution's points of order are aimed at the appropriations committees and the reconciliation instructions are aimed at the committees that permit spending through other processes. Reconciliation bills originate from reconciliation instructions developed in the budget resolution. They are drafted under the aegis of the budget committees acting on the guidance of the committees to whom reconciliation instructions were sent. Section 104 of the FY98 conference report (U.S. House Budget Committee, 1997) sent reconciliation instructions to eight standing committees in the Senate asking for a reduction of specified amounts of spending from the programs within their jurisdiction, one revenue reconciliation instruction to reduce taxes, and one pay-as-you-go instruction providing that the Committee on Finance could fund a children's health initiative costing not more than $2.3 billion in 1998 if it could reduce other expenditures by a similar amount.

In the House, reconciliation instructions were issued for two separate reconciliation bills: one for entitlement reform and the other for tax relief. Instructions were given to eight committees for each bill. In general, reconciliation instructions direct a committee to report changes in laws within its jurisdiction such that the total level of spending does not exceed a given amount, thereby reducing future spending in that area. Usually, reconciliation instructions indicate the dollar amount to be saved, leaving specific program changes to the particular committee. These may include changing tax laws and fees and various entitlement program changes, including benefit formulas, eligibility requirements, and shared cost percentages. Conversely, the reconciliation bill may include all of the budgetary process; in 1990 an omnibus reconciliation bill was passed that included reconciliation directives affecting taxes and deficit reduction, all the appropriations bills, and changes in the budgetary process. This package implemented a summit agreement made between the president and Congress. While reconciliation bills generally reduce spending, there are examples of savvy budget players being able to squeeze additional money for programs into reconciliation bills and making the increases stick because their votes were needed to pass the bill. For example, in 1987 a three-year increase for Medicaid was worked into the reconciliation bill by Representative Henry Waxman (Meyers, 1994, pp. 120–121).

As can be seen, Congress does not pass a budget per se; rather, it passes spending authority for specified purposes in appropriations acts each year. There are usually thirteen appropriations acts. They carry *budget authority,* which is the legal power to incur obligations that will result in immediate or future *outlays.* Outlays are the amount of money a program is actually expected to spend in a given year. Congress votes on budget authority and its staff estimate when the outlay will happen based on historical data. For example, most budget authority for salaries is spent in the year for which it is voted; however, a contract to repair a facility may be signed late in the fiscal year and the actual outlay of dollars may occur in the next fiscal year. Wildavsky (1988, p. 11) suggests that this practice of voting for budget authority has historical roots in when the country was large, infrastructure was primitive, and communications were slow, and Congress wanted to provide budget authority so that work could be begun and funds could be obligated through contracts or hiring of personnel and outlays would be paid as the work was completed. Once an obligation is made, the actual payment can occur in the current or the next fiscal year as appropriate. An additional complication is that appropriations bills can create budget authority for the budget year and for future budget years; thus, what an agency has to outlay (total obligational authority) depends not only on the budget for the new fiscal year but also on the obligational authority that has been passed in previous years to be spent in the new fiscal year.

The House initiates appropriations bills. The appropriations committees in each chamber have jurisdiction over the annual appropriations. Traditionally these committees have been divided into subcommittees, which hold hearings and review detailed budget materials developed by the agencies under the subcommittee's jurisdiction. Although the agency witnesses are most central to subcommittee deliberation, other witnesses also submit testimony before the subcommittee to support or amend some part of the agency request. Most witnesses at hearings seek budget increases: for example, James Payne compiled data showing that pro-spending witnesses at appropriations committee hearings outnumbered antispending witnesses by 145 to 1 (Meyers, 1994, p. 180).

In the defense arena, for example, the defense budget is first presented by the secretary of defense and the chairman of the Joint Chiefs of Staff. Then the secretary of the Navy, the chief of Naval Operations, and the commandant of the Marine Corps will appear on the Navy's budget. As questions get further into the details of the budget, budget officers and program managers from various levels are called to testify. In addition to hearings, written questions are submitted by congressmen and senators to the agencies, and congressional staff spend many hours on the telephone getting answers to questions. Many hours are also spent by analysts and managers within the agency trying to convince the committee staff and members to see the issue the way the agency sees it. Each department has a budget office, but each also has legislative liaison offices dedicated to servicing the information needs of Congress.

Congressional staff, for their part, work hard to ensure that the right issues get raised at hearings, that answers are given to the right questions, and that all sides of an issue are explored. This is important to staff later in the session; when they brief their legislator on an issue, before mark up or floor action, they can refer to what witnesses said in committee hearings.

At the beginning of each session of Congress, committee membership is organized to reflect the outcome of the last election. Committees are divided between majority and minority party members so that the majority party has control and the minority party is well represented, generally in proportion to the seats each party holds in the chamber. Staff for committees and subcommittees are similarly divided. This makeup is critical to the policymaking process. Congressional control does change, so completely excluding the minority would not be a good idea and in some years votes from the minority side are important to pushing a bill through when some members of the majority party cannot support it. The appropriations committees in particular like to get as much bipartisan agreement over issues in committee as they can in order to come out with a united front on complex budget issues. Indeed, some issues will even be presented as "nonpartisan," as just a matter of good fiscal management. Nonetheless, it is the majority chairman who controls the committee markup process, and if worst comes to worst he can ignore the minority members on some issues. To do so on all issues would mark him as an ineffective chairperson.

After the hearings, the subcommittee marks up the bill by approving or disapproving it or by modifying numbers and programs, writing instructions or limitations into the bill itself or into the report that will accompany the bill. The bill is then sent to the full committee. The full committee scrutinizes the bill, generally from a perspective of how the bill will fit in with the other bills in terms of the total dollar allocation given the committee by the budget resolution. The full committee then "reports out" the bill to the full chamber. Here the bill is scheduled for debate, amendments are offered and either accepted or rejected, and then the bill is voted on for final passage as amended. The same process ensues in the other chamber. When a bill has passed each chamber, a conference committee is appointed to resolve the differences between the two bills. The report of the conference committee will be taken back to each chamber and voted on. Once this is accomplished, the bill is sent to the president for approval or veto. When appropriations bills are not passed on time, Congress enacts a continuing resolution to fund the affected agencies so that they may continue to administer their programs. CRs must be presented to the president for approval or veto. In some years a portion or all of the government has been funded by an omnibus continuing resolution for the entire year.

In addition to appropriation acts, Congress also provides for spending in "permanent" laws. These include provision of budget authority for paying interest on the national debt and most entitlement programs, such as social security and Medicare. These laws do not need to be reenacted each year. In fact, although much time and effort is spent on the annual budgetary process, most of the total spending authority available in any year is provided by permanent laws and budget authority created in previous years that will be obligated in the current year. Consequently, most outlays in a year are not controlled through the appropriations process. For FY98, for example, 32.8 percent of total spending was classified as discretionary. The appropriations committees have almost all of the discretionary spending, but they also have spending responsibility that comes from previously enacted budget appropriations. For FY98, $274.4 billion of the House Appropriations Committee total of $791.4 billion had been enacted in previous years (34.6 percent) and would be spent without any further action by the committee. None of this was entitlement authority.

Almost all taxes and other receipts result from permanent laws. Tax bills are initiated in the House. The House Ways and Means Committee and the Senate Finance Committee have jurisdiction over the tax laws, including the financing of programs funded by those laws, such as programs financed by the social security taxes. These facts make these two committees very powerful. Appropriators have sometimes complained that they get all the blame for budget deficits, yet much of what has caused deficits—such as increases in entitlement payments and rising medical costs—is either outside their jurisdiction or outside the purview of the current budgetary process. Schick (1990, p. 125) observes that for Congress, budgeting in the 1980s was a frustrating and unpleasant chore: "Their misfortune has been to be blamed for both the spending cuts that the budget's dire finances force them to make and for the updrift in total spending that past commitments mandate."

The normal budgetary process runs from the president's budget to the Budget Resolution to the appropriations bills to the new fiscal year. Some programs are governed by permanent law, but others must be authorized annually. The Department of Defense has an annual authorization; thus it must annually present its programs before a substantive defense committee in each chamber, such as the Senate Armed Services Committee, and gain an authorization bill. This bill follows the same process as described earlier for an appropriations bill: hearings, markup, floor debate, amendment and passage, conference committee, vote on final passage, and presentation to the president for approval. In authorization bills, the issues involve the shape of the program; in evaluating defense bills, questions would be asked about strategic deterrence and nuclear weapons, about how conventional forces should be assembled, how many tanks the Army should have, how many ships and what type should be bought, and so forth. Authorizers see themselves as giving guidance to the appropriators (mainly the appropriations subcommittees that correspond to their authorization area), whom they see as being concerned with issues of timing and pricing in the current year. Authorizers may create new programs and suggest a cap for funding for the program, but they do not provide the funding. In some years, the turmoil of the budgetary process has left dollars for programs in the appropriations bill that were not in the authorization bill. This is a problem for the agency: the money is appropriated but the program is not authorized. One year, in order to maintain good relationships with the authorizing committees, Defense Department leadership agreed not to spend about $5 billion that had been appropriated but not authorized until the authorizers could find a bill in which to authorize it. In other instances, the agency takes the appropriations bill to be the last action of Congress on the matter, which implicitly assumes an authorization as it makes the appropriation. Authorizers do not necessarily agree with this logic.

The budget committees, the authorizing committees, and the appropriating committees each look at the defense function from a little bit different perspective, but some critics have argued that two sets of committees should be enough, because both must basically review the same things to come to the decisions they reach. When the budget committees suggest a total for the defense function, they do not do so by taking last year's budget and adding or subtracting 3 percent. Rather, they do much the same kind of review that the appropriations committees do. When the authorizers review defense programs and make suggestions, they are fully aware that there will be fiscal consequences, just as the appropriators are aware of the program consequences of fiscal decisions. Hence, some critics suggest that the process could be streamlined; others suggest that the oversight role of the authorizing committees is so critical that if the defense authorizing committees were abolished, the role would be assumed by other committees. Consequently, this change is unlikely to happen soon.

The final step in the legislative process occurs when the president signs an appropriations bill into law. The president may veto a bill to which he objects and Congress may override the veto with a two-thirds majority. As a practical matter, a majority of this size is often hard to achieve; thus presidential vetoes are rarely reversed. Even so, presidents signal well in advance when and with what they are displeased. A veto is not costless to a president. Although the act of vetoing may make him appear to be a strong leader, it also delays the start of whatever else was about to be funded, and the next version of the bill may be only marginally better than the one he vetoed. If the veto is over a small amount in a large appropriations bill, the tendency is for the president to accept the bad with the good; members of Congress have counted on this in the past and have presented the president with "Christmas tree" bills laden with small items for specific purposes in their districts (usually called "pork" by nonrecipients) that might stand no chance of making it through the process on their own merits. Some bills become "veto-proof" due to grand political factors. In the fall of 1995, about to extend the Bosnian peacekeeping operation, President Clinton, unhappy with some additions to the defense appropriations bill, realistically could not veto the bill for fear of the signals it would send within the Defense Department to the troops he was about to commit, and internationally to allies involved with the peacekeeping operation. During budget execution, presidents can try to manage portions of a bill with which they have a problem.

Within a fiscal year, the president has power to withhold spending under certain limited circumstances—to provide for contingencies, to achieve savings made possible through changes in requirements or through greater efficiency of operations, or as otherwise specifically provided in law. The Congressional Budget Act of 1974 specifies the procedures that must be followed if funds are withheld. *Deferrals,* which are temporary withholdings, take effect immediately unless overturned by an act of Congress. In 1995, a total of $17.8 billion in deferrals was reported to Congress and none was overturned. Deferrals control the pace of spending and must be obligated by the end of the fiscal year. Conversely, rescissions permanently cancel budget authority. They do not take effect unless Congress passes a law agreeing to them. If such a law is not passed within forty-five days of continuous session, the withheld funds must be made available for spending. From 1974 through 1993, Congress agreed with about one third of the rescissions proposed by the president, rescinding slightly less than a third of the total funds requested. Patterns do vary according to the relations between Congress and the president; in 1981, President Reagan asked for 133 rescissions and Congress approved 101, rescinding almost $11 billion of the proposed $15.3 billion (Schick, 1995, p. 176). In other years, presidents have been much less successful.

States vary in the power they give to governors in the budgetary process. All governors except the governor of North Carolina possess a veto power. In addition, forty-three governors have a line-item veto power that allows them to void part of an appropriations bill. In theory, the line-item veto allows for the reduction of foolish spending; but Abney and Lauth (1989) have found that governors use line-item vetoes for partisan and policy reasons. Moreover, the scope of the line-item veto differs. For example, in Illinois the governor may amend or rewrite legislation as part of the veto process; and in Wisconsin the governor may change wording as long as the law remains workable and the changes do not alter the purpose of the bill. Governors also may reduce expenditures during budget execution if revenues fall short of estimates. In these circumstances, governors in forty states may cut budgets during the spending year without legislative approval. In seven of these states, gubernatorial action is limited to across-the-board cuts; in the others, the governor may selectively reduce spending, except in seven states that limit the percentage that budgets may be decreased without legislative involvement (Abney and Lauth, 1989). The basis for this power is found in the requirement that states operate a balanced operating budget. In forty-three states, governors are required to propose a balanced operating budget. In thirty-six states, the budget enacted by the legislature must be in balance, and thirty-nine states require that the operating budget be executed so that it is balanced at the end of the fiscal year—although eleven of these states may carry over a deficit into the next fiscal year. These requirements are found in the constitutions of thirty-five states and in the statutes of thirteen others (Lauth, 1997, p. 270). Congress has given the president a line-item veto power, but as this is written its constitutionality remains to be tested. It seems clear that the line-item veto confers substantial additional legislative power upon the president; consequently, one would suspect that eventually Congress will feel a need to constrain this power.

Budget Execution

Although the act of budgeting is a planning process, budget execution is a management process. In budget execution, agencies obligate funds in pursuit of accomplishing their program goals. Following plans made in the budget preparation cycle, employees or contractors are engaged, materials and supplies are purchased, contracts are let and capital equipment is purchased in order to realize the programs, plans, and activities presented in the budget. There is a basic assumption that, once it is approved, the budget will be executed as it was built. Many also assume that this execution phase is a relatively simple task compared to preparing and passing the budget, because all it involves is returning to the budget-building documents and executing the plans described in them, as modified by the final version of the appropriations bill. The reality of administrative life is somewhat different. A substantial portion of budget execution is driven by the necessity of rescuing careful plans from unforeseen events and unknowable contingencies. At the close of the fiscal year, in the aggregate and on average, budget execution may appear to have been a matter of uninteresting routine dominated by financial control procedures, but it is unlikely to have appeared so uneventful to the department budget officer and his staff or to the manager charged with carrying out the program. The usual occurrence is for most of the budget year to unroll as planned, but for execution of a small percentage of the budget to consume a major investment of managerial and leadership effort.

All systems have set rules and procedures to help guide the jurisdiction through budget execution. In the federal government, once an appropriation is passed, the Treasury issues a warrant for the amount of money to be spent during the year. OMB apportions this amount to each agency. Each agency head then uses allotments to delegate to subordinates the authority to incur a specific amount of obligations. These allotments may be further subdivided into allocations by lower administrative levels. Following these allotments and allocations, obligations can be incurred (for example, a contract may be let) and outlays can be paid when the work or service is completed or the equipment is delivered. The apportionment, allotment, and allocation processes are the actual planning for when funds will be spent, by quarter or month and by administrative level.

In his classic text on budgeting, Jesse Burkhead (1959, pp. 340–356) expresses his belief that budget execution is an executive responsibility; he observes, however, that the history of the United States offers many instances in which the legislative body has intervened in execution to modify decisions it had previously made, to influence administrative actions, and to interpose independent checks on specific transactions (p. 342). Burkhead divides budget execution techniques into two classes: those concerned with financial controls and those concerned with administrative controls. Financial controls are directed at the various accounts used to record government transactions, for both receipts and expenditures. Administrative controls are concerned with executing and adjusting the budget plan that was developed and refined in the executive branch and reviewed and approved in the legislative branch. Burkhead suggests that the goals of budget execution involve preserving legislative intent, observing financial limitations, and maintaining flexibility at all levels of administration.

Bernard Pitsvada (1983) has illustrated some of the complexity of these administrative control systems at the federal level by examining the flexibility that federal agencies have in budget execution in terms of object classification, appropriations structure, contingency appropriations, emergency provisions, and reprogramming authority. Pitsvada observed that in budget execution, object classification generally leaves agencies with great flexibility to shift funds around to meet needs within or between object categories in order to meet shortfalls in one category with surpluses in another. Pitsvada adds that in general Congress intercedes with specific constraints only if an agency has "performed in a manner that displeases Congress" (p. 86). For example, in 1997 Congress tightened its reprogramming controls on certain defense accounts by lowering the amount of money that could be reprogrammed without asking for congressional consent.

Pitsvada suggests that the paradox of budget execution involves agencies, who feel they must have more flexibility to meet changing needs, and Congress, which feels that it is not performing its most vital constitutional power, the power of the purse, unless it exercises meaningful control over execution (1983, p. 100) The tension over the correct amount of control and flexibility in budget execution remains. Recently observers have suggested that too much control and controls of the wrong kind impair program efficiency (Thompson and Jones, 1994, pp. 155–193); but with the growth in size of the federal budget converting small percentage errors into large dollar errors, the necessity for controls that ensure fiscal propriety contains powerful practical and symbolic value. Where managers might prefer more flexibility, the public insists that public monies be safeguarded, even if this results in more control than might be strictly necessary.

Audit and Evaluation

The final phase of the budgetary process involves audit and evaluation. In this phase the disbursement of public money is scrutinized to assure officials and the public, first, that funds were used in accordance with legislative intent and no monies were spent illegally or for personal gain, and second, that public agencies are carrying out programs and activities in the most efficient and effective manner pursuant to legal and institutional constraints.

The first type of audit is called a *financial audit.* It concentrates on reviews of financial documents to ensure that products and services are delivered as agreed upon, that payment is accurate and prompt, that no money is siphoned off for personal use, and that all transactions follow the legal codes and restrictions of the jurisdiction. Such audits are generally carried out or supervised by agents external to the entity undergoing audit. These agents include, at the federal level, the General Accounting Office (GAO) and agency inspectors general, as well as internal auditing agencies (for example, the Navy Audit Service); at the state level, elected or appointed state auditors; and private sector accounting firms at all levels of government. There is also some accounting between levels of government as the federal government audits use of federal monies in state and local programs and as state governments audit certain local fiscal practices.

Financial audits evaluate honesty and correctness in handling money. As the role of government expanded after World War II, more effort was spent to measure the efficiency and effectiveness of government. This led to experiments with performance budgeting at different levels of government, and ultimately to *performance auditing.* In performance auditing the auditor attempts to ensure that the agency is conducting programs in a manner consistent with the laws and regulations that authorize the program, and to determine whether the agency has taken judicious action in resource deployment to attain programmatic ends. Basically, the auditor is attempting to judge efficiency in resource use and effectiveness in program delivery. Findings from such audits help policymakers to enhance program outcomes while minimizing the resources required to operate the programs. Often the same agencies responsible for financial audits also do performance audits, but because the focus in each audit is different, different personnel usually conduct each audit. The audit reports are fed back into the budgetary process and may lead to changes in the laws and rules that guide the program and in the managerial practices of the agency that administers it. Audit findings may also be reviewed in special hearings by oversight committees outside the budgetary process who want to ensure that agencies behave responsibly. Generally these audits are published and available to the public. Both financial audits and performance audits help to ensure that a jurisdiction is getting the most for its tax dollars. In so doing, they help maintain the vital element of trust in government and in those who disburse its monies and create and administer its programs.

CONCLUSIONS

Fundamentally, the budgetary process is a mechanism for making choices among competing claims for resources under conditions of scarcity. Technically, the fundamental task in budgeting is twofold: it predicts the future and evaluates the past. Visions of the future are complicated both by differing visions of what the future *should* and by arguments about what it *will* be given current understandings of causal relationships. Thus there is great uncertainty in going forward. Because government is a coercive arrangement and can extract money and time from its citizens and deliver goods and services unequally, budgeting tends to be a conservative process in which players examine in excruciating detail the information on decisions they are about to take. Consequently, the great problem in budgeting is information overload. Reformers have attempted to address this problem in a variety of ways: with the executive budget movement, with the creation of central budget bureaus and legislative staff agencies, with public hearings, and with published documents describing the budget. Much of this effort involves a sense that better information leads to a better budgetary process, and ultimately to better public policy.

Under the Government Performance and Results Act of 1993 (GPRA), the federal government has embarked on a performance measurement experiment that may lead to performance budgeting. Performance budgeting efforts date from the 1950s, but in this iteration, strategic planning and customer or clientele involvement have been added to activity groupings, input-output measurements, and the effort to measure outcomes and evaluate changes that might come from additional dollars. The strategic planning and customer involvement facets of this iteration are important changes. In the 1950s, performance budgeting seemed to focus on costs of activities, implicitly assuming that cost per unit numbers would eventually lead to increased centralization of the budgetary process and allow a few people to make good judgments about all activities by following the changes in a few key numbers. In the 1990s, under GPRA, this iteration of performance measurement and strategic planning seems more open to decentralizing goals throughout the organization and to forcing customer or client desires to percolate up into consideration at higher levels. The promise of a more useful and effective system seems tantalizingly close. This promise has attracted subordinate levels of government in the United States (Florida, Texas, and Arizona) and national levels elsewhere (New Zealand). The record of budget innovation suggests, however, that one ought not be too optimistic about this reform.

References

Abney, G., and Lauth, T. P. "The Executive Budget in the States: Normative Idea and Empirical Observation." *Policy Studies Journal,* 1989, *17,* 829–840.

Associated Press. "Clinton Budget to Seek Money for Welfare: Pentagon Spending Will Be Targeted. *Washington Times,* Jan. 15, 1997, p. 5.

Berner, K., and Daggett, S. *A Defense Budget Primer.* Washington, D.C.: Congressional Research Service, 1993.

Burkhead, J. *Government Budgeting.* New York: Wiley, 1959.

Clynch, E. J., and Lauth, T. P. (eds.). *Governors, Legislatures, and Budgets: Diversity Across the American States.* Westport, Conn.: Greenwood Press, 1991.

Curro, M., and Yocom, C. "The Federal Budget Process." Paper presented at Willamette University Conference on Modern Public Finance, Salem, Ore., Aug. 1996.

Domenici, P. "Make It a Two-Year Budget." *Washington Post National Weekly Edition,* Dec. 16, 1996, p. 22.

Gore, A., Jr. *Common Sense Government: Works Better and Costs Less.* Third Report of the National Performance Review. Washington, D.C.: Government Printing Office, 1995.

Kearns, P. "State Budget Periodicity: An Analysis of the Determinants and the Effect on State Spending." *Journal of Policy Analysis and Management,* 1994, *13,* 331–362.

Keith, R., and Davis, E. *Manual on the Federal Budget Process.* Washington, D.C.: Congressional Research Service, 1991.

Lauth, T. P. "The Balanced Budget Idea." In *The International Encyclopedia of Public Policy and Administration.* Boulder, Colo.: Westview Press, 1997.

Meyers, R. T. "Biennial Budgeting by the U.S. Congress." *Public Budgeting and Finance,* 1988, *8,* 21–32.

Meyers, R. T. *Strategic Budgeting.* Ann Arbor: University of Michigan Press, 1994.

Pitsvada, B. T. "Flexibility in Federal Budget Execution." *Public Budgeting and Finance,* 1983, *3*(2), 83–101.

Schick, A. *The Capacity to Budget.* Washington, D.C.: Urban Institute, 1990.

Schick, A. *The Federal Budget: Politics, Policy, Process.* Washington, D.C.: Brookings Institution, 1995.

Thompson, F., and Jones, L. R. *Reinventing the Pentagon: How the New Public Management Can Bring Institutional Renewal.* San Francisco: Jossey-Bass, 1994.

U.S. House Budget Committee. *Conference Report on the FY98 Budget Resolution.* Washington, D.C.: Government Printing Office, 1997.

U.S. Office of Management and Budget. *Budget of the United States Government, Fiscal Year 1996: Analytical Perspectives.* Washington, D.C.: Government Printing Office, 1995.

U.S. Senate Budget Committee. *Budget Newsletter,* Mar. 17, 1997.

Van De Water, P. "Baselines." In *The International Encyclopedia of Public Policy and Administration.* Boulder, Colo.: Westview Press, 1997.

Wildavsky, A. *The Politics of the Budgetary Process.* New York: Little, Brown, 1964.

Wildavsky, A. *The New Politics of the Budgetary Process.* Glenview, Ill.: Scott, Foresman, 1988.

CHAPTER TWO

Understanding the Role of Conflict in Budgeting

Irene S. Rubin

onflict is endemic to budgeting. The amount of money available is never sufficient to satisfy all requests, and it generates competition for scarce resources. Moreover, budget actors may not agree on key policies that are made through the budgetary process, such as who will bear the heaviest burden of taxation, which programs will be expanded or contracted, or whether it is acceptable to run a deficit. Occasionally tensions escalate, as they did in December 1995 and January 1996, when disagreements about how to balance the budget shut down the federal government. But the relative rarity of open conflict and disruption calls attention to the mechanisms in budgeting for handling competition and controversy. Because budgets must be passed regularly in order for government to carry on, budgeters have developed an array of techniques to suppress or manage disagreements and pass the budget more or less on time.

The resulting level of conflict may actually be too low for a democratic society. Visibly clashing interests may be necessary to engage the public, the press, and the elected officials, to make them pay attention to public issues before policy is determined. If interests have been obscured in the budget and people cannot see how the budget relates to their well-being or needs, they will fail to contest the outcomes. If citizens feel that their participation in budgetary decision making is unwelcome, they may ignore budget processes and then complain vociferously about the outcomes. Without some conflict, government institutions may not work as intended. A system of checks and balances, of shared power between institutions of government, is intended to prevent hasty action and ensure participation of relevant parties. Conflict is built into this process. The goal for public managers and budgeters should be to help articulate relevant policy disagreements but keep the resulting arguments moderate and constructive.

Controlling the level of conflict is not easy. Fiscal stress or spending cutbacks may intensify competition. The emergence of new interests or more powerful demands on the budget may exaggerate the level of tension. Divided government—a chief executive of one party and a legislative body dominated by the other party—can result in cascading efforts to block one another's proposals. Fear that disagreements may get out of hand may result in avoiding or suppressing conflict rather than managing it, thus exacerbating underlying problems of governance. The sources or level of conflict cannot always be contained, but conflict can often be channeled in constructive rather than destructive ways.

This chapter addresses conflict in the budget under four headings: intrinsic sources of conflict, routines and norms that hold down the normal level of conflict, factors that increase this base level, and approaches to conflict management that avoid the extremes of suppression or disruptive fighting.

INTRINSIC SOURCES OF CONFLICT IN BUDGETING

Demands on the budget routinely exceed resource levels. As a consequence, programs, regions, classes, and interest groups compete with one another for resources. Decision-making power is widely dispersed among a variety of budgetary actors who often disagree on who should get what from the budget. These decision makers often jockey for power to control allocations.

Competition Among Projects and Programs

Elected and appointed officials sometimes make competition among programs or projects or proposed items of expenditure an explicit part of the budget process. At the federal level, the budget process requires Congress to allocate spending between functions and between committees and subcommittees. At the state and local levels, a frequently used process called *target-based budgeting* requires competition and prioritization at the margins of the budget. Capital budgeting at the state and local levels frequently entails formal competition and choice between projects.

Representative Charles Stenholm (1996) described this competition at the federal level: "Next week the Budget Committee, on which I am privileged to serve, is scheduled to begin the process of putting together the budget resolution for fiscal year 1997. This process will require many tough choices as priorities are set among worthy programs. . . . But essentially all programs will be together in the same boat, competing for priority status as we seek to determine how best to allocate the revenues coming into the U.S. Treasury" [p. H3521]. At the state and local levels, target-based budgeting makes competition explicit at the margins of the budget. Program managers create a list of unfunded priorities, including items they need that were squeezed out of the maintenance-of-effort budget, and items they want, that will improve efficiency, expand services, reduce backlogs, or satisfy demands. The items on each list must be rank ordered and merged with similar lists coming from other departments and programs. The merged list of priorities is funded in order of importance until money runs out. Each request on the unfunded list thus formally competes with other unfunded requests (Rubin, 1991).

Budget choices can become highly emotional, with strong opinions on each side. Politicians argue about whether allocations should be increased for defense, police, or prisons, or whether they should be held constant and spending be increased on social services, education, health, and income support. Budget choices may become particularly emotional when they are viewed in terms of class. For example, some people consider tax breaks for business to be "corporate welfare," while others consider such breaks essential for economic growth.

Budgetary decision makers trying to determine what to cut and what to fund often disagree on what criteria to use. This lack of agreement goes well beyond choosing between programs. It also includes choices between capital and operating expenses, or more narrowly, between equipment and staff; prevention and suppression; government provision of services, contracting out, and privatization; and technical and political goals.

Conflict Among Strategies for Service Delivery

Decisions about how to deliver services are often made on emotional rather than technical grounds. For example, on one side may be people who believe that equipment should replace employees; on the other side are those who argue that machines take the jobs of people who need them. Similarly, some decision makers may support prevention strategies while others support suppression (of crime, drug use, disease, or illegal immigration). Prevention tends to be cheaper but less dramatic than suppression. Suppression calls for a higher level of skill and often higher levels of visibility and satisfaction. With good preventive programs some problems never occur, so the public never sees the problem, let alone watches professionals wrestle it to the ground. The result is often a tilt toward suppression even when prevention is more cost-effective.

One battleground in service delivery has been the choice between using public employees or contract workers. Whether contracting out will save money or not is a perennial budget question, but the matter may be decided on nonfinancial grounds. A mayor or a governor may want to build a national reputation as a privatizer, arguing for contracting at every turn. The legislature may be opposed to privatization, for equally political reasons. Or the roles may be reversed. Government employees and their unions often argue against contracting for fear of losing their jobs.

Bruce Wallin (1997) tells the story of a Republican governor in Massachusetts who was "eager to privatize" and a state legislature responsive to state employees that was skeptical of the governor's claims about the successes of contracting. After a series of proposals and blocking actions, the result was a gradually improved list of requirements before contracting could be chosen as the service delivery option. These requirements included certifiable savings, open competition for contracts, and maintenance of service quality.

COMPETITION AMONG ACTORS FOR CONTROL OF BUDGET ALLOCATIONS

Part of the reason for lack of agreement on priorities and service delivery modalities is that so many different actors with different interests have a hand in the decision making. They jockey for power over budget decisions.

Fragmented budgetary power leads to a series of built-in conflicts that typify budgeting at all levels of government. The executive and legislative branches have contested over time for control over the budget. Over the years, the executive's role has become larger, with increased responsibility for gathering, examining, and paring down departmental requests. This responsibility has often been delegated to the budget office, creating tensions within the executive branch between the budget office and the departments. On the legislative side of the budget equation, the fragmentation of budget power may lead to competition among committees or between committees and the leadership of each house. With respect to the role of the public, some citizens and interest groups feel that they should play a larger and more consequential role in budgeting than the role that professional budgeters and bureau chiefs are comfortable having them play.

Tension Between Executive and Legislative Branches

Academics often describe budget processes in the United States in which the executive proposes the budget and the legislature examines that proposal and accepts, rejects, or modifies it. In fact, however, the respective roles of the executive and the legislative branches in budgeting have often been contested and have shifted around considerably.

The colonial experience in the United States left behind public fear of powerful executives and a strong sentiment in favor of legislative power. Government was limited, budgets were simple. Departments made requests directly to legislative committees and requests for payment were approved by legislative committees. This legislatively dominated process can still be found in many counties, some smaller cities, and a few states.

As society became more urbanized and the role of government grew and budgets expanded, demand grew for more control over spending totals and more logic to the expenditures than could be provided by a disparate representative body with little expertise. Legislatures that had consisted primarily if not exclusively of property owners gradually came to include representatives of the working class as well, threatening the wealthy with taxation to serve the poor, build roads, and improve sanitation. The costs to the well-to-do seemed potentially confiscatory. Well-publicized instances of corruption furthered sentiment against legislative bodies. Reform movements shifted budgetary power increasingly to the executive branch, in the sometimes futile hope that the chief executive would not represent the poor against the rich, would not be corrupt, and would control costs. The executive branch was expected to collect budget requests, analyze them, cut them back, and present a balanced proposal to the legislative body. The legislative body was expected to review the proposal, rejecting it if necessary.

At the national level, Congress gave major budgeting power to the president in 1921. But some budgetary power shifted back to Congress in 1974, when it increased its ability to check the assumptions in the president's budget and come up with its own budget proposals if necessary. The change came about in part as a congressional reaction to a president who intentionally withheld spending that Congress had authorized. Congress increased its power to control such incursions on its prerogatives. A bit of budget power shifted back to the president in 1996, when Congress granted the president increased power to reduce congressionally approved spending.

The line-item veto act passed in 1996 gives the president "enhanced rescission" powers, which enable him to cancel or rescind dollar amounts of discretionary budget authority within an appropriation bill unless Congress votes to disapprove of the president's cancellation. If Congress disapproves, the president can then veto the disapproval bill. A two-thirds majority of Congress would be required to override the president's veto.

Presidents have long wanted the power to veto line items, supposedly to eliminate the "pork" that legislators include in appropriation bills. However, pork is hardly ever isolated in a line of the budget. Many governors have line-item vetoes, but such vetoes seldom make much financial impact on the budget. They do make it easier for the governors who have them to exert policy dominance over their legislatures. The governors are more likely to exert such control when the legislature is of the opposite party (Abney and Lauth, 1985; Gosling, 1986; Reese, 1997).

The line-item veto at the federal level is unlikely to lead to major reductions in spending but it does shift some power from Congress to the president. Senator Robert Byrd (1996), a long-time defender of congressional prerogatives, opposed giving the president such enhanced budgetary powers. He argued, "This so-called line-item veto act should be more appropriately labeled 'The President Always Wins Bill.' From now on, the heavy hand of the President will be used to slap down Congressional opposition wherever it may exist" (p. 2937). Although Byrd may have overstated the case, the question remains: Why did Congress give the president more budgetary power? The measure probably passed because of Congress's recent failure to pass a constitutional amendment to balance the budget despite widely publicized promises to do so, and because of the consequent need for Congress to appear to do something else that would strengthen the mechanism to balance the budget (Joyce and Reischauer, 1997). An increase in partisanship may also have been involved, with Democrats assuming that the measure would strengthen the Democratic president, and Republicans thinking parallel thoughts.

In some state and local governments, the movement to executive dominance over the budget stripped the legislative branch of most of its budgetary power. In recent years, especially at the state level, there have been efforts to restore some balance, giving legislatures some additional role in budgeting. At the local level, several patterns have appeared. In one pattern, the city council hires a manager to run the budget for them, and the council maintains considerable budget authority for itself. In the second pattern, a strong mayor continues to dominate the budget, with relatively limited powers for the council.

In some cities where the mayor dominates the budget, fear that a rival in the council will use budget information against the mayor has encouraged the mayor to keep budget information out of the council's hands. Such a policy may create tension between the executive and legislative branches. For example, in St. Louis, Geraldine Osborn, who was the chair of the ways and means committee of the board of aldermen, complained bitterly that she could get no information about contracts that the mayor claimed saved the city money (interview with author, Jan. 12, 1990). As a result, she held up the budget in an effort to get the information. The mayor in turn successfully took a referendum to the public to prevent the board of aldermen from delaying the budget.

Tension Between the Central Budget Office and Departments and Agencies

The model of executive dominance over the budget assumes that the chief executive, along with his or her budget staff, will solicit requests from the departments and examine them in detail before preparing the executive's budget proposal and handing it over to the legislature to review. Part of the budget officer's role in this model is to control departmental spending. Department heads often come to see the budget office as an opponent interfering with their vital work. From the budget office's perspective, the departments often play games, proposing to cut what cannot be cut and exaggerating needs.

One municipal fire chief summarized the tension in the following terms: "An overstated version would be [that] the departments view the budget office as color-coordinated suits; the budget office would view the departments as not understanding the whole picture. The reality is a lot softer than that. . . . There are days when we fight like cats and dogs. We are fighting cuts" (A. Brunacini, interview with author, Phoenix, Ariz., Dec. 10, 1990). The chief's reference to "suits" reflects the tension between those who wear hard hats and uniforms and do the work of the city and those who dress up, sit in an office, and make rules for those who actually do the work.

The fire chief's perception of the budget office as cutter and naysayer was confirmed by budget directors. One director, during an interview, stamped a scrap of paper with the word *no!* He said, "That is what the budget office is about." The interviewer responded, "It is not exclusively about *noes;* it's also about *yeses.*" "Yes," the director replied, "but it starts with no, to get the discussion going" (A. Sette, interview with author, Rochester, N.Y., Oct. 6, 1989).

Departments' response to this wall of *noes* has often been to strategize around the objection. An observer in Tampa argued that before the city changed its pattern of budgeting, the departments would routinely try to evade budget cuts as if they had no responsibility for budget totals. "The fire chief would close a fire station in a wealthy neighborhood, knowing it would [have to] be restored during the year" (R. Wehling, interview with author, Jan. 1990). In response, the mayor and budget office changed the budgetary process so that department heads had to make their own cuts and could no longer force the budget office to make these decisions for them. Roy Meyers (1994) has demonstrated that federal agencies, too, try to get around *no* through a variety of strategies that are eventually caught and curtailed by budget offices.

Part of the animus of department and program directors against the budget office is the sometimes excessive rule making that budget offices engage in to maintain financial controls. For example, one municipal budget director described one control function, slot control, that is frequently located in budget offices:

> We have a position authorization system. We are in control of the number of positions in the city and what level they are. What each costs. The number of positions is determined in the budget negotiations. We control when they can be filled and how much money can be spent for each new position. If a position is vacant, there are forms to fill out to fill it, it goes through the budget office for approval, and then goes to personnel. We are the beginning of the process [J. Stefan, budget director, interview with author, Tampa, Fla., Jan. 1991].

At the federal level, resentment against the Office of Management and Budget (OMB) became apparent during the National Performance Review (NPR) begun in 1993. During this process, officials from across many agencies met and discussed what they would like to see change about management in the federal government. They complained most bitterly about the General Services Administration, the agency that controlled rental of space and purchasing, and the Office of Personnel Management, the office that controlled testing and hiring and monitored civil service regulations. But agency staff also complained about the OMB because they blamed it for cutting their budget requests. Some agency officials also felt that the OMB apportionment process was heavy-handed.

Tension in Congress Between Legislative Committees and Between Committees and Leadership

Within the executive branch, agencies try to outwit the budget office to get additional resources and the budget office tries to catch the agencies doing it. Within legislative bodies, committees and subcommittees may jockey for increased power and committees may compete with legislative leadership for a role in budget negotiations. Power over budgeting shifts location over time.

For example, in 1974 the Congressional Budget Act created budget committees to draw up overall priorities, estimate revenue totals, and assign targets to other committees for spending and taxation. The new budget committees could have dramatically shifted power away from the appropriations and taxation committees, but in fact they were not set up as strong supercommittees. They were independent of the revenue and appropriations committees and hence were potential rivals, whose power was somewhat curtailed by the competition. As long as there were no major cuts, the budget committees did not exert much control over the other committees. By 1980 there was more emphasis on cutbacks, and the process of reconciling the budget committee's totals with other committees' subtotals gave the budget committees the ability to implement their budget resolutions. (For information on the period up to 1979, see Schick, 1980.)

During the 1980s, pressure to reduce deficits and ongoing disagreements over priorities between Congress and the president resulted in summit negotiations between the executive and legislative branches for multiyear budget targets. (For background on summits in the 1980s, see White and Wildavsky, 1989.) These agreements shifted budget power toward the leadership and away from the committees, including the budget committees. The power of the House Speaker compared to that of the committees was marked during the summit negotiations in 1995, but by the end of 1996 committees had begun to reassert some of their traditional budgetary power.

For example, Representative Bill Archer, chair of the House Ways and Means Committee, had yielded his role in the summit negotiations in 1995 and 1996 to House Speaker Newt Gingrich and Majority Leader Richard Armey. But on

December 27, 1996, he visited President Clinton in search of common ground for resumed negotiations. The visit was interpreted as a clear indication of his intention to play a direct role in the 1997 negotiations. Clint Stretch, director of tax legislative affairs at the accounting firm Deloitte & Touche, argued that the committees had to play a larger role in 1997 because the Republicans had a smaller majority and might need the support of Democrats, a support that could be forged only in committee (Chandler, 1996). (Another example of this conflict is discussed in the accompanying insert.)

Speaker Newt Gingrich Versus the Committees in the House

House Speaker Newt Gingrich centralized budgetary power in his own hands in 1995 using the budget reconciliation process to bypass committees if they were deadlocked or could not come up with proposals that suited him.

The reconciliation process was part of the 1974 Congressional Budget Reform Act but was not used until 1980. Under the 1974 act, the budget committees propose resolutions, which are approved by Congress, that contain spending and revenue targets for committees working on different parts of the budget. The committees are supposed to figure out ways to meet the targets in the budget resolution. The committees' separate proposals are rolled into one inclusive piece of legislation, often called the Omnibus Reconciliation Act.

Over the years, nonrelated legislation has crept into the Omnibus bill, often without adequate or any committee consideration. One reason this occurred was that "as necessary legislation, reconciliation bills were a way to guarantee that authorization legislation opposed by the other chamber would get to conference" (Smith and Deering, 1990, p. 202). In addition, in 1995 Speaker Gingrich, as part of a broader effort to implement a Republican agenda, took legislation away from several authorizing committees and had his own version put into the reconciliation bill. Some of the committee members who found themselves suddenly stripped of any influence were left sputtering with anger.

Congressman Lee Hamilton protested the threat to the power of the committees that design and modify legislation in particular subject areas:

I am here today because I am troubled by the pattern of abuse of the legislative process that has been developing during this Congress. . . . This reconciliation bill enters a new universe in its breadth, the sheer number and complexity of proposals, and the extent to which committees of jurisdiction—and thus, all Members of the minority—were shut out of developing this package. . . .

(1) This process places enormous power in the Leadership, who will consult only with those persons and groups they want to include. The Committee is bypassed, an entire House of the Congress is bypassed. All decisionmaking about the issues occurs behind closed doors in a group formed by the leaders of the majority. Final decisions are made by the Speaker. You have created a largely secret system. This is a system which reduces accountability. It is an entirely closed process. . . . Many members of both parties with significant expertise were simply not welcome to contribute to the process.

(2) This process bypasses and undermines the entire committee system. . . . The Commerce proposal is a case in point. Our Committee had no role in developing that proposal. We held no hearings on this proposal, there was no debate, we had no markup, no amendments were permitted, we did not vote. . . . The Committee is also stripped of its responsibilities when items that it has considered and moved through the House are included in the reconciliation package. Moving the Committee's foreign affairs reorganization bill or the Cuba bill through the reconciliation bill removes the Committee from meaningful participation in a conference. It puts these major foreign policy bills into a conference with a mix of 1000 other domestic items. The substance of these bills will not likely be discussed in a reconciliation conference. . . .

(5) . . . . I believe that the essence of democracy is process, and that the end does not justify the means, that the means is as important as the end. . . . You may get bills out of conference more quickly. But in the end we will not get better laws. And we will erode the foundations of this institution. . . [Hamilton, 1995, pp. E2079–E2080].

Source: Rubin, 1997, pp. 76–77.

Tension Between Community Members or Interest Groups and Professional Staff

Although the chief executive, the budget office, the department heads, and legislators are the key actors in the budgetary process and the ones most likely to compete or argue with one another over money, citizens and interest groups have also been important budget actors from time to time. They have often wanted more influence over budget priorities and allocations, and government officials have had mixed feelings about their participation. There has been tension between technical expertise on the one hand and representativeness and public accountability on the other.

Professionals in agencies often think that the budget should reflect their best technical estimates of needs, demands, and costs, and that opening the budget to citizens and interest groups is likely to cost more and introduce technically inefficient solutions. Budget staff are also likely to see citizen participation as stimulating demands that the government cannot afford to satisfy, resulting in deficit financing, excessive borrowing, or alienated citizens. Asking people what they want and then telling them they cannot have it is likely to rouse intense resentment. Citizens and interest groups may see their exclusion from the budgetary process as an indication that government is out of their control.

At the local level, these tensions often result in pro forma budget hearings, where the citizens are not really listened to or where the decisions have been reached before the hearing. This solution alienates citizens, who either cease to participate or put their efforts into referenda to limit taxation.

MECHANISMS FOR DEALING WITH CONFLICT

Budgeters—technical staff as well as elected and appointed officials—have developed a number of ways to deal with the intrinsically high level of conflict in the budgetary process. Some mechanisms limit the scope of conflict, some obscure the issues over which controversy might occur, and others discourage those who would challenge the status quo. Norms of behavior have evolved to minimize confrontations, and patterns of bargaining have emerged that emphasize consensus. Decision makers may allocate resources across the board, to avoid comparison between programs or interest groups. Resources are distributed so that everyone may get a little and no one feels left out. Administrators may take their programs out of the most intensely competitive part of the budget and put them into parts of the budget where they have fewer or no rivals for funding.

Incrementalism

One set of routines that minimizes conflict has been called incrementalism. In incremental budgeting, a distinction is made between the budgetary base, an amount that probably will not be questioned every year, and the proposed increase, which will be scrutinized. The limited scope of the examination reduces the number of items that potentially compete with one another. A second feature of incrementalism is the widespread use of simple formulas to allocate budget increases. One formula divides new money among departments and programs in the same proportion as their existing share of the budget. A department that received 10 percent of the entire budget would receive 10 percent of the new money. Another formula gives every department the same percentage increase. Such simple rules make comparisons among programs unnecessary and reduce competition.

Nondecision Making

If government does not make decisions or reopen decisions made in the past, it may avoid controversies. One way to deflect potentially contentious decisions is to promote the idea that discussion of the issue is inappropriate (Bachrach and Baratz, 1962, 1963). Another approach is to stop monitoring the severity of policy problems or to define them as not serious. A common variant is denying responsibility for a problem.

The legitimacy of complainants or claimants may be denied. Thus one city council member refused to fund a request from the shelter for abused spouses because, he said, "they are all a bunch of dykes." A mayor refused to listen to a citizen during a hearing because the citizen had been in the city for only three years and the problem being discussed had been going on for twelve years. A city manager and public works department head ignored a citizen's suggestion for a (less expensive) well instead of a water tower because it was a technical matter and the citizen lacked expertise.

Those who favor a particular policy that already exists may strive to keep the issue off the agenda for discussion. Calls for public hearings and examination of a city's economic development policy are met with responses from the policy's supporters, such as "If it ain't broke, and it ain't, don't fix it," and "Any breath of disagreement will scare away business; you can't discuss such issues publicly." Other versions of this argument are that we are doing the best we can (so don't complain) or we have spent a lot of time and work on this (so don't undo it by asking questions). Through such means, elected and appointed officials sometimes discourage discussion of controversial issues.

Decentralization

Another commonly used mechanism for handling conflict is decentralization of budgetary decision making. The more centralized budgeting is, the more different programs have to be in order to compete with one another. If decision making is decentralized, comparisons among items of spending can be made within a program or department, thus limiting the scope of comparisons. Decentralization of budget decisions can also help defuse the tension between the budget office and the program or department heads, because in a decentralized process the budget office does less irritating micromanaging.

Norms

Norms of budgeting have evolved to minimize the open competition between departments. It is generally not acceptable to say "we are better or more deserving than they are." Such statements would invite retaliation. As a result, the public and politicians would look more negatively at all the programs. Department and program heads usually avoid reference to competitors and concentrate instead on advertising their own program's strengths.

Obscuring Interests

Budgeters typically lay out the budget in such a way that it is difficult for one interest to see how it is faring in comparison to other interests. A chamber of commerce, which consists of owners of small businesses in a town, would have a hard time seeing in the budget whether small business owners were getting fewer public dollars than some other group. If individuals and interest groups do not know that they are getting less than others, they are less likely to make demands on the budget in order to catch up with rivals.

One reason that budgets obscure interests may be more historical than intentional. In the teens of this century, reformers advocated departmental budgets broken down by line items. These line items were to be associated with work plans. If a fire department planned to put out fifty fires in a year, it would probably need to pay so many firefighters so much in wages, it would have to maintain and heat so many fire stations, and it would have to feed so many horses to draw the fire trucks. Broken down this way, the costs could be compared with those of other departments and the relationship between work accomplished and spending needed could be established. Although clearly an advance at the time, line-item budgets by department obscured programs in the budget and made it unclear who benefited from public spending programs. Line-item budgeting has persisted in many units of government to the present day.

History is not the whole answer, however. Even modern budgets based on programs rather than on line items may not make it clear who benefits from which expenditure. Budgeters may define programs so that they crosscut several interests without showing how each interest benefits from the program. For example, an economic development program may suggest that the whole community benefits, without spelling out the dollars that go to labor for retraining, without estimating the dollar losses from tax incentives that go to new businesses, or without presenting the capital outlays made to increase profitability for land developers. One reason that programs are defined in this fashion is to help gather the greatest possible support for them. Another motivation is to prevent criticism of spending proposals that seem unfair. But even with the best of intentions, it is difficult for analysts to figure out with any precision who benefits from such programs. For example, how many jobs are created when a business gets a tax break? How many of those jobs can be attributed to the tax break or would have occurred anyway? Answers are elusive.

Regardless of whether budgeters have intentionally obscured interests in the budget, the effect has been to lower the level of conflict among interest groups and between interest groups and the government.

Rabbit Gardens

One way of handling the stress between legislative bodies and executives is for the executive to set aside small amounts of money for the legislature to allocate. Such set-asides are metaphorically similar to creating a vegetable garden for rabbits so that they will leave the main garden alone. Elected officials often feel that they have to bring some projects to their districts in order to be reelected. If chief executives make it easier for the legislators to be reelected, they can defuse some of the legislators' efforts to discredit the executive for political gain. The costs need not be great, the projects may be worthwhile, and the credit sharing drains some of the tension out of a natural antagonism.

Escaping Competition

Especially when fiscal stress intensifies and budgets are tight, the level of competition in some areas of the budget may become intense. Programs that have enough of their own resources or that can raise their own resources may try to get out of the competitive environment and set up on their own with earmarked revenues. If a program is set up as an enterprise fund and its revenues cover its expenditures, it is no longer in competition with other programs. Special-purpose governments and authorities also reduce competition. Typically, special-purpose governments and authorities have only one function, so there cannot be any budgetary tradeoffs between functions.

Escape from the competitive parts of the budget occurs at all levels of government. At the federal level, some programs are taken "off budget," that is, they no longer count toward aggregate totals and they usually escape from across-the-board cuts or other rules applied to "on-budget" programs. Some programs are taken off budget and then later restored to budget status. While the program's supporters want to be off budget, supporters of other programs want the base of cuts to be as broad as possible so that cuts in their programs do not have to be as deep. The decision to go off budget is likely to be contested.

Congressman Charles Stenholm argued strongly against a recent proposal to take the transportation trust funds out of the provisions of the Budget Enforcement Act. He argued that that decision would give transportation programs a priority above all other programs when in fact they should compete with other programs.

> At a time when programs for education, health, senior citizens, youth jobs, scientific research and so many other important programs are being cut or given increases well below inflation, I have a hard time justifying a $40 billion increase straight out of the gate for transportation spending.
>
> Finally, granting special status to the trust funds will undermine the principle of shared discipline which is so critical to building consensus for reaching a balanced budget. Supporters of all other federal programs, understandably, will be far less willing to accept cutbacks in their own programs if transportation, or any other specially anointed program, is exempt from sharing the burden. The credibility of the process will be severely undermined by the contrast of transportation spending receiving a full inflation increase plus as much as $20 billion beyond inflationary increases while other programs [are] losing in actual dollar terms [Stenholm, 1996, p. H3521].

Consensual Bargaining

The fact that budgetary power is widely shared among people who often have different interests means that some kind of bargaining must occur in order to produce a budget. Classical bargaining encourages each party to take an extreme position because the resolution is often to split the difference. Whoever has the most extreme initial position often gains the most. However, taking extreme positions risks failed negotiations. By contrast, bargaining in budgeting encourages moderate stances by ignoring the more extreme ones. The difference may be split between remaining actors or remaining positions. Because budgeting must come up with an agreement, stances that work against that agreement are often unwelcome. That is not to argue that budget negotiators never take extreme positions, only that there is a tendency in budgeting to punish rather than reward extreme positions because of the widely shared desire to complete the bargaining successfully.

For years during the 1980s, after Congress had rejected some of President Reagan's proposals, the president resubmitted the same extreme proposals. Congress treated the requests as "dead on arrival." The president's proposal lost its legitimacy because he proposed what he knew was not acceptable. His proposal was therefore ignored.

In the 1990s, a determined effort to balance the budget and eliminate particular programs resulted in deep cuts for some agencies and programs. Given the traditional roles of authorizing committees as advocates and appropriating committees as budget controllers, one would have expected the authorizing committees to take a more protective role of the programs and the appropriations committees to support cuts actively. In fact, very little of this tension was apparent. A congressional staffer explained why. "Although the appropriations committees are required by budget laws to come in under ceilings and the authorization committees are not so regulated, they [the authorization committees] would look foolish if they did not also adhere to the budget law. They would not only look foolish, but especially because their formal role in budgeting is limited, they would be putting themselves out of the realm of negotiations, outside of the decision making that would continue without them." In other words, taking a position too far outside an emerging area of consensus makes it likely that the committee will be ignored.

Many of the most difficult budgetary problems over the past fifteen years have been addressed in summit negotiations. Summits allow bargaining to go on in private, without the negotiators having to justify intermediate stances or explain compromises. The lack of need to play to a broader audience on a step-by-step basis also works toward taking moderate and realistic stances rather than extreme ones that appeal to particular constituencies. The negotiators can focus on finding common ground and working out a compromise acceptable to both sides that satisfactorily addresses the problem (Gilmour, 1995). The need for politicians to avoid blame, especially when dealing with stressful decisions such as budget cuts, also leads to strong incentives to come up with consensus decisions, thus avoiding extreme positions. In summit bargaining on deficit reduction, "decision makers may find themselves in a situation where they have a common interest in defusing the inevitable blame by arriving at a consensus solution. Thus no one has to stick their neck out: everyone provides political cover for everyone else, making it difficult for a future political opponent to raise the issue. When it works best, this approach may even yield political dividends—for taking the hard, gutsy stand (which everyone else is taking as well)" (Weaver, 1986, p. 389).

FACTORS THAT INCREASE CONFLICT

Even though conflict is routinely damped down in budgeting, a number of factors can exaggerate the level of tension. For some of these factors there are possible solutions, but in many cases these solutions are obscure or politically difficult to implement.

One major factor that increases the level of conflict is reduced resources without a commensurate reduction in the level of needs, demands, or expectations. Tax limitations, indexing, deep recessions, increased tax breaks, and erosion of the economic base can all reduce the level of revenues. If revenue is reduced without decreasing demands, conflict over limited resources is likely to increase. At the national and state levels, recessions reduce revenues while at the same time increasing the need for services, as more people lose their jobs, pay less or no taxes, require unemployment compensation, and increase their need for food stamps. The conflict-reducing strategies for this kind of situation are to borrow or draw down money from rainy-day funds.

Reducing need for public spending as revenues go down is often beyond the ability of government. Wear and tear on roads is not reduced when revenue growth tapers off; the need for drug rehabilitation facilities does not decrease because the money to fund them is not there. The result is likely to be intensified fighting about priorities. But while need may remain high, expectations can be lowered and the level of effective demand can be curtailed. Educating the public about the availability of resources and about what they can expect in the way of services from so many dollars of revenue can help alleviate conflict and moderate demands. Expectations can also be lowered for department heads and program directors. The budget process can curtail departmental demands by issuing caps for budget requests.

Just as a decrease in revenues can exaggerate conflict, so can an increase in demands. The population may age, increasing the number of people entitled to certain benefits. An aging population may need to spend more on medicine and thus drive up the costs of publicly provided medical insurance programs. When the costs of publicly provided health care increase and revenues do not grow proportionally, other programs have to compete for fewer dollars, intensifying the competition in the budget.

The budget process may either encourage or discourage the articulation of demands. At times it has been necessary to increase public participation in budgeting. As the city manager of Phoenix noted, one of the major changes in budgeting over time was the degree of openness of the budget process. When community needs were high and public trust was low, the city opened up the budgetary process and gave the council more input (F. Fairbanks, City Manager, Phoenix, Ariz., interview with author, Dec. 1990). The result was more pressure on the budget.

It is possible to open up the budget process and still keep expectations moderate. Dayton, Ohio, found itself in a financial crisis that required public approval of higher levels of taxation. To help develop public confidence that the city was responsive and well run, the budget office invited the public to participate in priority setting. Community priority boards were established. To handle their concerns that the public lacked sufficient knowledge, city staff educated the community council members about the budget process and revenue limitations. "Some staff people say, 'But we can't trust them.' OK, then train neighborhood leaders. The city selects potential neighborhood leaders and takes them through six months of work programs, and educates them. Many then run for city priority board. Then we do explicit training for the priority board. People gravitate from one level to another. Even if you don't like them, they aren't dummies" (P. Woodie, former director of the Budget Office, Dayton, Ohio, interview with author, Oct. 20, 1989).

In addition, city staff served as staff for the priority boards. Sums of money were set aside for the publicly demanded projects. If two or more groups could agree on priorities, they could get access to an additional pool of resources. Despite the openness of the process and the solicitation of budget requests, the process did not become excessively conflictual. One reason is that the sixty-five neighborhood groups were forced into coalitions in order to be eligible for funding. Another reason is that the priority boards' recommendations were not binding; department heads could turn down a community-recommended project if they had a good reason for doing so. The city council included the priority boards' recommendations, a community public opinion survey, a technical condition statement, and other input in making its recommendations. If at all possible, the community-recommended projects were funded, but everyone's concerns were considered.

If the budgetary process is decentralized to departments or community groups without sufficient a priori constraints on demands, the requests that result may far exceed resources, lead to excessive competition among requests, and create many angry losers. Conversely, centralizing the budget process can also exacerbate conflict. A highly centralized budget process forces trade-offs that would otherwise be made in departments to be made by the central budget office or in the chief executive's office. Rather than comparing a limited number of roughly comparable options, the budget office may be required to compare many incommensurate programs with different funding mechanisms, goals, constituencies, and degrees of effectiveness. Departments may push all their options forward, rather than winnowing them first, thus creating many more competing options from which to choose. Responses to this surfeit of competition include requiring the departments to winnow first and avoiding real choices between options by funding across the board at lower-than-requested levels.

Budget actors are likely to become more combative if the chief executive is of one political party and the legislative majority is of the other party. Political partisanship encourages thwarting of each other's proposals, credit taking and blame awarding, extreme public positions, and a general reluctance to compromise. In the 1995 negotiations between the Democratic president and the Republican Congress to agree on a plan to balance the budget by 2002, the two sides were reportedly close on the dollar amounts, but the negotiations foundered, possibly because the Republicans in Congress feared that the Democratic president would get all the credit for achieving a deal. Also, as noted earlier, chief executives at the state level are more likely to use a line-item veto to overrule the priorities of the legislators if the legislative majority is of the opposite party.

At the local level, an elected official's political party may be less obvious— many elections are formally nonpartisan, though the candidates may represent a point of view or political platform. In nonpartisan situations, the tensions between the legislative and executive branches may rise and fall depending on whether there is a viable candidate for mayor in the council. The potential rival may try to use budget information to attack the mayor. Mayors may respond by withholding potentially damaging budget information from the council.

A perception of unfairness can make budgeting more contentious. Tax increases that unduly burden one group are likely to generate controversy. Services that are perceived as disproportionately aimed at a particular group, such as subsidies for wealthy real estate developers or housing for one racial group, may provoke public outcry.

As suggested earlier, if the budget format makes it possible to compare winners and losers, the losers are likely to protest. Some budgets list goals, such as redeveloping the downtown area, revitalizing inner-city neighborhoods, housing the homeless, or holding the line on property taxes. If these goals are linked to programmatic spending in a clear way, it may be possible for the reader of the budget to figure out which interest groups have received what dollar amounts. To tone down the level of conflict, the goals can be phrased in such a way as to crosscut social cleavages. Thus, better housing for all may be a better goal for conflict reduction than more housing for the poor or minorities; job growth may be a better goal than renewing the downtown or revitalizing neighborhoods.

Finally, budgeting conflicts are made worse by the occurrence of huge, messy problems involving multiple, conflicting interests, such as the rapidly growing costs of health care or dying inner cities. For messy problems, the typical solution in the past has been either to ignore them, to define them as private rather than public problems, or to approach them incrementally, a small piece at a time. It is not clear that such problems can be solved through these low conflict options.

MANAGING FOR HEALTHY LEVELS OF CONFLICT

Many sources of conflict in the budget are not controllable. It is not possible to pick a level of conflict and achieve that level all the time. Nevertheless, the level of conflict in budgeting can often be increased or decreased. In many cases, the level of conflict is held down so far that real needs and priorities cannot be expressed. Fear of uncontrolled conflict and fear that newcomers will undo old deals often result in suppression and evasion of conflict, rather than its articulation and resolution. Suppression or evasion of conflict sometimes prevents government from addressing important public problems. Also, conflict avoidance techniques sometimes alienate citizens and reduce the legitimacy of government.

At the local level, governments often hold hearings on the budget after allocation decisions have been made. This practice reduces conflict because it does not allow citizens to express priorities that may differ from those of the staff and elected officials. But it also breeds cynicism and anger in citizens who feel manipulated. When public officials humiliate citizens or ignore their questions in an effort to keep controversial issues off the agenda, citizens may become infuriated (Lo, 1990). Fear of uncontrolled conflict also contributes to a policy of not sharing budgetary information, lest it be used against the officials who circulated it. Lack of budgetary information allows citizens to build up false beliefs about the inefficiency and waste in government. The goals ought to be widespread sharing of budgetary information, a budgetary process that encourages the articulation of interests, and management that handles potential conflicts constructively.

Public officials should seek citizens' opinions on what government should be doing. Some governments do not do this for fear that the public will make too many demands, or demands that are too expensive. But inappropriate requests can be minimized by an education process that outlines history, legal constraints, and revenue estimates in a convincing way. If citizens demand too many projects, one solution is to sequence them over a period of years. Not all demands can be met in the short run, but many demands are realistic, necessary, and appropriate and can be satisfied in the long run. If citizens were to articulate demands and governments were to satisfy them, citizens would likely feel that they control government far more than they do now.

Sometimes the sequencing of projects over time becomes symbolic, as when a city's capital budget lists the same project from year to year and never funds it. Aldermen put projects in the budget that will be located in their districts and then take some credit for getting the items in the budget, even if the projects are not funded. This practice can breed cynicism to the extent that it is understood; but it is not completely sleight of hand, because the projects will be funded if money becomes available, cut if there are insufficient funds, and put forward to another year for another chance at funding (Adams, 1988).

Even with appropriate sequencing of projects, as public budgets continue to tighten, the need for trade-offs increases. These trade-offs mean that one department or program is likely to gain resources at the expense of others, thus intensifying normal competition. If budgeters have not devised and publicized a credible set of criteria for cuts, departments may consider efforts to cut their proposals to be politically based. Consequently, they enter the fray armed with as much public and interest group support as they can muster to defend their budget. The result is a politicized conflict that may be difficult to resolve. Moreover, those who win this kind of contest are less likely to be efficient and effective managers and more likely to be managers who can quickly mobilize a set of supporters. It is usually better to create and gain support for a credible set of criteria for cutback. Such criteria will not eliminate the tendency to bring in constituents, but they may make constituent support one factor among many.

Sometimes what is needed is not a whole new set of criteria but a reconsideration or modification of the criteria that were used for the initial allocation. Any scarce resource can be budgeted, which is to say allocated in different ways among those who demand the resource. Doctors could allocate livers to transplant patients based on which patients are closest to death. Changing the criterion for allocation to give priority to those most likely to survive many years in good health would certainly hurt some potential recipients, possibly killing them; but the apparent logic of the latter criterion could mute the level of criticism. The same is true in budgeting dollars. The requirement is to come up with clear and reasonable criteria for allocations and publicize them widely.

A certain amount of open competition between programs based on such criteria is healthy. Administrators need to consider which programs suit the times, which ones are more urgent, which ones are more popular, which ones are more cost-effective. Issues, even difficult ones, can be decided in public settings as long as the number of issues presented at one time is not too large and enough information is circulated to allow informed choices. Although considering a lot of issues at one time is confusing, it can be advantageous to have several issues on the table at once, so that a loss in one area is balanced by a win elsewhere with respect to the same interest or clientele groups.

When difficult issues are addressed in public, it can also be helpful to structure the deliberation by creating groups representing the different interests and requiring them to work out a solution that at least minimally satisfies all of them. This structure reorients the energy that was going into maintaining the status quo into forging unexpected coalitions and working out solutions. Interest groups may be forced to listen to and understand the requirements of other interest groups for the first time. The normal pattern is for interest groups to act in isolation or with other similar groups. They seldom view themselves as part of a system or visualize the impact of their choices on others. As a result, their demands may become extreme, making resolution more difficult, unless some structure is imposed on their participation.

Setting up separate temporary organizations to deal with controversial budget matters has the additional advantage of taking the blame away from politicians. Thus a special base-closing commission determined which military bases would be closed, insulating legislators from harming their own districts or the districts of their allies.

If policymakers do not set up separate structures to make cuts and take the heat off politicians, they may seek other ways of avoiding blame. They may, for example, obscure the impact of cuts on programs. Decision makers sometimes fear that making clearer how a program has been hurt will activate supporters, creating sharp and open conflicts between supporters and detractors. The downside of obscuring the impact of cuts is that program managers may be unable to convince legislators that programs cannot absorb more cuts and still keep going at a satisfactory level. The temptation on the part of the elected officials to just keep cutting is enormous, because there seem to be no political costs.

There are budgetary paths around the problem of continuous erosion of programs. One is a contract of sorts for the level of services to be provided for a given level of program funding. A program manager's budget proposal says that for this much money the agency can provide this much service of such and such a quality, and for that much money it can provide that much additional service and that much additional quality. The chief executive and the legislature decide on the level they wish and fund that level. This kind of budget proposal makes the impact of cuts on programs very clear. Cuts made in this fashion still risk mobilizing program supporters to reverse the decisions, but they also create pressure to examine the impacts of cuts in greater detail and come up with strategies that could moderate the effects on clients or beneficiaries. Could clients of this program realistically be served by other programs instead? Is there another way of delivering these services that is more cost-effective? Can demand be moderated by the addition of fees or cost-sharing arrangements? If decision makers can anticipate that groups of beneficiaries will be hurt and hence may oppose a decision, they may be able to diminish the effects and calm the opposition.

CONCLUSION

Budgeting is intrinsically conflictual. As a result, budgetary actors have developed a number of mechanisms that routinely reduce the level of conflict. However, the level of conflict in the budgetary process can be jerked upward by a variety of circumstances, including fiscal stress and cutbacks, changes in budget processes that encourage new demands, and divided government or electoral rivals.

Fear of excessive levels of conflict and unwillingness to reopen issues that have been settled in ways that benefit one side to a dispute have often resulted in the suppression of conflict rather than its articulation and resolution. Keeping the level of conflict too low not only threatens democratic participation and the operation of democratic institutions, it also feeds citizen alienation and anger at government. More open sharing of information and opinions with greater attention to managing the resulting conflict is usually a better option than conflict suppression in a democratic society. Not all budget-related conflicts can be managed, but some can. With more open information and more visible conflict, budgeting is likely to be much more interesting to the public and they are more likely to participate in priority setting and performance evaluation.

The tools for managing conflict include moderating demands through fees and cost sharing; setting limits for budget requests; educating new participants so they are familiar with legal, financial, and technical constraints; and negotiating agreement on the criteria used for allocation. Other major ways of handling conflict involve creating special purpose structures to force those with opposing interests to discuss the problem and come up with mutually satisfactory proposals and to buffer elected officials from the heat of their decisions.

As budgeters gain confidence in their ability to keep conflicts within acceptable limits, they should become more comfortable in sharing information and soliciting citizen opinions. Problems are more likely to be articulated and solved, and citizens are more likely to feel that they control government and that it is working well.

References

Abney, G., and Lauth, T. P. "The Line-Item Veto in the States: An Instrument for Fiscal Restraint or an Instrument for Partisanship?" *Public Administration Review,* 1985, *45*(3), 372–377.

Adams, C. T. *The Politics of Capital Investment: The Case of Philadelphia.* Albany: State University of New York Press, 1988.

Bachrach, P., and Baratz, M. S. "Two Faces of Power." *American Political Science Review,* 1962, *56*(4), 947–952.

Bachrach, P., and Baratz, M. S. "Decisions and Non-Decisions: An Analytical Framework." *American Political Science Review,* 1963, *57*(3), 632–642.

Byrd, R. C. "Line-Item Veto." *Congressional Record,* Mar. 27, 1996, p. 2937.

Chandler, C. "Archer Meets Clinton, Says 'Common Ground' Sought on Budget." *Washington Post,* Dec. 29, 1996.

Gilmour, J. *Strategic Disagreement: Stalemate in American Politics.* Pittsburgh: University of Pittsburgh Press, 1995.

Gosling, J. J. "Wisconsin Item Veto Lessons." *Public Administration Review,* 1986, *46*(4), 292–300.

Hamilton, L. *Congressional Record,* Oct. 31, 1995, pp. E2079–E2080.

Joyce, P. G., and Reischauer, R. D. "The Federal Line-Item Veto: What Is It and What Will It Do?" *Public Administration Review,* 1997, *57*(2), 95–104.

Lo, C.Y.H. *Small Property Versus Big Government: Social Origins of the Property Tax Revolt.* Berkeley: University of California Press, 1990.

Meyers, R. T. *Strategic Budgeting.* Ann Arbor: University of Michigan Press, 1994.

Reese, C. "The Line-Item Veto in Practice in Ten Southern States." *Public Administration Review,* 1997, *57*(6), 510–516.

Rubin, I. S. "Budgeting for Our Times: Target-Based Budgeting." *Public Budgeting and Finance,* 1991, *11*(3), 5–14.

Rubin, I. S. *The Politics of Public Budgeting: Getting and Spending, Borrowing and Balancing.* (3rd ed.) Chatham, N.J.: Chatham House, 1997.

Schick, A. *Congress and Money.* Washington, D.C.: Urban Institute, 1980.

Smith, S., and Deering, C. J. *Committees in Congress.* (2nd ed.) Washington, D.C.: Congressional Quarterly Press, 1990.

Stenholm, C. *Congressional Record,* Apr. 17, 1996, p. H3521.

Wallin, B. "The Need for a Privatization Process: Lessons from Development and Implementation." *Public Administration Review,* 1997, *57*(1), 11–20.

Weaver, R. K. "The Politics of Blame Avoidance." *Journal of Public Policy,* 1986, *6*(4), 371–398.

White, J., and Wildavsky, A. *The Deficit and the Public Interest: The Search for Responsible Budgeting in the 1980s.* Berkeley: University of California Press, 1989.

CHAPTER THREE

Financial Management Reform in the Federal Government

L. R. Jones
Jerry McCaffery

Sound financial management and financial systems are critical to the successful performance of government. These systems include the following functions or subsystems: taxation, accounting, budget formulation, resource-allocation decision making, apportionment, allotment, obligation and execution of budgeted funds, cash management and investment, borrowing and debt management, fund management, auditing, and reporting on financial status and performance. Financial management systems support other important functions of government, such as long-range resource planning, human resource management, contracting, purchasing of capital assets, property management, inventory control and management, risk management, policy and program analysis, and evaluation. Financial systems are crucial to establishing and maintaining management control processes in both the public and private sectors.

Financial management systems allow a jurisdiction to carry out its programmatic missions. Accounting, budgeting, and auditing systems are maintained so that the activities of the jurisdiction are performed in a manner intended to avoid or to detect and correct fraud, waste, and misuse of funds. Financial management also entails management of information systems that support these efforts. Accounting information systems must be capable of producing financial reports that relate how revenues are collected, budgeted, expended, and invested; and of providing beginning and end-of-period account and fund balances. Financial statements are required to conform to generally accepted accounting and reporting standards and must stand the test of both internal and external audits. Financial reporting may attempt to relate resources to the performance and results of government actions, and to describe the extent of outcome achievement. Financial reporting is intended to be understandable to elected and appointed officials, government managers and the public.

This chapter provides a brief historical review of government financial management reform initiatives, and it reports on more recent and systematic efforts to improve federal financial management. It concludes with an analysis of selected impediments to effective reform. Despite the importance of financial management and decades of improvement at all levels of government, financial management reform often appears to be reactive, of low visibility, episodic, and dominated by ad hoc efforts to correct and punish instances of fiscal impropriety of one sort or another. Recent financial management reform initiatives, however, seem to be better conceived and organized, and more clearly understood and sponsored by elected officials (Jones, 1993; Jones and McCaffery, 1992a, 1992b, 1993, 1997).

In 1990, Congress passed the Chief Financial Officers (CFO) Act to improve federal financial management. Subsequently, Congress enacted the Government Performance and Results Act (GPRA, 1993) and the Government Management Reform Act (GMRA, 1994) to extend the mandate for financial management reform in the federal government and accelerate its implementation. These three pieces of legislation, together with the Federal Managers' Financial Integrity Act (FMFIA) of 1982 and the Inspector General Act of 1978, have established a framework for improved accountability and better, more timely provision of information to the president, Congress, and the public. The primary emphasis of the CFO Act is on preparation and audit of federal department and agency financial statements. In contrast, the focus of the GPRA is on strategic planning, customer satisfaction, and performance and outcome measurement. The GPRA has drawn substantial attention, particularly from those who want a more efficient government evaluated on the basis of the outcomes it achieves.

The intent in enacting the CFO Act, the GPRA, and related legislation has been to create a financial management structure and systems to improve financial management practice and to better support federal government resource decision making. These goals are in turn intended to facilitate the evolution of more responsible government and a public better informed about the actions and capacity of government.

REVIEW OF FINANCIAL MANAGEMENT REFORM IN THE FEDERAL GOVERNMENT

The improvement of financial management has been a continuing challenge. In 1802, President Thomas Jefferson lamented to his Secretary of the Treasury, "we might hope to see the finances of the Union as clear and intelligible as a merchant's book, so that every member of Congress and every man of any mind in the Union should be able to comprehend them . . . I hope . . . that by our honest and judicious reformations, we may be able . . . to bring things back to that simple and intelligible system on which they should have been organized at first" (Dollenmayer, 1990, p. 2). This was to be a forlorn hope.

The Constitution has little to say about financial management other than that no spending shall take place except as a result of appropriations voted by Congress. Charles McAndrew (1990, pp. 27–40) suggests that the first major effort to institute financial management controls was the passage of the Dockery Act in 1894, which established and strengthened the centralized accounting functions of the government in the Treasury Department by creating a single comptroller of the Treasury. This act simplified the settling of accounts and claims. The Dockery Act also required preparation of an annual combined statement of receipts and expenditures. Prior to this, legislation had been passed to remedy particularly egregious examples of bad financial management. The most important legislation of this type was the Anti-Deficiency Act passed in 1870 in the wake of post–Civil War financial abuses. It prohibited federal officials from making expenditures or incurring obligations in excess of available appropriations or in advance of new appropriations.

Federal financial management and budget reform has, over time, responded to developments at other levels of government and in the private sector. In the last third of the nineteenth century, a major factor in stimulating reform at all levels of government was the widespread occurrence of corruption, fraud, and waste in almost all facets of political life, from elections to hiring practices to rigging bids and contracts, securing kickbacks, and diverting money for personal uses. These widespread abuses, coupled with the need to create a basic infrastructure of services, led to a wave of Progressive Era reforms beginning in the 1890s and continuing through World War I. The reforms of this era affected virtually all aspects of government. Initially, reformers focused on city government (such as New York City) and state governments, but eventually the reform effort reached the federal level.

Under the presidential administrations of Theodore Roosevelt and Woodrow Wilson in particular, a variety of financial, accounting, and budgetary reforms were studied and reported to the presidents and Congress. In the 1880s the federal budget was often in a surplus position, but recessions, spending on the Panama Canal, the Spanish American War, and World War I led to deficits. These events and the rise of large and successful private sector organizations such as railroads led to reform efforts focused on strengthening the role of the president in managing the federal budget, culminating in passage of the Budget and Accounting Act of 1921. This act created a centralized executive budget procedure for the federal government, required the president to prepare and submit a unified executive budget proposal annually to Congress, and established the General Accounting Office (GAO) as an independent agency under a comptroller general to assist Congress in audit and oversight of the executive. The effect of the law was to separate budgeting, accounting, and auditing and to establish an independent auditing office as an arm of Congress. It should be noted that the federal government was late in establishing an executive budget process. Many state and local governments had, by the turn of the century, implemented such systems to balance the budgetary power of the legislative and executive branches of government.

A decade later, under the authority provided by the Economy Act of 1932, President Herbert Hoover issued an executive order prescribing the installation of accounting forms, systems, and procedures, in part as a response to the need for better management and financial control in a federal government reeling from the effects of economic depression. Subsequently, President Franklin D. Roosevelt implemented the Bank Acts of 1933 and a myriad of other actions to stabilize the federal government and the federal banking system. The Reorganization Act of 1939 moved the Bureau of the Budget (BOB) from the Treasury Department to the executive office of the president to assist him in preparation and execution of the budget and "changed it from an agency concerned with management improvement in a narrow sense to an agency concerned with program review" (Burkhead, 1959, p. 292).

The federal government incurred large deficits to finance World War II. The end of the war allowed for defense spending decreases, and pent-up consumer demand and a growing economy led to reestablishment of budget equilibrium after nearly two decades of fiscal stress. The postwar period saw a continuation of efforts to improve the organization of federal financial management. During this period, the Budget and Accounting Procedures Act of 1950 was a milestone in that it placed the responsibility for establishing and maintaining adequate systems of accounting and internal controls on the head of each executive agency (McAndrew, 1990, p. 28). The act also required full disclosure of financial results, adequate information for agency management, improved control and accountability of all funds, more reliable accounting results to serve as the basis for budget preparation and execution, and integration of the agency accounting structures with those maintained by the Treasury.

The Budget and Accounting Procedures Act of 1950 also required that executive agencies conform to accounting principles, standards, and requirements prescribed by the comptroller general. It required that the director of the BOB, the comptroller general, and the secretary of the Treasury continuously improve the federal government's accounting and financial systems. One result of this effort was the creation of the Joint Financial Management Improvement Program (JFMIP), which brought together the director of the BOB (now the Office of Management and Budget, or OMB), the comptroller general of the United States, the secretary of the Treasury, and the director of the Office of Personnel Management to better coordinate federal management functions. The JFMIP is credited with improving federal accounting, auditing, budgeting, financial management training and education, and cash management (Staats, 1981, p. 44).

The Budget and Accounting Procedures Act was amended in 1956 following the recommendations of the Second Hoover Commission and is perhaps best remembered for calling for cost-based budgeting for the federal government and for reaffirming agency accounting standards and principles developed by the GAO from 1950 to 1952. After 1956 it appears that, on balance, the GAO turned its attention away from helping executive agencies to develop accounting systems to approving systems that agencies had designed. The principle embraced was that, as specified by the 1950 act, agencies should be responsible for designing the systems they needed for their purposes, subject to GAO review. The GAO divided this review process into three areas: approval of principles and standards, approval of system design, and approval of systems in operation (Steinhoff, Skelly, and Narang, 1990, p. 56). Although leaving the responsibility for developing systems in the hands of the agencies conformed to the law, many agencies were not prepared to manage this responsibility. The effect was to leave the door open for proliferation of different accounting systems, principles, and standards while financial operating procedures were allowed to become outdated and inefficient. The GAO spent more time on approving principles and system design and less on reviewing operating systems.

Passage of general revenue sharing in the 1960s to send revenue from the federal to state and local governments brought with it an increased awareness of good financial management through its emphasis on the independent audit. The 1976 amendments to the General Revenue Sharing Act required all recipients of $25,000 or more in annual revenue sharing to have an independent audit of their financial statements not less than every three years. By the early 1970s, however, the creation of more than five hundred federal grant programs engendered as many problems as it attempted to solve. Administrative and reporting requirements were "inconsistent, overlapping, contradictory and very burdensome to the grantees" (McAndrew, 1990, p. 35).

OMB circular A-102, issued in 1971, provided a consistent set of guidelines for grant management and reporting for state and local governments. These guidelines simplified the auditing and reporting burden for state and local governments and also paved the way for passage of the Uniform Single Audit Act of 1984. This act simplified audit requirements, because it enabled a single audit for all funds received rather than requiring audits for each grant. This was a step forward in efficiency. More importantly, it made all state and local governments liable for audit. The act stated that audits were to determine and report "whether the entity has the internal control systems to provide reasonable assurance that it is managing federal financial assistance programs in compliance with applicable laws and regulations" (McAndrew, 1990, p. 36). These requirements were further clarified in OMB circular A–128 to explicitly include internal accounting and "other control systems," meaning administrative controls that had previously been off limits for independent auditors. What this meant was that acceptance of $25,000 or more in federal funds allowed the federal government to pass judgment not only on the proper use of the money but also on the adequacy of all financial management systems in the jurisdiction.

Although this chapter is concerned primarily with financial management rather than budgeting, budgeting is an important component of financial management. Consequently, it must be noted that in 1974 Congress enacted the Budget and Impoundment Control Act, which among other things moved the federal fiscal year three months forward to begin on October 1, created the Congressional Budget Office to assist Congress with budget and economic analysis, reorganized the congressional budget process by adding the budget committees and charging them with responsibility for passage and enforcement of the annual Budget Resolution and reconciliation process, and established the means for congressional review of presidential impoundment (rescission and deferral) of appropriations. Other significant budget legislation not reviewed in this chapter includes the Balanced Budget and Emergency Deficit Control Act of 1985 (the Gramm-Rudman-Hollings Act, or GRH), the GRH Reaffirmation Act of 1987, and the Budget Enforcement Act of 1990.

The passage of the Inspector General Act of 1978, amended in 1988, established offices of inspectors general (IGs) in departments and federal agencies. IGs were chartered to conduct and supervise audits and investigations of executive departments and major independent agencies; to provide a leadership role in promoting economy, efficiency, and effectiveness; and to detect and prevent fraud and abuse in programs and operations. IGs were also given the responsibility of seeing that audit work done by nonfederal auditors (on state and local governments, for example) complied with federal audit standards as specified in OMB circular A-73, "Audit of Federal Operations and Programs." The Inspector General Act is generally considered to have been a landmark piece of financial management legislation. In the first ten years of its existence, the actions of IGs were credited with more than $100 billion in savings and cost-avoidance measures in federal agencies (McAndrew, 1990, p. 30).

Perhaps the most important piece of financial management legislation in the 1980s was the FMFIA, which required each executive agency to make ongoing evaluations and issue reports on the adequacy of their systems of internal accounting and administrative control, and to identify weaknesses that could lead to fraud, waste, and abuse. Annual reports to the president and to Congress were required. Passage of this act was part of the President's Management Improvement Program (Reform 88) effort to modernize federal financial management. The program was launched in September 1982, against a backdrop of reports of wasteful spending, poor management, ineffective programs, and losses involving billions of dollars. When President Reagan took office in 1981, his advisors and OMB officials "discovered" thousands of antiquated, duplicative management systems that could not provide even elementary government-wide management information to the president (Wright, 1989, pp. 136–137). Weaknesses in systems made outright fraud more likely; inadequate, inaccurate, and archaic accounting procedures and systems made it difficult to distinguish inadvertent from deliberate errors.

Reform 88 and congressional efforts in the 1980s led to a number of financial management improvements. The Debt Collection Act of 1982 strengthened the federal government's ability to collect monies owed to it. Better management of federal credit programs became a goal of the OMB in the mid-1980s with OMB circular A-129, "Managing Federal Credit Programs." Since the late 1970s, Congress had taken an active interest in the timeliness of government payments to vendors, leading to passage of the Prompt Payment Act of 1982, which required the federal government to pay bills within thirty days after receiving an invoice or receiving the goods or services, and it prescribed penalties for late payment. In August of 1986, the GAO estimated that agencies paid about 24 percent of their invoices late and about the same amount early (Steinhoff, Skelly, and Narang, 1990, p. 56). A thirty–day bill-paying standard was established along with electronic funds transfer and direct deposit capability. Use of credit cards to pay for services provided to government was initiated. Further, 311 accounts in fifty agencies were converted to a nationwide lockbox system, and electronic collection of funds via the Fedwire Deposit System grew substantially, exceeding $280 billion in 1988 (Wright, 1989, p. 140).

Improved credit practices were also instituted, including use of credit reports to screen federal loan applicants. Federal loan program collection performance was improved through the use of salary and tax refund offsets, private collection firms, and prosecution for delinquent debt by the Justice Department. In 1984, an OMB requirement that each federal agency have a single, primary accounting system addressed the issue of duplicate and redundant systems, and aggressive efforts were made to convince smaller agencies to use systems at larger agencies.

Purchasing procedures have also been improved. Here perhaps the biggest change occurred in the Department of Defense (DOD) in acquisition stream-lining. This change involved introducing competitive bidding, decreasing the use of "military specifications" for products that did not need them (such as for paper clips, as opposed to bombs), and using commercial buying practices rather than cumbersome government contracting practices. This is an ongoing effort. By 1997, acquisition reform in pilot programs in the DOD had yielded savings of up to 50 percent by virtually eliminating military specifications and relying on commercially available products. Estimates were that such practices would save the DOD, and taxpayers, about $10 billion annually by the year 2000. These practices were also good for companies that did business with the federal government. In 1996, McDonnell Douglas said that acquisition reforms had saved the federal government about $40 million and the company a simi-lar amount, thus improving its shareholder value and allowing it to compete more effectively in the marketplace ("DOD Launches," 1997, p. 408).

Although the federal government had been a leader in office automation in the early 1950s, by the 1970s it had fallen far behind much of the private sec-tor. Throughout the 1980s the OMB and the GAO worked to push federal gov-ernment financial management systems back on track. This effort included issuance of a series of OMB circulars and GAO publications. For example, in 1984, OMB circular A-127, on financial management systems, directed agencies to meet two goals: single, integrated accounting systems and a reduction of the number of administrative subsystems performing the same function. The Gen-eral Services Administration introduced an off-the-shelf software schedule to help meet these goals, and in 1986 a government-wide standard general ledger was established (U.S. Office of Management and Budget, 1992, p. 14). None-theless, in his 1988 report on management of the U.S. government, President Reagan criticized the state of federal financial management systems and out-lined a comprehensive plan for modernization and improvement. This initiative called for development of modern, effective accounting systems based on the federal government standard ledger system to provide uniform financial infor-mation and implement more timely, comprehensive financial reporting. By the end of the decade, serious efforts had been made to improve federal financial management systems by law, by OMB circular, and by GAO guidance. A num-ber of high-level, high-visibility efforts pushed the reform agenda, including the Reform 88 initiative, the Presidential Council on Integrity and Efficiency in Gov-ernment (PCIE) and the Presidential Council on Management Improvement (PCMI), the Grace and Packard commission reports, and support from profes-sional groups, including the Association of Governmental Accountants, the American Society for Public Administration, and major accounting firms.

Most of the initiatives just noted were begun in the executive branch after consultation with appropriate committees of Congress, the GAO, and department and agency representatives. Initial policy typically was announced by executive order, OMB circular, or other directive based on presidential authority. Congress followed up on these initiatives with oversight hearings, the most important of which were convened by the House Government Operations Committee and the Senate Governmental Affairs Committee. Meanwhile, federal departments and agencies had an opportunity to experiment with alternative methods of implementation. Congress and the executive branch evaluated these alternatives, often with the aid of the GAO or agency IG audits. A consensus emerged from this process of experimentation in the 1980s that CFO legislation was needed to better coordinate and direct financial management reform. However, the decade of the 1980s ended without agreement between Congress and the executive branch on the specifics of such legislation. Reviewing these reform efforts, McAndrew wrote in 1990 that, "financial management remains a pathetic disaster in most federal departments and agencies" (p. 40). Although audit, IG action, and FMFIA reports found many material weaknesses in systems, departments failed to take corrective action and major scandals continued to shake the faith of the public in the federal government and its handling of money. The title of a 1989 GAO report is indicative of the situation: "Financial Integrity Act: Inadequate Controls Result in Ineffective Federal Programs and Billions in Losses."

Certainly the scope of federal financial management activities was broad enough to give the most determined reformer pause. By 1988, OMB and the Treasury Department had annual oversight responsibility for spending equal to one-fourth of the gross national product. They managed a $2 trillion cash flow, $900 million in annual contract payments, payroll and benefit systems for five million civilian and military personnel, and a budget with 1,962 separate accounts (Wright, 1989, p. 150). It is against this background that the CFO Act was drafted, debated, and passed.

CONGRESSIONAL ACTION LEADING TO PASSAGE OF THE CFO ACT OF 1990

Testimony given before the Committee on Government Operations in 1988 focused on three problem areas for financial management reform legislation: organizational fragmentation and a focus on short-term criteria, inadequate accounting systems and internal controls, and the absence of audited financial statements.

Focus and Fragmentation

The weight of the testimony suggested that decision makers at all levels of the federal government were not getting the financial information they needed to make policy and management decisions with sufficient knowledge of the ultimate financial impact of those decisions. Too many important decisions were made based on rudimentary cash flow projection and "checkbook balancing," with insufficient consideration given to the qualitative nature of expenditures and the future costs and liabilities (DioGuardi, 1989, p. 38).

Congressional testimony indicated that the financial decision-making process was inhibited because financial management functions were split within the executive branch between OMB, the Treasury, and the General Services Administration. Because these control agencies had overlapping responsibilities for oversight and direction of financial management operations, it had been difficult to sustain reform initiatives, despite repeated efforts by the OMB to assume this responsibility. Congress concluded, as had the executive branch, that a CFO of the United States was needed to provide centralized leadership for federal financial management.

Considerable debate ensued in Congress and within the executive branch over whether to locate the federal government's CFO in the OMB or in the Treasury. The final decision favored the OMB because it was the management and budget power center of the federal government and better situated to establish government-wide policies to achieve financial management reform. The Treasury was seen as best suited to continuing its operational support role for those efforts (U.S. House of Representatives, 1990, p. 16).

Accounting Systems and Internal Controls

By the end of the 1980s it was recognized that much of the federal government's financial systems and operations had become obsolete and did not meet generally accepted accounting standards (Bowsher, 1989, p. 58). Critics charged that the federal government was managing current financial challenges with yesterday's technology and that without modern accounting systems, financial managers could not perform their jobs well. Costs associated with servicing, upgrading, and replacing antiquated systems were estimated in the billions of dollars. Although accounting systems and internal controls had been strengthened somewhat by reform efforts, deficiencies continued to have serious consequences. For example, weaknesses in agency debt collection systems were significant and delinquencies in nontax debt owed to the federal government grew by 167 percent from FY81 through FY87. Moreover, financial audits routinely uncovered weak controls that permitted, for instance, more than $50 million in undetected fraudulent insurance claims at the Federal Crop Insurance Corporation and excessive rate charging by the Rural Telephone Bank. In reports required by FMFIA during this period, seventeen of eighteen agencies disclosed significant weaknesses in financial management and associated areas (Bowsher, 1989, pp. 59–60).

The Committee on Governmental Affairs concluded that the absence of timely, relevant, and comprehensive financial information and persistent internal control weaknesses compounded the difficulty of controlling government operations and costs. One approach presented in hearings suggested that the government adopt the same accounting principles employed by businesses and many governments—generally accepted accounting principles, or GAAP (Mautz, 1991, pp. 3–11). The federal government employed a cash-basis budgeting and accounting system to measure spending. It was argued that instituting GAAP rules would move the process toward capital budgeting and accrual accounting. GAAP had been developed to provide users of financial documents with improved understanding of financial data for reporting and decision making. "Most importantly, GAAP recognizes liabilities as they are incurred and associates the cost of assets with the period during which they are utilized or consumed" (DioGuardi, 1989, p. 45). Under GAAP, assets such as federal buildings or equipment would be recognized as capital items with specific values and rates of depreciation. The advantage advocated in congressional hearings from using GAAP was that decision makers would be given a more complete and accurate picture of government finance than they currently received from a cash-basis snapshot. For example, on a balance sheet using GAAP, the construction of a new building would not appear as a one-time debit with no future benefit, as it does on a cash basis. Instead, the full value of the building over its entire life would be recognized by budget decision makers.

GAAP also would make it more difficult for federal agencies (and Congress for that matter) to manipulate budget accounts by, for example, adding trust fund accounts in surplus into the unified budget to offset deficits in other areas of the budget. Other practices, such as the shifting of paydays from one fiscal year to the next to meet outlay ceilings, would not be necessary under accrual accounting. Proponents of GAAP financial statements argued that such "games" would be unnecessary and implausible because liabilities appear on the balance sheet, regardless of when they must be paid. Critics warned, however, that advocates of improved accounting practices failed to recognize the need to modify private sector procedures to fit the unique needs of government.

Audited Financial Statements

Testimony suggested that a key element of financial management reform would be strengthened and expanded financial reporting through the development of audited annual financial statements. Financial statements that provide a scorecard for an agency and subject them to the rigors of an independent audit would, it was argued, instill discipline in financial systems and strengthen accountability. For example, Comptroller General Charles Bowsher testified that financial statement audits ensure that "accounting transactions, accounting systems, financial statements and financial reporting to Treasury, OMB, the Public, and the Congress are properly linked" (Bowsher, 1989, p. 69).

Witnesses provided examples of the value of audited financial statements. The Social Security Administration published its 1988 annual report, which included audited financial statements that attempted full disclosure of financial information on agency administered programs. These financial statements attested to the financial soundness of the social security system. In another instance, audited financial statements were said to have proven their worth by detecting serious financial problems. For instance, when the GAO audited the Federal Savings and Loan Insurance Corporation using accrual-based accounting, it showed a $13.7 billion deficit, whereas the cash-based audit for the same period had reported a substantial surplus (Craig, 1989, p. 25).

In 1989, President Reagan said that although the federal government had once been a leader, "the government's financial systems and operations have eroded to the point that they do not meet generally accepted standards" (Steinhoff, Skelly, and Narang, 1990, p. 56). GAO and OMB studies of "high risk" programs in 1989 identified as many as seventy-eight different problems that posed potential federal liabilities reaching into the hundreds of billions of dollars (U.S. House of Representatives, 1990, p. 14). Other problems identified by Congress included failure of the Internal Revenue Service (IRS) to collect $63 billion in back taxes, an alleged $30 billion in unnecessary inventories bought by the DOD, and losses at the Federal Housing Administration estimated at over $4 billion. The identification of these problems helped muster support for the passage of the CFO Act; they are the kinds of problems it was designed to help prevent.

THE CFO ACT OF 1990

The CFO Act was intended to knit the budget and accounting functions together and to centralize all financial management functions at the department and agency level with a CFO reporting to the head of each agency or department. The act created a CFO for the federal government as an executive deputy director in the OMB whose task it is to take the lead on the development of system-wide efforts to improve federal financial management. The goal of the CFO Act was to dramatically change the shape of federal financial management, relying, like the Budget and Accounting Act of 1921 before it, on financial management practices prominent and proven in the private sector. Among these practices were the requirement for one CFO responsible for all financial functions to report to the head of the agency; an annual financial statement that is understandable in generally accepted accounting terms, which will bear the weight of an annual audit and IG certification; and a reduction in the number of separate department/agency accounting systems. The act also had mechanisms for continuing modernization of financial systems. It created the Office of Federal Financial Management (OFFM) in the OMB to spearhead implementation. Under the leadership of the controller, the OFFM also has become responsible for implementation of a large part of the GPRA, GMRA, and FMFIA. In accordance with the CFO Act, CFOs were appointed and confirmed by the Senate for twenty-four major departments and agencies. CFOs were also appointed for major agencies within large departments. Deputy CFOs have been appointed as well and a CFO Council has been established to determine objectives and policy and to oversee implementation. Subsequently, the CFO Council has become a major clearinghouse for policy guidance, leadership, and general oversight of the implementation of the CFO Act, primarily due to its membership of CFOs and deputy CFOs from the twenty-four CFO operating agencies, along with senior leadership from OMB and the Treasury.

The major initiative of the CFO Act was preparation of auditable consolidated financial statements for departments, agencies, and the federal government as a whole. The act assigned audit responsibility to the IGs of each department and agency. IGs may perform audits on their own, with GAO assistance and oversight if necessary, or they may contract with outside private sector accounting firms to assist in or conduct the audits. The GAO also has authority to outsource audits when appropriate.

Underlying the CFO Act is the need for a comprehensive set of federal accounting standards and principles. The Federal Accounting Standards Advisory Board (FASAB) was established by a "memorandum of understanding" among the three principal agency heads concerned with overall financial management in the federal government: the secretary of the Treasury, the director of OMB, and the comptroller general. The federal government has never had a body of "generally accepted accounting principles" ("FASAB Standards," 1996, p. 2). Recognizing that such standards were needed, and that compliance must be measured on a regular basis, FASAB was tasked to develop financial and cost-accounting standards. Congressional oversight for implementation of the CFO Act, the GMRA, and the GPRA and related legislation continues to be provided by the two oversight committees that sponsored much of this legislation: the House Government Reform and Oversight Committee and its subcommittee on government management, information, and technology; and the Senate Governmental Affairs Committee. However, substantial responsibility for oversight has been delegated to the GAO.

The FASAB has recommended a framework for federal financial reporting and the basic standards needed to implement it. By June 1995, the FASAB had completed work on the eight basic concept statements, accounting standards, and cost standards. These were approved by the OMB, the Treasury, and the GAO and issued by the OMB. Approval of the revenue accounting standard by the three principals marked the completion of the basic accounting and cost accounting standards called for by the National Performance Review (NPR). As issued by the OMB, these standards become GAAP for executive branch agencies. By issuing the standards, the OMB fulfilled its responsibility to prescribe the form and content of agency financial statements by modifying its existing "Form and Content of Financial Statements" guidance to incorporate the new standards.

Although it took a long time for the FASAB to complete its tasks of developing standards for financial and cost accounting, a number of very contentious issues, including appropriate means for accounting for depreciation of federal assets, had to be resolved. Furthermore, as is always the case with modification of standards, the FASAB had to spend a considerable amount of time putting out draft standards and guidelines for review and comment and responding to comments prior to their promulgation. The GAO played a very strong role in assisting the FASAB, pressing for closure in part as a result of Bowsher's desire to see standards issued prior to the completion of his tenure as comptroller general in September 1996.

Pursuant to the CFO Act, auditable financial statements have been prepared for selected departments and agencies. The Government Management Reform Act of 1994 extended the audit requirement from ten to twenty-four departments and agencies and to all types of accounts; required auditing within five months of the close of the fiscal year to make data more timely for the budgetary process; and directed an audit of the government-wide financial statement for FY97. Departments and the OMB have made substantial efforts to enable preparation of these statements and to improve and consolidate agency accounting systems. Considerable investments of time, money, and energy have been made to reengineer and refine agency accounting procedures and processes. In addition, the OFFM and OMB have expanded the scope of initiatives to improve federal financial management under the authority of the CFO and related legislation.

GOALS OF GPRA LINKED TO THE CFO ACT

The Government Performance and Results Act of 1993 was a product of the NPR directed by Vice President Albert Gore Jr. (Joyce, 1993; U.S. General Accounting Office, 1996b). It called for agency strategic planning, performance measurement, a focus on customer involvement, and the measurement of outcomes of governmental actions. Pilot programs were created and an implementation calendar was set that would lead the federal government toward comprehensive performance measurement and, perhaps, performance budgeting. To begin with, the GPRA expressed congressional will that performance measurement and reporting be introduced throughout the government. The GPRA provided a mechanism for assessing agency mission and program while downsizing and increasing efficiency. The essence of the CFO Act and the GMRA lay in systems that allow for the preparation of auditable financial statements. However, with the passage of the GPRA, the financial management reform mandate has grown to encompass a much more ambitious set of goals.

Preparation and auditing of financial statements generally falls under the scope of responsibility of accountants and auditors. However, reengineering financial systems requires the talent and experience of seasoned financial managers, often assisted by knowledgeable external consultants. Relation of costs to outcome measures in order to influence budgets not only requires the skills and participation of accountants, auditors, and financial managers; it also demands the close attention of policy and budget decision makers. It is perhaps an understatement to observe that the task of improving federal financial management has become much more complicated than proponents of the CFO Act initially envisioned. Fundamentally, the GPRA makes the critical and necessary connection between costs and policy and program; it recognizes the fundamental necessity to make financial data relate to program in a timely and useful manner.

In assessing the potential impact of the CFO Act, the GPRA, and the other laws noted, the intent is that, in the future, budget numbers will accurately relate to audited statements of government assets and liabilities. Better information should indicate to decision makers where to focus additional efforts to improve financial management. Better financial management should also lead to more informed public policymaking and more efficient resource utilization.

IMPEDIMENTS TO CURRENT
FINANCIAL MANAGEMENT REFORM

Why is federal financial management reform so difficult? The sheer size of the federal government is a factor, but that alone is not enough. If it were large but capable of reduction to simple routines, improving financial management would not be so laborious or have taken so long. The same logic would apply if federal financial affairs were a stationary target, which clearly they are not. The challenge of financing federal entitlement programs, including social security, Medicare, and numerous others created over the last forty years, clearly demonstrates the tremendous expansion of federal functions and responsibilities. If federal financial management requirements were the same as those of the private sector, financial management improvement would be much less onerous, at least in concept. However, government is different from the private sector and this has consequences for the way financial concepts and practices are defined and how systems are developed. It is no accident that a large part of reform involves deciding how to define the problem; hence the continuous creation of boards and study committees to develop concepts and coordinate improvement efforts related to interagency financial management. Impediments to reform are numerous. They range from the incentives that elected and career officials have to change financial management systems, to questions of resources, including the size of the job and cost and staffing limitations faced by agencies.

The following discussion is an analysis of selected impediments to reform, concentrating on the CFO Act and the GPRA as the major changes currently under implementation. While this list is not exhaustive, it does suggest that reform is unlikely to be easy and that our expectations should emphasize patience with respect to the amount of time needed to overcome these barriers.

Accounting System Weaknesses

Accurate and reliable accounting systems are critical to successful production of auditable financial statements. It is possible, however, that departments and agencies might not invest sufficient effort to improve accounting systems in order to produce accurate data on which financial statements would be based. This absence of investment is not predicted because departments would not want to make such an investment but because they lack the money.

In the 1990s, departments and agencies have invested to a considerable extent in improving their accounting systems. They also have in some instances provided detailed estimates of the costs of substantial improvement and consolidation. The president and Congress initially made an effort to address these funding demands. For example, the president's budget for 1992 requested $647 million for funding financial system upgrades, and Congress appropriated $628 million (U.S. Office of Management and Budget, 1992, p. 16). Since then, however, significant amounts have not been appropriated specifically for improving accounting systems, with the exception of funding for the IRS and the DOD.

With respect to the annual cost of implementing the CFO Act, the OMB and the CFO Council issued the following statement: "The CFO Act . . . requires . . . an estimate of the cost of implementing this government-wide five-year plan. For fiscal year 1997, the 24 agencies covered by the CFO Act estimated that the cost of maintaining, operating, and improving financial management activities will total approximately $7.15 billion" (U.S. Office of Management and Budget, 1997, p. iii).

Weaknesses in accounting systems still abound, and they are both a problem to be fixed and a barrier to fixing other problems. For example, current statutes dictate that excise taxes be earmarked for certain purposes, but according to the GAO, the IRS accounting system does not have the capability to segregate funds by type. Consequently it is possible that the Superfund Trust Fund and the Highway Trust Fund may be receiving more or less than is due to them. Another example is the inability of the IRS to match social security wage information and actual tax payments. The Social Security Administration receives payments based on wage information reported to the IRS, even if the taxes are ultimately not paid. This results in amounts going to the Social Security Fund from other tax sources, and although the IRS knows there is a discrepancy, it could not identify the amount in 1995 (Bowsher, 1995, p. 5). Other problems have included consistent underestimation of loss reserves in farm loans, in student financial aid, and in housing guarantees; more than $100 million of Medicare receivables under contractor supervision where collectibility was questionable; and liability for known environmental cleanup requirements that could range from $200 billion to $400 billion or more, not counting estimates for items like groundwater pollution where reliable data to solve existing problems do not exist (Bowsher, 1995, p. 10).

Insufficient funding to make improvements to accounting and related systems is a significant problem. In the 1995 *Federal Financial Management Status Report and Five-Year Plan* (U.S. Office of Management and Budget, 1995a), agencies identified 436 financial management systems currently in operation that needed to be replaced or upgraded in the next five years. The report states, however, that "agencies lack the funds to replace or upgrade many systems that need it, and consequently have no plans to improve them. Funding, personnel, and technology constraints make it difficult to implement all of the systems improvements that are needed" (U.S. Office of Management and Budget, 1995a, p. 5).

Improving financial systems, developing financial statements and accounting standards, and now implementing the GPRA are the top three priorities of the Chief Financial Officers Council established by the CFO Act to guide financial management reform. Table 3.1 indicates the magnitude of the accounting system problem. It shows the total number of federal financial management systems, the number of accounting system applications, the percentage of these systems for which major upgrading or replacement is planned, the percentage that comply with the standard general ledger requirements of the CFO Act, and the percentage that use off-the-shelf software. From 1992 to 1996, the total number of accounting systems was reduced by 7.6 percent and the number of applications by 9.6 percent, but the federal government still operates more than eight hundred financial management systems in 1180 financial

Table 3.1. Federal Financial Management Systems and Improvement Plans.

	1992	1993	1996
Total Number of FM Systems	878	816	811
Number of FM Applications	1,306	1,183	1,180
Percentage Planning to Replace or Upgrade	49	55	60
Percentage Complying with Standard Ledger	30	34	45
Percentage Using Off-the-Shelf Software	13	10	11

Note: Percentages calculated from total number of applications.

Source: U.S. Office of Management and Budget, 1995a, pp. 4–5; 1997, pp. 4–6.

management applications. In 1994, five of the twenty-four CFO agencies (DOD, Housing and Urban Development, the Department of Agriculture, the Department of Transportation, and the Treasury) accounted for 67 percent of the federal financial management systems and 53 percent of the applications (U.S. Office of Management and Budget, 1995a, pp. 4–5). One thing that reform has not meant is a quick decrease in the number of financial management systems and applications. Due to the complexity of federal operations, it is difficult to see such a decrease occurring in the near future given present trends.

These data indicate great turbulence in the environment as agencies plan to replace or make major upgrades on more than half of their applications. Moreover, these applications do not seem to lend themselves to off-the-shelf software: in 1996 only 11 percent of the applications used off-the-shelf software packages, and this percentage is only a slight decrease since 1992. Many large private sector firms use off-the-shelf packages and are satisfied with them. Federal government systems appear either to be too dissimilar or to demand too many agency-specific routines to use off-the-shelf software. This cannot help but increase the complexity and cost of reform efforts. The use of a government-wide general ledger standard was established in 1986 and the call for the use of off-the shelf software also dates from this period and OMB circular A-127. Table 3.1 indicates that only about 34 percent of the applications met the standard general ledger requirement in 1994 but this had increased to 45 percent by 1996. This is a substantial increase (33 percent) in an important area in a short period. Nevertheless, with more than 60 percent of the applications planned for replacement or major upgrading, a higher usage of off-the-shelf software would seem an important goal. The advantage of off-the-shelf software is that it is generally cheaper than custom-tailored applications, training costs are generally lower, and transferability is easier and cheaper, including the ability of employees to move from one agency to another, with reduced training needs and costs in the new agency.

These numbers may paint too pessimistic a picture, but it is clear that much work remains to be done, and a significant investment in modernizing systems, upgrading procedures, and training people has to be made. All of this will require additional funding and it is not clear that either the executive or Congress is willing to fund the improvements needed by departments to improve accounting systems in order to meet the requirements of the CFO Act. Further, more investment is needed to capture the types of performance data needed and to match it to costs as requested by the GPRA.

Limitations of Financial Statements

Financial statements for one year may confirm facts already known by department financial managers, but to use financial statement data effectively, trend data from multiple years is needed. Most departments do not possess reliable trend data outside of budgetary accounts. Even in this area, data are weak in many departments and agencies.

Although it is too early to draw a conclusion, financial statements have been prepared and audited for selected agencies. The OMB's 1997 *Federal Financial Management Status Report and Five-Year Plan* (U.S. Office of Management and Budget, 1997, p. 25) indicated steady progress in producing and auditing financial statements. Through fiscal year 1995, 106 entities had been audited and 64 (60 percent) were given a clean opinion, meaning that their statements were presented fairly in accordance with the basis of accounting adopted by the agency. Fifty-four entities (54 percent) were reported by auditors as having no material weakness in internal controls, meaning that the design or operation of one or more of the internal control elements reduced to a relatively low risk any errors or irregularities occurring in amounts material to the financial statement. If any errors or irregularities occurred, they would be detected in a timely manner by employees performing their assigned functions. In contrast, only three entities were audited and only one had a clean opinion in 1990 (U.S. Office of Management and Budget, 1995a, p. 16). From 1996 forward, under the GMRA fewer entities must issue audited, stand-alone financial statements. The number decreased from 106 entities under the CFO Act in 1995 to 43 under the GMRA for 1996 and forward, but the amount of federal assets, liabilities, and operations included in the statements subjected to audit coverage has increased dramatically (U.S. Office of Management and Budget, 1997, p. 25). Obviously these results will increase the aggregation of data and perhaps diminish comprehensibility and utility in evaluation and decision making. How this will work out remains to be seen.

Ability of Congress to Use Financial Statement Data

It may be argued that Congress passed the CFO Act for the "wrong" reason, that is, that the act represents an effort by oversight committees to increase their power to influence executive agency behavior relative to that of appropriation committees. Even if Congress intends to implement the CFO Act for the "right" reason (that is, to stimulate needed financial reform), and even if financial statement data were accurate, Congress appears to be institutionally incapable of making long-range financial decisions based on information in financial statements. The same observation may be made with respect to the use of performance measures and strategic plans mandated by the GPRA. It may be argued that financial statements will not replace the annual budget as the primary methodology for resource decision making in the nation's capital because the budget provides the money that keeps the wheels of politics rolling and financial reports do not provide budget justification. What members of Congress and their staffs care about most in budgeting is winning and losing battles over programs and money to operate them. Further, it may be argued that in many instances Congress appears not to have much interest in costs (Wildavsky, 1988, pp. 25–33, 102).

OMB and OFFM staff are attempting to deal with how to use data in audited financial statements and performance reports once they are available. OMB Director Franklin Raines, Comptroller Edward DeSeve, and other officials have made clear the intention to use department financial and performance data in budget proposal examination and, perhaps, in budget execution control. Although it is still true that neither OMB staff nor congressional oversight staff know yet exactly how they are going to use financial statement and performance data, the OMB is well on its way to integration of data. However, neither the president nor the OMB can force Congress to use data as they wish. Congress will have to be persuaded that it is in its interest to do so before any significant change in congressional practice will occur.

Some observers clearly view use of financial statement data in the appropriations process as critical to the ongoing implementation and utilization of the CFO Act, the GPRA, and the GMRA. For example, William Phillips of the accounting firm Coopers and Lybrand observed that it is important that Congress use financial statements when deliberating budget requests. To do so would require integration of the CFO Act into the budget process, and it would answer the concerns of agency managers that all of the effort spent on developing financial statements was worthwhile. Without this assurance, agencies would not spend the time and effort to improve their financial statements (Phillips, 1995, p. 52). That this is not an idle concern is emphasized by Senator Hank Brown, who suggested that financial statements providing only summary data might not be used by appropriations committees because their subcommittees cannot operate at a summary level. They have to have specific line items and dollar amounts for appropriations bills. Brown (1995, p. 44) added that unless financial statements had this detail, they would not be useful.

Management Capacity Within the Office of Management and Budget

Some question exists as to whether the management component of the OMB has sufficient capacity to fully implement the CFO Act. By making a commitment to use financial and performance report data in budget review, the OMB has implicitly recognized the validity of this criticism. Budget examiners and OMB senior officials will provide the incentive for departments to comply with the CFO Act and the GPRA through budget review. OMB use of financial and performance data is intended to be part of a comprehensive process of review, from policy development through program implementation and evaluation. To serve the president well, these responsibilities should be carried out in an integrated rather than a fragmented manner. In 1996, the GAO report titled *OMB 2000: Changes Resulting from the OMB 2000 Reorganization* analyzed the efforts of the reorganization under former Director Alice Rivlin that were intended to better integrate OMB's budget analysis, management review, and policy roles. The GAO found OMB staff to be giving greater attention to agency management issues, and clear support by top OMB officials for consideration of management issues in the context of budget examination (Stevens, 1996, pp. 4–5).

In 1993, OMB had decreased the size of the OFFM from forty-one to twenty. OFFM personnel have been assigned at least part of the time to the resource management offices (budget analysis offices), where they work with the budget examiners and analysts. Congress was clearly worried by these changes. Senator John Glenn asked Edward DeSeve about the downsizing of his OFFM staff. The senator worried that the OFFM would not be able to do its job. DeSeve replied that historically in the OMB one of the criticisms had been that the management side of the OMB never talked to the budget side. DeSeve suggested that sending the OFFM analysts into the budget divisions meant they would be working closely with budget analysts and this would help both the budget and the management side because the OFFM analysts could help interpret the new audited financial statements and stimulate their use in the budget process. Senator Glenn worried that OFFM analysts would be preempted by the budget divisions and that feedback of data to the OFFM would be impaired. DeSeve responded that he had been able to get timely information, and that the presence of OFFM analysts in budget examination had resulted in a recognition among the budget divisions of a need for better understanding of agency financial management practices (DeSeve, 1995; Glenn, 1995). Although it is too early to tell how this will play out, the budget function in the OMB is paramount and has a history of absorbing or ignoring nonbudgetary reform efforts. As noted, finding the dollars necessary to improve financial systems may be a significant barrier to reform, despite acceptance of the goals of the acts. Moreover, absence of funding could provide excuses for departments that fail to obtain clean opinions (no errors) in audits of their financial statements.

Ability to Implement Performance Measurement

It may be questioned whether performance measurement, as required by the GPRA, may be implemented well or at all by departments and agencies. Performance measurement is expensive to perform properly. If performance measurement were affordable and easy to accomplish, it already would have been, because the federal government has attempted to implement performance budgeting in one form or another since the 1950s, when Maurice Stans was director of the BOB under President Eisenhower. Stans spearheaded efforts to develop performance measures in the federal budget from 1958 to 1960.

Approximately seventy pilot performance measurement projects were submitted by twenty-seven agencies in 1995 in response to an OMB request for proposals to conduct performance measurement experiments under the authority of the GPRA. It is apparent that few agencies wanted to be left out of the performance measurement initiative. Given that the budget is eventually the primary leverage point available to the OMB to enforce the requirements of the CFO Act, the GMRA, and the GPRA, agencies apparently have perceived that they needed to be viewed as willing and eager to play in this new game. The results of these experiments are uncertain. A repackaging of measures already in use is one alternative. Preliminary reports from diverse agencies demonstrate successful implementation of portions of the GPRA mandate. These agencies include the Department of Transportation's Office of Budget and Program Performance, the Defense Logistics Agency, the Office of Strategic Planning in the Treasury, the Office of Policy and Strategic Planning in the National Oceanic and Atmospheric Administration (Department of Commerce), and the Bureau of Reclamation in the Department of the Interior. The GAO issued reports to help agencies implement GPRA that provided instructions on how to define mission and outcomes and develop performance measures (U.S. General Accounting Office, 1996a, pp. 96–118). The experience of these agencies shows that strategic and performance plans that include measurable indicators of performance can be prepared successfully. Moreover, agencies reported that they benefited from the experience—the goal was not mere compliance with GPRA and OMB directives. Strategic and performance planning enabled review and reformulation of agency missions, achieved greater clarity of objectives, and resulted in a better understanding of relationships between mission and outcomes.

The OMB envisions eventual development of definitive performance measures linked to accurate cost accounting, with results issued in what are referred to as accountability reports in conformance with NPR goals. This is a worth-while goal, one shared by many governments worldwide, and real progress has been made in some venues, such as New Zealand. The OMB recognizes that the leap from performance measurement, as required by the GPRA, to performance budgeting, which is not required, is fraught with problems, not the least of which is the need for accurate cost-accounting data. Because the FASAB produced and the OMB issued accounting principles and standards for the federal government in 1996, and because departments and agencies are training employees in compliance with these principles and standards, it will be a while before results of all this activity become apparent.

The risk that the OMB will tilt at windmills in attempting to implement performance measurement under a single template in federal organizations that are tremendously diverse in mission and operation seems to be low. OMB policy guidance appears to circumvent this problem. The OMB and the OFFM want to avoid creating a blizzard of paper containing useless information of the type that helped kill zero-based budgeting, and such a goal is probably attainable. Nevertheless, the utility of performance data will continue to be subject to interpretation. In the end, Congress bears the responsibility for determining whether performance measurement and budgeting pilots reveal sufficient promise to cause wider application across the federal government.

The OMB is attempting to integrate the tasks required by the CFO Act and the GPRA in a manner consistent with the goals of Vice President Gore's NPR. The OMB has asked departments and agencies to prepare financial statements and to develop performance standards and measures that could be reported both in financial statements and in budget proposals submitted to OMB. Spring reviews of strategic and performance plans, including performance measures developed by departments, were conducted by OMB in 1995, 1996, and 1997.

In September 1995, the OMB issued two important documents to guide departmental efforts: a memorandum on strategic planning and a new part two to the budget guidance circular A-11 (U.S. Office of Management and Budget, 1995b, 1995d). In the strategic planning memo, the director stated that the A-11 revision was to be the first step in a larger effort to link various GPRA requirements to the budgetary process. The addendum to A-11 provided instructions for preparation and submission of strategic plans. The OMB intends that performance measures be used in budget review. This supports the OFFM stewardship role to ensure that departments and agencies prepare both auditable financial statements, as stipulated by the CFO Act, and performance measures, as demanded by the GPRA. Budget examiners in the five resource management offices in the OMB are the principal points of contact responsible for analysis of agency budget submissions.

The OMB intends to review agency strategic plans, performance plans, and measures, and to use audited financial statement information to improve the integrity of the budgets they examine. Performance measures are required from agencies for FY99, but they have been included in some budget submissions for FY98. Pursuant to the new part two of A-11, OMB staff have attempted to assist agencies in developing measures and comprehensive plans for improving their financial systems and management practices. Strategic plans under preparation by departments and agencies are intended to indicate what initiatives need to be taken and in what order of priority. Department and agency strategic plans will not be identical in that each organization is laying out its own definitions of mission, performance plans and measures, and priorities.

The strategic plans and the performance measurement initiatives required by the GPRA are scheduled to be implemented in a two-step sequence, and it is the intention of the OMB to integrate the results to the greatest extent possible through what are called accountability reports in conformance with the NPR. Accountability reports are supposed to integrate audit and financial statement data with information contained in strategic and performance plans, including performance measures. The OMB has thus responded ambitiously to the formidable agenda provided by Congress and the vice president and it is up to departments and agencies to produce financial reports, strategic plans and performance standards, and measurement methods that will satisfy the OMB and Congress.

Nonetheless, funding to sustain improvement efforts is still a problem. Agency financial managers and IGs have concluded that downsizing and budget cuts were affecting operations. In 1995, only one-third of financial managers reported that their offices had received additional funding to implement CFO Act requirements (Phillips, 1995, p. 52). William R. Phillips of Coopers and Lybrand suggested that Congress needed to provide resources and protect those implementing the acts from "excessive downsizing": "It is important . . . that Congress protect the offices of the CFO and the offices of the inspector general from excessive downsizing cuts while still holding them accountable for improved financial management and reporting, customer service and cost-effective operations. These improvements are both necessary and important. Investing a few million now to implement the CFO act will yield billions of dollars of savings in the future" (p. 53).

CONCLUSIONS

Financial management reform in the 1990s is not confined to the legislation analyzed previously in this article. For example, in 1996 Congress passed the Federal Financial Management Improvement Act (FFMIA), which mandated that agencies should implement and maintain financial management systems in substantial compliance with standard general ledger and accounting principles and other system requirements. FFMIA also mandated a process by which agency heads, CFOs, IGs, and the OMB work to implement sound financial management systems. The CFO Council and the IGs are presently preparing draft guidance to implement this legislation. In the same year, Congress also passed the Debt Collection Improvement Act, thus creating incentives for the Treasury and other agencies to invest in improved electronic payment and debt-collection systems. This act requires all federal payments to be made by electronic funds transfer by January 1999. In connection with this legislation, the President's Management Council established an Electronic Process Initiatives Committee (EPIC) to integrate electronic business processes in procurement and finance. Additionally, the CFO Council is working with the EPIC on electronic funds transfer, high-volume buying and payment, and intergovernmental transfers (U.S. Office of Management and Budget, 1997, p. vi).

Although the outcomes of passage of the legislation just noted cannot be forecasted, these initiatives complement the other financial management improvement initiatives enacted within the last decade. What may be observed with greater certainty is that the CFO Act, the GPRA, and other legislation have increased attention to how financial and performance statement data may be used in detecting and resolving financial problems. What must be guarded against, however, is promising too much from financial statement data. It is a misrepresentation to declare that as a result of financial statement preparation and performance measurement, "Americans will soon know for the first time whether they are getting what they pay for," as stated in the third report of the NPR (Gore, 1995, p. 5). Financial statements do not provide enough of the right kinds of data to support such conclusions. Even if departments and the OMB are able to integrate financial and performance data in a way that relates to budget accounts, caution must be exercised to avoid sweeping claims of success. The road to federal government financial management and budget reform is littered with similar, politically motivated promises that tend to turn off Washington insiders who have watched as various initiatives have blossomed and withered with the passing of presidential regimes.

Departments are moving forward to complete the financial statements required by the CFO Act and the GMRA so as to eventually produce reports that receive clear audits. And as has been noted, the OMB intends to integrate financial statement data into budget review and accountability reports. Thus the primary goal of the CFO Act appear to be obtainable within a few years as departments refine their accounting and reporting methods. However, the issue of major accounting system improvement remains unresolved.

Although all departments and agencies are responding to the CFO Act, related legislation, and the GPRA with financial statements, strategic and performance plans, and performance measurement, executives and staff wonder about the extent to which Congress and the OMB are willing to provide the resources needed to implement the acts effectively. This is a significant issue given that many agencies are operating under conditions of fiscal stringency due to the budget squeeze on discretionary spending resulting from efforts to reduce the deficit, and an executive and congressional decision in 1994 to further downsize the federal workforce by 272,900 employees by 1999 (Rivlin, 1995, p. 176). This latter issue is particularly important. The size of the personnel reduction was based on the logic that half of the 700,000 federal financial management and related positions estimated to be engaged in "overseeing" work (managers, supervisors, and specialists in personnel, procurement, budget, and audit) could be eliminated if up-to-date information systems were put in place. It was also estimated, however, that 100,000 new positions would need to be created and filled by new people with new skills, or by retrained employees, thus leaving a net reduction of 250,000 equivalent full-time employees. This number was increased as the bill passed through Congress (Fosler, 1995, p. 193).

Departments and agencies face a dilemma in that they are being asked to do more and perform more efficiently while also developing and implementing major financial systems improvements with fewer people and a mismatch of skills. Administrators are placed in the difficult position of having to support rapid and ambitious change while accommodating budget reductions and organization-wide reinvention and reengineering initiatives. Change is taking place fast, but morale has suffered as line managers and employees have been confused by the magnitude of change and the intermingling of various reforms with downsizing initiatives. In some departments, staff are confused about what is expected from them and about which initiatives have highest priority. As Scott Fosler (1995, p. 193) comments, "The problem is that the position reductions have begun, but in very few instances have the new systems been developed or the new employees and skills put into place. Consequently, throughout the government one finds fewer employees attempting to operate cumbersome old systems, while simultaneously designing and implementing new systems, but without the training or access to skills required to do either."

To help remedy this situation, Fosler advocated a larger investment in training, observing that top-rated businesses commonly invest as much as 10 percent of their payroll in training and development, while the federal government, by contrast, spends less than 1 percent of payroll costs for these purposes (Fosler, 1995, p. 193). Many department and agency officials believe they are being asked to do too much too quickly. Congress, the president, the vice president (through the NPR), and the OMB have set out very laudable objectives and ambitious implementation schedules. However, the agencies that have to do the real work to fulfill the promises made to the American public for a more efficient and effective government complain that they are underresourced for this task. Officials lament that neither branch of government and neither political party appears willing to defend them against the onslaught of ambition embodied in the CFO Act, the GPRA, and the other financial management reform legislation enacted since 1982. As a result of passage of the 1997 Balanced Budget Agreement, caps (spending ceilings at current levels adjusted moderately for inflation for the next five years) have been put in place on all discretionary spending. Consequently, if departments and agencies want to find funding for information technology and for training staff to perform the tasks required by the CFO Act and the GPRA, in all likelihood they will have to make trade-offs against programs and support in their existing budgets. Such trade-offs may have to be made with personnel, such as cutting staff to fund acquisition of computers, software, and training.

References

Bowsher, C. A., Comptroller General of the United States. *Statement, Hearings, "Improving Federal Financial Management," House of Representatives, Committee on Government Operations, Subcommittee on Legislation and National Security, Sept. 22, 1988.* Washington, D.C.: Government Printing Office, 1989.

Bowsher, C. A., Comptroller General of the United States. Testimony, Committee on Governmental Affairs of the U.S. Senate, Dec. 14, 1995. *Federal News Service,* Dec. 15, 1995, p. 5.

Brown, H., Senator. Hearing, Committee on Governmental Affairs of the U.S. Senate, Dec. 14, 1995. *Federal News Service,* Dec. 15, 1995, p. 44.

Burkhead, J. *Government Budgeting.* New York: Wiley, 1959.

Craig, L. E., Congressman. *Statement, Hearings, "Improving Federal Financial Management," House of Representatives, Committee on Government Operations, Subcommittee on Legislation and National Security, Sept. 22, 1988.* Washington, D. C.: Government Printing Office, 1989.

DeSeve, E., Comptroller and Deputy Director, Office of Management and Budget. Testimony, Committee on Governmental Affairs of the U.S. Senate, Dec. 14, 1995. *Federal News Service,* Dec. 15, 1995, pp. 46–49.

DioGuardi, A., Congressman. *Statement, Hearings, "Improving Federal Financial Management," House of Representatives, Committee on Government Operations, Subcommittee on Legislation and National Security, Sept. 22, 1988.* Washington, D.C.: Government Printing Office, 1989.

"DOD Launches Acquisition Reform Week, Seeks to Further Cut Costs." *Defense Daily,* Mar. 17, 1997, p. 408.

Dollenmayer, J. "Landmarks in Federal Financial Management." *Government Accountants Journal,* Winter 1990, p. 2.

"FASAB Standards Completed and Signed by Principals." *Joint Financial Management Improvement Program News,* 1996, *8*(2), 2.

Fosler, R. S., President of the National Academy of Public Administration. Statement, Senate Committee on Governmental Affairs, May 17, 1995. *Federal News Service,* May 18, 1995, p. 193.

Glenn, J., Senator. Hearing, Committee on Governmental Affairs of the U.S. Senate, Dec. 14, 1995. *Federal News Service,* Dec. 15, 1995, pp. 46–49.

Gore, A., Jr. *Common Sense Government: Works Better and Costs Less.* Third Report of the National Performance Review. Washington, D.C.: Government Printing Office, 1995.

Jones, L. R. "Counterpoint Essay: Nine Reasons Why the CFO Act May Not Achieve Its Objective." *Public Budgeting and Finance,* 1993, *13*(1), 87–94.

Jones, L. R., and McCaffery, J. L. "Symposium: Federal Financial Management Reform, Part I." *Public Budgeting and Finance,* 1992a, *12*(4), 70–106.

Jones, L. R., and McCaffery, J. L. "Symposium: Federal Financial Management Reform, Part II." *Public Budgeting and Finance,* 1992b, *12*(4), 75–86.

Jones, L. R., and McCaffery, J. L. "A Symposium: Federal Financial Management Reform." *Public Budgeting and Finance,* 1993, *13*(1), 59–94.

Jones, L. R., and McCaffery, J. L. "Implementing the Chief Financial Officers Act and the Government Performance and Results Act in the Federal Government." *Public Budgeting and Finance,* 1997, *17*(1), 35–55.

Joyce, P. G. "Using Performance Measures for Federal Budgeting: Proposals and Prospects." *Public Budgeting and Finance,* 1993, *13*(4), 3–17.

Mautz, R. K. "Generally Accepted Accounting Principles." *Public Budgeting and Finance,* 1991, *11*(4), 3–11.

McAndrew, C. R. "Strengthening Controls for Better Government." *Government Accountants Journal,* Winter 1990, pp. 27–40.

Phillips, W. R. Testimony, Committee on Governmental Affairs of the U.S. Senate, Dec. 14, 1995. *Federal News Service,* Dec. 15, 1995, p. 52.

Rivlin, A. M. Testimony, Senate Committee on Governmental Affairs, May 17, 1995. *Federal News Service,* May 18, 1995, p. 176.

Staats, E. "Financial Management Improvements: An Agenda for Federal Managers." *Public Budgeting and Finance,* 1981, *1*(1), 44.

Steinhoff, J., Skelly, J., and Narang, J. "Modernizing Systems and Practices." *Government Accountants Journal,* Winter 1990, p. 56.

Stevens, L. N., Director, Federal Management and Workforce Issues, U.S. General Accounting Office. Statement, Subcommittee on Government Management, Information and Technology; Committee on Government Reform and Oversight of the House of Representatives, Feb. 7, 1996. *Federal News Service,* Feb. 8, 1996, pp. 3–4.

U.S. General Accounting Office. *Financial Integrity Act: Inadequate Controls Result in Ineffective Federal Programs and Billions in Losses.* Washington, D.C.: Government Printing Office, 1989.

U.S. General Accounting Office. *Executive Guide: Effectively Implementing the Government Performance and Results Act.* Washington, D.C.: Government Printing Office, 1996a.

U.S. General Accounting Office. *Managing for Results: Achieving GPRA's Objectives Requires Strong Congressional Role.* Washington, D.C.: Government Printing Office, 1996b.

U.S. General Accounting Office. *OMB 2000: Changes Resulting from the Reorganization of the Office of Management and Budget.* Washington, D.C.: Government Printing Office, 1996c.

U.S. House of Representatives. *Report, Chief Financial Officer Act of 1990.* Report 101–818, 101st Congress, 2d Sess., pt. 1, 1990.

U.S. Office of Management and Budget. *Federal Financial Management Status Report and Five-Year Plan.* Washington, D.C.: U. S. Office of Management and Budget, 1992.

U.S. Office of Management and Budget. *Federal Financial Management Status Report and Five-Year Plan.* Washington, D.C.: U.S. Office of Management and Budget, 1995a.

U.S. Office of Management and Budget. *Preparation and Submission of Annual Budget Estimates.* OMB Circular A-11, Part 2. Washington, D.C.: U.S. Office of Management and Budget, 1995b.

U.S. Office of Management and Budget. *Primer on Performance Measurement.* Washington, D.C.: U. S. Office of Management and Budget, 1995c.

U.S. Office of Management and Budget. *Strategic Plans, Budget Formulation and Execution.* Memorandum from the Director. Washington, D.C.: U.S. Office of Management and Budget, Sept. 1995d.

U.S. Office of Management and Budget. *Federal Financial Management Status Report and Five-Year Plan.* Washington, D.C.: U.S. Office of Management and Budget, 1997.

Wildavsky, A. *The New Politics of the Budgetary Process.* Glenview, Ill.: Scott, Foresman, 1988.

Wright, J. R., Jr., Deputy Director, Office of Management and Budget. *Statement, Hearings, "Improving Federal Financial Management," House of Representatives, Committee on Government Operations, Subcommittee on Legislation and National Security, Sept. 22, 1988.* Washington, D.C.: Government Printing Office, 1989.

CHAPTER FOUR

Budgetary Management in the United States and in Australia, New Zealand, and the United Kingdom

A. Premchand

A comparative study of budgetary institutions and practices has the potential of, on the one hand, contributing to our understanding of the nexus between economic policies, and on the other hand, supporting organizational agendas. Given the far-reaching consequences that budgets have in the current setting of societies, the need for a comparison of the various budgetary systems may be self-evident. Such a comparative study gains impetus from the ongoing globalization of economies and financial markets. The process of globalization has implications for the management of domestic issues. Two such major issues are the design of governmental budgetary systems and the means by which the dominant issue of management of fiscal deficits is being addressed by governments. Notwithstanding the importance of the subject, attention to comparative budgeting has been sporadic.[1]

Comparative studies encounter two types of issues. One type deals with the nature of changes taking place all the time in countries. Budgetary systems in several European countries have undergone major changes during the last three decades of the twentieth century. More changes are scheduled, reflecting the requirements of the Maastricht Treaty on European integration. Thus, any statements about the systems used in these or other countries may run the risk of

---

Note: The views expressed in this chapter are personal to the author and do not in any way represent those of the International Monetary Fund.

not being accurate in that recent developments may not as yet be fully known to the outside world. Similarly, in the United States much of the recent legislation relating to financial statements of agencies, government performance, and results is likely to yield beneficial effects only in the future. When these legislative provisions are fully implemented, the differences between the United States and the other countries covered in this chapter, which are believed to be at the cutting edge of the budgetary art, could be minimal.

The second issue concerns the choice to be made between theory and practice. It is often argued that without an undercurrent of theory a good deal of descriptive material would be of very little utility. Although this view is being debated at both an emotional and a factual level, the scope of this chapter is somewhat modest. It describes, first, how the numerous developments in the United States in the arena of government budgeting have over the years influenced the systems of other countries. This description is followed by a discussion of the features of reforms in budgeting in three other countries and how they compare with the ongoing efforts in the United States. The concluding sections of the chapter are devoted to a discussion of the difficulties associated with the current efforts at improvement and how some of these difficulties may be exacerbated by the unique constitutional structure of the government of the United States.

The theory implicit in this comparative study has three components. First, the lightning rod of changes in budgetary strategy and the quest for new approaches come more from economic factors and less from organizational philosophies. Second, as the economic context changes frequently due to both domestic and external factors, reforms in budgeting may not be implemented fully or carried forward to their logical conclusions; organizational inertia may also contribute to less-than-full implementation of the reforms and reaping of their benefits. Third, improvements in one country may be quickly replicated elsewhere, particularly when the economic problems encountered tend to have common origins. Such replication may involve extensive indigenization to suit the specific requirements of a country. Diffusion and extensive modification of the innovations may lead to the impression, more so in the context of the common nomenclature of innovations, that differences among countries are not significant. In reality, however, there may be differences at an operational or practical level.

PERVASIVE INFLUENCE OF THE U.S. BUDGETARY SYSTEM

In considering the differences between the U.S. and other systems, it is important to recognize how U.S. institutions, systems, and intellectual debates have had and continue to have a pervasive influence, in one form or another, on the rest of the world. This influence is to be ascribed to five factors. First, there are countries that at some stage in their history were under the administrative management of the United States and therefore came to have institutions and budget systems that are, for all intents and purposes, the same as those prevalent in the United States. These countries include the Philippines and Micronesia. The legislative framework in both of these countries follows that of the United States.

Second, there are countries that received technical assistance from the United States that in turn contributed to the establishment of budgetary systems similar to those in the United States. The organizational underpinning of the budgetary system of Thailand (which was drawn up by a Chicago-based consultancy service) is closely patterned (except in its legislative part) after the then Bureau of the Budget in the United States. Similarly, much of the reform undertaken in Italy in the late 1970s in the area of legislative involvement in budget formulation and implementation is based on the U.S. congressional budget reform of 1974.

Third, the budgetary innovations since the early 1950s—performance budgeting, program budgeting, the planning-programming-budgeting system (PPBS), management by objectives, management by results, zero-based budgeting, and program evaluation—were all tried first in the United States. Many countries in the industrial and developing world followed the budget innovations in the United States and made similar efforts, with vastly differing results. Despite the Cold War, even the Soviet Union followed the PPBS in the United States with considerable interest and adapted it for internal planning in the Ministry of Defense. Neither language nor custom nor the much discussed administrative culture would appear to have been barriers to the spread of these techniques and to their relatively quick acceptance.

Fourth, many countries that have become democracies during recent years have started introducing budgetary institutions and practices based on the U.S. experience. The Budgetary Process Act of the Soviet Union (1990) and several pieces of legislation enacted by the formerly centrally planned economies in Eastern Europe have drawn their inspiration, and in some cases the language of the legislation itself, from the United States. Many countries have simply absorbed the English terms into their respective languages. The Russian word, for example, for *sequestration* is also *sequestration*. Similar absorption has taken place in other countries, too. Some of the Latin American countries that have become democracies in the 1980s have set their sights on the U.S. legislative institutions so that the functioning of their own institutions could be suitably strengthened.

Fifth, in those countries where there has been no explicit adaptation of the U.S. government practices—notably New Zealand and the United Kingdom—academic theories developed in the United States have had substantive influence on the budget innovations introduced in those countries. Public choice theory, principal-agent theory, and transaction cost analysis have, despite the inconsistencies and irreconcilable differences among the groups that promote these theories, had a good deal of impact on those engaged in reform. These theories were instrumental in making these reformers aware of the fundamental limitations that characterized the workings of the government. This awareness in turn enabled them to look for alternatives and to design systems that were suited to their administrative capabilities. It is not farfetched to suggest that in terms of the sheer spread of ideas and generation of debate, the influence of these schools of thought is comparable to that of Marxian ideas, with the difference that the Marxian ideas were adopted by the lumpen proletariat and the working classes, while the ideas of the schools discussed here were accepted by the members of bureaucracy and the ruling elites. Even the so-called new managerialism is drawn from the corporate practices and the precepts frequently advocated by the business schools in the United States.

That the influence of the U.S. systems has been pervasive does not mean, however, that what is practiced in the United States is followed in other countries, particularly those considered in this chapter. The actual situation may be quite to the contrary. To illustrate the differences and to consider the relevance of other experiences, the remainder of this chapter is organized into two parts. The first part deals with recent innovations and the themes that arise at both a conceptual and a practical level in the United States and in Australia, New Zealand, and the United Kingdom. The second part deals with the relevance to the United States of the practices found in these three countries, and how some of the issues experienced in the United States may be addressed.

BUDGETARY PRACTICES IN VARIOUS COUNTRIES

A broad review of the institutional features of budgeting in various countries reveals five types of arrangements that reflect variations on a theme. The first group comprises the United States, Italy, and to a certain extent, the Russian Federation after 1991. The institutional arrangements in these countries reveal the dominant influence of the legislature, which has the power to reject the proposals of the executive and is empowered to craft its own legislation, which is then subjected to presidential approval or veto. Such a prominent role for the legislature often contributes to conflicts and legislative gridlocks between the executive and the legislature. A distinguishing feature of the Russian Federation needs to be noted here: after 1992 there was a mushrooming of extra-budgetary funds, and these revenues in 1992 amounted to 18 percent of the gross domestic product (GDP) (Åslund, 1995, p. 192). The ostensible purpose of these funds was to minimize the role of the legislature and to reduce the fiscal power and flexibility of the Ministry of Finance.

The second group comprises the United Kingdom and the member countries of the British Commonwealth (including Australia, New Zealand, and several developing Asian, African, and Caribbean countries). In these countries, the primary responsibility for the preparation and implementation of the budget is located in the executive, and the role of the legislature is to approve the proposals of government. The legislature has the power to reject the budget or modify any part of it (without increasing expenditures), but such nonapproval is viewed as a vote against the government, obliging it to resign. In general, however, the party whip and associated discipline prevent such a vote.

The third group of countries, comprising France and others, envisages a different role for the legislature in that it is expected to concentrate on new proposals and expenditures while continuing expenditures are approved in a routine way. Similarly, in Japan more attention of the legislature is devoted to new expenditures. A balanced budget was a requirement in Japan up to 1965. The interpretation of this requirement was, however, more pragmatic than legal in that it was a balance of receipts with outlays. For this purpose, the former approach included borrowing proceeds. In France, the legislature cannot increase expenditures or reduce revenues.

The fourth group comprises countries where the medium-term financial plan has a significant role to play in overall budgetary decision making, although the legislative approval is limited to one year. In Germany, the financial plan is more than a baseline projection in that it is a framework within which the subnational governments and federal spending agencies prepare their annual budgets. In Sweden, budget approvals are given for a period of three years and each government agency is subjected to an in-depth review once every three years. In most Nordic countries, investment budgets are approved for the duration of the projects. Similar procedures are found in Japan as well.

The fifth group of countries consists of those where either there is no legislature or, if there is one, it has little power except to debate. In China, for example, the budget is approved by the people's congress. This group is not, however, a deliberative body responsible for legislation. In several countries in the Middle East, budgets are approved through royal decrees and the public has little access to them. Furthermore, several policy directives are issued through decrees. This practice has had a revival in some formerly centrally planned economies. (Åslund, 1995, p. 138, notes that in the Russian Federation, 48,000 instructions were issued in 1993. Some of these obviously were financial regulations.)

UNIQUE FEATURES OF THE U.S. BUDGETARY PROCESS

At a practical level, three features of the U.S. budgetary process are being emulated in varying degrees by other countries. These features are emblematic of the areas in which progress may come in the future in unexpected forms.

To that extent, these features continue to be those associated with the United States.

First, the U.S. budgetary system reflects a close integration of economic concepts and analysis with the budget. Assumptions made on the basis of the expected rate of growth in the economy are of crucial importance, and once they are accepted, the approval of the budget estimates is more or less viewed as a routine exercise. Many industrial countries have made similar efforts, but more remains to be done. The U.S. budget represents more the calculus of economists than of the traditional budgeter. Indeed, the traditional budgeter depicted by Paul Appleby (1957) would now be considered extinct in the United States, having yielded his place to economists.

Second, the amount of documentation provided by the U.S. government as part of its annual budget is enormous, contains a good deal of detail, and sets a standard that others have been endeavoring to reach. The documentation is so elaborate that users often tend to look for the parts that are of direct interest, ignoring the larger elements of the canvas. Although special interests would always clamor for more decision-related information, it should be admitted that documentation in the United States represents the cutting edge of the art of budgeting.

Third, the U.S. budgetary process involves greater participation of citizens than the budgetary processes of other countries, with the exception of Switzerland. Many of the important proposals are frequently debated through specific propositions, referenda, or opinion surveys, and even voted upon by citizens before the proposals reach the congressional stage and set the tone for legislative action. This process of engagement by the knowledgeable citizenry actually reduces the gulf between the people and the government. As further advances are made in electronic communication, and as budgets become available to households through the electronic medium, a stage may very well be reached where the annual rite of approval of the budget could usher in an era of electronic participation by the citizenry. (For an interesting discussion of these possibilities, see Grossman, 1995.) Few countries are equipped to undertake this type of citizen participation.

From a political point of view, the American model is viewed as having strong tendencies toward pork barrel policymaking and the dominance of sectional interests. This view also reflects that the bureaucracy in the United States is less strong than, say, the bureaucracies in France, Germany, or Japan. Foster and Plowden (1996, p. 36) envisage a set of five models in this regard. In addition to the American model, they consider African, Italian, Japanese, and Westminster (United Kingdom) models. According to these authors, in the African model public decisions are for sale. In the Italian model public services are subject to corruption at the point of delivery. In Japan the bureaucracy is strong and is known for its interventionist but impartial framework. Finally, the authors contend that in the Westminster model the power of ministers has tended to increase during recent years, and that in the absence of a written constitution the probability of greater political manipulation of policies and decisions has increased. Any typology of this type is bound to have limitations in view of its dependence on selective traits and its tendency to indulge in exaggerated oversimplification as well as generalization.

CHANGING FISCAL TRENDS AND NEW MANAGEMENT PHILOSOPHY

During recent years, particularly since the seventies, changing fiscal trends have contributed to several innovations in budgetary management in industrial and other countries.

The most significant problem faced by several industrial and developing countries during the previous two decades has been burgeoning fiscal deficits. The growth in the deficits has in turn been due to the growth in public expenditures. Surveys conducted by the Organization for Economic Cooperation and Development (OECD) show that public expenditures in OECD countries claimed 28.5 percent of the GDP in 1960. By 1994, this share reached 41.4 percent. This trend has contributed to changes in fiscal policy, as well as to changes in the philosophy of public sector management. The new philosophy of public management, primarily drawn from the managerial school of thought, principal-agent theories, and transaction costs, envisaged three broad vectors of attack on the public sector. The first attack was aimed at a reorganization or restructuring of the government that had three components: downsizing, creation of small and compact units (agencies) that could be given the primary responsibility for policy implementation, and change in work processes through delayering of hierarchical structures and greater application of information technology.

The second attack was aimed at greater provision of managerial flexibility and a supporting structure of incentives. The greater freedom given to executives was to be tempered by a series of measures that sought to achieve greater accountability, with a view to preventing excessive pursuit of self-interest by managers that might prove to be costly for government. As a part of the accountability framework, a service provision contract and a performance guarantee were to be concluded with managers of the agencies. Together, these elements sought to consolidate the links between budgetary appropriations and outputs on the one hand, and between the buyer and the provider on the other.

The third attack envisaged the development of competition (internal markets within governments) and greater contracting out of services. The expectation was that competition would stir up the agencies from their traditional inertia and show greater enthusiasm in the economical provision and delivery of services. These ingredients have been translated into specific components of budgeting and expenditure management in Australia, New Zealand (the only country that has completely transformed its systems into the new pattern), the United Kingdom, and the United States. The framework of government budgeting emerging from the application of these various elements is depicted in Table 4.1. As a result of these approaches, together with improved buoyancy in the economy, stringent efforts to reduce new expenditure programs, and rigorous pursuit of economies in government transactions, by 1993 New Zealand had won the battle against deficits. The United States has seen, during more recent years, a tapering off in the level of its deficits, and a similar phenomenon is observed in Australia, too.

It is essential here to keep in view the changing composition of public expenditures, because it has a considerable influence on the content and course of government budgeting. A synoptic review shows that current transfers and interest payments have tended to dominate expenditures. For example, interest on public debt, barely 1 percent at the turn of the century in the United States, reached 15 percent of total expenditures by 1994. Social welfare programs, which were nonexistent in the early periods, now constitute the single largest amount of U.S. federal outlays. These outlays, which represent entitlement and associated categories, tend to be inflexible in terms of annual budget making because they are determined by law.

Another important feature deserves to be noted. Much of this expenditure is incurred by agencies or through third-party transactions, and very little may be directly incurred by the central or federal government departments. In New Zealand, for example, by 1995–96, the appropriations for nondepartmental bodies represented 84 percent of the budget. In the United States, the expenditure on the services delivered directly by the federal government in 1994 was only about 4 percent of the total. The other appropriations are accounted for by payments to individuals (58 percent), interest on the national debt (15 percent), contracts with private companies for goods and services (13 percent), armed forces (5 percent), and grants to state and local governments (5 percent). (See Kettl, Ingraham, Sanders, and Horner, 1996, for details on the United States; and Controller and Auditor General of New Zealand, 1996, for details on New Zealand.) It may be added that these data cannot always be compiled from the budgetary accounts in view of the somewhat limited nature of the classification used in the budgets, and therefore in the accounts. The changing expenditure portfolio illustrates that central and federal governments have become disbursing centers of money while actual delivery of the services may be managed by agencies in the government and those in the nonprofit, voluntary, or cooperative sectors.

Table 4.1. Emerging Framework of Government Budgeting.

Task	Focus	Instruments	Role of Ministry of Finance	Role of Agencies
Resource allocation	Specification of responsibility and provision of resources	Macroeconomic planning	These tasks are undertaken by the Ministry of Finance or a similar agency, such as the Office of Management and Budget.	
		Specification of budget ceilings		
		Corporate plans specifying goals	Overall coordination provided by the Ministry of Finance or OMB	Tasks undertaken by the agencies
Resource utilization	Achievement of stated results	Performance indicators		
		Buyer/provider contract	Guidance provided by the Ministry of Finance or OMB	Arranged by the agencies
		Service guarantee		These are ensured by the agencies
		Provision of incentives		These are designed to suit the individual requirements of each agency
		Regular monitoring		
Resource use accounting	Accountability	Accrual-based accounting and financial reporting systems	Overall guidance provided by the Ministry of Finance or OMB	Utilized for internal control by the agencies

RECENT BUDGET INNOVATIONS

The experience of Australia, New Zealand, the United Kingdom, and the United States in budget innovations is explained in terms of the various structural components shown in Table 4.2. The focus of the reform and the main ingredients of the reform packages may be briefly recapitulated before considering the relevance of the experiences of Australia, New Zealand, and the United Kingdom for the United States.

In Australia, the main program relevant to the purpose is the Financial Management Improvement Program (FMIP), which has been the guiding light since 1984 (Keating and Dixon, 1989; Keating and Rosalky, 1990; and McDonald, 1990). Its main components are corporate management, program management, organization design, improved management information systems, and program evaluation. The emphasis is on both improved resource allocation and effective resource utilization. In terms of resource allocation, and in conformity with the traditional and constitutional responsibility of a cabinet-type government, the departments are asked to concentrate on their priorities within each portfolio (a variant of the envelope budgeting that was prevalent earlier in Canada) and to review the issues across the portfolio. The departments are expected to formulate corporate plans and to devolve responsibility to the agencies. The Program Management and Budgetary System, an integral part of FMIP, concentrated on the development of program goals as well as performance measures and standards (the latter always lagging behind the former) and the refinement of information and evaluation systems.

The improvements envisaged in New Zealand (see Boston, Martin, Pallot, and Walsh, 1991) share many of the features just described in that there is greater emphasis on, for example, accountability for results, measurement of performance, increased delegation of financial powers to the spending agencies, and improved information and cost measurements. These elements continue to be common to most of the budget innovations introduced since the early 1950s. In three respects, however, the reforms introduced in New Zealand have extended the frontiers of budgeting and management in government. First, a new relationship between the owner or buyer on the one hand and the provider of services on the other was introduced. The minister of each department represented the owner or the buyer of outputs or services to be provided by a department. The budget became the instrument through which this financial contractual relationship came to be solidified. In theory this arrangement, while providing a much needed choice for the buyer, also enhanced accountability to the legislature.

Second, supporting this arrangement, budget classification was extensively revised and is being revised every year to shift the focus from inputs to outputs.

Table 4.2. Structural Components of Budgetary Systems in Australia, New Zealand, the United Kingdom, and the United States.

Category	Australia	New Zealand	United Kingdom	United States
I. Budgetary Policy Objectives	The framework for the conduct of fiscal policy is specified in the legislation (yet to be enacted) relating to the charter of Budget Honesty. The legislation requires that the strategy be based on sound fiscal management. As an integral part of this effort, an intergenerational report permitting an assessment of the sustainability of current policies is to be published at least once every five years. The legislation is a statement of an intent and creates no rights or duties that are enforceable through judicial proceedings.	The Fiscal Responsibility Act of 1994 requires the government to specify the short- and long-term fiscal objectives in conformity with the following principles: achievement of prudent levels of government debt through operational budget surpluses; maintenance of prudent debt levels; maintenance of adequate levels of government net worth; prudent management of fiscal risks, including pension liabilities; and pursuit of expenditure policies consistent with stable and predictable tax rates.	Policy is stated in the annual budget speech. During recent years, the slowdown of growth has complicated the process of fiscal consolidation. The ratio of public sector borrowing requirements to the GDP has been higher than estimates in 1995–96. The intent is to bring down the level of this borrowing and stabilize it.	Budgetary strategy is governed by the Budget Enforcement Act of 1990 (BEA), now extended through 1998. The present strategy is to achieve a balanced budget by fiscal year 2002. The proposals of the government are subject to approval by the congress. The BEA has a variety of provisions aimed at maintaining the deficit at the projected levels. The general government deficit has declined since 1992.

Table 4.2. Structural Components of Budgetary Systems in Australia, New Zealand, the United Kingdom, and the United States. (*continued*)

Category	Australia	New Zealand	United Kingdom	United States
	Policies are stated in the annual budget. In general, these aim at enhancing the competitive position of the country and generating stronger economic growth. The aims include a trilogy approach of not allowing the revenues, outlays, and debt to grow as percentages of GDP. During the early 1990s there was an increase in the public debt that reflected the recession. Government is committed to fiscal consolidation and maintenance of a low inflation rate.			

Table 4.2. Structural Components of Budgetary Systems in Australia, New Zealand, the United Kingdom, and the United States. (*continued*)

Category	Australia	New Zealand	United Kingdom	United States
II. Features of the Budgetary System				
A. Baseline Projections	Undertaken. Rolling expenditure planning has an important role in the measurement of out-year implications for current-year decisions.	Undertaken. They have a role in the determination of the fiscal outlook for the next year, which in turn determines the budget allocations for the next year.	This exercise, which has a history of three and a half decades, has an important role in the formulation of the annual budget. The average of this exercise has been changing over the years.	Baseline projections are provided for in the budget presented by the administration. The Congressional Budget Office also prepares its own baseline projections. The actual use of these projections in budgetary decision making is less precise than in other countries. In essence, they provide background information.
B. Budget Structure	In principle, the budgets hereafter will also be presented in accrual terms. As such, they will be operational and investment budgets.	Following the accrual system, the budget is divided into operational and capital budgets, with the latter including a capital charge. The format	With the full application of resource-use accounting early in the next century, the budget will be on an accrual basis. Thus there will be both an	The accounts of the governments will be on an accrual basis and financial statements will reflect the operational and capital budgets. The

Table 4.2. Structural Components of Budgetary Systems in Australia, New Zealand, the United Kingdom, and the United States. (continued)

Category	Australia	New Zealand	United Kingdom	United States
		for budgets and accounts is the same.	operational and a capital budget. Capital charge will also be included in the capital budget.	budget as presented by the administration and as approved by the legislature will continue along present lines. The administration's budget makes an analytical distinction between current, investment, and capital budgets, and the data are intended for information, not for legislative action.

Table 4.2. Structural Components of Budgetary Systems in Australia, New Zealand, the United Kingdom, and the United States. (*continued*)

Category	Australia	New Zealand	United Kingdom	United States
C. Budget Classification	Follows the familiar pattern of ministries/ departments, programs, and the details of their running costs.	The budgets are divided into two: operational and capital. A further split is made between departmental and nondepartmental (earlier known as payments on behalf of the crown) expenses. The operating budget consists of output classes (a variation of program classification), benefits and other unrequited expenses, borrowing expenses, and other expenses. Capital comprises capital contributions.	Divided into functional heads (ministries), with programs and details of running costs or current outlays on programs, including wages and other charges.	Divided into departments, programs, objects of expenditure, and sources of financing.

Table 4.2. Structural Components of Budgetary Systems in Australia, New Zealand, the United Kingdom, and the United States. *(continued)*

Category	Australia	New Zealand	United Kingdom	United States
III. Principal Features of Financial Management				
A. Budget Releases	Budget authority is available to agencies after the approval of the annual budget.	Budget authority and the requisite funding (on a monthly basis) are available to departments and agencies.	Budgetary authority is available to departments and agencies after the approval of the budget. The Pay Master General issues warrants on request.	Budgetary apportionments are made by the Office of Management and Budget to facilitate a smooth flow of expenditures.
	Pending the final approval of the budget, a vote-on-account is approved to provide provisional budgetary authority.	Pending the approval of the budget, provisional parliamentary authority is given.	A vote-on-account is approved by the legislature pending the approval of the budget.	During recent years, temporary budgetary authority is given for short periods in view of the extended delays in the approval of the annual budget.

Table 4.2. Structural Components of Budgetary Systems in Australia, New Zealand, the United Kingdom, and the United States. *(continued)*

Category	Australia	New Zealand	United Kingdom	United States
B. Payments	Payments are centralized in the Department of Finance. All documentation reaches there for final approval and payment. Use of electronic payments is extensive.	Payments are made by the respective departments and agencies. The Ministry of Finance monitors the cash status from the banks.	Payments are made by the respective departments. Use of electronic payments is extensive.	Payments are made by the Treasury Payments Service. By the end of the century all payments will be made on an electronic basis.
C. Control Basis	Primary tools of control are corporate plans, program management agreement that focuses on results and resource consciousness, running costs of programs, and program evaluation.	Emphasis is on outputs and performance agreements with the chief executives of departments and on parliamentary scrutiny. The output agreement between the minister and the chief executive is the basis for the accountability relationship.	A distinction is made between departments and agencies. The latter, headed by executives, are accountable for delivery of services within specified resource and time schedules. Departments are subject to conventional controls of inputs and outputs.	Performance orientation is sought through pilot projects that will be extended to the whole government (Government Performance and Results Act of 1993). The linkages between allocation of resources and delivery of service with specific performance standards remains to be achieved.

Table 4.2. Structural Components of Budgetary Systems in Australia, New Zealand, the United Kingdom, and the United States. (*continued*)

Category	Australia	New Zealand	United Kingdom	United States
D. Performance Orientation	This is built into the program design and monitoring.	The key elements are the Statement of Service Performance and the underlying contractual basis between buyer and provider.	Performance targets, including quality of service, are provided for departments and agencies.	As above, this remains to be achieved.
E. Efficiency Orientation	A fiscal dividend or specified savings are indicated to each agency. Part of the savings achieved may be retained by the agencies to be spent on approved purposes.	This is the responsibility of the chief executive, and performance agreements may have incentives aimed at promoting efficiency.	All departments are required to produce an efficiency plan showing how they intend to operate within the running cost constraints.	As a part of reengineering, the government departments, in an exercise separate from the budget, have been endeavoring to drop uneconomic practices and search for economies in their operations.
	Periodic evaluation by the Department of Evaluation is intended to facilitate the achievement of efficiency in resource use.			

Table 4.2. Structural Components of Budgetary Systems in Australia, New Zealand, the United Kingdom, and the United States. (*continued*)

Category	Australia	New Zealand	United Kingdom	United States
F. Financial Reporting	Internal reporting is substantially strengthened. Departments publish annual reports showing performance aspects. With the full implementation of the accrual system, financial statements will be published.	Departments have developed information systems. Financial statements are issued two times a year.	Over the years, steady efforts have been made to improve the departmental information systems. Performance information is published by the departments. With the full implementation of the accrual system, financial statements will also be issued.	Departments have been engaged in improving their integrated financial management systems, including their information systems. Departments are expected to furnish financial statements on an annual basis. Performance information is being developed.
G. Accountability	Departments publish annual reports indicating resource use and performance.	Departments furnish to the legislature reports on performance and resource use.	Departments publish annual reports showing progress in resource use and plans for the future.	Now a few agencies provide accountability reports. This pilot project will be extended to cover the whole government.

Table 4.2. Structural Components of Budgetary Systems in Australia, New Zealand, the United Kingdom, and the United States. *(continued)*

Category	Australia	New Zealand	United Kingdom	United States
IV. Role of Spending Agencies	Agencies prepare corporate plans and are responsible for the delivery of services. Agencies have some freedom in switching resources between personnel and other categories.	Agencies have full freedom, while being accountable for performance, to use the budgetary resources in a flexible manner.	Departments have limited freedom to switch resources among the running costs category. Agencies have more functional freedom, including determination of pay levels.	Pay levels are prescribed by government. Personnel strength may be specified in the enabling legislation. Within these parameters, departments and agencies have the freedom and the responsibility to implement the budget as approved by the legislature.

In essence, the reform envisaged two separate forms of appropriation to ensure that departments are held accountable only for those activities over which they have complete control. These two forms of appropriation were departmental (output categories) and nondepartmental. The emphasis on outputs would lead, it was expected, to a results orientation.

Third, far-reaching changes were also made in personnel management. In lieu of traditional approaches, variations of corporate practices were introduced in that each department was expected to be headed by a chief executive officer who would be appointed on a contractual basis. This practice in New Zealand is different from the practices in France, Japan, and Germany, which continue to have a strong civil service that plays a dominant role in the formulation and implementation of government policies. This raises the important issue of whether contract-based civil service offers a viable alternative to the traditional civil service. The experience of France and other countries shows that the real issue is the quality of policymaking. Does policymaking stand to gain through contract-based civil service? Available experience does not provide a conclusive answer. Singapore has introduced a system of budgeting for results based on the experience of New Zealand, but it has retained the structure of traditional civil service and has not appointed chief executive officers. In the United States, most agency heads are changed when there are changes in the administration. In most cases, the appointment of agency heads is subject to congressional approval. A few years ago, the post of chief operating officer was created in executive departments and agencies. This officer, who reports directly to agency heads, is responsible for overall management of agencies; he is also a member of the President's Management Council.

The reforms in the United Kingdom have many of the common budgetary themes that have come to characterize the 1980s and 1990s. These reforms thus emphasize rolling expenditure plans, formulation of corporate plans, planning by objectives, specification of efficiency goals, formulation of global ceilings, review of functions as a part of annual budget review, specification and monitoring of performance measures, and appropriate strengthening of the parliamentary accountability framework. In two respects, these reforms sought to provide additional dimensions. First, a number (and this number has been growing over the years) of task-oriented agencies have been created. The heads of these agencies, who were on contractual appointments, were given the freedom to manage the given resources while being accountable for the specified performance. Second, the agency heads were given, though gradually, financial powers to determine the pay scales of the agency employees. The establishment of task-oriented agencies was seen as a significant step in the organization of government to improve the delivery of services. Each organization is headed by a chief executive who is personally responsible for the work of departments, including agencies. Ministers retain the right to investigate and intervene in the work of the agencies whenever deemed necessary. In addition, the British Treasury was reorganized to reduce layers and to promote team work (United Kingdom, 1996).

Some of the features referred to here have already become ingredients of the legislation enacted over the last few years in the United States as well. Departments are expected, after the pilot projects are completed, to have strategic plans and performance standards. These features are expected, however, as noted earlier, to become operational at the turn of the century.

THE MAJOR CHALLENGES OF BUDGETARY INNOVATION

The principles and practices just discussed and illustrated in detail in Table 4.2 revolve around the establishment of small agencies with specific tasks, resources, managerial flexibility, and a framework of accountability. The principles and the associated management philosophy of this approach have, however, become controversial even in their application to the private sector, where they originated. Indeed, some consider that the new approaches have tended to treat management as an end in itself instead of as a service to organizations and their customers, and they believe that these approaches have had the effect of eroding the organizations and the society. Management as a discipline has a long pedigree in controversy, and general approval is a difficult goal to achieve. Although discussion of principles is essential, it is even more important to consider the issues in the application of those principles. In particular, it is important to raise the issue of whether the uniqueness of government has been recognized and modifications have been made in the application of private sector practices to the public sector. Rituals should not be mistaken for efficiency; instead they need to be analyzed.

In applying the principles of corporate practice to government and in considering the budget innovations introduced in the four countries, three areas need to be considered: control culture versus management culture, the creation of agencies as shadow government, and the provider-purchaser link.

Control and Management Culture

The hitherto existing, and in many ways continuing, expenditure management systems are based on institutionalized distrust, which as history shows was far from successful in achieving the desired results. The new management approach is anchored in trust and flexibility, albeit with an enhanced accountability. Critics of this approach reveal a skepticism about the trustworthiness of the civil service and express fears about the abuse of powers and doubts about the adequacy of regulations controlling bureaucratic behavior. In their view, public servants may, in the exercise of newly endowed entrepreneurial zeal, cut corners, be less compliant with the rules, and given the generally weak structures of legislative accountability, not to mention lack of full transparency, end up being all-powerful technocrats.

It is further suggested that the new philosophy is based on performance, and in that context the top layers of administration may resort to control by numbers. Where measurement becomes the religion of management, the top levels in an organization may do "nothing but exercise financial control and so drive everyone else crazy" (Mintzberg, 1996). The tyranny of rules, a feature associated with the previous approaches, may yield to a tyranny of numbers. Although performance agreement may provide, in theory, a degree of autonomy, in practice it may be replaced by a performance-oriented control and by situations in which financial controllers may, through the constant exercise of oversight, become an irritant rather than a lubricant contributing to the smooth functioning of the system. To some this scenario is reminiscent of the number-dominated centralized administration associated with centrally planned economies. Finance ministries endowed with the new power may extend their oversight in the name of economic management and surveillance.

Some experiences lend credence to these beliefs. The alternative does not necessarily lay in continuing a discredited approach. Rather, it underlines the imperative need to address the details of the application of the new approaches so that more inclusive patterns of management may be fostered.

Elsewhere, experience shows that line managers in many government departments have been reluctant to accept the new authority on the plea that they are not yet ready to manage their own funds. This illustrates the erosion that has taken place over the years in the financial management capacities of agencies as a result of the centralized and dominating influences of the central agencies. Centralized management has reached its limits. But the growth of a management capability in the spending agencies may not be easy as they continue to find comfort in the dependency syndrome. This feature has, however, less relevance for the United States, which has promoted a more decentralized system for the last seven decades.

Creation of Agencies: A Shadow Government?

The new management philosophy seeks, with a view to institutionalizing manager autonomy, the establishment of freestanding agencies to carry out specific activities within available resources. This is based on the belief, in part generated by the experience of the private sector, that government is too big and too diverse to be managed as one unit. Although the approach has several merits, its application gives rise to problems. First, if these agencies are expected to be fiscally self-reliant, it may be appropriate, after determining who should do what, to delink these agencies from the government. If, conversely, agencies are expected to be partly reliant on government budgetary transfers, it would be necessary to specify the commercial and noncommercial objectives of these agencies as well as the rate of return expected.

Second, many governments have created, even before the emergence of the new management philosophy, autonomous agencies (distinct from the public enterprises) that are for the most part dependent on government finances while having autonomy and pursuing goals that may be independent from those of the government. The experience of some countries shows that a few of these agencies have sometimes engaged in domestic and foreign borrowing that was guaranteed by government. Not infrequently, governments had to redeem these guarantees. The agencies may even compete with one another, and the general experience is that there are coordination weaknesses among the agencies and between the agencies and government. Not infrequently, there is little information on the activities and the financial status of autonomous agencies in the government. This has contributed to the view that a shadow government beyond the control of the government and the legislature has emerged.

Provider-Purchaser Link

An ingredient of the new approaches to expenditure management is the explicit provision of a provider-purchaser link. Thus the legislature buys the outputs from the government, and within the government the minister buys from the department, the department buys from the agencies, and the agencies buy from contractors. In each case there is an intent to specify the outputs (outcomes or effectiveness are considered to be somewhat remote and there may not be explicit causal links between outputs and outcomes) in return for the funding provided. These outputs are specified in the form of a performance agreement or contract that would solidify the relationship. The outputs may be based on detailed benchmarks drawn either from within the government or from comparable operations in the private sector. This agreement seeks to usher in a regime of management-by-results based on agreement on the goals, objectives, and outputs and their quality indicators. The agreement system aims at achieving a greater congruence between the goals of the government in its capacity as the owner-principal (and representative of the public interest) and the goals of the agency or department engaged in the provision of the services.

The application of this principle to the government requires an explicit consideration of the unique features applicable to governments. Apart from the generally recognized difficulties in measuring outputs in government, experience shows that outputs may frequently be underestimated initially so that greater efficiency may be shown at the end of the year. Quality is often difficult to judge despite the development of numerous indicators, and the relationship between quality and budgetary outlays is far more nebulous than is recognized. In addition, governments may not be able to provide stable external environments that may be implicit in the budget strategy. In an open economy, many external factors are beyond the direct control of the government, which is more often than not at the receiving end. External uncertainty may force the government, as the owner and as the macromanager, to intervene and renegotiate the contract. If once-presumed resources are not available, the scale of outputs could be reduced (but that would contribute to unutilized infrastructure in the agencies and to higher costs). Or the insistence on outputs could induce a short-term behavior aimed at achieving the targets one way or another.

A performance contract also implies a high degree of specificity of outputs so that its enforceability may be strengthened. If such a contract is viewed as legally binding or justiciable in a court of law, then the principal-agent relationships, as applied to government, would be far different from what they are now. At the same time, it is essential to recognize that the new links provide a new management dimension to the agencies and make them resource conscious while also being goal oriented. The links should also contribute to a lowering of the costs of administration. The new approaches would require different skills in the civil service in that the members of the service would have to be capable of formulating goals, targets, output measures, and indicators, and they would have to be responsive to environmental and policy developments.

OTHER ISSUES FOR BUDGETARY INNOVATION

In addition to the preceding philosophical aspects, there are other, technical aspects that merit consideration in applying the practices of Australia, New Zealand, and the United Kingdom to the United States.

Fiscal Policy Objectives

One of the major differences between New Zealand and the United States is the way in which the medium and long-term objectives of budgetary policy are stated. This difference in the approach is partly attributable to the respective ways in which the rulers or governments are subject to control by the ruled. New Zealand, being a former colony, essentially bestowed the powers on the government as a representative of the people, but one that drew its inspiration, and in some sense its legitimacy, from the Crown. The financial powers of the government are in turn located in the Ministry of Finance, or Treasury, as it was and continues to be known. In the American tradition, however, the people themselves were and are the supreme source of power and the final political authority. Government is not imposed from anywhere but is authorized by the people, and the sovereign law-making power is the people. It is for this reason that in the United States all matters, including financial matters, are legislated and laws are enacted. In the British type of government, which follows more closely the tradition of civil law, some of the same purposes are served by an executive order.

Accordingly, no specific legislation is enacted stating the budgetary objectives in the United Kingdom except through the annual budgetary legislation. Australia formulated a Budget Honesty legislation along the lines of the experience of New Zealand. New Zealand made a significant departure from its own tradition by enacting the new reforms through legislation (the Public Finance Act of 1989) and in continuation of this new convention has enacted the 1994 Fiscal Responsibility Act. This act lays down the principles of prudent fiscal policy. Because the term *prudence* can mean several things to as many people, the act went on to state that prudence consists in achieving relatively low levels of public debt (to be below 30 percent of GDP in the short term and below 20 percent in the longer term) through balanced budgets and the maintenance of adequate levels of government net worth. The intent is to achieve stable fiscal policy, which in turn will lead to stable tax rates. The Australian legislation specifies that the budget statement should also include data on intergenerational aspects at least once every five years, while indicating the strategic priorities and the short-term fiscal objectives, as well as expected outcomes or targets for key fiscal measures, for the budget year and the following three years. Moreover, comprehensive fiscal information is to be provided before elections. Where temporary measures are taken to address economic downturns, it is required that the process of their reversal be identified.

The issue remains, however, whether the pursuit and implementation of fiscal policies would stand to be gained through legislation of the type envisaged in Australia and New Zealand. Here again, experience does not provide any unqualified support to this proposition. Many state governments in the United States are bound by their legislation to create balanced budgets. In practice, however, in many states activities were assigned to autonomous agencies in order to maintain balanced budgets. Could this have been prevented through greater transparency in accounts? The answer is not conclusive at this stage.

The formulation of an explicit expenditure strategy for the medium term is, however, an important step forward. Whether such a strategy should be enacted by legislature or whether it should be a part of the annual budget strategy depends on the constitutional and legal traditions of a country.

Buyer-Provider Contract Between Ministries and Civil Service

In conformity with their intent to install a system oriented to the achievement of results, the New Zealand reforms provided for a contract or an agreement between the responsible minister and the chief executive of the department. In principle, the minister has the choice to buy policy advice either from the department or from outside. The performance agreements have three parts.

Part One specifies the key results areas of the government's strategic concerns, and the expected results are specified in verifiable terms of outputs. Part Two sets out the detailed information on the outputs to be purchased. Part Three provides information on departmental compliance with statutory responsibilities and government responsibilities. This innovation signifies a radical departure from the previous tradition of the civil service and the relationships between the minister and his civil servants.

Is this a practice that needs to be emulated by other governments? On this matter, opinions are far more divided than in any other area. To start with, many contend that the distinction between policy formulation and policy implementation is not appropriate. In fact, in many cases what gets implemented becomes the policy, given the numerous slippages between policy formulation and implementation. Are policies formulated exclusively either by ministers or by civil servants? The extensive research carried out in this area suggests that much depends on the situation, on the personalities, and more significantly, on what the policy is about. (See Aberbach, Putnam, and Rockman, 1981. See also Stewart, 1993, and Thain and Wright, 1995.) In highly technical matters, such as the modernization of the defense forces, there would be many technical inputs. Decisions, however, cannot be made only on the merits of technical viewpoints, but need to be tempered by the political objectives and related costs. Ministers are appointed to bring about change, to explain the nature and need for change to the people, and to win their acceptance. But change cannot be perceived without an idea of the content. In all these areas, there is a constant interaction between the minister and the civil service, and the final product, however deliberate in design, is an indivisible one in which the footprints of all participants cannot always be separated. In what is admittedly a collaborative effort, any exercise at separating the building blocks could have serious consequences. Furthermore, when the minister seeks to get the specified outputs from outside, which would have the desired effect of making the purchase a contestable one, it could also have the unfortunate consequence of serious erosion of the department's credibility. Also, there may be several areas in which anticipation of future events can at best be very tentative.

The application of this approach to the United States and its possible benefits are, however, issues on which there is likely to be more skepticism than ready acceptance. The pattern of accountability in the United States is different than in other countries, and there is no collective responsibility of the cabinet in the same way as in British-type democracies. It could also be argued that the real buyer is not the secretary of a department but the legislature, which represents the people. The absence of a contract does not, however, mean the absence of performance; under the existing legislation, every department is expected to indicate their expected performance at the beginning of the year and then fulfill it.

The issue also arises whether these agreements have any major weight in the overall scheme of budgetary management given that the departments are responsible for only a small portion of the total expenditure on directly delivered services. The performance agreements would have greater applicability between the departments and the autonomous agencies. The agreements would also have greater relevance where much of the federally funded work is carried out by the state or local governments. In this regard, the U.S. budget for FY96 envisaged a performance partnership with the other levels of government (see U.S. Office of Management and Budget, 1995, p. 167). The form and content of this partnership remains to be specified. Such an indigenous device, when fully developed, could have a more far-reaching impact than the buyer-provider agreement between the minister and the civil service.

Performance Measurement

Performance measurement is now an accepted ingredient of budgetary management. There is little debate about its relevance or application. What is debated is the best way to secure it. Essentially, the performance should reflect those activities over which the entity or the organization has full operational control. Such control tends to be diffuse, however, where the services are provided by third parties. In these cases the role of the agencies is to fund the operations and monitor the way in which the services are provided to the public. The controls exercised by the agency relate to the release of monies and to the specification of various features in the contracts. In these cases, a substantial distance emerges between those responsible for funding and those responsible for the delivery of the services. In this regard, the experience of New Zealand does not offer any new insights. Measures are often fuzzy. Relevant cost information is not available. Narrative notes provided for in the budget tend to be too general, skimpy, and lacking in focus. These shortcomings point to the need for a more careful review of the way in which the performance measures are developed.

The emphasis on management by performance and results, while shifting the emphasis from the conventional inputs to the outputs, does not promote a resource consciousness. Rather, from the point of view of the agencies, the promised results imply a specified relationship between resources and results, and each time that higher results are expected, it will be assumed that higher budgetary allocations are available. The thrust of management would then be not on a more effective utilization of the given resources but on seeking more resources commensurate with expected results. The manager would not have the incentive to change the dynamics of delivery unless the implicit equation between resources and results is itself changed. In due course this could lead to a creeping built-in pressure for higher allocations.

Institutional Aspects

The reforms introduced in Australia, New Zealand, and the United Kingdom have two major implications for the ministries or departments engaged in budgetary management and for the structure of the government itself.

The Ministry of Finance or its equivalent in these countries is a powerful organization. It is responsible for rolling expenditure planning, for determining global ceilings for allocations, and for approving the performance measures. Viewed from the spending agencies and depending on the situation, the finance ministry is seen as a friendly critic or as an avoidable menace. Be that as it may, the ministry's assigned role is to facilitate the formulation and implementation of policies during the year. The nearest counterpart to this role in the United States is the Office of Management and Budget (OMB). The budget in the United States is increasingly becoming a compact between the legislature and the spending departments. Even in regard to macroeconomic policies, the role of the OMB is often overshadowed by the Congressional Budget Office. Although the Budget Enforcement Act of 1990 does permit a sort of portfolio management (between defense and nondefense spending, between entitlements and discretionary spending), the agencies are the ones that are responsible for operations and performance. This is not to say, however, that government does not have instruments it can use to prevent spending whenever there is a lack of congruence between resources and spending. It can enforce rescissions, reconciliation, and sequestration. Thus there are instruments for government through which an emerging fiscal crisis can be anticipated and averted. The role of the Finance Ministry, however, is far more significant in an unspecified way in that by convention it is viewed as the financial conscience of the government. That financial conscience is fragmented in the government of the United States.

The second implication relates to the creation of small task-oriented agencies, which are given specific tasks to be performed for the monies allotted. The relevance to the United States of this approach is somewhat doubtful in view of the fact that there are already more than 35,000 autonomous public authorities at various levels of government (federal, state, and local) engaged in transportation, economic development, housing, water supply, sewage and waste disposal, power, urban development, education, hospitals, and prisons. (This estimate is taken from Axelrod, 1992.) The agencies in most cases have autonomy to conduct their financial operations. They may also borrow from both the government and the public; although they were intended to be self-financing, this test, if applied, is unlikely to show many winners. More significantly, there is a problem in terms of accountability. Axelrod (1992, p. iii) observes that "many public authorities are quagmires of political patronage, corruption and mismanagement" and that they are unaccountable for their activities. A more recent experience in the United Kingdom also shows that there are major gaps in the chain of accountability (Jenkins, 1996). Given this experience, the creation of more agencies, particularly at a time when governments are being streamlined to be lean and, it is hoped, efficient, is rendered even more moot than it has been. This does not mean that there is no need to adapt some of the corporate practices to the requirements of governments. Such an adaptation does not necessarily require, as a precedent, the creation of small agencies.

TECHNICAL ASPECTS OF BUDGETARY PROCESSES

There are four operational aspects of other countries' experience that are of some value. The first aspect relates to the availability of an approved budget at the beginning of the fiscal year, or in the absence of an approved budget, the use of a technique that provides continuous funding for all the operations of the government. During recent years, the United States has experienced considerable difficulty in passing an approved budget on time. In fact, by the time all the requisite legislation is completed, more than half the fiscal year is completed. To avoid this situation, and with a view to ensuring funding for all the continuing activities, many countries have created legislation to the effect that governments may spend amounts not exceeding the amounts spent for the same period during the previous year. A similar technique could prevent governments from coming to a stop for want of a budget.

Second, the legislature in the United States spends far too much time determining the next year's estimates and relatively little time on what has been actually achieved during the previous budget year. It does make special inquiries in matters that are of topical interest, but an in-depth review of achievements has not formed its focus. With a view to establishing a balance between what is needed and what has been accomplished, Sweden has been experimenting with a system of triennial allocations. Under this procedure, government is divided into three parts, and each year one part is taken up for intensive evaluation. The intent has been to cover the whole government over a three-year period. Because the time frame has been extended due to operational reasons, the legislature is permitted to gain a better perspective on what has been achieved and to determine the future of the allocations in light of the assessment. In principle, periodic review of spending authorizations ("sunset legislation") would provide such an opportunity to the United States. In practice, however, legislation covers too many fields and does not provide a coherent opportunity to review the activities of an agency. In extenuation, it should be realized that budget appropriations for more than two years would be equivalent to robbing a future Congress of an opportunity to use its prerogatives. This has to be tempered by a recognition that even now, for a vast majority of the federal outlays—in particular, entitlements—legislative authority is available on an extended basis.

Third, the issue arises whether the budget classification needs to be changed to output categories as is done in New Zealand. Recalled that one of the considerations to be kept in view in the formulation of programs has been that they should have identifiable and measurable outputs. To that extent, explicit recognition of outputs is to be welcomed. In practice, however, this may not mean a major change. For example, "policy formulation" in program-oriented budgets is not very different from the "policy advice" found in the output-oriented budgets. That said, it should also be noted that the program classification utilized in the United States may need to be updated in view of the extensive change in the range of activities undertaken by the U.S. government. Moreover, there is also a need to synchronize, to the extent possible, the classification of programs with the revised system of national accounts.

Finally, the changing composition of government expenditures implies that more attention needs to be paid to operational agencies, including third parties, where much of the delivery of services is taking place. For far too long, attention has been focused on the operations of the federal government. What is needed is equal emphasis on the strengthening of the internal controls of the agencies. They represent the foundations of the government and therefore need to be looked into with greater care than has been the case so far.

CHOICE AND OUTLOOK

The choices in regard to the new initiatives have already been made. The traditional systems did not yield the desired results. It is therefore appropriate that new approaches are given a full opportunity to demonstrate that their conceptual superiority would yield, without adding to cost, improved services from governments. Public authorities have to engage in drawing operational designs for the architecture of budgeting and financial management indicated in the new approaches. In doing so, adequate safeguards have to be provided so that managerial autonomy is not misused, and so that the full benefits of competitive tendering accrue to governments. Contracting out needs to be seen not as a mere substitute for government by the corporate sector but as a part of a larger effort of continuous evaluation of government work processes.

The bottom lines in government for which budgetary management has responsibility are the following two questions: *Are services being provided in a more cost-effective way under the new approaches?* And as the Plowden Committee in the United Kingdom remarked in 1961 in regard to whether the management systems are addressing the central problem, *How can the growth of public expenditure be brought under control and contained?* The new approaches and practices discussed in this chapter and the program of action envisaged for implementation in the United States offer a reasonable assurance to answer these questions in the affirmative. The effectiveness of these approaches is dependent not only on short-term gains but also on sustaining those gains over the medium and long term. In turn, this approach may suggest that financial management improvement requires continuous and dedicated effort.

Note

1. The literature in this regard is not considerable and much of it is not yet accessible to the general public. The pioneering effort in this area is Sundelson (1937), who offered a detailed study of the laws of the budgetary systems in various countries. This effort was followed, after the Second World War, by studies performed by the United Nations (1952, 1966). Although the UN studies were largely aimed at meeting the needs of the developing countries, they also contained, in the initial stages, case studies of selected industrial countries. Later, the Organization for Economic Cooperation and Development issued two studies (1987, 1995) containing descriptions of the budgetary systems in its member countries. More recently, the UN has issued several reports and studies that deal primarily with the developing countries (1991, 1992). In addition, there are a few studies of the comparative picture. Important among these are Premchand (1983, 1990, 1993); Premchand and Burkhead (1984); Dean and Pugh (1989); and Leeuw, Rist, and Sonnichson (1994). For the countries in the European Community, Von Hagen (1992) offers a brief description of their systems. Recently, as a result of the efforts of international financial institutions, more attention has been devoted to a comparative analysis of budget institutions and fiscal outcomes. In this genre are studies by Alesina (Alesina and Perroti, 1996; Alesina and others, 1996), Von Hagen and Harden (1996), and Campos and Pradhan (1996).

References

Aberbach, J. D., Putnam, R. D., and Rockman, B. A. *Bureaucrats and Politicians in Western Democracies.* Cambridge, Mass.: Harvard University Press, 1981.

Alesina, A., and Perroti, R. "Budget Deficits and Budget Institutions." Unpublished working paper. Washington, D.C.: International Monetary Fund, 1996.

Alesina, A., and others. "Fiscal Adjustments in OECD Countries: Composition and Macroeconomic Effects." Unpublished paper. Washington, D.C.: International Monetary Fund, 1996.

Appleby, P. "The Role of the Budget Division." In A. Schick (ed.), *Perspectives on Budgeting.* Washington, D.C.: Society for Public Administration, 1987. (Originally published 1957.)

Åslund, A. *How Russia Became a Market Economy.* Washington, D.C.: Brookings Institution, 1995.

Axelrod, D. *Shadow Government.* New York: Wiley, 1992.

Boston, J., Martin, J., Pallot, J., and Walsh, P. (eds.). *Reshaping the State: New Zealand's Bureaucratic Revolution.* New York: Oxford University Press, 1991.

Campos, J. E., and Pradhan, S. "The Impact of Budgetary Institutions on Expenditure Outcomes." Unpublished paper. Washington, D.C.: World Bank, 1996.

Controller and Auditor General of New Zealand. *First Report for 1996.* Wellington: Office of the Controller and Auditor General of New Zealand, 1996.

Dean, P. N., and Pugh, C. *Government Budgeting in Developing Countries.* London: Routledge, 1989.

Foster, C. D., and Plowden, F. H. *The State Under Stress.* Bristol, Pa.: Open University Press, 1996.

Grossman, L. K. *The Electronic Republic: Reshaping Democracy in the Information Age.* New York: Penguin, 1995.

Jenkins, S. *Accountable to None: The Tory Nationalization of Britain.* Harmondsworth, England: Penguin, 1996.

Keating, M., and Dixon, G. *Making Economic Policy in Australia, 1983–88.* Melbourne: Longman Cheshire, 1989.

Keating, M., and Rosalky, D. "Rolling Expenditure Plans: Australian Experience and Prognosis." In A. Premchand (ed.), *Government Financial Management: Issues and Country Studies.* Washington, D.C.: International Monetary Fund, 1990.

Kettl, D. F., Ingraham, P. W., Sanders, R. P., and Horner, C. *Civil Service Reform: Building a Government That Works.* Washington, D.C.: Brookings Institution, 1996.

Leeuw, F. L., Rist, R. C., and Sonnichson, R. C. *Can Government Learn?* New Brunswick, N.J.: Transaction, 1994.

McDonald, P. W. "Results-Oriented Management: Australia Public Sector Financial Management, Accounting and Budgeting Reform." In A. Premchand (ed.), *Government Financial Management: Issues and Country Studies.* Washington, D.C.: International Monetary Fund, 1990.

Mintzberg, H. "Musings on Management." *Harvard Business Review,* July-Aug. 1996, p. 62.

Organization for Economic Cooperation and Development. *The Control and Management of Government Expenditure.* Paris: Organization for Economic Cooperation and Development, 1987.

Organization for Economic Cooperation and Development. *Budgeting for Results: Perspectives on Public Expenditure Management.* Paris: Organization for Economic Cooperation and Development, 1995.

Plowden Committee. *Control of Public Expenditure.* London: HMSO, 1961.

Premchand, A. *Government Budgeting and Expenditure Controls.* Washington, D.C.: International Monetary Fund, 1983.

Premchand, A. (ed.). *Government Financial Management: Issues and Country Studies.* Washington, D.C.: International Monetary Fund, 1990.

Premchand, A. *Public Expenditure Management.* Washington, D.C.: International Monetary Fund, 1993.

Premchand, A., and Burkhead, J. (eds.). *Comparative International Budgeting and Finance.* New Brunswick, N.J.: Transaction, 1984.

Schick, A. (ed.). *Perspectives on Budgeting.* Washington, D.C.: Society for Public Administration, 1987. (Originally published 1957.)

Stewart, J. "The Limitations of Government by Contract." *Public Money and Management,* July–Sept. 1993, pp. 7–13.

Sundelson, J. W. *Budgetary Methods in National and State Governments.* Albany, N.Y.: J. B. Lyon, 1937.

Thain, C., and Wright, M. *The Treasury and Whitehall.* Oxford: Clarendon Press, 1995.

United Kingdom. *Next Steps Review.* London: HMSO, 1996.

United Nations. *Budgetary Structure and Classification of Accounts.* New York: United Nations, 1952.

United Nations. *Government Accounting and Budget Execution.* New York: United Nations, 1952.

United Nations. "The Budgetary System and Procedures of African Countries." Unpublished paper. Addis Ababa: United Nations, 1996a.

United Nations. *Government Budgeting and Economic Planning in Developing Countries.* New York: United Nations, 1996b.

United Nations. *Government Financial Management in Least Developed Countries.* New York: United Nations, 1991.

United Nations. *The Control and Management of Government Expenditure: Issues and Experience in Asian Countries.* New York: Economic and Social Commission for Asia and Pacific, 1992.

U.S. Office of Management and Budget. *Budget of the United States Government, Fiscal Year 1996: Analytical Perspectives.* Washington, D.C.: Government Printing Office, 1995.

Von Hagen, J. "Budgeting Procedures and Fiscal Performance in the European Communities." *Economic Papers,* Oct. 1992, *96.*

Von Hagen, J., and Harden, I. "Budget Process and Commitment to Fiscal Discipline." Unpublished working paper. Washington, D.C.: International Monetary Fund, 1996.

PART TWO

CREDIT MARKETS, THE ECONOMY, AND BUDGET BALANCING

CHAPTER FIVE

Understanding and Using
Government Financial Statements

John H. Engstrom

This chapter examines financial reporting by state and local governments by discussing the sources and meaning of so-called *generally accepted accounting principles* (GAAP), by examining the content of the *comprehensive annual financial report* (CAFR), by looking at the interaction between the CAFR and the budget, and by examining some of the uses of financial statements, both externally and internally. It is not possible, of course, to cover all aspects of financial reporting in a chapter of this length; readers interested in learning more are advised to read *Essentials of Accounting for Governmental and Not-for-Profit Organizations* (Engstrom and Hay, 1996) or another of the major textbooks in the field.

A basic understanding of financial reporting is essential for government financial managers. A great deal of information is available from the CAFR that will assist in planning, controlling, and evaluating financial performance. The CAFR, which should be prepared by all units of state and local government, formally disseminates information about the government's financial condition, results of operations, cash flows, and budgetary compliance. The report takes on special significance because the statements are to be prepared according to common standards (the GAAP) and are attested to by independent auditors who conduct audits according to *generally accepted auditing standards* (GAAS) and *generally accepted government auditing standards* (GAGAS). The CAFR is intended to be used by the financial community (investors and creditors) to make decisions about rating and investing in bonds, by legislative and oversight bodies to make policy decisions, and by the general public (including the media) to make voting and business decisions.

Financial reporting for the federal government is significantly different than that for state and local governments and is in the process of major change. For many years, the Department of the Treasury issued cash-basis reports, indicating compliance with federal budgeting. Now, because of the Federal Financial Management Improvement Act of 1996, each federal agency and the federal government as a whole are required, for the first time, to report audited financial information in accord with uniform standards issued by the Federal Accounting Standards Advisory Board. Federal government accounting is significantly different than accounting for state and local governments and is not covered in this chapter.

SOURCES AND MEANING OF GENERALLY ACCEPTED ACCOUNTING PRINCIPLES

The Securities and Exchange Commission (SEC) has authority to establish accounting and reporting standards for private sector entities that sell stock to the public. The SEC generally has delegated the setting of accounting standards in the private sector, initially to the American Institute of Certified Public Accountants (AICPA), and more recently to the Financial Accounting Standards Board (FASB). No national legislative mandate exists for governmental accounting; until 1984, standards that did exist were promulgated by the Municipal Finance Officers Association, later renamed the Government Finance Officers Association (GFOA). In 1984, an independent Governmental Accounting Standards Board (GASB) was created, with authority to establish standards of accounting and reporting for state and local governments.

The Financial Accounting Foundation (FAF) is the parent organization of both the FASB and the GASB. The FAF has the responsibility to raise funds for both the FASB and the GASB and to appoint members. The FASB has authority to establish accounting principles for all private sector organizations, including nongovernmental, not-for-profit organizations, such as private colleges and universities and voluntary health and welfare organizations. The GASB has the authority to establish accounting principles for state and local governments, including government-related organizations, such as public colleges and universities. This authority comes as a result of actions taken by the AICPA, which has indicated that when its members, the auditors, issue an opinion on financial statements, they are certifying that the statements are (or are not) in accordance with GAAP (American Institute of Certified Public Accountants, 1997). If an auditor issues an "unqualified opinion" on the financial statements of an entity, that entity will be presumed to be following GAAP; auditors must justify any departures.

A complex set of rules known as the "GAAP hierarchy" has been established by the FASB, GASB, AICPA, and other organizations. Essentially, it lists authoritative sources of guidelines in order of importance; that is, the first category of sources is the most important. If an issue is not resolved by those sources, then the second category would be followed, and so on. The first category is statements and interpretations issued by the GASB. The second category is statements of position and audit guides of the AICPA (when approved by GASB), and GASB technical bulletins. Three additional categories include certain minor pronouncements of the GASB and AICPA, widely prevalent practices, and other sources, such as textbooks.

The GASB is a private sector entity, supported by contributions, through the FAF, from state and local governments, public accounting firms, and other firms and organizations. It has a seven-member board, with one member full-time and the other six part-time. The staff is headed by a research director. GASB statements are the primary pronouncements; in addition, the GASB may issue interpretations (of statements), technical bulletins, and "Q&A's" (from the staff). GASB follows an extensive due process, which includes written responses to due process documents, formal public hearings, task forces, informal meetings, and focus group sessions. Due process documents include "invitations to comment," "preliminary views," and "exposure drafts." To date, the GASB has issued thirty statements, four interpretations, and a number of technical bulletins. It began by issuing *Concepts Statement 1: Objectives of Financial Reporting* (1987), which adopted prior pronouncements of the National Council on Governmental Accounting, a committee of the GFOA.

As the next section illustrates in more detail, the current financial accounting and reporting model is a disaggregated, fund-based model that generally provides users with the ability to trace funds flows, but it does not provide an overall picture of the financial position and results of operations of the entire government. The entire financial report is the CAFR, which includes three main sections: introductory, financial, and statistical. The financial section includes (but is not limited to) the general purpose financial statements (GPFS), which consists of five basic combined statements and the accompanying notes.

Current reporting uses two models of accounting. One model, called the financial resource flows measurement focus and modified accrual basis of accounting, reflects mostly current assets and liabilities and provides measurements somewhere between the accrual and cash basis of accounting. This approach is used for the general, special revenue, debt service, and capital projects funds (the governmental funds), as well as for agency and expendable trust funds. The other approach, used by enterprise, internal service, nonexpendable trust, and pension trust funds, uses an economic resource measurement focus and the accrual basis of accounting, similar to the accounting used by business enterprises. One of the statements, a "budget-actual" statement, presents budgetary compliance information for the general and other governmental funds that have a legally adopted annual budget on the budgetary basis of accounting, which may be different than modified accrual.

The GASB is currently in the process of making major changes to the reporting model. A recent "preliminary views" document, *The Governmental Financial Reporting Model* (Governmental Accounting Standards Board, 1996b), along with some additional due process documents, suggests a model that will provide a "dual-perspective" approach. The *entity-wide perspective* will address the unmet need of providing information on the financial condition and results of operations of the government as a whole; it will be consolidated and use the accrual basis of accounting. The *major fund perspective* will be similar to the current reporting model. A great deal of controversy surrounds the new model. It will be some time before it is adopted, and even more time before it is effective. The following sections describe the current model.

THE COMPREHENSIVE ANNUAL FINANCIAL REPORT

Each state or local government unit is encouraged by the GASB to prepare a CAFR. As mentioned earlier, the CAFR has three main sections: introductory, financial, and statistical. Some CAFRs also add the *single audit report,* which may be included with the CAFR or issued separately for those state and local governments that have more than $300,000 in federal grants.

The Introductory Section

The introductory section of a CAFR normally includes a title page, a table of contents, a letter of transmittal, a list of principal officials, and an organizational chart. If a state or local government received a certificate of achievement for excellence in financial reporting from the GFOA in the previous year, then that certificate is displayed in the introductory section. (A financial statement that receives a GFOA certificate passes an extensive review by financial reporting experts and GFOA staff; the program is credited with improving financial reporting significantly.)

The most important part of the introductory section is the letter of transmittal, which is signed by the chief financial officer and, sometimes, by the chief executive or operating officer. According to the GFOA (1994), the letter of transmittal is an opportunity for management to discuss, in easily understandable language, the financial report and the financial condition of the government. The letter should include:

- A formal transmittal of the financial report

- Acknowledgment that the government is responsible for the report

- A discussion of the financial reporting entity (the primary reporting government and any component units, such as a library, for which it is financially accountable)

- A discussion of the local economy

- Major initiatives and service efforts and accomplishments

- Internal controls

- Budget information

- A financial overview, including general government, enterprise, and fiduciary operations

- Debt administration

- Cash management

- Risk financing

- Discussion of the independent audit

- A list of any awards

- Acknowledgments to the finance department and others

The Financial Section

According to the GASB's *Codification of Governmental Accounting and Financial Reporting Standards* (Governmental Accounting Standards Board, 1996a, Section 2200.108), the financial section should include the auditor's report, the GPFS (five combined statements and the notes), any required supplementary information, and combining and individual fund and account group statements and schedules.

The Auditor's Report. The first item in the financial section is a letter from an independent auditor. The letter should contain a paragraph indicating the *scope* of the audit—whether it covers the entire financial section or only the GPFS. A second paragraph should indicate that the audit was conducted in accord with GAAS and GAGAS, and it should contain a short description of the nature of the audit. A third paragraph should express an opinion on the fairness of the financial statements. This paragraph may indicate that the opinion is *unqualified*—for example, it might say that the financial statements "present fairly, in all material respects, the financial position of the City of _____, and the results of its operations and cash flows of its proprietary and similar trust funds for the year [then ending], in conformity with generally accepted accounting principles." By "material" auditors normally mean that the omission or incorrect statement of the item would make a difference to the financial decisions made by the users of the financial statements. Conversely, the opinion may be *qualified* as to some material item (such as insufficient fixed-asset records, and so forth); an *adverse* opinion may be issued ("These statements do not present fairly . . ."); or a *disclaimer* may be issued ("We are not able to express an opinion due to . . ."). If a government's financial report receives a qualified, adverse, or disclaimed opinion, readers of the statements will not have the same confidence in the report as if it were unqualified.

Depending on the state, the independent auditor may be a state auditor, a certified public accountant (CPA) firm contracting with the state auditor to audit local governments, or a CPA firm contracting directly with the local government. The auditor's report should be addressed to the governing board and to the state (in some cases). A separate management letter is normally issued, but it is not normally included in the CAFR.

The General Purpose Financial Statements. The GPFS are five combined statements and their accompanying notes. Actually, GAAP permit the GPFS to be reported separately, without the remainder of the CAFR. In this sense, the GPFS are considered to be "liftable"—that is, the combined statements and the notes can be considered sufficient, unless one wishes to include the additional information contained in the combining and individual funds statements, the statistical section, and the introductory section. Due to the importance of these five statements, each is discussed and illustrated here.

- The *combined balance sheet: all fund types, account groups, and discretely presented component units* lists the assets, liabilities, and fund equity of the governmental unit. The combined balance sheet for the City of De Kalb, Illinois, as of June 30, 1996, is presented in Exhibit 5.1. The fund types are classified at the top of the statement. The *governmental* funds type includes the *general, special revenue, debt service,* and *capital projects* funds. *Proprietary* fund types include *enterprise* and *internal service* funds. *Fiduciary* funds (*trust and agency* funds) include *expendable trust, nonexpendable trust, pension trust,* and *agency* funds. The *general fixed asset account group* includes those fixed assets used by the general government (the fixed assets of proprietary funds are included in the funds), and the *general long-term debt account group* includes the long-term debt to be paid out of general government resources (the debt to be paid out of proprietary funds is included in those funds). A discretely presented component unit is a legally separate government (in this case, the De Kalb Public Library) for which the primary government (the City of De Kalb) has financial accountability. The combined balance sheet indicates that the unreserved fund balances of all the governmental fund types is positive, as are the unreserved retained earnings of the proprietary fund types.

Note that the combined balance sheet is organized into three sections: assets and other debits, liabilities, and equity and other credits. According to the GFOA (1994), an asset is "a probable future economic benefit obtained or controlled by a particular entity as a result of past transactions or events" (p. 313). Liabilities are "probable future sacrifices of economic benefits, arising from present obligations of a particular entity to transfer assets or provide services to other entities in the future as a result of past transactions or events" (p. 340). Note that for the governmental funds most of the assets are current; that is, it is anticipated that those assets will be converted into cash in the near future. Fixed assets of governmental funds are included in the general fixed asset account group. Conversely, all of the assets of proprietary funds, and of the nonexpendable and pension trust funds, are recorded directly in the funds.

Note that the last items in this section are called "other debits." These include the amount to be provided and the amount available to repay general obligation long-term debt. These accounts offset the long-term liabilities in the general long-term debt account group and provide an indication of the amount set aside in the debt service or other governmental funds for debt payment.

Liabilities in the government funds (general, special revenue, debt service, and capital projects) are mostly current; that is, these liabilities will be paid or extinguished with currently available resources. Long-term liabilities related to government funds are reported in the general long-term debt account group. Conversely, all of the liabilities of the proprietary, nonexpendable trust, and pension trust funds are recorded directly in the accounts of those funds.

The difference between assets and liabilities is called *fund equity.* The term used for governmental funds and for trust funds is *fund balance.* Note that fund balance may be either *reserved* or *unreserved.* Fund balance that is reserved is committed due to some past transaction or transactions. In the City of De Kalb, reserves are established for prepaid items, debt service, long-term receivables, and the employees' retirement system. Many other governments have a reserve established for *encumbrances*—that is, for those purchase orders that are outstanding at the end of the year. The unreserved fund balance is significant for analysts and budgeters. It is the amount, for those funds that have annual budgets, that is available for appropriation. As the City of De Kalb report shows, unreserved fund balance may be designated for certain items; in the case of De Kalb, a designation is established in the general fund and in capital projects funds for capital improvements. However, a designation is just that: a determination by the government that certain of the available balances are set aside. That designation can be undone by action of the government.

Proprietary funds equity accounts are called *contributed capital* and *retained earnings.* These accounts, similar to those of business enterprise, distinguish between the net resources that have been contributed by the government and those that have been earned over time.

Exhibit 5.1. City of De Kalb, Illinois, Combined Balance Sheet: All Fund Types, Account Groups, and Discretely Presented Component Units, June 30, 1996.

	Government Fund Types				Proprietary Fund Types	
	General	Special Revenue	Debt Service	Capital Projects	Enterprise	Internal Service
Assets and Other Debits						
Assets						
Cash and investments	$3,348,653	$676,168	$2,278,902	$6,146,446	$1,719,253	$945,862
Receivables (net, where applicable, of allowances for uncollectables)						
Property taxes	805,030	153,255	—	1,695,027	—	—
Accounts	—	—	—	—	760,974	—
Accrued interest	33,136	—	17,377	26,121	4,100	1,881
Other	719	17,362	—	—	—	117,727
Prepaid items/ expenses	34,628	1,060	—	6,075	12,019	894
Due from other governments	1,305,137	174,006	—	412,827	—	—
Due from other funds	668,505	266,000	—	475,229	882,129	162,000
Advance to other funds	—	—	—	655,000	—	—
Deferred compensation plan investments	—	—	—	—	—	—
Fixed assets (net, where applicable, of accumulated depreciation)	—	—	—	—	8,582,694	—
Long-term receivables— revolving loans	—	140,630	—	747,813	—	—
Other Debits						
Amount available for debt service	—	—	—	—	—	—
Amount to be provided for retirement of general long-term debt	—	—	—	—	—	—
Total Assets and Other Debits	$6,195,808	$1,428,481	$2,296,279	$10,164,538	$11,961,169	$1,228,364

Fiduciary Fund Types	Account Groups		Total Primary Government (Memorandum Only)	De Kalb Public Library	Total Reporting Entity (Memorandum Only)
Trust and Agency	General Fixed Assets	General Long-Term Debt			
$23,089,636	$—	$—	$38,204,920	$880,915	$39,085,835
462,974	—	—	3,116,286	529,487	3,645,773
—	—	—	760,974	—	760,974
366,641	—	—	449,256	2,166	451,422
—	—	—	135,808	—	135,808
132	—	—	54,808	5,908	60,716
—	—	—	1,891,970	—	1,891,970
—	—	—	2,453,863	—	2,453,863
—	—	—	655,000	—	655,000
4,288,681	—	—	4,288,681	—	4,288,681
—	30,000,429	—	38,583,123	276,129	38,859,252
—	—	—	888,443	—	888,443
—	—	2,295,279	2,295,279	—	2,295,279
—	—	23,586,493	23,586,493	14,691	23,601,184
$228,208,064	$30,000,429	$25,881,772	$117,364,904	$1,709,296	119,074,200

(*continued*)

Exhibit 5.1. (*continued*)

	Government Fund Types				Proprietary Fund Types	
	General	**Special Revenue**	**Debt Service**	**Capital Projects**	**Enterprise**	**Internal Service**
Liabilities						
Accounts payable	$188,997	$300,744	$1,000	$762,111	$223,321	$3,835
Claims payable	—	—	—	—	—	225,799
Accrued payroll	332,488	—	—	—	24,474	—
Contracts payable	—	19,114	—	94,898	8,592	—
Other payables	176,219	—	—	—	8,450	—
Deferred property taxes	1,070,075	169,653	—	2,052,685	—	—
Other deferred revenue	4,010	5,770	—	—	108,926	—
Due to other funds	60,000	13,424	—	2,218,307	—	162,000
Advance from other funds	—	—	—	655,000	—	—
Due to other governments	—	—	—	127,774	360,042	—
Due to participants	—	—	—	—	—	—
Due to bondholders	—	—	—	—	—	—
Compensated absences payable	223,843	—	—	—	131,817	—
Capital lease payable	—	—	—	—	—	—
General obligation bonds payable	—	—	—	—	—	—
General obligation bond anticipation notes payable	—	—	—	—	—	—
Total liabilities	2,055,632	508,705	1,000	5,910,775	865,622	391,634
Equity and Other Credits						
Contributed capital	—	—	—	—	2,270,429	—
Investment in general fixed assets	—	—	—	—	—	—
Retained earnings, unreserved	—	—	—	—	8,825,118	836,730
Fund balances						
Reserved for prepaid items	34,628	—	—	6,075	—	—
Reserved for debt service	—	—	2,295,279	—	—	—

Fiduciary Fund Types	Account Groups		Total Primary Government (Memorandum Only)	De Kalb Public Library	Total Reporting Entity (Memorandum Only)
Trust and Agency	General Fixed Assets	General Long-Term Debt			
$9,413	—	—	$1,489,421	$10,257	$1,499,678
—	—	—	225,799	—	225,799
—	—	—	356,962	16,440	373,402
—	—	—	122,604	—	122,604
—	—	—	184,669	—	184,669
—	—	—	3,292,413	640,516	3,932,929
—	—	—	118,706	—	118,706
132	—	—	2,453,863	—	2,453,863
—	—	—	655,000	—	655,000
—	—	—	487,816	—	487,816
4,288,681	—	—	4,288,681	—	4,288,681
87,829	—	—	87,829	—	87,829
—	—	2,014,590	2,370,250	16,323	2,386,573
—	—	246,963	246,963	—	246,963
—	—	14,805,219	14,805,219	—	14,805,219
—	—	8,815,000	8,815,000	—	8,815,000
4,386,055	—	25,881,772	40,001,195	683,536	40,684,731
—	—	—	2,270,429	—	2,270,429
—	30,000,429	—	30,000,429	276,129	30,276,558
—	—	—	9,661,848	—	9,661,848
—	—	—	40,703	—	40,703
—	—	—	2,295,279	—	2,295,279

(*continued*)

Exhibit 5.1. (*continued*)

	General	Government Fund Types			Proprietary Fund Types	
		Special Revenue	Debt Service	Capital Projects	Enterprise	Internal Service
Reserved for long-term receivables	—	140,630	—	1,402,813	—	—
Reserved for employees' retirement system	—	—	—	—	—	—
Unreserved						
Designed for capital improvement	1,300,000					
Undesignated	2,805,548	779,146	—	2,844,875	—	—
Total equity and other credits	4,140,176	919,776	2,295,279	4,253,763	11,095,547	836,730
Total Liabilities, Equity and Other Credits	$6,195,808	$1,428,481	$2,296,279	$10,164,538	$11,961,169	$1,228,364

The equity account, investment in general fixed assets, reflects the balance of the fixed assets in the general long-term debt account group. This balance is supported by detailed property records, and some of that detail is reported elsewhere in the CAFR.

It should be noted that agency funds do not have equity accounts; they have only assets and liabilities. Finally, note the term *memorandum only* used in the totals columns. This is an indication that the totals do not really mean much; they are simply aggregations of the balances of the funds and account groups. Interfund eliminations have not been made, and many accountants feel that the totals column includes many unlike items. A government is not required to present a totals column; if one is presented, the term *memorandum only* is required.

The combined balance sheet for the City of De Kalb reflects a positive unreserved fund balance or retained earnings for all funds. The notes reveal, however, that some of the individual funds have deficit fund equity balances. A large portion of the unreserved fund balance of the general fund has been designated for capital improvements. A total of $2,295,279 has been reserved in a debt service fund for the payment of debt; a like amount is shown as "avail-

Fiduciary Fund Types	Account Groups		Total Primary Government (Memo-	De Kalb Public	Total Reporting Entity (Memo-
Trust and Agency	General Fixed Assets	General Long- Term Debt	randum Only)	Library	randum Only)
—	—	—	1,543,443	—	1,543,443
23,822,009	—	—	23,822,009	—	23,822,009
—	—	—	6,429,569	749,631	7,179,200
23,822,009	30,000,429	—	76,063,709	1,025,760	77,089,469
$28,208,064	$30,000,429	$25,881,772	$116,064,904	$1,709,296	$117,774,200

able" in the general long-term debt account group. Also note that the enterprise funds have more than $8 million in retained earnings and no long-term debt.

• The *combined statement of revenues, expenditures, and changes in fund balances: all governmental fund types and discretely presented component units,* reflects the revenues, expenditures, other financing sources and uses (such as operating transfers, which are normal, recurring transfers between funds), prior period adjustments, and residual equity (unusual, nonrecurring) transfers of the general, special revenue, debt service, and capital projects funds, as well as those for any expendable trust funds and component units that are accounted in the same way as the governmental funds. Note that the proprietary funds are not included. The governmental funds use *modified accrual accounting:* revenues are recognized when measurable and available to pay current expenditures, and expenditures are recognized when goods and services are received, except for debt service expenditures, which are recorded as expenditures when due. Exhibit 5.2 reflects this statement for the City of De Kalb and the De Kalb Public Library. Note the revenue source classifications and the expenditure classifications as well as the transfers between funds. The general fund reports

Exhibit 5.2. City of De Kalb, Illinois, Combined Statement of Revenues, Expenditures, and Changes in Fund Balances: All Governmental Fund Types and Discretely Presented Component Units, for Year Ended June 30, 1996.

	Governmental Fund Types		
	General	Special Revenue	Debt Service
Revenues			
Taxes	$10,492,059	$337,006	$ —
Licenses and permits	249,707	—	—
Intergovernmental	20,893	1,786,078	—
Charges for services	599,944	185,796	—
Fines and forfeits	451,306	—	—
Interest	211,671	12,008	21,733
Miscellaneous	196,349	67,398	—
Total revenues	12,221,929	2,388,286	21,733
Expenditures			
Current			
General government	3,783,361	836,780	—
Public safety	5,786,715	21,086	—
Highways and streets	2,733,410	1,047,274	—
Culture and recreation	—	795,356	—
Capital outlay	—	11,039	—
Debt service			
Principal retirement	—	—	904,203
Interest and fiscal charges	—	—	1,205,321
Total expenditures	12,303,486	2,711,535	2,109,524
Excess (Deficiency) of Revenues over (under) Expenditures	(81,557)	(323,249)	(2,087,791)
Other Financing Sources (uses)			
Operating transfers in	1,287,727	516,429	1,973,544
Operating transfers out	(556,540)	(362,000)	—
Sale of fixed assets	6,083	—	—
Proceeds from general obligation bonds	—	—	4,320,836
Payment to escrow agent	—	—	(1,998,551)
Proceeds from bond anticipation notes	—	—	—
Total other financing sources (uses)	737,270	154,429	4,295,829

Capital Projects	Total Primary Government (Memo-randum Only)	De Kalb Public Library	Total Reporting Entity (Memo-randum Only)
$3,307,825	$14,136,890	$612,567	$14,749,457
—	249,707	—	249,707
248,908	2,055,879	81,139	2,137,018
—	785,740	7,080	792,820
—	451,306	21,361	472,667
276,481	521,893	51,929	573,822
141,581	405,328	19,632	424,960
3,974,795	18,606,743	793,708	19,400,451
—	4,620,141	709,077	5,329,218
—	5,807,801	—	5,807,801
—	3,780,684	—	3,780,684
—	795,356	—	795,356
5,342,218	5,353,257	56,773	5,410,030
—	904,203	—	904,203
—	1,205,321	—	1,205,321
5,342,218	22,466,763	765,850	23,232,613
(1,367,423)	(3,860,020)	27,858	(3,832,162)
146,027	3,923,727	—	3,923,727
(2,291,454)	(3,209,994)	—	(3,209,994)
—	6,083	—	6,083
—	4,320,836	—	4,320,836
—	(1,998,551)	—	(1,998,551)
500,000	500,000	—	500,000
(1,645,427)	3,542,101	—	3,542,101

(continued)

Exhibit 5.2. (*continued*)

		Governmental Fund Types	
	General	Special Revenue	Debt Service
Excess (Deficiency) of Revenues and Other Financing Sources over (under) Expenditures and Other Financing Uses	655,713	(168,820)	2,208,038
Fund Balances, July 1	4,473,205	1,070,687	87,241
Prior period adjustment	11,258	17,909	—
Fund Balances, July 1, Restated	4,484,463	1,088,596	87,241
Residual equity transfer in (out)	(1,000,000)	—	—
Fund Balances, June 30	$4,140,176	$919,776	$2,295,279

a large excess of revenues and other financing sources over expenditures and other financing uses, but it also reports a $1 million equity transfer to a capital projects fund. Also note the changes in the fund balances of the other fund types. It should be mentioned that a government has only one general fund; other fund types may each have several funds within them. For example, the City of De Kalb has ten special revenue funds; one would look to the combining statements in the CAFR to see the status of the individual funds. As indicated earlier, revenues are recognized when measurable and available to finance expenditures of the current period.

Expenditures are reported by character (current, capital outlay, and debt service) and by function (general government, public safety, and so forth). Most of the time the functional expenditures are aggregations of departmental expenditures; for example, public safety would include the police and fire departments and protective inspections. Expenditures are recognized when goods and services are received, as described earlier in the chapter. The term *expenditure* has a different meaning than the term *expenses,* commonly used in business reporting. According to the GFOA (1994), expenditures are "decreases in net financial resources" and include "current operating expenses requiring the present or future use of net current assets, debt service and capital outlays, and intergovernmental grants, entitlements and shared revenues" (p. 329). Expenses, which are reported by businesses and by enterprise, internal service,

Capital Projects	Total Primary Government (Memo- randum Only)	De Kalb Public Library	Total Reporting Entity (Memo- randum Only)
(3,012,850)	(317,919)	27,858	(290,061)
6,266,613	11,897,746	721,773	12,619,519
—	29,167	—	29,167
6,266,613	11,926,913	721,773	12,648,686
1,000,000	—	—	—
$4,253,763	$11,608,994	$749,631	$12,358,625

nonexpendable trust, and pension trust funds, are recorded when incurred and represent the use of economic resources, which are "matched" with the revenues generated. For example, an expenditure of the general fund might include the acquisition of a police car. Conversely, an enterprise fund would not record an expense at that stage for a car used by a utility fund; depreciation expense would be charged over the useful life of the car.

Other financing sources and uses include operating transfers in or out, sales of fixed assets, proceeds of general obligation bonds and notes, and payments to escrow agents. These funds-flow movements can be significant and should be traced to the combining and individual fund and account group statements. Prior period adjustments are normally made to correct accounting errors, and note disclosure would normally be made. Equity transfers are unusual and nonrecurring transfers between funds. In the case of the City of De Kalb, $1 million was transferred from the general fund to a capital projects fund. An analyst or a person involved in the budgetary process would want to know more about this transfer.

• The *combined statement of revenues, expenditures, and changes in fund balances—budget and actual: all governmental fund types,* shown in Exhibit 5.3, compares the final budget and actual revenues, expenditures, and other financing sources and uses for the general fund and for all other government fund types that have a legally adopted annual budget. This statement is prepared

Exhibit 5.3. Combined Statement of Revenues, Expenditures, and Changes in Fund Balances—Budget and Actual: All Government Fund Types, for Year Ended June 30, 1996.

| | General | | | Special Revenue | |
	Budget	Actual	Variance Favorable (Unfavor- able)	Budget	Actual
Revenues					
Taxes	$10,529,171	$10,492,059	(37,112)	$320,750	$337,006
Licenses and permits	252,000	249,707	(2,293)	—	—
Intergovernmental	30,000	20,893	(9,107)	1,715,000	1,786,078
Charges for services	520,000	599,944	79,944	195,000	185,796
Fines and forfeits	391,081	451,306	60,225	—	—
Interest	92,721	211,671	118,950	19,000	12,008
Miscellaneous	201,300	196,349	(4,951)	30,370	67,398
Total revenues	12,016,273	12,221,929	205,656	2,280,120	2,388,286
Expenditures					
Current					
General government	3,758,024	3,783,361	(25,337)	1,352,900	836,780
Public safety	6,321,463	5,786,715	534,748	20,100	21,086
Highways and streets	2,912,314	2,733,410	178,904	907,154	1,047,274
Culture recreation	—	—	—	230,240	795,356
Capital outlay	—	—	—	140,738	11,039
Debt service					
Principal retirement	—	—	—	—	—
Interest and fiscal charges	—	—	—	—	—
Total Expenditures	12,991,801	12,303,486	688,315	2,651,132	2,711,535
Excess (Deficiency) of Revenues over (under) Expenditures	(975,528)	(81,557)	893,971	(371,012)	(323,249)
Other Financing Sources (Uses)					
Operating transfers in	1,727,727	1,287,727	(440,000)	77,000	516,429
Operating transfers out	(691,779)	(556,540)	135,239	(402,000)	(362,000)
Sale of fixed assets	10,000	6,083	(3,917)	—	—
Proceeds from general obligation bonds	—	—	—	—	—

	Debt Service			Capital Projects		
Variance Favorable (Unfavorable)	Budget	Actual	Variance Favorable (Unfavorable)	Budget	Actual	Variance Favorable (Unfavorable)
$16,256	—	—	—	$3,211,998	$3,307,825	$95,827
—	—	—	—	—	—	—
71,078	—	—	—	410,000	248,908	(161,092)
(9,204)	—	—	—	—	—	—
—	—	—	—	—	—	—
(6,992)	21,400	21,733	333	60,000	276,481	216,481
37,028	—	—	—	178,840	141,581	(37,259)
108,166	21,400	21,733	333	3,860,838	3,974,795	113,957
516,120	—	—	—	—	—	—
(986)	—	—	—	—	—	—
(140,120)	—	—	—	—	—	—
(565,116)	—	—	—	—	—	—
129,699	—	—	—	6,523,555	5,342,218	1,181,337
—	904,203	904,203	—	—	—	—
—	1,330,070	1,205,321	124,749	—	—	—
(60,403)	2,234,273	2,109,524	124,749	6,523,555	5,342,218	1,181,337
47,763	(2,212,873)	(2,087,791)	125,082	(2,662,717)	1,367,423	1,295,294
439,429	2,174,583	1,973,544	(201,039)	—	146,027	—
40,000	—	—	—	($2,173,269)	(2,291,454)	(118,185)
—	—	—	—	—	—	—
—	4,320,836	—	—	—	4,320,836	—

(continued)

Exhibit 5.3. (*continued*)

	General			Special Revenue	
	Budget	Actual	Variance Favorable (Unfavor- able)	Budget	Actual
Payment to escrow agent	—	—	—	—	—
Proceeds from bond anticipation notes	—	—	—	—	—
Total other financing sources (uses)	1,045,948	737,270	(308,678)	(325,000)	154,429
Excess (Deficiency) of Revenues and Other Financing Sources over (under) Expenditures and Other Financing Uses	70,420	655,713	585,293	(696,012)	(168,820)
Fund Balances, July 1		4,473,205			1,070,687
Prior period adjustment		11,258			17,909
Fund Balances, July 1, Restated		4,484,463			1,088,596
Residual equity transfer in (out)		(1,000,000)			—
Fund Balances, June 30		$4,140,176			$919,776

on the same basis as the budget if the annual budget is prepared in a manner different than the GAAP. For example, if the budget is on a cash basis, this report would be on a cash basis. One difference between the budgetary basis and the GAAP that is often found in practice is that encumbrances (purchase orders and contracts) are often reported as expenditures when issued under the budgetary basis and reported as expenditures only when received under the GAAP. Any differences between the budgetary basis and the GAAP should be illustrated in this statement or described in the notes. The notes to the financial statements and the combining statements reveal more detail about the excesses of expenditures over appropriations at the legal level of control.

As indicated earlier, this statement is prepared on the same basis as the budget if the budgetary basis of accounting is different than the GAAP. In the case

Variance Favorable (Unfavor- able)	Debt Service			Capital Projects		
	Budget	Actual	Variance Favorable (Unfavor- able)	Budget	Actual	Variance Favorable (Unfavor- able)
—	(1,998,551)	(1,998,551)	—	—	—	—
—	—	—	—	—	500,000	500,000
479,429	4,496,868	4,295,829	(201,039)	(2,173,269)	(1,645,427)	381,815
527,192	2,283,995	2,208,038	(75,957)	(4,835,986)	(3,012,850)	1,677,109
		87,241			6,266,613	
		—			—	
		87,241			6,266,613	
		—			1,000,000	
		$2,295,279			$4,253,763	

of De Kalb, no differences exist. The same categories—revenues, expenditures, other financing sources and uses, and so forth—are used as in Exhibit 5.2. This statement is required for the general fund and for all other governmental funds that have a legally adopted annual budget. In the case of De Kalb, all of these funds have legally adopted budgets, so all are included. There are a number of instances in which negative figures are reported, even at the fund level, for expenditures. The notes disclose the individual funds that have exceeded appropriations at the legal level of control.

Following is an example of a budget-actual statement, which is a legal compliance document that reports to the public the comparison between the final budget and actual results. This statement, like the others, is included in the audit scope, so auditors are required to verify the budget and actual figures on the budgetary basis.

The following funds had an excess of actual expenditures and expenses (exclusive of depreciation and amortization) over budget for the fiscal year:

Fund	Excess
Foreign Fire Insurance Tax	$986
Airport	$565,116
Motor Fuel Tax	$215,053

• *The combined statement of revenues, expenses, and changes in retained earnings/fund balances: all proprietary and similar trust funds* is the fourth of the five combined statements. This statement reflects the net income and other changes in fund equity of the proprietary (enterprise and internal service), pension trust, and nonexpendable trust funds. These funds use full accrual accounting—essentially the same system used in the accounts of business enterprise. This statement is a reflection of whether or not these funds break even, or whether a subsidy is needed, using a full-cost allocation of expenses, including depreciation of fixed assets. Exhibit 5.4 reflects this statement for the City of De Kalb, which has no nonexpendable trust funds and no separately displayed component units that use full accrual accounting. Note that enterprise funds and pension trust funds show a positive net income for the year before operating transfers while internal service funds show a loss.

Under the full accrual basis used by the funds in this statement, revenues are recognized when earned, regardless of when the cash will be received. Expenses (not expenditures) are recognized when incurred, regardless of when payment will be made. As mentioned earlier, expenses do not include the acquisition of capital assets but record depreciation. In like manner, expenses do not include the payment of debt service principal.

The format shown in Exhibit 5.4 is generally required by GASB. Operating revenues are shown by source. Operating expenses are shown by major category, including depreciation. Operating income is a significant number to financial analysts because it indicates the amount generated by the central operations of the fund. Nonoperating revenues and expenses are those that are not central to operations and include interest. Operating transfers in and out are also shown. In the case of De Kalb, the enterprise funds have a significant net income before operating transfers, but the operating transfer-out results in a small net loss. The add-back of depreciation that reduces contributed capital (instead of retained earnings) is a technical adjustment that is required when some of the depreciation is on fixed assets acquired with contributed capital. In addition, the internal service funds show a loss for the year. This reflects losses for all three self-insurance funds (workers' compensation, health insurance, and liability and property insurance); however, all three continue to have positive retained earnings balances. Finally, the statement ends with a reconciliation of the equity account, retained earnings.

Exhibit 5.4. City of De Kalb, Illinois, Combined Statement of Revenues, Expenses, and Changes in Retained Earnings/Fund Balances: All Proprietary and Fiduciary Fund Types, for Year Ended June 30, 1996.

	Proprietary Fund Types		Fiduciary Fund Type	Totals (Memorandum Only)
	Enterprise	Internal Service	Pension Trust	
Operating Revenues				
Charges for services	$3,196,081	$1,444,462	—	$4,640,543
Contributions	—	—	741,981	741,981
Interest	—	—	1,348,018	1,348,018
Gain on sale of investments	—	—	258,127	258,127
Miscellaneous	16,463	45,615	—	62,078
Total operating revenues	3,212,544	1,490,077	2,348,126	7,050,747
Operating Expenses				
Administration	—	1,740,299	—	1,740,299
Operations	2,286,800	—	—	2,286,800
Depreciation	317,301	—	—	317,301
Benefits and refunds	—	—	940,988	940,988
Miscellaneous	—	—	53,948	53,948
Total operating expenses	2,604,101	1,740,299	994,936	5,339,336
Operating Income (Loss)	608,443	(250,222)	1,353,190	1,711,411
Nonoperating Revenues				
Interest income	80,532	51,046	—	131,578
Gain on sale of investments	7,384	—	—	7,384
Total nonoperating revenues	87,916	51,046	—	138,962
Net Income (Loss) Before Operating Transfers	696,359	(199,176)	1,353,190	1,850,373
Operating Transfers (out)				
Operating transfers (out)	(713,733)	—	—	(713,733)

(*continued*)

Exhibit 5.4. (*continued*)

| | Proprietary Fund Types | | Fiduciary Fund Type | Totals (Memo- |
	Enterprise	Internal Service	Pension Trust	randum Only)
Total operating transfers (out)	(713,733)	—	—	(713,733)
Net Income (Loss)	(17,374)	(199,176)	1,353,190	1,136,640
Other Changes in Retained Earnings- Fund Balances Add back depreciation that reduces con- tributed capital	39,939	—	—	39,939
Increase (Decrease) in Retained Earnings- Fund Balances	22,565	(199,176)	1,353,190	1,176,579
Retained Earnings-Fund Balances, July 1	8,802,553	963,688	22,468,819	32,235,060
Prior period adjustment	—	72,218	—	72,218
Retained Earnings-Fund Balances, July 1, Restated	8,802,553	1,035,906	22,468,819	32,307,278
Retained Earnings-Fund Balances, June 30	$8,825,118	$836,730	$23,822,009	$33,483,857

• The fifth and last of the combined statements is the *statement of cash flows,* which is required for enterprise, internal service, and nonexpendable trust funds. In Exhibit 5.5, cash flows are shown separately for operating, non-capital financing, capital and related financing, and investing activities. This statement enables financial analysts and others to trace cash flows that would not be apparent from the previous statement, including borrowing and invest-ing activities.

De Kalb had two choices regarding how to report cash flows from operations. The first method, called the *direct method,* has categories such as "cash received from customers," "cash paid to suppliers," and so forth. De Kalb chose, how-ever, *the indirect method,* which begins with the operating income figure shown in the *statement of revenues, expenses, and changes in retained earnings/*

Exhibit 5.5. City of De Kalb, Illinois, Combined Statement of Cash Flows: All Proprietary Fund Types, for Year Ended June 30, 1996.

	Proprietary Fund Types		Totals (Memorandum Only)
	Enterprise	Internal Service	
Cash Flows from Operating Activities			
Operating income (loss)	$608,443	$(250,222)	$358,221
Adjustments to reconcile operating income to net cash provided (used) by operating activities			
Depreciation	317,301	—	317,301
Changes in assets and liabilities			
Accounts receivable	(12,431)	—	(12,431)
Other receivables	—	(45,493)	(45,493)
Prepaid expenses	(6,690)	61,399	54,709
Intergovernmenal receivables	—	2,148	2,148
Accounts payable	126,488	(2,022)	124,466
Accrued payroll	3,231	—	3,231
Claims payable	—	40,694	40,694
Contracts payable	8,592	—	8,592
Other payables	(1,500)	—	(1,500)
Intergovernmental payables	(5,866)	—	(5,866)
Deferred revenue	(5,421)	—	(5,421)
Compensated absences	14,360	—	14,360
Net cash provided by (used in) operating activities	1,046,507	(193,496)	853,011
Cash Flows from Noncapital Financing Activities			
Interfund receivables	(326,208)	(10,000)	(336,208)
Interfund payables	(105)	10,000	9,895
Operating transfers (Out)	(713,733)	—	(713,733)
Net cash provided by (used in) noncapital financing activities	(1,040,046)	—	(1,040,046)
Cash Flows from Capital and Related Financing Activities			
Fixed assets purchased	(248,299)	—	(248,299)

(continued)

Exhibit 5.5. (*continued*)

	Proprietary Fund Types		Totals (Memorandum Only)
	Enterprise	Internal Service	
Net cash provided by (used in) capital and related financing activities	(248,299)	—	(248,299)
Cash Flows From Investing Activities			
Proceeds from sale and maturities of investment securities	411,134	202,000	613,134
Purchase of investment securities	(202,000)	—	(202,000)
Interest on investments	88,018	51,589	139,607
Net cash provided by (used in) investing activities	297,152	253,589	550,741
Net Increase (Decrease) in Cash and Cash Equivalents	55,314	60,093	115,407
Cash and Cash Equivalents, July 1	199,439	146,919	346,358
Cash and Cash Equivalents, June 30	254,753	207,012	461,765
Cash and Investments			
Cash and cash equivalents	254,753	207,012	461,765
Investments	1,464,500	738,850	2,203,350
Total Cash and Investments	1,719,253	945,862	2,665,115
Noncash Transaction			
Developer contributed mains	479,000	—	479,000

fund balances, and with making adjustments for noncash items and for changes in balances in asset and liability accounts. Exhibit 5.5 shows that De Kalb had a positive cash flow from operations for the enterprise funds and a negative cash flow from operations for the internal service funds.

Cash flows from noncapital financing activities reflects operating transfers between funds, changes in interfund receivables and payables, and (if it applies) borrowings for noncapital activities. The purpose of this section of the report is primarily to reflect such borrowings. An analyst would be concerned if a large borrowing took place to finance a current deficit in one of these funds.

Cash flows from capital and related financing activities reflect cash flows from borrowings, any interest paid on such borrowings, and any fixed assets acquired. As mentioned earlier, De Kalb does not have long-term debt in its enterprise funds. Cash flows from investing activities reflect cash flows from purchasing and selling investments and from interest income on investments. Generally, cash flows are to be reported gross on this statement, so users can trace the activities of the government related to cash. It should be noted that this statement differs from a similar statement required for business enterprises in that four categories are required instead of three, a number of the transactions (for example, interest receipts and payments) are reported in different categories, and the operating section for the indirect method begins with operating income, not with income as is reported for business enterprises.

The notes to the financial statements are integral to understanding the numbers presented in the five combined statements. To highlight the importance of the notes, each of the five statements has, at the bottom of the page, a required sentence: "See accompanying notes to financial statements." Most state and local government financial reports have extensive notes. For example, the City of De Kalb's CAFR devotes twelve pages to the five combined statements and thirty-four pages to the notes. The GASB *Codification* (1996a) lists those note disclosures that are essential to fair presentation of the GPFS, as well as a number of suggested disclosures. *Governmental Accounting, Auditing, and Financial Reporting* (GFOA, 1994) presents example disclosures. The most important of the notes is a summary of significant accounting policies, which describes the accounting choices made as well as a description of the measurement focus and basis of accounting. Other items that would be found in the notes and not in the five combined statements include the unfunded actuarial pension obligation, a summary of interfund transfers, deficit fund equity balances in individual funds, and excesses of expenditures over appropriations in individual funds at the legal level of control. The notes are written as if the five combined statements and their notes were issued separately.

Combining and Individual Fund and Account Group Statements and Schedules. For each fund type that consists of more than one fund, a complete financial section of a CAFR also includes combining statements that have one column for each fund in the fund type. Added across, these columns total the amounts presented in the combined statements. Exhibit 5.6 reflects a *combining statement of revenues, expenses, and changes in retained earnings for the enterprise funds* for the City of De Kalb. Note that the totals column presents the same numbers as the enterprise fund column in the combined statement shown in Exhibit 5.4. In addition, individual fund statements and schedules are often included in this section, especially to show more detail and to make comparisons with the previous year for the general fund.

The Statistical Section

The final section of the CAFR is the statistical section. The GASB *Codification* (1996a) presents a number of statistical tables that are helpful for analysts and others. Most of these tables include ten years' information. Included are revenue and expenditure detail, property values, tax rates and tax collections, debt information, and demographic and economic statistics.

INTERACTION BETWEEN THE CAFR AND THE BUDGET

As already noted, GAAP are defined by the GASB, the AICPA, and other groups in the GAAP hierarchy. As indicated earlier, two bases of accounting are used for governmental units. The modified accrual basis is used for the governmental (general, special revenue, debt service, and capital projects), expendable trust, and agency funds as well as for those component units that are more governmental than proprietary, such as the De Kalb Public Library. Full accrual accounting is required for proprietary (enterprise and internal service), nonexpendable trust, and pension trust funds, as well as for those component units that are more proprietary in nature, such as a transit system or a stadium authority. Budgets will always be prepared and passed in public session for the general fund; others will require formally adopted legal annual budgets in accord with state or local law. Those budgets may or may not be in accord with GAAP, again depending on state or local law.

Under modified accrual accounting, revenues are recognized when measurable and available to finance the expenditures of the current period. This places modified accrual accounting someplace between cash and accrual accounting. Property taxes are to be recognized as revenues for the accounting period levied, but no revenues should be recognized that are not expected to be collected more than sixty days beyond the end of the fiscal year. Sales taxes and income taxes can be accrued as long as the amounts are reasonably estimable and will be received soon enough to pay the liabilities of the current period. In practice, many governments do not accrue these revenues in advance of

Exhibit 5.6. City of De Kalb, Illinois, Enterprise Funds, Combining Statement of Revenues, Expenses, and Changes in Retained Earnings, for Year Ended June 30, 1996.

	Water	Refuse	Totals
Operating Revenues			
Charges for services	$2,328,372	$867,709	$3,196,081
Miscellaneous	16,463	—	16,463
Total operating revenues	2,344,835	867,709	3,212,544
Operating Expenses Excluding Depreciation			
Personal services	582,710	—	582,710
Commodities	157,461	647	158,108
Contractual services	320,579	861,991	1,182,570
Other services/expenses	172	—	172
Equipment/improvements	363,240	—	363,240
Total operating expenses excluding depreciation	1,424,162	862,638	2,286,800
Operating Income (Loss) Before Depreciation	920,673	5,071	925,744
Depreciation	317,301	—	317.301
Operating Income (Loss)	603,372	5,071	603,443
Nonoperating Revenues			
Interest income	80,532	—	80,532
Gain on sale of investments	7,384	—	7,384
Total nonoperating revenues	87,916	—	87,916
Income (Loss) Before Operating Transfers	691,288	5,071	696,359
Operating Transfers in (out)			
Operating transfers in	—	—	—
Operating transfers out	(678,733)	(35,000)	(713,733)
Total operating transfers in (out)	(678,733)	(35,000)	(713,733)
Net Income Loss	12,555	(29,929)	(17,374)

(*continued*)

Exhibit 5.6. (*continued*)

	Water	Refuse	Totals
Other Changes in Retained Earnings			
Addback depreciation that reduces contributed capital	39,939	—	39,939
Increase (Decrease) in Retained Earnings	52,494	(29,929)	22,565
Retained Earnings, July 1	8,773,007	29,546	8,802,553
Retained Earnings (Deficit), June 30	$8,825,501	$ (383)	$8,825,118

collection. When an asset (a receivable, such as property taxes receivable) is recognized during a fiscal year but the revenue is not, a liability, called *deferred revenue,* is recognized. Other revenue source categories, such as fines and forfeits, license and permit fees, and so on, are normally recorded when received in cash, on the basis that these revenues are not measurable prior to collection, or on the basis of materiality.

Under GAAP, expenditures are to be recognized when the goods or services are received, not when the cash is paid. Three exceptions to this rule exist. First, debt service payments, both principal and interest, are recorded as expenditures when due and payable. Second, inventories may be recorded as expenditures either when received (the purchases method) or when used (the consumption method). Third, goods or services received that will not be paid for with currently available resources will not be charged as expenditures. For example, compensated absences that have been earned by employees but that are not going to be paid soon out of available resources are recorded as a liability in the general long-term debt account group. It should be noted that expenditures are not charged when encumbrances have been issued under GAAP.

Budgetary accounting may differ from GAAP due to basis differences, perspective differences, and timing differences. A *basis difference* is a difference in the basis of accounting. For example, GAAP requires the modified accrual basis of accounting for the general fund. A local government's state government may require the cash basis for budgeting purposes, for one or more revenue or expenditure items. A *perspective difference* results from the structure of financial information for budgetary purposes. For example, one government may not organize certain expenditures on the basis of fund, or organizational unit, for budgetary purposes. Compensated absences, for example, might be charged to a separate account rather than to the fund, department, and function where the salary is recorded; GAAP will require compensated absences to be reported with the salaries. Finally, *entity differences* may exist. For financial reporting purposes, the appropriated budget might include certain departments and agencies that are not a part of the primary government, or the appropriated budget might not include all of the expenditures of a fund, department, or function.

The Budget-Actual Statement on the Budgetary Basis

As indicated earlier, a budget-actual comparison is required in the CAFR for the general fund and for all other governmental funds that have a legally adopted annual budget. The budget-actual comparison is required in the GPFS (the combined statement of revenues, expenditures, and changes in fund balances—budget and actual, shown in Exhibit 5.3) and in the combining and individual fund and account group statements.

Regardless of whether the differences between GAAP and the budgetary basis are due to basis, perspective, or timing, the "actual" as well as the "budget" column in all budget-actual statements must be on the budgetary basis. Differences between the budgetary basis and GAAP are to be explained in the notes to the financial statements, or if the difference can be shown, on the face of the budget-actual statement. It is helpful if the budget-actual statement indicates in the heading whether the statement is prepared on the GAAP basis. It should be noted that the City of De Kalb does use the GAAP basis for budgeting, as can be seen from the fact that all revenues and expenditures are the same in the budget-actual statement (Exhibit 5.3) as in the statement of revenues, expenditures, and changes in fund balances (Exhibit 5.2).

The Accounting System for Both
Budgetary and GAAP Reporting

The GASB *Codification* (1996a) indicates that GAAP reporting is essential; all but the budget-actual statements are to be prepared in accordance with GAAP. GASB also indicates, however, that legal compliance reporting is essential.

As a result, it is imperative that a governmental unit establish an accounting system that will accommodate reporting on both the budgetary and GAAP bases. Generally, a government will design its accounting system on the budgetary basis for use in interim internal reporting, for management use, and for reporting to the governing body. Typically, revenues will be compared with estimated revenues by the governing board and others to determine if resources will be available as expected. Expenditures and encumbrances will also be compared with appropriations, by department heads, top management, and the governing board, to determine compliance and to determine whether budgetary impoundment or other actions are necessary. At year's end, the information from the accounting system is used to prepare the year-end budget-actual statements required for the CAFR, as described earlier. Adjustments are then made, as necessary, to prepare GAAP financial statements.

One common example of an adjustment that might be necessary is related to encumbrances. The budgetary system might include encumbrances of the current period as a deduction from appropriations, along with current-period expenditures. For example, assume that the appropriation for the equipment budget of the public safety function was $1 million, that current year expenditures were $920,000, and that current year but unfilled purchase orders amounted to $70,000. The budget-actual statement would reflect expenditures and encumbrances of $990,000 and a positive balance of $10,000, when comparing appropriations with expenditures and encumbrances. The GAAP operating statement, however, would reflect $920,000 as expenditures in most cases.

Care must be exercised in developing account codes so that budget-actual comparisons are easily made, normally from a computerized system. Account codes for the budget and the actual for each revenue source and expenditure classification should be similar, with the only difference being that one is budget and the other is actual. When the budget is originally passed or later amended, the amounts are loaded into the budgetary accounts. Without going into the details of debits and credits here, it should be noted that the codes for the budgetary accounts will have opposite signs to the actual accounts, facilitating comparisons in the reporting process. Again, both the budget and actual recording during the year will normally be on the budgetary basis; adjustments will be made at year's end for purposes of preparing the financial statements in accord with GAAP.

USERS AND USES OF FINANCIAL STATEMENTS

The GASB (1987, p. 30) lists three primary users of financial statements:

- "Those to whom government is primarily accountable (the citizenry)"
- "Those who directly represent the citizens (legislative and oversight bodies)"
- "Those who lend or who participate in the lending process (investors and creditors)"

Further, the GASB indicates the following regarding the uses of financial statements (1987, p. 32):

Financial reporting by state and local governments is used in making economic, social, and political decisions and in assessing accountability primarily by:

a. Comparing actual financial results with the legally adopted annual budget
b. Assessing financial condition and results of operations
c. Assisting in determining compliance with finance-related laws, rules, and regulations, and
d. Assisting in evaluating efficiency and effectiveness.

The last use is not met by current financial statements. GASB has a project on service efforts and accomplishments that in the future should result in disclosures of inputs, outputs, and outcomes.

Two of these uses of financial statements are discussed here: analysis of debt by the financial community, and use by government employees and elected officials for budgetary control and planning.

Analysis of Debt by the Financial Community

Probably the most intensive use of the financial reports of state and local governments is by municipal financial analysts who are involved in the municipal bond market. These include those who rate bonds (such as Moody's Investors Service, Standard & Poor's, and Fitch Investors Service) as well as investors, underwriters, financial advisers, bond attorneys, and bond insurers. Although a great variety of municipal debt exists, it is generally categorized in two ways: as debt that is supported by the general taxing power of the government (general obligation or tax supported debt), and as debt that is supported only by the revenues of certain revenue streams (limited obligation debt, often revenue bonds supported by a single enterprise, such as a utility or airport). Ratios for these two classifications of debt have been developed by the bond-rating agencies and by others in the financial community. The ratings agencies use these ratios, and other background information—much of it nonfinancial, such as population changes—to develop bond ratings. Investors, insurers, and others in the municipal bond market use the ratings of the ratings services, as well as their own techniques, to make financial decisions regarding municipal debt. Governments with strong financial numbers are able to sell debt with much lower interest charges or to obtain bond insurance at a lower cost.

Four examples of computations of ratios for the City of De Kalb are net direct debt per capita, net debt to the equivalent fair value of property, the operating ratio for enterprise funds, and the unreserved fund balance of the general fund divided by the general fund revenues. The *net direct debt per capita* represents the net general obligation debt divided by the population. The net debt comes from the combined balance sheet (see Exhibit 5.1):

General obligation debt (bonds and notes)	$23,620,219
Minus the "amount available"	2,295,279
Net general obligation debt	21,324,940
Divided by the population	36,950
Net debt per capita	*$577.13*

Moody's *1997 Medians: Selected Indicators of Municipal Performance* indicates that the median net debt per capita for cities the size of De Kalb is $765, so De

Kalb is in a favorable debt position. One would want to consider overlapping debt, accrued compensated absences, and the unfunded pension obligation to round out consideration of tax-supported debt per capita.

Direct net debt as a percentage of the fair value of property is a measure of the residual revenue source for local governments—property taxes—to back the debt. In De Kalb's case, the assessed valuation of property is presented in the statistical section of the CAFR. Fair value is three times the amount shown. The calculations would be as follows:

Net debt	$21,324,940
Divide by the fair value of property	$857,069,280
Net debt to fair value of property	*2.49 percent*

Moody's indicates a median of 1.6 percent, so De Kalb is in a worse position when comparing debt with property values.

The *operating ratio for enterprise funds* would be important for municipalities issuing revenue bonds for enterprise activities. Although De Kalb has no revenue bonds payable, the computation is presented here; it determines the operating and maintenance expenses minus depreciation divided by the operating revenues. These figures are all reflected in the enterprise fund column of Exhibit 5.4:

Operating expenses	$2,604,101
Minus depreciation	317,301
Net	$2,286,800
Divided by operating revenues	$3,212,544
Operating ratio	*71.2 percent*

In this case, the smaller the ratio, the better. Moody's indicates a median ratio of 63 percent for water and sewer funds. The combining statement of revenues, expenses, and changes in retained earnings (not shown and including columns for water and sewer and sanitation funds) indicates that the operating ratio for De Kalb's water and sewer fund is 60.7 percent, which is below Moody's median. The sanitation fund, which accounts for a contract with a private hauler, has an expected much higher operating ratio of 99 percent.

Finally, the *unrestricted fund balance divided by the revenues-general fund* presents the short-term liquidity of the general fund. Exhibit 5.1 reflects the unreserved fund balance and Exhibit 5.2 reflects the general fund revenues:

Unreserved fund balance-general fund	$4,105,548
Revenues, general fund	$12,221,929
Percentage	*33.6 percent*

De Kalb's liquidity position is strong. Analysts would be concerned if the unreserved fund balance were to fall below 5 to 10 percent.

Use of the Accounting System
by Government Employees and Elected Officials

Information from the accounting system and financial reports can be very useful to government officials in the budgeting process and in other ways, including to provide budgetary control, to provide historical information for the budgetary process, and for benchmarking.

To Provide Budgetary Control. Accounting information systems have traditionally been used to provide budgetary control during a fiscal year, and this need will continue. Consider the preparation of information for interim reports on expenditures for use by department heads and others. Assume that a police department had an annual appropriation of $12 million for the fiscal year ending June 30, 1998. During July 1997, the first month of the fiscal year, the department had the following transactions:

1. Issued purchase orders for supplies and equipment amounting to $300,000

2. Received goods related to purchase orders amounting to $250,000, though due to discounts, the invoices amounted to $245,000

3. Incurred salary and other expenditures, not encumbered, amounting to $700,000

The appropriations expenditure and encumbrances ledger, or computer printout, for the police department would appear as follows:

Date	Appropriations	Encumbrances	Expenditures	Available Balance
7/1/97	$12,000,000			$12,000,000
July		300,000		11,700,000
July		(250,000)	245,000	11,705,000
July			700,000	11,005,000
7/31/97	$12,000,000	$ 50,000	$945,000	$11,005,000

In practice, each of the individual transactions would be posted. The subsidiary report indicates that after one month the police department was within budget so far (assuming a constant draw). Obviously, in order to use the accounting system to control the budget, budget and accounting categories should be the same.

To Provide Historical Information. Another traditional use of accounting information in the budgetary process is to generate historical information to be presented along with budgetary plans. This use has especially been the case with line-item budgeting. Formats have been designed that show, for example, historical expenditures for the past few years, the anticipated expenditures for the coming year, and the requested expenditure for future years. Assume the following for the police department's expenditures request:

Category	Actual Actual (FY95–96)	Actual (FY1995–96)	Budgeted (FY1996–97)	Estimated (FY96–97)	Requested (FY97–98)
Salaries	$6,000,000	$6,300,000	$6,500,000	$6,450,000	$6,600,000
Equipment	1,250,000	1,500,000	1,750,000	1,800,000	2,000,000
Other	3,300,000	3,600,000	3,750,000	3,550,000	3,600,000

For Benchmarking. A less traditional use of financial statements is to generate financial information that is useful in assessing the overall financial condition of the governmental unit, compared with the past (by developing trends) and compared with other, similar governments. This can be done by taking information directly from the financial statements, especially the statistical section, or by computing ratios, some of which are the same as those used by the financial community. Trend information can, of course, be developed in-house. Information from other governments is now becoming available for comparisons. For example, the GFOA's *Financial Indicators Database* (1996), available from the Government Finance Officers Association (180 North Michigan Avenue, Chicago, IL 60601), provides selected information, but with a two-year time lag. Moody's Investors Service provides medians for some of their ratios (Moody's Investors Service, 1997). Professor Ken Brown (1996a, 1996b) has developed a ten-point financial condition test that pulls information from the GFOA database and then presents ten ratios for a number of cities.

The statistical section of the CAFR of the City of De Kalb indicates that the population in 1996 was 36,950, an increase of 7.8 percent in ten years. The estimated market value of property in 1995 was approximately $857 million, an increase of 95 percent in ten years. The city's property tax rate was very low ($0.76 per $100 of assessed value, which is one-third of market value) and had declined over the previous ten years. The net general obligation debt per capita increased from $187 in 1987 to $577 in 1996, and the net general obligation debt to assessed value increased from 4.37 percent in 1987 to 7.46 percent in 1996. Both of these ratios decreased, however, from 1995 to 1996. The governmental revenues per capita, which must be computed and include the general, special revenue, and debt service funds, amounted to $396. The expenditures per capita amounted to $463; according to the combined statement of revenues, expenditures, and changes and fund balances (Exhibit 5.3), operating transfers made up most of the difference. The combined balance sheet (Exhibit 5.2) shows that the unreserved fund balance was 66 percent of the total assets, a very comfortable margin.

SUMMARY AND CONCLUSIONS

This chapter has provided a background in the preparation and use of financial statements. Information was presented on governmental accounting, with special reference to the development of GAAP. The comprehensive annual financial report was introduced using the CAFR of the City of De Kalb, Illinois, as an example. Emphasis was placed on the unique terminology used by accountants in the reports. A number of differences and similarities between the CAFR and the budget were noted. Finally, the uses of financial reporting were discussed, including analysis by the financial community and governmental officials.

Government financial managers should have a basic understanding of accounting and financial reporting. Without that understanding, the annual financial report will be merely a required document that has little relevance to financial management. With that understanding, financial managers will be able to evaluate better the financial condition and performance of their governments and will be able to use the CAFR and the accounting system in planning, controlling, and evaluating financial performance.

References

American Institute of Certified Public Accountants. *Professional Standards,* Vol. 1. New York: American Institute of Certified Public Accountants, 1996.

Brown, K. W. "The 1996 Edition of the Ten-Point Test of Financial Condition with Comparative Ratios for Cities." Springfield, Mo.: Solstice Productions, 1996a.

Brown, K. W. "Trends in Key Ratios Using the GFOA Financial Indicators Databases 1989–1993." *Government Finance Review,* 1996b, *12*(6), 30–34.

City of De Kalb. *Comprehensive Annual Financial Report: Fiscal Year Ended June 30, 1996.* De Kalb, Ill.: City of De Kalb, 1996.

Engstrom, J. H., and Hay, L. E. *Essentials of Accounting for Governmental and Not-for-Profit Organizations.* (4th ed.) Burr Ridge, Ill.: Irwin, 1996.

Government Finance Officers Association. *Governmental Accounting, Auditing, and Financial Reporting.* Chicago: Government Finance Officers Association, 1994.

Government Finance Officers Association. *Financial Indicators Database.* Chicago: Government Finance Officers Association, 1996.

Governmental Accounting Standards Board. *Concepts Statement 1: Objectives of Financial Reporting.* Norwalk, Conn.: Governmental Accounting Standards Board, 1987.

Governmental Accounting Standards Board. *Codification of Governmental Accounting and Financial Reporting Standards as of June 30, 1997.* Norwalk, Conn.: Governmental Accounting Standards Board, 1996a.

Governmental Accounting Standards Board. *Preliminary Views: The Governmental Financial Reporting Model.* Norwalk, Conn.: Governmental Accounting Standards Board, 1996b.

Moody's Investors Service. *1997 Medians: Selected Indicators of Municipal Performance.* New York: Moody's Investors Service, 1997.

CHAPTER SIX

The Changing World of State and Local Debt Finance

Merl Hackbart
James R. Ramsey

S tate and local budgets, both operating and capital, have experienced increased fiscal pressures in recent years. Operating budget pressures have come from the need to finance unfunded mandates and required expenditure growth at a time of taxpayer resistance to revenue increases. Capital budgets have been under fiscal stress as states and cities have experienced reductions in federal funding for critical infrastructure projects at a time when many roads, water systems, sewer systems, and so forth need to be repaired and replaced. Economic growth in many communities has required expanded expenditures to support the infrastructure necessary to accommodate this growth. Capital budgets are also under increased fiscal pressure due to technological advances requiring large capital expenditures on information and telecommunications systems—a rapid growth area of capital expenditures. A recent *Wall Street Journal* article reported that $1 out of every $4 of business capital investment involves computer and communications hardware ("Inflation Stays Low," 1996).

State and local governments utilize various fund sources to finance capital expenditures. These sources include cash appropriations from the operating budget or from undesignated fund balances, federal funds, gifts, endowment income, leasing arrangements, and borrowing. When state and local governments finance capital projects by issuing bonds, the federal government subsidizes the cost of the construction and the acquisition of the capital project through the exemption granted on the interest income paid by state and local governments. This subsidy allows state and local governments to borrow at interest rates that are lower than the financing costs for private individuals, businesses, and the federal government. As a result of this subsidy, borrowing is an important source of funding for state and local capital projects.

This chapter explores the municipal bond market and debt management issues currently facing state and local governments. The most important and distinguishable characteristic of state and local bonds is the exemption of the interest paid on them from federal income taxes. The chapter therefore begins with a discussion of the concept of the tax exemption. This discussion is important because many of the tax law changes over the past decade have limited the types of projects that qualify to be financed by tax-exempt bonds. Also, current federal tax reform discussions would have a significant impact on the value of the subsidy to state and local governments.

The credit characteristics of bonds sold by state and local governments, and changes in these credit characteristics in recent years, are presented next. They are followed by a review of the trend in the municipal markets to "enhance" an issuer's credit through the acquisition of municipal bond insurance or other credit-perfection methods. The role of the rating process is then discussed, along with the key determinants of state and local government ratings. The chapter concludes by identifying recent trends in the municipal finance markets, including the use of tax-exempt leasing and other financing means to acquire technology and other information systems that have become an integral part of state and local budgets in recent years, and that will continue to require large expenditures of public funds in the future.

THE TAX EXEMPTION ON STATE AND LOCAL BONDS

The most distinguishable characteristic of bonds sold by state and local governments is the exemption of the interest paid on these securities from federal income taxation. This tax exemption has been granted through the tax laws enacted by Congress over time; it is statutory and not constitutional. In a landmark 1988 case, the Supreme Court (*South Carolina* v. *Baker*) ruled that Congress granted the exemption of interest income on state and local bonds and as a result Congress had the authority to take away this exemption. (Interestingly, the original case dealt with a challenge by the South Carolina state treasurer to the authority of Congress to require municipal governments to issue registered bonds instead of coupon bonds. The Supreme Court ruled that Congress had such authority, and although the issue of the tax exemption of state and local bonds was not raised in the original case, the Court sent a stark reminder to the municipal markets that Congress could take away this tax-exempt treatment of such bonds.)

The potential loss of the tax exemption is a continuing concern for state and local policymakers because it is the tax exemption that allows state and local governments to finance needed capital projects at a reduced interest cost. But since the mid-1980s, Congress and the Department of the Treasury have, through both legislative and administrative actions, narrowed the range of projects that may be financed on a tax-exempt basis. As a result, the interest on some state and local borrowings is now subject to federal income taxes. The Tax Reform Act of 1986 identified two types of municipal bonds: *governmental bonds* and *private activity bonds* (PABs). PABs are issued for the benefit of individuals (for example, student loan bonds and mortgage revenue bonds) or businesses (such as industrial revenue bonds). They are subject to the alternative minimum tax calculation for individuals and corporations. Thus not all municipal bonds are tax-exempt. Governmental bonds used for public purposes—for government office buildings, roads, parks, and so on—have retained their tax exemptions. The Treasury, through the Internal Revenue Service (IRS), interprets and implements such legislation through the promulgation of administrative regulations and rulings that are critical to the determination of the tax-exempt procedures to which state and local governments adhere. (For a fuller discussion, see Marlin, 1994, and Poterba, 1989.)

To illustrate the nature of the subsidy, Table 6.1 shows two investment alternatives that may be faced by a hypothetical investor. Alternative A is the purchase of a tax-exempt municipal bond. If the hypothetical investor purchases a $100,000 municipal bond with a 6 percent interest, the investor's annual interest income will be $6,000. We assume that the investor is in the 39.6 percent marginal tax bracket; however, for Alternative A the tax bracket of the investor is immaterial because the interest income is exempt from federal income taxation. Thus the investor's after-tax income is $6,000.

Compare this result with that of Alternative B: the purchase of a bond with a credit quality equivalent to that of Alternative A but issued by a private corporation. If the interest rate on this investment is 8 percent and the investor

Table 6.1. The Value of the Tax Exemption.

	Investment A Tax Exempt Bond Interest Rate 6%	Investment B Taxable Bond Interest Rate 8%
Principal Invested	$100,000.00	$124,172.12
Pretax Income	6,000.00	9,933.77
Marginal Tax Rate	39.6%	39.6%
Tax Due	-0-	3,933.77
After-Tax Income	6,000.00	6,000.00

invests $124,127.12, then the investor's pretax interest income is $9,933.77. Because the investor is in the 39.6 percent marginal tax bracket, the tax liability to the federal government is $3,933.77, so the investor's after-tax income is $6,000. It can be seen that despite the higher interest rate earned on the private corporation bond, the investor had to invest an additional $24,127.12 to have the same after-tax income as with investment alternative A.

This example illustrates the value of the tax exemption to an investor. The investor achieves the same after-tax income on an a smaller investment amount than would be available on a larger investment amount when the interest income or dividend income are taxable. The value of the tax exemption to the investor is also a function of the investor's tax bracket; the higher the individual's tax bracket, the greater the value of the tax exemption. That is, the taxable equivalent yield on a 6 percent tax-exempt bond is 9.93 percent for an individual in the 39.6 percent federal income tax bracket and 7.06 percent for an individual in the 15 percent federal income tax bracket. The formula for calculating the taxable equivalent yield for a state or local bond is taxable equivalent yield = interest rate on tax-exempt bond/(1 − marginal tax rate).

This outcome leads to the conclusion that investors, particularly individuals in higher tax brackets who desire tax-exempt income, are willing to lend money to state and local governments at an interest rate lower than the rate at which they are willing to lend money to private individuals, corporations, or the U.S. government. Table 6.2 compares the borrowing cost for the U.S. government with that of a state or local government with an AA rating (a relatively secure financial investment). It also shows the relationship between interest costs and maturity. This relationship is referred to as the *yield curve.* Because an investor will normally expect a greater return on investments of greater maturity, the *normal* yield curve is positively sloped. Economic uncertainty may result in an *inverse* yield curve, or periods when interest rates on short-term maturities are greater than those on long-term maturities.

In addition, Table 6.2 shows the ratio of state and local borrowing costs to those of the federal government. For example, for a one-year security, an AA-rated state or local issuer can borrow at 66 percent of the borrowing cost for the U.S. government. This ratio between state and local borrowing costs and the federal government's borrowing costs is called the *spread,* and this spread relationship changes over time given the supply and demand characteristics for state and local government securities and other factors such as changes in federal and state tax laws. A Treasury bond is considered to be of the highest credit quality; differences in credit quality will have an impact on spread relationships.

For example, within a state there may be budget periods in which fewer new bonds are authorized. A lack of supply would drive up the price of and lower the yield on new issues. As a result, the spread relationship between tax-exempt bonds for the state and Treasury securities could be increased. A decrease in federal income tax rates would make tax-exempt securities less attractive to investors and would decrease spreads relative to Treasury securities. Factors that affect the supply and demand characteristics of one type of security relative to the other type of security will have an impact on the spread relationship. Although these spread relationships will change over time, it is important to note that the tax exemption on municipal bonds allows state and local governments to borrow at a lower rate of interest than other borrowers.

This exemption of the interest paid on state and local government securities provides an important financial incentive to state and local governments to finance capital projects through the issuance of municipal bonds. For example, a state financial manager considering alternatives for financing the acquisition of a $5 million computer system has two options: pay for the computer with a cash appropriation or pay for the computer by issuing a tax-exempt bond. Suppose the source of cash is the undesignated fund balance of the state. The state can leave its cash invested in a U.S. government security yielding 6.28 percent interest rate for a five-year maturity and borrow to finance the $5 million at a 4.50 percent interest rate (Table 6.2). Financially the state is better off investing its undesignated fund balance at a taxable rate and financing the acquisition of the computer system at a tax-exempt rate, because its borrowing cost is less than its investment rate.

The ability of a state or local government to borrow at a lower interest rate than is earned on invested funds is called *arbitrage*. Due to some abusive practices by state and local governments that intentionally borrowed in the tax-exempt manner to earn arbitrage rather than to finance public purpose projects, federal tax law changes have been enacted to restrict the ability of state and local governments to earn arbitrage. Still, understanding the differences in the taxable and tax-exempt markets is important to public financial managers.

In addition to the financial reason that state and local governments access the capital markets, there are also several practical reasons for borrowing to

Table 6.2. Comparison of Municipal and U.S. Treasury Interest Rates.

Years to Maturity	Local or State Government Interest Rate	Treasury Interest Rate	Spread Ratio of Municipal/ Treasury Rates
1	3.65	5.52	66
2	4.05	5.91	68
5	4.50	6.28	72
10	5.00	6.54	76
30	5.55	6.80	82

Source: The Bond Buyer, 1996. Used by permission.

finance capital projects. Capital expenditures are generally expensive and difficult to finance from recurring revenue sources. As a result, state and local governments borrow the amount needed to finance the capital project and then make debt service (principal and interest) payments out of recurring revenues as part of the operating budget. This is analogous to the individual who finds it difficult to finance the purchase of his or her home from current income. For this reason, most people borrow to purchase homes and then amortize the debt out of their annual incomes. Hence, borrowing offers a practical method for state and local governments to finance large, expensive capital expenditures.

A third reason for financing capital projects through the issuance of tax-exempt securities is to avoid "tax friction." If state and local governments attempt to finance capital projects on a pay-as-you-go basis, some years will require large tax increases to fund major new capital expenditures. Borrowing allows state and local governments to smooth out their tax collections and avoid significant variations that are required as part of a pay-as-you-go system of finance.

A strong case can therefore be made for state and local governments to access the credit markets as a means of financing capital projects, infrastructure projects, and technology and information systems. A critical policy issue then becomes, how much debt is affordable? The excessive issuance of debt may squeeze necessary operating expenditures from the budget. Also, a high debt burden can create fiscal problems for state and local governments in periods of economic downturn, because the payment of debt service is nondiscretionary. In a period of economic weakness with slow revenue growth, state and local governments will be constrained in their ability to fund ongoing, recurring expenditures because the payment of debt service has first claim on available dollars. The issuance of bonds is appropriate for financing capital projects when the issuance of debt is maintained at affordable levels (Hackbart and Ramsey, 1993; Bahl and Duncombe, 1993). As a result, bond financing is an important component of a capital financing program for state and local governments.

CREDIT CONSIDERATIONS AND TRENDS OVER TIME

The credit that secures bonds sold by state and local governments consists of either a general obligation (G.O.) credit or a revenue bond credit. A G.O. bond is secured or backed by the full faith and credit of the issuer. That is, the issuer pledges, or covenants, to the buyer of the bond that the issuer will use all available resources and assets to ensure the repayment of the principal and payment of the interest on the bonds being sold. This pledge can even extend to increasing taxes to ensure payment of the debt service on the bonds.

A revenue bond, conversely, is backed by the revenues generated by the project being financed with the proceeds of the bond issuance. For example, if a city issues a revenue bond to finance a golf course, the revenues generated from the golf course provide the only debt service payment security to the investors. Projected revenues to be generated by the project and projected costs of the golf course will therefore be important to the potential investors comparing investment alternatives.

The credit quality on an issuer's general obligation bonds will be greater than the credit quality on revenue bonds sold by the same issuer for similar projects. As a result, the interest rate on general obligation bonds will generally be lower than the interest rate on revenue bonds. For example, in October 1996, the interest rate index on revenue bonds was 6.01 percent and the interest rate index on general obligation bonds of equal rating was 5.75 percent (*The Bond Buyer*, 1996). Thus the spread is twenty-six points; it changes over time with changes in supply and demand characteristics of both G.O. bonds and revenue bonds. It represents the premium required by the investor to buy bonds of less credit quality.

Table 6.3 provides data on the volume of state and local bonds, both revenue and G.O., issued between 1987 and 1995. It is interesting to note that the number of G.O. bonds as a percentage of total municipal bonds issued has increased. This is a reversal of a trend of earlier years whereby issues relied more heavily on revenue bonds than on G.O. bonds. The increased trend toward G.O. bonds in recent years may be due to tax law changes (primarily the Tax Reform Act of 1986) that have attempted to reduce the supply of municipal bonds. The greatest effect of such supply restrictions has been on revenue bonds sold to finance private activities, such as industrial revenue bonds. A *cap,* or maximum amount of private activity bonds, is calculated each year for each state. This cap

Table 6.3. G.O. and Revenue Municipal Bonds Issued by Year.

Year	Total Bonds Issued	Revenue Bonds	% of Total	General Obligation Bonds	% of Total
1987	$105,026,700	$74,495,500	70.93	$30,531,200	29.07
1988	117,315,700	86,443,200	73.68	30,872,500	26.32
1989	125,004,900	85,503,600	69.20	38,501,300	30.80
1990	127,828,000	87,525,500	68.47	40,302,500	31.53
1991	172,443,700	115,333,500	66.88	57,110,200	33.12
1992	234,623,200	154,141,500	65.70	80,481,700	34.30
1993	291,853,600	200,281,200	68.62	91,572,400	31.38
1994	164,559,300	108,773,100	66.10	55,786,200	33.90
1995	159,369,600	98,822,300	62.01	60,547,300	37.99

Source: The Bond Buyer, 1996. Used by permission.

often limits the number of such bonds that can be issued by all issuers in the state, hence limiting supply.

State and local governments have, over time, created special districts, special bond authorities, and other quasi-governmental entities to finance capital projects (Leigland, 1993). In many cases these proxy financing entities have been created due to statutory or constitutional limitations on the amount of G.O. debt that can be sold by a state or local government. Special debt authorities may also allow for the issuance of debt without direct taxpayer authorization and approval. A 1990 study by the Council of State Governments examined the growing trend in the creation of special debt-issuing entities. This study included a fifty-state survey that indicated that there has been a 50 percent increase in the number of state-level entities or authorities issuing revenue-backed debt (Hackbart, Leigland, Rieherd, and Reed, 1990).

A *hybrid credit* is a moral obligation bond. The project being financed with the proceeds of the bond is the security to the bondholder. However, the issuer provides the investor with a commitment that the issuer will do whatever possible to make up any revenue shortfalls that may exist in the revenue streams derived from the project. This commitment is not legally binding but represents a moral pledge of the issuer. Various types of moral obligation credits exist in the market. Moral obligation credits are not as strong as general obligation credits, but they are stronger than revenue bond credits.

The creation of special debt authorities, the use of revenue bonds, and the use of moral obligations may have led to an increased use of credit enhancements, such as municipal bond insurance, as means of propping up the credit of the issuer. That is, to lower the cost of financing capital projects, issuers have purchased insurance policies and other forms of credit enhancement as replacements for the issuer's credit. (For a fuller discussion, see Satz and Perry, 1993, and Kidwell, Sorenson, and Wachowicz, 1987.) Table 6.4 shows the increase in revenue bonds that either have been insured or have some other type of credit enhancement.

A bond issuer will enter into numerous covenants with the bondholder. Such covenants are contractual obligations between the bond issuer and the bondholder. These contractual agreements provide important assurances to the investor as part of the investor's decision to lend money to a state or local government. For example, covenants pertaining to the maintenance of a project financed with the proceeds of tax-exempt bonds are common. Issuers will make covenants in regard to the amount of future debt they can incur. These covenants are contained in either the bond resolution or the trust indenture that governs the transaction. The provider of a credit enhancement to an issuer may require covenants beyond those normally made by the issuer. Such additional covenants are a cost of obtaining a credit enhancement and must be evaluated by the issuer along with the financial costs of the enhancements. Purchase of

Table 6.4. Trend Toward Increased Credit Enhancement of Revenue Bonds.

Year	Credit Enhanced Bonds	Credit Enhanced as % of Revenue Bonds	Revenue Bonds Issued
1987	$38,299,200	51.41	$74,495,500
1988	49,685,600	57.48	86,443,200
1989	47,282,400	54.66	86,503,600
1990	53,305,000	60.90	87,525,500
1991	67,495,400	58.52	115,333,500
1992	94,833,900	61.52	154,141,500
1993	123,747,600	61.79	200,281,200
1994	78,283,200	71.97	108,773,100
1995	83,286,300	84.28	98,822,300

Source: The Bond Buyer, 1996. Used by permission.

bond insurance also appears to be promoted by "market segmentation," in which certain portfolio managers strongly prefer very low risk investments (Below, 1994).

The decision to seek a credit enhancement should be determined by a financial analysis that compares the price of the insurance premium or other credit enhancement cost to the net discounted present value of the savings that is expected to be realized as a result of the improved credit quality. Table 6.5 provides an example of a financial analysis performed to determine the financial viability of the purchase of a credit enhancement. In this example, an issuer is faced with issuing a $10 million bond for which the credit is that of the issuer, or a bond that is credit-enhanced. The annual debt service savings for the credit-enhanced bond is $32,200, or $644,000 over the life of the bonds, and the net discounted present value of this stream of savings is $385,700. Therefore, if the issuer can purchase a credit enhancement for less than $385,700, the decision to credit enhance should be made. If, however, the cost of the credit enhancement is more than this amount, credit enhancement is not financially viable.

State and local governments issue bonds in the marketplace in one of two ways. They may sell their securities via either a competitive sale or a negotiated sale. In the case of a *competitive sale,* the issuer structures the bond issue and markets it to potential buyers—normally underwriting syndicates, that is, one or more investment banking firms or banks that bid to purchase the bonds from the issuer. The bids are in the form of an interest rate on the bonds. They are usually received through a sealed-bid process at a specific point in time. The

Table 6.5. Analysis to Determine Whether or Not to Credit-Enhance.

	Issuer-Credited Bond	Credit-Enhanced Bond
Bond Size	$10,000,000	$10,000,000
Bond Rating	A	AAA
Average Interest Rate	6.5%	6.0%
Maturity	20 years	20 years
Average Annual Debt Service	$872,200	$840,000
Present value savings due to credit enhancement	$385,700	

issuer awards the sale of the bonds to the syndicate that has submitted the bid with the lowest rate, to minimize the future interest rate costs to the issuer.

In a competitive sale it is common for an issuer to employ various advisers and experts to assist in the structuring and marketing of the bonds. Among these advisers are often an investment banking firm that serves in the role of financial adviser, who provides financial and marketing expertise to the issuer. In some instances the investment banking firm that serves as the issuer's financial adviser may also be part of an underwriting syndicate that submits a sealed bid to purchase the bonds through the competitive sale process. Most smaller bond issues are sold through the competitive bid process. Also, issuers that go to market on a frequent basis and issuers with an accepted credit security in the market also often borrow through the competitive bid process.

Alternatively, a state and local government may issue their bonds through a *negotiated sale process*. In this case the issuer selects an investment banking firm or bank or a group of investment banking firms or banks to serve as the underwriting syndicate. The issuer determines in advance with whom it will negotiate the sale of the bonds, most often selected through a competitive process such as a *request for proposal* (RFP). The criteria for the RFP usually emphasize the firm's experience in similar types of transactions and the perceived financial and marketing expertise that the firm will provide to the issuer.

The issuer and the lead firm in the underwriting syndicate then determine through a negotiation process what the interest rate on the bonds will be. Negotiated sales are more common for issues of large magnitude and for issuers who are not frequent borrowers in the credit markets. As a general rule, the more complex a bond issue is in terms of credit or special features, the more likely it will be that a negotiated sale process will result in a lower interest cost to the issuer.

A policy decision must be made by the issuer as to the appropriate method for selling tax-exempt bonds. This decision may be governed by statutes or other legal requirements. For example, numerous cases exist in which issuers of a particular type of bond (such as school districts) are required by state law to market all bonds via a competitive sale.

The investment banking firm that is employed by the issuer can assist in the determination of the appropriateness of obtaining credit enhancement on a proposed issuer. The investment banking firm will normally have experience dealing with municipal bond insurance companies, with banks that issue letters of credit, and so on; and the investment banking firm can perform the analysis outlined earlier, which is critical to the process of deciding whether it is in the issuer's best interest to seek a credit enhancement. It should be noted also that on a competitive sale the issuer may elect to make the bond issue eligible for a credit enhancement (such as municipal bond insurance); that is, the issuer may provide financial, budget, economic, and other information to the municipal bond insurance company, and the municipal bond insurance company in turn determines whether they will provide an insurance policy to the issuer. In the case of a competitive sale, however, the decision to insure or not insure can be left to the winning syndicate in the bidding process. The winning syndicate would then pay the cost of the insurance premium to insure the bonds. This process of making a bond eligible for credit enhancement on competitive issues has become more commonplace in recent years. In other transactions, the issuer decides unilaterally whether a credit enhancement is financially viable.

RATINGS AND RATING CONSIDERATIONS

As noted earlier, the bonds issued by state and local governments may be sold in the public marketplace by either a competitive or negotiated sale process, or through a private placement (Leonard, 1996; Lamb and Schott, 1987). Regardless of the sale method, the majority of municipal bonds are eventually sold to retail and institutional investors. Issuers generally need broad market acceptance in order for their bonds to achieve an attractive interest rate. The attainment of one or more credit ratings from the rating services may enhance the marketability of the bonds (Hsueh and Kidwell, 1988). But note that not all issuers may benefit from obtaining a rating, because some issuers borrow only small amounts that can be effectively marketed locally without ratings. Also, some issuers borrow on an infrequent basis and find that the advantages of obtaining a credit rating are not worth the cost.

There are three major rating agencies that perform credit analysis on state and local governments: Moody's Investors Service, Standard and Poor's, and Fitch Investors Service. The issuer pays these rating agencies to perform a credit review of the issuer and to assign to the issuer a rating that can be used in the marketing of the bonds. Potential buyers of the bonds rely on the credit analysis of the rating agencies to provide guidance on the credit quality of the bonds. For example, an issuer of a large issue or a frequent issuer of bonds will often rely on investors from other regions of the country—investors who are not always familiar with the issuer or its credit characteristics. The rating can be used by the issuer to communicate such credit qualities to investors and to broaden the market of potential buyers.

Although the credit considerations on a general obligation credit and a revenue bond issue are different, the rating agencies generally perform four evaluations of the issuer in their credit review process: an economic analysis, a financial analysis, a demographic analysis, and a review of the issuer's management characteristics.

The economics of the issuer is an important consideration in the determination of the issuer's ability to repay bond monies. Employment growth and income trends are reviewed. The rating agencies also look at diversification of the issuer's economic base, because a diversified economic base can withstand economic uncertainty better than a narrowly defined economic base (Cluff and Farnham, 1984; Morton, 1976). A review of the issuer's finances includes both current and past budgets, financial statements, revenue-estimating and budgetary practices, provisions for rainy-day funds, and any unfunded liabilities that may exist for the issuer.

In the demographic analysis, a declining population may be an indicator of the issuer's difficulty in servicing future debt; conversely, the population of a state or city may be increasing, yet the increase may be represented by increases in the elderly population or by a growing younger population. The "graying" of the population represents unique challenges for state and local governments. For example, many state and local governments provide "homestead exemptions," or property tax relief, to individuals over the age of sixty-five. Also, those state and local governments that utilize individual income taxes to finance state and local services often exempt the pension income of their retired population from state income taxes and local occupational taxes. The graying of the population thus affects an issuer's ability to pay.

Finally, the management strength and capabilities of an issuer are important in the assignment of a rating by the major rating agencies. The investor's reaction to management changes in the corporate world is often reflected in changing stock prices. Although the "value" of state and local governments is not determined in the marketplace, the rating agencies realize that management is an integral part of the overall willingness and ability of an issuer to service its debt. Rating agencies often need to meet with key government officials to assess strategic and operational plans and to develop an understanding of the organizational strength of the state and local government. A difficult-to-define but critically important management characteristic is the "political will" of the government's leadership to make difficult budgetary decisions as the need arises—for example, to make tax increases or spending cuts in response to changes in economic activity—and thus to "do the right thing" in the eyes of the rating agencies.

Issuers today are finding that ongoing communication with the rating agencies is becoming a critical component of a debt management program. State and local finance officials are providing quarterly reports of economic and financial activity to the rating agencies, and often these officials make trips to New York to visit with the rating agencies. On an annual or biannual basis, rating agencies are invited to visit the issuer. These frequent meetings and forums for communication enhance the rating agencies' understanding of the credit characteristics of an issuer and generally make for a more efficient market.

The rating process is complex and involves extensive detailed analysis by the rating agencies of the four areas just discussed to determine the credit of a state or local government. Again, this rating of the state and local government is one of the many important determinants of the borrowing cost to the issuer and hence affects the issuer's ability to carry out its capital budget.

FUTURE ISSUES IN STATE AND LOCAL MANAGEMENT

The 1980s was a period of great change in the credit markets. New investment products were created, volatility in the bond markets became commonplace, and leverage and debt financing became a more prominent aspect of the financial management programs of federal, state, local, and private corporations. A number of other challenges have emerged from these changes, and a number of trends have developed for state and local financial managers.

Financing Information and Technology Systems

The conventional wisdom of public finance is that capital projects that will result in multiyear benefits are appropriate for bond financing. The bond financing of capital projects allows a match of the life of an asset with the payment of debt service over time by the future users or beneficiaries of the capital asset. A fundamental rule of prudent financial management is that the life of the bond issue used to finance capital projects should be matched with the projected life of the capital asset. For example, a road that is expected to have a useful life of twenty years is appropriate for financing with a twenty-year bond issue. Given this conventional wisdom of municipal debt management, municipal bonds most often have been used to finance buildings, roads, infrastructure projects, and other major capital expenditures (Ramsey and Hackbart, 1996).

At the same time, the acquisition of telecommunication systems, computer hardware and software systems, and networking systems are becoming more critical to the effective management of state and local governments. Historically, large equipment expenditures have been funded on both a cash basis and a lease basis by state and local governments. Lease financing has taken on added importance in an era of tight budgets when cash is not available. In the past these equipment-leasing arrangements have most often been provided by the vendor. Given that vendors of telecommunications equipment, computer hardware and software systems, and networking systems are for-profit companies, they cannot borrow on a tax-exempt basis as can state and local governments. Therefore, the financing costs incorporated into these lease arrangements represent the cost of capital to the company—a taxable cost of capital. As discussed earlier, and as shown in Table 6.2, the ability to issue tax-exempt bonds allows state and local governments to borrow at lower interest rates than for-profit companies. Prudent financial management requires state and local governments to take advantage of this cheaper cost of capital.

An emerging trend in state and local finance is the question of how to finance the increased demand for information and technology systems. Tax-exempt leasing, master leases, and other short-term financing approaches offer affordable methods for purchasing such acquisitions. In the case of a master lease, a state or local government negotiates a financing program whereby funds are available to provide for the acquisition of equipment projects throughout the budget year on a tax-exempt basis. As a department or program of a state or local government acquires equipment, the funding source for the equipment is a "draw" against the financing program. The advantages to the state and local government of such financing programs include the ability to finance these projects at a lower interest rate than through the vendor's financing, the substitution of the credit of the state or local government for the credit of one of its agencies or departments, administrative ease (a master financing program can be put in place), and economies of scale (the finance department of the state or local government can put in place tax-exempt financing programs at lower overhead and administrative costs than can be negotiated on a department-by-department basis).

The financing of equipment involves some of the same issues as the financing of major capital projects. For example, what is the affordable amount of lease financing that can be incorporated into the operating budget for which recurring revenues are available to finance recurring lease payments? (Lease payments of this nature represent a recurring commitment of resources and in a sense may compete with other recurring expenses such as salaries and operating expenses.) A second issue is the question of the technological life of the asset. A computer hardware system may have a physical life of ten years or longer, but the true useful life of the equipment will often be much shorter. That is, given rapid changes in technology, hardware and software may become functionally obsolete in three or four years. A lease-financing program that extends beyond this period would commit the budget to paying for equipment that is no longer useful and that needs to be replaced before the equipment is depreciated. Matching the life of the lease to the technological life of the project ensures that in the future the budget will not be required to support two systems—the obsolete system and its replacement.

Joint or Pooled Financing Programs

As previously discussed, a recent trend in the municipal markets has been the creation of debt authorities to borrow on behalf of state and local governments. In addition, many states have intergovernmental cooperation laws that allow various local governments to come together for a specific purpose and to function with the same powers as those of a single governmental entity—including the ability to incur debt.

As a result, there is an increasing use of quasi-governmental entities that have been created for the purpose of financing capital projects for a group of local governments or other units of government. These local government entities often do not have the staff or expertise to access the credit markets individually. Further, these quasi-governmental entities are often created for the sole purpose of providing financing to the group, or "pool," of cooperating governments. Pool financings allows for cost of issuance and other administrative costs to be spread over a larger number of participants and hence allows for the realization of economies of scale.

For example, in Kentucky several school districts joined together and utilized the state's Intergovernmental Cooperation Act to form a debt authority to finance the acquisition of school buses for the participants. School buses are capital assets that may be appropriate for debt financing with a life of seven to ten years. By joining together to form a pooled financing program, lower interest rates can be obtained than if the buses were financed on a district-by-district basis.

Pool financing on behalf of governmental entities provides advantages but also challenges. The credit supporting a pool financing program is, from a rating and market perspective, only as strong as the weakest credit among the program participants. As a result, most pool financings must resort to the acquisition of credit enhancements as discussed earlier. The involvement of third-party credit enhancers adds a level of cost and administrative burden; in addition, as previously noted, the issuer is often required to agree to covenants demanded by the credit enhancer as a condition of providing the credit enhancement. For example, in some pool financings the municipal bond insurance company or letter-of-credit provider reserves the right to approve individual projects eligible for financing from the pool. The pool participants and the issuer set up to borrow on behalf of the participants are removed from this decision-making process.

Because of historical abuses of pool financings, tax laws over the years have changed, making pool financings more difficult to undertake—especially blind pool financings whereby projects are not identified prior to the issuance of bonds. The role of the state, if any, also becomes an issue for policymakers. Because local governments are creations of the state, pooled financing programs that give the appearance of being statewide or state sponsored create the perception that the state's credit is behind the bonds being sold. Also, if a problem results from such a financing program, the market may perceive a problem with the credit of other local governments and hence the program will have an impact on the borrowing costs of other local governments. Therefore, at least in some states, state-level policymakers are struggling with the issue of whether state oversight, either approval or reporting, should be required. Still, pool financing can offer financial advantages to governmental units, and a challenge facing financial managers is the need to ensure that such financings are properly structured and managed in order to offer maximum benefit to the pool's participants.

Cash Flow Borrowings

State and local governments have long used tax and revenue anticipation notes (TANS and RANS) for many years. The "spring borrowing" of New York State, a major market cash flow borrowing, has long dominated the market. This borrowing allows the state to use the proceeds of the cash flow notes to make state payments to local school districts at the start of the school districts' fiscal year. Taxes are then collected throughout the year to repay the notes. Other state and local governments also experience a mismatch between their expenditure requirements and their revenue collections and have utilized the proceeds of tax and revenue anticipation notes to smooth out these cash flow differences.

The federal arbitrage laws, a component of the IRS code, contains provisions to be met to qualify for the issuance of short-term tax-exempt cash flow securities. To qualify for cash flow borrowing, the issuer must size the borrowing such that the amount of the notes cannot exceed the cumulative cash flow deficit that would otherwise be paid by such tax or revenue sources during the period for which the obligation is outstanding, plus one month's reasonably required cash balance, minus amounts available from other sources. Amounts available from other sources are available to the extent that accounts may, without legislative or judicial action, be invaded to pay such expenditures without a legislative or judicial requirement that such amounts be repaid.

A "safe harbor" also exists for determining when short-term tax-exempt issues are treated as spent for purposes of the arbitrage rebate requirement. The safe harbor provides that if at any time during the six-month period after issuance the cumulative cash flow deficit of the issuer exceeds 90 percent of the note proceeds, then the net proceeds and the interest earnings are treated as having been spent for purposes of the borrowing and are therefore exempt from the six-month exception to the arbitrage rebate requirement.

Assuming a cumulative state cash flow deficit of $200 million, a state could expect to borrow funds at short-term tax-exempt rates, or 3.65 percent (Table 6.2). A state investment portfolio for the same maturity has a current yield of 5.55 percent (Table 6.2). The difference between the financing rates translates into approximately $4.5 million in annualized net savings.

The increased fiscal stress that state and local governments continue to face has enhanced the necessity for prudent financial management practices such as cash flow borrowings. Revenue constraints along with increased expenditure demands require all units of government to better manage their revenue and expenditure cash flows. Further, changes in federal cash-management laws and various accounting practices make many of the past practices utilized to manage cash flow unavailable to state and local governments today. As a result, more state and local governments are finding that borrowing for cash flow purposes represents prudent financial management. Even small issuers are finding cash flow borrowing to be important. Unfortunately, many city and county governments do not have the staff or expertise to structure cash flow borrowings. Further, the cost of issuance for small cash flow borrowing programs offsets many of the advantages that can be derived from such programs. As noted earlier, quasi-governmental entities organized on behalf of numerous small issues allows cash flow borrowings to become a reality for the smallest units of government.

Tax Reform

In recent years, tax reform has become a major public policy issue at all levels of government. Tax reform discussions at the federal level can have significant implications on the financing costs of state and local governments. As previously noted, the interest paid on the bonds sold by state and local governments is exempt from federal income taxes and this exemption represents an important subsidy to state and local governments. Most of the recent tax reform proposals at the federal level would decrease this subsidy. The loss of this subsidy would have a significant impact on the financing of capital projects by state and local governments.

Since passage of the Tax Reform Act of 1986, several specific, major federal tax reform proposals have been discussed. Each of these proposals would reduce the subsidy that state and local governments currently receive as a result of the tax exemption on the interest of the bonds they sell. State and local governments must begin to plan for addressing this loss in subsidy, which may result if tax reform continues to move forward. For example, the tax reform proposals that have received the most attention are the replacement of individual income tax with a consumption tax and the replacement of the current progressive individual income tax structure with a flat-rate income tax. In the case of a consumption tax, interest on tax-exempt bonds becomes taxable given the loss of tax-exempt status on all forms of income. In the case of the flat-rate tax, the financial advantage of tax-exempt bonds over taxable bonds is significantly reduced, especially for high-income individuals.

Tax reform has also become a public policy issue for state and local governments. In general, because federal income tax rates are significantly higher than state and local income tax rates (in those states and cities where income taxes exist), state and local tax reform is less of a threat to the tax-exempt status of municipal bonds. Rather, the continued devolution of spending responsibilities is placing increased fiscal pressures on state and local budgets. Increased expenditure pressure, without corresponding revenue growth, creates a credit challenge for state and local financial managers. The need to maintain long-term structurally balanced budgets is critical to maintaining a strong credit rating and the ability to access the credit markets at reasonable financing costs.

Interest-Rate Risk Management

Historically, state and local governments would borrow for capital projects by issuing fixed-rate bonds with a long-term maturity. If interest rates declined in the future, the issuer would issue refunding bonds to capture the savings available due to the lower rates. An issuer would issue advance-refunding bonds if the lower interest rate were available prior to the "call" date on the original bonds, and current-refunding bonds if the lower interest rate were available after the call date on the original bonds. The call date is the first opportunity that an issuer has to rebuy their bonds from the investor. Call provisions are established as a covenant in the bond resolution or trust indenture.

During the 1980s the spread between long maturities and short maturities and the increased market demand for short-term and variable-rate securities led to increased sales of such issues by state and local governments. For example, an issuer might be faced with a decision to sell a twenty–year bond with a fixed rate of 6 percent or a shorter-term maturity with an interest rate of 4 percent. Choosing the latter offers significant debt service savings to the issuer—important savings given budget constraints. These savings could quickly disappear, however, with an increase in interest rates.

State and local governments also became aware of the "opportunity costs" associated with interest rate volatility on the asset side of their balance sheets. For example, a public funds portfolio manager might buy a six-month Treasury security and find that its value declined with an increase in interest rates. Or, as often happens, if interest rates declined during the budget year, the portfolio manager would not be able to earn the forecasted interest income for budget purposes.

Thus, during the 1990s, state and local financial managers began to focus more attention on the management of interest rate risks—on both the liability and the asset sides of the balance sheets. Interest rate swaps and other types of derivative products became alternatives that were analyzed and in some cases utilized by financial managers. Unfortunately, financial managers (both public and private sector) did not always understand the products they were using to manage risks, and financial managers ended up increasing market exposure by speculating as to future interest rate movements. High-profile public fund losses, such as those in Orange County, California, and elsewhere, created a perception that hedging risks was inherently bad. (In 1991, the treasurer of Orange County, California, boosted interest earnings on county funds by borrowing and investing in derivatives. In the fall of 1994, in a rising interest rate environment, the county was faced with losses of $1.5 billion as a result of this strategy. Such losses affected the financial position of the county and its bond rating.) In addition, the risk management mistakes of the past have contributed to efforts at greater oversight and regulation of the municipal markets.

In reality, a well-defined interest-rate risk management program is important to a comprehensive and prudent financial management program. The Government Finance Officers Association (GFOA) adopted a recommended practice for the use of risk management techniques by the state and local governments. The GFOA's recommendations advise governments to be aware of the special risks incurred as a result of the use of derivatives. Also, many derivative products do not have a history of successful use through both increasing and declining interest rate periods. State and local governments often have not had the internal control systems necessary for the use of such products. Still, interest rate volatility will continue to present both opportunities and challenges to state and local governments, and the development of an interest-rate risk management program should be an important part of a financial management program.

Increased Federal Oversight and Regulation of Municipal Markets

The municipal bond market has historically been an unregulated over-the-counter market. A formal, organized market, such as a stock market exchange or commodity market exchange, for the buying and selling of tax-exempt bonds does not exist. In addition, the municipal market has largely been left alone by federal regulators. State and local governments are required to comply with the laws and regulations of the IRS to ensure the tax-exempt status of the bonds. Other federal oversight, however, has been minimal.

Given well-publicized defaults and abusive financial management practices (such as those in Orange County), a trend in recent years has been for increased oversight and regulation of the tax-exempt markets. This oversight and regulation has been resisted by state and local issuers, but numerous examples of federal oversight can be identified. For example, the Securities and Exchange

Commission (SEC) has taken an active interest in the municipal market in recent years. Given the inability of the SEC to regulate directly the issuance of bonds by state and local governments, it has attempted to regulate the municipal market through its regulatory authority over investment banking firms who underwrite and sell municipal securities. For example, SEC rule 15(C)2–12 requires that an investment banking firm cannot purchase or underwrite municipal securities unless certain disclosure guidelines are adhered to by state and local bond issuers. SEC 15(C)2–12 became effective in July 1995 and applies to any new offering with a par amount of $1 million or more. This new SEC rule requires most debt-issuing municipal entities to file annual financial reports. Further, SEC rule 15(C)2–12 identified material events that must be reported in a timely fashion to each nationally recognized repository of municipal security information or to the municipal security rule-making board and to the appropriate state information depository.

It is anticipated that there will be continued efforts for increased federal oversight and review of the municipal market. In fact, at any point numerous legislation is before Congress that would extend federal oversight to state and local governments.

SUMMARY AND CONCLUSIONS

The tax-exempt bond market provides an important source of capital to state and local governments. The tax exemption on state and local bonds provides state and local governments with an important subsidy that they have used to help fund their capital budgets. A number of significant policy issues and challenges will continue to face state and local governments in the years ahead, as they attempt to continue to utilize the tax-exempt market as a source of funds for capital projects, infrastructure projects, and information systems and technology projects.

References

Bahl, R., and Duncombe, W. "State and Local Debt Burdens in the 1980s: A Study in Contrast." *Public Administration Review,* 1993, *53*(1), 31–40.

Below, S. "Existence of Municipal Bond Insurance: Theory and Evidence." Unpublished doctoral dissertation, University of Kentucky, 1994.

Cluff, G. S., and Farnham, P. G. "Standard and Poor's vs. Moody's: Which City Characteristics Influence Municipal Bond Ratings?" *Quarterly Journal of Economics and Business,* 1984, *24,* 72–94.

Hackbart, M., Leigland, J., Rieherd, R., and Reed, M. *Debt Duty: Accountability and Efficiency in State Debt Management.* Lexington, Ky.: Council of State Governments, 1990.

Hackbart, M., and Ramsey, J. R. "Debt Management and Debt Capacity." In R. B. Lamb, J. Leigland, and S. Rappaport (eds.), *The Handbook of Municipal Bonds and Public Finance.* New York: New York Institute of Finance, 1993.

Hsueh, L. P., and Kidwell, D. S. "Bond Ratings: Are Two Better Than One?" *Financial Management,* 1988, *17*(1), 47.

"Inflation Stays Low, with the Aid of Some Luck." *Wall Street Journal,* Dec. 16, 1996, p. 1.

Kidwell, D. S., Sorenson, E. H., and Wachowicz, J. "Municipal Bond Insurance." *Municipal Finance Journal,* 1987, *8*(1), 21–31.

Lamb, R. B., and Schott, H., Jr. "Price Efficiency of Competitive Bidding on New Issues in the Municipal Securities Market." *Municipal Finance Journal,* 1987, *8*(1), 9–19.

Leigland, J. "Overview of Public Authorities and Special Districts." In R. B. Lamb, J. Leigland, and S. Rappaport (eds.), *The Handbook of Municipal Bonds and Public Finance.* New York: New York Institute of Finance, 1993.

Leonard, P. A. "An Empirical Analysis of Competitive Bid and Negotiated Offerings of Municipal Bonds." *Municipal Finance Journal,* 1996, *17*(1), 40.

Marlin, M. "Did Tax Reform Kill Segmentation in the Municipal Bond Market?" *Public Administration Review,* 1994, *54*(4), 387–390.

Morton, G. T. "A Comparative Analysis of Moody's and Standard and Poor's Municipal Bond Ratings." *Review of Business and Economic Research,* 1976, *11*, 74–81.

Poterba, J. M. "Tax Reform and the Market for Tax-Exempt Debt." *Regional Science and Urban Economics,* 1989, *19*, 537–562.

Ramsey, J. R., and Hackbart, M. "State and Local Debt Policy and Management." In G. J. Miller, *Handbook of Debt Management.* New York: Marcel-Dekker, 1996.

Satz, M., and Perry, J. "Municipal Bond Insurance." In R. B. Lamb, J. Leigland, and S. Rappaport (eds.), *The Handbook of Municipal Bonds and Public Finance.* New York: New York Institute of Finance, 1993.

CHAPTER SEVEN

State and Local Government Budgeting

Coping with the Business Cycle

Michael Wolkoff

lthough the sustained economic growth of the 1990s has reduced concerns about the hazards of economic cycles, a somewhat longer historical perspective reveals that such optimism is premature at best. Indeed, no professional economist seriously believes that cyclical variability is a phenomenon of the past. In fact, the U.S. economy has consistently exhibited periods of economic expansion and decline, and even within the past twenty-five years, it has undergone four expansions and contractions.

It is important to realize that the cyclical variability actually experienced by state and local governments exceeds what is portrayed by national statistics. An examination of the disaggregate data reveals that the performance of regional and local economies is sufficiently uncorrelated (or negatively correlated) that nationally calculated indices of economic performance understate subnational variability. Simply put, not all jurisdictions experience national average economic performance. Thus, even when most jurisdictions are experiencing growth it is likely that some jurisdictions are struggling against adverse economic events.

Successfully coping with the business cycle is of great importance to budget officials and political leaders. Voters pay close attention to the ability of the president and Congress to responsibly manage the government through the annual budget exercise. The president's success in managing economic growth and unemployment has been shown to dominate other determinants in predicting reelection success (Fair, 1994).

Although such governmental watchdogs as the Congressional Budget Office distinguish the full-employment budget position from cyclically driven deficits or surpluses, the electorate has for the most part confined its attention to a much less technical and easily understood measure: whether the budget has been balanced. A balanced budget also lies at the heart of the concerns of state and local budget officials, for here, too, voters have scrutinized the rising costs of governmental services. But state and local officials seeking to achieve budget balance face much greater challenges than their counterparts at the federal level. Most important are the state constitutional requirements that bind state and local officials to submit balanced budgets. Unlike the federal government, which has the luxury of running annual budget deficits, subnational units are given relatively little time flexibility to shape long-term solutions in order to adjust budget imbalances. Furthermore, many state and local governmental units are constrained to the extent to which they can use debt to meet current obligations. Although on occasion these constraints have been circumvented, there is little question that state and local governments enjoy less flexibility than federal budget makers (Briffault, 1996).

Compounding this problem is that it is far more difficult to achieve state and local budget balance because smaller and less diverse local economies provide minimal cushion against cyclical variability. At the national level, weak performance in one sector or region can be balanced by better performance in another sector or region. State and local economies are much less diverse, with far fewer opportunities to balance decline in any sector with growth in another.

Ironically, both greater variability in economic-base performance and tighter balanced budget requirements place greater demands on units of government that are far less equipped to offset the underlying sources of economic variation. While federal officials can manipulate a number of policy levers to counteract cyclical effects, state and local officials have far fewer effective options. For example, federal officials have attempted to stabilize aggregate demand by trying to influence nominal interest rates through expansionary or contractionary monetary policy. But monetary policy is a function reserved for the federal level and is consequently unavailable to the state and local sector. Although fiscal policy can be implemented by the state and local sector, it is of limited usefulness. Local economies are too leaky for the stimulative impact of fiscal policy to have much effect. Household mobility, fluid labor markets, and exported sales all ensure that the effects of fiscal policy efforts will not be contained within the political boundaries of the jurisdiction initiating the policy, thereby reducing the impact of any local fiscal policy action. All this argues that state and local officials can do little to influence the economic winds that blow sharply across their bow. For the most part, local and state officials must treat cyclical changes as exogenous, and they have little option but to do the best they can to manage their effects.

This chapter examines the cyclical vulnerability of state and local budgets, and what officials can do about it. First, the linkage between national cycles and local economic performance is explored; then the connection between local economic activity and the state and local public sector is established. The bulk of the chapter examines a number of policy responses that might be chosen to manage cyclical vulnerability. And finally, a conclusion is offered.

ECONOMIC CYCLES

Considerable controversy exists within the economics profession over the root causes of economic cycles, but all professional economists would agree that the performance of the U.S. economy has shown considerable variation from year to year. Figure 7.1 provides evidence of this variability from 1970 to 1996. In the post-1970 period, for example, the growth in the national economy as measured by the growth rate of real (inflation-adjusted) gross domestic product (GDP) has gone through four periods of expansion and contraction. This variation is consistent with the economy's history over a much longer period. Even today, after twenty-plus quarters of sustained growth, there is no controversy over the inevitability of an eventual downturn in national growth rates. What debate does exist is over when such a turning point will occur, how long and how deep the next recession will be, and what might be done about it.

Irrespective of national aggregate economic trends, it has long been recognized that national economic performance can mask the sum of its many parts. Engerman's work on regional economies (1965) documented substantial variation in economic performance across locations, which can be explained in part by differences in industrial composition. Different jurisdictions have different economic bases for a variety of reasons; some are due to locational advantages, including access to markets, or to the presence of raw materials, or perhaps even to historical happenstance. As technology evolves and reliance on certain raw materials changes, or as tastes get altered, locational advantages dissipate or grow, thereby leading to different sectors growing at different rates. These explanations remain valid today despite shifts in the relative importance of different employment sectors and the changing relative advantages of certain regional locations.

Table 7.1 provides recent evidence on locational differences in economic performance. The annual unemployment rate in ten major Standard Metropolitan Statistical Areas (SMSAs) is contrasted with the contemporaneous national unemployment rate. Unemployment rates are generally a trailing indicator of

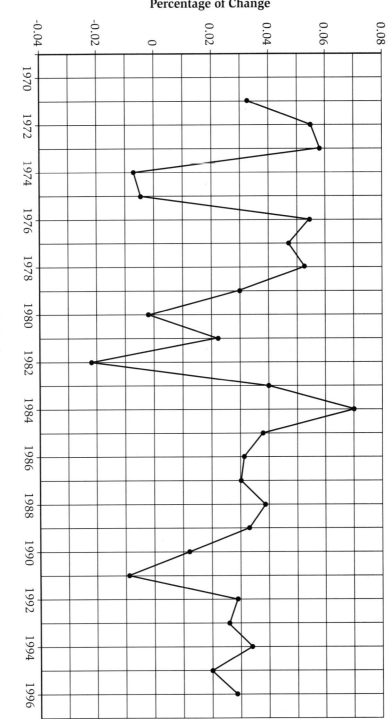

Figure 7.1. Percentage of Change in Constant Gross Domestic Product.

Table 7.1. Unemployment Rate in Ten Largest Metropolitan Areas.

SMSA	Unemployment Rate by Year						
	1989	1990	1991	1992	1993	1994	1995
Los Angeles, Long Beach, CA	4.7%	5.8%	8.0%	8.7%	9.7%	9.4%	7.9%
Chicago, IL	5.5	5.9	6.9	7.8	7.1	5.5	5.1
New York, NY	5.4	6.2	8.1	10.3	9.4	8.1	7.6
Washington, DC, MD, VA	2.7	3.4	4.5	5.2	4.5	4.1	4.2
Philadelphia, PA, NJ	3.8	4.6	6.4	7.0	6.8	5.9	5.9
Detroit, MI	7.1	7.5	9.3	9.7	7.1	5.7	5.0
Houston, TX	5.9	5.2	5.6	6.8	7.2	6.4	5.7
Atlanta, GA	5.1	5.1	4.7	5.8	5.2	4.7	4.3
Boston, MA	3.4	5.1	7.7	8.5	6.0	5.2	4.7
Dallas, TX	5.5	5.1	6.0	7.0	6.0	5.3	4.6
U.S. Average	5.3%	5.5%	6.7%	7.4%	6.8%	6.1%	5.6%

Source: U.S. Department of Commerce, Bureau of the Census.

economic performance, so it is no surprise that unemployment rates peaked in 1992, a year after real growth in GDP had recovered. Nevertheless, it is clear from the table that economic recovery is not experienced uniformly by all jurisdictions. Indeed, there is considerable variation in unemployment across jurisdictions in any year and within jurisdictions across time. These data are meant to be illustrative. Had a set of more diverse local governments (such as big cities versus small cities) been compared, the observed variation would have been even greater.

Figure 7.2 demonstrates this variation as well as the differing sensitivity of different jurisdictions to national economic trends. It graphs the expected unemployment rate for the ten largest SMSAs under two different assumptions about the national rate of unemployment, which is used as a proxy for aggregate cyclical movements. The predictions come from a regression model, which estimates the sensitivity of unemployment rates in large SMSAs to national trends for the 1990s. To obtain these estimates, deviations of the annual unemployment rate in the ten largest SMSAs are regressed from the national average unemployment rate in a model that picks up the region's fixed effect and the interaction between the national level and the region's response. The model is statistically significant and the F tests reject the hypothesis that local unemployment rates are unrelated to national trends. Furthermore, the model rejects the hypothesis that all SMSAs respond identically to national unemployment shifts.

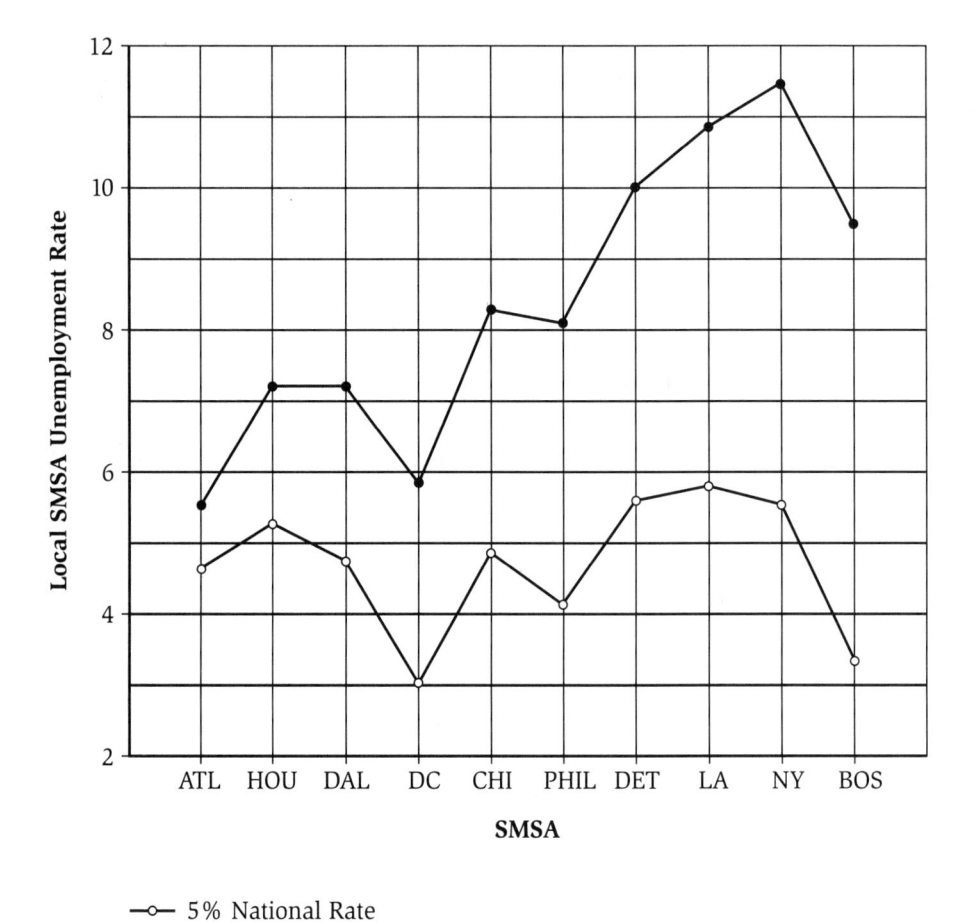

Figure 7.2. Cyclicality of Standard Metropolitan Statistical Area Unemployment Rates.

Figure 7.2 is constructed to show the increasing sensitivity of local economies to changes in the national economy, with increasing SMSA cyclical sensitivity displayed from left to right across the figure. The larger the gap is between
the two lines on the graph, which show the predicted local unemployment rate
based on national rates of 5 percent or 8 percent, the more sensitive is the local rate to changes in the national rate. For example, compare the experience
of Atlanta (ATL) to Boston (BOS). Atlanta's unemployment rate is predicted to
increase less than 1 percent if the national rate changes from 5 percent to 8 percent. In contrast, Boston is predicted to experience a 6 percent change in the
local unemployment rate, approximately double the simulated 3 percent shift
in national unemployment. Clearly Boston has had a far more cyclical economy
than Atlanta during this period. In addition to illustrating these cyclical differences, the figure also provides evidence of the differences in levels of economic

activity across jurisdictions. Washington, D.C., for example, experienced relatively low unemployment rates during this period, particularly in contrast to the New York City metropolitan area, for which the model predicts the highest unemployment rate if the national unemployment rate were to reach 8 percent.

Variations in local unemployment rates reflect differences in local industrial structures. Table 7.2 shows variation in industrial structure at a regional level. It presents shares of employment in seven key industry groupings: mining and construction; manufacturing; transportation and public utilities; wholesale and retail trade; finance, insurance, and real estate; services; and government. As might be expected, metropolitan employment is concentrated in services and trades, with relatively little employment in mining and construction (with the notable exception of Houston). On average, smaller local economies exhibit even less diversity in employment than cities. These variations in employment structure lead to different experiences as national economic conditions change.

LINKING ECONOMIC CYCLES TO THE PUBLIC FISC

There should be little doubt that state and local fiscal fortune is connected with economic performance. When economic times are good, revenue coffers are readily filled because employment levels are high and consumer expenditures are increased, leading to higher yields from income, sales, and business taxes. Economic prosperity also leads to reductions in a variety of governmental transfer programs as the demand for welfare, unemployment insurance, job training, and similar programs declines. A variety of data confirm this relationship. Gramlich (1991) and Kusko and Rubin (1993) point to the cyclically changing state and local budget surplus reported in the National Income and Product Accounts. Similarly, surveys of individual state budget conditions by the National Association of State Budget Officers reveal declining year-end budget balances coinciding with national economic recessions, and growing balances with periods of robust growth (Poterba, 1994). Because forty-eight states operate under some sort of constitutional requirement that they operate a balanced budget (National Association of State Budget Officers, 1992), the connection between economic cycles and the public fisc is of great importance.

Jurisdictions will differ in the sensitivity of their public fisc to cyclical changes depending on a number of factors. First, as discussed earlier, the local or regional industrial structure will exhibit different degrees of cyclical sensitivity. Second, jurisdictional expenditure responsibilities will differ in their connectedness to economic performance. Third, jurisdictions will experience economic cycles differently depending on the composition of their revenue sources.

During recessions, greater demands are placed on local governments. Public assistance and unemployment insurance programs expand, expenditures on

Table 7.2. Employment Shares by Industry in Ten Largest Metropolitan Areas.

	Mining and Construction	Manu-facturing	Transportation and Public Utilities	Wholesale and Retail Trade	Finance, Insurance and Real Estate	Services	Government
Los Angeles, Long Beach, CA	3.1%	16.9%	5.4%	22.0%	6.4%	32.1%	14.1%
Chicago, IL	4.1	16.9	5.8	23.3	8.1	30.0	11.8
New York, NY	3.0	8.8	5.9	17.2	13.5	34.9	16.7
Washington, DC	5.1	3.8	4.6	19.3	5.7	36.3	25.2
Philadelphia							
Detroit, MI	4.1	16.9	5.9	23.2	8.1	30.0	11.8
Houston, TX	10.7	10.7	6.9	23.8	5.7	29.1	13.1
Atlanta, GA	4.9	11.6	7.7	27.0	6.5	29.2	13.1
Boston, MA	3.1	12.3	4.2	22.0	8.6	38.2	11.6
Dallas, TX	5.0	14.4	6.5	25.6	8.3	28.6	11.6

Source: U.S. Department of Commerce, Bureau of the Census.

fire and crime control increase, and the use of public facilities swells as formerly affordable private sector substitutes are discarded. The reverse is true during periods of economic growth. The precise effect depends on the current package of services offered and the socioeconomic mix of the jurisdiction's residents. In part these differences may also reflect state mandates as to the service responsibilities of local governments.

The connection between state and local revenue structures and cyclical movements has long been recognized as a potential source of fiscal destabilization (Rafuse, 1965). For instance, income taxes are particularly sensitive to changes in economic conditions, providing local budgets with increasing revenue when economic times are good, but falling short when economic activity slows down. In contrast, the impacts of revenue are dampened in jurisdictions that rely on property taxes because changes in personal income do not lead directly to property value changes. Although income-elastic tax structures have definite advantages during periods of economic growth, more stable tax structures have their own comparative advantages. For example, jurisdictions seeking to enter the public debt market must establish their ability to pay back both principal and interest over periods stretching up to thirty years. Lenders look for revenue structures that provide some assurance that funds will be available through all phases of the economic cycle.

Table 7.3 contains data on own-source revenue for state and local governments. For all state and local governments, revenue dependence is balanced fairly evenly between property, sales, and income taxes as well as fees and charges. Other taxes and miscellaneous income play smaller roles. The pattern for differing levels of government differs markedly, however. School districts are the jurisdictions most dependent on property taxes, raising more than 80 percent of own-source revenue in this way. In contrast, state governments raise less that 2 percent of their revenue from property taxes. States do, however, rely on income taxes to a greater extent than other jurisdictions, while for county governments income taxes are virtually an untapped source of revenue. It is clear from the table that different types of jurisdictions experience cyclical movements differently because of their revenue structures. Furthermore, the true amount of variation is understated in this table. Missing is the additional within-group variation that occurs for each level of government and revenue source. For example, although states are most dependent on income taxes, five states do not levy income taxes at all. Thus, different cyclical responses can be found within types of jurisdictions, too.

For many years analysts have viewed the selection of revenue sources as a choice between growth and stability. Officials could trade off greater certitude for faster growth, but in general few combinations would permit both. More recent work has begun to call this conventional wisdom into question. Analysts now recognize that trend in growth is not the same as variability around the trend line. In particular, it has been shown that taxes that have higher long-term

Table 7.3. Percentage of Distribution of Own-Source Revenue, 1991–1992.

	State and Local Government	State	County	Munici-pal	Town-ship	School Districts	Special Districts
Property	22.47%	1.53%	44.31%	32.16%	73.93%	81.37%	15.78%
Sales	16.46	24.62	8.90	9.70	0.00	0.59	6.83
Income	17.55	29.03	1.67	8.22	1.97	0.66	0.00
Other taxes	13.59	20.20	4.76	11.06	3.62	0.91	0.74
Charges	17.24	12.12	26.21	23.85	11.66	9.15	57.74
Miscella-neous income	12.70	12.50	14.15	15.01	8.82	7.32	18.91

Source: U.S. Department of Commerce, Bureau of the Census.

income elasticities need not vary more over the business cycle than taxes with lower elasticities (Dye and McGuire, 1991). Apparently the combination of long-term growth and short-term stability is possible (Sobel and Holcombe, 1996). Although at the aggregate level these results show significantly higher short-run elasticity differences between corporate income taxes and nonfood retail sales than all other sources tested (the short-run elasticities for personal income, retail sales, adjusted gross income, and motor fuel are not statistically distinguishable), analysis at the individual state level might provide somewhat different results.

DEALING WITH BUDGETARY IMBALANCE

Cyclical economic performance can lead to budgetary imbalance by affecting both the revenue and expenditure functions. Regardless of the source of an imbalance, state and local governments have a limited number of options for dealing with it. Essentially, four different generic strategies are available to budget officials: they can budget unduly pessimistically, they can make use of savings devices, they can practice financial legerdemain, or they can implement contingency plans.

Pessimistic Estimates Versus Structural Balancing

Perhaps the most conservative approach for dealing with prospective budget imbalances is for a strategic chief executive to develop a pessimistic budget plan (Larkey and Smith, 1989). Under this scenario the proposed budget would presume the least favorable economic circumstances for the budgeted period. Such a budget would never run a deficit due to cyclical changes but would run surpluses each year in which the economy was not in a trough. It would meet state constitutional requirements prohibiting a proposed budget with a deficit.

If all that mattered was complying with constitutional requirements concerning deficits, this approach might be attractive. But the budget can be balanced at many levels, including service provision levels far below what the citizenry demands, so budget balance by itself is not a sufficient reason for choosing this mode of operation. Rather, this approach must be evaluated by taking a closer look at its implications and at what is gained and lost by establishing such a *de minimus* spending plan.

This budget strategy has two major consequences. First, the balance of power is shifted in favor of the individual or group responsible for revenue estimation, which in many jurisdictions is accountable to only the chief executive. Second, the level of service provided under these arrangements is less than what is sustainable (and likely desired) given the average long-run resources of the community. Perhaps most important, this approach vests tremendous power in the budget setter. Because this strategy is designed to run a surplus in all years except when the economy stalls, control over the disbursement of this surplus creates multiple opportunities for the executive to reward constituencies through either program additions and enhancements or tax relief or both. Furthermore, because decisions about how the surplus should be dispensed typically involve less visibility (public hearings, scrutiny) than the initial budget-setting process, there is more opportunity for the chief executive to implement his own agenda.

This potential transfer of budget power to the budget setter provides the legislature with ample incentive to take a less conservative view about future economic conditions, even if it means that the budget runs the risk of being in deficit if such optimistic projections are not realized. There is a limit, however, to this expansive behavior. The legislature generally has limited technical capability, which hampers its ability to provide alternative economic forecasts. Despite this relative imbalance of power and expertise, it is likely that budgets will be set at levels above that which would be funded under the most pessimistic economic forecasts. Consequently, budget deficits inevitably result when the economy underperforms; then a mechanism must be developed to bring the budget back within the constitutional balance requirement.

Constitutional balanced budget requirements cannot prevent a budget plan from being plunged into deficit by cyclical economic effects. But what degree of unbalance are jurisdictions willing to tolerate? In part this is a question about how sensitive the local public fisc will be to cyclical changes. But it also speaks to the issue of where the budget estimate sits between the peaks and troughs of economic performance that might be experienced.

A jurisdiction that has the average long-run capacity to fund budgeted service levels is said to have a budget in structural balance (Proctor, 1992). Figure 7.3

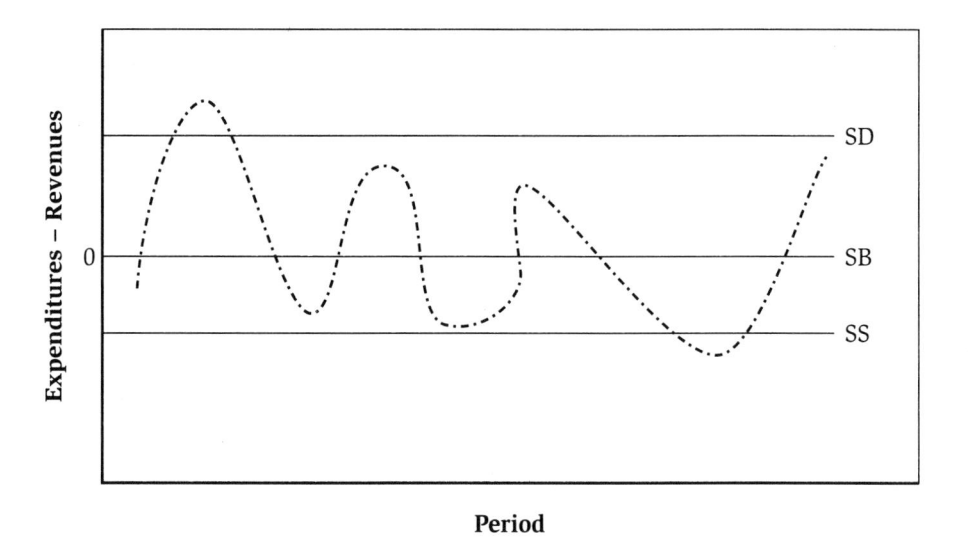

Figure 7.3. Structural Budgeting.

illustrates the concept of structural balance. The curved dashed line represents the familiar cyclical pattern of peaks and troughs in the expenditure-revenue balance experienced by a hypothetical local unit of government each year. Line SB represents a structurally balanced budget, line SS represents a budget in structural surplus, and line SD represents a budget in structural deficit.

This picture makes clear that it is unlikely that fund balances in any given year will be zero; instead it is likely that the actual revenues and expenditures will be different from their budgeted amounts. These differences will in part represent cyclical effects, but they may also result from forecast error, because it simply is not possible to predict perfect budgetary performance as far in advance as required by the budgetary process. If such errors are random, then there will be no systematic overprediction or underprediction over time. In contrast, a budget constructed so that the combination of forecast errors and cyclical perturbations results in balance only during good economic performance can be considered out of structural balance.

To pursue this issue further, return to Figure 7.3. The budget represented by line SB is constructed so that cyclical deviations from trend are approximately symmetrical. Furthermore, the spending and revenue plan represented by line SB exhibits structural balance; it is a plan that can be sustained throughout the economic cycle because cyclically induced deviations from trend create surpluses that balance negative shocks. In contrast, a policy of pessimistic estimating and budgeting (as just defined) would set spending at the minimum of the cycle (line SS). This type of budget would rarely run deficits, because it is structurally balanced far below the sustainable spending level.

Budget SD represents a third alternative. Here, budget balance is achieved only when economic conditions are particularly good. Once things sour, the budget deficits that are created far outweigh the limited savings possible from accumulations in fruitful years. To continuously meet constitutional budget requirements, a jurisdiction budgeting under scenario SD would have to either reconstitute its economy so that it would not suffer the troughs exhibited in Figure 7.3, or it would have to go through a budget-balancing exercise that lowers spending or increases revenue in years of weak economic performance. Balanced budget spending at level SD simply is not sustainable over the entire cycle. Therefore, budget SD does not achieve structural balance.

Rainy Day Funds

Long-term structural budget balance does not satisfy the no-deficit requirement imposed by state and local constitutions. To do so requires a mechanism that would allow a jurisdiction to save positive balances in good economic years in order to fund deficits when the economy performs poorly.

A potentially effective method for achieving balance each year is the use of rainy day funds. There has been near universal adoption of such funds at the state level (National Association of State Budget Officers, 1995). What limited evidence there is indicates far less use at the local level (Wolkoff, 1987). Wolkoff's 1987 survey has not been updated, reflecting the difficulty in enumerating the budgetary decisions of thousands of localities across the nation. Aggregate data available through the National Income and Product Accounts does indicate changes in state and local fund balances over time, but whether these funds are segmented in special rainy day accounts is unknown.

Not all rainy day funds are similarly sized or similarly constituted. The National Association of State Budget Officers (1985) has given a clear guideline for the size of state rainy day funds, recommending that they should be set at 5 percent of budgeted outlays. Although this guideline has been adopted by a number of analysts, there appears to be no analytic rationale for choosing this level. As Vasche and Williams (1987) point out, a number of considerations should be contained in the calculus for deciding optimal fund balance, and quantitatively assessing the value of these various considerations is a formidable task. The exercise is highly unlikely to find that the same size fund would be optimal for all communities. Rather, fund balances will vary across the budgetary cycle and across jurisdictions.

No single approach has emerged for triggering changes in the balances of rainy day funds. State-level mechanisms for adding to such balances vary from constitutionally defined requirements in some states to legislative prerogatives in others. For example, South Carolina and Michigan both determine contributions to the fund on the basis of a formula. In South Carolina, once fund balances decline sufficiently, new contributions are mandated. In Michigan, sufficiently rapid growth of personal income triggers fund contributions. Similarly, fund withdrawal mechanisms differ across jurisdictions. They occur primarily in two different ways: either the chief executive can dispense rainy day funds by administrative order, or such disbursements require legislative approval. Michigan is an exception; in this state, fund dispersal is formula-driven, based on declines in state personal income.

For a number of reasons, the Michigan approach seems quite sensible. It permits governmental units to budget for cyclical shocks when they are best able to do so. Requiring rainy day contributions at the same time that the locality is enjoying revenue growth helps instill the type of fiscal discipline that can sustain continued structural balance. Irrespective of whether fund balances prove to be ample, this procedure for changing fund levels appears to avoid some of the perverse incentives that are created by other institutional forms.

Financial Legerdemain

Too often the constitutional requirement prohibiting deficits evokes a set of budgetary responses that can have quite negative long-term consequences. For example, various unsound accounting tricks can redefine budget years or reassign collection periods (Morris, 1980).

Such short-run fixes can be irresistible for elected officials. Yet these temporary solutions merely put off the difficult choices to the succeeding budgetary period, resulting in a series of forward borrowings and leaving each year's budget makers with fewer and fewer resources to meet that year's requirements. Moving revenue collections into an earlier budget period leaves the period from which they are taken without those revenues but with no smaller expenditure obligation. The symmetrical strategy of shifting expenditures into a later period yields the same result. In this case, no additional revenues are available to pay for the increased expenditure responsibility. Another form of budgetary deception is to move into the capital budget operating budget items that need not be balanced in the current year. Such an action also has cascading long-term consequences as borrowing costs increase to fund items that should rightfully appear in the expense budget. Because bond-rating agencies view funding of the expense budget through borrowing as a fiscally unsound practice, there is a clear price to pay in pursuing this strategy. A third class of actions involves selling off government-owned assets. This strategy has proved attractive to all levels of government despite its drawback of reducing the wealth of the community and thereby lowering its long-term fiscal viability.

Another common form of financial manipulation is to make use of monies that are designated for other purposes. States and localities typically have a variety of funds, each with its own sources of revenue and nominal purpose.

Creative accounting, including redefinition of acceptable fund use, can lead to transfers from such designated funds to the general account, particularly when the general account falls short of resources to handle budgeted expenditures.

Contingency Spending and Taxing Plans

As an alternative to case-by-case decision making, some governmental units have institutionalized taxation and spending policies that are automatically implemented depending on economic conditions (Gold, 1983). So-called contingency policies are pre-agreed-upon courses of action that are triggered by economic events. For example, if revenue collections fail to meet expectations, a contingent tax increase would result in the levying of an additional tax, through either rate-base adjustment or a new instrument. Similarly, faster revenue growth than expected would result in a tax rollback. Such reductions could actually result in rebates to taxpayers, or alternatively, revenue overruns could be placed in a stabilization-type fund. Contingency planning can also be used on the expenditure side of the budget, which is typically more common. Some states (for example, Arkansas) pursue this approach exhaustively and designate all proposed appropriations as contingent upon defined funding levels for a given revenue structure. If the revenue yield falls short of its potential, only a subset of expenditure programs would be funded. Numerous other possibilities exist, ranging from funding succeeding years' capital budget items from last year's surplus to designating increases in funding for specific programs if revenue exists.

An important consideration in designing contingency spending and taxation plans is the explicit statement as to whether the implementation of contingency policies are one-time events or considered to be part of the new tax or expenditure base. For this reason the use of contingent funds for one-time appropriations, such as debt reduction or capital outlay, has the advantage of nonrecurrence. The alternative approach of including contingent decisions in the longer-term base creates problems because it alters the requirements for long-term structural balance.

Unfortunately, one drawback of contingency spending and taxation plans is that they may tend to exacerbate any local cyclical effects. Although there is some dispute as to whether local policies can have significant stabilization effects, contingency plans can result in procyclical policies. When revenue yields are low, taxes are increased or programs are shrunk. When revenue yields are high, taxes are reduced or programs are added.

To this point in the chapter, minimal attention has been paid to the types of decisions and judgments that are made on a daily basis by those charged with the budgeting function. As these budget officers would stress, the numerous day-to-day policy decisions they make, ranging from the rate at which supplies are replenished to enforcing a hiring freeze or reducing opportunities for overtime, all have significant impacts on the ability of a jurisdiction to live within its budget plan.

Although these decisions may require action, they are not viewed as specific policy responses to cyclical economic impacts; rather, they are made irrespective of the institutional arrangements available to counteract cyclical effects. Furthermore, there are typically limits to the extent that these informal mechanisms can enforce budgetary discipline. For example, the decision to leave a position vacant becomes a decision to offer a permanently lower level of service if the position goes unfilled for too long. Similarly, unless efficiency adjustments are made, the restriction of overtime hours means that work product will be generated in a less timely manner. These types of adjustments may provide some budgetary relief and they may provide the jurisdiction with some greater flexibility to operate, but they should be viewed within the short-term context. When revenue and expenditure adjustments are institutionalized for longer periods, they involve a resetting of budgeted priorities.

ENDOGENOUS STRATEGIES

To this point the focus has been on ways that state and local governments can respond to cyclically induced fiscal problems. These strategies were aimed at managing events that could be only partially anticipated. But what about the possibility of influencing the frequency or intensity of the events themselves? There are three generic strategies that jurisdictions can use to get off the cyclical roller coaster.

The first strategy seeks to reduce the variance in economic performance between budget periods. This requires a reexamination of the jurisdiction's revenue structure. Jurisdictions make various trade-offs in their choice of how monies are to be raised, ranging from considerations of whether stable revenue growth should be emphasized even if it means higher burdens on the poor to whether elastic revenue sources should be relied on even if they are more cyclically prone. Some of these choices are purposeful in that they directly acknowledge differential growth, stability, and burden. But other choices reflect historical artifact and convenience. Short-term convenience is particularly tempting when electoral cycles and economic cycles are out of phase. Nevertheless, an analysis that goes beyond the immediate political setting would call for a more explicit recognition of the costs of cyclical variance.

The tools by which cyclical deviations could be dampened are not difficult to identify. The key would be to choose a combination of revenue sources that either were less cyclically prone individually or that offset each other cyclically so that all revenue flows did not simultaneously experience the same exaggerated hills and valleys. In general, property taxes have proven to be more stable than other revenue sources and therefore would be attractive for this purpose. Of course, yield stability is only one of a number of desiderata that should be used in determining tax structure. Whether stability implications are sufficiently considered will depend in part on whether alternative institutional arrangements are present to minimize cyclical effects.

A second strategy is to use policies to counter the cyclical effects of existing tax and expenditure structures. Such local and regional countercyclical efforts have long been viewed suspiciously. Musgrave's assignment of the stabilization function to a central governmental authority (1959) shaped the thinking of multiple generations of public finance economists and virtually ruled out serious consideration of subnational stabilization efforts. Recently, Musgrave's view has been reexamined and strong counterarguments have been offered to support such efforts. This new view holds that local multipliers are larger and jurisdictional borders are less leaky than was previously believed (Gramlich, 1987) . As a consequence, policies deployed for countercyclical reasons may be much more effective than was once thought (Fox and Murray, 1996). Although monetary policy still would not be feasible, a variety of fiscal initiatives could have stabilization effects.

A third strategy is to use governmental policies to alter the jurisdiction's growth path. This approach might be viewed as the flip side to the conservative budget view described by Larkey and Smith (1989). Rather than setting government spending at the minimum point of revenue yield realized at the bottom of the cycle, economic growth raises revenue yield so that its new minimum provides sufficient resources for existing spending. Basically, governmental policy allows the economy to grow its way out of cyclical instability. There have been no shortages of efforts to use governmental policy to influence economic development, and this is not the place to review that broad and extensive literature (Bartik, 1991). Perhaps here it is best merely to caution that such a strategy is effective in terms of reducing cyclicality only if governmental spending can be constrained so that it does not capture all of the growth yield.

CONCLUSION

Although this chapter focuses on the particular challenges that the economic cycle creates for state and local budget officials, it is important to recognize that these challenges are not necessarily unique, and that the types of responses formulated to deal with these problems could also serve to solve other challenges facing budget officials. In a very real sense, cyclical economic forces are no different that other exogenous (and perhaps endogenous) shocks to the budgetary system.

Think of it this way: it is highly likely that budgetary officials are well aware of the sensitivity of their public fisc to the economic environment. What is unknown is when an economic shift will occur, how intense it will be, and how long it will last. Turning points in cycles have been notoriously difficult to predict, and history is only the weakest of guides to forecasting their intensity. But how is that any different than forecasting the need for snow removal, or for police overtime because of a particularly gruesome set of crimes, for the coming year? (It may be argued that the expenditure response may be more endogenous than the economic cycle or the need for snow removal, although it is certainly a reasonable position that we could wait for nature to melt the snow, just as we might hold back on creating a dedicated detective task force, waiting for natural life-cycle effects to reduce the likelihood that a criminal will strike again.) The problem is that all three situations exhibit year-to-year variation in budget requirements, and it cannot be predicted with certainty whether the budget will be affected positively or negatively in the coming year, or how much of an impact there will be.

Thus, although an analyst may be able to isolate a specific set of factors as being responsible for changes in budgetary conditions, this is not the same as having a unique set of policies for restoring fiscal balance. Budget officials must still conform to a set of constitutional requirements, a set of procedural guidelines, and they must be responsive to political realities when shaping responses. The types of actions officials may take will depend on the timing and magnitude of the unexpected shock, the political environment at that time, and the tools available.

Effective budgetary policy calls for flexibility in dealing with the new budgetary environment. Such flexibility is required when budgetary outcomes differ from what was planned, whether as the consequence of shifting economic conditions, environmental or meteorological events, or political changes. Whatever the source of change, flexibility is aided by the various institutional arrangements suggested in this chapter.

References

Bartik, T. J. *Who Benefits from State and Local Economic Development Policies?* Kalamazoo, Mich.: Upjohn Institute for Employment Research, 1991.

Briffault, R. *Balancing Acts: The Reality Behind State Balanced Budget Requirements.* New York: Twentieth Century Fund Press, 1996.

Dye, R. F., and McGuire, T. J. "Growth and Variability of State Individual Income and General Sales Taxes." *National Tax Journal,* 1991, 44(1), 55–66.

Engerman, S. "Regional Aspects of Stabilization Policy." In R. Musgrave (ed.), *Essays in Fiscal Federalism.* Washington, D.C.: Brookings Institution, 1965.

Fair, R. *Testing Macroeconometric Models.* Cambridge, Mass.: Harvard University Press, 1994.

Fox, W. F., and Murray, M. N. "Intergovernmental Aspects of Growth and Stabilization Policy." Paper presented at the National Tax Association's Eighty-Eighth Conference, San Diego, California, Oct. 1996.

Gold, S. D. "Preparing for the Next Recession: Rainy Day Funds and Other Tools for States." Legislative Finance Paper no. 41, National Conference of State Legislators, Dec. 1983.

Gramlich, E. M. "Subnational Fiscal Policy." In J. Quigley (ed.), *Perspectives on Local Public Finance and Public Policy.* Greenwich, Conn.: JAI Press, 1987.

Gramlich, E. M. "The 1991 State and Local Fiscal Crisis." *Brookings Papers on Economic Activity,* 1991, *2,* 249–287.

Kusko, A. L., and Rubin, L.S. "Measuring the Aggregate High-Employment Budget for State and Local Governments." *National Tax Journal,* 1993, *46*(4), 411–424.

Larkey, P. D., and Smith, R. A. "Bias in the Formulation of Local Government Budget Problems." *Policy Sciences,* 1989, *22,* 123–166.

Morris, C. R. *The Cost of Good Intentions.* New York: McGraw-Hill, 1980.

Musgrave, R. A. *The Theory of Public Finance.* New York: McGraw-Hill, 1959.

National Association of State Budget Officers. *State Balanced Budget Requirements: Provisions and Practice.* Washington, D.C.: National Association of State Budget Officers, 1992.

National Association of State Budget Officers. *Budget Stability: A Policy Framework for States.* Washington, D.C.: National Association of State Budget Officers, 1995.

National Association of State Budget Officers and National Governors' Association. *Budgeting Amid Fiscal Uncertainty: Stabilization Funds and Other Strategies.* Washington, D.C.: National Association of State Budget Officers and National Governors' Association, 1985.

Poterba, J. M. "State Responses to Fiscal Crises: The Effects of Budgetary Institutions and Politics." *Journal of Political Economy,* 1994, *102*(4), 799–821.

Proctor, A. J. *Structural Balance.* New York: New York State Financial Control Board, 1992.

Rafuse, R. W., Jr. "Cyclical Behavior of State-Local Finances." In R. Musgrave (ed.), *Essays in Fiscal Federalism.* Washington, D.C.: Brookings Institution, 1965.

Sobel, R. S., and Holcombe, R. G. "Measuring the Growth and Variability of Tax Bases over the Business Cycle." *National Tax Journal,* 1996, *49*(4), 535–552.

Vasche, D., and Williams, B. "Optimal Governmental Budgeting Contingency Reserve Funds." *Public Budgeting and Finance,* 1987, *7*(1), 66–82.

Wolkoff, M. "An Evaluation of Municipal Rainy Day Funds." *Public Budgeting and Finance,* 1987, *7*(2), 52–63.

CHAPTER EIGHT

The Federal Budget and Economic Management

Van Doorn Ooms
Ronald S. Boster
Robert L. Fleegler

This chapter discusses the budget as a tool of macroeconomic management in addressing problems of unemployment, inflation, and economic growth. These are *macro* considerations, involving the *aggregate* economy, which is affected by the overall levels and broad composition of taxes and spending. Individual tax and spending provisions in the budget, of course, have myriad economic effects on households, firms, and specific economic sectors, but these do not concern us here. Our basic conclusion is that policymakers can use the budget effectively to influence economic growth, but they will find it less effective, and perhaps even counterproductive, as an instrument for managing inflation and unemployment. Our discussion represents a mainstream, "new Keynesian" view. (For a rigorous analytical exposition of new Keynesian macroeconomics, see Dornbusch and Fischer, 1994; for a less technical account, see Schultze, 1992. Unfortunately, there is insufficient space in this article to discuss alternative macroeconomic perspectives in detail. For a controversial look at supply-side economics, see Bartley, 1992; for an understanding of real business cycle theory, see Huh and Trehan, 1991; and for a cogent treatment of rational expectations theory, see Lucas and Sargent, 1981.)

Note: The authors thank Josh Lewis and Grant Kronenberg for their valuable assistance on this project.

DEFINITIONS AND DISTINCTIONS

In popular discourse, the terms *fiscal policy* and *budget policy* are used interchangeably. According to their economic meanings, however, *fiscal policy* denotes choices regarding a budget's total revenues, expenditures, and deficit, particularly when these aggregates are calculated on a structural or high-employment basis (terms explained shortly); and *budget policy* is concerned with choices about the broad composition of such aggregate revenues and expenditures. *Stabilization policy* refers to the use of fiscal and monetary policies to affect economic activity, unemployment, and inflation in the short term, while *growth policy* denotes their use to affect long-term changes in the economy's productive capacity. Finally, *monetary policy* refers to the actions taken by the Federal Reserve Board (the Fed) to change the growth of the money supply and thereby the level of short-term interest rates. Although monetary policy is not a subject of this chapter, reference to it is required for the discussions of stabilization and growth.

Economic stabilization is concerned with the problems of unemployment and inflation in the short term—that is, over the course of months or, at most, a year or two. Stabilization policy—either fiscal or monetary—affects inflation and unemployment by directly or indirectly changing the level of *aggregate demand* (total spending) and thereby the level of economic activity, or output. The fundamental measure of this output is *real gross domestic product* (GDP)— the total annual production of goods and services in the United States, adjusted for inflation. Unemployment and inflation are principally determined by the relationship between GDP and *potential GDP*, the output that the economy has the capacity to produce without increasing inflation.

Economic growth is the increase in the economy's productive capacity—potential GDP—over the long term, a period measured in years or decades. Productive capacity, of course, will determine future living standards on the basis of the consumption of both privately and publicly produced goods and services.

Growth policies affect potential GDP by increasing future supplies of *productive factors*—labor, skills, machines, and structures—and the technology that determines how productively these factors are used. They do this by shifting the composition of GDP, such as the balance between investment and consumption goods, through changes in aggregate taxes and expenditures. Faster growth will require a reduction in goods and services devoted to consumption and an increase in investments that increase the long-term supply of productive factors or improve the technology with which they are used.

Figure 8.1 shows GDP and potential GDP from 1960 to 1996 and illustrates the relationship between stabilization and growth. Potential GDP rose along a

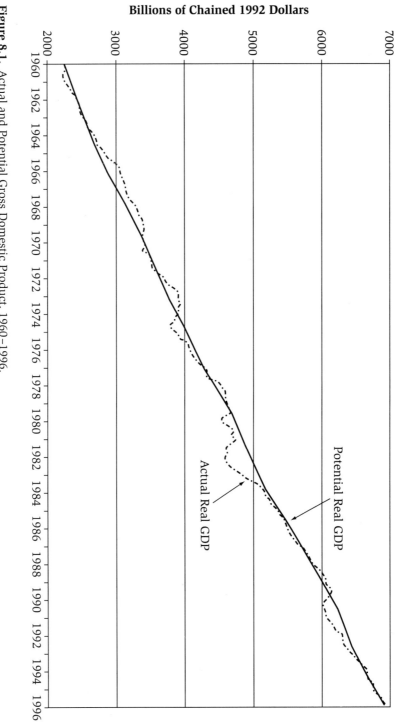

Billions of Chained 1992 Dollars

Actual Real GDP

Potential Real GDP

Figure 8.1. Actual and Potential Gross Domestic Product, 1960–1996.

Sources: Congressional Budget Office; U.S. Department of Commerce, Bureau of Economic Analysis.

smooth trend during this period, while actual GDP fluctuated around this trend. From the bottom of the recession in 1982 to the end of the subsequent economic expansion in 1990, GDP rose by 34 percent, an average rate of 3.7 percent per year, while potential GDP rose by only 23 percent, or 2.4 percent per year. GDP could increase faster than potential GDP because the economy had significant idle capacity in 1982 and succeeding years. The increase in GDP can usefully be seen as both a rise in potential GDP and a reduction in the gap between GDP and its potential.

Stabilization is concerned with this GDP gap (capacity utilization) and with its implications for inflation and unemployment; growth is concerned with the increase in potential GDP. In concept, the goal of stabilization policy is to manage aggregate demand (explained shortly) such that GDP is close to its potential, in that output and incomes will be high and unemployment low, but not above it so that inflation will rise. The goal of growth policy is to raise the slope of the upward trend of potential GDP by increasing the supplies of productive factors and by improving technology. Increases in GDP that reduce the GDP gap, such as the increase that occurred from 1982 to 1990, are often popularly referred to as growth. We follow standard economic usage in reserving that term for long-term changes in potential GDP. Failure to recognize the distinction often leads to the erroneous conclusion that rapid increases in output that close the gap between actual and potential GDP can be sustained without inflationary consequences after GDP reaches its potential.

UNEMPLOYMENT, INFLATION, AND GROWTH

Involuntary unemployment has costs for both individuals and society. At the personal level, it means reduced income and consumption, increased anxiety, and if prolonged, reduced self-respect and increased family problems. For society, high unemployment means fewer resources for private or public uses, and it may contribute to crime and other socially destructive behavior (Freeman, 1996). Unemployment is also a source of inequity, because low-income workers spend more time unemployed than those with higher incomes. Finally, prolonged high unemployment may perpetuate and augment itself, a process called *hysteresis*. The chronic high-unemployment rates in some European countries suggest that these economies have adapted to high unemployment in ways that make its reduction more difficult. This difficulty may result from, for example, the erosion of job skills through disuse, policies that reduce work incentives, or labor market regulations that impair flexibility in wages and employment practices (Organization for Economic Cooperation and Development, 1994, pp. 67–69).

The costs of inflation are less obvious than the costs of unemployment and have been debated more often. Some economists have argued that anticipated inflation would have few costs that could not be corrected through comprehensive indexing of wages and prices. Quite apart from the practical difficulties with indexing, however, there appears to be a deep-seated public antipathy to inflation. First, because inflation in practice has been largely unanticipated, it has often produced large redistributions of wealth and income, both among households and businesses and across generations. Second, even when inflation affects prices and wages similarly, workers may perceive that price inflation reduces their purchasing power without crediting wage inflation for increasing it. Inflation also engenders uncertainty, a sense of loss of control, and difficulty in planning for the future. High inflation, such as that in the double-digit range, may also reduce investment, economic growth, and the efficiency of the price system.

A major cost of inflation is that regardless of what economic theory and analysis may suggest, rising inflation is usually followed by higher unemployment. This is because the Fed normally reacts to the emergence of significant inflationary pressures with monetary restraint, often severe enough to cause a recession. The public reaction during 1968 to 1982, although now little remembered, indicates that high and rising inflation is not politically viable in our society. The Fed's policies of monetary restraint reflect, in addition to the public's antipathy to inflation, its conviction that inflation harms the economy in the long run.

The question posed by economic growth is how much consumption should society sacrifice in the present to make investments that will increase incomes and consumption in the future? Economics provides little guidance on this issue. Nevertheless, three concerns have led many analysts to conclude that the recent growth of potential GDP of just over 2 percent per year is too low. First, there is a public sense of diminished expectations resulting from the near stagnation of average real wages during the last twenty to twenty-five years. This stagnation stems from the sharp drop in productivity growth from the nearly 3 percent annual average during the quarter century following World War II to about 1 percent since 1973. Second, the increasing inequality of earnings and incomes, given the stagnating average, has for the first time reduced real incomes for a significant portion of the U.S. population, especially for less educated and less skilled workers. (For a more detailed analysis of these trends, see Committee for Economic Development, 1996.) Finally, there is a growing belief that the rapidly approaching retirement of the baby boomers will put pressure on the living standards of both retirees and workers unless stronger growth produces a larger economic pie to be divided between them. (For a more detailed analysis of these trends, see Committee for Economic Development, 1995, 1997).

STABILIZATION GOALS

The Employment Act of 1946 (PL 79–304) and the 1978 Humphrey-Hawkins legislation (PL 95–523) established a responsibility of the federal government to promote maximum employment and price stability. The broad statutory language leaves ample room for disagreements, based on differences in either economic analysis or value judgments, about what such goals might mean in practice. Nevertheless, a rough operational consensus on these stabilization goals has developed among economists and policymakers.

The central concept informing this consensus is that *unemployment and inflation are independent in the long run.* Contrary to the widely accepted view of thirty to forty years ago, we cannot "buy" permanently lower unemployment by accepting higher inflation, nor does lower inflation require permanently higher unemployment. This is so even though low unemployment is strongly associated with high inflation in the short run, and vice versa (see Figure 8.2). This change in view has dramatically altered the approach to stabilization policy.

First, we must recognize that full employment does not imply zero unemployment. In a dynamic economy there will always be individuals searching for first jobs, searching for new jobs upon reentering the labor force, changing jobs as the location of employment changes, and quitting jobs to search for better ones. Such *frictional* unemployment is not only inevitable but may also be widespread, and to some extent desirable, in a dynamic and rapidly changing economy. In addition, even in a booming economy with very strong overall demand for labor, some long-term *structural* unemployment remains among those who lack necessary job skills or are located in regions of declining prosperity and weak labor demand. Unemployment in excess of these frictional and structural components, related to a general weakness of demand for labor, is called *cyclical.* Conceptually, full employment (or high employment) means that unemployment is entirely frictional or structural, and that cyclical unemployment is zero.

Frictional and structural unemployment are not fixed magnitudes, however. They ultimately depend not only on underlying demographic, social, and economic factors, such as the age, experience, skills, and location of the unemployed, but also on the demand for labor. (For example, frictional and structural unemployment fell to extremely low levels during World War II, when labor demand was exceptionally high due to requirements for war production.)

How then do we operationally define *full employment?* A definition emerges from the empirical observation that when labor markets are tight and the unemployment rate is low, the rate of wage inflation rises (from whatever its initial rate was); similarly, at high rates of unemployment, wage inflation falls. At some intermediate unemployment rate, the demand for and supply of labor will

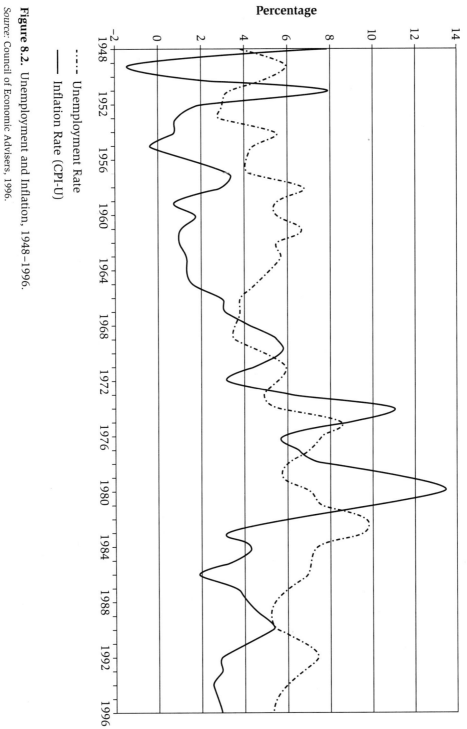

Figure 8.2. Unemployment and Inflation, 1948–1996.

Source: Council of Economic Advisers, 1996.

Percentage

-·-·- Unemployment Rate

——— Inflation Rate (CPI-U)

be in balance, in the sense that wage inflation continues at the same rate. Full employment is thus operationally defined as a *nonaccelerating inflation rate of unemployment* (NAIRU), which is the lowest unemployment rate attainable without continually rising inflation. (The underlying rationale is that this is the lowest politically sustainable rate of unemployment, because continually rising inflation would not be tolerated by the public or the Fed.) *Potential GDP*, in turn, is operationally defined as the output that would be produced at the full employment level associated with the NAIRU.

Economists use historical relationships between unemployment, inflation, and output to estimate the NAIRU and the potential GDP associated with it. (They also estimate the high-employment budget revenues and expenditures associated in turn with that potential GDP.) Accurate estimates are difficult to make, however, because it is difficult to disentangle fundamental relationships from more transitory ones. The fact that inflation did not rise when unemployment fell to and then below 5 percent in 1995 to 1997 suggests that recent estimates of the NAIRU in the 5.5 to 6 percent range are too high and those of the potential GDP are correspondingly low. Some economists believe, however, that a number of transitory phenomena, such as the strong dollar, have been responsible for this apparent decline in the NAIRU.

The choice of an inflation goal has thus been a matter of considerable controversy. If inflation and unemployment are independent in the long run, why not pursue zero inflation? Some policymakers do in fact favor an explicit goal of price stability for the Fed, and zero inflation goals have been adopted by monetary authorities in some other countries. Nevertheless, most policy discussions, as well as the observed behavior of the Fed, suggest that a more modest goal has been generally accepted and pursued. Fed Chairman Alan Greenspan has noted that inflation should be low enough that it does not significantly affect household and business economic decisions, and in practice policymakers appear to be reasonably comfortable with the 2 to 3 percent inflation experienced during the 1990s.

There are several likely reasons for this. First, the official price measures probably overstate inflation to some degree, and in any case the costs of inflation noted earlier appear to be small at the low rates recently experienced. Second, forcing inflation down to zero may entail substantial short-term costs in higher unemployment and lost output, and policymakers are reluctant to pay either the economic or political price. Finally, at inflation rates near zero the independence of inflation and unemployment noted earlier may break down—in which case a further reduction in inflation would require higher long-term unemployment. Price inflation allows real wages to fall and reduces unemployment if money wages are unchanged. At zero or very low inflation, however, real wages cannot fall unless nominal wages are reduced. Such reductions in money wages may be strongly resisted, prolonging higher unemployment. (See upcoming discussion of wage flexibility, as well as Akerlof, Dickens, and Perry, 1996.)

STABILIZATION POLICY

The need for stabilization policy arises from two observed features of the economy. First, aggregate demand does not increase smoothly along a full-employment path near potential GDP but instead fluctuates, sometimes falling below and sometimes rising above that level. When aggregate demand is insufficient to purchase all the economy's potential output, unemployment will tend to rise and inflation will tend to fall; the opposite occurs when aggregate demand is excessive. Second, the adjustment of employment and inflation to insufficient aggregate demand is slow. This sluggish adjustment in turn reflects two closely related problems: the downward flexibility of wages (and many prices) is limited, and inflation has significant inertia. This inertia arises because price and wage increases lead firms and workers to expect, plan, and implement future increases, which perpetuates the inflationary process.

Fluctuations in aggregate demand arise regularly from private spending decisions. Consumer spending, which comprises two-thirds of aggregate demand, and especially spending on autos and other durable goods, shifts to reflect changing sentiment about job or income prospects, price and wage expectations, and so on. Residential construction responds to these factors, as well as to changes in interest rates. Business investment spending on plant, equipment, and inventories fluctuates with expectations about future sales and the costs of capital. Export sales change with foreign business conditions and exchange rates.

Demand fluctuations also originate in the public sector, either directly, through changes in government spending, or indirectly, through changes in tax policy or monetary policy that affect household and business spending. The large reduction in military spending at the end of World War II led to recession in spite of rapid growth in private consumption and investment expenditures. The simultaneous escalation of spending on the Vietnam War and domestic Great Society programs in 1966 to 1968, when aggregate demand was already above potential GDP, set off rising inflation. The large tax cuts of the early 1980s boosted consumer spending and recovery from the deep 1981 to 1982 recession. Virtually every episode of rising inflation since World War II has led the Fed to curtail private spending by reducing money growth and raising interest rates.

If wages were entirely flexible, a drop in aggregate demand, and thereby in the demand for labor, would cause an immediate fall in wages. At lower wages, businesses would hire more labor, restoring full employment. In the real economy, however, wages are "sticky downward," adjusting slowly and incompletely to such declines in labor demand. As a result, when demand falls, "sticky" wages remain too high to bring the supply and demand for labor into balance. The result is involuntary unemployment—fewer jobs available than individuals who wish to work at the going wage—that may persist for extended periods.

Once it has been incorporated into economic decision making, inflation can be reduced only by large and/or prolonged reductions in aggregate demand. For this reason, reducing high inflation entails large costs in higher unemployment and lower output (see Figure 8.2). This cost-of-inflation reduction can be expressed in terms of the *sacrifice ratio*—the fraction of a year's potential GDP that must be sacrificed to reduce inflation by one percentage point. Current estimates put this ratio at about 4 percent, so that a reduction in inflation from, say, 6 percent to 5 percent would require the GDP to remain at 4 percent below its potential for a year (or 2 percent below its potential for two years, and so on). Thus, in the deep recession and prolonged disinflation of the early 1980s, inflation was reduced by about 6 percentage points, from about 9 percent to 3 percent, over six and a half years, at a cumulative GDP loss of 26 percent (Dornbusch and Fischer, 1994, p. 547).

USING FISCAL POLICY TO STABILIZE THE ECONOMY

When discussing fiscal policy, it is important to distinguish between changes in budget revenues and spending that result from planned, legislated, discretionary policy actions, and those that result automatically from changes in economic activity. When the economy weakens and employment and income levels fall, tax revenues decline and some expenditures, such as unemployment compensation, increase. The budget deficit therefore rises. Similarly, when the economy strengthens, these processes reverse and the budget deficit declines. Although these automatic budget effects have important consequences, they must be distinguished from discretionary policy changes.

The concept of the *high-employment budget* can be used to identify discretionary changes in fiscal policy. At any moment, we can estimate what federal revenues, spending, and the resulting deficit would be if the economy were at full or high employment, with the unemployment rate at the NAIRU and GDP (by definition) at its potential. This deficit is called the high-employment or *structural* deficit—that is, the deficit produced by the structure of tax and spending programs and not by any revenue and spending effects of subpotential (or above-potential) economic activity (see Figure 8.3). If GDP is below potential, the actual deficit will be larger than this structural deficit by the amount

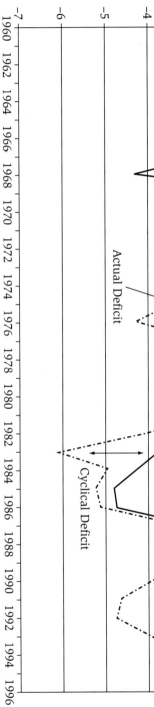

Figure 8.3. Actual and Structural Budget Deficits, 1960–1996, as a Percentage of Gross Domestic Product.

Source: Congressional Budget Office, 1997a.

of the *cyclical* deficit. Similarly, if the economy is exceptionally strong and the GDP is above its potential, the actual deficit will be less than the structural deficit, with a negative cyclical deficit. The size of the structural deficit (standardized as a percentage of potential GDP) is commonly used as a measure of the expansionary or contractionary "posture" of fiscal policy, and changes in this standardized deficit are used as a measure of fiscal policy changes.

Automatic Stabilizers

When GDP changes, certain automatic revenue and expenditure changes occur that help to stabilize aggregate demand without discretionary policy changes. For example, if business investment increases or federal defense spending drops, the impact of this initial spending change may be multiplied as it affects incomes and thereby subsequent spending decisions. (For instance, if military procurement declines, reducing employment and wages in aircraft production, the consumption spending of the workers affected also declines. This leads to further rounds of reductions in employment, income, and spending.) The automatic stabilizers moderate these secondary spending effects and thereby dampen the total change in aggregate demand.

Several mechanisms in the budget act as automatic stabilizers. The most important is the tax system, in particular the income tax. When wages (or profits or other taxable incomes) fall as a result of a decline in GDP, the taxes on these incomes also fall. The after-tax incomes of the workers affected will therefore fall by less than the original GDP decline. This will moderate the workers' subsequent reduction in their consumption spending. The government budget, in effect, absorbs part of the income decline, which is reflected in a fall in revenues and an increase in the cyclical deficit. A similar, smaller stabilization effect occurs in some spending programs. The most important and obvious is unemployment compensation, which pays out more benefits as unemployment increases, but similar effects occur in other entitlement programs, such as food stamps and Medicaid, in which the number of beneficiaries responds automatically to changed economic conditions.

Estimates by the Congressional Budget Office (1997a) indicate that each dollar change in GDP on average changes federal revenues by about $0.27 and spending by about $0.05, so the cyclical deficit automatically changes by about $0.32 and private spendable incomes change by the remaining $0.68. When aggregate demand falls, such an automatic rise in the deficit is a measure of the additional fiscal stimulus provided by the budget to dampen subsequent reductions in aggregate demand. In a recession, this stimulative effect can be quite large. For example, in 1983, just after the trough of the deep 1981–1982 recession, when the unemployment rate averaged 9.6 percent and GDP was 6.7 percent below its potential, the cyclical budget deficit was $68 billion, or 1.8 percent of potential GDP. Clearly, if tax and spending programs had been structured in a manner that eliminated the cyclical deficit in the early 1980s, the decline in aggregate demand, production, employment, and incomes would have been substantially larger. For this reason, many observers have expressed concern about the effects on economic stabilization of a constitutional amendment to require a balanced budget (Greenstein, 1997).

Discretionary Stabilization Policy

As noted, the automatic stabilizers moderate the effects of initial changes in aggregate demand but do not reverse or offset them. A more ambitious agenda for stabilization policy is to make discretionary changes in fiscal or monetary policy intended to partially or completely offset such deviations of aggregate demand from its desired high-employment, low-inflation level. In principle, an unwanted surge in aggregate demand, which threatens to trigger an inflationary boom, can be offset by restrictive monetary or fiscal policies or both. Monetary restraint would reduce the growth of the money supply, raise interest rates, and thereby reduce private spending, especially on interest-sensitive residential housing, consumer durables, and business investments. The rise in interest rates would also raise the value of the dollar, which would reduce exports as well as production that competes with imports. Alternatively, fiscal restraint could reduce government spending directly, raise taxes, or both, to discourage private consumption spending. In the opposite case, when aggregate demand is expected to be insufficient, expansionary monetary or fiscal policy, by reversing these actions and effects, could support total spending and offset the decline in aggregate demand.

This oversimplified picture of discretionary stabilization policy roughly characterizes the view held thirty to forty years ago, when many mainstream economists were optimistic about using fiscal and monetary policy to fine-tune aggregate demand and thereby achieve an appropriate balance between unemployment and inflation. (There were, nevertheless, vigorous disagreements about what balance was appropriate.) Since then, both economic events and developments in economic theory have led economists and policymakers to become less ambitious regarding stabilization policies, and about fiscal policy in particular. Some of these developments have affected both monetary and fiscal policy and led to a more cautious approach to both, although monetary policy remains actively employed in economic stabilization. Others have highlighted problems peculiar to fiscal policy that have greatly restricted its use for these purposes.

Problems with Using Discretionary Policies

Optimism among economists about the prospects for economic stabilization grew after World War II, as refined Keynesian theory became the standard macroeconomic paradigm (Stein, 1996). In the 1960s, this theory found its way into national thinking and policy with the advent of "new economics" during the Kennedy administration, which carried over into the Johnson and Nixon eras. Walter Heller, the chairman of President Kennedy's Council of Economic Advisers, wrote in 1967 that "we now take for granted that the government must step in to provide the essential stability at high levels of employment and growth that the market mechanism, left alone, cannot deliver" (p. 9).

This optimism was soon overtaken by events. First, as noted earlier, inflation began to accelerate in the mid-1960s, when large structural deficits drove aggregate demand above potential GDP. The initial rise in inflation was seen as a confirmation of Keynesian theory, in that the government, unwilling to choose between "guns and butter," had failed to cut spending or raise taxes. The buildup of inflationary inertia, however, proved stubbornly resistant to the stronger fiscal and monetary restraint that finally came at the end of the decade; unemployment rose, but inflation also remained high. The U.S. economy had begun to encounter *stagflation*—the coexistence of high rates of both unemployment and inflation.

Confidence was waning that discretionary policy could "buy" lower inflation inexpensively with a brief rise in unemployment, which led to several years of experimentation with *incomes policies,* which attempted to restrain prices and wages directly through administrative actions. The final blow to the simple trade-off view was delivered by the "oil shock" of 1973 (repeated in 1978), when a near doubling of oil prices led to escalating inflation and, simultaneously, deep recession. During this period the economy was also hit with other supply shocks, such as grain shortages and a still largely unexplained permanent collapse in productivity growth that had the same cost-raising effect as the oil shocks. This unpleasant new world of stagflation was summarized in the concept of the *misery index*—the sum of the national inflation and unemployment rates—which rose through the 1970s and finally reached 21 percent in 1980.

While these economic events were undermining public confidence in the new economics, developments in economic theory were attacking its very foundations. In the mid-1960s, Edward Phelps (1967) and Milton Friedman (1968) independently developed the basic structure of the theory described earlier that denied any long-term relationship between unemployment and inflation. In this view, which has since been incorporated into mainstream economic theory, if stabilization policies held unemployment below an equilibrium, or "natural" rate, determined by the characteristics of the labor market, inflation would rise, not to some new constant rate but *continuously.* Inflation could then be stabilized at a higher rate if unemployment rose to the natural rate, but would not fall unless unemployment was pushed above that rate and held there. The implications for the old view of stabilization policy were devastating: unemployment permanently below the natural rate could not be bought with a limited increase in inflation. Policies that attempted to do this would leave the economy with no improvement in unemployment and with permanently higher inflation, which could then be reduced only by a prolonged period of higher unemployment.

Not only did the new theory appear to accord with the facts of stagflation, but the struggles of policymakers to conquer stagflation instilled a new humility and caution. Efforts to reduce inflation during the 1970s and early 1980s revealed that the sacrifice ratio was very high—a warning that policy mistakes that allowed inflation to rise would carry a heavy cost. In addition, the new experience with supply shocks brought a realization that the "cruel dilemma" of stabilization policy was even harsher than suspected. A supply shock that brought both high inflation and high unemployment left policymakers with a painful political choice: accept the unacceptably higher inflation, or push the economy further into recession. It was no longer easy to be optimistic about stabilization policy.

These difficulties were compounded by other obstacles to effective stabilization policies. One was a sharpened awareness of the enormous uncertainty about future (or even current) economic conditions to be addressed by policy, and about the impact that specific policy actions would have on those conditions. Large financial resources and much effort went into the development of econometric forecasting models to address this uncertainty, but the results, while useful, fell short of the high hopes with which the new techniques had first been introduced.

In addition, economic theory had begun to insist upon the importance of expectations in affecting economic behavior. In its extreme form, the doctrine of *rational expectations* held that stabilization policies, if expected by the public, would be impotent because individuals would adjust their behavior to nullify the impact of the policy. For example, real wages would not fall to restore full employment if workers and employers expected the government to respond to unemployment by stimulating demand and thereby maintaining upward pressure on prices and wages. Although the extreme form of the theory has not been supported by the evidence, it is now widely accepted that expectations significantly limit the conduct of stabilization policy. In particular, for policies to be effective in reducing inflation at an acceptable cost in higher unemployment, they must be consistent and credible—a consideration that obviously limits the flexibility of policymakers in making ad hoc changes to policy when economic circumstances change.

A final limitation on the effectiveness of discretionary stabilization policy concerns the long and variable time lags between the initial awareness of the need for policy change and the ultimate effects of such a change on economic activity and prices. These lags are often classified into *inside lags* and *outside lags*; the former are delays inside the policymaking process, between the initial consideration of a policy change and the implementation of policy actions; the latter are delays in the time between the policy action and its economic effects.

Monetary and fiscal policy have very different lags. Monetary policy normally has quite short inside lags; the Fed's policymaking body, the Federal Open Market Committee, meets every six weeks to consider the need for policy changes, and its decisions to intervene in the government securities markets to change money growth and short-term interest rates can be implemented immediately. In contrast, the outside lags for monetary policy are long and variable. Production most sensitive to interest rates—those of inventories, construction, and consumer durables expenditures—tend to be affected first, but even these sectors, in the aggregate, experience less than half the full impact of an interest rate change within the first year. For exports and particularly for business investment, the effects are delayed several years; for total aggregate demand, more than half the impact would be delayed beyond two years (Schultze, 1992, p. 186).

Because of these long lags, monetary policy must be directed not at current economic conditions but at the highly uncertain conditions expected far in the future. If the Fed waits until it has conclusive evidence that inflation is rising before taking anti-inflationary action, inflation may rise significantly and acquire substantial inertia before the policies take hold. Policymakers are then confronted with the high economic costs of bringing inflation back down. These long lags also mean that the effects of today's policy changes will stretch far into the future, when they may be inappropriate as conditions change. For these reasons, policy mistakes tend to have high costs, and large policy changes are therefore dangerous. As a result, monetary policy often proceeds by "leaning against the wind"—that is, by making sequential, small adjustments to interest rates designed to dampen future changes in aggregate demand and inflation as evidence of such changes begin to appear on the horizon.

Additional Problems

The outside lags for fiscal policy, and especially for spending changes, tend to be somewhat shorter and less variable than for monetary policy. A reduction in actual outlays for defense spending, for instance, will have quite rapid effects on economic activity and incomes in sectors supplying defense equipment, with secondary effects rippling out over the economy within a few months. (In the case of changes in taxes or transfer payments, however, the effects may be longer and less certain, because they depend on the spending decisions of taxpayers and payment beneficiaries.) The inside lags for fiscal policy, however, are usually quite long because legislation authorizing expenditures must be agreed upon by the president, the House, and the Senate in a protracted legislative process, and additional time is then required for such new spending authority to generate actual outlays. Although emergency fiscal legislation has sometimes been passed relatively quickly during recessions, the delayed economic effects of such policies have often occurred well into the subsequent economic expansions, thus overstimulating rather than stabilizing aggregate demand. These institutional considerations mean that fiscal policy, unlike monetary policy, cannot easily be administered gradually in small doses, nor can it be quickly modified as new information becomes available.

Discretionary fiscal policy is complicated by additional problems that arise from its inherently political nature. First, fiscal policy is often plagued by disagreement over the form it should take; during the 1980s and early 1990s, Democrats favored stimulus spending packages, while Republicans favored tax reductions. Second, it is politically very difficult to enact fiscal restraint, and expansionary tax cuts and spending programs are not easily withdrawn, especially after they acquire strong interest-group support. This became dramatically apparent when policymakers attempted to reduce large structural budget deficits as the economy approached full employment in the late 1980s. Furthermore, it is usually undesirable to operate spending programs or tax policy on a "start-stop" basis that depends on the state of the economy.

Finally, the increasing globalization of the U.S. economy in recent years, combined with the international movement from fixed to flexible exchange rates, has reduced the effectiveness of fiscal policy. With flexible exchange rates, fiscal policy actions affect interest rates, and hence exchange rates, in ways that counteract the fiscal policy. For example, an expansionary fiscal policy raises aggregate demand, thereby raising interest rates. The higher interest rates attract foreign capital, causing an appreciation of the dollar that makes U.S. exports more expensive abroad and imports cheaper domestically. As fewer exports are purchased and produced, and as consumers switch their purchases from U.S.-made goods to the cheaper imports, aggregate demand falls, reducing the impact of the initial fiscal policy. In this manner, part of the impact of policy changes is shifted from domestic aggregate demand to the trade balance. A striking instance of this occurred in the early 1980s, when the sharp rise in U.S. structural budget deficits increased domestic demand and inflation less than commonly expected, but dramatically increased the U.S. trade deficit.

In the 1980s and early to mid-1990s, chronic large structural budget deficits effectively eliminated discretionary fiscal policy as an expansionary tool. Financial market reactions to still-larger deficits posed a threat of higher interest rates that would nullify the policy actions. And the prospect of enlarging seemingly intractable deficits had little political appeal for policymakers. These factors, along with some of the other problems noted earlier, were important in defeating the stimulus package proposed by newly elected President Clinton in 1993.

As a result of these difficulties in using discretionary fiscal policy, the responsibility for stabilization policy has increasingly fallen to the Fed. This does not imply that fiscal policy should never be used for stabilization, but rather that it cannot be used effectively for fine-tuning aggregate demand through frequent adjustments. The difficulties generally outweigh the benefits in dealing with short and moderate recessions, such as that in 1990–1991. Nevertheless, if the economy experienced a deep and protracted slump in aggregate demand, such as that of the Great Depression, or sustained excess demand, such as that during the Vietnam War, monetary policy would require assistance from the heavy artillery of fiscal policy to stabilize demand without major distortions to the economy. Barring such unusual conditions, fiscal policy's major role relates to the issue of economic growth, to which we now turn.

GROWTH POLICY

As noted earlier, concerns about U.S. economic growth are both backward-looking and forward-looking. Looking back, there is concern about the sharp slowdown in the growth of productivity and average real wages that began in the early 1970s and about the growing inequality of earnings and incomes associated with it. Looking forward, there is increasing concern about the coming demographic transition, when the large cohort of baby boomers begins to retire in about a decade and significantly raises the number of elderly, consuming retirees in relation to younger, producing workers. This transition will require a large increase in the transfer of incomes from young to old, to the extent that the increase has not been prefunded through higher saving by the baby boomers during their working lives. Future production will have to be large enough to provide for both workers and retirees without jeopardizing the living standards of either. It is widely believed that annual growth in productive capacity higher than the 2 to 2.5 percent of the last twenty-five years will be required to achieve this.

Productive capacity at any time is determined by the economy's *factor inputs*—labor hours, human capital (education and skills), and physical capital (machines and structures)—and by the efficiency, or productivity, with which these factors are used. Productivity is related to the effectiveness with which factors are combined, but principally to the "state of technology" resulting from new scientific knowledge and innovation. Faster growth of productive capacity, then, requires faster growth in factor inputs, productivity, or both. For the ultimate purpose of analyzing the growth of per capita income and thereby living standards, we are interested in the growth of output per worker, or labor productivity.

Although estimates differ regarding the relative importance of physical capital, human capital, and technological change in raising labor productivity, virtually all studies attribute the most important role to technological progress.

Edward Denison's *growth accounting* (1985) suggests that advances in knowledge contributed roughly 44 percent of the increase in output per worker during 1929–1982. Increases in the average education of workers, an important component of human capital, contributed roughly 26 percent. About 15 percent of the increase was attributed to increases in capital per worker, and 33 percent to other factors, the most important of which were scale economies and improved resource allocation, principally the reallocation of labor to high-productivity jobs. (These estimates refer to contributions to potential output per employed worker. They add up to more than 100 percent principally because declining hours per worker reduced output per worker. See Denison, 1985, p. 114; also see Greenwood, Hercowitz, and Krusell, 1997.)

Although the low GDP growth during the last several decades is related to a slowdown in productivity growth, rather than to slower growth in factor inputs, the drop in productivity growth itself is largely unexplained. Nevertheless, it is widely agreed that either increases in factor inputs or more rapid technological change, or both, can raise economic growth. Because labor force growth is largely predetermined by demographic factors, with the notable exception of immigration, the broad choices for growth policy revolve around strategies to increase physical capital, human capital, and technology.

USING FISCAL AND BUDGET POLICIES TO INCREASE ECONOMIC GROWTH

Fiscal policy and budget policy, as defined here, offer quite different strategies for raising economic growth. Fiscal policy, by addressing the size of the full-employment budget deficit, affects the amount of national savings that becomes available for private capital formation. Budget policy, by altering the broad composition of taxes and spending, affects the size of public capital formation. It also affects the development of human capital and technology, insofar as these are related to public support, either directly through public expenditures or indirectly through the tax system. Budget policy can also affect private capital formation by changing incentives for private saving and investment.

Fiscal Policy: Private Capital Formation

Federal growth policy has in recent years been directed primarily toward reductions in the budget deficit to increase the stock of private physical capital. Except when the economy has significant unemployed resources, the production of more private machines and structures requires that fewer other goods and services be produced and consumed—in other words, that national saving be increased. (However, as discussed later, if the additional resources for private investment are diverted from public investment, national saving and investment would not increase.) Government deficits that are financed by borrowing from the public absorb private saving that could otherwise be used for private capital formation. Deficit reduction, in effect, reallocates resources from other uses to private investment.

The relationship between deficit reduction and private investment is not dollar-for-dollar. First, the increase in public saving may cause some reduction in private saving as private incomes are reduced. (An extreme view asserts that the decline in private saving would fully offset the increased public saving, but there is little evidence for this.) Second, some of the improvement in public saving will be reflected in larger net foreign investment rather than domestic capital formation, producing an improvement in the trade balance. This, however, will also raise future U.S. living standards by raising capital income from abroad, or by reducing debt service payments to foreign owners of capital in the United States.

The primary attention to deficit reduction and increases in national saving as a growth strategy springs from three sources. First, the concept of balancing the budget has a political appeal that transcends its economic justification in terms of growth. Second, there appears to be a broader consensus on the effectiveness of deficit reduction to raise private investment than on the effectiveness of some of the alternative budget policies discussed shortly. A third, very important reason is concern about the sharp downward trend in the proportion of resources directed to national saving and investment in recent years.

As Figure 8.4 shows, in recent decades private saving has steadily fallen, and public dissaving from growing budget deficits has increased. The resulting collapse in net national saving has produced a substantial decline in the country's net domestic investment. This decline has been less than the decline in saving only because the United States has borrowed heavily from abroad. This growing foreign indebtedness, however, like reduced domestic investment, reduces future U.S. incomes because it increases the interest and dividends that must be paid abroad.

During the last decade, the picture of public saving has greatly improved. The structural budget deficit has fallen substantially, from nearly 5 percent of potential GDP in the mid-1980s to only 0.3 percent in fiscal year 1997. In addition, legislation was enacted in 1997 that purports to balance the budget by 2002. Nevertheless, the long-term outlook for the deficit and national saving remains unfavorable because of the projected explosion in federal retirement and health care expenditures when baby boomers begin to retire. The Congressional Budget Office projects that under the policies in place in early 1997, expenditures on social security, Medicare, and Medicaid will double as a proportion of GDP by 2030, from the current 8 percent to 16 percent. The deficit

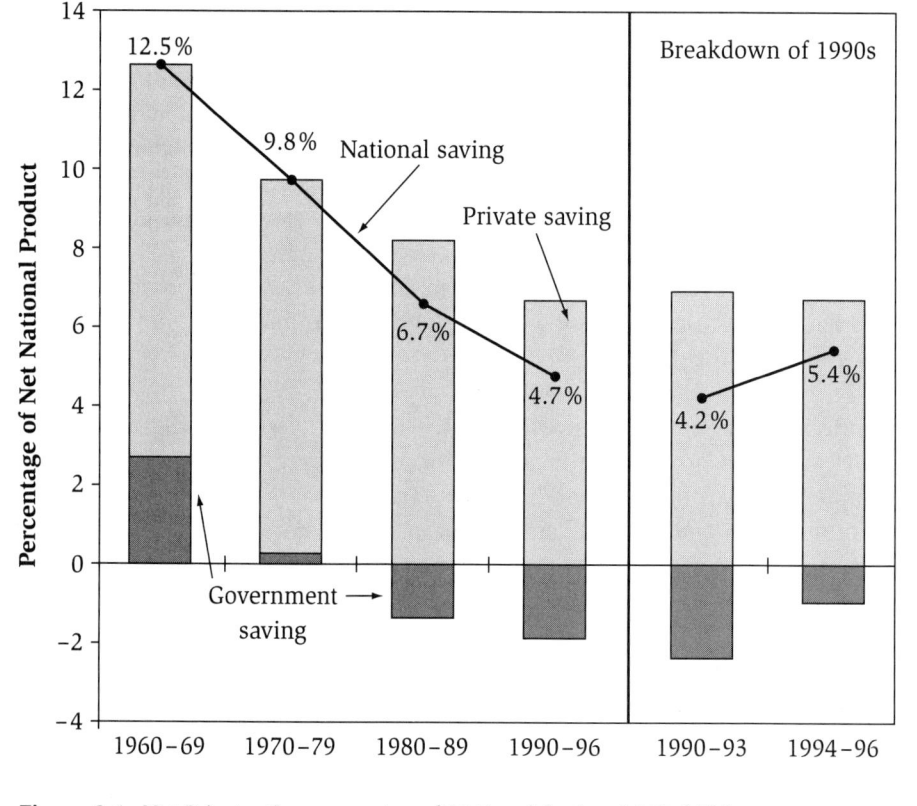

Figure 8.4. Net Private, Government, and National Saving, 1960–1996.

Note: Net national saving is the sum of net private saving and net government saving.

Source: U.S. Department of Commerce, Bureau of Economic Analysis.

would rise correspondingly from 2 percent of GDP in 1996 to 11 percent (Congressional Budget Office, 1997b, p. xv).

Budget Policies: Physical Capital, Human Capital, and Technology

National output can be classified into goods and services currently consumed and those that form investments to enhance productive capacity in the future. Federal expenditures can be usefully divided in the same way between those that raise consumption (public or private) and those that increase investment. Similarly, federal tax policy can be structured in ways that promote or discourage private investment relative to private consumption. The broad composition of expenditures and taxes can therefore significantly affect the proportions of national output devoted to investment and consumption.

In this way, budget policies can enhance or retard economic growth quite apart from the size of the budget deficit *per se*. In practice, of course, the size of the structural deficit and the composition of taxes and expenditures change simultaneously. Hence, both deficit reduction and how the deficit is reduced are important for growth. Deficit reduction achieved by cuts in public investment, or by tax increases that reduce private saving and investment, may not raise national saving, investment, and growth—which is the economic purpose of deficit reduction.

Space is not available here to discuss in any detail the many possible budget policies related to growth, but a broad sketch of the major types of such policies can be outlined.

Public Investments in Physical Capital. The most obvious and direct budget policy affecting growth is the redirection of public expenditures from consumption to investment, either directly or through grants to the states. Highway, aviation, water, and environmental programs are major examples. The budget does not distinguish between consumption and investment expenditures, but classifications by the U.S. General Accounting Office (1997) indicate that about 7.5 percent of total federal outlays are devoted to investments "directly intended to enhance the private sector's long-term productivity." Before 1996 the Department of Commerce also made no distinction between federal investment and consumption purchases in the National Income and Product Accounts (NIPA). According to the NIPA, in 1996, 18.6 percent of GDP consisted of investment in structures and equipment.

The role of public investment in economic growth is somewhat controversial. Although there is broad agreement that public investment in transportation, communications, education, sanitation, and similar activities has historically been very important to U.S. growth, there is also skepticism about the productivity of many public investment projects, which are often established on the basis of political considerations rather than economic criteria subject to market tests. (For a somewhat dated but useful summary of this debate, see Congressional Budget Office, 1984.)

Private Saving and Investment. Tax policies are regularly proposed to raise private saving and investment and thereby accelerate economic growth. Policies to raise directly returns to private business investment have included the investment tax credit, accelerated depreciation of business investment expenditures, and preferential tax treatment of capital gains. Expenditures on residential housing, a major component of private investment, have long received favorable tax treatment, principally through the mortgage interest deduction. Other tax measures enacted or proposed to increase private saving include different varieties of individual retirement accounts (IRAs) and other exclusions of saved income from the tax base. Among these exclusions, employee pensions, including individual 401(k) plans, have been most important.

The effectiveness of tax incentives in raising national saving and investment depends on two considerations that are often overlooked, especially by the special-interest groups that promote these policies. First, when the economy is operating near capacity, additional investment requires either additional domestic saving or borrowing from abroad to provide the required resources. Unless spending is cut or taxes are raised to generate such saving, policies to stimulate investment will create excessive aggregate demand. To prevent a rise in inflation, the Fed must then raise interest rates, with the likely result that the tax-favored investments will merely crowd out other domestic or foreign investments.

The second consideration has to do with the effects of private saving incentives on public (and thereby national) saving. Even if IRAs and other tax incentives succeed in raising private saving, which itself is controversial, the related revenue loss and increased deficits create a reduction in public saving. The net effect on national saving depends on the balance between the two, and is uncertain (Hubbard and Skinner, 1996; Poterba, Venti, and Wise, 1996; Engen, Gale, and Scholz, 1996).

The lesson of both these considerations is clear: the unintended consequence of a change in budget policy may be an offsetting change in fiscal policy. The budget policy, to be effective, may require a coordinated fiscal policy change.

Public Investments in Human Capital. As noted earlier, studies have consistently found that investments in human capital have played an important role in economic growth. The President's Council of Economic Advisers recently put human capital's contribution to productivity growth over the past three decades at about 20 percent, and it appears likely that education and skills are becoming increasingly important in applying new technology to production (Council of Economic Advisers, 1996, p. 31; see also Committee for Economic Development, 1996, and references cited therein). As a result, some policymakers, including President Clinton, have strongly emphasized budget policies directed at increasing education and training.

Although this strategy is sound in principle, major obstacles arise in practice. One obstacle is that the federal government plays little direct role in education spending, especially in K–12 schooling, which is primarily funded by state and local governments or private sources. Tax policies that operate indirectly to subsidize education costs are an alternative approach, but the impact of these in increasing the actual quantity of education delivered, or its quality, are open to question. (Tuition tax credits may have the principal effect of subsidizing students who would attend college in any case, or of raising the cost of education; see Reischauer and Gladieux, 1996.) Another serious problem is that in many instances additional funding may not be the most important requirement for improving the quality of K–12 education. There is increasing evidence that reform of educational management is needed, including the implementation of more rigorous standards and stronger incentives for student achievement and effective instruction (Hanushek and others, 1994, pp. 25–49; Burtless, 1996; Committee for Economic Development, 1994, p. 39). For this reason, it is not clear that additional financial resources can be effectively used to improve performance, even in some low-income school districts where schools undeniably lack adequate facilities and teachers.

Public Investments in Technology. As noted earlier, technological advance has been the most important source of higher productivity and incomes over the long term. There is a strong rationale for public support of research and development (R&D) that presents a case of market failure. Because private investors are often unable to capture the full returns from R&D investments, the benefits of such investments to society are substantially greater than their private returns. (One careful study finds private returns averaging 20 to 30 percent and social returns averaging roughly 50 percent; see Nadiri, 1993.) As a result, the private sector substantially underinvests in R&D. The case for public support is strongest in basic scientific research, where firms are least likely to reap the rewards. The federal government funds about 58 percent of basic research, principally through universities, compared with only 36 percent of applied research and 29 percent of development costs (National Science Board, 1996, pp. 108–110).

Although there it is wide agreement that the budget should support basic research, and that development expenditures should normally be funded by private firms, there is deep disagreement about the appropriate federal role in the intermediate area of applied research. President Bush's administration was largely opposed to such expenditures, while the Clinton administration has proposed large increases, especially in public-private joint ventures.

The economic and political considerations in this controversy are in conflict. Economically, it appears that the private sector underinvests in applied as well as basic research; estimated private returns on commercial and industrial R&D investments are roughly 25 percent, about twice those on plant and equipment investment (Schultze, 1992, p. 303). Nevertheless, as with highways, dams, and other public investments, one has little confidence that our competitive political process will select the most productive investments or terminate those that prove to be economically unsound. The federal government's experience with large-scale commercial ventures in synthetic fuels, nuclear energy, air transportation, and solar power have not been encouraging (see Cohen and Noll, 1991). The influence of politics on the allocation of R&D investments is also evident in the fact that the United States spends roughly 60 percent of its civilian

R&D budget on health, environment, and space exploration, compared with about 10 to 25 percent in Germany, Japan, France, and the United Kingdom (National Science Board, 1996, p. 153).

The potential economic gains from larger federal expenditures on R&D thus seem unlikely to be realized without reforms in the process of selecting and conducting R&D projects. Indeed, for the foreseeable future, even the maintenance of current efforts may be in political jeopardy. The policies proposed to achieve a balanced budget may reduce real federal support for basic research along with the rest of domestic appropriations, paying little regard to differences between investment and consumption expenditures and their implications for economic growth.

Nonbudgetary Policy Instruments. Economic growth is also affected by instruments such as regulatory and trade policies that are not reflected in the budget, apart from relatively minor administrative costs and revenues. Such policy instruments are sometimes less visible than public expenditures and tax subsidies and often more politically palatable. Space limitations preclude a more complete discussion here, but it is worth noting that because nonbudgetary instruments do not have to compete with other programs for scarce budget resources, they are likely to become increasingly important as efforts to balance the budget continue.

COORDINATION OF FISCAL AND MONETARY POLICY

The fiscal policy actions of the president and Congress profoundly affect the monetary policy options available to the Fed, and the actions it takes. While in theory the reverse is also true, in practice the Fed largely adapts to the constraints imposed by fiscal policy because its policy decisions are more frequent, more flexible, and less constrained by political considerations. Although the Fed vigorously protects its de facto independence, there is regular and close sharing of information, analysis, and discussion between senior officials of the Fed and the administration. The fiscal and monetary policy mix that results from their independent but coordinated actions has major implications for both economic stabilization and economic growth.

In principle, economic policies should be coordinated to achieve a coherent set of economic objectives and not work at cross-purposes. In the most straightforward case, fiscal and monetary policies are often used in parallel to pursue a single economic stabilization goal of expansion or restraint. Thus, when the structural budget deficit was increased to promote recovery from the recessions of 1957–1958, 1969–1970, and 1981–1982, the Fed accommodated the expansive fiscal policy by keeping interest rates low. Conversely, during periods of rising inflation, such as 1968–1970, 1973–1974 and 1978–1980, efforts were made, sometimes too little and too late, to reduce the structural deficit in support of the Fed's anti-inflationary monetary policy.

The coordination problem becomes more complex when more than one economic goal is involved, for example, in the simultaneous pursuit of economic stability and more rapid growth. A rule governing policy choices in general is the so-called Tinbergen Rule—that the pursuit of multiple policy goals requires an equivalent number of policy instruments. In the stabilization-growth context, this means that in principle different combinations of monetary and fiscal policy that produce the desired level of aggregate demand are available to policymakers, and one such combination can be selected that produces the desired rate of economic growth.

More specifically, an expansive (loose) fiscal policy, with large structural budget deficits, requires a relatively restrictive (tight) monetary policy, with high real interest rates, to keep aggregate demand from rising above potential GDP and pushing up inflation. High interest rates restrain private investment demand, while large budget deficits normally imply larger public or private consumption or both. Such a mix of high-consumption and low-investment policy will tend to raise current living standards at the expense of economic growth. Conversely, a tight fiscal policy of low structural deficits or surpluses will allow monetary policy to follow a more expansive, low-interest-rate path; such a policy restrains consumption in favor of higher investment and growth.

The mid- to late 1980s provide a dramatic illustration of a low-growth policy mix. After the deep recession of 1981–1982, the economy began a seven-year expansion. The large structural deficits produced by the tax cuts and accelerated defense buildup that began in 1981, although enacted for quite different reasons, helped the economy recover after the Fed relaxed its intense monetary restraint in 1982. These large structural deficits persisted, however, and even grew as the economy expanded, notwithstanding the tax increases of 1982 and 1984 and modest efforts at spending restraint.

This very expansionary fiscal policy forced the Fed to keep interest rates unusually high, crowding out business investment. In addition, the high interest rates produced a sharp rise in the dollar that curtailed exports, encouraged imports, and impaired production and employment in U.S. export- and import-competing industries. Finally, as the economy approached full employment in 1988–1989 and inflation began to rise, the Fed tightened policy markedly, leading to recession in 1990. It is uncertain, of course, whether a tighter fiscal policy during the 1980s could have averted the recession, but there is little doubt that the expansive fiscal policy required monetary policy to be more restrictive and less conducive to growth. By the end of the decade, personal consumption expenditures were a larger portion of our national income than at any other time in the postwar period.

Although the principle of policy coordination is attractive, in practice the president, Congress, and the Fed are likely to have different policy goals. Elected officials not surprisingly put great weight on the short-term level of economic activity and employment; indeed, jobs considerations strongly affect other, noneconomic policies, such as defense base closings, in addition to economic policy. Inflation is politically powerful when it rises sharply, as we learned in the 1970s, but it is out of sight and largely out of mind, especially in Congress, when it is tranquil. Stronger economic growth clearly benefits future voters at the expense of the current electorate—not a situation designed to inspire fiscal restraint by elected officials, in spite of the lip service paid to the "welfare of our grandchildren."

As a result, the Fed usually does most of the worrying about the long term, especially with regard to the heavy potential costs entailed in allowing inflation to rise. Although the Fed's actual policy actions indicate that it usually formulates policy with an eye on both inflation and unemployment, it clearly has the institutional responsibility of being the "inflation fighter." Policy coordination therefore often involves a public drama in which the president or Congress criticizes the Fed for excessive concern about inflation, and jawbones it to undertake a more expansionary monetary policy. These publicized policy differences may appear larger than they are in operation due to the Fed's conviction that the costs of inflation control in terms of lost output and unemployment will be lower if the Fed's determination to fight inflation is unquestioned.

The coordination of fiscal and monetary policy may also take the form of implicit bargains between fiscal and monetary policymakers. During the various deliberations on deficit reduction plans in the late 1980s and early 1990s, it was commonly understood that if Congress and the president enacted a program of fiscal restraint, the Fed, at the very least, would have more leeway to pursue a less restrictive monetary policy, even though the Fed could not admit to this publicly. Similarly, the Fed apparently eased monetary policy aggressively at the end of 1991, when the economic recovery appeared to languish, in part to forestall a fiscal expansion by a Congress and administration looking ahead to the 1992 elections (Dornbusch and Fischer, 1994, p. 141).

The policy mix is of course more than merely a balancing of fiscal and monetary policy. As noted earlier, any desired fiscal policy, roughly characterized by a given structural budget deficit, allows for many choices regarding the budget policies that compose it. The ultimate selection of a budget policy mix will reflect political preferences involving both aggregate levels of taxes and spending and their composition. The budget wars of the 1980s and 1990s have been fought principally over the policy mix. As a rough characterization, Republicans, with a preference for smaller government, lower spending, and lower taxes, have advocated spending reductions for fiscal restraint and tax reductions for fiscal expansion, although the latter have often been presented as supply-side rather than demand-enhancing measures. Democrats, less enthusiastic about reducing the size of government and cutting programs, have supported tax increases for fiscal restraint and stimulus spending programs for fiscal expansion. Under two-party government, mix-and-match compromises have often been the order of the day, as in the 1990 and 1997 budget agreements. Furthermore, these fiscal policy changes have been directed almost entirely at the long-term issue of resource allocation and growth rather than at economic stabilization.

CONCLUSION

Economic theory and experience provide three primary lessons for policymakers interested in using the federal budget to manage the economy. First, the budget can be an effective policy tool for promoting long-term economic growth because higher national saving from deficit reduction as well as public investments in human and physical capital and technological progress can increase the economy's productive capacity. Second, the budget plays an important role in moderating fluctuations in economic activity through its automatic stabilizers. Finally, however, discretionary fiscal policy is not a very effective tool for short-term economic stabilization and may in fact be counterproductive. As a result, monetary policy, in spite of its imperfections, has become, and is likely to remain, our primary instrument for economic stabilization.

References

Akerlof, G. A., Dickens, W. T., and Perry, G. L. "The Macroeconomics of Low Inflation." *Brookings Papers on Economic Activity*, 1996, *1*, 1–59.

Bartley, R. L. *The Seven Fat Years.* New York: Free Press, 1992.

Burtless, G. (ed.). *Does Money Matter? The Effect of School Resources on Achievement and Success.* Washington, D.C.: Brookings Institution, 1996.

Cohen, L. R., and Noll, R. G. *The Technology Pork Barrel.* Washington, D.C.: Brookings Institution, 1991.

Committee for Economic Development. *Putting Learning First: Governing and Managing the Schools for High Achievement.* New York: Committee for Economic Development, 1994.

Committee for Economic Development, *Who Will Pay for Your Retirement?* New York: Committee for Economic Development, 1995.

Committee for Economic Development. *American Workers and Economic Change.* New York: Committee for Economic Development, 1996.

Committee for Economic Development, *Fixing Social Security.* New York: Committee for Economic Development, 1997.

Congressional Budget Office. *How Federal Spending for Infrastructure and Other Public Investments Affects the Economy.* Washington, D.C.: Government Printing Office, 1984.

Congressional Budget Office. *The Economic and Budget Outlook, Fiscal Years 1998–2007.* Washington, D.C.: Government Printing Office, 1997a.

Congressional Budget Office. *Long-Term Budgetary Pressures and Policy Options.* Washington, D.C.: Government Printing Office, 1997b.

Council of Economic Advisers. *Annual Report of the Council of Economic Advisers.* Washington, D.C.: Government Printing Office, 1996.

Denison, E. *Trends in American Economic Growth, 1929–1982.* Washington, D.C.: Brookings Institution, 1985.

Dornbusch, R., and Fischer, S. *Macroeconomics.* (6th ed.) New York: McGraw-Hill, 1994.

Engen, E., Gale, W., and Scholz, J. "The Illusory Effects of Saving Incentives on Savings." *Journal of Economic Perspectives,* 1996, *10*(4), 113–138.

Freeman, R. "Why Do So Many Young American Men Commit Crimes and What Might We Do About It?" *Journal of Economic Perspectives,* 1996, *10*(1), 25–42.

Friedman, M. "The Role of Monetary Policy." *American Economic Review,* 1968, *58,* 1–17.

Greenstein, R. "The Balanced Budget Constitutional Amendment: An Overview." Washington, D.C.: Center on Budget and Policy Priorities, 1997.

Greenwood, J., Hercowitz, Z., and Krusell, P. "Long-Run Implications of Investment-Specific Technological Change." *American Economic Review,* 1997, *87*(3), 342–362.

Hanushek, E. A., and others. *Making Schools Work: Improving Performance and Cutting Costs.* Washington, D.C.: Brookings Institution, 1994.

Heller, W. *New Dimensions of Political Economy.* New York: Norton, 1967.

Hubbard, R., and Skinner, J. "Assessing the Effectiveness of Saving Incentives." *Journal of Economic Perspectives,* 1996, *10*(4), 73–90.

Huh, C., and Trehan, B. "Real Business Cycles: A Selective Survey." *Economic Review, Federal Reserve Bank of San Francisco,* Spring 1991.

Lucas, R., and Sargent, T. (eds.). *Rational Expectations.* 2 vols. Minneapolis: University of Minnesota Press, 1981.

Nadiri, M. I. *Innovations and Technological Spillovers.* Working Paper no. 4423. Cambridge, Mass.: National Bureau of Economic Research, 1993.

National Science Board. *Science and Engineering Indicators, 1996.* Washington, D.C.: Government Printing Office, 1996.

Organization for Economic Cooperation and Development. *OECD Jobs Study, Part 1.* Paris: Organization for Economic Cooperation and Development, 1994.

Poterba, J. M., Venti, S., and Wise, D. "How Retirement Saving Programs Increase Saving." *Journal of Economic Perspectives*, 1996, *10*(4), 91–112.

Reischauer, R., and Gladieux, L. E. "Higher Tuition, More Grade Inflation." *Washington Post*, Sept. 4, 1996, p. A15.

Schultze, C. *Memos to the President*. Washington, D.C.: Brookings Institution, 1992.

Stein, H. *The Fiscal Revolution in America*. (2nd ed.) Washington, D.C.: American Enterprise Institute, 1996.

U.S. General Accounting Office. *Budget Trends: Federal Investment Outlays, Fiscal Years 1981–2002*. Washington, D.C.: U.S. General Accounting Office, 1997.

CHAPTER NINE

The Rhetoric and Reality of Balancing Budgets

Naomi Caiden

W hat could be more commonsensical than balancing the budget? The rhetoric fills speaker and listener alike with the satisfaction of moral rectitude. But rhetoric fades too easily into platitude as the task of moving from wish to reality reveals conceptual problems and practical difficulties. The simplicity, neutrality, and moral certainty of budgetary balance dissolve into complexity and ambiguity.

In the United States, the model of budgetary balance at the state and local levels turns out, on close examination, to be seriously flawed. At the federal level, it might be difficult to determine whether the budget was really balanced, and constitutionally enforced balance would probably result in many kinds of subterfuge. In addition, strict insistence on budget balance from year to year would negate or vitiate certain strengths of the federal government, such as countercyclical fiscal policy or reliable disaster assistance. At all levels of government, balancing budgets involves, rather than substitutes for, political judgments on what and who should gain or lose in the budgetary conflict. Budgetary balance should also be only one criterion in the making of public policy for the welfare of society. And because a balance between income and expenditures says nothing about the levels of either income or expenditures, such a balance would not necessarily fulfill the wishes of conservative advocates for smaller government. Given a climate hostile to raising taxes, however, these advocates use the balanced budget banner to gain support for what is really an agenda for limitations on government programs. All of this is not to say that balancing budgets might not be a good idea; the idea just raises more questions than it resolves, and because of its obvious merit as a slogan, it may even prevent questions from being raised at all.

Just what should be balanced? When should it be balanced? Who should balance it and who should decide if in fact it is balanced? How should it be balanced? And why should it be balanced? Even at state and local levels of government, where balance is frequently mandated, answers to these questions have required political choices. At the federal level, the enactment of a constitutional amendment to enforce budgetary balance would involve not only practical difficulties but also issues of fiscal policy and institutional balance.

The idea of balancing revenues and expenditures is almost implicit in the concept of the budget itself. Some of the earliest budgets and accounts that we know about were those of autonomous medieval city states where an alert citizenry kept a wary eye on municipal finances in the hands of a city manager. Nation states were slow to balance their books, preferring rather to juggle them. Real national budgets that financed expenditures with appropriate revenues on an annual basis did not emerge until after the end of the Napoleonic Wars. From that point on, budgetary balance was an accepted part of the idea of the budget. In Aaron Wildavsky's phrase, it was a "norm" the observance of which (together with the related norms of annularity and comprehensiveness) safeguarded budgetary viability. "The norm of balance," he explained, "established an equilibrium between spending and taxing" (Wildavsky and Caiden, 1996, p. 259). He further linked the balance between spending and taxing with limits on spending and taxing, to characterize a world itself in an equilibrium of mutual dependence in which everyone knew where he or she stood.

Of course, it was never quite like that. Long before Keynesian theory came along to shatter the norms of budgeting, national budgets had often breached the bounds of balance. In the United States, the executive budget enacted in 1921 was an outcome of the alarm at growing federal deficits. Wars inevitably produced a spate of borrowing. Although federal expenditures remained relatively low, their lack of growth might be attributed less to conscious observance of a budgetary norm than to a variety of political factors that limited potential demands on government and kept taxes low.

The pressures of the Great Depression of the 1930s and the clear inability of local and state governments to deal with its effects overwhelmed the priority of having a balanced federal budget. Keynesian theory affirmed the notion that the relationship between revenues and expenditures should vary with the state of the economy, and fiscal fine-tuning took the place of budgetary balance, although in practice the surpluses that should have accompanied periods of economic growth did not materialize.

By the end of the 1970s, concern about federal deficits emerged once more, and the following decade saw more or less desperate attempts to stuff the genie back into the bottle. In the 1990s, almost every year saw an effort to amend the U.S. Constitution to enforce a balanced budget. Many states and localities had long been mandated by constitution or statute to balance their budgets, and critics of the federal deficit inevitably pointed to them as appropriate examples to follow.

WHAT SHOULD BE BALANCED?

The constitutions of thirty-five states require balanced budgets and another thirteen states have statutory requirements. It would thus seem that most states are forced by mandatory balanced budgets to live within their means.

But as Louis Fisher (1992, p. 1) has pointed out, "The facts are otherwise. States and all average Americans do not live within their means. They borrow." The balanced budget requirement usually refers only to a state's general fund, "the fund into which general tax receipts are credited for discretionary appropriation" (U.S. General Accounting Office, 1993a, p. 19). General fund spending in 1990 was only 54 percent of total state spending and ranged from only 21 percent of total state spending in Wyoming to 74 percent in Hawaii (p. 19). Another recent study found that in FY93 only 48 percent of state spending was from general funds (Briffault, 1996, p. 12). States typically use a variety of other funds, including capital, enterprise, and trust funds. Although these too may be required to balance, governments may gain that balance either by issuing bonds or, if necessary, by borrowing from other funds. Richard Briffault (1996) suggests that the considerable fluctuations in the use of the general funds from state to state indicate that current as well as capital expenditures are covered through capital or special funds that allow borrowing. "In short," he concludes, "the byzantine structure of state finances can undermine the discipline of balanced budget requirements that, on paper, seem quite severe" (pp. 12–13).

Although twenty-five states include their capital budgets under a balanced budget requirement, this has not prevented them from issuing long-term debt to finance major capital projects. According to Census Bureau figures, between 1951 and 1991 "outstanding, short- and long-term state and local debt, primarily for capital construction, soared from $24 billion to $911 billion" (Axelrod, 1995, p. 117). Much state and local borrowing is carried out through thousands of public authorities, set up for a variety of purposes, which are able, in Donald Axelrod's words, "to evade constitutional limits on debt and con the voters by making state and local budgets look smaller than they actually are" (p. 140). In this way, states have been able to issue a variety of tax-exempt bonds and other debt instruments to bypass constitutional debt limits and voting requirements as well as balanced budget provisions.

Although the forms differ, the general principle behind these actions is similar. A state, city, or county sets up an authority, which then issues debt such as revenue bonds or certificates of participation (Johnson and Mikesell, 1994, pp. 41–54). The trick is to create a flow of revenue that will pay back the capital and interest on the bond. In its simplest form, for example, a stadium's capital cost might be repaid over several years of ticket sales. More often, the stream of revenue comes from the parent jurisdiction itself, which "leases" the library, police station, student dormitory, or prison so that the rent goes to pay off the bond.

A popular variant is tax increment financing, which is used to divert local tax revenues from general purposes to "redevelopment." Suppose a developer wishes to raise capital for a shopping center. The company might go to the local city and persuade it to declare that a certain area is "blighted." The city would then set up a redevelopment authority, or use an existing one, which would issue a tax-exempt bond the proceeds of which would provide the capital for the public infrastructure for the shopping center. At the same time, the assessed value of the area, which of course was very low, would be frozen for the period of the bond. During that period, reassessment would take place in increments, which would be paid by the property owner, and the proceeds would pay off the bond.

Leasebacks may be quite complicated. For example, in the early 1980s, the City of Palmdale, California, created the Palmdale Civic Authority (PCA) as a financing device to build the city library. For the use of the library the PCA charged the city rent equal to the principal and interest payments on its bonds. Actually, the rent payments came from the Palmdale Community Redevelopment Agency, which signed an agreement with the city and PCA to pay them out of the tax increment from one of its redevelopment projects, which in turn was based on mortgage revenue bonds (Caiden and Chapman, 1982, p. 124; for further examples of the use of public authorities, see Walsh, 1978; Henriques, 1980; Di Lorenzo, 1983; and Axelrod, 1992).

Public authorities may also be used to remove whole functions, such as waste disposal or water supply, from the budget and so make balance easier. But the price of changing payment through taxes to payment by fees may be high. Axelrod has in no uncertain terms excoriated the practice of creating public authorities that are unaccountable to the public. The consequences of this practice have been documented in

> multibillion-dollar defaults; monumental spending sprees; the bailout of failed and bankrupt authorities; outright corruption, theft, and political patronage; manipulation of funds from various sources to confuse the voters; subversion of statutory missions by some public authorities; regressive fees that hit the poor; misuse of industrial bonds designed to create jobs; evasion of constitutions and

laws; fragmentation of government; failure to monitor the performance and costs of public authorities; erosion of budget control; and a bonanza for brokers, bond attorneys and financial advisers [Axelrod, 1995, p. 141].

In FY90, according to the Census Bureau, state spending for capital was 9 percent of total state general spending (U.S. General Accounting Office, 1993a, p. 19).

If the concept of the balanced budget were to be applied to the federal government, it would obviously be necessary to make separate provisions for capital and investment expenditures. The difficulty would be determining just what should be included in either the capital or operating budgets. There have been a number of different proposals, which differ widely in their coverage. The federal government invests two quite different kinds of capital. The first kind is its own direct spending on such items as office buildings or weapons systems. The second is investment in services designed to increase economic growth, such as highways, education, and research, much of which is actually carried out through grants to states and localities. Should a broader or narrower definition be adopted? Should investment be financed by borrowing? How should grants to other entities be treated (U.S. Office of Management and Budget, 1995, pp. 108–112)?

We might expect that the same incentives that have led state governments to create off-budget mechanisms to circumvent budget-balancing requirements would probably also operate at the federal level. The federal government already operates more than forty quasi-autonomous corporations, several of which, according to one recent study, "are really little more than accounting tricks designed to hide federal spending and debt" (Briffault, 1996, p. 26). Social security is also legally off budget, although because it is currently in surplus it is almost always included in both government and news references to the budget, a somewhat ambiguous position, which might change if the surplus becomes a deficit (Schick, 1995, p. 28).

What should be balanced, therefore, is a tricky question. The purest interpretation of the term *balance* suggests that governments should not be allowed to borrow at all, and that all government funds should be self-balancing. Faced with this constraint, most state and local governments have worked out ways to avoid it in order to meet their capital requirements. Surely it is unrealistic to expect that all expenditures should be met from current income. Governments are in debt—but so are households and businesses, and the U.S. economy is built on credit. The days of regarding all credit as usury and immoral are long gone, and credit plays an important role in both the public and the private sectors to finance purchases that would otherwise be unattainable. This argument might also be extended to intangible investment in human and social capital, which may be as critical for national development as fixed capital construction.

WHEN SHOULD THE BUDGET BE BALANCED?

Among the most elementary definitions of *budget* is that it is a plan. It states openly and ideally, in quite detailed terms, what monies legislators have agreed that a government may raise and spend in the coming year. But what if, for reasons beyond its control, the government gets it wrong and revenues are less than predicted, or expenditures are more, or both? At what point does the budget have to be in balance?

State practices differ and their obligations are often unclear. Although forty-four states require that governors present legislatures with a balanced budget, only thirty-one state constitutions actually require that legislatures pass one. Many of these constitutions are worded vaguely, referring to "estimated expenditures" and "anticipated revenues." Nothing may be said about year-end balance, and at least twenty constitutions either allow a deficit to be carried over to the following year or allow it to be financed by borrowing (Briffault, 1996, pp. 10–11; Axelrod, 1995, p. 176). In recent years, seven of the ten largest states have done just this, in effect negating the intent of budget-balancing provisions.

Governments do not have to stand still helplessly and watch their budgets spiral out of control. In thirty-six states the governor has a restricted power to cut spending with or without legislative approval (Axelrod, 1995, p. 176). The states may impound funds, as Massachusetts did with the approval of the courts in 1978, or they may transfer dedicated funds to the general fund to maintain balance, as Louisiana did in 1987; its action was upheld by the courts (Fisher, 1992, p. 5). But other cases have negated or restricted such power. An interesting recent case arose in December 1996 in the City of Los Angeles, where the mayor took $31 million from the airport enterprise fund to help balance the city's general fund, only to have the federal government promptly withhold federal funds from the city's Metropolitan Transit Authority in retaliation (Simon, 1996, p. B1).

The powers of state governors to take action to reduce spending during the fiscal year vary. In some states, reductions are limited to a certain percentage of the budget, such as 5 percent of an appropriation in Connecticut or 25 percent of most executive branch appropriations in Maryland (U.S. General Accounting Office, 1993a, p. 22). There may be no restrictions on a governor's authority, or the governor may only cut across the board or be required to consult with the legislature (see National Conference of State Legislatures, 1992). Missouri's constitution explicitly gives the state governor power to reduce agencies' expenditures to less than their appropriations whenever revenues are less than forecasted: "The governor may control the rate at which any appropriation is expended during the period of the appropriation by allotment or other means, and may reduce the expenditures of the state or any of its agencies below their appropriations whenever the actual revenues are less than the revenue estimates upon which the appropriations were based" (art. 4, par. 27). Michigan's constitution has a similar provision requiring approval of the state's house and senate appropriations committees: "The Michigan constitution authorizes the governor, with the approval of the House and Senate appropriations committees, to reduce expenditures whenever it appears that actual revenues for a fiscal year will fall below the revenue estimates on which appropriations for that period were based" (art. 5, par. 20; quoted in Fisher, 1992, p. 6). Such executive powers are extraordinary, and it would be highly unlikely for Congress to grant them to any president.

Where gaps have appeared during the budget cycle, state officials have often been resourceful in resolving them. A 1993 General Accounting Office (GAO) report documents actions taken by the states. In twenty-five states that reported that they had closed gaps during budget enactment, revenue increases were used for about one-third of the dollar amount, while spending cuts accounted for almost half. Later in the budget cycle, spending cuts predominated (60 percent of the dollar value of budgets for thirty-two states). But more than one-third of the gaps in dollar terms were resolved through "other actions," including rainy day funds, interfund transfers, personnel actions, deferred payments, accounting changes, changes in pension fund contributions, or short-term borrowing (U.S. General Accounting Office, 1993a, pp. 25–29).

Can deficits be carried over to the following year? The situation is not entirely clear. A 1992 survey found that thirteen states were permitted to carry over deficits into the next fiscal period (Briffault, 1996, p. 11). Briffault estimates that at least twenty state constitutions and possibly more permit either carryover or borrowing to finance a deficit (p. 10). The 1993 GAO survey reported that between FY90 and FY93, ten states had carried over deficits, borrowed to finance deficits, or both, but only three were states requiring year-end budgetary balance (U.S. General Accounting Office, 1993a, p. 36). For example, at the end of FY92, Connecticut converted two years' worth of budget deficits (nearly $1 billion) into bonds payable over the next five years. Massachusetts had to borrow $1.5 billion to finance its 1990 deficit, and for three consecutive years in the early 1990s, New York issued short-term deficit notes amounting to more than $2 billion (U.S. General Accounting Office, 1993a, p. 36; see also Briffault, 1996, pp. 16–18, for details on California, New York, Louisiana, Connecticut, and Massachusetts).

Prediction is particularly difficult where governments face uncertainties related to open-ended, and sometimes inflation-indexed, entitlements, such as Medicaid, unemployment payments, or welfare. Although finance departments typically underestimate revenues in order to hedge against unexpected economic downturns, they may still find their revenues inadequate as the fiscal year unwinds. Fluctuations in interest rates may also be difficult to predict. Conversely, states have sometimes deliberately overestimated revenues and underestimated expenditures to come up with a plausible balanced budget (Briffault, 1996, p. 19).

The situation of federal budgetary balance is especially problematic. The federal budget, and hence the deficit, is particularly vulnerable to economic fluctuations because of the large proportion of entitlements it contains. The gap between enacted deficit limits and the eventual actual deficits was one stumbling block to the success of the Balanced Budget and Emergency Deficit Control Act of 1985 (the Gramm-Rudman-Hollings legislation) during the four years it was in operation. Once the budget was agreed to, there was no stipulated mechanism to bring the deficit back into line (although sequestrations were possible during the year) (Wildavsky and Caiden, 1996, p. 128).

The difficulties of deficit projection may be seen in the efforts of the Congressional Budget Office to predict the federal deficit in recent years (see Table 9.1). The changing figures reflect changing assessments of the economic situation, as well as "technical reestimates." The sensitivity of the federal budget is acknowledged in every budget by a section that documents the effects of changes in assumptions about key economic indicators on revenues, expenditures, and the deficit (see Table 9.2). For example, the president's FY96 budget noted that the effect of a 1 percent lower growth rate for real gross domestic product than predicted in 1995, including higher unemployment, would result in a deficit increase of $8.2 billion in 1995 and $21.0 billion in 1996, with correspondingly greater increases in the following years (U.S. Office of Management and Budget, 1995, p. 8).

In the epic struggle between the president and Congress at the end of 1995, the issue of assumptions took center stage. When agreement was reached that the budget should be balanced in the year 2002, the argument turned on whether administration or Congressional Budget Office assumptions should be used in the calculation. The differences between them were actually minute— 0.1 percent for inflation and 0.2 percent for real economic growth—but these discrepancies, combined with differences in estimated allocation of income between employee compensation and corporate profits, would, over a period of seven years, result in a difference of more than $400 billion in deficit projections (Wildavsky and Caiden, 1996, p. 327). Given the notorious lack of accuracy in medium-term economic projections, estimates of future budgetary balance based on such projections may be something of an illusion.

But the issue of entitlements is more than just a matter of timing, or of determining whether the budget is really balanced. What would happen if during the fiscal year entitlement outlays were determined to have outstripped

Table 9.1. Congressional Budget Office Deficit Projections (in Billions of Dollars).

	1990	1991	1992	1993	1994	1995	1996	1997	1998	1999	2000
January 1992	220	269	352	327	260	194	178	226			
Summer 1992			331	268	244	254	290				
January 1993		270	290	310	291	284	287	319	357		
September 1993					253	196	190	198	200		
January 1994				255	223	171	166	182	180	204	
August 1994			290		202	162	176	193	197	231	
January 1995				203	162	176	207	224	222	253	
April 1995					177	211	232	231	256	276	

The actual deficit for FY95 was later assessed at $164 billion.

Sources: U.S. Congressional Budget Office, 1992, 1993, 1994, 1995a, 1995b.

Table 9.2. Sensitivity of the Budget to Economic Assumptions (in Billions of Dollars).

Budget Effect	1995	1996	1997	1998	1999	2000
Real Growth and Unemployment						
Effects of 1 percent lower real GDP growth in calendar year 1995 only, including higher unemployment						
Receipts	−7.0	−15.2	−17.4	−17.6	−18.1	−18.7
Outlays	1.2	5.8	7.7	9.6	11.6	13.8
Deficit increase (+)	8.2	21.0	25.1	27.2	29.7	32.5
Effects of a sustained 1 percent lower real GDP growth rate during 1995–2000, including higher unemployment						
Receipts	−7.0	−22.4	−40.6	−59.6	−79.9	−101.4
Outlays	1.2	7.0	15.1	25.0	38.8	51.8
Deficit increase (+)	8.2	29.4	55.6	84.6	118.2	153.2
Effects of a sustained 1 percent lower annual real GDP growth rate during 1995–2000, with no change in unemployment						
Receipts	−7.0	−22.7	−41.6	−61.9	−83.8	−107.3
Outlays	0.3	1.3	3.5	7.1	12.3	19.4
Deficit increase (+)	7.3	24.0	45.1	69.0	96.2	126.7
Inflation and Interest Rates						
Effects of 1 percentage point higher rate of inflation and interest rates during calendar year 1995 only:						
Receipts	7.7	16.0	16.4	15.4	15.8	16.2
Outlays	5.9	13.9	10.9	9.1	7.6	7.1
Deficit increase (+)	−1.7	−2.1	−5.5	−6.3	−8.1	−9.2
Effects of a sustained 1 percentage point higher rate of inflation and interest rates during 1995–2000:						

Receipts	7.7	24.0	41.5	58.7	77.0	96.3
Outlays	5.9	20.4	33.8	46.2	58.8	71.1
Deficit increase (+)	−1.7	−3.7	−7.7	−12.6	−18.3	−25.2
Effects of a sustained 1 percentage point higher interest rate during 1995–2000 (no inflation change):						
Receipts:	0.7	1.8	2.4	2.7	2.9	3.3
Outlays	5.5	16.8	24.9	31.7	38.3	44.8
Deficit increase (+)	4.9	14.9	22.5	28.9	35.3	41.5
Effects of a sustained 1 percentage point higher rate of inflation during 1995–2000 (no interest rate change):						
Receipts	7.0	22.2	39.1	56.0	74.1	93.0
Outlays	0.4	3.6	8.9	14.5	20.5	26.3
Deficit increase (+)	−6.6	−18.6	−30.2	−41.5	−53.6	−66.7
Interest Cost of Higher Federal Borrowing						
Effect of $100 billion additional borrowing during 1995	3.6	7.0	7.3	7.6	8.0	8.5

Source: U.S. Office of Management and Budget, 1995.

available resources? Theoretically, Congress and the president should vote to increase revenues by a commensurate amount. But suppose they declined to do so? Would this mean that entitlement benefits would have to be cut, or cease altogether? And could recipients sue for their reinstatement? The notion of entitlement might be profoundly altered if social security and similar outlays became dependent on whether Congress chose to finance them or not.

Another problem of timing arises from the question of when payments to the government and by the government are actually recorded. If a government recognizes income and expenditure only when money is actually received or paid out, it may be argued that the picture of its real position will be seriously distorted: it may balance its budget in the short term by simply delaying payment on outstanding commitments. For this reason there is a solid body of opinion favoring accrual accounting over cash accounting. In 1987, the Government Accounting Standards Board recommended for state and local governments a system of modified accrual accounting in which revenues are recognized and recorded when they are measurable, available, and collectible in the fiscal year, and all expenditures for which the government is liable within the fiscal year are counted in that fiscal year (Axelrod, 1995, p. 257). Most state and local governments follow this practice in their accounting systems but retain a cash basis for budgeting, so that while the budget shows a balance, the financial reports may reveal sizeable deficits (Axelrod, 1995, p. 258). There is a clear incentive to accelerate revenues into the current period while deferring expenses to the next. Governments may also delay payments to employees, vendors, and other governments until after the beginning of the next fiscal year (Briffault, 1996, pp. 19–20). A related practice is to reduce contributions to public employee retirement trust funds. According to Briffault, "a common state practice is to recalculate upward the projected yields on trust fund investments in order to reduce the amount the state needs to pay into the fund to provide future retirees' benefits" (p. 21). Public employee pension funds are typically underfunded. States have also used asset sales as a means of "realizing paper increases in income, or reductions in costs, that do not reflect real changes in the actual wealth or expenses of the state" (Briffault, 1996, p. 22). Budget balance has also often been achieved through interfund transfers and borrowing (p. 23).

In the federal government, accrual accounting has been a statutory requirement for nearly forty years, but its implementation, according to Axelrod (1995, p. 257), has been "partial and fragmentary." The Gramm-Rudman deficit-reduction legislation of the 1980s gave rise to numerous charges of smoke and mirrors, and state experience suggests that a constitutional amendment would be likely to elicit similar accounting gimmickry.

WHO DECIDES IF THE BUDGET IS BALANCED?

Making a law is one thing; enforcing it is another. There are virtually no formal provisions for enforcing state balanced-budget rules (Poterba, 1996, p. 12). The literature on balancing budgets is biased in favor of the virtue of the executive branch of government that stretches right back to the advocates of executive budgeting. In general, in the states there is an expectation that executives should propose balanced budgets and that they should take action if it appears that outlays are outrunning revenues to cause an unbalanced budget by the end of the year.

Courts have played little role in enforcing balanced budget rules. As we have seen, many of the state constitutional budget-balancing rules require presentation or legislative passage of a balanced budget, but they do not cover the issue of budgets unbalancing during the fiscal year. In 1980, the Court of Appeals of New York ruled that the governor had no power to impound appropriations even if the purpose were to balance the budget (*County of Oneida* v. *Berle,* 404 N.E. 2d 133 [N.Y. 1980], in Fisher, 1992, p. 6). In 1990 the Supreme Court of Massachusetts, notwithstanding constitutional provisions, held that the governor lacked authority to withhold school-aid funds, but the case hinged on specific statutory authority that did not extend to those funds (*Town of Brookline* v. *Governor,* 553 N.E. 2d 1277 [Mass. 1990], in Fisher, 1992, p. 6). Other cases have been brought by parties harmed by actions taken to cut their budgets in order to balance state budgets, and the state courts have intervened and made decisions on budgetary matters.

Conversely, there do not appear to have been cases in which the state has been sued to enforce balanced budget provisions. In only three states were state officials personally liable and subject to fines, removal from office, or even jail terms if the state budget was not balanced, and apparently these sanctions do not appear to have been invoked (U.S. General Accounting Office, 1993a, p. 23). Automatic enforcement mechanisms are also rare. In California, a "trigger" mechanism was enacted that would automatically reduce budget-year appropriations when forecasted general fund revenues were insufficient to fund the state's general workload budget. Following the use of this mechanism in the 1991–1992 budget (a reduction of $800 million), the trigger mechanism was suspended, however (U.S. General Accounting Office, 1993a, p. 21).

Obviously one of the main attractions to its proponents of a federal balanced budget amendment to the Constitution is its potential enforcement through the courts. Theoretically, a budget might be challenged, beyond the jurisdiction of president or Congress, as unconstitutional. The forms of constitutional amendment proposals have varied over the years, and the extent to which the Supreme Court would be involved as an enforcement body is unclear. Opponents of constitutional amendments have contended that their effect would be to draw the Court into deciding political and economic questions that it was not designed to address. Proponents, conversely, have been placed in the peculiar position of diminishing both the importance of judicial intervention as an enforcement mechanism and the willingness of the judicial branch to intervene, even though presumably the chief attraction of a constitutional provision, as opposed to a statute, is its liability to interpretation by the Court. Thus, the report of the Senate Committee on the Judiciary on S.J. Res. 58, a proposal discussed in 1981, expressed confidence that the "courts will not involve themselves, as a normal matter, in reviewing the operations of the budget process" (U.S. Senate, 1981, p. 62). The committee based this view on the belief that there would rarely be "standing" for a group or individual to challenge actions in breach of the amendment, and that the courts would not treat "political questions" as falling within the jurisdiction of the judiciary. One of the most recent versions of the amendment actually tried to incorporate this view into the document itself, which provided that "the congress shall enforce and implement this article by appropriate legislation, which may rely on estimates of outlays and receipts. The judicial power of the United States shall not extend to any case or controversy arising under this article except as may be specifically authorized by legislation adopted pursuant to this section" (U.S. House of Representatives, 1996, sec. 6).

Whether this effort to exclude the courts would itself be constitutional, and whether more recent cases have expanded notions of standing and judicial activism remain issues for speculation. But in the absence of special enforcement power, the case for a constitutional amendment seems weakened. State experience has shown that the courts have been willing to intervene in budgetary matters, and that their role has been, rather than to enforce budget balance, to protect those who would challenge adverse budget balancing decisions. The courts have also been seriously involved in other kinds of cases in which they have directed states, counties, cities, school districts, and other governmental agencies to take actions irrespective of the budgetary impact of those actions. To believe that the courts would desist from action because an issue is "political" seems highly unlikely. Such views also promote the idea that balancing the budget is an exercise somehow outside the sphere of political life. Any discussion, at any level, of how to balance the budget in practice should surely put such views to rest.

HOW SHOULD THE BUDGET BE BALANCED?

To discuss the "how" of budget balancing is to discuss the whole gamut of choices facing politicians, administrators, and the public every year. The task may be easy or, as it has been in recent years, difficult. During the early 1990s, widespread recession in the United States turned budgeting into an ordeal, and several states ran year-end deficits, which were only resolved by the carryovers, borrowing, and fiscal gimmickry described in previous sections of this chapter. But balance their budgets they did, and Briffault (1996, pp. 60–62) concludes that they did so not so much because of statutory or constitutional mandates but because they had little practical alternative given the compulsions of credit markets and the expectations of public opinion. As the economy improved in mid-decade, budget balancing should have become easier. The federal government deficit dropped dramatically, and most states found themselves in a better position. But for a number of reasons some state and local governments still found that they were unable to close the gap between revenues and expenditures by their usual methods. (This discussion is based on U.S. General Accounting Office, 1993a; all page numbers refer to this source, unless otherwise cited.)

The difficulty of balancing a budget may depend in large measure on whether the deficit is cyclical or structural. A *cyclical deficit* arises from the dynamic of the economic cycle. In a recession, revenues may be expected to dip and demands for expenditures may be expect to increase. When the recession is over, other things being equal, the deficit should disappear. In contrast, a *structural deficit* denotes a permanent imbalance between revenues and expenditures. Even in good times, in the absence of policy action to amend the situation, a serious deficit persists.

The distinction between cyclical and structural deficits is of course not absolute. A cyclical deficit may turn into a structural deficit in an area that fails to recover from a recession. Similarly, an economic boom may mask serious structural problems that become apparent only when the economy turns sour. Nevertheless, the distinction is useful in explaining the predicament of state and local government in the 1990s.

The effects of the dynamic of the business cycle on state and local finances are not difficult to trace. As the recession of the early 1980s faded, year-end surpluses grew in response to real growth in GDP of about 3.3 percent a year (p. 5). But as real GDP growth dropped, first to 2.5 percent in 1989 and then to negative 1.2 percent in 1991, increased spending pressures, particularly in "safety net" programs such as Medicaid and Aid to Families with Dependent Children (AFDC), ate up fund surpluses. Revenues were lower, and even prosperous areas found themselves in difficulty. For example, Santa Clara, California, one of the wealthiest urban areas in the country, had experienced fast economic growth in the 1980s, and property tax revenues had expanded between 10 to 14 percent each year, as the population grew. As economic growth slowed in the 1990s, the property tax growth rate diminished, and demands for entitlements grew (p. 39). A similar story comes from Stamford, Connecticut, another wealthy city. An economic boom in the 1980s almost tripled population, and property taxes expanded. With the stagnation of economic growth in 1989, assessed property values declined, and unemployment and general assistance case loads increased, as did the numbers of hard-core drug users and individuals with high service needs (p. 450).

These and similar jurisdictions responded to rebalance their budgets in a number of ways. Several had built up reserves in previous years, which could now absorb some of the stress. In Nashville, Tennessee, for example, the FY87 combined general funds balance was equivalent to nearly 11 percent of the combined general fund budget, but two years later this reserve had dropped to 2 percent (p. 52). Fresno County in California also used its general fund balance to balance its budgets (p. 38).

But this strategy was rarely enough and it was necessary to both enhance revenues and restrain expenditures. Nashville-Davidson MetroGovernment's budget grew by an average of more than 12 percent annually between FY87 and FY89, but from FY89 to FY92, it grew only 0.8 percent. MetroGovernment raised property taxes and motor vehicle sales taxes, and transferred sales tax revenues from school debt service to school operations and from the general fund to school operations. It reduced expenditures through a hiring and wage freeze, by privatizing and cutting back some services, by deferring capital projects, and by reducing nonmandated programs (which were later reinstated).

All of these measures were marginal, designed to cope with what was viewed as a temporary situation. It was assumed that a rising tide would raise all ships. By the end of 1996, this view seemed borne out: twenty-seven states had cut personal or corporate taxes, revenue collections were higher than budget estimates, and the 4 percent increase in general fund spending estimated for the following year was the third smallest in nineteen years. State year-end balances from FY95 and FY96 were at their highest levels since 1980 (*Wall Street Journal*, 1996, p. A10). But recessions often reveal more serious imbalances between revenues and expenditures, and lack of governmental capacity to meet service demands. When the recession ends, the structural gap persists because of underlying causes affecting revenues or expenditures or both.

A case in point is the state of California, although its ability to produce a surplus in the FY97 budget might appear to denote otherwise. California has a large and diverse economy, which traditionally was expected to bounce back after recessions. But it also has a growing population and rising demands for public services, particularly education, corrections, health, and public assistance. By the early 1990s, projections for "workload" or baseline budgets were clearly outrunning those for revenues. The revenue base was itself relatively inflexible because of a number of measures passed in referenda, such as Proposition 13 (which restricted local property taxes) and others that restricted use of funds and taxing capacity (see Savage, 1992).

The state coped with its financial crisis in a number of ways, including cutbacks in higher education, reductions in income security payments, and most notably, adjusting the formula for allocation of local property tax revenues and shifting certain county revenues to the state, thereby divesting itself of part of its deficit. The effect was to place additional pressures on county budgets, several of which were themselves in trouble. For example, by 1992–1993, Fresno County, a primarily agricultural county, had found that service demands were exceeding its capacity to meet them. Compared with the state as a whole, the county had "more overcrowded housing, a lower median family income, lower per capital income, a higher poverty rate and a higher civilian unemployment rate than the state" (p. 36). A decade of high population growth, including a large component of refugees and migrants, helped fuel dramatic demands for county services for police and corrections, AFDC, Medicaid, and public assistance. Property tax revenues slowed and intergovernmental revenues were primarily dedicated to specific health and welfare programs, the costs of whose administration fell on county general revenues, leaving fewer dollars for law enforcement and judicial services (p. 38). In both 1992–1993 and 1993–1994, state budgetary actions resulted in serious general fund losses to the county.

Quite different circumstances resulted in a structural budget gap in Memphis, Tennessee. Between 1987 and 1992, the general economic situation was not unfavorable, and revenues grew by nearly 15 percent. But at the same time expenditures outstripped revenues, increasing by more than 18 percent, because Memphis attracted the poor and others with high service needs from surrounding rural areas. For example, between 1986 and 1992, AFDC expenditures grew from $28 million to $76 million. Costs for providing services in an aging inner city were also high, because of the high operating and maintenance costs of deteriorating infrastructure. Meanwhile, both property tax and sales tax bases were weakened by a decrease in residential population during the 1980s, even though the daytime working population increased (pp. 48–49).

Structural budget imbalance, in the worst scenario, results from structural economic changes, which undermine the local economy. Population and business activity desert the jurisdiction, leaving behind poverty and decay in what has become a familiar dynamic. Over the past forty years, Detroit, for example, has experienced a steady loss of residents and jobs: between 1972 and 1987, the number of businesses in the city declined by nearly half, and population declined nearly 15 percent between 1980 and 1990 (p. 54). The poor were left behind. In 1989 about a third of the population lived below the poverty level, and nearly half of these were children under eighteen. Less than half the population were in the workforce in 1993.

The effects on city finances were disastrous. In thirty of the forty-three years between 1950 and 1993, the city ran a deficit. The smaller, poorer population bore an increasing tax burden, paying at the highest tax levels in the state.

Meanwhile, federal and state aid declined. Although federal revenues accounted for more than 23 percent of the total city budget in 1980, they were only 8.3 percent in 1991. Conversely, state revenues grew over the same period from 17 percent to 23 percent, but because state revenue sharing funds were based on population, a decade of population decline were likely to result in significant losses in state aid in the coming years.

The ability of localities to expand their tax bases is also sometimes restricted legally. The city of Hartford is limited by the Connecticut prohibition on imposing new taxes, such as a commuter tax. Memphis cannot profit from employment in the city because Tennessee prohibits imposition of an income tax (p. 48). California cities, unable to raise property taxes because of Proposition 13, resorted to a wide variety of fees and charges, but a new initiative (Proposition 218) has now severely limited their ability to do so. In any case, economics may make tax increases impracticable. In Hartford, for example, where the tax base is eroding, taxpayers are overburdened relative to surrounding cities. Its business property tax is more than three times higher than that of an adjoining city, and according to the city manager, tax increases were responsible for business flight in the late 1980s. Similarly, Memphis is constrained in raising taxes by its proximity to Mississippi and Arkansas, and it already suffers "tax leakage" when residents cross the border to avoid higher sales taxes (p. 48).

Balancing the budget is even trickier when politicians promise tax cuts. Not only does such a promise mean that budget balance must be achieved entirely by reducing expenditures, but expenditures have to be cut even deeper to accommodate revenue losses. New Jersey Governor Christine Todd Whitman, for example, came into office in 1993 on a promise of massive income tax cuts and a balanced budget. How could this be done? Governor Whitman began by making a complicated series of actuarial changes to the state pension fund, which saved about $1 billion a year—and will probably result in problems for taxpayers in about twenty or thirty years. She raised fees for state services and cut state aid to municipalities. She transferred special projects money (the educational facilities fund and the temporary disability insurance fund) into general revenue and, as a visible sign of thriftiness, turned off 5,500 lights on streets, above highway signs, and at freeway interchanges throughout New Jersey.

The New Jersey strategies exemplify the choices open to budget balancers in states and localities throughout the United States: sleight of hand, moving funds from one place to another, raising fees of various kinds, and making cuts, including deferring maintenance, closing facilities, laying off employees, cutting programs and services, cutting employees' salaries, and increasing caseloads. The issue is the extent to which these efforts to maintain budget balance increase efficiency or defeat their purpose by actually costing taxpayers more, diminish the quality of life, evade accountability, aggravate deteriorating economic and social conditions, and are even downright dangerous. For example, cutting law enforcement and judicial services in the face of growing juvenile crime, as in Fresno County (p. 38), seems at the very least shortsighted. In Los Angeles, a new downtown jail facility stood empty for two years due to alleged inadequacy of operating funds while convicted individuals served little or even no jail time. The chronic gap in the Los Angeles County budget in 1995–1996 was bridged by huge layoffs from county hospital facilities used by a large indigent population without health insurance, and the cuts were only mitigated by federal intervention. Cuts in maintenance for streets, bridges, schools, vehicles, equipment, and buildings result in problems in safety and loss of efficiency. Layoffs increase caseloads, delays in services, and inability to fulfil tasks properly. Vehicles go unrepaired, inspections are not made, homicides are not investigated or followed up, garbage is not picked up, mental health patients are not monitored, and probation violations are not dealt with.

Balancing the budget, then, particularly where a structural imbalance persists, in bad times and good, requires hard political choices. Where the situation re-presents itself from year to year, these choices are made ad hoc: the budget for that year is balanced but the underlying situation is not resolved by such measures as load shifting, revenue grabbing, random fees and charges, neglect of maintenance, and downgrading of vital public services. Such measures, especially where they are combined with resistance or inability to increase revenues, speak not to the capabilities of public decision makers but rather to their incapacity. Balancing the budget is a simplification that evades rather than engages the major institutional and political questions currently confronting government: the nature of the relationships among the different levels of government; the quality and kinds of services that should be supplied and financed collectively; the means by which public capital projects should be chosen, financed, and maintained; the extent of societal responsibility for those who are unable to care for themselves; and the justifications for subsidy of the unemployed and working poor in a capitalist society.

Balancing the budget is both a norm and a value. Where it is placed above other values, in a position of absolute priority without mitigation, it has been responsible for a good many distorted decisions, such as overbuilding of shopping malls and stadiums in an effort to increase tax revenues, interjurisdictional competition for tax bases, loss of needed public services, deterioration of valuable public infrastructure, and self-defeating cuts that damage organizational capacity and may cost more in the long run. In a time of recession, balancing the budget increases unemployment and aggravates the slowdown in the local economy. Where a structural gap exists, balancing the budget prevents the kinds of remedial action that may be necessary to restore the dynamic to a local area. Yet for state and local governments, the legal, and to some extent the moral, imperative remains. So what is to be done? How can the deleterious effects of balancing the budget be mitigated to preserve local responsibility and capacity? Enter the federal government, whose capacity to live with an unbalanced budget may enable states and localities to balance theirs.

WHY BALANCE THE BUDGET?

Balancing the federal budget has become a premise, the highest priority for federal fiscal policy. In the words of Representative John Kasich (Republican, Columbus, Ohio), Chairman of the House Budget Committee, the Republican victory in the 1994 congressional elections "permanently stamped the idea of the need to balance the budget in America on the federal government of the United States. . . . We will ultimately get it done. . . . Now it's a matter of detail" (Hook, 1996).

After decades of emergence and disappearance, a proposal for a constitutional amendment to balance the federal budget narrowly failed to pass Congress in 1995 and 1996. There have been a number of different proposals which have varied in their stringency, their inclusiveness, and the ease with which they would allow increases in taxes to balance the budget. The common element is the need for a supermajority to permit a deficit, that is, to allow outlays to be greater than revenues.

Several of the arguments against a constitutional balanced budget amendment have been covered in the preceding sections. The analogy with states' provisions is misleading because of states' extensive use of capital and other budgets to evade such provisions, and because of the haziness of many of them. It is unclear what might happen if the federal budget became unbalanced during the year, particularly where entitlements are concerned. The role of the courts in enforcement is undetermined, and if they were to intervene, their qualification to make budgetary decisions is open to doubt. Yet politicians of all stripes and colors seem enthralled by the rhetoric of balancing the budget—not now, perhaps, but in a few years' time, say, in 2002. And they mean really, seriously, no jiggery-pokery this time. Why? Well, one reason is the will of the people. According to Kasich, "the reason why we're going to have a balanced budget is because the American people have basically said, you bunch of rumdums, the least you can do is balance the budget because I have to work to balance mine" (Hook, 1996).

Quite apart from the question of when "the American people" actually said that (rumdums?), we might note a curious inverse correlation: budget balancing hysteria grew at precisely the time that the federal deficit was rapidly diminishing. From a high of about $290 billion in 1992, the federal deficit shrank to just over $107 billion in FY96. This was the smallest budget deficit since 1981, representing 1.4 percent of national income, a figure lower than any deficit since the time of President Nixon, and well below the deficits of most industrialized nations (Cassidy, 1996, p. 10). The decline appeared to be due largely to improvement in the economy and to revenue measures taken in 1993. The federal deficit was predicted to amount to $34 billion for FY97. At this rate, a balanced federal budget would likely become a reality in our time, even before the 2002 date set by president and Congress in an unprecedented budget balancing agreement in 1997.

But "aha," say the critics: the deficit may be diminishing now, but what about in ten years' time, or in twenty years' time? How big will the federal deficit be then? The small deficits of today, they say, are the huge deficits of the future. The scenario was painted most persuasively by the GAO at the beginning of the 1990s. Its projections were alarming. They showed that, assuming current spending and tax policies, deficits would explode to 20 percent of GNP by the year 2020. The culprits were retirement costs, health spending, and interest payments (Bowsher, 1992, pp. 1, 4). The social security surplus would disappear by 2017, and by 2020 Medicare and Medicaid outlays would have grown from 2.8 percent of GNP in 1990 to about 7 percent. Meanwhile, interest costs would have grown to consume more than 30 percent of federal spending (p. 5).

The consequences for the economy would be dire. The deficit would gobble up national savings, with obvious repercussions in investment and economic growth. Already by 1990 the deficit was absorbing 58 percent of national savings and only an inflow of foreign capital was sustaining investment (Bowsher, 1992, p. 1). In mid-decade, the picture looked no different: "Left unchecked through 2025, growing deficits would result in collapsing investment, a declining capital stock, and, inevitably, a declining economy" (U.S. General Accounting Office, 1995, p. 4).

The compelling case for balancing the budget, then, rests on the deficit's alleged propensity to consume national savings and hence subtract from private investment. As Paul Posner (1996, p. 2), director of budget issues for the Accounting and Information Management Division of the GAO, warned that "chronic deficits have consumed an increasing share of a declining national savings pool, leaving that much less for private investment. Lower investment will ultimately show up in lower economic growth. Future generations of taxpayers will pay a steep price for this lower economic growth in terms of lower personal incomes and a generally lower standard of living at a time when they will face the burden of supporting an unprecedented number of retirees as the baby boom generation reaches retirement."

Is the case so compelling? Economic doctrine is also subject to fads and fashions. White and Wildavsky (1989, p. 7) remind us:

> When the deficit panic began, it was due to the deficit's supposed inflationary effect. When the deficit burgeoned and inflation shrank, however, the panic did not decline. One can, of course, say that inflation subsided because of the

Federal Reserve's tight monetary policy. But if so, why did inflation not return with the unprecedented deficits of the recovery? Nobody really knows, and politically it does not matter. As Herbert Stein put it, budget deficits cause bad things, so whatever bad things are happening are blamed on deficits. In 1980 the deficit was blamed for inflation, and in 1982 for high interest rates and unemployment. By 1985 the deficit was said to cause the trade deficit, high real interest rates, an unbalanced recovery, and the strong dollar. In 1987 it was blamed for the stock market crash . . . the trade deficit, and the weak dollar. The evolution of its supposed evils suggests that the massive disapproval of deficits has been supported by no consistent logic of cause and effect. The cause is constant but the alleged effects keep changing.

A group of nearly forty prominent economists and seven Nobel Prize winners in related fields are now on record as opposing a constitutional balanced budget amendment.

Are federal deficits really so terrible that they must be constitutionally outlawed forever? Since World War II, the federal budget has been a powerful instrument of fiscal policy. It has become fashionable to deride Keynesian economic theory, and indeed deficits persist in both good times and bad. But the built-in countercyclical nature of the federal budget undoubtedly has mitigated the extent and depth of economic recessions over the past half-century. Even without positive policy, in times of economic downturn, tax revenues diminish and government payments increase, pumping resources into the economy ("Simon's Simple Pie," 1994). As an article in *The Economist* has put it, "Forcing the budget to balance every year is bad economics. It would require higher taxes in recessions, to offset the drop in revenues and higher spending on benefits. A sensible rule should, at a minimum, allow the deficit to fluctuate counter-cyclically (as it would if tax rates were held constant throughout)" ("Balancing the Government's Books," 1994, p. 73). Requiring a balanced budget irrespective of economic conditions would end the support of households and probably result in deeper and longer recessions.

One of the key reasons for the federal government assuming such a pivotal role during the depression of the 1930s was the financial incapacity of state and local governments. Only the federal government was in a position to prime the economic pump and come to the rescue of bankrupt regions and localities, because it was unhampered by the necessity for budget balance. Conditions are quite different today, but the role played by the federal government in local economies is still enormous, including infrastructure, defense spending, entitlements of various kinds, health outlays, and disaster assistance. A study conducted by the Center on Budget and Policy Priorities estimated that policies to balance the budget by 2002 would result in an annual loss to the states of $96 billion—the equivalent of one-quarter of projected revenues from state sales taxes, personal income taxes, and corporation taxes (Healy, 1995, p. A17).

Perhaps state governors and legislatures would be willing to forgo federal aid in the interests of moral rectitude, though the effects of such cuts are likely to be disproportionate—that is, poor states would probably lose more because they receive more. But is this spirit of self-sacrifice based on real necessity and moral virtue or on misconception?

Yet the moral argument in favor of budget balance still persists. Somehow it still seems more virtuous to balance the books. Is this really so? Should budgetary balance be the overwhelming criterion for public policy, one that overrides all other considerations? A budget deficit is simply an accounting number, not a measure of a country's well-being. Instead we should look to indicators such as the level and growth rates of per capita income, which bear no simple relation to the size of the government's deficit. Where current deficits sustain investment in the broad sense of the word—in children, education, research and development, and infrastructure, for example—they add to rather than subtract from national well-being, both now and in the future.

To this argument the objection may be made that federal deficits are being fueled by expenditures on the elderly or on poor people. One might easily counter that objection because deficits are fungible, and they are also fueled by high levels of expenditure on defense. But even if the poor and the elderly are beneficiaries of borrowed largesse, surely these expenditures are also worthwhile, as long as they reduce societal poverty, contribute to the flow of consumption, and alleviate current burdens (Eisner, 1996, p. 89).

All this is of course not to argue that federal budget policy and process are perfect or that deficits are necessarily desirable. Political debates about the size and role of the federal government, entitlement spending, intergovernmental relations, debt policy, and the scope and place of every one of the myriad programs supported from the public purse will continue to swirl. But a rigid and absolute priority for federal budget balance rests on doubtful if not spurious grounds.

What about the long term? It would of course be sensible to make provision for future commitments and to ensure that there is a reasonable balance between resources and expenditures at the time they are needed. The current fear is that entitlements, particularly for health programs and social security, in future years will far outrun existing arrangements for paying for them. There are reasons for doubting this impending crisis (see, for example, Cassidy, 1997, p. 3); but assuming that this scenario is correct, how would mandating a balanced budget through the Constitution correct the situation? Presumably it would force politicians to make provisions for funding. But most balanced budget amendment proposals have rarely discussed serious adjustments to these programs. It would seem more likely that changes would take place through agreements outside the budget framework altogether on measures such as raising the age of retirement, adjusting indexing measures, increasing payroll taxes, or raising the ceiling on social security contributions. It is doubtful whether a constitutional amendment relating to the current year's budget would contribute significantly to the long-term policymaking required to make such decisions, particularly where assumptions about the future are sufficiently uncertain and easily manipulable to come up with predetermined outcomes.

Why would a measure with so many arguments against it gain such currency and acceptance at the highest political levels? One answer is that simple rules of thumb are easier to grasp than complicated policy measures or complex political arguments. Perhaps it is easier to be "good" than to be "clever." Once opinion has reached a groundswell, even sensible politicians hesitate to declare that the emperor has no clothes. Given the tide of rhetoric and hysteria, we should maybe ask whether the debate about balancing the budget is really about balancing the budget. In the mid-1990s, even as politicians earnestly affirmed their faith in budgetary balance, they made their task harder by a variety of proposals to cut taxes. A balanced budget does not in fact imply anything about the level of revenues and expenditures. Yet the debate has been couched in the language of smaller government and cuts in expenditures. Perhaps there is public support for these policies, and perhaps there is not. In any case, arguments on both sides would gain greater clarity if their merits were debated more honestly, rather than hidden under the veil of complex, vague, and uncertain proposals to balance the budget.

References

Axelrod, D. *Shadow Government.* New York: Wiley, 1992.

Axelrod, D. *Budgeting for Modern Government.* New York: St. Martin's Press, 1995.

"Balancing the Government's Books." *Economist,* Feb. 12, 1994, p. 73.

Bowsher, C. A. *Budget Policy: Long-Term Implications of the Deficit.* Testimony Before the Subcommittee on Deficits, Debt Management and International Debt; Committee on Finance, U.S. Senate, June 5, 1992 (GAO/T-OCG-92-4). Washington, D.C.: Government Printing Office, 1992.

Briffault, R. *Balancing Acts: The Reality Behind State Balanced Budget Requirements.* New York: Twentieth Century Fund Press, 1996.

Caiden, N., and Chapman, J. "Constraint and Uncertainty: Budgeting in California." *Public Budgeting and Finance,* 1982, *2*(4), 111–129.

Cassidy, J. "Hoover Rides Again: The False Pieties of Balancing the Budget." *New Yorker,* Dec. 9, 1996, p. 10.

Cassidy, J. "Spooking the Boomers." *New Yorker,* Jan. 13, 1997, pp. 30–35.

Di Lorenzo, T. *Underground Government: The Off-Budget Public Sector.* Washington, D.C.: Cato Institute, 1983.

Eisner, R. "A Balanced Budget Crusade." *Public Interest,* Winter 1996, pp. 85–92.

Fisher, L. Statement Before the U.S. House of Representatives, Committee on the Budget, on the Balanced Budget Amendment, May 11, 1992.

Healy, M. "GOP Goal to Balance the Budget Likely to Pinch States' Pockets." *Los Angeles Times,* Feb. 6, 1995, p. A17.

Henriques, D. *The Machinery of Greed.* San Francisco: New Lexington Press, 1980.

Hook, J. "John Kasich: The GOP's Point Man in the Balanced Budget Debate." *Los Angeles Times,* Dec. 15, 1996, p. M3.

Johnson, C., and Mikesell, J. "Certificates of Participation and Capital Markets." *Public Budgeting and Finance,* 1994, *14*(3), 41–54.

National Conference of State Legislatures. *Legislative Authority over the Enacted Budget.* Denver: National Conference of State Legislatures, 1992.

Posner, P. *Budget Issues: Deficit Reduction and the Long Term.* Testimony Before the U.S. House of Representatives, Committee on the Budget, Mar. 13, 1996 (GAO/T-AIMD-96-66). Washington, D.C.: Government Printing Office, 1996.

Poterba, J. M. "The Effect of Budget Rules on Fiscal Policy." *National Bureau of Economic Research Reporter,* Spring 1996, pp. 12–13.

Savage, J. D. "California's Structural Deficit Crisis." *Public Budgeting and Finance,* 1992, *12*(3), 82–97.

Schick, A. *The Federal Budget: Politics, Policy, Process.* Washington, D.C.: Brookings Institution, 1995.

Simon, R. "U.S. Likely to Take Back $31 Million from MTA, Staff Says." *Los Angeles Times,* Dec. 7, 1996, pp. B1, B3.

"Simon's Simple Pie." *New Yorker,* Feb. 28, 1994, pp. 6, 8.

U.S. Congressional Budget Office. *Economic and Budget Outlook.* Washington, D.C.: Government Printing Office, 1992.

U.S. Congressional Budget Office. *Economic and Budget Outlook.* Washington, D.C.: Government Printing Office, 1993.

U.S. Congressional Budget Office. *Economic and Budget Outlook.* Washington, D.C.: Government Printing Office, 1994.

U.S. Congressional Budget Office. *Economic and Budget Outlook.* Washington, D.C.: Government Printing Office, 1995a.

U.S. Congressional Budget Office. *Economic and Budget Outlook: Update.* Washington, D.C.: Government Printing Office, 1995b.

U.S. General Accounting Office. *Balanced Budget Requirements: State Experiences and Implications for the Federal Government.* Briefing Report to the Chairman, U.S. House of Representatives, Committee on the Budget (GAO/AFMD-93-58BR). Washington, D.C.: Government Printing Office, 1993a.

U.S. General Accounting Office. *State and Local Finances: Some Jurisdictions Confronted by Short- and Long-Term Problems* (GAO/HRD-94-1). Washington, D.C.: Government Printing Office, 1993b.

U.S. General Accounting Office. *The Deficit and the Economy: An Update of Long-Term Simulations* (GAO/AIMD/OCE-95-119). Washington, D.C.: Government Printing Office, 1995.

U.S. House of Representatives, Committee on the Judiciary. Joint Resolution presented by Mr. Wyden, Mr. Dorgan, Mr. Daschle, Mr. Reid, Mr. Ford, and Mr. Hollings, May 22, 1996.

U.S. Office of Management and Budget. *Budget of the United States Government, Fiscal Year 1996: Analytical Perspectives.* Washington, D.C.: Government Printing Office, 1995.

U.S. Senate Committee on the Judiciary. Report on S.J. Res. 58, July 10, 1981.

Wall Street Journal, Nov. 13, 1996, p. A10.

Walsh, A. H. *The Public's Business.* Cambridge, Mass.: MIT Press, 1978.

White, J., and Wildavsky, A. "How to Fix the Deficit—Really." *Public Interest,* Winter 1989, pp. 3–24.

Wildavsky, A., and Caiden, N. *The New Politics of the Budgetary Process.* (3rd ed.) Reading, Mass.: Addison-Wesley, 1996.

PART THREE

TAXATION
IN BUDGETING

CHAPTER TEN

The Major Tax Bases

Jane G. Gravelle

T his chapter focuses on the economics of the tax base. Topics discussed include the categorization of tax bases by type, the use of different tax bases
over time and by jurisdiction, the decision about who bears the burden
(shifting and incidence), and the efficiency, equity, and revenue yield of alternative taxes.

TYPES OF TAX BASES

Tax bases fall into four basic categories: income, consumption, wages, and
wealth. All taxes effectively have one or more of these bases. It is not always
easy to fit taxes exactly in these categories, and some taxes combine bases. For
example, a capital gains tax is commonly thought of as a tax on income, but it
is imposed only if a transaction (a sale) occurs. Similarly, an inheritance or estate tax is commonly thought of as a tax on wealth, but it is imposed only if
wealth is transferred. Severance taxes on the production of oil, gas, and miner-
als have elements of several taxes.

For purposes of economic analysis, it is useful to distinguish between taxes
imposed on the basic production inputs of capital and labor. (Capital can be

---

Note: The views in this chapter do not necessarily represent those of the Congressional Research
Service or the Library of Congress.

broadly defined to include land and deposits of natural resources.) General income taxes fall on the returns of both capital and labor, wage taxes fall on labor earnings, and wealth taxes fall on capital. Consumption taxes, in the long run, are equivalent to wage taxes, although at the time they are imposed they also include existing wealth in the tax base (which will be subject to tax when turned into consumption goods).

Although taxes can be characterized in these broad ways, they come in many different forms and varieties. They may be either general or selective; for example, consumption taxes may include both broad retail sales taxes and narrow levies on specific goods such as gasoline, alcohol, and tobacco. Similarly, wealth taxes can be applied either to wealth generally or to specific types of wealth, such as real property. Taxes may be imposed either as direct taxes (imposed on the person meant to bear the burden) or as indirect taxes (paid by one person but effectively shifted to someone else). Taxes may be either personal (adjusted to the individual's ability to pay) or *in rem* (imposed on activities or objects independently of the characteristics of the owner). *In rem* commodity taxes may be imposed per unit, as is the case of certain excise taxes, or they may be *ad valorem* (based on dollar value), as in the case of retail sales taxes.

Personal taxes may incorporate features such as graduated rates, exemptions, ceilings, and adjustments for family size, to relieve the tax on those with fewer resources—all adjustments that are not feasible for *in rem* taxes. For that reason, the flexibility of personal taxes in accommodating distributional preferences is an important consideration, and personal taxes dominate the federal tax system. *In rem* taxes are the major state and local taxes. (Some states have, however, used income tax credits, termed *circuit breakers,* to provide relief from property taxes for low-income individuals.)

USE OF TAX BASES ACROSS JURISDICTIONS AND OVER TIME

The use of tax bases is markedly different across jurisdictions, and taxes have changed substantially over time.

Reliance on Different Tax Bases by Level of Government

Federal taxes are dominated by income (54 percent) and wage (payroll) taxes (37 percent). Local taxes are primarily based on property taxes (75 percent). The dominant bases of state taxes are sales and excise taxes (49 percent) and income taxes (39 percent) (data are from Fleenor, 1995, pp. 182, 232). States and localities also carry on specific activities of a private-business nature (such as liquor stores and utilities), where the receipts cannot be clearly specified as taxes or as a particular type of tax. These latter receipts are sometimes reported as revenues and sometimes as spending offsets. This chapter focuses on coercively obtained receipts.

Table 10.1 shows the receipts (other than grants) by different levels of government for different types of taxes. Income taxes are the most important, accounting for more than a third of total taxes. The payroll tax is second largest, followed by sales taxes and then the corporate income tax.

A small part of the individual income tax falls on capital and a part of sales and excise taxes was originally a lump sum tax on old capital (as discussed subsequently). As a result, about a quarter of taxes are on capital income and about three-quarters are on labor income, roughly the factor shares of incomes in the economy. Thus, overall the burden of taxes on capital and labor are about equal. Taxes at the federal level, however, tend to fall somewhat more heavily on labor income, because of the payroll tax.

Changes in the Federal Tax Base over Time

The level of federal taxes has changed relatively little over time, but the federal system has gradually come to rely more on wage taxes. In large part, this trend reflects the increased reliance on payroll taxes and the growing size of the programs—social security and Medicare—that these taxes fund. At the same time, the corporate tax has shrunk in importance. Excise taxes, while never important, have also declined over time. These variations over time in

Table 10.1. Taxes as a Percentage of Gross Domestic Product by Type of Tax: Federal, State, and Local.

Type of Tax	Federal	State	Local	Total
Individual Income	7.9	1.7	0.2	9.9
Corporate Income	2.0	0.4	—	2.4
Payroll	6.7	—	—	6.7
Sales and Excise	1.1	2.7	0.5	4.3
Sales	—	1.8	—	—
Excise	0.8	0.9	—	—
Customs	0.2	—	—	—
Property	—	0.1	2.8	2.9
Estate, Gift, Inheritance	0.2	0.1	—	0.3
Other	0.3	0.5	0.2	1.0
Charges	—	1.7	2.1	3.8
Utilities, Liquor Stores, Insurance	—	2.3	1.2	3.5
Total Taxes	18.4	5.5	3.7	27.6
Total Receipts	18.4	9.5	7.0	34.9

Note: Author's calculations based on data for FY94 for federal taxes and from Council of Economic Advisers, 1996, pp. 280, 370. State tax data (FY93) and local tax data (FY92) from Fleenor, 1995, pp. 182, 232. Missing entries due to lack of consistent data for a single year.

the size and composition of federal taxes relative to gross domestic product (GDP) are shown in Figure 10.1.

Some, although not all, of the reason for the reduction in the corporate tax is the decrease in effective tax rates for corporate income due to tax legislation. Tax burdens fell in the 1960s with the adoption of investment credits and accelerated depreciation. The investment credit was repealed temporarily on several occasions in the late 1960s and early 1970s, was reinstated at higher rates in the mid-1970s, and was repealed in 1986 in conjunction with lower statutory tax rates. At the same time, higher inflation rates increased tax rates somewhat during the 1970s, offsetting some of the statutory changes. When inflation slowed in the 1980s, the lower taxes enacted in 1981 were reinforced through accelerated depreciation. Accelerated depreciation was scaled back and the investment credit was repealed in 1986, but offsetting rate reductions were made.

The decline in excise taxes reflected the repeal in the 1960s of many of these taxes and the failure of others, imposed on a per unit basis, to keep pace with inflation.

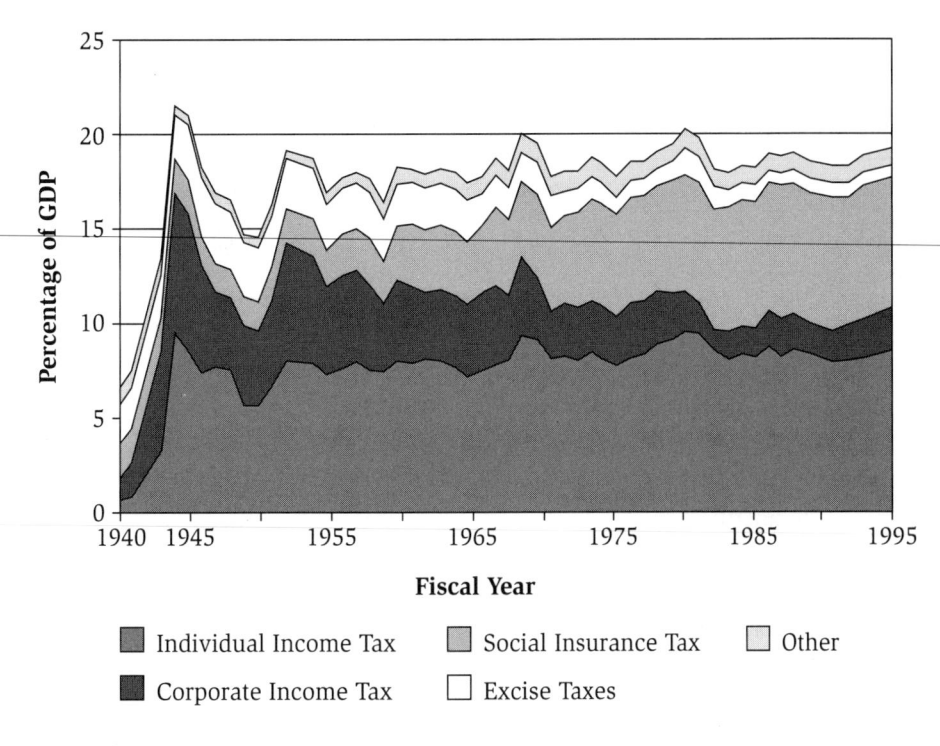

Figure 10.1. Federal Receipts as a Percentage of Gross Domestic Product, Fiscal Years 1940–1996.

Source: Brumbaugh, 1996.

Changes in the Total Tax Base over Time

Although federal taxes remained relatively constant in the post–World War II period, state and local taxes rose as a share of GDP until about 1970; they have since remained relatively constant. This pattern of state and local taxes relative to GDP and compared with federal taxes is shown in Figure 10.2.

Much of the rise in state and local taxes reflects increases in state taxes, particularly income taxes. Property taxes, which in 1950 accounted for 46 percent of state and local taxes, accounted for 32 percent in 1992. Sales taxes maintained roughly the same share, rising from 32 percent to 35 percent. Income taxes, however, rose from 5 percent of the total to 21 percent (Fleenor, 1995, pp. 182, 232).

Earmarking

One budgeting phenomenon that has influenced the nature of the tax base over time is the earmarking of taxes for particular uses. A common earmarked tax is the gasoline tax, which is usually dedicated to highway construction and maintenance. The rationale for this earmarking is clear: the gasoline tax is an indirect way of charging drivers for the use of the roads.

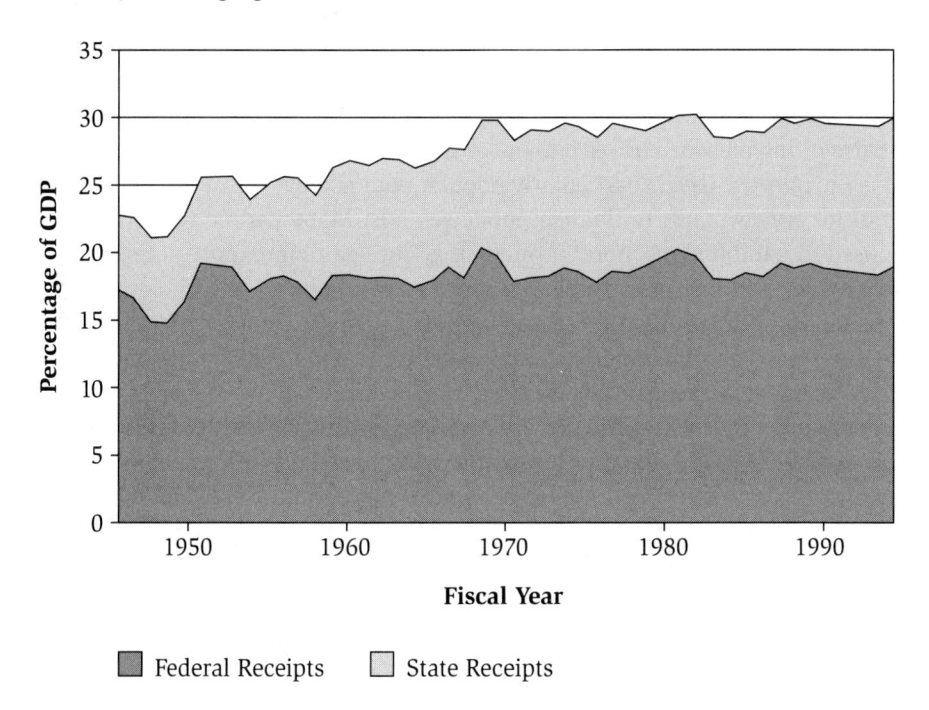

Figure 10.2. State and Local Taxes and Federal Taxes as Percentage of Gross Domestic Product.

Source: Brumbaugh, 1996.

An earmarked tax, the benefits of which are closely tied to the tax, may be efficient because it mimics the private markets in some way. Because roads can be worn out and congestion occurs, individual drivers impose costs on others when they drive. If the roads were entirely free, motorists would drive too much as a group because they would not have to pay the social costs of driving. The gasoline tax, if set correctly, can correct this tendency to overuse the roads.

Earmarking may also be appropriate to correct for spillover effects. Private automobiles cause pollution and congestion; a tax that raises the cost of gasoline would therefore be appropriate to reflect these additional social costs. It would also be appropriate to earmark these revenues for alternative transportation, which reduces congestion and pollution, such as mass transit.

Some taxes are earmarked to cover damages and liabilities directly. The federal government has, for example, a series of liability taxes, such as taxes on petroleum and chemicals, which go to the superfund used to clean up hazardous wastes; taxes on coal, to fund black lung disability payments; and vaccine taxes to fund an injury compensation fund. Whether these taxes are efficient or not depends on the link between the product and the damages. For example, the superfund taxes are imposed on current products to correct past damages, which severs the link between payment and liability. The vaccine tax is a way of providing no-fault insurance and therefore substitutes for a potentially costly private litigation system. (Because vaccination has positive spillovers, however, such a system might be better funded from general revenues.)

Earmarking may also be used to make taxes more palatable, by tying them to a specific purpose that is particularly popular with taxpayers. An example is the use of lottery revenues to finance public schools. Many people who might be opposed to gambling on moral grounds may find gambling more acceptable if receipts are used for some purpose deemed particularly worthy. Of course, because money is fungible, the earmarking of a tax to a particular spending purpose does not guarantee that spending will be increased by the amount of the tax; general revenues that might have been spent on education, for example, may be diverted to other uses when lottery revenues are dedicated to public schools.

At the federal level, the most important earmarked tax is the payroll tax, dedicated to social security and Medicare. As these programs have grown relative to other expenditures, the share of tax raised by payroll taxes has grown as well, altering the nature of total federal taxes. The link between a wage tax and old-age retirement is not straightforward as is the link between gasoline taxes and road expenditures; other transfers in the federal budget are financed out of income tax revenues.

BURDEN AND INCIDENCE

Despite popular discussions to the contrary, tax burdens do not necessarily fall on the individual who is legally liable for the tax or who is the intended target. Nor do they fall on the entity who is actually depositing the tax money. (Most individual taxes are withheld by businesses.) In any case, firms do not bear the burden of taxes; rather, their owners, creditors, employees, or customers (or the owners, creditors, and employees of their suppliers) do. Much economic analysis has been devoted to measuring the incidence of taxes, or who actually bears the burden of taxes through some real reduction in purchasing power. This process occurs through tax shifting, and taxes imposed on businesses are commonly referred to as being shifted backward to factors of production (labor and capital) and forward to consumers (via higher prices). (Rosen, 1995, pp. 273–302, presents a comprehensive discussion of tax shifting and incidence.)

Fundamental Precepts of Tax Shifting

There are several fundamental precepts of tax shifting and incidence. First, legal liability should not matter except in the short run, before adjustments are made. Thus the fact that one-half of the payroll tax is imposed on the employer and one-half on the employee does not mean that the burden of the tax is different for each party. If the employee tax falls on wages, the employer tax should do so as well, because there is no economic difference between the two taxes. For example, suppose the supply of labor is fixed, as some evidence suggests. A tax imposed on the employee will reduce wages directly, while a tax imposed on the employer will increase the employer's cost and cause him to offer a lower wage, which employees will accept. Similarly, a uniformly applied retail sales tax and a uniformly applied value-added tax (which is a sales tax imposed at each stage of production) are economically identical in the long run.

Second, incidence can be measured through either the sources side or the uses side of transactions. A tax could reduce wages (through the sources side) or raise prices and make purchases more expensive (through the uses side). These distinctions do not matter to fundamental incidence. There are equivalent uses and sources for every tax.

Incidence depends on behavioral responses, and the incidence of some types of taxes is much more difficult to ascertain than the incidence of others. There are generally agreed-upon expectations for the incidence of broad-based uniform taxes—expectations that hinge on the likelihood of a minimal response of labor supply and savings to changes in wage and interest rates. (See Engen, Gravelle, and Smetters, 1997, for a survey of this evidence.)

Wage (Payroll) Tax

A uniform tax on labor income reduces wage income to workers as long as the labor supply is fixed. With unchanged labor, the firm continues to pay the same gross (tax-inclusive) wage and the net wage falls relative to the amount of the tax.

If labor supply responded to taxes, second-order effects would alter wages, rates of return, and output. If labor supply contracted (it could, however, expand due to income effects), wages would go up and the rate of return would fall, shifting some of the burden onto capital. This effect would be transitory, however. Over time, the reduction in income would reduce savings and the capital stock, and in standard growth models the rate of return would ultimately return to its previous value. In any case, the evidence suggests that the labor supply is relatively insensitive to changes in the after-tax wage, so labor income taxes can be presumed to fall on labor income.

One complication of the payroll tax is that it is tied to future social security benefits, which may moderate the behavioral response (to the extent that the payment of tax increases the benefits, it is not a tax).

Income and Wealth Taxes

A uniform tax on income can be thought of as a simultaneous tax on labor income (as discussed earlier) and capital income. A capital income tax would fall on capital income if the savings rate were unresponsive to changes in the rate of return, and most evidence supports this view. If it were responsive, the tax would shift partially to labor as the capital stock contracts, causing wages to fall and the rate of return to rise. This process would occur slowly, but there would be a permanent effect on wages.

Note the different patterns of response over time. If labor supply changes because of a change in wage taxes, it is likely to adjust relatively quickly, producing an initial decline in the rate of return that gradually recovers over time. (In the end, of course, there is less overall income, and thus a smaller tax than originally contemplated.) If saving changes, the change in capital income taxes will have a minimal but growing effect on wages initially, but the long-run effect will be permanent.

In theory, a capital income tax could also directly affect labor supply by altering the consumption of leisure over time. There is no direct empirical evidence of such an effect, however.

A wealth tax can generally be thought to fall on capital; that is, there are economic similarities between taxes on wealth and taxes on capital income.

General Consumption Tax

One could characterize the consumption tax on the sources side as a wage tax plus a lump sum tax on existing capital. If, for example, a sales tax or value-added tax were imposed and the nominal price level in the economy did not change, consumption prices would not rise. Rather, the tax would be shifted backwards to reduce wages and to reduce the value of capital assets. The tax does not, however, fall on income from new capital investments.

There are some real differences between backward and forward shifting of a consumption tax. Some people in the economy receive transfers of income. If the price level does not increase or if the transfers are automatically indexed to inflation, individual consumption out of transfers will not bear the tax. When the overall price level does not increase, the tax burden on assets falls only on equity claims to assets so that individuals who hold debt and consume out of debt will not bear the tax.

Partial Consumption Taxes

A partial consumption tax, such as an excise tax, is typically legally imposed on the manufacturer. But no one is likely to expect that the stockholders pay the tax except in the very short run. Rather, the imposition of the tax sets into motion several effects. The manufacturer will try to raise prices, perhaps by cutting back production. But the resources released from the manufacture of the taxed commodity will be employed in producing other goods.

If the overall price level in the economy does not change, prices of other products will fall. In that case, taxes as an aggregate cannot be passed forward in price; rather, they must be passed backward. A standard effect of any consumption tax is that the tax falls on wages and on old capital. Wages will fall in the economy in an amount proportional to the tax as a percentage of all commodities (which may be very small for a very narrow tax), and the value of capital assets will also fall by the same percentage.

An example may be helpful. Suppose that half of the output in the economy is the good to be taxed, and the other half is another good, both selling for a dollar per unit, and a tax of 10 percent is levied on the good. Holding the original shares constant, this tax is equivalent to an overall sales tax of 5 percent. Holding shares constant, the taxed commodity will rise in price to $1.05 and the untaxed commodity will fall in price to $0.95. Wages will fall by 5 percent (as will the value of capital). A worker who buys only untaxed commodities will be unaffected by the tax, because the commodity price has fallen; but workers who buy the taxed product will find their consumption affected by both lower wages and higher prices, equivalent to the rise in price of the taxed commodity by 10 percent.

One can achieve the same real outcome if the overall price is allowed to rise to accommodate the tax. In that case, wages and asset prices do not fall but the price of the taxed commodity rises by 10 percent explicitly.

As in the case of a general sales tax, there are some consequences of backward and forward shifting. Backward shifting benefits individuals who receive transfers or own debt, and individuals who consume less than the average share of the taxed commodity will actually benefit from the excise tax because the price of their consumption goods will fall. (Indexed transfers will also be exempt under forward shifting.)

The incidence of a retail sales tax is similar to the incidence of a partial consumption tax because most state sales taxes exempt a lot of consumption from the tax.

There are some other nuances of a partial consumption tax. Substitution of untaxed for taxed commodities can have effects on demands for labor and capital, if firms differ in their capital-labor ratios. These effects are typically thought to be relatively small. As a result, the standard assumption about partial consumption taxes is that the burden of the tax falls on the consumer of the commodity.

Partial Factor Taxes

A common example of a partial factor tax is the corporate income tax, which applies only to equity capital in the corporate sector. In addition, taxes on different types of investments differ for other reasons (for example, the return to owner-occupied housing is not taxed, and investment subsidies alter tax burdens across assets).

The corporate tax (or rather the excess of the corporate and personal taxes applied to corporate income over taxes on noncorporate income) has been the subject of extensive analysis (see Harberger, 1962, for the seminal analysis in this area, and Gravelle, 1994, pp. 75–93, for a survey). The conclusion that virtually all of the analyses lead to is that the tax, although initially borne by stockholders, is probably subsequently spread to all capital, assuming a fixed aggregate supply of capital. Thus, a partial tax could be treated in the same way as a general tax.

This effect occurs because as the after-tax return in the corporate sector falls, capital migrates from corporations to noncorporate firms, lowering the latter's price and the rate of return. (The noncorporate sector produces more output and does so with a higher capital-labor ratio.) In the corporate sector, the rate of return rises as corporate prices rise and the capital-labor ratio declines. These shifts can change the aggregate demand for labor, affecting the wage rate. Depending on the substitutability of capital and labor in the two sectors and on the substitutability of products, the corporate tax could fall either more or less than 100 percent on capital (that is, labor could benefit or be burdened); a central and reasonable case, however, is that the tax falls on capital.

The corporate tax also has excise effects, however, because it raises the price of corporate products relative to noncorporate products. Differentials arising for other reasons, such as investment subsidies, also have excise tax effects.

Arguments have been made that corporate taxes fall on labor in a small, open economy because capital can migrate but labor cannot. The required conditions are extreme (a small economy and perfect substitutability of investments and products). For reasonable empirical estimates of substitutability and given the large size of the United States, the corporate tax is still likely to fall largely on capital (Gravelle, 1994, pp. 232–235).

Property Taxes

The property tax is a partial tax on wealth, which is similar to an income tax; hence the property tax is likely borne by owners of capital. The tax also has excise tax effects, causing products with a high property tax component (such as housing and products that rely heavily on structures as a factor of production) to rise in relative price.

There is a complication to the residential property tax, because it is a local tax. Individuals can choose which jurisdiction to live in, and individuals with tastes for government services will choose high-tax, high-benefit jurisdictions, while individuals who do not prefer government services will choose low-tax, low benefit jurisdictions. This link between taxes and benefits causes the tax to take on some characteristics of a direct payment for goods and services (the Tiebout hypothesis; 1956).

ECONOMIC EFFICIENCY AND OPTIMAL TAXATION

All taxes, except one that is imposed on a flat, per head basis, have behavioral effects that are generally harmful because they distort choices. This distortion is costly to economic welfare, and because it adds to the direct burden of the tax, it is also referred to as the excess burden. (The loss in welfare due to a distortion from any type of policy is also called a deadweight loss; see Rosen, 1995, pp. 302–327, for a more detailed discussion and survey of the assumptions about the incidence of typical taxes.)

For example, suppose the marginal tax rate on wages is raised while the tax payments are kept fixed (say, by increasing the exemption level). This change would cause people to reduce work effort because their wage for an additional hour of work will have decreased. The welfare cost is the difference between the value of the consumption forgone in the economy because of the reduced work effort and the value of additional leisure people enjoy. Note that the cost is not simply the loss of output, because the value of the substitute, leisure, must be accounted for.

This distortion can be approximated, for a tax of T, by the formula $ET^2/2$, where E is the elasticity (percentage change in quantity divided by a percentage change in price). The welfare cost rises proportionally with the elasticity—for example, if the elasticity is doubled, the welfare cost is doubled. The cost rises more than proportionally with the size of the tax. For example, if the tax rate is doubled, the welfare cost is quadrupled; if the tax rate is tripled, the welfare cost is multiplied by a factor of nine.

This simple formula is an approximation based on a linear function. A linear function means, for example, that the fall in consumption when prices rise is a straight line rather than a curve. When taxes are large, nonlinear functions can make a significant difference. Moreover, the formula refers to the tax rate applied as a percentage of net-of-tax amounts—as in a sales tax. Income and payroll taxes are percents of the gross-of-tax amount. A 25 percent tax rate of the gross-of-tax type, is a 33 percent tax of the net-of-tax type (because 25 percent is one-third of the after-tax amount of 75 percent). This point is important because a proportional change in a gross-of-tax rate is a much larger proportional change in the net-of-tax rate and thus produces a much larger potential efficiency cost.

Although the excess burden must be worked out by taking account of elasticities, type of tax, and use of nonlinear functions, this simple rule of thumb does serve to remind us that the welfare cost of high taxes can be significant. Moreover, it suggests that the distortionary cost of increasing taxes can be very large relative to the additional revenues. A doubling of the tax may less than double revenues, but it will more than double the distortionary costs. Of course, if the elasticity, or behavioral response, is low, then even a large tax will not have a large distorting effect.

Which Types of Taxes Are More Efficient?

Of the types of taxes that are politically feasible, a broad-based consumption tax is generally thought to be the most neutral. The only distortion in such a tax system is that between consumption and leisure (because leisure is not included in the tax base). Moreover, a consumption tax effectively imposes a one-time lump sum tax on existing wealth, and lump sum taxes have no distorting effects. This aspect of a consumption tax makes it more neutral than a wage tax, which does not benefit from the lump sum tax and must therefore impose higher tax rates in order to raise the same amount of revenue.

Also in favor of the broad-based consumption tax is the evidence suggesting that there is not a very large elasticity associated with the supply of labor. Because labor-leisure choice is the only distortion associated with the tax, a small elasticity implies a small distortion.

It is not entirely clear, however, that a broad-based income tax might not be more neutral, or at least that a tax system composed of some combination of income and consumption taxes might not be more neutral. Because the consumption tax base is smaller than the income tax base, tax rates on wages are higher under a consumption tax than under an income tax. If the distorting effect of introducing a tax on capital income is less onerous than the higher taxes on wage income, raising at least some revenues from income taxes may be desirable.

Because the wage tax does not benefit from the lump sum payment, an income tax is likely to be even more appropriate in combination with a wage tax than a wage tax alone for minimizing distortions.

One important limitation of an income tax is that it is difficult to develop a tax on investment income that is uniformly applied to all capital income. It is probably not practical to tax the imputed income from investing in owner-occupied housing, and it is difficult to estimate economic depreciation precisely.

Progressive taxes, which are feasible with income, wage, and even consumption taxes, tend to be more distortionary than flat rate taxes because the exemptions contract the tax base and require higher marginal tax rates.

Finally, for both factor taxes and consumption taxes, one can distinguish between a uniform tax and a differential tax. Differential taxes can cause distortions between different commodities and different investments. Nevertheless, an argument can be made on efficiency grounds for differentially taxing commodities. Those commodities that are necessities, such as food and medical care, tend to be the least responsive to taxes and thus create the smallest distortions. (A case could also be made for taxing consumption goods that are complementary with leisure as an indirect way of taxing leisure.)

Although this discussion suggests that flat rate taxes, perhaps targeted towards consumption of necessities and recreational goods, may be ideal for an efficient tax, there are formidable barriers to enacting such taxes. Such taxes would perform poorly by most standards of fairness (discussed subsequently), and would probably be quite difficult to administer.

Some of the most significant tax distortions across assets in the current tax system are not necessary, however. The double tax on corporate equity income causes distortions in the allocation of capital, the choice of debt versus equity finance, and the payout of dividends. There are numerous ways to relieve or even eliminate this tax differential.

Arguments are often made for special tax treatment because of the spillover effects of certain types of consumptions or investments. If so, imposing taxes or providing subsidies or exemptions from general taxes is efficient. The most familiar of the taxes imposed on goods with negative spillover effects are probably those on alcohol or tobacco; pollution taxes could also correct distortions. Some types of expenditures, such as investments in research and development and human capital are probably undersupplied in a market economy (although whether tax subsidies are superior to direct provision of funds is another question).

Many of the pleas for special treatment rest on relatively shaky ground. These include arguments for favoring investment in owner-occupied housing (to encourage good citizenship), in oil and gas exploration (to protect national defense), and in equipment (because of embodied technical advance). In general these arguments are not based on careful quantitative estimates (owner-occupied housing); they may be shortsighted and inferior to alternatives (such as oil and gas exploration); or they are likely not to be true (equipment investment).

A tax that is capitalized in asset value can also be imposed without distorting behavior. A tax will be capitalized if the supply is fixed, and therefore the tax can induce no behavioral response and no distortion. The most well-known tax of this type is a tax on unimproved land. Another tax that some economists argue is capitalized (and others argue is not) is the tax on corporate dividends. Some taxes, such as property taxes, may be capitalized in the short but not the long run; these taxes are distorting.

Finally, taxes that are tied to benefits do not impose their full tax burden or their full distortionary effect. Examples, include the payroll tax, which is tied to social security benefits, and the residential property tax, which is associated with local public benefits.

Distinguishing Between Efficiency and Economic Growth

In the popular debate about taxes there is often some confusion about the difference between the effect of taxes on economic growth and their effect on efficiency. It is important not to confuse these effects. Growth comes at the price of less leisure (if due to increased labor supply) and less consumption (if due to increased savings). These changes are efficient only if the benefits exceed the costs.

For that matter, lowering taxes could actually decrease growth. Higher wages could lead people to work less rather than more (because they can now afford to do so), but their choice of leisure versus consumption would be more consistent with their preferences, given their new income. If rather than lowering tax rates we simply gave individuals a lump sum amount to offset their wage taxes, labor supply would fall even more because individuals could afford to work less via the income effect but would have no offsetting incentive at the margin to work more. Thus, lowering the tax rate increases labor supply over what it otherwise would have been had the relief been granted through a lump sum rebate.

DISTRIBUTIONAL ISSUES

A critical issue for taxation, especially in the context of budgeting, is the relative "fairness" of the current tax policy compared to alternative policies.

Benefit Principle Versus Ability to Pay

Two common standards for determining the distribution of a tax are the benefit principle and the ability-to-pay principle. As discussed earlier, the benefit principle is associated with taxes such as the gasoline tax and perhaps more loosely with the payroll and residential property taxes.

Most taxes are justified on the basis of ability to pay, which simply means that taxes should be levied in accordance with financial capacity, which is most commonly measured by income. Ability to pay has both a vertical equity dimension and a horizontal equity dimension.

Vertical equity refers to the treatment of individuals with different incomes. Although the ability-to-pay standard indicates that high-income individuals should pay more than low-income individuals, it does not clarify whether taxes should be regressive (taking a larger fraction of lower incomes than higher incomes), proportional (taking the same fraction of all incomes), or progressive (taking a larger fraction of higher incomes than lower incomes), except that a tax should not be so regressive that it takes a larger absolute amount from lower income individuals.

Horizontal equity indicates that individuals with the same ability to pay should pay equal taxes. In most cases this issue is straightforward. The most complicated issue is how to treat different types of families and different family sizes. Larger families have less ability to pay than smaller ones (and income taxes include allowances for dependents), but how much less is not easy to ascertain. This issue is further complicated in the federal income tax system because the tax law can benefit or penalize individuals for getting married (even though their living arrangements may not change), an issue that raises issues not only of equity but also of behavioral choice. This marriage benefit or penalty occurs because families are taxed, not individuals—a treatment that is probably appropriate to distinguishing ability-to-pay but that creates problems for a tax system that must rely on legal rather than actual living arrangements.

Horizontal inequities can also occur because taxes apply differentially (such as excise taxes that apply to different commodities) or because general taxes, such as income taxes, are not applied on a broad base. According to the Haig-Simons definition of income that is generally accepted by economists, income is the sum of consumption and changes in net wealth. This definition is also equal to wages plus the earnings on all assets. The main deficiencies of the income tax with respect to this definition, are the exclusion of wage income earned in the form of fringe benefits (such as health insurance) and the failure to tax many types of imputed or unrealized income. For example, the imputed income from owner-occupied housing is not taxed, favoring homeowners over renters. Unrealized income, such as accrued capital gains, is not taxed. At the same time, there is a failure to adjust many types of capital income for inflation.

Distributional Effects of Alternative Taxes

Only taxes levied directly on individuals can be adjusted for income, and only levies on families can adjust for total family income and family characteristics. Currently, only the individual income tax can make full family income adjustments. The income tax is designed to be progressive across incomes, and also to provide relief for family size.

Payroll taxes could be graduated, at least with respect to the individual worker's income, but they are not. In fact, the payroll tax base is capped, so the tax is actually regressive at the higher income levels. In addition, the tax applies only to wage income, which constitutes a smaller part of the income of higher income individuals. (When the entire population rather than the working population alone is considered, however, the payroll tax at the bottom of the income scale tends to rise because of the low-wage incomes of the elderly and of the poor who receive a substantial portion of income from transfers.)

Consumption taxes are proportional with respect to consumption but tend to be regressive with respect to income, because consumption as a fraction of income falls as income rises. Some tax scholars argue that the annual perspective used in most distributional analyses makes the consumption tax look too burdensome on the poor, who tend to have a disproportional amount of individuals who consume large amounts relative to income because of transitory income losses or lifetime characteristics (over the life cycle, consumption is high relative to income at the beginning and end of life).

Presuming that property taxes fall on wealth, the property tax is likely to be progressive because higher income individuals have greater wealth.

Are U.S. Taxes Progressive, Proportional, or Regressive?

A study by Brookings Institution tax scholars Joseph Pechman and Benjamin Okner (1974) that used tax data for 1966 provided a dramatic and easily understandable picture of how the total tax burden is distributed across income classes. In *Who Bears the Tax Burden?* the authors showed that under a variety of incidence assumptions the total tax burden in the United States was roughly proportional across most of the population. Tax burdens rose at the very lowest income levels and at the very highest.

Pechman and Okner used a variety of incidence assumptions, including a base case with assumptions similar to those described earlier. Their findings were a result of a federal tax system that was progressive throughout, although the progression was mild across much of the income spectrum, combined with a state and local tax that was regressive initially and then progressive, but also relatively proportional throughout the middle of the income spectrum.

These findings reflected the mix of tax types. The federal government relied almost entirely on progressive income taxes and payroll taxes that look like an inverted but relatively flat U. The corporate tax tends to be proportional across most of the income range but high at the highest levels. Sales and excise taxes used by the states are regressive, because the rates are flat and lower income individuals consume more of their income. The property tax, like the corporate tax, is relatively flat across the income spectrum, except that it rises at the highest level.

Pechman and Okner also examined a less progressive variant that attributed some of the property, corporate income, and payroll taxes to consumption; the higher tax rates on the lower income classes were more pronounced and there was little progression at the top.

Using a very different type of approach, which estimated income on a lifetime basis and determined incidence endogenously through a sophisticated lifecycle model, Fullerton and Rogers (1993) came to similar conclusions about the tax system for 1984. Although they found the tax proportional through most of the distribution, with an uptick at the top, unlike the Pechman and Okner studies, they found no high effect at the bottom.

Unfortunately, there is no up-to-date study of the overall current tax system (including state and local as well as federal taxes) using the Pechman-Okner approach of looking at current incomes, and even the 1984 study is somewhat dated. The federal tax has undoubtedly become less progressive since 1966 because of the declining importance of the corporate income tax and the increasing importance of the payroll tax. The state and local tax system has grown, but much of that growth has been in state income taxes, which tend to be slightly progressive. These trends thus seem to be offsetting.

The findings for 1984 have probably been altered since then at the federal level by changes that lowered federal tax burdens at the lowest income levels and raised them at the highest levels. These changes included the 1986 tax reform revisions, which increased personal exemptions and standard deductions so as to remove individuals at the poverty level from the income tax and the higher tax rates adopted in 1993.

The Congressional Budget Office (CBO) has prepared distributional estimates for federal taxes alone, otherwise using methodology similar to that of Pechman and Okner. They do assume that the corporate tax falls half on wages and half on all capital, but the corporate tax has become relatively unimportant in the federal revenue system. These estimates are similar to estimates prepared by Gale, Houser, and Scholz (1996).

Table 10.2 illustrates the CBO's findings over time, showing how the tax system became first less progressive and then more progressive since the mid-1980s (when distribution was studied by Fullerton and Rogers). A comparison

Table 10.2. Total Average Federal Tax Rates for Families.

All Families by Income Quintile	Average 1996 Income	1977	1980	1985	1990	1996[a]
Lowest	$8665	9.2%	8.1%	10.4%	8.9%	5.0%
Second	21,578	15.5	15.6	15.9	15.8	14.9
Third	35,536	19.5	19.8	19.2	19.5	19.7
Fourth	53,020	21.9	22.9	21.7	22.1	22.6
Highest	123,749	27.2	27.6	24.1	25.5	28.1
Top 10%	171,047	28.9	28.7	24.4	26.0	29.2
Top 5%	247,596	30.6	29.7	24.4	26.2	30.2
Top 1%	651,274	35.4	31.9	24.5	26.3	32.7

[a]Projected

Source: Congressional Budget Office data, reported in Esenwein, 1996, p. 9.

of the 1996 and 1985 data shows relatively little difference except at the lowest income levels.

Taken together, these distributional studies indicate that the federal tax system is progressive, and that overall taxes are roughly proportional across most income brackets, except at the very highest income levels, where rates tend to be higher. There has probably not been a great deal of change except at the lower and upper income levels, with both effects tending to flatten out the system further. As a result, the tax system can be viewed as roughly proportional and having little effect on the distribution of income across the income classes.

TAX ELASTICITY AND BUDGETARY EFFECTS: DYNAMIC REVENUE ESTIMATION

Tax elasticity (the percentage change in tax revenues for a given percentage change in output) used to be a very important issue at the federal, state, and local levels. If taxes and expenditures tended to grow uniformly with income growth, then there would be no need to be concerned about revenues outstripping or lagging behind expenditure needs.

Prior to the 1980s, the federal tax system was characterized by an elastic base. Revenues from the individual income tax, because it was a graduated tax, tended to rise faster than output. Inflation exacerbated this effect—even if real output were not changing, inflation would cause revenues to rise as a percentage of output. This phenomenon was referred to as "bracket creep."

States tended to experience the opposite effect. States that relied heavily on per unit excise taxes found their revenues lagging behind as prices went up because of inflation. Inflation, and other economic factors, also created a need for a constant reassessment of value for the local property taxes. If localities did not reassess property values each year, property tax revenues would lag as the market value rose, while the assessed value stayed constant.

Federal policymaking, including tax policymaking, was profoundly affected by the elasticity of the income tax. (The payroll tax, a proportional tax, tended to rise with output, and excise taxes, which tend to lag output, were relatively unimportant sources of revenue.)

When inflation was low and the major problem with business cycles was from excess or lagging demand, the income tax acted as an automatic stabilizer, rising and putting the brakes on the economy when growth was too rapid, and declining and acting as a fiscal stimulus during recessions.

The cyclical effects of the income tax became a problem in the 1970s, which were characterized by recessions induced by supply contractions and accompanied by high levels of inflation. During "stagflation" (when there were high rates of both unemployment and inflation), the growth in real income tax exacerbated the recessions and slow growth due to external shocks; and a sustained level of high inflation could cause the income tax to put on the brakes when the economy was lagging.

The additional revenues produced by the income tax during rapid growth or high inflation periods produced a *fiscal dividend.* Although such funds could have been spent, most of the response to the fiscal dividend was to enact periodic tax cuts. These cuts, however, were often not of the precise nature appropriate to offset the effects of inflation, and they therefore changed the tax system in many ways. For example, the personal exemption was unaltered for many years, causing the tax burden to rise on larger families relative to smaller families. Inflation caused the tax burden to shift toward lower income individuals who were pushed up through the tax brackets, and the offsetting cuts were rarely designed to offset these effects.

The transformation of the income tax from one with a high elasticity to one with relatively stable revenue yield as a percentage of output arose from two important pieces of tax legislation. The 1981 Kemp-Roth Act, after allowing a three-year tax cut, provided for indexation of the rate brackets for inflation. With the exception of the personal exemption and a few minor items that were not indexed, the system was insulated from inflation. The 1986 Tax Reform Act completed most indexation (for example, the personal exemption) and greatly flattened the rate structure by effectively adopting two rates for most taxpayers. These revisions not only purged the income tax of most remaining influences of inflation (which had come down substantially in any case), but also dramatically slowed the rise in revenues with real growth in incomes, due to the flatter rate structure.

Federal taxes currently keep pace with inflation, due to a very slight tendency of the income tax to rise because of rate graduation and an offsetting tendency for excise tax receipts to fall.

With the loss of the fiscal dividend, periodic discretionary tax cuts are now no longer needed and revenues do not rise merely because of inaction. In fact, the 1981 tax cuts were eventually partially offset by tax increases (including two bills that followed the original legislation very quickly in 1982 and 1984). These and later tax increases probably would not have been necessary had the fiscal dividend remained. In general, it has been very difficult politically to raise revenues to combat the budget deficits that grew rapidly in the 1980s. Various budget acts designed to reign in growing deficits have led to major constraints on tax policymaking. Many critics believe that the combination of revenue needs and the desire of many politicians to provide tax breaks has led to a tax policy that is largely revenue driven and that is frequently characterized by budget gimmicks that are designed to avoid revenue losses over the budget horizon.

These revenue constraints on tax policy have also intensified the interest in, and in some quarters, the pressure for, dynamic revenue estimates that account for behavioral feedbacks (see Auerbach, 1996, for a discussion). Revenue estimators have increasingly included microeconomic responses (the most visible of these is the assumed increase in realizations of capital gains with lower rates). Large-scale responses such as increases in savings and labor supply have not yet been included, but there is much discussion of this issue. In January 1995, joint hearings were held before the budget committees of the House and Senate; most witnesses cautioned, however, against adopting this form of dynamic estimating. Although most economists would prefer that behavioral responses be incorporated in revenue estimates, many believe that these responses are too small to be of concern, and many also fear potential political influences on revenue estimation, including the exaggeration of supply response to make tax cuts appear less costly.

Like the federal revenue estimators, most state revenue estimators do not tend to incorporate supply side behavioral responses in their revenue forecasts. California, however, has formally adopted such a system, and some states, such as Massachusetts, have informally explored these options.

During 1996, the Joint Committee on Taxation undertook an extensive modeling study, with nine modeling teams estimating the effects of an identical major policy change (a shift to a flatter tax, based on either income or consumption). The results varied dramatically, due to model structure or the explicit or implicit behavioral responses built into the models, suggesting that at this point there is little consensus about the effects of tax revisions in the economic models. Engen,

Gravelle, and Smetters (1997), who participated in the study, explain some of the features in various models that account for supply responses.

PROPOSALS FOR REFORM

Several recent tax proposals have focused on consumption taxes and in most cases propose a flat, or at least a flatter, tax base.

These proposals include direct consumption taxes, retail sales taxes, value-added taxes, and the flat tax (a value-added tax with the wage portion, net of an exemption, collected from individuals and the old wealth portion collected from businesses). Direct consumption taxes would be imposed on individuals in the same way as the individual income tax, but with consumption rather than income as a base. Much of the flat tax would be collected from individuals, but the value-added taxes and sales taxes would be collected only from businesses. There have also been some proposals to flatten the rates and broaden the base of the existing income tax.

These tax proposals, advanced to encourage economic growth and in some cases to simplify tax compliance for individuals, face some serious barriers. All proposals except a direct graduated tax would inevitably shift the tax burden from the rich to the poor; this effect would be especially pronounced with the flat-rate indirect taxes such as the value-added tax and the sales tax. They would make the overall tax system regressive.

Consumption taxes, regardless of their form, also impose a lump sum tax on existing wealth and thus increase the burden of tax on older individuals who have accumulated wealth. Many people would view this sudden shift in tax as unfair, and they suggest transition relief; but transition relief would shrink the consumption tax base and require higher tax rates during the transition period.

The direct consumption tax suffers from a problem with increased complexity, particularly if transition and other relief is allowed. Moreover, the tax rates would have to be quite high to match current tax distributions.

The value-added tax and sales tax proposals would shift the collection of huge amounts of revenue from individuals to businesses, causing a substantial amount of disruption in the economy and requiring a one-time price accommodation to avoid the most serious dislocations. The retail sales tax is also very difficult to administer at high rates, because firms must distinguish between intermediate and final sales and would have a powerful incentive to cheat.

The flat tax avoids many of these problems, although it is still less progressive than the current income tax. And while the flat tax would not require a price accommodation, it would also impose the entire lump sum tax on old capital on equity claims; such a tax could be extremely high (even confiscatory) for heavily leveraged investments.

All of the tax proposals, moreover, face opposition from special-interest groups that are harmed, or perceive that they are harmed, by the shift, including housing suppliers, real estate agents, and owners, insurance companies, state and local governments (who lose the tax subsidy for borrowing), charitable organizations, and firms that are slow-growing or heavily leveraged.

References

Auerbach, A. J. "Dynamic Revenue Estimation." *Journal of Economic Perspectives,* 1996, *10,* 141–157.

Brumbaugh, D. *The Level of Taxes in the United States, 1940–1996: A Fact Sheet.* Report no. 96-812. Washington, D.C.: Library of Congress, 1996.

Council of Economic Advisers. *Economic Report of the President, February 1996.* Washington, D.C.: U.S. Government Printing Office, 1996.

Engen, E., Gravelle, J. G., and Smetters, K. "Dynamic Tax Models: Why They Do the Things They Do." *National Tax Journal,* 1997, *50,* 657–682.

Esenwein, G. A. *The Size and Distribution of the Federal Tax Burden, 1950–1995.* Report no. 96-386. Washington, D.C.: Library of Congress, 1996.

Fleenor, P. (ed.). *Facts and Figures on Government Finance.* Washington, D.C.: Tax Foundation, 1995.

Fullerton, D., and Rogers, D. *Who Bears the Lifetime Tax Burden?* Washington, D.C.: Brookings Institution, 1993.

Gale, W. G., Houser, S., and Scholz, J. K. "Distributional Effects of Fundamental Tax Reform." In H. J. Aaron and W. G. Gale (eds.), *Economic Effects of Fundamental Tax Reform.* Washington, D.C.: Brookings Institution, 1996.

Gravelle, J. G. *The Economic Effects of Taxing Capital Income.* Cambridge, Mass.: MIT Press, 1994.

Harberger, A. C. "The Incidence of the Corporation Income Tax." *Journal of Political Economy,* 1962, *70,* 215–240.

Pechman, J. A., and Okner, B. A. *Who Bears the Tax Burden?* Washington, D.C.: Brookings Institution, 1974.

Rosen, H. *Public Finance.* (4th ed.) Burr Ridge, Ill.: Irwin, 1995.

Tiebout, C. M. "A Pure Theory of Local Expenditures." *Journal of Political Economy,* 1956, *19,* 416–424.

CHAPTER ELEVEN

Addressing Tax Expenditures in the Budgetary Process

Bruce F. Davie

The United States's first *tax expenditure,* a special provision designed to accomplish some objective other than simply raising revenue, was enacted soon after taxes were imposed in colonial New England. To encourage wool production, sheep were excluded from the base of the property tax. Ever since, American tax systems at all levels of government have been full of such provisions.

This chapter begins by introducing the tax expenditure concept, primarily within the context of federal taxation of corporate and individual income but also with respect to other taxes and other levels of government. Using tax expenditures as substitutes for (and sometimes complements to) spending programs is then discussed, along with the use of tax expenditures to influence individual and corporate behavior. The chapter's third section presents criteria for evaluating tax expenditures. Its fourth section analyzes techniques for incorporating tax expenditures into budgetary processes. The final section states three findings and draws a conclusion for consideration by both elected officials and professionals engaged in budget making and program analysis.

Note: The views expressed in this chapter are those of the author and should not be attributed to the U.S. Department of the Treasury.

THE TAX EXPENDITURE CONCEPT

The term *tax expenditure* was popularized by Stanley Surrey, the Treasury Department's assistant secretary for tax policy during the Kennedy and Johnson administrations beginning in the late 1960s (Forman, 1986). Academicians, practitioners, and politicians had certainly been aware previously of the many subsidy-like provisions of the federal income tax, but Surrey was the first public official to prepare estimates of the revenue losses associated with these provisions. These estimates were first presented in testimony by secretary of the Treasury Joseph Barr before the Joint Economic Committee on January 17, 1969, just days before the end of the Johnson administration (U.S. Congress, Joint Economic Committee, 1970). The Nixon administration did not actively pursue the effort to identify, measure, and publicize tax expenditures, but it did, in response to congressional pressure, agree to have Treasury staff work with the staff of the Joint Committee on Taxation (JCT) to produce tax expenditure estimates on an ongoing basis. In the Congressional Budget and Impoundment Control Act of 1974 (Public Law 93-344), Congress took steps to integrate the analysis of tax expenditures into the federal budgetary process, in part by mandating that the president's budget should include a set of projections of tax expenditures (U.S. Office of Management and Budget, 1975, 1996). These projections have been prepared by the Department of the Treasury and published annually as part of the Budget of the United States Government by the Office of Management and Budget. The JCT also publishes a similar list and set of estimates annually (see, for example, Joint Committee on Taxation, 1996b). These two sources have been used to create Table 11.1. (Footnotes within the table indicate items that are on one list but not on the other, items that are not considered tax subsidies under reference tax criteria, and additions to the list resulting from legislation enacted during 1996. The list will have to be revised substantially to reflect provisions of the Taxpayer Relief Act of 1997. All of the relief in this act took the form of new tax expenditures, such as child credits and tuition credits, and expansion of existing tax expenditures. Similar lists have been developed for individual state income taxes and for income taxes in other countries.)

The 1974 act defined tax expenditures as "those revenue losses attributable to provisions of the federal tax laws which allow a special exclusion, exemption, or deduction from gross income or which provide a special credit, a preferential rate of tax or a deferral of tax liability" [Congressional Budget Act, sec. I(b)(3)]. This definition is not self-executing. At best, applying the term *special* requires informed judgment; at worst, it opens possibilities for endless dispute. The act's legislative history indicates that *special* meant a deviation from the "normal" structure of individual and corporate income taxes, without defining the normal structure. The difficulty in precisely defining tax expenditures can be illustrated by examining each of the operative indicia mentioned in the statutory definition.

**Table 11.1. Tax Expenditures in Federal Income Taxes: Estimates by Budget Function,
Fiscal 1997 and 1997–2001 (in Billions of Dollars)**

Tax Expenditure Item	FY97 Individual	FY97 Corporate	1997–2001 Total
National Defense			
Exclusion of benefits and allowances to armed forces personnel	2.1	—	7.9
Exclusion of military disability benefits	0.1	—	0.5
International Affairs			
Exclusion of income earned abroad by U.S. citizens	1.7	—	9.3
Exclusion of certain allowances for federal employees abroad	0.2	—	1.0
Exclusion of income of foreign sales corporations	—	1.5	7.9
Inventory property sales source rules exception	—	3.7	18.8
Deferral of income from controlled foreign corporations[1]	—	1.0	5.6
Interest allocation rules for certain financial operations[2]	—	0.1	0.5
General Science, Space, and Technology			
Expensing of research and experimentation expenditures[1]	*	2.4	14.0
Credit for increasing research activities	*	0.3	1.6
Energy			
Expensing of exploration and development costs:			
Oil and gas	*	0.2	1.0
Other fuels	*	*	0.2
Excess of percentage over cost depletion:			
Oil and gas	0.1	0.5	3.0
Other fuels	*	0.2	1.4
Credit for alternative fuels production	0.3	1.0	6.5
Exception from passive loss limitation for working interests in oil and gas properties[2]	0.1	—	0.3
Capital gains treatment of royalties on coal[2]	*	—	0.1
Exclusion of interest on state and local IDBs for energy facilities	0.1	*	0.9
Credit for solar and geothermal energy facilities	*	0.1	0.5
Credit for electricity from wind and biomass	*	*	0.6
Alcohol fuel credit[3]	—	*	*
Credit for electric vehicles	*	*	0.1

(continued)

Table 11.1. (*continued*)

Tax Expenditure Item	FY97 Individual	Corporate	1997–2001 Total
Deduction for clean-fuel vehicles and refueling properties	*	*	0.1
Exclusion of conservation subsidies provided by public utilities	*	—	0.1
Expensing of tertiary injectants[4]	*	*	0.1
Credit for enhanced oil recovery costs[4]	*	*	0.4
Natural Resources and Environment			
Expensing of exploration and development costs, nonfuel minerals	*	*	0.3
Excess of percentage over cost depletion, nonfuel minerals	*	0.2	1.5
Special rules for mining reclamation reserves	*	*	0.2
Exclusion of interest on state and local IDBs[†] for pollution control and sewage and waste disposal facilities	0.5	0.2	3.2
Capital gains treatment of certain timber income[2]	*	—	0.1
Expensing of multiperiod timber growing costs	*	0.2	1.0
Credit and seven-year amortization for reforestation expenditures	*	*	0.1
Credit for preservation of historic structures	*	0.1	0.5
Exclusion of contributions in aid of construction for water and sewer utilities	—	*	0.2
Agriculture			
Expensing of soil and water conservation expenditures	*	*	0.2
Expensing of fertilizer and soil conditioner costs	*	*	0.2
Expensing of certain dairy and cattle breeding costs	0.1	*	0.8
Exclusion of cost-sharing payments[4]	*	*	0.1
Exclusion of loans forgiven solvent farmers as if insolvent	0.1	—	0.3
Capital gains treatment of certain income[2]	0.1	—	0.7
Cash accounting rules[4]	0.2	0.1	1.1
Commerce and Housing			
Financial institutions:			
Exemption of credit union income	—	0.9	4.7
Excess bad debt reserves of financial			

Table 11.1. (*continued*)

Tax Expenditure Item	FY97 Individual	FY97 Corporate	1997–2001 Total
institutions	—	*	0.2
Insurance companies:			
Exclusion of interest on life insurance savings	20.4	1.2	115.8
Small life insurance company taxable income adjustment	—	0.1	0.5
Special treatment of life insurance company reserves	—	1.8	10.3
Deduction of unpaid property loss reserves for property and casualty insurance companies	—	2.5	15.5
Housing:			
Exclusion of interest on state and local government bonds for owner-occupied housing	1.5	0.5	10.4
Exclusion of interest on state and local bonds for rental housing	0.7	0.3	5.1
Deduction of mortgage interest on owner-occupied homes	41.3	—	220.2
Deduction of property taxes on owner-occupied homes	15.6	—	86.0
Deferral of income from post 1987 install-ment sales[2]	0.7	0.2	5.1
Deferral of capital gains on home sales	18.6	—	95.0
Exclusion of capital gains on home sales for persons over age 54	4.9	—	26.3
Exception from passive loss rules for $25,000 of rental loss[2]	4.5	—	17.6
Accelerated depreciation on rental housing[1]	0.8	1.2	9.0
Credit for low-income housing	1.8	1.0	17.9
Commerce:			
Permanent exceptions from imputed interest rules	0.2	*	1.1
28% maximum rate on capital gains (other than agriculture, timber, iron ore, and coal)[1]	10.5	—	65.5
Capital gains exclusion of small corporation stock[2]	0.0	—	0.1
Exclusion of capital gains at death	15.5	—	91.5

(*continued*)

Table 11.1. (*continued*)

Tax Expenditure Item	FY97 Individual	FY97 Corporate	1997–2001 Total
Carryover basis of capital gains on gifts	1.5	—	8.1
Ordinary income treatment of loss from small business corporation stock sales[2]	0.1	—	0.3
Accelerated depreciation of buildings other than rental housing[1]	1.4	3.2	15.0
Accelerated depreciation of equipment[1]	5.9	22.8	152.9
Expensing of depreciable business property[1]	0.4	0.6	4.9
Amortization of start-up costs[1]	*	0.2	1.1
Graduated corporation income tax rate[1]		4.1	21.5
Exclusion of interest on small issue IDBs	0.3	0.1	1.4
Expensing of magazine circulation expenditures[4]	*	*	0.1
Special rules for magazine, book, and record returns[4]	*	*	0.1
Deferral of gain on nondealer installment sales[4]	0.3	0.4	4.3
Completed contract rules[4]	*	0.2	1.1
Cash accounting, other than agriculture[4]	0.1	*	0.6
Deferral of gain on like-kind exchanges[4]	0.3	0.5	4.6
Exception from net operating loss limitations for corporations in bankruptcy proceedings[4]	—	0.5	2.5
Credit for employer-paid FICA taxes on tips[4]	0.1	0.1	1.3
Deferral of gain on involuntary conversions resulting from presidentially-declared disasters[4]	*	—	0.1
Transportation			
Deferral of tax on capital construction funds of shipping companies	—	0.1	0.5
Exclusion of reimbursed employee parking expenses	1.2	—	6.9
Exclusion for employer-provided transit passes	*	—	0.4
Exclusion of interest on state and local government bonds for high-speed rail[4]	*	*	0.3
Community and Regional Development			
Investment credit for rehabilitation of structures (other than historic)	*	*	0.4
Exclusion of interest on state and local government bonds for docks, airports,			

Table 11.1. (*continued*)

Tax Expenditure Item	FY97 Individual	FY97 Corporate	1997–2001 Total
convention centers, and sports mass-commuting facilities	0.7	0.3	5.6
Exemption of certain income of mutuals and cooperatives[2]	—	0.1	0.3
Tax incentives for empowerment zones, enterprise communities, and Indian reservations	0.1	0.1	2.1
Education, Training, Employment, and Social Services			
Education and training:			
Exclusion of scholarship and fellowship income[1]	0.8	—	4.6
Exclusion of interest on state and local student loan bonds	0.2	0.1	1.4
Exclusion of interest on state and local debt for private nonprofit educational facilities	0.6	0.2	4.7
Exclusion of interest on savings bonds used for higher education	*	—	0.1
Parental personal exemption for students aged 19 to 23	0.8	—	4.4
Deduction for charitable contributions to educational institutions	2.1	0.9	17.0
Exclusion of employer-provided educational assistance[2]	0.1	—	0.1
Deferral of tax on earning of qualified state tuition programs[5]	0.1	—	1.0
Employment:			
Work opportunity job credit[5]	*	0.1	0.4
Exclusion of employee meals and lodging (other than military)	0.7	—	3.7
Exclusion of parsonage allowances	0.3	—	1.6
Exclusion of miscellaneous fringe benefits[4]	5.5	—	30.9
Special provisions for employee ownership plans[4]	*	0.7	4.4
Exclusion of cafeteria plan benefits[4, 6]	5.0	—	32.2
Exclusion of employee awards[4]	0.1	—	0.7
Exclusion of voluntary employees' beneficiary association income[4]	0.5	—	2.7

(*continued*)

Table 11.1. (*continued*)

Tax Expenditure Item	FY97 Individual	FY97 Corporate	1997–2001 Total
Social services:			
Credit for adoption expenses and exclusion			
of employer-provided adoption assistance[5]	0.4	*	1.5
Exclusion of employer-provided child care	0.8	—	5.2
Credit for child and dependent care expenses	2.8	—	14.5
Credit for disabled access expenditures	*	*	0.1
Expensing for disabled access expenditures	*	*	0.1
Deduction for charitable contributions, other			
than education and health	15.3	0.8	88.8
Exclusion of certain foster care payments	*	—	0.1
Health			
Exclusion of employer contributions for			
medical and long-term care insurance			
premiums and medical care	51.5	—	298.0
Medical savings accounts	0.1	—	1.2
Deduction for medical and long-term care			
expenses	4.3	—	27.6
Exclusion of interest on state and local debt			
for private nonprofit health facilities	1.3	0.4	9.6
Deduction for charitable contributions to			
health-related institutions	1.6	0.6	12.3
Special deduction for Blue Cross and Blue			
Shield companies	—	0.4	2.0
Exclusion of medical care and CHAMPUS			
medical insurance for military dependents,			
retirees, and retiree dependents[4]	0.6	—	3.0
Income Security			
Exclusion of railroad retirement system benefits	0.4	—	2.3
Exclusion of workers' compensation benefits	3.8	—	20.0
Exclusion of public assistance benefits[1]	0.5	—	2.5
Exclusion of special benefits for disabled coal			
miners	0.1	—	0.5
Net exclusion of pension contributions and			
earnings:			
Employer plans	70.5	—	380.7
Individual Retirement Accounts	9.3	—	51.8
Keogh plans	3.7	—	20.9
Exclusion of employer-provided death benefits	0.2	—	1.0

Table 11.1. (*continued*)

Tax Expenditure Item	FY97		1997–2001
	Individual	Corporate	Total
Exclusion of other employee benefits:			
Premiums on group term life insurance	1.7	—	8.9
Premiums on accident and disability			
insurance	0.2	—	1.0
Trust income to finance supplementary			
unemployment benefits[2]	*	—	0.1
Additional deduction for the blind	*	—	0.1
Additional deduction for the elderly	1.3	—	6.8
Tax credit for the elderly and disabled	*	—	0.1
Deduction for casualty losses	0.1	—	0.5
Earned income credit[7]	3.5	—	19.5
Social Security			
Exclusion of social security benefits:			
OASI[‡] benefits for retired workers	17.3	—	94.3
Disability insurance benefits	2.4	—	14.0
Benefits for dependents and survivors	4.0	—	22.4
Veterans' Benefits and Services			
Exclusion of veterans' disability compensation	1.8	—	9.1
Exclusion of veterans' pensions	0.1	—	0.6
Exclusion of GI bill benefits	0.1	—	0.6
Exclusion of interest on state and local debt			
for veterans' housing	0.1	*	0.4
General Purpose Fiscal Assistance			
Exclusion of interest on public purpose state			
and local debt	10.5	3.6	78.9
Deduction for state and local income and			
personal property taxes	27.3	—	150.4
Tax credit for business income from Puerto			
Rico and U.S. possessions	—	3.2	18.2
Interest			
Deferral of interest on saving bonds	1.4	—	8.0

* Less than $50 million.

† Industrial Development Bonds.

‡ Old-Age and Survivors Insurance.

[1] Not considered a tax expenditure.

[2] Not included on the list published by the Joint Committee on Taxation.

[3] In addition, $0.54 per gallon excise tax exemption for alcohol fuels results in a reduction in excise tax receipts, net of income tax effects, of $0.5 billion in 1997 and $2.6 billion for 1997–2001.

(*continued*)

Table 11.1. (*continued*)

⁴Not included on the list published in the FY97 budget.

⁵Provision enacted in 1996 and hence not on the list published in the FY97 budget.

⁶Estimates include amounts for employer-provided health insurance, child care, and dependent care also included in other items.

⁷Estimates are for effects of the earned income tax credit (EITC) on receipts. EITC outlays are estimated at $21.6 billion in 1997 and $117 billion for 1997–2001.

Source: Adapted from Office of Management and Budget, 1996, and U.S. Congress, Joint Committee on Taxation, 1996b.

Exclusions. Income can be very broadly defined as the monetary value of the increase in a taxpaying unit's ability to consume during an accounting period (a year, for example), or equivalently, as the unit's actual consumption plus net additions to its wealth. Several exclusions from this broad definition of income have traditionally been left off the list of tax expenditures because a normal income tax would not be expected to include such income in the tax base, either as a matter of administrative convenience or because of intractable problems of measurement. The failure to list exclusion of accrued but unrealized capital gains as a tax expenditure is an example of an exclusion that is part of the structure of the normal tax as a matter of administrative convenience. The rental value of owner-occupied homes and the value of homegrown food are examples of exclusions attributable to problems of measurement. Note also that tax expenditures are, as a matter of practice, identified only with respect to legal economic activity. The de facto failure to tax income generated in the underground economy results in revenue losses, but these are not considered to be tax expenditures. Other statutory exclusions are clear-cut, such as those for interest received on state and local government bonds, workers' compensation benefits, and untaxed social security benefits in excess of individual contributions.

Exemptions. Exemptions are related to the individual taxpaying unit. They are considered to be part of the normal tax structure as a matter of administrative convenience. An example is setting a threshold level of income below which the taxpayer is not subject to tax. More importantly, personal exemptions for taxpayers and their dependents are also not regarded as tax expenditures because a normal tax is expected to differentiate tax liabilities on the basis of family size and structure. Because the extra personal exemptions for those over sixty-five and for the blind were converted into additional standard deductions by the Tax Reform Act of 1986, the only "special" exemption currently listed as a tax expenditure for individuals is the one parents may claim for children aged nineteen to twenty-four who are full-time students. For corporations, the exemption for credit unions is the only listed tax expenditure of this type. Exemptions for nonprofit corporations have never been regarded as tax expenditures (though for a contrary view, see Surrey and McDaniel, 1985).

Deductions. Deductions are related to the use of income by taxpayers. Deductibility of the cost of earning income is, of course, regarded as part of a normal tax structure. Special deductions either adjust the normal tax structure's measure of income on ability-to-pay grounds or create incentives for taxpayers to engage in certain forms of economic activity. The difference between the two types of deductions is in their voluntary or involuntary nature. For example, the deductions for payment of state and local income taxes and for medical expenses in excess of 7.5 percent of adjusted gross income recognize expenses involuntarily incurred that reduce the ability to pay income taxes. Conversely, deductions for the purchase of clean-fuel vehicles are clearly intended as an incentive.

Tax credits. Credits against tax liabilities provide both incentives for taxpayers to engage in certain activities and, in the case of the earned income tax credit (EITC), a mechanism for transferring income to certain low-income families. As incentive devices, credits are to be preferred over deductions because their intensity does not depend on the taxpayer's marginal tax rate. Credits for payment of foreign taxes have never been regarded as tax expenditures but rather as legitimate devices for avoiding the international double taxation of income.

Preferential rates. Tax expenditures also arise from applying reduced rates of tax to income from particular sources, to income of certain taxpayers, or to certain amounts of income. The maximum rate of 28 percent, reduced to 20 percent by the Taxpayer Relief Act of 1997, on capital gains received by individuals is an example of reducing rates on particular types of income. Tax rates below the maximum rate in a progressive set of marginal tax rates on individual income have not been regarded as resulting in tax expenditures. As of 1996, there are no tax expenditures that result from reduced tax rates applied to particular individual taxpayers. A proposal has been made, however, for a flat 15 percent tax rate on the income of residents of the District of Columbia. The generally applicable reduced rate of tax on the first $10 million of corporate income is the only case of a preferential corporate rate. Graduated individual income tax rates are regarded as a mechanism by which the normal tax achieves its distributional objectives. Corporations with incomes below $10 million are not necessarily owned by low-income individuals.

Deferrals. Taxpayers would always prefer to pay their taxes later rather than sooner because of the time value of money. Provisions allowing taxpayers to defer payments (or that charge an intentionally low interest rate on deferred payments) beyond the deferrals necessary for administrative convenience are the final category of tax expenditure. As indicated earlier, deferring the recognition of capital gains until realization has always been regarded as part of a normal tax and not as a tax expenditure. Accelerated depreciation and not taxing the profits of controlled foreign corporations until those profits are repatriated to their U.S. shareholders are examples of deferrals.

Thresholds and aggregations. As a laborsaving convention, the Treasury and JCT staffs do not list provisions unless the revenue loss rises above a particular threshold. In 1996, the Treasury listed items only if the revenue loss was at least $5 million in a year, and the JCT listed items only if the revenue loss rounded up to at least $100 million over five years. Table 11.1 adopts the $100 million rule, thus excluding a few items on the Treasury list, but not on the JCT list. Table 11.1 would be pages longer if it listed every provision of the Internal Revenue Code that meets the definition of tax expenditure, along with every such noncode provision. The noncode provisions would include transition rules provided when tax rules are changed; these are tucked away in revenue acts rather than amended to the code.

Some tax code provisions could be considered as single tax expenditures or as several different tax expenditures. Take the exclusion from income of the interest on bonds issued by state and local governments. The revenue loss from this provision could be considered a single amount but, in practice, estimates are made separately for tax-exempt bonds related to different functional areas, such as bonds for owner-occupied housing. How items are split apart or aggregated reflects the judgments of the revenue-estimating staffs and is in part responsible for some of the minor differences in the lists developed by the Treasury and the JCT.

Negative tax expenditures. There are a few tax code provisions that can be thought of as deviating from a normal tax and leading to revenue gains rather than losses. It has been suggested over the years that these items should be included in tax expenditure lists as *negative tax expenditures.* An example is the failure to allow a deduction for gambling losses in excess of gambling winnings for a person engaged in the business of gambling. Another is the limitation on the deductibility of *passive activity losses,* that is, losses from rental activities or from trades or businesses in which the taxpayer does not materially participate, to the extent that these losses result from real costs, such as interest payments, rather than from tax expenditures such as accelerated depreciation.

Much more important to the definition of tax expenditures and to the possibility of negative tax expenditures is the treatment of the separate tax on corporate income. The United States is said to have a "classical" income tax, that is, one that treats individuals and corporations as separate taxpaying entities. As a result, profits are taxed both at the corporate level and at the individual level when paid out as dividends or reflected in realized capital gains. Many other countries provide some mechanism for integrating individual and corporate income taxes to avoid or mitigate the double taxation of corporate income. If integration of the individual and corporate taxes were regarded as part of the normal structure of income taxation, the double tax that results under U.S. practice could be listed as a negative tax expenditure.

The U.S. practice of treating the separate taxation of individuals and corporations as part of the normal tax structure has led to a number of ad hoc decisions regarding deviations from the classical norm. No tax expenditures have been identified as resulting from the several ways in which corporate income is allowed to flow to individuals without a corporate-level tax being imposed. Thus, treating subchapter S corporations as though they were partnerships is not listed as a tax expenditure, nor is the flow-through treatment of mutual funds, real estate investment trusts, or cooperatives.

The conceptual possibility of negative tax expenditures must be distinguished from the possibility that some estimates of tax expenditures may be negative. That is, any tax expenditure that involves deferral of tax liabilities means that, relative to normal tax treatment, revenues are lost with respect to a particular cohort of transactions in early years and tax payments are larger in later years. Accelerated depreciation is an example of such a deferral provision. If investment is always increasing, the estimates for the provision will always be positive; that is, the extra taxes paid with respect to earlier cohorts of transactions will be more than offset by the revenue losses from contemporary cohorts. But if the underlying stream of transactions is declining over time, the revenue gains from payment of deferred taxes may more than offset the revenue losses from deferrals associated with new transactions, thus producing a negative estimate.

Accounting rules. Any income tax uses accounting rules to identify business outlays that should be capitalized rather than allowed as a current expense. Capitalized outlays must be further segregated into those that can be amortized over time, those that can be depreciated, and those that are neither amortized nor depreciated but become part of the taxpayer's basis. In addition, inventory accounting rules must be specified and determinations must be made as to which taxpayers are required to use accrual accounting and which may use cash accounting. These rules are intended to match as closely as possible the timing of the taxpayer's income and the expenses associated with earning that income without creating excessive compliance burdens on either tax administrators or taxpayers. Because this process is a matter of art rather than science, separately identifying the accounting rules designated as part of the normal tax and the deviations constituting tax expenditures are matters on which reasonable technicians can disagree. The treatment of depreciation and of research and development expenditures has led to some controversy in this regard; these were two of the items involved in the Treasury's 1982 decision to redefine tax expenditures as tax subsidies that were exceptions to the "reference tax."

Defining Tax Expenditures in Terms of the Reference Tax

In 1982, the Treasury argued for a revised definition of tax expenditures: only tax provisions that are "similar to" an outlay program should be called tax expenditures or tax subsidies. First, such a provision must be "special in that it applies to a narrow class of transactions or taxpayers. Second, there must be a 'general' provision to which the 'special' provision is a clear exception" (U.S. Office of Management and Budget, 1982). The general provisions made up the *reference tax* and included, for example, depreciation allowances generally available to taxpayers, graduated rate schedules for the corporate as well as the individual income tax, and all tax accounting rules. If allowable depreciation is accelerated relative to a standard, such as economic depreciation, it was argued, the depreciation provision is nonetheless not a tax subsidy because the economic depreciation standard was not a basic provision of the Internal Revenue Code. Moreover, a direct outlay program could not replicate the economic effects of accelerated depreciation.

The treatment of research and development (R&D) expenditures is another example of the difference between defining tax subsidies relative to a reference tax rather than a normal tax. The expensing of R&D is a basic tax accounting rule and hence part of the reference tax. There is no tax treatment of R&D to which expensing is an exception. Nonetheless, the "traditional" tax expenditure lists always included the tax benefits of expensing R&D costs over the hypothetical alternative of five-year amortization. Some R&D undoubtedly resembles a capital expenditure that is expected to provide value to a firm over several years. Other R&D expenditures generate economic value for only a few months, and some never contribute to the generation of income. Using five-year amortization as a feature of the normal tax is essentially arbitrary.

Note the similarity between R&D spending and advertising. Some advertising is clearly intended to enhance a corporate image and have a lasting impact. Conversely, for example, advertising this week's price of broccoli has no lasting value. The failure of the tax code to require any part of advertising expenses to be capitalized and amortized over time has never been listed as a tax expenditure. In effect, the tax accounting rule that allows all advertising to be currently deductible has been regarded as part of both the reference and the normal tax.

Defining Tax Expenditures in the Context of Other Taxes

Tax expenditures can be identified in systems of taxation other than income taxes. All that is necessary is reasonable agreement as to the tax's normal structure and its special features.

Broad-based consumption taxes. Retail sales taxes, value-added taxes, and expenditure taxes (for which taxpayers file returns, the tax base is income minus current net additions to savings, and progressive rates are applied) are all examples of broad-based consumption taxes. Tax expenditures can be identified with respect to such tax systems (though a returns-based expenditure tax has never been implemented).

If a retail sales tax generally applied to final sales of all tangible goods, including food, but exempted certain commodities (infant formulas, for example) or certain classes of purchasers (nonprofit organizations, for example), those exemptions could be identified as tax expenditures and the revenue losses estimated. If casual sales (such as yard sales) and sales by very small vendors are excluded as a matter of administrative convenience, those exemptions should not be regarded as tax expenditures.

Tax expenditures can be incorporated into a value-added tax regime. Where a value-added tax adopts multiple rates, the identification of tax expenditures is not clear cut. A lower-than-normal rate applied to food, for example, would seem to be a fundamental part of the tax regime and not a tax expenditure. Conversely, a low rate applied only to fish as a way to encourage the fishing industry should then be called a tax expenditure.

In a European-style credit-invoice value-added tax system, exemptions lead to reduced revenues only if they apply at the stage of final consumption. For example, as long as fish retailers are fully subject to the tax, the fishermen's value added is effectively taxed at the retail level. Indeed, exempt fishermen can be disadvantaged because no credit can be claimed for the taxes they pay on their purchases of boats, nets, fuel, and so on. This feature of a value-added tax has been alluded to by its American supporters, who anticipate keeping tax expenditures to a minimum in a value-added tax regime. But this feature ignores the use of zero rating to create tax expenditures. If fishermen are zero rated, they receive a rebate on the tax applied to their purchases of intermediate goods, including their boats; their value added plus the value added that is embodied in their purchases are never taxed.

A returns-based expenditure tax seems as vulnerable to the proliferation of tax expenditures as an income tax. Some items, such as expensing (deducting in the year of acquisition) certain amounts of business investment, that constitute tax expenditures under an income tax regime would not be tax expenditures under an expenditure tax. Expensing of business investment, for example, is an inherent feature of an expenditure tax. But nothing in the basic structure of an expenditure tax would preclude allowing, say, a deduction for charitable contributions or an extra personal exemption for the elderly.

Gift and estate taxes. Since publication of the budget documents for FY90, a listing of tax expenditures associated with the gift and estate (unified transfer) tax has been presented. The executive branch was under no legislative mandate to present such a list of items and estimated revenue losses; they were simply presented for informational purposes. The two big items are the credit for state death taxes and the deduction for charitable contributions. The exclusion for transfers to surviving spouses has been treated as part of the "reference" structure of the unified transfer tax. Estimates from the budget for FY97 are presented in Table 11.2.

Excise taxes. Exemptions from generally applicable excise taxes and lower rates for certain transactions can be thought of as tax expenditures. The only such item referred to in the Treasury and JCT lists is the reduced excise tax rates for gasohol, a mechanism for subsidizing the production of ethanol-based fuels. The excise revenue estimates appear as footnotes to the related income tax credit for producing alcohol fuels. An attempt has been made to identify all the tax expenditures associated with federal excise taxes (Davie, 1994), but neither the Treasury nor the JCT regularly estimates these tax expenditures.

Table 11.2. Tax Expenditures in Federal Unified Transfer (Gift and Estate) Taxes by Budget Function, Fiscal 1997 and 1997–2001 (in Billions of Dollars).

Tax Expenditure Item	FY97	1997–2001 Total
Agriculture		
Special use valuation of farm real property	0.1	0.4
Tax deferral for closely held farms	0.1	0.4
Commerce		
Special use valuation of real property used in closely held businesses	*	0.1
Tax deferral for closely held businesses	*	0.1
Education, Training, Employment, and Social Services		
Deduction for charitable contributions to educational institutions	0.6	3.4
Deduction for charitable contributions (other than education and health)	1.8	10.1
Health		
Deduction for charitable contributions to health-related institutions	0.6	3.2
General Government		
Credit for state death taxes	3.4	19.9

*Less than $50 million.

Source: Office of Management and Budget, 1996, p. 84.

Payroll taxes. Some tax expenditures are found in the payroll tax provisions of the Internal Revenue Code. Several tax expenditures associated with the income tax also create tax expenditures for Social security, Medicare, and unemployment compensation payroll taxes. Specifically, employer-paid fringe benefits, such as health insurance premiums, excluded from employee income are also excluded from payrolls taxable under the Federal Insurance Contributions Act (FICA). Certain classes of workers are also excluded. The concept is not clear-cut, however (Forman, 1993). Excluding certain earnings or fringe benefits from the defined tax base may reduce future benefits, which suggests that any estimate of the revenue loss should be adjusted for its effect on future outlays. Just how to do so is unclear.

Property taxes. Local governments frequently use property tax abatements and reduced rates as elements of social and economic policy. These can be identified as tax expenditures and the resulting revenue losses can be estimated. Special features, such as reduced rates for the elderly or temporary exemptions to attract new businesses, are distinguishable from generally applicable rules such as different ratios of assessed to market values for residential property than for commercial property.

MEASURING TAX EXPENDITURES

The measurement convention adopted as the tax expenditure concept evolved identifies the revenue loss associated with each provision. Such estimates are easily confused with the revenue that would be gained if the provisions were repealed. This section explains the important differences between the two types of revenue and some of the technical issues involved. The logical problems associated with aggregating estimates of tax expenditures are also discussed (U.S. Congress, Joint Committee on Taxation, 1992).

Measuring Revenue Losses

Take a big-ticket item, the deductibility of home mortgage interest, for example. The dollar measure of this tax expenditure is estimated from a model of the individual income tax based on a data file of sample returns. The model is programmed to answer the question, How much would individual tax liabilities increase if taxpayers who itemize were not allowed to claim mortgage interest as a deduction? Interactions with other features of the tax systems are taken into account. This point is illustrated in Table 11.3. If home mortgage interest were not deductible, the hypothetical taxpayers would claim standard deductions instead. Their mortgage interest deductions of $7,000 for 1996 exceed the standard deduction of $6,700 for joint filers. If this were their only itemized deduction, the associated tax expenditure would be determined by increasing their taxable income by $300. Other itemized deductions increase the base for measuring the tax expenditure to the lesser of their mortgage interest or the excess of their total deductions over the standard deduction. In a more complicated example, interactions with the alternative minimum tax (which effectively requires a minimum tax payment by taxpayers who otherwise would pay little or no tax) would also have to be accounted for.

Note that tax expenditure measures are always estimates and never "actuals." Even for a previous year, estimates must be made from tax models. An amount analogous to the dollar amount spent for a particular purpose is never known with certainty.

No behavioral change is anticipated in making these estimates. For example, if home mortgage interest were not deductible, homeowners would use more equity in financing their homes, with the result that less interest and dividend income would be reported, offsetting the effect of eliminating the deduction. Moreover, the estimates do not anticipate any other changes in the tax system,

Table 11.3. Example of Measuring Tax Expenditures: Effect (in Dollars) of Taxpayer Relief Act of 1997 on Hypothetical Married Couple with Daughter, Aged Twelve, and Son, Aged Eighteen, Enrolled in First Year of College, Tuition $4,000.

	Tax Law and Parameters for			
	1996		1999	
Adjusted Gross Income		$65,000		$65,000
Deductions Equal to the Greater of				
Standard deduction	6,700		7,300	
Itemized deductions:				
Mortgage interest	7,000		7,000	
Charitable contributions	500		500	
Property taxes	1,500		1,500	
State income taxes	2,000		2,000	
Total		11,000		11,000
Personal Exemptions				
Four	2,550	10,200	2,800	11,200
Taxable Income		43,800		42,800
Income Tax Before Credits Equal to Greater of				
15% of taxable income	6,015		6,525	
Plus 28% of taxable income				
in excess of	40,100		43,500	
Total		7,051		6,420
Child credit ($500 for each child under 17)		n/a		500
Tuition credit (HOPE scholarship) for first two years of college, first $1,000 of tuition plus 50% of second $1,000		n/a		1,500
Income Tax After Credits		5,820		4,420
Tax Expenditures				
Mortgage interest (tax on excess of itemized over standard deduction, 3,700 at 28% and 600 at 15% in 1996; at 15% in 1999)		1,126		585
Charitable contributions (500 at 28% in 1996; at 15% in 1999)		140		75
Property taxes (1,500 at 28% in 1996; at 15% in 1999)		420		225
State income taxes (2,000 at 28% in 1996; at 15% in 1999)		560		300

Table 11.3. (*continued*)

	Tax Law and Parameters for	
	1996	1999
Tax Expenditures (*cont.*)		
Child credit	n/a	500
Tuition credit	n/a	1,500
Nominal total	2,246	1,185
Total with Interactions (tax on excess of itemized over standard deduction plus credits)	1,126	2,585

such as a higher standard deduction or lower rates, that might be in place if mortgage interest were not deductible.

Estimating Revenue Gains from Repealing Provisions

In popular and political discussions of tax policy, lists of tax expenditures are often searched for "loophole closers" that could be enacted to fund additional government expenditures, reduce deficits, offset the revenue cost of new tax expenditures, or offset a rate reduction or other broad-based tax cut. If this is the purpose to which a list of tax expenditures is put, then estimates of the revenue gained from repealing individual provisions would be more helpful. Such estimates should, at least for major items, take behavioral responses into account (Joint Committee on Taxation, 1992). The problem is that *repeal* can have several different meanings. Again taking the deductibility of home mortgage interest as an example, repeal could be prospective, that is, it could apply to homes purchased (or mortgages closed) after an assumed effective date. Repeal could be "cold turkey," that is, beginning after an assumed date no deductions could be allowed for taxable years. Repeal might also be phased in over a number of years by allowing a declining fraction of home mortgage interest to be deducted, or the allowed size of a mortgage on which interest is deductible might be phased down. Because repeal is not an unambiguous term, establishing a new set of estimates on that basis would require agreement on a convention to use, such as cold turkey as of the next January 1, to actually make the estimates. Estimates based on hypothetical repeals require considerably more effort because behavioral responses must be modeled for each item.

Interactions, Aggregations, and Stacking Orders

The structure of the normal tax has a major influence on the measurement of tax expenditures. High tax rates magnify estimates for exclusions, exemptions, deductions, and deferrals. Estimates for tax credits fall if changes to the normal tax reduce liabilities to the point where taxpayers cannot use credits for which they are otherwise eligible. Some of these interactions are illustrated in the example provided in Table 11.3. Increasing standard deductions, personal exemptions, and taxable income levels that mark the break point between different marginal tax rates, as a result of inflation indexing, erodes the measured value of particular tax expenditure items. As in Table 11.3, part of the effect may be a reduction of the marginal tax rate used to measure revenue loss.

Interactions between the structure of the normal tax and the measurement of tax expenditures were highlighted by passage of the Tax Reform Act of 1986. One analysis concluded that the act reduced tax expenditures by $190 billion, or about 40 percent, with about 60 percent of the reduction attributable to rate reductions and the rest to base broadening through eliminating or trimming back specific tax expenditure provisions (Neubig and Joulfaian, 1988). Tax policy took the opposite direction in 1997 by adding several new tax expenditures and expanding existing provisions.

The revenue loss (or revenue gain from repeal) for a group of tax expenditure items, such as those related to a particular spending function or those that make up a package of reform proposals, can be more or less than the sum of the estimates for the individual items. Interaction among provisions and with other features of the tax code are likely to be pervasive. Consider two tax expenditure items that are special deductions: home mortgage interest and property taxes on owner-occupied housing. Taken together, the estimated revenue loss (or the revenue gain upon repeal) would be less than the sum of the two separate estimates because of the interaction with the standard deduction. Conversely, a combination of exclusion items will be more than the sum of the individual estimates because taxpayers will be pushed into higher marginal tax brackets.

If estimates are to be presented for the individual parts of a package so that they add to the total for the entire package, some stacking order must be used to present estimates of the individual items. The procedure is to estimate each item as if all the changes to the law listed above it were in effect. The estimate for the individual item put at the top of the stacking order could, in principle, be either larger or smaller if moved down the list. Despite all these technical problems regarding aggregation of tax expenditure estimates, popular discussion of tax policy is full of statements in the following form: "In addition to spending $X billion for A, tax expenditures for this purpose total $Y billion." No amount of caveats in the technical literature about tax expenditures prevents the repetition of such statements.

Forecasts and Present-Value Estimates

Both Treasury and JCT estimates of tax expenditures are forecast ahead for five fiscal years. One reason that the two sets of estimates may differ is that they are based on separate economic forecasts. The Treasury estimates are intended to be consistent with the administration's forecast of future outlays and receipts, while the JCT bases its estimates on a macro forecast provided by the Congressional Budget Office.

Sometimes it is important to answer the question, How much revenue loss is associated with this year's activity that is the benefit of a particular form of preferential tax treatment? The answer will depend on the time pattern of the revenue consequences. Some provisions, such as credits, bunch practically all of the revenue consequences into the year in which the economic activity takes place, and others spread out the consequences over many years. In contrast, the revenue loss resulting from issuing tax-exempt bonds may be spread out over thirty years. Present-value calculations can be used to compare two or more tax expenditures with different time patterns of revenue loss. The tax expenditure section in the federal budget documents of recent years has included, for about twenty items in which timing is important, present-value estimates for the revenue losses associated with economic activity in the calendar year.

For deferral provisions the present-value analysis is particularly important because the effect of postponed tax collection is captured. Consider the two flavors that individual retirement accounts (IRAs) come in. Some taxpayers are eligible to take current deductions for contributions to IRAs during their working years. Withdrawals from such accounts during retirement years are fully taxable. Other taxpayers can make nondeductible contributions, in which case withdrawals are tax free. The first group would cause an immediate revenue loss and increased future taxes. The second group would cause a postponed loss, yet the two could be equivalent in present-value terms.

Outlay Equivalents

Some tax expenditures are intended to accomplish policy objectives that alternatively might have been pursued through a direct spending program. To compare such tax code provisions with hypothetical spending programs, a measure of their magnitude other than revenue loss is needed. An appropriate measure would be the outlay amount required to deliver to recipients the same benefit as the tax expenditure. In general, this "outlay equivalent" differs from the measure of revenue loss because outlays usually result in taxable income and because the equivalent benefit would be the net-of-tax income received. For example, if a $1,000 tax credit is provided to purchasers of electric cars, an outlay program could be directed to the same policy goal of encouraging use of alternatively fueled vehicles by giving grants to purchasers (or sellers) of electric cars, but the grants would be taxable income to the recipients. If the recipient were in the 33 percent tax bracket, the grant would have to be $1,500 to deliver a net-of-tax benefit of $1,000. Since 1982, the Treasury has published estimates on an outlay-equivalent basis in the tax expenditure part of the budget documents (U.S. Office of Management and Budget, 1982).

Distributional Analysis

The distribution of tax expenditures by income class is information that the makers of tax policy would sometimes like to know and at other times like to conceal. Much of the heated debate between congressional Republicans and the Clinton administration over tax law changes in 1997 centered on the distributional consequences of modifying existing tax expenditures and creating new ones. Distributional estimates provided separately by the Treasury and the JCT differed significantly, partly because different concepts of income were used to classify taxpayers and partly because the Treasury focused on the fully phased-in effects of policy changes and the JCT focused on effects over a five-year period (Gravelle, 1997).

The annual JCT pamphlet on tax expenditures presents distributions for several major individual income tax items. Taxpayers are classified into nine income classes. The income classifier used is adjusted gross income (AGI) plus elements of economic income that are excluded by various tax expenditure provisions, including those items treated as preferences under the alternative minimum tax. The employer share of payroll taxes is also included in income for this purpose. The items selected for distributional analysis are those that appear directly on individual returns, such as mortgage interest and charitable deductions. The distribution shown for the EITC includes the outlay portion of that refundable credit. The distribution over income classes of the revenue gain from repeal of one of these provisions could be quite different from the distribution of the revenue loss. Moreover, the benefits from a tax expenditure provision that accrue to persons other than the taxpayer are not reflected in the analysis. Tables distributing among income classes the revenue loss from deducting charitable contributions do not reflect the gains to those who benefit from the activities of charitable organizations. Distributional analysis needs to be done carefully and used with caution.

USES OF TAX EXPENDITURES

Almost every year Congress adds to, subtracts from, or modifies the details of tax code provisions on the list of tax expenditures. State legislatures and city councils engage in similar statutory activity affecting the tax expenditures associated with their tax systems (whether a list of them has been compiled or not). Without judging the efficacy of individual items, is there some way to make sense of this dimension of U.S. tax policy? One attempt is to categorize tax expenditures on the basis of the apparent fiscal intent of the individual provisions.

As Substitutes for Spending Programs

Clearly, most of the items listed in Table 11.1 can be viewed as substitutes for direct outlay or lending programs. There are at least three reasons why the legislative process responds to a programmatic objective with a tax expenditure. First, tax expenditures are thought to be self-executing without requiring implementation by a government agency. The strength of the argument varies enormously from item to item. All expenditures require a certain amount of effort by tax administrators; some, such as the low-income housing tax credit, require administrative action on the part of state or local government agencies; and still others convert what would be public administrative costs, in the case of direct spending programs, into burdens on taxpayers in the form of certifications required to claim tax benefits. Taxpayers, of course, willingly endure these burdens to gain tax relief.

Second, tax expenditures give legislators opportunities to respond to perceived social and economic problems (and rent-seeking political pressures) without annually involving the authorization-appropriations process. This power makes tax-writing committees more popular and powerful than if their role were strictly limited to imposing taxes.

Third, tax expenditures have programmatic permanence that often cannot be achieved through direct spending programs. One legislature cannot easily commit the next legislature to continue a spending program; additional appropriations are usually required. Tax expenditures stay in place until they are repealed. The similar technique on the outlay side of the budget of permanent appropriations has been used sparingly, but for major forms of spending, such as social security benefits and interest on the public debt.

Refundable tax credits carry tax expenditures to the logical extreme of surrogate spending programs. With refundability, the effectiveness of the tax provision is not dependent upon taxpayers having tax liabilities to reduce. The EITC, introduced in 1975, was for many years the only tax expenditure to incorporate refundability among its features. For FY97, it is expected to reduce income tax liabilities by $3.5 billion and additionally pay refunds of $21.6 billion.

The congressional appropriations committees were quick to appreciate the significant threat to their jurisdiction represented by refundable credits. In 1978, congressional rules were changed to subject any cash payments resulting from refundable tax credit (other than the EITC) to the appropriations process. As of the end of 1996, no additional refundable tax credits had been enacted. The Taxpayer Relief Act of 1997 did allow the new $500 child credit to be refunded in certain circumstances for taxpayers with three or more children without requiring a special appropriation.

As Complements to Spending Programs

A few tax expenditures are so inextricably interwoven with programs appearing on the outlay side of the federal budget that they are best thought of as complements to these programs. The tax expenditure estimates do not provide a full measure of the cost of the programs of which they are a part. The deferral of tax on savings bond interest is the clearest example of this. The rest of the costs of the savings bond program appear on the outlay side of the budget as accrued interest. Historic rehabilitation tax credits, for example, are allowed only if projects are reviewed and certified by the National Park Service, whose administrative costs appear as outlays.

As Unique Policy Tools

Although most tax expenditures are substitutes for, or complements to, outlay programs, several important expenditures have no programmatic surrogates, or at least no direct spending or lending programs can easily be imagined as doing what these tax expenditures do. Deductibility of charitable contributions is the classic example. A program making payments to thousands of churches and charitable and educational institutions that benefit from this tax provision is hard to envision. Employer-provided fringe benefits, such as medical insurance and pensions, are encouraged by excluding employer contributions from employee income. Whole sections of the Internal Revenue Code and attendant regulations govern the detailed characteristics of "qualified" employer health insurance and pension plans. Direct government provision of health care and retirement income exists in a variety of ways, and could be used more extensively as an alternative to employer-sponsored plans. But if the principle of organizing private pensions and health insurance through employers is accepted as a given, direct subsidies for such plans are hard to envision.

The deferral of taxes accomplished by accelerated depreciation is the equivalent of an interest-free loan from the government. The investment tax credit, first introduced in 1962 and finally repealed in 1986, was the equivalent of the government sharing in the cost of new equipment. A government agency making loans or sending out checks every time a business acquires a piece of equipment or puts a building in service is inconceivable. (Ronald King, 1993, argues that these tax provisions were part of a progrowth strategy designed to move the politics of taxation away from zero-sum distributional battles.) A programmatic equivalent of preferential tax rates on realized capital gains is even harder to imagine. These cases indicate how limiting it is to define tax expenditures simply in terms of provisions that hypothetically could be structured as spending programs.

EVALUATING TAX EXPENDITURES

Economists traditionally use concepts of efficiency, equity, and simplicity of administration to judge taxes. These concepts can also be used to evaluate tax expenditures. (References to some of the literature evaluating individual tax expenditures can be found in U.S. Senate Budget Committee, 1996.)

Efficiency Criteria

Tax expenditures can be judged efficient if their benefits exceed their costs. In assessing costs, both the private and public costs of administering and complying with the provision have to be added to the revenue losses. The revenue losses can be thought of as being offset by other taxes that impose excess burdens. Martin Feldstein (1997) has argued that the deadweight burden caused by incremental taxation needs to be considered in measuring such costs. Measuring benefits is difficult, too. Clearly articulating the objectives of a tax expenditure provision and establishing an appropriate measure of accomplishment are nontrivial exercises. The space constraints of this chapter prevent examining anything other than a single example of the conceptual difficulties.

A 20 percent tax credit is allowed for qualified rehabilitation expenditures with respect to any certified historic structure, defined as buildings on the National Register of Historic Places or certified by the National Park Service as significant to a historic district. The buildings must be used in a trade or business (including rental housing).

To avoid allowing credits for minor renovations, the rehabilitation credit rules require qualifying expenditures to be at least equal to the taxpayer's basis (cost minus prior claims for depreciation) in the property. If reasonable and appropriate rehabilitation expenditures were just a little less than basis, the taxpayer has a strong incentive to spend more (say, by gold plating the faucets) to qualify the entire amount for the credit. This rule works well if an empty shell of a building is being rebuilt, but it may deny credits when, for example, the historically important part of a large building is its lobby. Additional rules distinguish a rehabilitation from a new building and specify how much of an old building has to be retained to claim the credit.

Dollars spent on qualifying rehabilitations would be one measure of the provision's results. Another measure would be the number of buildings (or square feet of floor space) rehabilitated. The objective could be specified more precisely as rehabilitation that would not be undertaken without the credit of buildings particularly important to the nation's cultural heritage. This latter specification requires someone to exercise judgment about the relative importance of particular projects. As this example suggests, defining a measure of benefits from a tax expenditure can be a daunting analytical task.

Equity Criteria

The distribution of tax expenditures by income class has been a traditional way to examine their equity consequences. The annual JCT publication contains such distributions for nine of the major tax expenditures appearing on individual returns. Because some of these items, such as deductions for medical expenditures, casualty losses, and state and local taxes, entered the tax code as attempts to perfect the ability-to-pay concept, their distribution by income class is not terribly significant. Their contribution to horizontal inequity (that is, the variance of tax liabilities within an income class) is intentional. The fundamental equity question is whether such adjustments are appropriate in measuring ability to pay. For tax expenditure items intended to induce certain types of investments, such as the rehabilitation credit, a finding that resulting tax reductions are concentrated in the upper-income classes would surprise no one.

The equity consequences of tax expenditures are best examined in the context of the distributional dimensions of a tax system as a whole. Here the appropriate question is, Are the results of the tax code in its entirety acceptable in terms of vertical and horizontal equity? Often the answer has been no. If persons with high levels of economic income end up paying little or no tax, the results have been judged unacceptable. Rather than repealing tax expenditures in some wholesale fashion, the legislative response typically has been to impose limits: phasing down itemized deductions at higher levels of income, denying deductions for certain "passive activity losses," and imposing a minimum tax in situations where regular tax liabilities are "too small."

A special problem of equity arises whenever the rules governing one of these provisions are changed: Should the new rule apply to current holders of assets, to new holders of old assets, or only to new assets? The answer will determine the extent of windfall losses and gains because tax expenditure provisions often affect asset values. The political process is sympathetic to those who have made investment decisions in good faith and in reliance on old rules. Tax expenditure provisions are hardly ever changed in ways that inflict serious capital losses on holders of existing assets. A clear example of this is tax-exempt bonds. Bonds that carry a low but exempt rate of interest have market values supported in part by tax exemption. When Congress has restricted the purposes for which such bonds can be issued, the changes have always been made prospective, allowing both old and new holders of bonds issued under the old rules to continue to receive tax-free interest.

Simplicity Criteria

Using the tax system to accomplish some specific objective is often defended on the grounds that no new bureaucracy need be created to administer the program. But tax expenditures are seldom truly simple. At one end of the simple-to-complex continuum are provisions such as the additional standard deduction for those sixty-five and over and the deduction for property taxes, which are based on simple facts or a limited number of well-defined transactions. At the other end of the continuum are items such as the low-income housing tax credit (LIHTC), the longest single section in the Internal Revenue Code, which must replicate the terms and conditions of what would alternatively be a complicated direct spending program. In general, narrow purposes and limitations intended to constrain revenue losses result in complex provisions requiring the administrative involvement of the Internal Revenue Service (IRS), other federal agencies, and in some cases, such as the LIHTC, state and local government agencies.

Several tax expenditure provisions require third-party reporting to taxpayers, the IRS, or both. For example, in an effort to improve compliance with respect to the deductibility of home mortgage interest, financial institutions receiving such interest are required to report the amounts. Such reporting requirements add to the cost and complexity of tax expenditures.

Because so many tax expenditures have been criticized as inefficient, inequitable, or lacking simplicity (or all three), several techniques for their control through the budgetary process have been considered by both academics and public officials.

TAX EXPENDITURE BUDGETS AND CONTROLS

In principle, a government's budgetary process should control tax expenditures as well as spending programs. In practice, no government has a budgetary process that directly does so.

Budgeting for Tax Expenditures

What have come to be called *tax expenditure budgets* are simply estimates for a list of items, categorized into the same functional groupings used for spending programs. Amounts spent for particular purposes can be known with certainty. This is not so with tax expenditures. Estimates remain estimates, even for prior years. Limiting tax expenditures in the aggregate or within individual functional categorizes requires tax code amendments. Tax expenditure budgets do, however, serve as valuable sources of information during the budgetary process, helping to give a more complete picture of government activity.

Because tax expenditure estimates cannot be used in a simple, mechanical fashion in a budgetary process, such as imposing an across-the-board reduction, there is no significant consequence to having a particular item on the list or not. If there were, there would be no end to controversy over the definition of tax expenditures, how to apply the definition to particular tax code provisions, and how to do the estimates.

Techniques for Controlling Tax Expenditures

Although tax expenditure budgets have not proven to be a useful device for controlling the revenue losses associated with individual items, a number of legislative techniques have been used in structuring individual tax code provisions to control costs and target benefits. Examples include limiting the home mortgage interest deduction to mortgages of $1 million or less and limiting deductible charitable contributions generally to 50 percent of AGI. Setting thresholds is another technique. Medical expenses are deductible only to the extent that they exceed 7.5 percent of AGI, and uninsured casualty losses to the extent that they exceed 10 percent. Indirect limits have been used to offset the aggregate effect of broad groups of tax expenditures. Sunsets, caps, and certifications are among the direct constrains imposed.

Sunsets. Tax provisions designed to encourage certain activities are often enacted for limited periods, or "sunsetted." Some observers of tax policy argue that sunsets force policymakers to reevaluate provisions before extending their life. Others point out that taxpayer uncertainty about the future of particular provisions vitiates the incentives the provisions were designed to provide. It would be better, they say, to establish a provision permanently and repeal it later if proven unsuccessful. The tax credit for research and experimentation expenditures, commonly called the R&D credit, is an example of a provision that has been turned on and off several times as sunset dates have been passed and subsequent renewals enacted.

Caps. Limits on the revenue losses resulting from some provisions of the Internal Revenue Code have been put in place. The most precise limits apply to the LIHTC, which provides tax credits over ten years to owners of newly constructed rental units for low-income tenants. Annual state-by-state limits of $1.25 per capita are placed on the amount of first-year credits that state housing agencies may allocate to various projects. A similar device is used to limit the revenue loss from tax-exempt bonds issued for a variety of allowable private purposes. An annual volume cap, equal to the greater of $50 per capita or $150 million, on the amount of such bonds can be issued in each state. States have established various mechanisms for allocating the available volume among competing uses.

Certifications. Third-party certifications are used as a device to limit some tax expenditures. For example, as already noted, historic rehabilitation credits may not be claimed unless the National Park Service or a comparable state agency certifies that the quality of the restoration is acceptable. The work opportunity credit, enacted in 1996, may not be claimed unless the eligibility of the persons for whom their employer is claiming the credit has been certified by state employment agencies. For projects to qualify for the enhanced oil recovery credit, petroleum engineers have to certify that these projects meet certain requirements.

Indirect Limits. Concern about the erosion of the revenue base by tax expenditures and the implications for tax equity have led to imposition of indirect limitations on the extent to which taxpayers can reduce liabilities through the use of such expenditures, thereby introducing new layers of complexity. Limiting the deductibility of "passive losses," phasing out itemized deductions at upper-income levels, and applying the alternative minimum tax constrain the aggregate fiscal impact of tax expenditures without eliminating or seeming to trim back particular items. (The estimates in Table 11.1 take these indirect constraints into account.) Political concerns about individuals with high levels of economic income who pay little or no tax and corporations reporting profits to stockholders and losses to the IRS have led to the imposition of these constraints. The complexity of these provisions is a high price to pay for not reducing tax expenditures directly.

Line-Item Vetoes. Presidents gained a new weapon against the proliferation of tax expenditures with enactment of authority to exercise line-item vetoes of provisions of tax legislation that affect a limited number of taxpayers (U.S. Congress, Joint Committee on Taxation, 1996a). President Clinton exercised this new power with respect to two provisions of the Taxpayer Relief Act of 1997. Court tests and further congressional action were expected. Some time is likely to elapse before the utility of this technique for controlling tax expenditures is established.

CONCLUSIONS

Three findings emerge from this review of tax expenditures. First, tax expenditures seem inevitable in complex economies with tax systems determined by popularly elected legislatures. Second, direct and indirect techniques used in tax statutes to control the fiscal consequences of tax expenditures create additional complexity. Third, efforts to limit tax expenditures through a formal budgetary process using dollar amounts in some mechanical fashion, such as setting specific limits on tax expenditures related to categories of direct spending, are doomed to failure because of the definitional vagueness of the concept and the inability to measure revenue consequences with precision.

As long as these findings are valid, a conclusion follows. Continuing efforts to identify, measure, and analyze the tax expenditures associated with all forms of taxation provide information useful to the ongoing process of revising tax statutes and thus determining the receipts side of government budgets. Such information can inform legislative initiatives that both broaden tax bases and simplify tax systems by repealing or revising provisions whose objectives no longer reflect policy priorities or whose consequences are demonstrably unintended.

References

Davie, B. F. "Tax Expenditures in the Federal Excise Tax System." *National Tax Journal,* 1994, *47*(1), 39–62.

Feldstein, M. "How Big Should Government Be?" *National Tax Journal,* 1997, *50*(2), 197–213.

Forman, J. B. "Origins of the Tax Expenditure Budget." *Tax Notes,* Feb. 10, 1986, pp. 537–545.

Forman, J. B. "Would a Social Security Tax Expenditure Budget Make Sense?" *Public Budgeting and Financial Management,* 1993, *5,* 311–335.

Gravelle, J. G. *Distributional Effects of the Proposed Tax Cut.* Report no. 97-669E. Washington, D.C.: Congressional Research Service, Library of Congress, 1997.

King, R. F. *Money, Time and Politics: Investment Tax Subsidies and American Democracy.* New Haven, Conn.: Yale University Press, 1993.

Neubig, T. S., and Joulfaian, D. *The Tax Expenditure Budget Before and After the Tax Reform Act of 1986.* Office of Tax and Analysis Paper no. 60. Washington, D.C.: Office of Tax Analysis, U.S. Department of the Treasury, 1988.

Surrey, S. S., and McDaniel, P. R. *Tax Expenditures.* Cambridge, Mass.: Harvard University Press, 1985.

U.S. Congress, Joint Committee on Taxation. *Discussion of Revenue Estimation Methodology and Process* (JCS-14-92). Washington, D.C.: Government Printing Office, 1992.

U.S. Congress, Joint Committee on Taxation. *Draft Analysis of Issues and Procedures for Implementation of Provisions Contained in the Line Item Veto Act (Public Law 104-130) Relating to Limited Tax Benefits* (JCL-48-96). Washington, D.C.: Government Printing Office, 1996a.

U.S. Congress, Joint Committee on Taxation. *Estimates of Federal Tax Expenditures for Fiscal Years 1997–2001* (JCS 11-96). Washington, D.C.: Government Printing Office, 1996b.

U.S. Congress, Joint Economic Committee. "Testimony of Treasury Secretary Joseph Barr." *Hearings on the 1969 Economic Report of the President Before the Subcommittee on Economy and Government of the Joint Economic Committee,* 91 Cong., 2 Sess., 4–94, 1970.

U.S. Office of Management and Budget. "Special Analysis F: Tax Expenditures." *Special Analyses, Budget of the United States Government, Fiscal Year 1976.* Washington, D.C.: Government Printing Office, 1975.

U.S. Office of Management and Budget. "Special Analysis G: Tax Expenditures." *Special Analyses, Budget of the United States Government, Fiscal Year 1983.* Washington, D.C.: Government Printing Office, 1982.

U.S. Office of Management and Budget. "Tax Expenditures." *Budget of the United States Government, Fiscal Year 1997: Analytical Perspectives.* Washington, D.C.: Government Printing Office, 1996.

U.S. Senate Budget Committee. *Tax Expenditures: Compendium of Background Material on Individual Provisions* (S. Put. 104-69). Washington, D.C.: Government Printing Office, 1996.

CHAPTER TWELVE

Practical Methods
for Projecting Revenues

Stuart Bretschneider
Wilpen L. Gorr

In this chapter, we explore forecasting as applied to projecting revenues in the budgetary process. First we examine the purpose of forecasting in the budgetary process and discuss evaluation of forecasts and forecasting processes. This examination is followed by a critical review of current practices and some prescriptions of practical methods for generating revenue forecasts. We prescribe thoughtful use of data and time-series plots, simple univariate methods (Holt smoothing and time trend regression), time-series multiple regression models, the recording of special-event data, expert knowledge and judgment for handling special events, and maintaining a database that includes forecast errors. Next we describe how forecasting systems operate in organizations, giving specific attention to forecasting revenues for budget development and execution. We also provide evidence that forecast performance is not solely the result of the forecasting methods used but is also a function of the underlying phenomena being forecast, the characteristics of the organizations that generate and use the forecast, and the politics associated with the budgetary process.

REVENUE FORECASTING AND THE BUDGET CYCLE

Figure 12.1 depicts a typical annual budget cycle, highlighting the placement of forecasting activities. Most state and local governments initiate their budget cycle with early revenue projections that typically occur six months before the

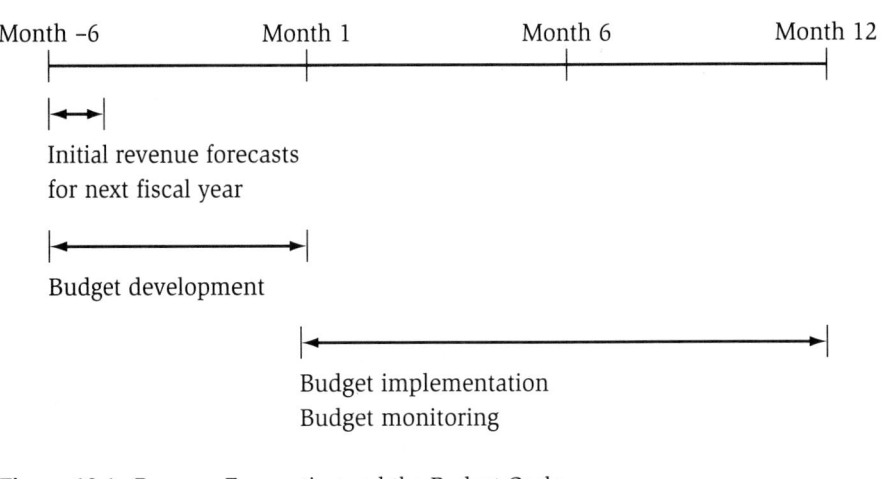

Month –6   Month 1   Month 6   Month 12

Initial revenue forecasts
for next fiscal year

Budget development

Budget implementation
Budget monitoring

Figure 12.1. Revenue Forecasting and the Budget Cycle.

start of budget implementation. In a survey of state governments, Klay and Grizzle (1986) found that a six-month lead time was the modal response, with approximately one-third of the responding states reporting that such projections took place less than six months before implementation, and another third stating that they occurred more than six months before implementation. Because of the extensive lead time generally associated with initial projections, revisions can occur several times prior to the final enactment of the budget law. In addition to forecasting for and within a budget cycle, many governments forecast over a three- to five-year period for strategic planning purposes. In total, then, there are three primary revenue forecasting activities that differ in terms of forecast horizon:

Budget forecast monitoring is done in the short run, with a horizon of a few months to a year ahead. For example, in the seventh month of a budget cycle the forecaster needs to prepare forecasts by revenue stream one month ahead, two months ahead, and up to five months ahead. Then the seven months of actual data plus the five months of forecasts can be added together for each revenue stream and compared to the target annual forecasts published in the budget. Questions to be answered during the monitoring process include *Does it look like revenue collections will proceed as forecast in the annual budget?* and *Will there likely be a shortfall or surplus?*

The *annual budget forecast* is based on annual data and projected from twelve to eighteen months ahead of the end of the fiscal year to be forecast. Because the budgeting process begins up to six months prior to the new fiscal year, the first task is to use the budget forecast monitoring system to fill out the current year's monthly data to yield an estimated current annual data point for each revenue stream. Then the annual data time series for each revenue stream can be forecast one year ahead. Questions to be answered are *What is the upper limit on the sum of budget allocations for the coming year?* and *What will be the effect of a change in tax policy?*

The *budget planning forecast,* a three- to five-year forecast, is based on annual data. This kind of forecast is used for strategic decision making, to examine the long-range consequences of changes in the economy and in government policies. Questions for budget planning include *What are the effects of a tax-rate freeze? How will the loss of federal grants affect revenues?* and *What will be the impact of large commercial or housing development projects?*

REVENUE FORECASTING METHODS

Current forecasting practices used by governments vary dramatically. Typically, larger governments that have highly complex revenue systems and great amounts of resources use complex statistical approaches relative to smaller jurisdictions, which rely on human judgment. Three broad classes of forecasting methods are used in state and local revenue forecasting: human judgment, time-series extrapolative methods, and regression-based models. Within each of these classes there are simple as well as complex techniques. Human judgment includes a single person making an educated guess as well as a board of economic advisers pooling their judgment using a formal process. Time-series extrapolative approaches span the use of straight-line extrapolation as well as complex autoregressive integrated moving-average (ARIMA) models. Finally, the most common approaches use multiple regression models that include variables forecast at the national level, such as gross national product and personal disposable income, as correlates of revenues at the state or local level. A few states have developed more complex causal forecast models, often using multiple interrelated relationships. Finally, because forecasting is truly a pragmatic activity, many forecasters combine analytic techniques with judgment to generate forecasts.

The empirical literature on forecasting methods has grown to be quite large over the past twenty years. Although a great number of complex forecasting methods have been devised, as noted earlier, fortunately one of the major results of comparative research on forecasting methods has been that simple methods are generally as accurate as or even more accurate than complex methods. This fact has struck a blow to methodologists, but it is good news for practitioners. Our first decision, therefore, on structuring this section of the chapter was to limit it to simple forecasting methods.

Our second decision was that this section would not delve into technical details but would instead identify and discuss major concepts on forecasting methods and make general prescriptions. Technical details are encoded into software and there are many sources of technical knowledge. The goal here is to provide guiding principles on which methods to use and under what circumstances.

Our third decision was to recognize that federal revenue forecasters are likely better equipped—in terms of staff, expertise, established methods, and so on— for revenue forecasting than state revenue forecasters, who in turn are likely better equipped than local government revenue forecasters. Although the material covered in this section will benefit any public sector revenue forecaster, the chapter is targeted more at state-level forecasters and even more at local government forecasters. More specifically, this section does not cover the simultaneous equation econometric models commonly used in macroeconomic, federal revenue, and some state revenue forecasting.

Fourth and last, this section deals only with initial technical forecasts and not with any of the issues related to adjustments for good management practices (that is, conservative forecasting) or for political purposes. There seems to be no limit to human ingenuity in adjusting forecasts. Whatever the motive for such adjustments, it is necessary to start with an accurate technical forecast.

Regardless of the complexity of the forecasting method or the level of government considered, there are three major dimensions for classifying revenue forecasting methods:

- Forecast horizon of short-term versus long-term forecasts
- Randomness and stable versus dynamic environments
- Objective versus subjective forecasting methods

Forecast Horizon

As forecasts look farther into the future, they are generally less accurate. As time passes there are more opportunities for change and for the unforeseen to occur. Experiments have forecast many time series over many origins (starting points) and many horizons (lengths of series). The results reveal a tendency for the first-step-ahead forecast (the period after the origin) to be the most accurate, the second-step-ahead forecast to be the second most accurate, and so on. Of course there are exceptions in which distance forecasts are more accurate than nearby ones.

Accuracy is always important in forecasting, but less so for long-term forecasting, in which exploration of alternative scenarios through "sensitivity analyses" and "what-if analyses" are needed to inform policymakers. Strategic planning forecasts need to be based on causal models with policy-relevant independent variables that can be manipulated, forecast, and understood in terms of the economy and government actions.

Randomness

There are two kinds of randomness to deal with in forecasting. The first kind is the variance of the error term of a well-specified statistical model in a stable environment. Many unexplained forces act randomly on the revenue stream of interest and cause period-to-period fluctuations best thought of as random draws from a distribution centered on zero. Randomness is the reason that forecast models are means or conditional means. Forecasts are more likely to be accurate when extrapolating from a mean level rather than from the last data point itself, because any data point has a random component that is not reliable. If, therefore, you make your budget forecast by adding a percentage change to the most recent year's tax collections, you are probably making an unnecessary error! It is generally more accurate to add a change to the most recently fitted mean value from a good model.

The second kind of randomness results from structural or pattern changes in revenue time series caused by policy changes or major economic events, such as major plant closings. The basic patterns that such events generate are impulse (a one-time large deviation—not really a pattern change but the threat of such a change), step-jump, time-trend slope change, or turning point (such as a positive time trend turning into a negative one). Structural changes can occur in univariate time series of a revenue stream, or in the coefficients of a multiple regression model for a revenue stream.

These situations produce the exceptions to the rule of using a mean as the basis of forecasts. If the economy has just experienced a step-jump change or turning point and you are convinced of it, you may be better off using the most recent data point as the model. Any mean estimate incorporating historical data, without manual adjustments (to be illustrated shortly), will be biased to the irrelevant past.

The causes of structural changes are discrete (or special) events that are too large to be considered part of the error term of random noise. Special events may be due to government policies (such as elimination of certain exemptions in a tax base), administrative changes (such as replacement of faulty water meters), or external economic changes (such as the closing of a factory). Special events should be collected and put into a database, along with time-series data (Gorr, 1986). If the same special event has an impact on other governmental units, you might want to compare notes with them to confirm that you have entered a new era.

The smaller the economy that is generating tax and fee revenues, the smaller will be the aggregation of receipts and the greater will be the chances that special events will occur and cause time-series pattern changes. A local government may have step jumps when a factory opens or closes, when properties are reassessed, when a shopping mall opens, and so on. Local governments therefore tend to have more special events and time-series pattern changes than state governments; furthermore, state governments tend to have more pattern changes than the federal government. The business cycle of the federal economy, in contrast, changes relatively smoothly.

When a structural change occurs, forecasters have to recognize it and change the parameters of the underlying forecast model, or discard old, irrelevant data belonging to an earlier economic regime. The way this can be done while forecasting is through visual examination of time-series plots for each revenue stream.

We strongly recommend that you always examine time-series plots of actual data, estimated values, and forecasts on the same time-series graph, using one graph for each revenue stream. If you do not do this, you are making a serious mistake, especially if you are using forecasting software, which can produce bizarre results for data with pattern changes. The number of data points available and relevant to examine are at most only fifteen or twenty-five per annual time series, so you can easily see and think about each data point and the entire series.

Univariate Time-Series Models

The first kind of objective model to examine and use is the *univariate* or *extrapolative time-series model*. A univariate model uses the revenue stream or base of interest as the dependent variable, and a time index (such as 1, 2, 3, and so on) and seasonal indicators (such as $I_1 = 1$ for January, 0 otherwise; $I_2 = 1$ for February, 0 otherwise; and so on for monthly data) as the independent variables. The components of univariate models include constant (or level at a given point in time), slope for a linear time trend (constant change per time period), sometimes coefficients for time (perhaps squared or to other powers of time), seasonal indicators, and an error term.

For budget monitoring and annual budget forecasts, univariate forecasts will likely be as accurate as or more accurate than any other type of forecast. The reason is that an economy is like a large ship—hard to turn quickly from its current course. The univariate methods accurately capture the current course as a mean function for extrapolation. Nevertheless, forecasters may prefer to use regression or other multivariate models, especially for large revenue streams that have public scrutiny, because such models have built-in explanatory powers through interpretation of independent variable trends.

To use a univariate time-series model you need at least five or six annual data points from a stable time series (Lee, 1990) or two to three years of monthly data. If there are special events, you can make some manual adjustments to regression or smoothing. To forecast, one simply extrapolates by substituting future values of the time index and seasonal indicators in the estimated model. If there are known special events in the forecast period, you can collect relevant data, make back-of-the-envelope estimates of its effects, and adjust forecasts.

There are a great many sophisticated univariate forecast models. For example, there are the *Box Jenkins models,* which are difficult to use and understand but generally do not offer superior forecast accuracy; *the Multi-State Kalman Filter,* which is a sophisticated Bayesian model for modeling pattern changes but performs poorly in practice; *Parzen's model,* which incorporates long- and short-term components and does seem to perform well with sufficiently large sample sizes; and so on (Makridakis and others, 1982). Most sophisticated univariate models are generally inappropriate for revenue forecasting, because revenue time series are typically short, with sample sizes that are too small for estimation of the many parameters of complex models.

There is a large literature on combining forecasts by simply averaging the forecasts from different models (see Clemen, 1989, for a literature review). A combination of many data sets and forecasts is often more accurate than any single forecast. Our belief is that the revenue forecaster is better off using one of a few alternative simple forecast models, because it is then possible to adjust forecasts for special events.

For both the monitoring and annual budget forecasting problems, we recommend that you use two simple models: *time trend regression* and *Holt's two-parameter, time-trend exponential smoothing model* with seasonal factors (Makridakis and Hibon, 1979). You may even consider using these two models for budget planning. The regression model estimates a single model for all input data points used. Holt's model is self-adaptive and "drifts" or changes the estimated model to follow pattern changes, but with some lag. Figures 12.2 and 12.3 use simulated data to illustrate the two recommended models (these data look a lot like real revenue data that we have forecast). Figure 12.2 provides the simulated actuals, estimates, and forecasts for a step-jump case using three forecast models. Figure 12.3 does the same for a turning point case. Details for generating the simulated data in Microsoft Excel are in the chapter's Appendix A. Equations and procedures for calculating the Holt model, also implemented in an Excel spreadsheet, are in Appendix B. The regression estimates were made in Excel using the regression data analysis tool.

The top graph of Figure 12.2 illustrates what could happen if a forecaster were to use a straight-line regression model, ignoring the step jump up at time period 7. The single straight-line estimate passes through all twelve historical data points as best as it can, fitting best at the end points of the time series. The estimated model appears to fit the data well for time periods 10 through 12, but in fact it has too large a slope. Hence the forecast for time periods 13 through 15 (seen as the dashed line for these time periods) is too high, yielding a forecast mean square error (MSE) of 14.6 over the three forecasts.

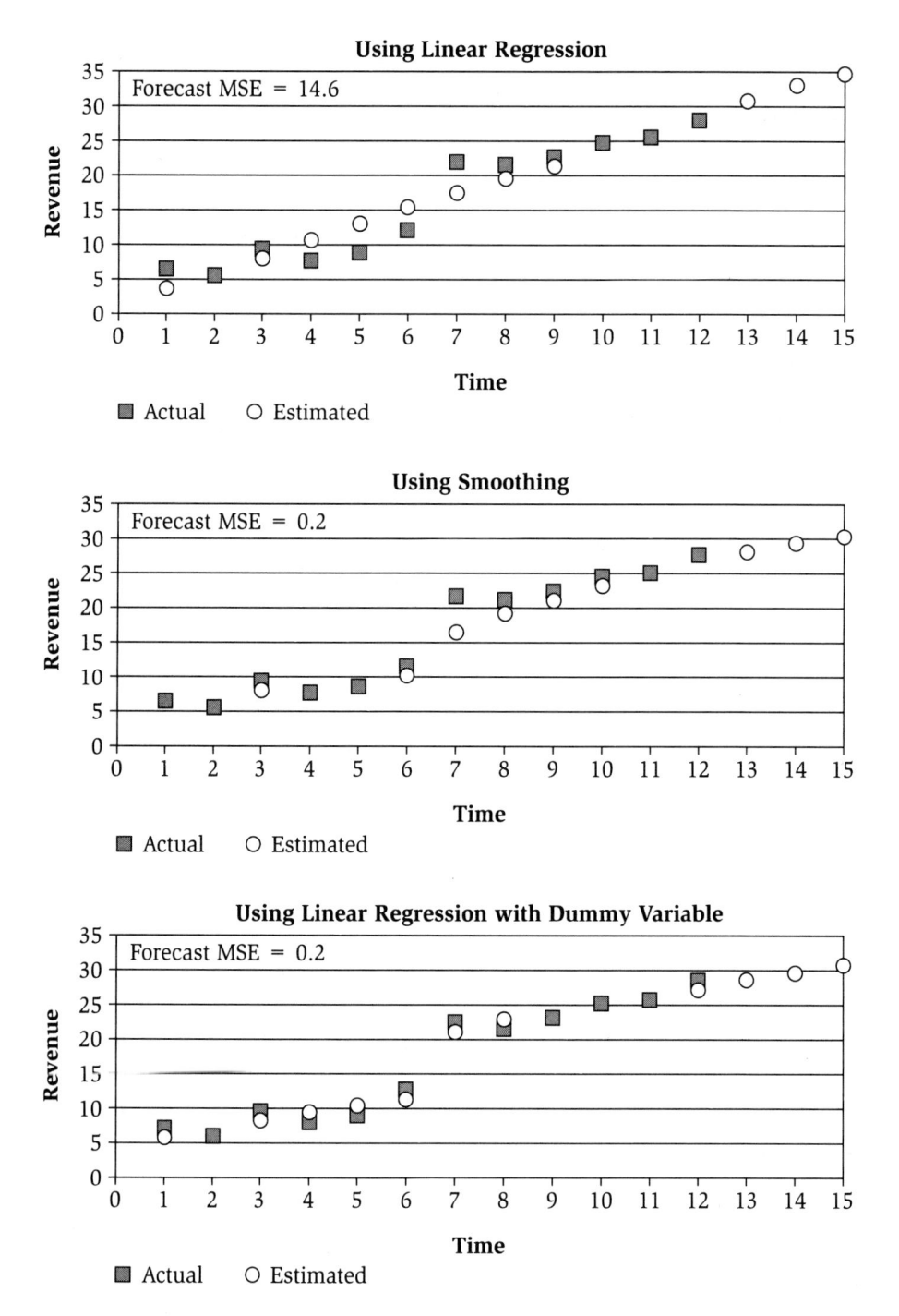

Figure 12.2. Univariate Forecasts: Step-Jump Case.

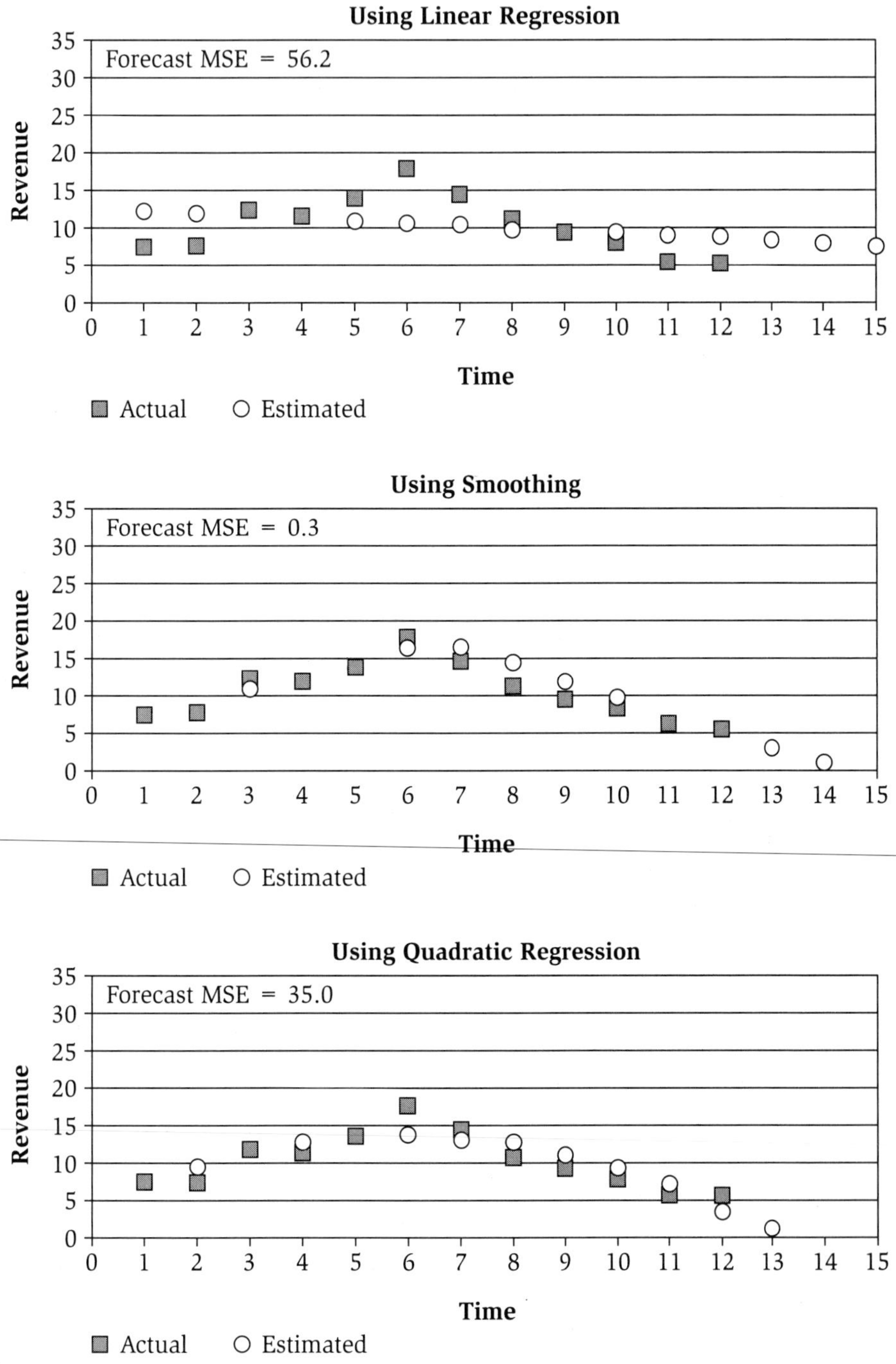

Using Linear Regression
Forecast MSE = 56.2
Revenue
35
30
25
20
15
10
5
0
0 1 2 3 4 5 6 7 8 9 10 11 12 13 14 15
Time
Actual
Estimated
Using Smoothing
Forecast MSE = 0.3
Revenue
35
30
25
20
15
10
5
0
0 1 2 3 4 5 6 7 8 9 10 11 12 13 14 15
Time
Actual
Estimated
Using Quadratic Regression
Forecast MSE = 35.0
Revenue
35
30
25
20
15
10
5
0
0 1 2 3 4 5 6 7 8 9 10 11 12 13 14 15
Time
Actual
Estimated

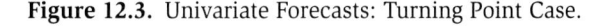

Figure 12.3. Univariate Forecasts: Turning Point Case.

The middle graph illustrates estimates and forecasts for Holt's smoothing. Values for smoothing constants used here were 0.5 for the level and 0.05 for the slope. Values were chosen by varying these two values as parameters while observing the data and fitted values on a graph. The low value for the slope smoothing constant uses the observation that the slope is not affected by the jump, but the high value for the level smoothing factor is necessary to adapt the model level quickly after the jump. The major observation to make here is that Holt adapts itself to the step jump, two periods after the jump, and then makes an accurate forecast with mean squared error 0.2.

Finally, the last graph in Figure 12.2 adds a second independent variable to the regression model that is 0 for time periods 1 through 6 and 1 thereafter. This allows the regression model to estimate the step jump accurately (forecast MSE = 0.2). This model also forecast accurately even for historical data that ends at time period 7 for forecasting time periods 8 through 10, although this result is not displayed in the figure. So, if as a forecaster you know that income has taken a step jump up at time period 7 because of a new factory opening, and if you believe that the time trend will be unaffected (perhaps as a conservative estimate), you could start forecasting using an estimated model as early as time period 7 as the forecast origin in the new economic regime. A forecast at time origin 6 needs an estimate based on the special event of time period 7, obtained by contacting the personnel division of the new factory, getting data on payrolls, number of employees transferring in, and so on, to estimate the step up.

When only one of the two parameters of the time trend change (intercept or slope), some special-event knowledge and simple regression are attractive approaches for forecasting. If the case were different and the slope were to change, too—to increase, for example—after time period 7, then Holt smoothing becomes attractive. You cannot change both the intercept and the slope at the same time in a regression model, but you can do so with Holt. (An alternative to using regression in this case with a forecast origin of period 11 or 12 and later is to discard data before time period 7; you need at least 5 or 6 data points for a straight-line, annual time series.)

The second case, the turning point, shown in Figure 12.3, is a good application for Holt smoothing. The top graph of the figure is, again, the consequence of using the wrong model. A simple straight line fits and forecasts very badly (forecast MSE = 56.2). The middle graph illustrates the smoothing model, with both smoothing constants at 0.5, allowing rapid modification of both the level and slope parameters. Here Holt lags the actual data a bit after the turning point but locks onto the right trend by time period 10 and makes an accurate forecast (MSE = 0.3). The last panel modifies the regression model by adding a quadratic term (using t^2 as a second variable). Here the fitted model is a parabola and seems to fit fine. Yet it produces an intrinsically bad forecast model, because an overturned parabola decreases at an increasing rate and the simulated data are linear and decrease at the same rate. Hence the regression model underforecasts badly (forecast MSE = 35.0).

MULTIVARIATE TIME-SERIES MODELS

Let us take the case of forecasting a state's auto sales tax collections. A univariate time-series model estimates and forecasts total auto sales tax collections as a function of time alone. Now suppose that you have information that auto prices are going to decrease significantly, say by 10 percent, because of increased competition. How do you factor that information into a univariate forecast? Of course you think that auto sales and taxes will increase, but by how much? The univariate model gives no clue on how to estimate the magnitude of increase.

If, however, you have a multivariate time-series model that includes a weighted average price index of new cars, you would have a direct means of forecasting the impact of a price decrease. There are, however, other independent variables that affect car sales. Suppose your state has an increasing number of registered drivers—that too is a factor. Suppose household income is increasing but interest rates are increasing as well. Finally, suppose the average age of cars inspected in your state, lagged by six months, is increasing. How might all these factors combine to affect revenues? You reason that auto sales taxes increase as the number of drivers increases, increase with increasing income, decrease with increasing interest rates, and increase with increasing lagged auto age. Using historical time-series data on sales revenues, auto price index, number of registered drivers, disposable household income, interest rates, and lagged auto age, a regression model would estimate a coefficient translating each independent variable into a component of auto sales and therefore of tax collections.

This sounds very good so far. Suppose you have estimated such a model. To use it for forecasting, you have to forecast each independent variable. You can use industry sources to provide a judgmental decrease in prices; you can calculate a forecast price index; you can build univariate time-series models for number of drivers and auto age and forecast them yourself; and you have access to forecasts of disposable income and interest rates from a macroeconomic forecasting service. With all of these inputs assembled, you then simply plug your forecast independent variables into your estimated regression equation to make forecasts. In explaining your forecasts, which show a marked increase in auto sales taxes, you can use your decomposition of auto sales taxes by independent variables with the expected changes in each independent variable to make a convincing argument.

What can go wrong with this approach (Armstrong, 1985)? First, your model may simply explain too little of the overall variation in your data to provide useful forecasts. If randomness is large and explained variation is low, then your forecast will be fairly constant, even with sizable changes in independent variables, and forecast accuracy will be low.

Second, even if your model explains a lot of the variation in historical data, you need estimates for your independent variables that accurately provide the marginal change in sales tax collections for changes in each independent variable. Unfortunately, the historical data you used to estimate your model are not from an experiment in which each independent variable is varied one by one, holding all other independent variables constant. Instead the independent variables are likely collinear—in the past, several independent variables changed together in related ways. Hence the information available in observational data is likely insufficient to separate the individual effects of each variable, making coefficient estimates unreliable. You can run standard diagnostics to see if such multicollinearity exists.

Third, you need accurate forecasts for independent variables. The forecasting problem is compounded by having to forecast all independent variables, but that is fine as long as you can do it accurately. The record of macroeconomic forecasts (which are based on simultaneous equation models) is mixed at best, even at the national level. Ashley (1988) examined the accuracy of such forecasts during the turbulent early 1980s and found that "most of the forecasts of most of the variables are so inaccurate beyond a couple of quarters ahead as to be essentially useless as inputs to forecasting models. On average one would be better off eliminating X as an explanatory variable altogether" (p. 364).

Fourth, even if you have a good model with accurate marginal estimates for independent variables, there may be too little change in independent variables to make a difference in forecast accuracy. It might be just as accurate to forecast auto sales taxes using a univariate forecast model. As stated earlier, an economy is like a large ship under way: it takes a lot to move it off its current course. All factors may just net out into a smooth time trend that a univariate model does very well on. So, simple extrapolation may be as accurate as or more accurate than a regression model. As forecast horizon increases, so do the chances of relatively large changes in independent variables, and therefore so do the relative merits of a multivariate forecast. It may also be harder, however, in this case, to forecast the independent variables accurately.

What if the underlying structure of your model changes? Suppose the effects of a lot of variables change as car leases become a major new way of obtaining cars. The problems are much the same as with adjusting univariate models, but instead of two parameters to change (level and time trend slope) you have several to consider (six in this case). In the short run, it may be better to switch to an adaptive univariate model that has only two parameters to change that you can start tracking sooner. You can also judgmentally change multiple regression coefficients—at least there are only six of them and you can easily examine and modify them with predictable outcomes.

In summary, while in some cases (such as for state sales tax revenues) multivariate forecasting seems to improve forecast accuracy, it also requires a lot of skill and thoughtful analysis.

MANAGING UNCERTAINTY IN REVENUE FORECASTING

Empirical evidence suggests that most governmental units have historically generated conservative forecasts that tend, on average, to be below actual receipts (Feenberg, Gentry, Gilroy, and Rosen, 1989; Gentry, 1989; Cassidy, Kamlet, and Nagin, 1989; Bretschneider and Gorr, 1987, 1992b; Bretschneider and others, 1989; Larkey and Smith, 1984; Kamlet, Mowery, and Su, 1987; Gorr and others, 1992; Shkurti and Winefordner, 1989). Several theories have been put forth in explanation. One theory is that budget managers have asymmetrical loss functions for forecast errors, leading to conservative forecasts (Larkey and Smith, 1984; Bretschneider and Schroeder, 1988). This view notes that shortfalls are more costly than surpluses, leading to the argument that an optimal strategy for managing uncertainty in revenue projections is to announce a forecast that is a little less than the expected level of revenues. The empirical effect of this strategy is to generate a pessimistic bias in revenue projections (Bretschneider and Gorr, 1987; Bretschneider and others, 1989).

An alternative argument is that most error and bias in revenue projections is generated by economic cycles and that no systematic managerial efforts are present to bias revenue projections (Cassidy, Kamlet, and Nagin, 1989). Though there has been some debate about the extent to which buffering is motivated by political concerns (Larkey and Smith, 1984) rather than economic cycles (Cassidy, Kamlet, and Nagin, 1989), there is significant empirical evidence that revenue projections incorporate some form of buffer into the process. Bretschneider, Bunch, and Gorr (1992) found similar consistent revenue forecasting bias in local government forecasts. Gorr, Kamlet, Lee, and Bretschneider (1992) found little support for either weak or strong economic rationality in local school board revenue forecasts. They instead found empirical support for organizational and managerial influences that created pessimistic revenue forecast biases.

Bretschneider and Gorr (1992b) attempted to consider more complex political, economic, and organizational forces on bias in revenue forecasting. Supporting work by Larkey and Smith (1984) and by MacManus and Grothe (1989) found that fiscal stress (a form of economic uncertainty) interacted with political cycles and that power dramatically altered the shape and character of revenue forecast bias. Conservative states tended to overforecast revenues when fiscal stress was latent, but once fiscal stress becomes manifest, these states became extremely conservative and underforecast revenues. This flip-flop was not symmetrical; the conservative response to manifest fiscal stress was significantly greater than the overforecasting done during only latent levels of stress. This work also found that policy associated with how forecasts are produced does not automatically generate underforecasts of revenue. An underforecast of total revenues is seen by some as a good management practice because it builds in a buffer or cushion, while others argue that such a practice is a form of governmental deception played on the public.

Another approach to dealing with uncertainty in initial revenue forecasting is to monitor actual receipts during the budget execution phase and revise revenue forecasts using the more recent information. Repeated and revised revenue forecasts are used to prepare decision makers for the necessary actions associated with managing the results of various forecast errors as they become evident. This process of revision occurs during budget execution and has led to the prescription to forecast both early and often. As the forecast horizon decreases and the amount of actual collected revenues becomes better known, both bias and magnitude of forecast error should decrease.

FORECASTING ORGANIZATIONS

Figure 12.4 provides a general model for understanding the elements of a forecasting system that is particularly associated with the budgeting process. No one uniform organizational approach to revenue projection exists in government. In small political jurisdictions one individual may be responsible for all forecasting activities, while in larger units several distinctive organizations may have some responsibility for generating revenue projections (Klay and Grizzle, 1986; Mocan and Azad, 1995).

Nevertheless, the major elements of a good revenue projection process need to include data management, model identification, estimation and use, organizational factors, and evaluation. Although many of these activities cross the organizational boundary between the formal forecasting system and the rest of the organization, the core internal technical functions include model identification and selection and forecast evaluation.

Data Management

By data management we mean the formal procedures the governmental unit uses for collecting, organizing, and maintaining data. Financial information systems track all receipts and expenditures on the basis of a transaction accounting

Organizational Environment

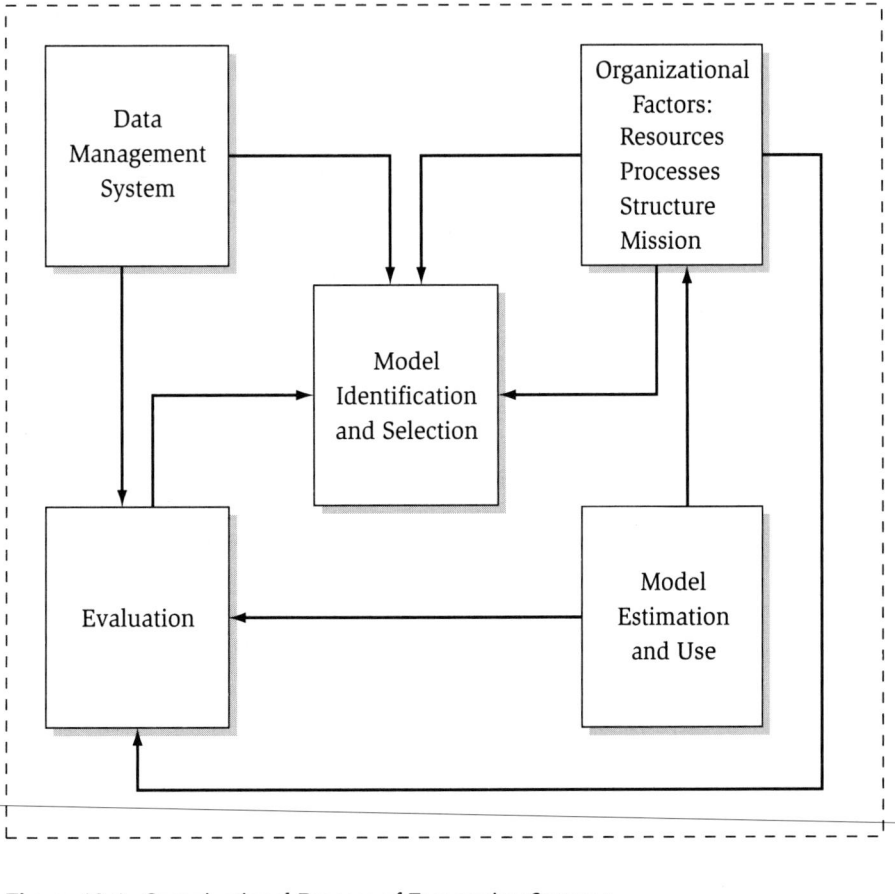

Figure 12.4. Organizational Process of Forecasting Systems.

system. Data preparation for forecasting requires aggregation by revenue stream and time period (such as monthly income tax collections). Although this requirement appears straightforward, financial systems often fail to store extensive historical records of revenues that are valuable for forecast model estimation, to use consistent rules for aggregation and measurement of revenues by category for more than a few years, and to store any history of forecasts, assumptions made, and resulting forecast errors necessary for evaluation. The reason for the inadequacy of government financial information systems is that they were designed primarily to support standard financial control and budgeting functions, while forecasting was at best a secondary consideration. Consequently, it is not surprising to find that these systems often do not provide the necessary inputs for the forecasting function.

Data requirements increase when considering multivariate forecasting methods that require independent variables (such as household income, interest rates, and so on). Many large cities and states purchase macroeconomic data and forecasts from various sources, such as Wharton Econometrics or Chase Econometrics. They may also obtain data from other government sources, such as the National Bureau of Economic Research, the Census Bureau, and the Bureau of Labor Statistics. Some states, such as Arizona and Wisconsin, have also made major investments in measuring various aspects of their economies in order to apply multivariate methods to revenue projection.

Model Identification and Selection

The formal identification and selection of a particular approach to forecasting is typically the responsibility of technical staff in the forecasting system. Although in reality the forecasts actually used in formal budget documents are hybrids modified by complex organizational and political processes, here we are focusing on the initial technical forecast that is typically generated before any political or institutional review and adjustment.

Although data requirements are an important aspect of model selection, other criteria are also important. Bretschneider and Gorr (1992a) provided twenty-five specific criteria organized into eight categories (see Exhibit 12.1). Although technical forecast accuracy is important, other criteria play a significant role in the selection process. Explainability is the extent to which the inputs required to generate the forecast are deemed reasonable. For example, are the model assumptions clear and reasonable, and are the data used accurate? Comparative criteria imply that to judge the quality of a forecast it is necessary to answer the question, Compared to what? Forecasts clearly are accompanied by uncertainty. It is therefore useful to evaluate the manner in which the forecasting process manages this uncertainty. For example, does it include a range, the width of which is a useful measure of the uncertainty in the forecast? Can the forecast be manipulated in reasonable ways? For example, can monthly forecasts be easily aggregated to year-end totals? Can forecasts be adjusted for information that was outside the forecasting model? How expensive is the forecasting process relative to its accuracy? Coordination criteria reflect the extent to which the forecasting system permits multiple individuals and units to access forecast results in common and consistent ways. Finally, it is important to understand that although forecasts are judged on accuracy, they must also be used to consider the impacts of policy alternatives during budget development. Can the forecasting approach predict the effects of a tax rate change? Can expenditure forecasts predict the effects of changes in eligibility requirements for social welfare programs? Clearly, evaluation of forecasts and forecasting systems require significant prior thought and should be integrated into the forecasting

Exhibit 12.1. Criteria for Evaluation of Forecast Outcomes.

Explainability	Dependability of method to others
	Reasonableness of assumptions
	Using sensible and accurate data
	Input data and assumptions being linked to output forecasts
Technical Forecast Accuracy	Systematic bias (e.g., mean error)
	Accuracy (e.g., mean square error)
	Existence of serial correlation
	Sophistication of technique (state-of-the-art)
Comparative Criteria	Simple benchmarking
	Multiple benchmarking
Managing Uncertainty	Present low, middle, and high forecasts
	Evaluate scenarios
	Identify outliers
	Identify structural change
Manipulability of Forecasts	Aggregate and disaggregate forecasts
	Adjust inputs
	Adjust forecasts
Cost Criteria	Manpower costs
	Computer costs
Coordination Criteria	Use of standard data (intra- and inter-agency)
	Use of standard methods
	Coordination and timing data collection and forecasting
	Standard forecast reporting
Utility Criteria	Multiple uses for forecasts
	Policy alternative evaluation

system. Having developed these various criteria, it is important to understand that with the exception of cost, accuracy has been the only criteria considered in most empirical studies.

Numerous experimental studies have demonstrated the superior forecast accuracy of simple extrapolative forecasting methods over multivariate forecast models in many contexts (see Ashley, 1983, 1988; Makridakis and others, 1993a, 1993b). Unfortunately, although many authors have examined biases in revenue forecasts, relatively few have directly examined the effect of revenue forecast methods on accuracy. One field study is Bretschneider and others (1989), which examined 136 sales tax forecast errors from twenty-eight states from 1975–1976 through 1984–1985. On average, use of judgmental methods reduced the mean absolute percentage budget forecast error by 2.1 percent, univariate forecasts increased it by 5 percent, multiple regression reduced it by 4.3 percent, and simultaneous equation models increased it by 1.7 percent. These results provide some support for using judgment and multiple regression models for state sales taxes. We suspect that smaller volume state revenue streams and many local government revenue streams would be most accurately forecast using a combination of extrapolative methods and special-event adjustments.

You can assess your own situation by conducting some forecast experiments. Namely, run univariate extraploative and multivariate methods in parallel using a rolling horizon design. With time-series data in hand, use the minimum number possible of oldest data points to estimate models and hold out the next three to five observations for forecasting. Compute forecasts and forecast errors with all models. Then add some more observations as historical data, reestimate models and forecast into a new holdout sample. Keep doing this until you use up all historical data. Besides getting some comparisons of alternate forecast methods, this exercise is good for budget staffs to use to become intimately familiar with their data, alternative methods, and expectations on forecast errors. Often revealing is to include actual forecasts published in past budgets (and initial technical forecasts) for comparison. We bet that practically any objective forecasts that include special-event handling will be more accurate than the budget forecasts used historically.

Organizational Factors

As depicted in Exhibit 12.1, organizational factors influence the model identification and selection process. Forecasting is a human process and therefore cannot be divorced from human and organizational contexts. The organizational structure, resources, and processes define the forecasting system. Resources and structure determine how the forecasting process will assess information for model selection, as well as what resources it can bring to bear in the process. Jones, Bretschneider, and Gorr (1997) found, for example, that the nature of the forecasters' advanced training had an influence on several aspects of the model identification and evaluation process. They found that when the forecaster had been trained as an economist, the forecasting system was much more likely to include a formal evaluation process. We also know that larger governmental units commit great resources to the forecasting task and that different organizational cultures affect the extent and nature of cooperation between executive and legislative forecasting units (Bretschneider and others, 1989).

A great deal of the empirical research on forecast bias and accuracy has examined the extent to which organizational factors influence the forecasting system (Bretschneider and Gorr, 1987; Bretschneider and others, 1989; Cassidy, Kamlet, and Nagin, 1989; Feenberg, Gentry, Gilroy, and Rosen, 1989; Gentry, 1989; Mocan and Azad, 1995). One of the major findings has been that forecasts generated in states having multiple forecasting organizations (that is, both a legislative and an executive agency) tend to have less bias than those that are generated by a single unit. Another result from this stream of work is the suggestion that when multiple forecasts are reconciled within the process in a cooperative manner, forecast bias is reduced. This work also indicates that forecasts generated by external experts tend to have greater bias than those generated internally.

In recent years the legislative branches of governments have become more involved in generating revenue projections. One recent survey found that twenty state legislatures forecast general fund revenues (85 percent of total state receipts) and another eighteen monitored the forecasts generated by other units, including departments of finance and taxation, comptroller's offices, governor's offices, joint state and house revenue committees, or consensus groups (Mocan and Azad, 1995). In many governments where both executive and legislative branches are actively involved in forecasting, some form of reconciliation occurs, often within the legislative debates over the budget bill (Bretschneider and others, 1989; Mocan and Azad, 1995).

Model Estimation and Use

Once a model is selected and technical forecasts are generated, the process of use extends outside the forecasting system back into the larger organization. Technical forecasts are fed directly into the political and institutional process of budgeting. It is common for technical forecasts to be reviewed and revised by external experts and political forces. These results are often modified first, as the estimates move through the executive branch, into a budget request laid before the legislature, and then again during the legislative debate and discussion as they become incorporated into the actual budget bill.

Little research exists on the organizational and political process of adjustment. Such research would require storing intermediate forecasts and other process data, and such data are not routinely collected. Most of the empirical research cited in this chapter has been based on ad hoc surveys of forecasters or on examination of final budget documents.

CONCLUSIONS

Revenue collections are uncertain and must be forecast for budget monitoring, design, and planning. This chapter has reviewed the field of revenue forecasting and its special nature, and has made prescriptions on how to forecast revenues.

As the old adage goes, any time you make a forecast, you make an error. The issue is how to make the smallest errors possible while clearly understanding the methods used and being able to explain and defend the forecasts made. A complexity rarely discussed but confronted directly in this chapter is how to deal with the special events that commonly disrupt revenue time-series patterns and produce large forecast errors. We feel that this chapter makes a valuable contribution to this issue, by prescribing visual examination of time-series plots, simple methods, and manual modifications to estimates. We hope you will use data well, use simple methods that you can command, and work hard at collecting and using special-event data.

We have also reviewed the empirical research on forecasting. Although most of this work has looked at state governments, many of the issues addressed apply at the local level as well. Here the focus has been on forecasting bias and on understanding how organizational and political factors tend either to increase or decrease bias. We have also considered forecasting as a system, and the various components that make up a good system. Clearly the prescription to integrate special-event information into the forecasting process requires the implementation of an information system that is up to the task. This information system is the backbone of the forecasting system because it is the basis of the data, the special-event information, and the ability to evaluate the forecasts. The information system also supports the important monitoring function that occurs during budget implementation, where the notion of frequent forecasting becomes important.

APPENDIX A: SIMULATED DATA
FOR STEP-JUMP AND TURNING POINT CASES

The general model is

$$Y_t = a + bt + e_t$$

where

Y_t = revenue at time t = 1, 2, . . . , 15

a = intercept, the mean value of Y_t at time zero

b = time trend slope, the mean increase in Y_t with each increase of t

$e_t \sim N(0,1)$, the random error term, is normally distributed with mean 0 and standard deviation 1 (95 percent of errors between 2 and +2).

The step-jump case model has a = 5 for t = 0, . . . , 6, a = 15 for t = 7, . . . , 15, and b = 1 for all t. There is a step jump up by 10 units at time 7. The turning point case has a = 5 and b = 2 for t = 0, . . . , 6 and a = 29 and b = 2 for

$t = 7, \ldots, 15$. Time period 6 is a turning point from an increasing trend with slope 2 to a decreasing trend with slope 2.

The 15 data values generated for the step-jump case and time periods 1 to 15 are 6.72, 5.98, 9.45, 7.89, 8.97, 12.06, 21.73, 21.23, 22.64, 24.50, 25.00, 27.66, 27.80, and 30.5. Similarly, the data values for the turning point case are 7.72, 7.98, 12.45, 11.89, 13.97, 18.06, 14.73, 11.23, 9.64, 8.50, 6.00, 5.66, 2.80, 0.29, and 0.50.

APPENDIX B: ESTIMATION OF THE HOLT SMOOTHING MODEL

Data points for $t = 1, \ldots, 12$ are used to estimate models, and one- through three-step-ahead trace forecasts are made from origin $t = 12$ for time periods 13 through 15. Details of the Holt procedure are as follows:

$F_{t+m} = L_t + mS_t$, the forecast model for the mth-step ahead forecast with forecast origin t,

$L_t = \alpha(Y_t + (1\ \alpha)(L_{t\,1} + S_{t\,1})$, the smoothed estimate of Y_t at time t,

$S_t = \beta(L_t\ L_{t-1}) + (1\ \beta)S_{t\,1}$, the smoothed estimate of the time trend slope at time t,

α = smoothing factor for the model level, and

β = smoothing factor for the slope

Initial values for the slope term, S_t, are the average first difference for the data in $t = 1, \ldots, 5$ or 6. The initial value for the level term, L_t, is the Y_1, the first data point. The forecaster has to choose values for α and β.

References

Armstrong, J. S. *Long-Range Forecasting from Crystal Ball to Computer.* New York: Wiley, 1985.

Ashley, R. "On the Usefulness of Macroeconomics Forecasts as Inputs to Forecasting Models." *Journal of Forecasting,* 1983, 2, 211–223.

Ashley, R. "On the Relative Worth of Recent Macroeconomic Forecasts." *International Journal of Forecasting,* 1988, 4, 363–376.

Bahl, R. "Revenue and Expenditure Forecasting by State and Local Governments." In J. Petersen, C. Spain, and M. Laffey (eds.), *State and Local Government Finance and Financial Management.* Washington, D.C.: Government Finance Research Center, 1980.

Bretschneider, S. "Estimating Forecast Variance with Exponential Smoothing." *International Journal of Forecasting,* 1986, 2, 349–355.

Bretschneider, S., Bunch, B., and Gorr, W. L. "Revenue Forecast Errors in Pennsylvania Local Government Budgeting: Sources and Remedies." *Public Budgeting and Financial Management,* 1992, *4,* 721–743.

Bretschneider, S., and Gorr, W. L. "State and Local Government Revenue Forecasting." In S. Makridakis and S. Wheelwright (eds.), *The Handbook of Forecasting: A Manager's Guide.* (2nd ed.) New York: Wiley, 1987.

Bretschneider, S., and Gorr, W. L. "Alternatives to Forecast-Error-Based Evaluation: Communicability, Manipulability, Credibility, and Policy Relevance." Paper presented at the 1992 Federal Forecasters Conference, Washington, D.C., Sept. 11, 1992a.

Bretschneider, S., and Gorr, W. L. "Economic, Organizational, and Political Influences on Biases in Forecasting State Tax Receipts." *International Journal of Forecasting,* 1992b, *7,* 457–466.

Bretschneider, S., Gorr, W. L., Grizzle, G., and Klay, W. "Political and Organizational Influence on the Accuracy of Forecasting State Government Revenues." *International Journal of Forecasting,* 1989, *5,* 307–319.

Bretschneider, S., and Schroeder, L. "Evaluation of Commercial Economic Forecasts for Use in Local Government." *International Journal of Forecasting,* 1988, *4,* 33–43.

Cassidy, G., Kamlet, M. S., and Nagin, D. "Empirical Examination of Bias in Revenue Forecasts by State Government." *International Journal of Forecasting,* 1989, *5,* 321–331.

Clemen, T. T. "Combining Forecasts: A Review and Annotated Bibliography." *International Journal of Forecasting,* 1989, *5,* 559–583.

Feenberg, D. R., Gentry, W., Gilroy, D., and Rosen, H. S. "Testing the Rationality of State Revenue Forecasts." *Review of Economics and Statistics,* 1989, *42,* 429–440.

Frank, H. "Municipal Revenue Forecasting with Time-Series Models: A Florida Case Study." *American Review of Public Administration,* 1990, *20*(1), 45–59.

Frank, H. *Budgetary Forecasting in Local Government: New Tools and Techniques.* Westport, Conn.: Quorum/Greenwood, 1993.

Frank, H., and Gianakis, G. "Raising the Bridge Using Time-Series Models." *Public Productivity and Management Review,* 1990, *14*(2), 171–178.

Frank, H., and McCollough, J. "Municipal Forecasting Practice: 'Demand' and 'Supply' Side Perspectives." *International Journal of Public Administration,* 1992, *15*(9), 1669–1696.

Galbraith, C. S., and Merrill, G. B. "The Politics of Forecasting: Managing the Truth." *California Management Review,* 1996, *38*(2), 29–43.

Gentry, W. M. "Do State Revenue Forecasters Utilize Available Information?" *National Tax Journal,* 1989, *42,* 429–439.

Gorr, W. L. "Special Event Data in Shared Databases." *MIS Quarterly,* 1986, *10*(3), 239–250.

Gorr, W. L., Kamlet, M., Lee, Y., and Bretschneider, S. "Economic and Managerial Rationality in Local Government Revenue Forecasting: Case Study of Pittsburgh Area School Districts." H. John Heinz III School of Public Policy and Management Working Paper 92-41, Pittsburgh, Carnegie-Mellon University, 1992.

Howard, J. "Government Economic Projections: A Comparison Between CBO and OMB Forecasts." *Public Budgeting and Finance,* 1987, *7*(3), 14–25.

Jones, V. D., Bretschneider, S., and Gorr, W. L. "Organizational Pressures on Forecast Evaluation: Managerial, Political, and Procedural Influences." *Journal of Forecasting,* 1997, *16,* 241–254.

Kamlet, M. S., Mowery, D. C., and Su, T.-T. "Whom Do You Trust? An Analysis of Executive and Congressional Economic Forecasts." *Journal of Policy Analysis and Management,* 1987, *6*(3), 365–384.

Klay, W. "Revenue Forecasting: An Administrative Perspective." In J. Rubin and T. Lynch (eds.), *Handbook on Public Budgeting and Financial Management.* New York: Dekker, 1983.

Klay, W. "The Organizational Dimension of Budgetary Forecasting: Suggestions from Revenue Forecasting in the States." *International Journal of Public Administration,* 1987, *7*(3), 241–265.

Klay, W., and Grizzle, G. "Revenue Forecasting in the States: New Dimensions of Budgetary Forecasting." Paper presented at the National Conference of the American Society for Public Administration, Anaheim, Calif., Apr. 4, 1986.

Larkey, P. D., and Smith, R. A. "The Misrepresentation of Information in Government Budgeting." In L. Sproull and P. D. Larkey (eds.), *Advances in Information Processing in Organizations,* Vol. 1. Greenwich, Conn.: JAI Press, 1984.

Larkey, P. D., and Smith, R. A. "Biases in the Formulation of Local Government Budget Problems." *Policy Sciences,* 1989, *22,* 123–166.

Lee, Y. "Conceptual Design of a Decision Support System for Local Government Revenue Forecasting." Unpublished Ph.D. dissertation, School of Urban and Public Affairs, Carnegie Mellon University, 1990.

MacManus, S., and Grothe, B. "Fiscal Stress as a Stimulant to Better Revenue Forecasting and Productivity." *Public Productivity Review,* 1989, *12*(4), 387–400.

Makridakis, S., and Hibon, M., "Accuracy of Forecasting: An Empirical Investigation." *Journal of the Royal Statistical Society,* 1979, *142,* 97–125.

Makridakis, S., and others. "The Accuracy of Extrapolation (Time-Series) Methods: Results of a Forecasting Competition." *Journal of Forecasting,* 1982, *1,* 111–153.

Makridakis, S., and others. "The M2 Competition: A Real-Time Judgmentally Based Forecasting Study." *International Journal of Forecasting,* 1993a, *9,* 5–22.

Makridakis, S., and others. "Commentary." *International Journal of Forecasting,* 1993b, *9,* 23–29.

McCollough, J., and Frank, H. "Incentives for Forecasting Reform Among Local Finance Officers." *Public Budgeting and Financial Management,* 1992, *4*(2), 407–429.

Mocan, H. N., and Azad, S. "Accuracy and Rationality of State General Fund Revenue Forecasts: Evidence from Panel Data." *International Journal of Forecasting,* 1995, *1,* 417–427.

Rubin, I. S. "Estimated and Actual Urban Revenues: Exploring the Gap." *Public Budgeting and Finance,* 1987, 7(4), 83–94.

Shkurti, W. J., and Winefordner, D. "The Politics of State Revenue Forecasting in Ohio, 1984–1987: A Case Study and Research Implications." *International Journal of Forecasting,* 1989, *5,* 361–371.

CHAPTER THIRTEEN

The Politics of Taxation

Sheldon Pollack

Budgeting addresses one of the fundamental questions of politics: How shall the resources of the government be employed? A budget is a map or blueprint for what political scientists refer to as the authoritative allocation of resources by the state. But for the U.S. government, the budget is only one side of this allocation; public finance is the other. How the government raises the revenue that finances its various activities ultimately dictates who pays what, when, and how. The nature, structure, and incidence of a system of public finance all have an impact on how the various economic and social interests of civil society will share the burden of government, that is, who will pay for the appropriations authorized in the budget. The design of a system of public finance determines how the economic burden will be distributed and hence raises political issues of the utmost importance.

In the twentieth century, the income tax has been the principal source of revenue of the U.S. government. The great revenue brought in by this tax financed two worldwide military campaigns and made possible (along with payroll taxes) the establishment of a social welfare state in the 1930s. The post–New Deal U.S. state has been funded largely through the income tax. Because of the centrality of income taxation to public finance, the politics of the income tax is

Note: The author wishes to thank David Beam for his many useful comments and suggestions on this chapter.

the politics of revenue in the United States. The particular structure of the income tax is thus a constant concern of federal policymakers as well as of an army of Washington lobbyists representing special interests who are jockeying for political favors bestowed through the tax code. The many exemptions, deductions, credits, and social policies written into the tax laws express political decisions and bargains—just as appropriations in the federal budget express political decisions and bargains over the funding of particular public policies and programs. As such, the federal income tax is a *political instrument* that effects an authoritative allocation of resources.

Although the tax laws (like the budget) allocate resources among various economic, social, and regional interests, the politics of taxation is quite distinct from the politics that prevails over the budgetary process in the appropriations and budget committees. Tax policy is expressed in its own distinct language— the arcane language and technical jargon of tax law. Likewise, the politics of taxation takes place in its own distinct political arena—the House Ways and Means Committee and the Senate Finance Committee. Although tax policy proposals commonly originate in the White House, and although congressional leadership and committee staff (that is, the staffs of the Joint Committee on Taxation, the Ways and Means Committee, and the Finance Committee) have considerable influence over the course and success of tax policy initiatives, the tax laws are mostly the product of the agreements and bargains struck by and among the most powerful members of the tax committees. The chairs of the tax committees play a dominant role in shaping tax bills through their markup of legislative proposals. Presidents may set the agenda for tax policy by initiating legislative proposals, but tax bills are largely the handicraft of the tax committees.

Because tax policy is made by elected politicians, decisions inevitably reflect compromise, consensus, and coalition building as well as partisan politics. Elected politicians must carefully cultivate support for their revenue policies (especially those that increase taxes) because they are ultimately accountable to the electorate. Furthermore, tax policy is highly susceptible to the pressures and influence of powerful, organized interest groups in the districts of congressional policymakers. This was recognized by T. S. Adams in his 1927 presidential address to the annual meeting of the American Economic Association: "Modern taxation or tax making in its most characteristic aspect is a group contest in which powerful interests vigorously endeavor to rid themselves of present or proposed tax burdens. It is, first of all, a hard game in which he who trusts wholly to economics, reason, and justice, will in the end retire beaten and disillusioned" (Adams, 1928, p. 1).

It is this politics of taxation—the "hard game" played by presidents, committee chairmen, congressional leadership, and powerful organized interests— that is the subject of this chapter. What, then, are the motives, goals, and interests of the politicians who formulate U.S. tax policy?

POLITICS AND REVENUE

The revenue policy of any state inevitably reflects a complicated calculus of decision making. Policymakers take into account numerous interests and goals dictated by the overall constitutional structure of the regime. As political scientist Sven Steinmo (1993, p. 10) has put it: "Politicians want to be reelected, bureaucrats want to manage a stable and efficient tax policy, and interest groups want to promote the well-being of their constituents. But how these general desires get translated into specific policy preferences and specific political strategies depends upon the rules of the game; and the rules of the game are written by the institutions through which the game is played." Thus, to make sense of the politics of taxation in the United States, it is first necessary to understand the rules of the game—namely, the political processes and institutions through which the tax laws are made.

The political institutions and procedures for legislation established under the U.S. Constitution are important but do not alone define the rules of tax policy-making. The extraconstitutional party system that evolved in the early nineteenth century has also had an important impact on the legislative process. The officials who write the tax laws are politicians who must periodically seek reelection. Their very claim to office is dependent upon winning election in their local district or home state. Elections link congressional policymakers to their constituents. Much has been written by political scientists about how this "electoral connection" influences the behavior of members of Congress, who introduce legislation and seek credit for the introduction of favorable legislation, and about how the actual distribution of government benefits constituents in their home districts (Mayhew, 1974; Fiorina, 1977). It is because of the electoral connection that the tax legislative process is so susceptible to the pressures and entreaties of interest groups located in the local districts or states of the most important members of Congress.

Although this side of the politics of taxation is important, tax policy is much more than the product of interest group politics. The politicians who are in control of the tax legislative process pursue other political interests and goals as well through the tax laws. Because U.S. tax policy is made within the context of a competitive party system, it is highly partisan. The same elected politicians who represent local districts must also operate within Congress as members of their political party. Although members of Congress do not always vote with their party, party affiliation remains the single most important factor in predicting voting behavior (Schneider, 1979). In the 1980s and 1990s, voting on major tax legislation has pretty much followed strict party lines as Democrats and Republicans have used the tax code to implement much of their respective partisan agendas and have consistently voted against each other's partisan proposals.

The U.S. political culture is also important in defining the environment for the tax legislative process. Endemic to this political culture is a strong, native strain of antitax politics that surfaces from time to time. Individual politicians or entire political parties express this antitax rhetoric periodically. In the twentieth century, the Republican party has generally carried the antitax banner; Democrats too, however, have found this a useful campaign theme. Occasionally the antitax message prevails and is translated into public policy—as in the major tax bill of 1981 and to a lesser extent the tax legislation enacted in 1997.

Finally, Congress is charged under the Constitution with the great responsibility and burden of raising the enormous revenue required to pay for the activities of the federal government. A good deal of the time of members of the tax committees is spent scrambling to find the revenue to fund the proposals authorized in the budget. This is especially the case in light of the requirement for "revenue neutrality" imposed on the tax and budget committees under the so-called pay-as-you-go (or PAYGO) rule in the Congressional Budget Act of 1974, as amended by the Budget Enforcement Act of 1990 [2 U.S.C.A., secs. 633(c), (f), and 902]. Every bill that gives away revenue through some new, special tax preference must be accompanied by offsetting savings. This requires the tax committees to come up with new revenue or to cut entitlement spending, most of which is Social Security and Medicare. Accordingly, a constant and unrelenting search for revenue is behind much of the politics of taxation. Political and electoral constraints make raising revenue a very difficult feat for politicians. Policymakers must carefully build support for any tax increase, putting together broad coalitions and cultivating acceptance among the electorate.

To summarize, tax policy is made within the confines of political institutions (Congress and its committees) and strongly influenced by the electoral connection (elections and party competition). Policymakers act within a complex environment, motivated by competing goals and interests defined by the constitutional structure and influenced by the antitax tradition of the U.S. regime. Within this context, members of Congress and the tax committees use the tax code as an instrument to further what are, in essence, three main functions—raising revenue, serving constituents, and implementing partisan policies. Tax policy is often at odds with itself because congressional policymakers use the tax laws for these disparate and often conflicting purposes. (These functions are explored further in coming sections of this chapter.)

Elsewhere I have argued that because the tax laws are used in this manner, contemporary U.S. tax policy has become increasingly unstable and unpredictable, highly partisan, and exceedingly complex (Pollack, 1996), which has had undesirable consequences for U.S. tax policy. The highly erratic pattern of tax policymaking and the explosion in the volume and complexity of tax legislation and regulations enacted in the 1980s and 1990s bear witness to this. Conversely, it must be acknowledged that the income tax remains remarkably successful in satisfying so many of the political interests of policymakers at once, while at the same time raising the enormous revenue that it does—an amazing $919 billion in 1997.

REVENUE AND PREDATION

Officials of any state face a common concern: raising revenue to fund the various activities of the state, ranging from military campaigns to social welfare programs. The particular method employed varies from regime to regime, but one way or another officials must extract revenue from civil society to support the state. In authoritarian regimes, raising revenue may take the guise of outright seizure—the state plundering civil society. Elsewhere, where civil society is better organized to resist state predation, state officials must negotiate for revenue with the major social and economic interests. This requires state officials to offer a tacit *quid pro quo*—protection, order, and public goods in exchange for revenue. In such cases, revenue is generally raised through regular, institutionalized methods of extraction.

Modern states use a variety of such methods, such as custom duties, user fees, and tariffs. In some cases, state-owned economic business enterprises generate revenue for the government. Taxation, however, is the primary method used by modern states to finance their activities; all the other methods of public finance merely supplement the revenue raised by taxation in its various forms. Everywhere the underlying relationship between taxation and the modern state is the same: "Taxes are the source of life for the bureaucracy, the army, the priests and the court, in short, for the whole apparatus of the executive power" (Marx, [1852] 1977, p. 320).

That the state must raise revenue to survive is obvious, but some theorists carry this observation one step further. They argue that state officials seek to *maximize* state revenue as predatory rulers. For example, economists Geoffrey Brennan and James Buchanan (1980) portray the state as an unrelenting Leviathan constantly seeking to maximize its own revenue. They base their analysis on the single premise that the state behaves like a monopolist seeking to maximize its own profit. The state as monopolist imposes taxation so as to maximize its revenue, ignoring the excess burden (or deadweight social loss) imposed on society and the private economy. From this perspective, the goal of politics becomes one of circumscribing constitutional boundaries around the state to limit the Leviathan's self-aggrandizing tendencies. Political scientist

Margaret Levi (1988) offers a similar and in many ways more sophisticated political theory of predatory rule, arguing that "rulers are predatory in that they try to extract as much revenue as they can from the population" (p. 3).

Although there is a certain appeal to the notion that revenue maximization motivates state officials, in practice predation theory just does not explain very much about the politics of taxation in the United States—or more properly, it explains only one aspect of the politics of taxation. Unlike the French and English monarchs of the sixteenth century (bona fide revenue predators), national political elites in the United States have always lacked both the institutional power and the political will to engage in predatory revenue policy. As a result of the peculiar institutional development of the American state, the national government lacked significant centralized powers until well into the twentieth century (Skowronek, 1982). At its inception, the American state was expressly designed through its original constitutional structure to *deny* the federal government easy access to revenue. Under the first, ill-fated constitution of the states—the Articles of Confederation (1777–1789)—the national government was itself denied the power of direct taxation. Rather, it was dependent upon the state governments to collect and pay revenues, which the states often did not do. Although the U.S. Constitution of 1789 strengthened the central government's fiscal powers, those powers were still limited, especially with respect to raising revenue. So, lacking the institutional power to raise revenue, much less to engage in predatory revenue policy, the nineteenth century American state relied on a hodgepodge system of excise taxes and custom duties, supplemented by the occasional sale of public lands, to fund its rather minimal activities. Actually, this system was adequate in financing the limited activities of the federal government—until the Civil War, when the administrative capacities of the federal government were expanded far beyond its traditional nineteenth-century functions. To supplement federal revenue, an income tax was enacted in 1860. It was allowed to expire soon after the war.

Throughout the nineteenth century, the U.S. government was largely financed by tariffs—commodity-based consumption taxes on imported goods and materials. The tariff was a highly successful source of revenue that regularly produced annual budget surpluses for the federal government (Savage, 1988). Nevertheless, political and regional pressure mounted to replace the tariff with an income-based tax, and opposition to the tariff emerged as the defining political issue of the era. "During the 1880s and 1890s, the two competing political parties came to base their economic appeals on sharply conflicting ideological views of the tariff and of taxation in general" (Brownlee, 1996, p. 35). Calls for a graduated income tax first appeared in the 1877 and 1878 platforms of the Greenback party, and again in the 1880 platform of the National Greenback party. The Grangers, the Knights of Labor, and the Farmers Alliance favored an income tax, as did the Populist party in each of its platforms. From

1874 to 1894, no fewer than sixty-eight bills proposing an income tax were introduced in Congress.

The constituents of the political parties understood that replacing the tariff with an income tax meant shifting the burden of public finance away from southern and midwestern agrarian interests and onto northern manufacturing interests and wealthy individuals. The intensity of the politics reflected the salience of the issue for the interests, groups, and regions that were affected. A new federal income tax was finally enacted in 1894, largely at the instigation of Populists in the Democratic party. The politics of the federal income tax of 1894 (which was subsequently held unconstitutional by the U.S. Supreme Court) and that surrounding the subsequent ratification of the Sixteenth Amendment in 1913 were highly partisan and reflected the economic and regional cleavages.

Ironically, the enactment of a new federal income tax, a minor revenue bill attached to the Underwood-Simmons Tariff Act of 1913, proved anticlimactic once the constitutional question was resolved. Reflecting political compromise, the income tax of 1913 applied to only a few of the wealthiest citizens. This was accomplished through a generous $3,000 personal exemption that rendered only a relatively small and well-defined stratum of the citizenry subject to the income tax. For 1913, the first half year under the tax, only 0.8 percent of the population had sufficient income to subject them to taxation; only 358,000 individuals filed income tax returns reporting net taxable income. For these people, the tax was imposed at 1 percent on personal income above $3,000, increasing to 6 percent on income over $500,000. With a 1 percent surtax, the maximum marginal tax rate reached 7 percent. In 1913, the corporate and individual income tax together raised only $28 million. In 1914 (the first full year of the tax), the income tax provided just 7.37 percent of total receipts of the federal government.

Although the new income tax was initially only a minor supplement to the tariff, the increased demand for revenue during World War I forced congressional policymakers to expand the tax. This was easily accomplished by reducing personal exemptions and raising tax rates. In addition, corporate rates were raised and an excess profits tax was enacted. By the end of the war, the top marginal tax rate soared to 77 percent on income over $1 million. Personal exemptions were lowered to $1,000 for single taxpayers and $2,000 for married taxpayers. These changes in the rate structure of the income tax shifted the burden of the tax from being exclusively on the very wealthy to include middle-income taxpayers. (Even still, at the height of the war only a minority of the citizenry was ever subject to the tax; no more than 20 percent of the population was required to file tax returns.) When the steeply graduated income tax was applied to a wider spectrum of the population, it produced revenue beyond anything previously imagined. By 1918, revenue from the wartime income tax and excess profits tax supplied 63.1 percent of total federal receipts, and revenue from the tariff and all other excise taxes declined to 28.7 percent. The income tax supplanted the tariff as the principal source of federal revenue.

Tax rates were reduced significantly during the 1920s during successive Republican administrations. President Warren G. Harding left tax policy mostly to his treasury secretary, Andrew W. Mellon, who led his famous campaign for a return to "tax normalcy." Although tax rates were lowered throughout the 1920s, budget surpluses were actually generated, and the relative contribution of the income tax to total federal revenue increased. By the end of the decade, tax rates and federal expenditures had been returned to prewar levels and the federal income tax was pretty much what it had been in 1913. This situation changed dramatically with the onset of the Second World War.

It is often said that World War II transformed the federal income tax from a "class" tax into a "mass" tax. Before the war, only a few wealthy citizens were subject to the income tax. By the end of the war, the vast majority of U.S. citizens had become taxpayers. The Revenue Act of 1942 lowered personal exemptions to only $500 for individuals and $1,200 for married couples. This expanded the application of the tax to the vast majority of the citizenry. Evidence of expansion of the tax base was the number of tax returns filed by individuals, which increased nearly eightfold from 1940 to 1945. The number of individuals subject to the income tax increased over the course of World War II, eventually reaching more than 74 percent of the population. In addition, the Revenue Act of 1942 raised the normal personal income tax from 4 percent to 6 percent and added a progressive surtax ranging from 13 percent on income over $6,000 to 82 percent on income over $200,000. By 1944, the top marginal tax rate rose to 94 percent for individuals (on income in excess of $2,000,000) and 40 percent for corporations (in addition to the excess profits tax).

As income tax rates were increased and exemptions lowered during the war, the volume of revenue collected increased dramatically. Total receipts from the income tax rose sevenfold, and revenue derived from both corporate and individual taxes combined increased to $34 billion for 1945. The impact of World War II on the structure and function of the federal income tax can be summarized as follows: tax rates increased, personal exemptions were lowered, revenue increased, and a majority of the population became subject to the tax. Most significantly, the changes made to the tax code to finance World War II were not withdrawn after the wartime crisis ended, as had been the case following the World War I. In 1950, 59 percent of the population was subject to the individual income tax; the figure increased to 81 percent by 1970. Revenue from the individual income tax, which provided more than 45 percent of federal receipts at its wartime peak in 1944, has since remained at a constant 40 to 45 percent of federal receipts.

Since World War II, the income tax has been the cornerstone of the system of public finance in the United States. For fiscal year 1997, the corporate income tax provided 11.5 percent of federal revenue and the individual income tax provided 46.7 percent, collectively totaling $919 billion—significantly exceeding prior budget revenue estimates. Revenue from the income tax was supplemented by wage taxes (34.2 percent), the federal estate and gift tax (1.3 percent), excise taxes (3.6 percent), and miscellaneous user fees (2.7 percent). These other sources of revenue are hardly insignificant, and in an era of budget deficits and revenue neutrality all sources of revenue must be pursued. But it is the income tax that finances the activities of the modern American state. This is especially the case given that the revenue raised by federal wage taxes (imposed at a total rate of 15.3 percent on the $68,400 wage base and at 2.9 percent on wages above that amount for 1998) is specifically earmarked for the various social security programs. Separating social security from the rest of the activities of the federal government, the income tax provides some 88 percent of the revenue for those programs.

Most interesting, although the income tax has enormous capacity to raise revenue, policymakers obviously do not use the income tax to *maximize* revenue for the state, except during the revenue crises experienced during most wars. In peacetime, policymakers find it irresistible to use the income tax for political purposes—which typically means introducing legislation to *reduce* taxes for favored interests and groups or implementing public policies through tax preferences that likewise reduce taxation for favored investments or programs. Such unabashed political use of the federal income tax makes little sense from the perspective of the state's purported interest in maximizing revenue. It makes all the sense in the world, however, relative to the perspective, interests, motives, and goals of individual congressional policymakers. Their political interests dictate in favor of using the income tax to cultivate support among constituents and to implement public policies through the tax code. This results more often in pork barrel tax legislation than in revenue predation.

Although revenue concerns constantly press upon federal policymakers, their behavior hardly comports with a model of revenue predation. The expanding tax expenditure budget, more than twenty years of budget deficits, and a national debt of $5.5 trillion bear witness to this. It is not that policymakers are inept as revenue predators. Rather, they are subject to considerable political pressure from constituents to help alleviate the impact of the highly progressive rate structure of the income tax. As politicians, policymakers are highly skilled at using the tax laws to assist constituents in order to enhance their own political standing. The politics of taxation necessarily involves raising revenue, but raising revenue requires the consent and support of constituents and political parties. As Irene Rubin (1997, p. 66) has put it, "The politics of taxation is not a politics of coercion, it is a politics of persuasion." It should be added that the politics of taxation is also a politics of accommodation—distributing benefits to supporters and constituents through the tax code. Rather than would-be

Leviathans, federal policymakers are rational politicians who use the tax laws for a variety of political purposes.

PARTISAN POLITICS AND THE INCOME TAX

One of the main uses of the income tax by politicians is as a means for implementing their partisan agendas. This use of the federal income tax reflects the fact that early in the history of the nation the major political parties cultivated their own very distinct fiscal and tax policies. In the nineteenth century the parties were sharply divided over the use of tariffs. Later the conflict was over income taxation. Since the modern income tax was enacted in 1913, Democrats and Republicans have disagreed on many substantive issues of tax policy—even while finding considerable bipartisan agreement over a wide range of policies (the oil and gas depletion allowance, the deduction of charitable contributions, and increases in social security benefits, to name a few). When each party has been in control of the legislative process, is has enacted a good deal of its partisan agenda through the tax laws.

Democrats are responsible for a wide assortment of partisan tax policies: tax credits for low-income earners, housing, and education; the deduction of home mortgage interest to encourage home ownership; tax preferences for employee stock ownership plans (ESOPs) and retirement plans to benefit labor; limits on executive compensation; and preferential tax treatment for employer-provided health insurance. Democrats favor a steeply progressive income tax with high rates for the wealthy and tax preferences for the constituents of the Democratic party—labor, unions, the poor, and so on. A significant portion of the social welfare state of the United States is funded through "indirect spending" via the tax expenditure budget (Howard, 1997). Republicans have pursued a similarly wide range of social and economic policies through the tax code. Their tax policies are designed to implement some of the most fundamental tenets of the Republican party: broad income tax cuts to stimulate the economy, preferential tax treatment for capital gains, tax-favored economic enterprise zones as a cure for urban blight, and various tax credits and expenditures aimed at encouraging savings, investment, and the accumulation of capital. The list goes on and on. The most significant difference between the tax policies of congressional Democrats and Republicans lies in the particular policies they choose to write into the tax laws, rather than in whether or not to use the tax laws to implement policies.

Why have policymakers in both parties found the tax code such an inviting vehicle for implementing public policies? The tax legislative arena has proved to be generally more accessible and hospitable to the personal interests, ambitions, and goals of individual congressmen than the arena of budgeting and appropriations. It is simply easier to provide constituents with benefits through the tax code than through direct budgetary expenditures (Reese, 1980, pp. 198–201). Tax expenditures are often highly technical and hence are less visible to the public (and the media) than direct budgetary expenditures. The members of the tax committees are particularly advantaged in providing such tax preferences to constituents; higher levels of campaign contributions are evidence of the importance of such strategic committee assignments (Manley, 1970; Strahan, 1990). Once adopted, programs enacted through the tax code typically have an indefinite life rather than requiring annual authorization as budgetary programs do. For these reasons, partisans on both sides of the aisle find the tax code to be a convenient instrument for implementing their favored public policies. As a result, the tax laws, ostensibly designed to raise revenue, provide all sorts of economic incentives that reduce the tax burden for those who engage in favored behavior. Public policies executed through tax preferences erode the tax base and reduce revenue for the Treasury. They also are a less efficient means of funding public policies, because tax benefits are distributed too broadly, with some of the economic incentives going to those who would have engaged in the favored activity without the tax preference. Furthermore, the revenue loss from tax preferences is difficult to predict and control because statutes are open-ended invitations to an unlimited number of taxpayers to take advantage of the favored tax treatment. Notwithstanding these shortcomings, the use of the tax laws by congressional policymakers in pursuit of their own political agendas is an integral component of the normal politics of taxation.

TAXATION AND CONSTITUENCY SERVICE

Beyond the expenditures that implement partisan agendas, the tax preferences that congressional policymakers find most conducive to satisfying their ambitions and goals as elected politicians are those targeted to their own constituents. Politicians use the income tax to cultivate support from the dominant economic and social interests in their districts and states. The congressperson as ombudsperson introduces amendments to the income tax that are intended to protect and enhance the economic well-being of local interests and constituents. In this way the income tax code is also used as a nonpartisan vehicle for politicians, Democrats and Republicans alike, to curry favor with constituents, resulting in numerous special-interest provisions buried within the arcane language of the income tax code. A significant portion of the eight hundred or so major sections of the federal income tax are dedicated not to raising revenue but rather to implementing policies that effectively reduce federal revenue by allowing special deductions, exemptions, or credits for favored groups, interests, or policies.

The tax expenditure budget that Bruce Davie describes in Chapter Eleven provides evidence of the use of the tax code by congressional policymakers as a tool for implementing public policies and distributing benefits to constituents via special tax preferences. Because policymaking through tax expenditures is relatively easy and conducive to the political and electoral needs of representatives and senators, it has become a common mode of congressional policymaking in the postwar era. Stanley Surrey and Paul McDaniel (1985) calculated that the volume of government spending through tax expenditures increased by 179 percent from fiscal year 1974 to fiscal year 1981 (Surrey and McDaniel, 1985). Reform efforts in 1986 went far in eliminating many special tax preferences and reduced the rate of growth in the tax expenditure budget. The spending spree picked up steam again, however, in the late 1980s and early 1990s. A recent study by the U.S. General Accounting Office (1994) estimated that tax expenditures totaled almost $402 billion in 1993 and would continue to increase annually by 4 percent. That projection turned out to be fairly accurate. According to the president's budget for FY96, the revenue loss attributable to federal income tax expenditures was $533 billion—a 5.2 percent increase over 1995. For fiscal year 1997, the total revenue loss attributable to tax expenditures was $554 billion—a 4.1 percent increase over 1996. Projections for fiscal year 1998 put the figure at $567 billion, showing a modest reduction in the rate of increase in the tax expenditure budget. Although measurement of the total revenue loss attributable to tax expenditures is problematic (as Bruce Davie explains in Chapter Eleven), these figures provide evidence of the overall tendency of policymakers to spend through tax expenditures.

One revealing example of how the tax laws are used by politicians to curry favor with local interests can be found in the legislation crafted by congressional Republicans in 1995 to implement their partisan agenda. A massive tax bill was included in the omnibus revenue bill known as the Seven-Year Balanced Budget Reconciliation Act of 1995. Even while trying to implement their party's policy agenda (the so-called Contract with America), the politicians on the tax committees could not resist the opportunity to introduce some special provisions designed to advance the economic well-being of constituents. For instance, Republicans on the Ways and Means Committee included in the House draft three provisions for the funeral industry. Although these were minor provisions with limited revenue impact (collectively losing only $500,000 in annual revenue), the only justification for including them in the bill was that four committee members had particularly close ties to family-run funeral businesses. Senate Republicans had their own list of special-interest provisions buried in the tax bill. Indeed, every Republican on the Senate Finance Committee, except for conservative presidential candidate Phil Gramm of Texas, had inserted a special-interest provision into the Senate bill. Beneficiaries (and their respective supporters on the committee) included newspaper companies (Robert Dole of

Kansas), small gas and electric companies (William Roth of Delaware, the home of the Delmarva Power & Light Company), water utilities and real estate developers (Charles Grassley of Iowa), college football coaches (Orrin Hatch of Utah, a close friend of Brigham Young University's football coach), life insurance companies (Alfonse D'Amato of New York), and independent gasoline marketers (Don Nickles of Oklahoma).

None of these special-interest provisions actually made it into law, because President Clinton vetoed the bill in December 1995. But proposals such as these circulate every time a tax bill is crafted and many eventually find their way into the tax code. The Taxpayer Relief Act of 1997 reads like a Christmas list of special tax provisions targeted at constituents of the Republican party. For example, the legislation reduced the maximum tax on capital gains for individuals to 20 percent (a perennial goal of Republicans since the preferential rate for capital gains was repealed in 1986), lessened the burden of the corporate alternative minimum tax and eliminated it altogether for small business corporations, and increased current exemptions to the federal gift and estate tax—as well as creating an entirely new $700,000 exemption for owners of small businesses and farms. The Republican bill also included provisions expanding the availability of individual retirement accounts (IRAs) and creating the new Roth IRA (named after Senate Finance Committee chairman Roth, who now has the dubious honor of being the only individual having a section of the tax code named after him). Because any tax bill requires a broad, nonpartisan coalition behind it, Republicans were forced to make concessions to Democrats. The Clinton administration was behind several new education tax credits, a provision that effectively eliminates tax on the sale of a home, and proposals to shut down certain "abusive" financial transactions designed by Wall Street investment firms to allow clients to defer gain realized on stock and securities. These provisions had originally been proposed by the Clinton administration in 1995 in response to the Republican party's Contract with America tax bill and were included in the 1997 tax bill as a compromise to secure the president's support (or at least tacit acceptance) of the bill.

None of this is to suggest that Republicans are any more prone than Democrats to use the tax laws for constituency service. The Democrats, who controlled Congress and the tax committees for decades before 1994, used the tax laws for the very same purposes, favoring their own constituents and implementing their own partisan agenda through the tax code. Both sides of the political spectrum appear equally enamored of the electoral benefits derived from using the tax code to provide nonpartisan constituency service to the home district. The point is that even those who campaign on a strong antitax theme are all too ready to use the tax laws to distribute benefits to their own constituents.

In the context of the two-party system in place since World War II, consensus is required to enact the kind of massive, omnibus tax legislation that has become commonplace. This consensus is achieved through a wide dispersal of benefits to produce majoritarian coalitions of convenience. A nonpartisan pattern of trading votes for tax benefits (logrolling) insures passage. This practice has been the norm for postwar tax legislation. The resulting tax policy has left the tax code riddled with a dizzying array of tax credits, preferences, and deductions which in turn create pressure on the rate structure of the income tax as policymakers struggle to make up the revenue shortfall attributable to the tax expenditures. The overall result is a steeply graduated rate structure, a broad tax base, and numerous tax expenditures granting relief to constituents of both political parties. The result is a "piecemeal, complicated, inconsistent, and inequitable tax structure that periodically needs overhauling" (Rubin, 1997, p. 30). Occasionally reform legislation is passed. More often, the rhetoric of tax reform is invoked by politicians who wish to distance themselves from their own creation—the tax code. In short, it is an understatement to say that contemporary U.S. tax policy is a highly complex, almost schizophrenic enterprise.

ANTITAX POLITICS IN THE UNITED STATES

Another foundation of U.S. tax policy is a deeply rooted tradition of antitax politics in American political history, beginning with the antitax protests during the American Revolution and the Whiskey Rebellion of 1794 (a regional rebellion in western Pennsylvania against collection of the first federal excise tax, which was imposed on distilled spirits). The antitax populism behind the Proposition 13 movement—a revolt against local California property taxation— was a powerful political force throughout the early 1970s (Hansen, 1983; Sears and Citrin, 1982); it was largely an expression of grassroots resistance organized by nonpoliticians and directed at the formal political system. But in many cases, the antitax sentiment is orchestrated from above by politicians who use the theme to secure office for themselves and their party. Many candidates expose antitax rhetoric to get elected; few run, and fewer still get elected on the slogan of *raising* taxes. This lesson was learned all too well by presidential candidate Walter Mondale, who told his supporters at the 1984 Democratic convention of his sincere belief that taxes would need to be raised in coming years—and was thereafter trounced in the general election by antitax Republican Ronald Reagan.

In the postwar era, antitax themes have been particularly strong in the national political arena, especially within the Republican party. After World War II, the GOP and its business constituency found a hospitable political climate in which to pursue an antitax campaign. Reducing the steep wartime tax rates still in place was the dominant Republican issue in the 1946 elections. Republican candidates campaigned for a 20 percent overall cut in income tax rates.

They succeeded with this theme and took control of both chambers of Congress for the first time since 1930. The new Republican leadership in Congress then sought to implement broad tax cuts. The Democratic Truman administration strongly and persistently opposed any such tax cuts. Three times Truman vetoed Republican tax bills. The compromise bill that finally became law, the Revenue Act of 1948, lowered the maximum individual income tax rate to 82 percent from the historic wartime high of 94 percent.

During the 1980s, antitax politics again became a potent force within the Republican party. During the presidential campaign of 1980, Ronald Reagan endorsed a proposal for tax rate reduction introduced in 1977 by Representative Jack Kemp and Senator Roth. The Kemp-Roth proposal had called for a 33 percent reduction in individual tax rates and a lesser reduction in the corporate rate. In the spring of 1981, newly elected President Reagan introduced his own legislative proposal for tax rate reductions styled on the Kemp-Roth proposal. Reagan's proposal ran into opposition from congressional Democrats. By midsummer 1981, however, the new president brought together a bipartisan conservative congressional coalition to enact the Economic Recovery Tax Act of 1981. Although the 1981 tax cuts were less than those proposed under Kemp-Roth, they still constituted at the time the most significant tax rate reductions in the history of the federal income tax, reducing the maximum marginal tax rate for individuals to 50 percent from 70 percent (roughly where it had stood since the Kennedy tax cuts enacted in 1964). During the second Reagan administration, the maximum marginal tax rate for individuals was further reduced to 28 percent under the historic Tax Reform Act of 1986.

The antitax rhetoric expressed by Reagan Republicans during the 1980s has resurfaced as a powerful force in the Republican party in the 1990s. Following their success in the 1994 midterm elections, Republicans took control of both chambers of Congress for the first time since 1954. A strong antitax wing of the GOP emerged in control of the House. Following the GOP landslide in 1994, Representative Bill Archer (Republican from Texas) was appointed chairman of the House Ways and Means Committee and instigated a campaign to repeal the income tax altogether. Ever since, Archer has repeatedly expressed his contempt for the federal income tax: "I personally would like to tear the income tax out by its roots and throw it overboard." Archer favors replacing the income tax with some form of consumption-based tax similar to a European-style value-added tax.

The most politically viable proposal for replacing the income tax surfaced even before the 1994 elections. Representative Richard K. Armey (Republican from Texas), House majority leader in the 104th and 105th Congresses, introduced a proposal for a flat tax. Under Armey's proposal, a 17 percent tax would be imposed on the wages of an individual in excess of relatively high standard deductions and generous dependent allowances. None of the traditional deductions of the current income tax system would be allowed. Business activity would be taxed at the same rate, with a deduction allowed for wages paid. Thus the tax on individuals would be progressive to the extent that average tax rates rose in proportion to the individual's income, and the overall tax base would be consumption rather than income because the return on capital investment would not be taxed. Armey's flat tax is virtually identical to the broad-based consumption tax proposed more than a decade ago by Stanford University academics Alvin Rabushka and Robert Hall (1985).

In the fall of 1997, the antitax wing of the GOP turned against the agency charged with administering the tax laws—the Internal Revenue Service (IRS). Tapping what they perceived to be a strong undercurrent of antitax sentiment, Republican leaders focused popular discontent with the tax laws on the IRS. Out on the campaign trail, Republican politicians took to blaming the IRS for the excessive complexity of the tax laws (dubbed the IRS Code) and for the burden of taxation itself—conveniently ignoring that it is Congress and not the administrative agency that writes the tax laws. In September 1997, Senate Finance Committee chairman Roth conducted televised committee hearings investigating alleged abuses of taxpayers by the IRS. In dramatic testimony, IRS agents (concealing their identities) testified before the committee on the alleged abusive conduct of the agency in its collection activities. The hearings were a great public relations success for antitax Republicans, who viewed the publicity as the first step in a full assault on the income tax itself. Soon after the hearings, the Ways and Means Committee approved a bill proposing new safeguards for taxpayers litigating with the IRS and restructuring the agency by putting it under the control of an independent supervisory board made up of nongovernmental executives. The bill sailed through the House in early November 1997 by a vote of 426 to 4 and was enacted into law in 1998.

Although they are only one faction within their own party, members of the antitax wing of the Republican party have attracted much attention for their cause and have organized a viable national political movement against the income tax. In the 1990s, antitax politics also has been particularly successful at the state level, with twenty-seven states enacting tax reduction legislation in 1997 alone. With publisher Steve Forbes contemplating entering the GOP presidential primaries again in 2000 (having campaigned in 1996 on his own version of the flat tax) and with House Ways and Means Committee chairman Archer promising extensive committee hearings in 1998 to "educate" the public on the need to replace the income tax (whether with a flat consumption-based tax or a national sales tax), the antitax message of the Republican party is sure to dominate the policy agenda in the immediate future.

The antitax rhetoric of the GOP imposes significant restraints on all policymakers—even Democrats, who might otherwise be tempted to raise taxes for the federal government. Indeed, there has been enormous political pressure on all politicians in the United States to reduce taxes even in the face of the significant budget shortfalls experienced in the 1980s and 1990s—a lesson learned all too well by President Clinton. Clinton was forced to offer his own tax-cut proposals in an effort to quiet the thunder of Republicans in the wake of their significant electoral successes in the 1994 midterm elections, during which antitax rhetoric again ran rampant. Later, Clinton sheepishly disavowed the extent to which his own 1993 tax legislation raised taxes (which it did—on those taxpayers with incomes above $250,000). In 1997, the Democratic president gave in and accepted a proposal from congressional Republicans for $95 billion of net tax cut over five years.

The persistence of this deep-rooted antitax ideology has had a significant impact on the development of tax policy. Ironically, although broad-based tax reduction is a fundamental tenet of the Republican party and cutting marginal tax rates is dogma to the proinvestment, supply-side wing of the GOP, all such tax cuts run counter to what is most advantageous to congressional policymakers *qua* politicians—namely, tax cuts targeted to constituents. As much as Republican politicians like cutting taxes in general, they (and their Democratic colleagues) have a greater interest in granting tax relief to constituents in their home districts and to those organized interests and groups that constitute their respective party coalitions. This helps explain why the 1995 Republican tax bill vetoed by President Clinton and the tax legislation enacted in 1997 included, despite all the antitax rhetoric, so many special tax preferences benefiting constituents of *both* political parties.

PLURALISM, INCREMENTALISM, AND THE INCOME TAX

How then to explain the complex politics of taxation in the United States? Pluralism is the most common model advanced by political scientists to generally describe U.S. politics. The pluralist model assumes that policymaking is decentralized, that political power is widely dispersed within civil society, and that the policymaking apparatus is readily accessible to numerous social and economic interests. Pluralist theory holds that policymakers are subjected to pressures from a wide range of organized groups, and that those who are most intensely affected by particular issues will organize and lobby policymakers hardest with respect to those issues. Overall, congressional policymakers respond to such lobbying by enacting policies that accommodate the best organized and most strategically situated interests—those with access to the decision-making institutions. Policy decisions are the outcome of bargaining among the groups that are organized and represented in the decision-making process. Pluralist power structures tend to produce a distinctive politics to the extent that numerous interest groups potentially possess the power to influence specific and narrow aspects of policymaking, but no single group is capable of dominating the entire policymaking process.

The politics-as-usual of taxation is generally portrayed as typical of a pluralist politics. Indeed, the pluralist model is highly descriptive of policymaking for the income tax during most of the twentieth century. The model focuses on Congress and the tax committees and assumes that a dynamic interest-group politics drives tax policy. Groups have organized around narrow economic interests and lobbied for relief from the relatively high marginal tax rates that have prevailed since the 1940s. Policymakers respond to the appeals of special interests (especially those located in their own home districts) for special tax preferences. Political scientist David Truman took as a given that well-financed special-interest groups with a great stake in outcomes will prevail in the tax legislative arena (Truman, 1971, pp. 361, 422). In the politics of the income tax, outside interest groups (both public and private) have ready access to the policymaking process. As a result of the openness of the congressional policymaking process, the preferences of many competing interests are successfully translated into tax policy. Many of the institutional barriers that congressmen relied on in the 1950s and 1960s to shield themselves from the pressures of special-interest groups (most particularly, the centralized control of the tax legislative process by Wilbur Mills, longtime and powerful chairman of the House Ways and Means Committee) were weakened by the post-Watergate reforms enacted in the mid-1970s, which had the unintended effect of exposing congressional members to greater lobbying and pressures exerted by such groups. In the 1980s, the tax policymaking process became even more receptive to interest-group politics. Indeed, during the decade it seemed that policymakers accommodated at one time or another virtually every organized interest group with its own special tax provisions.

Normal pluralist politics usually results in a process of incremental development for the income tax. Pluralist structures of political power tend to produce incremental policymaking because interest-group pressures most often lead to incremental modifications of existing policies. The pluralist-incrementalist model has thus been successfully applied to describe the normal policymaking of the federal income tax (Conlan, Wrightson, and Beam, 1990). Tax policy is said to advance through incremental or gradual departures from existing law rather than through radical advances. According to one astute observer of U.S. tax policy, "The tax code offers a variety of easily grasped levers. In this sense, it is an incrementalist paradise, susceptible and seductive to political tinkerers" (Witte, 1985, p. 245). In incremental policymaking, special provisions enacted for organized interests and groups are preserved in the tax laws, while new policies (very often at cross-purposes with old ones) are continually added.

This model explains a good deal about how the tax laws develop and why the tax expenditure budget increases each year. It also helps explain why tax policy is incoherent, with many provisions in the tax code expressing policies that are in conflict with other provisions. Congress enacts a provision that bestows special tax treatment on a favored group or interest and then (perhaps because of a change in the party that controls Congress) enacts other tax code provisions favoring diametrically opposed interests. The result is that some provisions benefit labor and others benefit business. Occasionally Congress is pressured by public opinion and media reports to enact provisions designed to limit a taxpayer's ability to make use of these special tax credits and deductions. For example, the alternative minimum tax was created to ensure that those taxpayers who make use of the overly generous tax preferences pay some income tax. Rather than repeal the original preferences, congressional policymakers found it more advantageous politically to enact new, complicated provisions to restrict the benefits derived from those preferences—thereby giving the appearance that Congress was doing something about special interests without actually taking a position adverse to those interests. This approach is typical of the pluralist tax politics that prevails in the United States.

Notwithstanding the descriptive power of the pluralist-incrementalist model, the model does not explain all of the politics and development of the federal income tax, especially that witnessed in recent decades. Partisanship and ideology have resurfaced as strong, even dominant forces shaping contemporary tax policy. This was the case in 1981 when supply-side economics dominated tax policy, in 1993 when Democrats passed by the slimmest of margins a 10 percent surtax on taxpayers with the highest income, and again in 1995 when anti-tax Republicans took control of the tax committees. In these cases, political ideologies dominated the tax-policymaking process, producing policies very much at odds with what would be predicted by the incrementalist-pluralist model. Although the normal politics of the income tax (such as use of the tax code for constituency service) is well described by the pluralist model, the most important tax legislation enacted in recent decades expresses a political use of the income tax by policymakers to advance their partisan agendas. Nonincremental tax policymaking has become commonplace in the past two decades.

Certainly, the most difficult tax legislation to explain from the perspective of pluralism and incrementalism is the Tax Reform Act of 1986. In his January 1984 State of the Union address, President Reagan called upon the Treasury Department to produce a study of tax reform. In response, the Treasury generated a series of tax reform proposals. For tax experts in the Treasury, "reform" meant eliminating all the special tax expenditures that Congress had inserted into the tax code for political reasons. Unexpectedly, the political movement for tax reform gained momentum, and Congress reluctantly took up the cause. Eventually, the White House and the tax committees were occupied for nearly two years with the campaign for tax reform. Even more surprising, the effort bore fruit in the fall of 1986 with the enactment of the Tax Reform Act of 1986.

This act has been widely hailed as the most significant tax-reform legislation in the history of the federal income tax (Witte, 1991, p. 4; Shaviro, 1990, p. 5). By virtue of the sheer volume of revisions and amendments to the tax laws that it implemented, the 1986 act was the most massive restructuring in the eighty-year history of the federal income tax. For this reason alone the 1986 act is impossible to explain from the perspective of pluralism and incrementalism. What accounts for such a dramatic departure from politics-as-usual for the income tax? Some have described the 1986 act as the product of unusual circumstances and the extraordinary convergence of ideas and political interests (Conlan, Wrightson, and Beam, 1990; Kingdon, 1995, pp. 213–217). In a distinctly unique moment in political time, conservatives and supply-siders in the Reagan administration who favored tax rate reduction found common ground with liberal Democrats in Congress who supported the reform proposals of tax experts in the Treasury Department. Likewise, politicians who normally were not in the vanguard of the tax reform movement (in particular, then Ways and Means Committee chairman Dan Rostenkowski and Senate Finance Committee chairman Robert Packwood) were swept along by the tax reform movement because they feared being perceived by the public as obstacles to reform.

Whatever the merits of this description of the politics behind the 1986 act, it remains difficult (if not impossible) to predict when political interests, reform efforts, and "ideas" will again converge to produce a tax reform bill. Tax reform disappeared from the policy agenda after 1986. Nevertheless, the repeated political use of tax expenditures creates new pressure for tax reform. Eventually, the complexity of the tax laws and the revenue loss attributable to the increase in tax expenditures stimulates interest in pruning and simplifying the tax code. But when and under what circumstances are such reform efforts likely to succeed? Such radical departures from the normal politics of the income tax lie outside the pluralist-incrementalist model.

A good deal of the politics surrounding the 1997 tax bill can be explained by the pluralist-incrementalist model. Existing provisions were amended and modified (such as changing the taxation of capital gains, reducing the impact of the alternative minimum tax on corporations, and so on) to produce slightly better tax results for constituents of the Republican party. Through trade-offs and compromises, the Democratic administration secured perks of its own—such as phasing out tax credits for education for high-income taxpayers. Overall, the resulting legislation added significantly to the complexity of the income tax by introducing many new and complicated concepts and computations to the tax laws. However, even while Congress was considering this bill that added to the complexity of the tax code and conferred so many tax benefits on the constituents of both political parties, political rhetoric against the income tax ran rampant. Several highly partisan proposals for "fundamental tax reform" (that is, for repealing the income tax altogether) have attracted unexpectedly strong support in Congress. At times it appears that another dramatic departure from the typical pattern of pluralist tax politics and incremental development is just over the horizon.

It remains to be seen whether the 1997 tax act was a return to the normal politics of the income tax or whether it was a harbinger of radical tax reform. Accordingly, we should not be too comfortable with the pluralist-incrementalist model and dismiss 1986 as a mere aberration. Although pluralism and incrementalism describe a good deal of tax politics most of the time, legislation such as that enacted in 1986 as well as that favored by Archer and Armey, lies outside the model. Because the tax laws are used not only to raise revenue but also to implement the partisan agendas of the two major political parties, contemporary tax policy is a highly complicated, erratic, and ultimately unpredictable enterprise.

CONCLUSION

The U.S. tax laws are used by policymakers for a variety of political purposes that are dictated by the constitutional structure of the U.S. regime. Under the democratic electoral system, it is politicians who make tax policy. Congressional tax policymakers serve as ombudspersons for their constituents and as leaders of the two political parties that control Congress. On top of this, the same policymakers are charged with raising the enormous revenue required to finance the activities of the U.S. government. The revenue function of the income tax is at odds with the instrumental, political uses of the tax.

The structures of the political system impose conflicting demands on tax policymakers, impelling them both to raise revenue and to implement policies that are functionally equivalent to direct budgetary expenditures. When the income tax is used by policymakers to implement public policies and to cull favor with local constituents, the Treasury is inevitably deprived of revenue. On top of all this, a strong antitax ideology pervades U.S. politics—most typically given voice by the Republican party. At various moments, such as in the late 1940s and early 1980s, this antitax rhetoric has prevailed in the political contest between the two major parties. The victory of the Republican party in the 1994 elections was driven by this antitax ideology and has altered the dynamics of the tax-policymaking process in favor of tax reductions—and will perhaps one day even lead to the abandonment of the income tax altogether. But even those politicians who rant and rave most against the income tax find it irresistible as a tool for achieving their own political purposes. This attitude dictates that the income tax will be around for a long time, serving both as the primary source of revenue for the federal government and as an important political tool of U.S. policymakers.

References

Adams, T. S. "Ideal and Idealism in Taxation." *American Economic Review,* 1928, *18*(1), 1–8.

Brennan, H. G., and Buchanan, J. *The Power to Tax: Analytical Foundations of a Fiscal Constitution.* Cambridge: Cambridge University Press, 1980.

Brownlee, W. E. *Federal Taxation in America: A Short History.* New York: Cambridge University Press, 1996.

Conlan, T. J., Wrightson, M. T., and Beam, D. R. *Taxing Choices: The Politics of Tax Reform.* Washington, D.C.: Congressional Quarterly Press, 1990.

Fiorina, M. P. *Congress: Keystone of the Washington Establishment.* New Haven, Conn.: Yale University Press, 1977.

Hansen, S. B. *The Politics of Taxation: Revenue Without Representation.* New York: Praeger, 1983.

Howard, C. *The Hidden Welfare State: Tax Expenditures and Social Policy in the United States.* Princeton, N.J.: Princeton University Press, 1997.

Kingdon, J. W. *Agendas, Alternatives, and Public Policies.* (2nd ed.) New York: Harper-Collins, 1995.

Levi, M. *Of Rule and Revenue.* Berkeley: University of California Press, 1988.

Manley, J. *The Politics of Finance: The House Committee on Ways and Means.* New York: Little, Brown, 1970.

Marx, K. "The Eighteenth Brumaire of Louis Bonaparte." In D. McLellan (ed.), *Karl Marx: Selected Writings.* London: Oxford University Press, 1977. (Originally published 1852.)

Mayhew, D. R. *Congress: The Electoral Connection.* New Haven, Conn.: Yale University Press, 1974.

Pollack, S. D. *The Failure of U.S. Tax Policy: Revenue and Politics.* University Park: Pennsylvania State University Press, 1996.

Rabushka, A., and Hall, R. E. *The Flat Tax.* Stanford, Calif.: Hoover Institution Press, 1985.

Reese, T. J. *The Politics of Taxation.* Westport, Conn.: Quorum/Greenwood, 1980.

Rubin, I. S. *The Politics of Public Budgeting: Getting and Spending, Borrowing and Balancing.* (3rd ed.) Chatham, N.J.: Chatham House, 1997.

Savage, J. D. *Balanced Budgets and American Politics.* Ithaca, N.Y.: Cornell University Press, 1988.

Schneider, J. E. *Ideological Coalitions in Congress.* Westport, Conn.: Quorum/Greenwood, 1979.

Sears, D. O., and Citrin, J. *Tax Revolt: Something for Nothing in California.* Cambridge, Mass.: Harvard University Press, 1982.

Shaviro, D. "Beyond Public Choice and Public Interest: A Study of the Legislative Process as Illustrated by Tax Legislation in the 1980s." *University of Pennsylvania Law Review,* 1990, *139*(1), 1–123.

Skowronek, S. *Building a New American State: The Expansion of National Administrative Capacities, 1877–1920.* New York: Cambridge University Press, 1982.

Steinmo, S. *Taxation and Democracy: Swedish, British, and American Approaches to Financing the Modern State.* New Haven, Conn.: Yale University Press, 1993.

Strahan, R. *New Ways and Means: Reform and Change in a Congressional Committee.* Chapel Hill: University of North Carolina Press, 1990.

Surrey, S. S., and McDaniel, P. R. *Tax Expenditures.* Cambridge, Mass.: Harvard University Press, 1985.

Truman, D. *The Governmental Process.* (2d ed.) New York: Knopf, 1971.

U.S. General Accounting Office. "Tax Policy: Tax Expenditures Deserve More Scrutiny" (GAO/GGD-AIMD-94-122). Washington, D.C.: Government Printing Office, 1994.

Witte, J. F. *The Politics and Development of the Federal Income Tax.* Madison: University of Wisconsin Press, 1985.

Witte, J. F. "The Tax Reform Act of 1986: A New Era in Tax Politics?" *American Politics Quarterly,* 1991, *19*(4), 438–457.

PART FOUR

THE INFORMATIONAL FOUNDATIONS OF BUDGETING

CHAPTER FOURTEEN

The Bases of Accounting for Budgeting and Financial Reporting

James L. Chan

The federal government is bankrupt, declared the Citizens for Budget Reform in its *USA Annual Shareholders' Report* (Fox, 1996, p. 1) on the basis of the following "simple balance sheet math":

$$\text{Assets} - \text{Liabilities} = \text{USA Net Worth}$$
$$\$22 \text{ trillion} - \$51 \text{ trillion} = -\$29 \text{ trillion}$$

Among the reported assets are "hard assets" such as cash and equipment, along with the power to tax and to borrow and above all the power to create money. The reported liabilities include, besides the national debt, $23 trillion in entitlements.

Because of the way assets and liabilities are defined in the example just presented, professional auditors would not give a clean opinion to these numbers. But the numbers are in the public domain regardless of their validity. If they are not to be given much credence, we might turn to the official numbers put out by the U.S. government itself.

Unfortunately the official numbers are also problematic. Table 14.1 shows the summary statistics from the *U.S. Government Annual Report, Fiscal Year 1995* (U.S. Department of the Treasury, 1996b) and the prototype *Consolidated*

Note: The comments of Allen Schick, Jean Harris, Jonathan Pingle, and anonymous reviewers are gratefully acknowledged. The author alone is responsible for any remaining errors.

Table 14.1. U.S. Government Financial Position at the End of FY95
(in Billions of Dollars).

	Assets	Liabilities	Net Position
CFS	$1,298	$5,811	−$4,513
Annual Report	89	3,674	−3,585
Difference	$1,209	$2,137	−928

Source: U.S. Department of the Treasury, 1996a and 1996b.

Financial Statements of the U.S. Government, 1995 Prototype (U.S. Department of the Treasury, 1996a). Were the U.S. government's assets closer to $1,000 billion or $100 billion, and were its liabilities closer to $6 trillion or $4 trillion? A major source of the differences between these two sets of numbers is the different measurement rules currently used in federal financial reporting.

This chapter analyzes the measurement rules (the basis of accounting) used in government financial reporting and budgeting. A framework is developed for analyzing the crucial concept of *accrual.* The chapter suggests that the conventional dichotomy of cash versus accrual is too crude. After contrasting the budgeting and accounting perspectives on the accrual basis, some numerical examples are given to illustrate how the extent of accrual results in different numbers in financial statements and budgets. This is followed by a description of the extent to which the accrual basis is required by governmental accounting policy boards. Finally, the implications of the accrual basis for budgets are examined.

DEGREES OF ACCRUAL

Basis of accounting refers to the measurement rules that instruct accountants and budget scorekeepers about ways to deal with the effects of an entity's transactions or events. Accountants typically frame the issue in terms of the *timing* of registering the effects of those transactions or events. Accordingly, there are two primary bases of accounting: the *accrual basis* and the *cash basis.* The cash basis records the transactions or events "when cash is received or paid"; the accrual basis recognizes those effects "when the transactions or events take place," according to the Governmental Accounting Standards Board (Governmental Accounting Standards Board, 1996b, para. 3b). Actually, accrual is not merely a matter of timing; it involves the complex issue of tracing the delayed financial effects of budgetary decisions and related actions. Unfortunately, discussions about accrual are often complicated by the different approaches used by budgeting and accounting professionals in interpreting those effects.

Budgeting and Accounting Perspectives

Budget analysts tend to assume a periodic operational perspective while accountants are trained to think about financial position in a double-entry framework. Budget discussions often seem fixated on the effects of decisions on the deficit—the excess of financial resource outflows over inflows during a period. Accountants also deal with such *flow measures,* but they are equally concerned about the balance sheet and the relationship between resources and debts—stock measures—at some points in time, most notably at the end of a fiscal year.

There are several other differences between budget and accounting analyses. First, budgeting is oriented to the future while accounting looks backward. Both time perspectives are necessary because government requires both planning and feedback based on actual performance. Whereas a budget makes promises, financial statements report whether those promises were kept. These roles give rise to the complementary and yet competitive relationship between accounting and budgeting.

Second, budgeting tends to focus on discrete periods while accounting is concerned with the continuous carryover effects from one period to the next. Politicians and the public alike focus on the bottom line of a budget—the annual deficit figure. Under the cash basis, the budget deficit for year t+1 is the projected deficiency of cash receipts to finance the cash outlays:

Equation 1

$$\text{Deficit}_{(t+1)} = \text{Outlays}_{(t+1)} - \text{Receipts}_{(t+1)}$$

To the extent that not all purchases for goods and services were paid for and not all revenues were collected during the year in question, there would be carryovers in the form of payables (a liability) and receivables (an asset) that would require reporting in the balance sheet at year's end. The issues surrounding the accrual basis turn on the question of what to do with these interperiod effects.

Placing the deficit on an accrual basis would require recognition of the stock measures, that is, payables and receivables, as follows:

Equation 2

$$\text{Deficit}_{(t+1)} = [\text{Outlays}_{(t+1)} + \Delta\text{Payables}_{(t+1)}]$$
$$- [\text{Receipts}_{(t+1)} + \Delta\text{Receivables}_{(t+1)}]$$

The delta in $\Delta\text{Payables}_{(t+1)}$ and in $\Delta\text{Receivables}_{(t+1)}$ refers to change during the year (t + 1). A comparison of the one-period budget model in Equation 1 and the accounting model in Equation 2 shows that the carryover effects are explicitly dealt with by accrual accounting but ignored by cash budgeting. To avoid confusion, the term *expenditure* has not been used. The budget literature, implicitly using the cash basis, often equates outlays with expenditures and refers to $\Delta\text{Payables}_{(t+1)}$ as *accrued expenditures*. Accounting, conversely, would regard the whole amount $[\text{Outlays}_{(t+1)} + \Delta\text{Payables}_{(t+1)}]$ as an expenditure by assuming an accrual basis of accounting. On the revenue side, formally recognizing receivables can give rise to extremely complex conceptual, measurement, and procedural problems.

Besides the cash and accrual bases, there exist also the *budgetary bases* of accounting. One of these bases may be called the *cash plus obligations basis* and the other may be called the *expenditure plus obligations basis*. Both were conceived to gauge the extent to which appropriations have been spent. At this point we need to distinguish between obligations and liabilities. *Obligations* are rooted in appropriations. An *appropriation* is legal authorization to spend— that is, to incur obligations, or legally binding contractual promises, that would immediately or eventually lead to cash outlays (U.S. General Accounting Office, 1993, pp. 61–62). As evidenced by contracts or orders for goods or services, obligations reduce the amount of appropriation available for future spending. Thus, at the end of fiscal year (t + 1):

Equation 3

Available Balance of Appropriation$_{(t+1)}$
$$= \text{Appropriation}_{(t+1)} - [\text{Outlays}_{(t+1)} + \text{Obligations}_{(t+1)}]$$

This method of budget calculation, however, overlooks the possible existence of obligations that have become liabilities, confirmed by the receipt of goods and services, a matter of considerable interest to accountants. Thus there arises the expenditure-plus-obligations budgetary basis, which would modify Equation 3 as follows:

Equation 4

Available Balance of Appropriation$_{(t+1)}$
$$= \text{Appropriation}_{(t+1)} - [\text{Outlays}_{(t+1)} + \Delta\text{Payables}_{(t+1)} + \text{Obligations}_{(t+1)}]$$

It is hoped that the sample equations just presented illustrate the point that financial numbers are virtually meaningless unless we know the measurement rules behind them. Often the terminology is not consistent and the rules are ambiguous, particularly to those trained in another specialty. The next section explains the accountant's mind-set.

Accounting Equation

The accountant's view of the world is encapsulated in the *accounting equation:*

Equation 5
$$\text{Assets}_{(t+1)} = \text{Liabilities}_{(t+1)} + \text{Net Assets}_{(t+1)}$$

The accounting equation is the conceptual model used by accounting to analyze transactions. Such an analysis provides numbers that are subsequently recorded and summarized and eventually reported in financial statements. The accounting process need not concern us here. What is important is that Equation 5 states that an entity's economic resources at a point in time—such as the end of period $t+1$—are either borrowed or owned by the entity itself. Net assets are variously called the *owner's equity* or *stockholders' equity* in a business, or the *fund balance* in the governmental and nonprofit context.

Alternatively, the accounting equation may be rewritten as follows:

$$\text{Equation 6}$$
$$\text{Assets}_{(t+1)} - \text{Liabilities}_{(t+1)} = \text{Net Assets}_{(t+1)}$$

This formulation puts the emphasis on *net assets,* or the residual. An entity is solvent if its net assets have a positive number, that is, when its assets exceed its liabilities. In contrast, if liabilities exceed assets, the net assets number is negative. Regardless of the presentation, it is quite obvious that the balance sheet emphasis influences the accounting perspective, so much so that the statement describing the results of operations of a period is sometimes viewed as representing changes in financial position.

At this point we can go no further without resolving the issue of what are assets and liabilities, that is the *measurement focus* of the balance sheet.

Measurement Focus

The measurement focus characterizes how broadly the concepts of assets and liabilities are construed. As explained earlier, the cash basis of accounting measures the results of operations in terms of the receipts and disbursements of cash. The accrual basis, in contrast, adopts a broader view of assets and takes liabilities into account as well. But how broadly?

An entity's *assets* are the economic resources that are capable of providing measurable future benefits. They include resources the entity owns as well as resources over which it has effective operating control, such as capital equipment financed by debt. Benefits are operationalized as future net cash inflows (as in the case of receivables) or as the reduction of future net cash outflows (as in the case of prepayments for services). The "measurable" qualification would rule out the accounting recognition of resources that produce benefits for which accountants have not developed acceptably precise and reliable measures. Furthermore, the transaction or event that establishes the entity's claim or control over the resource should have occurred. This requirement contrasts with the economist's approach of stating asset value in terms of the present value of future benefits.

Accounting policies interpret these basic criteria, resulting in the inclusion of some economic resources as assets and the exclusion of others. This filtering process is called *accounting recognition,* which is analogous to the legal concept of admissible evidence. There is considerable subjectivity in applying the basic recognition criteria. Consider research and development (R&D) as an example. Under the rules of the Financial Accounting Standards Board (FASB), a business cannot regard any of its R&D spending as an asset. But an experimental balance sheet depicting national wealth includes federal R&D spending as an asset (U.S. Office of Management and Budget, 1996b, p. 27). Similarly, by using the recognition criteria embodied in current generally accepted accounting principles, most accountants would leave investment in human capital, as measured by educational expenditures, off the balance sheet. Nor would they consider projected receipts, tax base, or the power to tax as assets.

After the assets are recognized, they can be classified as either financial resources or nonfinancial resources (See Figure 14.1). A *financial resource* is a claim against others' assets (such as receivables) or services (such as prepaid insurance). The timing of claims further separates financial resources into *current financial resources,* convertible into cash within one year, and *noncurrent financial resources.* Capital assets (such as buildings and equipment) are considered to be *nonfinancial resources* if they are held for future use.

Liabilities require measurable future economic sacrifices in terms of cash outflows or service delivery. Liabilities are usually classified as *current* (due within one year) and *noncurrent* or *long-term* on the basis of their maturity (see Figure 14.1). It is generally easier to identify liabilities because they are usually evidenced by or traced to past events or contracts. That is usually the case in the private sector and in commercial transactions involving government. The line, however, between a government's legal obligations and its social or moral responsibilities is often blurred. In the case of federal social insurance programs, even the government's legal obligations are debatable. Nevertheless, few

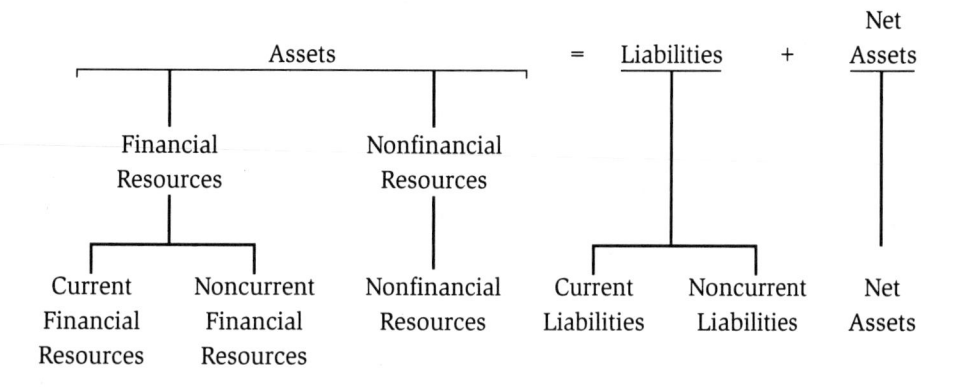

Figure 14.1. Measurement Focus.

accountants would take the resource requirements of national needs and discount them to arrive at a liability measure. For accountants, the starting point is a past event, from which they trace forward consequences that will require future costs.

Degree of Accrual

The degree of accrual is determined by the range of assets and liabilities encompassed in constructing revenue and spending measures. The expansion or contraction of the accounting measurement focus makes accrual an elastic concept. For example, accrual can be stretched to a breaking point by including educational capital as an asset and moral responsibility as a liability. These are extreme interpretations, however. In practice, judicious adjustments of the scope of assets and liabilities results in more refined measures of accrual.

Currently, government accounting distinguishes between full accrual and modified accrual. Upon closer examination, the modified accrual concept is ambiguous because the modification may be so mild that it resembles modified cash; conversely, the modification can be so extensive that it may amount to almost full accrual. Thus it is proposed that the ambiguous modified accrual basis be separated into two categories: the *weak* form and the *semistrong* form. This will lead to more rigorous definition and precise measures of revenue and spending.

Revenue Recognition

In terms of Equation 6, revenues are gross changes in net assets. The best accounting standards do not permit the use of the cash basis in recognizing revenue. Specifically, borrowed cash results not in revenue but in a liability. This may sound like a truism but bond proceeds are often included in government budgets as a part of the money available to finance operations. This practice runs the risk of blurring the distinction between borrowing and raising revenues through exercising the government's taxing authority or by providing goods and services. These activities often result in increased assets. The cash basis would regard cash receipts as revenues. The weak modified accrual basis would include cash and current financial resources as revenues. This is equivalent to what is called the modified accrual basis in the current government literature, which uses the "measurable and available" criteria. The semistrong modified accrual basis would include noncurrent financial resources as well. The full accrual basis of revenue recognition goes beyond the resource availability concern; it addresses the fundamental political and social relationship between the government and the public.

Accruing revenue may rest on legal grounds: a government can recognize revenues as soon as it acquires a legal claim on the taxpayer's resources. The moment a taxable transaction takes place, the government is entitled to whatever taxes or fees are due to it under existing laws. The second type of full accruals would treat governments like a business: no service, no revenue. In other words, governments would not be allowed to claim credit for revenues until and unless they have earned them. No revenue would be recognized until and unless governments have sold the goods or provided the services; cash received in advance of delivery or sale of goods gives rise to a liability, that is, revenue is deferred. This may sound like a rather radical idea, but it is consistent with the theory behind the current emphasis on service efforts and accomplishment in state and local governments and in the federal government's Government Performance and Results Act of 1993. Needless to say, many theoretical and practical problems remain to be solved if either level of the full accrual basis is to be implemented. The purpose here is to raise the possibilities and not to deal with implementation issues. Indeed, the terminology does not even exist to describe the various types of accrued revenues.

Spending Measure Recognition

Spending reduces net assets. The terms *cash outlays* or *disbursements* seem to adequately describe spending on the cash basis. Beyond that, the technical vocabulary is rich but ambiguous. The terms *expenditures* and *expenses* are often used interchangeably, but they really should not be. The term *expenditures* is associated with the modified accrual basis of accounting. Because expenditures, as changes in net assets, are defined in terms of assets and liabilities, the types of assets and liabilities shown in Figure 14.1 will affect the definition of expenditures. Specifically, the decreases in current financial resources as well as increases in current liabilities give rise to *expenditures I*—a weak modified accrual concept. Spending that reduces noncurrent financial resources or creates long-term liabilities may then be called *expenditure II*— a semistrong modified accrual concept. When the term *expenditure* appears in the government accounting literature, it typically refers to what we call expenditure I. The designation expenditure II can accommodate the trend toward the recognition of more and longer-term liabilities. Finally, the full accrual basis uses the concept of *expenses,* which can include the cost of nonfinancial assets used in producing goods or services, depreciation being a prime example.

Having analyzed revenue and spending measures in considerable depth it is time to relate these variables of financial operations to financial positions expressed in the form of the accounting equation. Recall Equation 6:

$$\text{Assets}_{(t+1)} - \text{Liabilities}_{(t+1)} = \text{Net Assets}_{(t+1)}$$

This section has discussed revenues, expenditures, and expenses in terms of assets and liabilities as follows:

$$\text{Assets}_{(t)} - \text{Liabilities}_{(t)} = \text{Net Assets}_{(t)}$$

Equation 7

| $+$ | $-$ | $+$ | $\text{Revenues}_{(t+1)}$ |

Equation 8

| $-$ | $+$ | $-$ | Expenses/ $\text{Expenditures}_{(t+1)}$ |

resulting in

Equation 9

$$\text{Assets}_{(t+1)} - \text{Liabilities}_{(t+1)} = \text{Net Assets}_{(t+1)}$$

In this way, the operating statement as symbolized by Equations 7 and 8 may be viewed as a bridge between two successive balance sheets depicted by Equations 6 and 9. Similarly, a budget, which projects resource inflows and outflows, links two pro forma statements of financial position. The financial accounting model is therefore more complete than the budget model in that it embodies both flows and stock measures. In comparison with the typical one-period budget model, the accounting model continuously traces the changes in assets and liabilities. It is therefore particularly useful in tracking the future consequences of current operations. As such, it is a necessary and useful complement to the one-period budget model.

ILLUSTRATIONS

Several illustrations of the concepts just presented are now provided. Throughout the examples, C stands for the cash basis, WM stands for weak modified accrual, SM stands for semistrong modified accrual, and F stands for full accrual. All the cases presented are analyzed from the government's perspective.

Case 1

Mr. Policeman worked for the City of Riverside. For FY97, he received $40,000 in salary and overtime pay, plus $4,000 in short-term fringe benefits ($3,000 of which had been received by year's end). In addition, he was entitled to some long-term benefits: $2,000 of vacation and sick-leave pay, as well as $6,000 in employer-contributed retirement pension and other postemployment benefits.

Analysis. The headings in Table 14.2 represent the elements of the accounting equation, which we will use to assess Mr. Policeman's impact on Riverside's finances under the four bases of accounting discussed earlier. The cost of Mr. Policeman's service increases from $43,000 under the C basis to expenditure I

Table 14.2. Personal Services and Operating Debt.

Basis of Accounting	Cash +	Current Financial Resources +	Noncurrent Financial Resources +	Non-financial Resources =	Current Liabilities +	Non-current Liabilities +	Net Assets
C	−43,000				=		−43,000
WM	−43,000				= 1,000		−44,000
SM	−43,000				= 1,000	8,000	−52,000
F	−43,000				= 1,000	8,000	−52,000

of $44,000 due to the recognition of $1,000 of short-term liability under the WM accrual basis. Another $8,000 in long-term liabilities raises the cost to expenditure II of $52,000 under the SM accrual basis. Because no diminution of capital assets is involved in this case, the full accrual basis is equivalent to the SM accrual basis. It should be noted that the WM basis added $1,000 in short-term liabilities, and the SM and F bases added another $8,000 in long-term liabilities to the amount recognized under the C basis. The acknowledgment of this $8,000 of *operating debt* related to services delivered represents the information value added of accrual accounting.

The budgetary implication of this analysis can be seen in attempting the answer to the question, How much should Riverside have levied in taxes to cover the cost of public safety provided by Mr. Policeman? The amounts would similarly range from $43,000 to $52,000, depending on the extent to which the city's budget policy required the FY97 taxpayers to bear the cost of Mr. Policeman's service during that period. Cash budgeting would leave a legacy of unfunded liabilities; accrual budgeting might induce higher current taxes to fund both cash payments and some or all of the delayed costs.

Case 2

For FY97, the Department of Transportation of the City of Metropolis received a $1.10 million appropriation to buy a fleet of twenty trucks: ten trucks of type A at the estimated cost of $50,000 each and ten trucks of type B at $60,000 each. Purchase orders were issued during the year. By year's end, four type-A trucks were received and payment of $200,000 was made. Six type-A trucks costing $300,000 were also received. Metropolis issued a short-term note of $40,000 and a long-term note of $260,000. None of the type-B trucks were received.

Analysis. This case is illustrated in Table 14.3. Again, the net assets column reflects the magnitude of the spending measures under different bases. Under the cash basis, $200,000 is recognized. The WM basis takes into account the $40,000 in current payables, thus raising the capital expenditure I to $260,000. The recognition of another $260,000 in long-term liabilities under the SM basis boosts the capital expenditure II to $500,000. As in Case 1, the modified accrual

Table 14.3. Capital Spending and Capital Debt.

Basis of Accounting	Cash +	Current Financial Resources +	Noncurrent Financial Resources +	Non-financial Resources =	Current Liabilities +	Non-current Liabilities +	Net Assets
C	−200,000						−200,000
WM	−200,000				+40,000		−240,000
SM	−200,000				+40,000	+260,000	−500,000
F	−200,000			+500,000	+40,000	+260,000	0

basis increases the visibility of liabilities—a capital debt of $300,000 in this case. There still exists, however, a major deficiency in the accounting system: there is no recognition on the balance sheet of the fact that the city now has ten trucks. The F basis cures this defect by placing ten type-A trucks on the balance sheet as assets at the cost of $500,000 total, along with the associated capital debt. The impact of the F basis on net assets is dramatic: compared to the SM basis, the net assets are $500,000 more, because the expenditures for the ten trucks received are viewed as having increased the city's capital assets. After the trucks are placed into service, the F basis will recognize their depreciation as an expense in the net assets column.

The accounting in Table 14.3 is appropriate but the disclosure, even under the F basis, is not complete. Ten type-B trucks still on order are not reported. As explained earlier, financial accounting does not consider undelivered orders as liabilities. It acknowledges their existence by reserving the fund balance (another name for net assets in governmental accounting) for the amount of the orders and offsetting that by reducing the amount of unreserved fund balance. Even though there is no net change in the total fund balance, information on the reserved fund balance would alert users to potential future cash outlays.

In addition to producing data for external reporting, the accounting system of Metropolis should also facilitate the city's budgetary control. Specifically, the accounting system should disclose the fact that the Department of Transportation has exhausted its appropriation for truck purchases by using the expenditure plus obligation budgetary basis (Equation 4): available balance in the appropriation = $1,100,000 − $200,000 + ($40,000 + $260,000) + $600,000 = $0.

Case 3

In January 1997, the City of Paradise Valley levied various taxes totaling $1 million for FY97, which ends on December 31, 1997. By the closing date, $800,000 was collected; another $150,000 was due by the end of February 1998, with the remainder of $50,000 due thereafter.

Analysis. The recognition of revenues is recorded in the net assets column of Table 14.4. Under the C basis, the $800,000 collected is recognized as revenue.

Table 14.4. Revenue Recognition.

Basis of Accounting	Cash +	Current Financial Resources +	Noncurrent Financial Resources +	Non-financial Resources =	Current Liabilities +	Non-current Liabilities +	Net Assets
C	+800,000						+800,000
WM	+800,000	+150,000					+950,000
SM	+800,000	+150,000	+50,000				+1,000,000
F	+800,000	+150,000	+50,000		?	?	?

The WM basis counts the $150,000 current receivable as revenue, raising the total revenue to $950,000. The SM basis adds another $50,000 of long-term receivables as well, bringing total revenue to $1 million. There is insufficient information in this case to determine what the amounts of revenue-driven liabilities would be under the F basis.

Accrual is an elastic two-edged sword: the more it is stretched, the more longer-term assets are recognized, but also the more longer-term liabilities are recognized. Whereas budgeting tends to focus on outlays and obligations for control purposes, financial statements based on the accounting model present a more complete framework that encompasses both flow and stock measures, and a broader range of assets and liabilities. Departing from the cash basis, one could modify the accrual basis weakly to include revenues and expenditures that have short-term financial implications, or one could modify the accrual basis strongly and expand the range of assets and liabilities being considered to include long-term items. The extent to which accrual should be extended is a policy question. The next two sections examine the extent to which accounting standards boards have sought to apply accrual to government.

STATE AND LOCAL GOVERNMENT ACCOUNTING STANDARDS

Since 1984, the Governmental Accounting Standards Board (GASB) has been responsible for setting generally accepted accounting principles (GAAP) for state and local governments in the United States. These principles determine the form and content of general-purpose external financial reports that serve primarily the general public, governing boards and oversight bodies, and investors and creditors. This section focuses on the key measurement rules embodied in the GASB standards issued to date (Governmental Accounting Standards Board, 1996a).

Current Policy

The GASB requires state and local governments to use the full accrual basis to account for their commercial activities. For activities financed by governmental funds—the general fund, special revenue funds, capital projects funds, and debt service funds—the board prohibits the cash basis and has to date generally endorsed only what in this chapter has been called the weak modified accrual basis. Accordingly, expenditures are cash outlays and increases in short-term liabilities attributable to services received. Revenues claimed through the exercise of governmental power are conceptually recognizable when the government's claim is established (such as when a taxable transaction occurs). Current standards, however, call for recognition to the extent that such revenues (such as property taxes, income taxes, and sales taxes) are measurable and available to finance the operations of the period intended. In effect, revenues are receipts plus short-term receivables—increases in net current financial resources. Practical difficulties (such as lack of information and procedures) may further push the recognition of some revenues (such as fines, licenses, and permits) toward the cash basis.

The GASB has been struggling with the issues of accrual accounting since the board's inception. It has been pushing governments in the direction of recognizing and reporting more long-term liabilities, such as employee pensions; other postemployment benefits; claims, judgments, and compensated absences; and capital lease obligations. Though significant, these disclosures would not have an impact on current budgetary decisions because of the disconnection between these long-term liabilities and the short-term perspective of governmental funds.

In other words, when governmental funds use the weak modified accrual basis, noncurrent financial resources and capital assets, along with long-term liabilities, are excluded from their balance sheets. This omission is partially compensated by the disclosure of general fixed assets and general long-term debts adjacent to the balance sheets of the funds. As noted earlier, there are two types of liabilities: capital debt and operating debt. The capital debt in the general long-term debt disclosures is offset by the general fixed assets. There are, however, no assets to offset the operating debt, which was incurred to provide services in the current or past periods. Placing these operating debts, which are in effect deferred costs for current services, outside the responsible funds is an attractive option to politicians and public managers under pressure to produce balanced cash budgets. But this practice raises the question of intergenerational equity: future taxpayers will be asked to pay for services received earlier by others.

Proposed Policy

To achieve the objective of intergenerational (operationalized to be interperiod) equity, the GASB in 1990 issued a standard requiring the operating statements of governmental funds to move effectively from the weak modified accrual basis to the strong modified accrual basis of accounting. This policy shift was announced in GASB's Statement No. 11, titled *Measurement Focus and Basis of Accounting: Governmental Funds Operating Statements*, and was to be effective for fiscal years beginning June 15, 1994. In the board's view, the operating statements would help users find out "the extent to which current-year revenues were sufficient to pay for current-year services" (Governmental Accounting Standards Board, 1996b, para. 27). The adoption, however, of a flow-of-financial-resources measurement focus, rather than a current-financial-resources measurement focus, would mean that an increase in long-term operating debt would be counted as an expenditure (or expenditure II in the lexicon of this chapter) in the operating statement. The other implication, which was not addressed by Statement No. 11, was that long-term operating debt would be moved from the general long-term debt disclosures to the general fund or special revenue funds. As every accounting student knows, for the two sides of the accounting equation to remain equal, increases in long-term liabilities unaccompanied by compensating increases in assets would require an offset through a decrease in net assets or fund equity. To the extent that a government has an appreciable amount of pensions payable and vacation and sick leave liabilities, the incorporation of those monies into a fund might lead to the reporting of a sizable negative fund equity. Whereas in the past public officials could conveniently ignore off-fund disclosures, it would be hard to overlook a visible negative fund equity.

Statement No. 11 was not entirely a bitter pill. It made the recognition of a higher level of revenue possible by pushing the accrual of revenue to earlier points. Namely, tax revenues would be recognized when the underlying events generating the revenues had occurred and the government had demanded payment (such as by setting a due date). For example, a property tax would be recognized when levied, income tax would be recognized when taxable income was earned, and sales tax would be recognized when the taxable transactions had occurred. Revenues from nontax, nonexchange transactions (such as fines, licenses, and permits) would be recognized when the underlying events had occurred and the government held a legally enforceable claim. (As before, earned revenues would be recognized after the government had provided the services.)

Statement No. 11 represented a revolutionary step. Not only would its implementation move government from weak modified accrual to strong modified accrual, but it would also reach for the goal of full accrual. Sophisticated analysts and public officials ran simulations to see how their government financial picture would be portrayed, but apparently they did not like the projected scenarios and began to oppose Statement No. 11. After considerable debate, and bowing to its constituents' concern that the costs associated with implementing Statement No. 11 would outweigh the benefits, the GASB (through Statement No. 17, issued in 1993) indefinitely postponed the effective date of the standard.

In retrospect, one could reasonably predict that given the political and economic incentives to postpone costs to the future, the GASB was swimming against the current by subscribing to the objective that "the intent of balanced budget laws is that the current generation of citizens should not be able to shift the burden of paying for current-year services to future-year taxpayers" (Governmental Accounting Standards Board, 1996c, para. 60).

The New Reporting Model

In the wake of the failed attempt to adopt a strong modified accrual basis in accounting for core governmental functions, the GASB has taken a different tack in advancing its agenda. It now advocates the coexistence of the weak modified accrual basis and the full accrual basis in the same reporting model. In this dual-perspective model (Governmental Accounting Standards Board, 1997), the governmental funds would continue to be accounted for on the weak modified accrual basis in the fund-perspective financial statements. The full accrual basis, however, would be used in preparing entity-wide (that is, consolidated) financial statements. Specifically, capital assets would be displayed on the entity-wide balance sheet—now called the statement of net assets—and depreciation expense would be included in the expenses reported in a statement of activities.

Although the GASB has crafted an artful compromise to create the best of both worlds (status quo in the fund-perspective statements and revolutionary changes in the entity-wide statements), the new model sends a mixed message. Yes, governments will be obliged to move toward full accrual, but that move would not be expected to have real budgetary consequences. Because state and local governments usually budget by fund, they could overlook the entity-wide liabilities that do not belong to any specific funds.

FEDERAL ACCOUNTING STANDARDS

The budget has traditionally dominated federal financial management. In this environment, accounting—or more precisely, budgetary accounting—functions as a budget execution tool. Budgetary accounting measures and controls the use of budgetary resources as provided by law, and records receipts and other collections by source. Budgetary accounting systems track the use of each appropriation through the various stages of budget execution—apportionment, allotment, obligation, and outlay—after funds are appropriated. The close relationship between budgeting and accounting was clearly evident in GAO Title II, the compilation of federal accounting rules used until the early 1990s, when the Federal Accounting Standards Advisory Board (FASAB) was established.

The FASAB also recognizes a close link between budgeting and accounting. Its "budgetary integrity" objective states that federal financial reporting "should provide information that helps the reader determine how information on the use of budgetary resources relates to information on the costs of program operations and whether information on the status of budgetary resources is consistent with other accounting information on assets and liabilities" (U.S. Office of Management and Budget, 1993b). Accounting, however, at least in the context of general purpose external financial reporting, has emerged as complimentary, rather than subordinate, to the budget. Specifically, the basis of accounting used in external reporting need not be the same as the one used in the federal budget. In principle, federal financial accounting should use the full accrual basis, modified as necessitated by circumstances. Differences that exist between the accounting and budgetary bases are to be explained and reconciled.

Differences exist because the FASAB's basic approach is the accountant's balance sheet perspective described previously. Not only do the FASAB standards require a balance sheet, but in many ways the stewardship reporting requirements enunciated by the FASAB exceed the scope and measurement capability of full accrual under current generally accepted accounting principles used outside of the federal government. The stewardship objective calls for the disclosure of such resources as the following:

- Heritage assets (such as the Washington Monument); federal mission property, plant, and equipment (such as weapon systems), and federal land not used in operations

- Federal grants for physical properties that are subsequently owned by state and local governments, as well investments in human capital (such as educational and training programs) and research and development

- The projected future costs of providing services, assuming no policy change

By opting for disclosure rather than accounting recognition, the federal government defers the resolution of some of the most intractable measurement problems imaginable in accounting.

Compared to the kind of accounting envisioned by the FASAB standards, the federal budget's measurement method borders on being primitive. The federal deficit is the difference between receipts and outlays (Equation 1). Thus it operates essentially on the cash basis. As Schick explains (1995, pp. 27–31), there are a half-dozen measures of "deficit." But most of these measures are concerned with the types of entities or expenditures included, rather than with the measurement rule. Outlays are the last step of the spending process that originates from the budget authority granted by Congress. Budget authority is apportioned to agencies, usually for a period, by the Office of Management and Budget and is then allotted to the agency's subdivisions. Budget authority is then actually available for obligations in terms of contractual commitment to another party. Later, when contracted goods or services are received, the related obligation becomes a liability. The liquidation of a liability results in cash outlays (Schick, 1995, pp. 165–185).

To manage federal spending properly, the federal government's accounting systems need to possess the capacity to track the changing status of budget authority at various stages of budget execution. Traditionally, the budget system tends to keep track of obligations and outlays, while the accounting system, designed on the accrual basis, monitors accrued expenditures (that is, liabilities) and is consistently urged to measure cost (expense). As shown later in the chapter, considerable progress has been made, at least in terms of accounting standards, to integrate budgeting and accounting systems. Even though the literature is not unambiguous, it seems fair to consider outlay plus obligations to be the prevailing budgetary basis of the federal budget.

Specific Standards

Since its establishment in 1990, the FASAB has exhibited an increasing willingness to embrace the accrual basis of accounting. It began by attempting to conceptualize certain assets, namely cash, fund balance with the Treasury, accounts receivable, interest receivable, advances and prepayments, and investments in Treasury securities, as financial resources. These resources, when offset by current liabilities, such as accounts payable and interest payable, become net financial resources. Acceptance of this modest step turned out to be unexpectedly difficult in an environment in which accounting rules prevailed.

After this initial inertia, the movement toward full accrual gained considerable speed. Furthermore, the FASAB seemed to have learned from the GASB's lesson: it was fully cognizant of the balance sheet effect of accruals. In fact, a majority of standards deal with assets and liabilities. On the asset side, recognition is made of inventory and related property, direct loans, and property, plant, and equipment. On the other side of the balance sheet, liabilities are recognized for a wide range of obligations such as loan guarantees, federal debt, pensions and other retirement benefits, insurance and guarantees, capital leases, and contingencies. Furthermore, the FASAB took on the task of articulating standards for revenue recognition and cost measurement (U.S. Office of Management and Budget, 1993b). Following is a summary of the major standards.

Revenue recognition. The FASAB distinguished between exchange revenues and nonexchange revenues. In principle, nonexchange revenue should be recognized when "specifically identifiable, legally enforceable claims to others' assets" are established. The FASAB imposed the measurability criterion, but it does not use the availability criterion; instead, probable recognition is added as a criterion. The FASAB acknowledged that, in reality, taxes and duties are accounted for on a modified cash basis, which seems to be even weaker than weak modified accrual, even though ideally accrual is desirable (U.S. Office of Management and Budget, 1996a, pp. 61–67).

Cost measurement (expense recognition). Federal agencies are required to accumulate and report cost of activities regularly and to establish "responsibility segments" for matching costs with outputs. In particular, the statement advocates the use of full-cost accounting, which includes direct and indirect costs, including allocated costs thereof, and the reporting entity's own costs as well as the cost of goods and services received from other entities (U.S. Office of Management and Budget, 1995a).

Asset recognition. Federal accounting has taken decisive steps to put assets other than cash (and its equivalence, fund balance with the Treasury) on the balance sheet. Accounting for direct loans was given special impetus in light of the 1990 Credit Reform Act. The FASAB decided to follow the lead of legislation by stating direct loans at the present value of their estimated net cash inflows. Finally, fixed assets that are used in providing general government services are admitted to the balance sheet. Those assets that involve very difficult identification and measurement problems—such as federal missions property, plant, and equipment; heritage assets; and federal land—are subject to what is called "supplementary stewardship reporting." That is, they are to be identified and measured in physical terms but not in terms of cost or economic value (U.S. Office of Management and Budget, 1993a, 1993c, 1995a).

Liability recognition. Besides addressing the conventional liabilities such as accounts payable, interest payable, and salaries and wages payable, federal accounting standards also tackled other relatively controversial federal liabilities. Political wisdom and technical problems combined to keep the megaliabilities associated with social insurance programs (such as social security) from accounting recognition as liability on the balance sheet. Nevertheless, the financial risk exposure of the federal government is considerable. Three types of events that give rise to federal government liabilities are transaction-based events, government-related events, and government-acknowledged events. In substance, these events amount to contractual obligations, legal obligations, and social obligations (U.S. Office of Management and Budget, 1995c, 1996).

Taken as a whole, the body of federal accounting standards solidly put the federal government's financial reporting on the full accrual basis.

ACCRUAL BUDGETING?

The current relationship between accounting and budgeting may be described as a kind of "constructive engagement." In other words, there exists an ongoing dialogue between accountants and budget analysts, and results of operations are presented and reconciled on both the accrual and budgetary bases. This approach reflects the recognition that accrual accounting and cash budgeting each serves a legitimate purpose and should be allowed to coexist. The FASAB explains this relationship as follows (U.S. Office of Management and Budget, 1996a, pp. 79–80):

Differences inherent in the different objectives of the budget and the [general purpose] financial statements must remain. The obligation basis for the budget differs from the costs-incurred [accrual] basis for the financial statements. This difference must continue in order for both types of information to serve their purposes. Some budgetary resources are used to invest in assets and therefore are not reflected in operating costs. Also, an entity may incur costs that were covered by previously provided budgetary resources (for example, depreciation), costs not yet covered by budgetary resources (for example, accrued annual leave), or costs covered by budgetary resources of other entities (for example, some pension costs). Continuing these differences in accounting reports is essential if financial statements are to report cost information that can be related to entities' outputs and if the statements are to report other information on the resources over which the entities are accountable. These remaining differences need to be explained in the financial statements to increase the utility of the financial statements.

The reconciliation approach implies that the accrual basis is no better than the cash basis. To claim so would understate the acceptance level of the accrual basis. There is universal acceptance in principle that the accrual basis of accounting is essential for the fair presentation of an entity's financial position and performance; as such, it is sanctioned by GAAP. However, as explained in the previous sections, there is considerable variation in the way accrual is applied in government. This section explores the implications of accruals for the budget.

To some extent, there is already some application of the accrual concept in budgeting. The recognition of obligations, in addition to outlays, as chargeable to an appropriation is a kind of accrual. The objective of this budgetary accrual—a preemptive measure—is to prevent overspending. It is quite different from accounting accruals, which are concerned with capturing all the future impact of a past action. To facilitate the analysis, the focus here will be on the effects of the accrual concept on budget deficit (Equation 1), which is often regarded as the bottom line of budget deliberations.

For illustrative purposes, the balance of this section will address the implications for the deficit of accruing long-term operating debt, accruing capital expenditures, accruing human capital and research and development expenditures, and accruing the cost of direct loans and loan guarantees.

Accruing Long-Term Operating Debt

Recall Case 1 involving Mr. Policeman. Long-term operating debt refers to the cost of services deferred for more than one year into the future for payment. A prime example is liability for employee pension benefits. When such costs are deferred, the cost of services on the strong modified accrual basis is greater than the amount of cash outlays during the period. If appropriations are made on the basis of the amount of projected cash outlays, unfunded liabilities will continue to arise. Consequently, the cash basis understates the deficit by the amount of increase in unfunded liabilities. If revenues are levied to cover only such appropriations to balance the (cash) budget, the current generation is undertaxed by the amount of unfunded liabilities. Additional revenues would have to be raised in the future to pay for past services. Such a funding method violates the notion of intergenerational equity.

Intergenerational equity would require the balancing of multiyear cash budgets instead of annual cash budgets. Take the year $(t+1)$ as an example, and let COS stand for the cost of services. To the extent that the COS of a period is not entirely paid for, the taxation and spending transactions are incomplete at the end of that year; thus there are future consequences to be reckoned with. Projected revenues $(t+1)$ should be set to equal projected COS $(t+1)$ on the SM accrual basis, including both cash payments and all liabilities attributable to the services rendered in that period. This practice would result in what is conventionally called cash surplus during the periods of service delivery. The accumulated cash surplus is intended to be used for liquidating the similarly accumulated liabilities in the postemployment periods. Assuming accurate projections, in the end the cash inflows should match the cash outflows.

In summary, the cash basis understates the deficit by the amount of deferred COS. When some COS are deferred to the future for payment, accrual budgeting, compared with cash budgeting, will result in higher current taxes and lower future taxes, other things being equal. The cash surpluses (excess) in the earlier years will be used to make up for the cash deficit (deficiency) in later years. The government balances its multiyear budget by basing its taxes on the accrual basis COS.

Accruing Capital Expenditures

Assume that during a certain fiscal year the government runs a cash deficit of $20 million—the total projected outlays of $120 million exceed projected receipts of $100 million. Suppose the budget includes $20 for purchasing capital equipment. One may then conclude that the cash budget deficit is caused entirely by the capital investment and that the government's operating budget is actually in balance. A relevant budget policy question is, How should the $20 million of capital budget spending be financed? Running a cash deficit is one option; another option is to borrow the $20 million based on the principle of "no service, no taxes."

As Case 2 explained, the cash basis and the modified accrual bases of accounting will all treat the $20 million as capital expenditures in the sense of using financial resources. This is the conventional treatment of capital budgets, which show capital spending and its financing sources. The full accrual basis, however, will treat the $20 million as an asset and the associated borrowing as capital debt. Under accrual budgeting, these capital-related transactions would be reported in three places: in the balance sheet as an addition of capital assets, in the cash flows statement as a cash outlay in the investing activities section of the cash flows statement, and in the cash flows statement but in the financing section as borrowings for financing the capital acquisition (see Table 14.5).

This approach is consistent with state and local government practices of separating the overall budget into an operating budget and capital budget, requiring the operating budget to be balanced, and financing capital spending by debt. A conventional (that is, cash basis) budget is in effect a pro forma cash flow statement. Accrual budgeting would require, in addition, a pro forma balance sheet and a pro forma operating statement to communicate the additional information.

Accruing Human Capital and R&D Expenditures

Does the idea of accruing capital expenditure as assets extend to accruing investment in human capital (that is, health and education) and R&D expenditures made by government? Probably not, for these reasons:

- The measurement of the economic value of human capital and R&D spending is not precise enough to survive the auditor's skepticism and the political credibility test.

- The government does not own or exercise effective control over any of the resulting assets even if any were recognized.

- The sunk costs cannot be used to pay off debt.

Hence these expenditures, as well as many other federal capital expenditures, are not capitalized. Nevertheless, the budget classification would make clear the long-term investment nature of these expenditures.

Accruing the Costs of Loans and Loan Guarantees

Loans and loan guarantees is one area in which accrual budgeting has made definite progress. In 1967, the President's Commission on Budget Concepts recommended that the unified budget distinguish between expenditure accounts and the loan accounts and place net lending (loan disbursements net of loan repayments) in the latter. In so doing, the commission appropriately distinguished between loan disbursements (which create a financial asset) and other expenditures, and between loan repayments (which reduce existing financial

Table 14.5. Pro Forma Financial Presentation Under Accrual Budgeting (in Millions of Dollars).

Balance Sheet		Operating Statement		Cash Flow Statement	
Capital Assets	$20	Revenues	$100	Operations	$0
Capital Debt	$20	Operating Expenses	−100	Capital Investment	−$20
Equity	$0	Surplus or Deficit	$0	Financing	+20
				Net Cash Flows	$0

assets) and receipts. Nevertheless, the net result for the united budget was the same: net lending contributed to the unified (cash) budget deficit. It was not until almost twenty-five years later that the 1990 Credit Reform Act put federal credit programs on a type of accrual basis.

The kind of accrual required by the 1990 Credit Reform Act calls for the recognition of the government's future cost of extending credit or guarantees *when such decisions are made.* The purpose of this accrual is to provide the relevant information to policymakers early enough to make a difference in, for example, deciding between direct loans and loan guarantees and between direct loans and grants. The recognition takes place before the event (that is, before default) happens but after the credit decision is made. This kind of *prospective accrual*—in contrast to *retrospective accrual* in accounting—is preventive in the sense that the full cost of a decision is communicated to inform the credit decision. As such, decision relevancy is the primary criterion for deciding to accrue or not to accrue. The secondary criterion is to enforce budget discipline. For example, under the Credit Reform Act, making loan guarantees is no longer free in the sense that no immediate cash flow takes place. (Conversely, direct loans look less costly because only the default and interest subsidy costs are scored rather than the entire amount of the loan being treated as an outlay.)

Under the Credit Reform Act, accrual budgeting scored a victory. Significant as the effort was, it nevertheless has resulted in incremental progress rather than a paradigm shift. This is so far an isolated case of integrating accrual budgeting into an overall cash budgeting system. To put the entire federal budget on the accrual basis would require a revolutionary change.

AN ACCRUAL BUDGET

Currently the federal budget is conceptually one single document listing receipts minus disbursements. An accrual-based budget would require three documents:

A *prospective balance sheet,* for reporting, among other things, loans receivable and capital assets on the asset side, as well as long-term operating debt and capital debt on the liabilities side. Contingent liability for guarantees would be estimated and reported.

A *prospective operating statement,* to project revenues (rather than just receipts) and expenses (rather than outlays). The advantage of the expense concept is that it can encompass not only cash outlays but also, for example, the cost of loan defaults and interest subsidies.

A *prospective cash flow statement,* to show the planned net cash flows from current operations and the net cash flows from investing and financing activities. This statement would correspond to the present cash-basis budget.

In essence, the current budget may be thought of as having an operating component and an investment component. The operating component relates to the net cash flows from operations, while the investment component features information about the cash outflows for investing activities and the cash inflows from financing.

In summary, a comprehensive accrual budgeting reform package would integrate the balance sheet perspective of the accountant and the operations perspective of the budget analyst. These two perspectives are complementary. Full accrual, however, with its emphasis on long-term assets and liabilities, raises uncomfortable questions about intergenerational distribution of the costs and benefits of fiscal policy.

It is unlikely that full accrual will be embraced by the federal budget anytime soon. (Remember that it took almost a quarter of a century to change the budget scoring rules on direct loans and loan guarantees.) Accruals are inherently difficult because they deal with remote and uncertain future benefits and costs. However difficult the measurement problem, the concept of accrual—that one cannot overlook the long-term consequences of current decisions and actions—was endorsed by the Hoover Commission in the 1950s and reiterated by the President's Commission on Budget Concepts in the 1960s. Incremental progress in accrual budgeting has been made in parts of the federal budget, such as in the full funding of military pensions and in the Credit Reform Act. As accounting moves from weaker to stronger forms of accrual, the fiscal and therefore the political stakes are higher. When it comes to the mega-accruals of social security obligations and federal land and natural resources, accrual is no longer a technical accounting exercise. Accrual has become too important to be left to the accountant!

References

Fox, H. W. *USA Annual Shareholder's Report.* Rockville, Md.: Citizens for Budget Reform, 1996.

Governmental Accounting Standards Board. *Codification of Governmental Accounting and Financial Reporting Standards as of June 30, 1996.* Norwalk, Conn.: Governmental Accounting Standards Board, 1996a.

Governmental Accounting Standards Board. "Measurement Focus and Basis of Accounting: Governmental Fund Operating Statements." Statement no. 11, May 1990. In Governmental Accounting Standards Board, *Codification of Governmental Accounting and Financial Reporting Standards.* Norwalk, Conn.: Governmental Accounting Standards Board, 1996b.

Governmental Accounting Standards Board. "Objectives of Financial Reporting: Concepts Statement no. 1, May 1987." In Governmental Accounting Standards Board, *Codification of Governmental Accounting and Financial Reporting Standards.* Norwalk, Conn.: Governmental Accounting Standards Board, 1996c.

Governmental Accounting Standards Board. *Basic Financial Statements—and Management's Discussion and Analysis—for State and Local Government.* Exposure draft. Norwalk, Conn.: Governmental Accounting Standards Board, 1997.

President's Commission on Budget Concepts. *Report of the President's Commission on Budget Concepts.* Washington, D.C.: Government Printing Office, 1967.

Schick, A. *The Federal Budget: Politics, Policy, Process.* Washington, D.C.: Brookings Institution, 1995.

U.S. Department of the Treasury. *Consolidated Financial Statement of the United States Government, 1995 Prototype.* Washington, D.C.: Government Printing Office, 1996a.

U.S. Department of the Treasury. *U.S. Government Annual Report, Fiscal Year 1995.* Washington, D.C.: Government Printing Office, 1996b.

U.S. General Accounting Office. *Glossary of Terms Used in the Federal Budgetary Process.* Exposure draft. Washington, D.C.: U.S. General Accounting Office, 1993.

U.S. Office of Management and Budget. "Accounting for Direct Loans and Loan Guarantees." Statement of Federal Financial Accounting Standards no. 2. Washington, D.C.: Government Printing Office, 1993a.

U.S. Office of Management and Budget. "Objectives of Federal Financial Reporting." Statement of Federal Financial Accounting Standards no. 1. Washington, D.C.: Government Printing Office, 1993b.

U.S. Office of Management and Budget. "Accounting for Inventory and Related Property." Statement of Federal Financial Accounting Standards no. 3. Washington, D.C.: Government Printing Office, 1993c.

U.S. Office of Management and Budget. "Managerial Cost Accounting Concepts and Standards for the Federal Government." Statement of Federal Financial Accounting Standards no. 4. Washington, D.C.: Government Printing Office, 1995a.

U.S. Office of Management and Budget. "Accounting for Property, Plant, and Equipment." Statement of Federal Financial Accounting Standards no. 6. Washington, D.C.: Government Printing Office, 1995b.

U.S. Office of Management and Budget. "Accounting for Liabilities of the Federal Government." Statement of Federal Financial Accounting Standards no. 5. Washington, D.C.: Government Printing Office, 1995c.

U.S. Office of Management and Budget. "Accounting for Revenue and Other Financing Sources." Statement of Federal Financial Accounting Standards no. 7. Washington, D.C.: Government Printing Office, 1996a.

U.S. Office of Management and Budget. *Budget of the United States Government, Fiscal Year 1997: Analytical Perspectives.* Washington, D.C.: Government Printing Office, 1996b.

CHAPTER FIFTEEN

Cost Measurement and Analysis

Fred Thompson

M anagerial accounting is a design science that uses a set of languages and behavioral controls to solve specific organizational problems. This chapter describes how managerial accounting defines and measures costs; major concepts are covered in both the text and a glossary at the end of the chapter. The chapter also discusses how methods of managerial accounting are linked to issues of organizational structures and processes.

Economists and accountants mean two different but related things when they speak of *cost*. Economists define cost in terms of opportunities that are sacrificed when a choice is made. Hence, to an economist costs are simply benefits lost. They are subjective, seen from the perspective of a decision maker rather than that of a detached observer (Buchanan, 1969, pp. 38–39), and prospective. Moreover, cost is a stock concept—costs are incurred when decisions arc made.

Accountants define cost in terms of resources consumed. Hence, from an accountant's standpoint costs are objective, seen from the perspective of a detached observer, and retrospective. Accountants usually define costs as flows. Costs reflect changes in stocks (reductions in good things, increases in bad things) over a fixed temporal interval.

Note: I wish to thank my friends and colleagues Michael Barzelay, Earl Littrell, Larry Jones, and especially Nathalie Halgand for their excellent advice and to acknowledge that any remaining errors and omissions are entirely due to my stubborn failure to heed that advice.

To distinguish between these two concepts of cost I refer to what economists do as *cost estimation* and what accountants do as *cost measurement* (Fisher, 1971). This chapter emphasizes cost measurement.

Of course both concepts have a lot in common. Both accountants and economists would agree that, for want of a better yardstick, costs should be measured in dollars. Both would agree that cost necessarily means cost *to do* something; it is meaningless to talk about cost without identifying a cost object (or cost objective, as the Cost Accounting Standards Board, 1992, calls it). The corollary to this concurrence is that there are as many different costs as there are cost objects.

Cost measurement is the special domain of managerial accountants. The vast majority of accountants, however, are financial accountants. They prepare and interpret *general purpose financial statements*: balance sheets, income statements, sources and uses of funds statements, and so on. In the public sector, many financial accountants focus on fiscal accountability, that is, ensuring that government spending is lawful and consistent with legislative intent, which implies a preoccupation with the timing and purpose of cash outlays rather than with cost.

Generally speaking, financial accountants deal with things that all entities have in common: assets and liabilities, capital, revenues and expenses, sources and uses of funds, cash flows, use of standardized definitions, categories, and arrays. In contrast, managerial accountants deal with things that are unique to an organization: its costs and cost objectives; its products, activities, policies, and procedures; its customers; and its strengths and weaknesses, opportunities and threats.

WHY MEASURE COSTS?

Why measure costs? There are two generic answers to this question: *to facilitate decisions* and *to influence decisions* (Demski and Feltham, 1976). Because time runs in only one direction, both uses of cost information are problematic. In the first use, estimates of the costs of the alternatives under consideration are provided to decision makers *before* a decision is made. In the second use, cost is measured *after* decisions have been made and implemented. Measured costs are used to evaluate managerial performance, with the purpose of influencing management choices. Consequently, managers must be informed as to how their performance will be measured and how the measurement will affect outcomes they care about, such as promotion, pay, esteem, and so on.

APPROACHES TO COST MEASUREMENT

Cost measurement is fundamentally a simple process. In most cases, cost analysts begin by measuring resources consumed (cost items). Next, they match (or assign) cost items to cost objects. Finally, they account for the prices paid (historical cost) to acquire cost items and adjust those prices to reflect economic reality.

Nearly anything of interest to a decision maker can be a cost object. Because organizations exist, however, to benefit customers or clients by means of their products and services, organizational decision makers should be especially interested in product and service costs. Sometimes a final product consists of several intermediate ones, each of which is produced in one or more organizational units, which implies several layers of cost objects.

Matching Cost Items to Cost Objects

There are four ways a cost item can be matched (or assigned) to a cost object: direct matching, averaging (apportioning), allocating, and allocating and then apportioning. Cost items that benefit an individual cost object—such as a department, an activity, a process, a service, or an individual's efforts—may be directly matched to the cost object in question. Cost items that are exhausted to produce one cost object are always direct costs. Cost items that benefit one cost object at a time but are not used up to produce that cost object must be averaged or apportioned, in this instance over time. Cost items that are exhausted to benefit two or more cost objects must be allocated to each on some basis so that each bears its fair share of the cost of the item. Cost items that benefit two or more cost objects at a time but are not used up as a result must be both allocated and apportioned. The distinction between exhaustible items and nonexhaustible items is roughly equivalent to the financial accountant's distinction between current (or short-term) and fixed (long-term) assets.

These distinctions can be illustrated by the production of mutton and wool. To produce mutton and wool one must acquire sheep, grazing land, and grain, and hire shepherds. Each leaf of grass or gram of oats will be consumed by one and only one sheep. In theory, then, we could treat each sheep as a cost object and directly match it to the items it consumed (although if this were not a 4-H project the measurement costs of doing so would be prohibitively high, because it would be necessary to fence in the sheep and monitor their consumption). There is a difference, however, between grass and grain. Grain is purchased by the kilo, grass by the hectare. The cost of grain can be matched directly to the cost object; the cost of the land used must be averaged or apportioned by calculating the rent per hectare for the period in question and then, if the cost object in question were kept in a pen one-tenth of a hectare in size, by dividing the rent by ten. If the cost objects were kept in a herd, the cost analyst could average the land rent in much the same way, simply by dividing the rent by the number of sheep or the total weight gain of the herd, in which case the rent could then be allocated back to each animal, if the analyst had a reason for doing so (this approach is called process costing). The cost of the shepherd could be handled in much the same way. Alternatively, the time the shepherd devoted to an individual sheep—getting it off a rock or out of a tree—could be assigned to the sheep in question (job order costing), and the rest of his time could be apportioned over the whole herd. Note that the main differences between process costing and job order costing are that in process costing costs are first assigned to cost pools and then to cost objects, whereas in job order costing costs are directly assigned to cost objects.

Things get a bit trickier if the cost analyst wants to know the cost of mutton. This is because the cost items used in sheep production jointly benefit the production of both mutton and wool. The analyst must allocate the cost of bringing the herd to market to its constituent products, perhaps on the basis of the total revenue obtained for each product, in which case a cost per kilo of mutton produced could be measured by apportioning the allocated cost by the total kilos of mutton sold.

My categories are somewhat heterodox, to be sure. Most accountants merely distinguish between direct and indirect costs: direct costs can be traced to a single cost object; indirect costs arise where resource consumption benefits several cost objects. The Cost Accounting Standards Board, for example, says that costs are assigned to accounting periods. They are then allocated to cost objects within the accounting period. They may be either directly or indirectly allocated. This classification, however, leaves the distinction between apportionment and allocation hopelessly confused; as I explain later, this distinction is a lot more important now than it once was.

Adjusting Prices Paid to Acquire Cost Items
to Reflect Economic Reality

Where a cost item is supplied by an efficient market and immediately exhausted (kilowatts of electricity, for example), the price paid to acquire the item measures cost satisfactorily. Some cost items are not instantaneously exhausted, however. Materials and supplies, work in progress or in transit, and finished goods awaiting delivery are held in inventory; plant and equipment are consumed very slowly. Land and capital are used rather than consumed.

Nonexhaustible items play a significant role in the delivery of services by government. For example, the federal government's investment in property, plant, and equipment exceeds $1 trillion. Consequently, Statement No. 6 of the

Federal Accounting Standards Advisory Board (FASAB), *Accounting for Property, Plant, and Equipment* (U.S. Office of Management and Budget, 1995), directs that "general PP&E shall be reported in the basic financial statements: the balance sheet, and the statement of net cost. The acquisition cost of general PP&E shall be recognized as an asset. Subsequently, except for land which is a non depreciable asset, that acquisition cost shall be charged to expense through depreciation. The depreciation expense shall be accumulated in a contra asset account: accumulated depreciation." The FASAB further directs that depreciation expense should reflect the estimated useful life of the asset in question minus its estimated salvage-residual value, taking into account factors such as physical wear and tear and technological change (such as obsolescence); and that any changes in estimated useful life or salvage-residual value shall be treated in the period of the change and future periods. In other words, Statement No. 6 moves the federal government toward and, in some respects, beyond commercial accounting practices, which probably represents a considerable advance over the status quo (although to my mind it does not go nearly far enough; see Littrell and Thompson, forthcoming).

Product Costing

Where the problem of measuring the consumption of nonexhaustible cost items has been satisfactorily dealt with, product costing in organizations that produce a single product or perform a single service or activity is straightforward. Full costs are the sum of all exhaustible and nonexhaustible cost items used for a cost object. Full unit costs are total costs apportioned over the total number of units of products produced or services or activities performed.

Where there are several layers of cost objects (such as when a final product or service consists of several intermediate services, each of which is produced in one or more organizational units) and processing is sequential or seriatim, product costing is equally straightforward. The cost object of one organizational unit is a merely a cost item for the next unit in line. This means that where a single product, service, or activity is concerned, measured cost provides a reliable basis for estimating the cost of replicating the cost object (decision facilitating) and an unambiguous basis for evaluating managerial performance against a target, benchmark, or standard (decision influencing). That is to say, measured product or service cost is a highly useful guide to decisions about product provision (retainment or divestment) and pricing; alternate mixes of cost items; the rate, volume, and timing of production; and even alternative processing sequences, although in these instances counterfactual estimates must be derived from other measures. Where there are two or more layers of cost objects, measured product cost is also a useful guide to decisions about whether to make or buy cost objects (see Horngren and Foster, 1991; Kaplan,

1982). Indeed, whenever these issues can be decided on the basis of direct costs, measured cost will satisfactorily perform the decision-facilitating function as well as the decision-influencing function.

The utility of product cost measurement becomes problematical only where cost items are shared by two or more cost objects. These can be either final products or layers of cost objects. Where the service delivery process is dominated by joint-cost items, cost measures that serve the decision-influencing function will rarely, if ever, also satisfactorily serve the decision-facilitation function. This means that different costs are required for different purposes (see Kaplan, 1988).

Financial accountants usually denied this fact, perhaps because it implied that their transactional accounting records were insufficient bases for managerial decision making. They often tried to enforce the fiction that allocated costs were satisfactory proxies for both opportunity costs and responsibility costs. For a long time they got away with it. This was possible for three reasons: most production processes could be traced to a single cost item (direct labor or machine hours, materials, and so on), managers were held responsible only for controllable cost items (that is, those items that could be significantly influenced by the actions of the manager), and given joint cost items, the only alternative to cost allocation was statistical cost estimation. Because statistical costs often cannot be tied directly to an entity's system of dual-entry transactional accounting records, financial accountants have been inclined to distrust their validity.

Cost Allocation

Traditional cost allocation is a two-step process: direct cost matching and indirect cost allocation. Indirect costs are lumped together as overheads (that is, any cost item not directly associated with a final cost object), pooled in cost centers, and distributed to cost objects. This step involves the selection of a basis of allocation (that is, a measure of activity associated with the pool of common costs being distributed) and a method of allocation.

Cost accountants rely on three methods to allocate cost pools to cost objects. The simplest is known as *single-step allocation*. Under this method, analysts allocate each cost pool to all the cost objects that use its services, but not to any others. For example, building maintenance and housekeeping services performed by a state department of administrative services could be allocated to various other departments and agencies based on the number of square meters of office space they occupy. Where there are several layers of cost objects, cost accountants usually rely on the *two-stage* or *step-down method of allocation*. Under this method, the cost pools are trickled down to other pools and cost objects using a variety of allocation bases. Usually analysts begin with the cost pool that serves the greatest number of other pools or final cost objects and spreads its costs over the others. They continue in this fashion with all other pools until all costs have been allocated to final cost objects.

For example, the allocation process could begin with depreciation of buildings and fixtures. These costs would be distributed across all remaining cost pools. The amount to be distributed from the next pool (building maintenance and housekeeping services) would now include not only its own costs but also the amount allocated to it from the previous step. This total would then be allocated to all the remaining pools, and so forth.

Two important aspects of the step-down method are that no reverse allocation takes place (that is, once a pool's costs have been allocated, that pool receives no additional allocations from other pools) and that pool costs are allocated both to other pools and to final cost objects (or the administrative units directly responsible for their delivery) but final cost objects (or the administrative units directly responsible for their delivery) are not allocated to other final cost objects (or the administrative units directly responsible for their delivery). Because no reverse allocation takes place, the sequence of the steps in the step-down method is an important cost-measurement decision. Although the effect of different step-down sequences is rarely great, in a few circumstances the choice may have a huge influence on the measured costs of final products.

This problem can be mitigated by using the *reciprocal method.* Under this method, cost pools are not stepped down. Rather, the accountant develops a set of simultaneous equations that measure and allocate each pools costs based on its use by all other cost pools, not just those below it in a step-down sequence. Sometimes this process can become quite complex. For example, the cost model developed by the National Center for Higher Education Management Systems provides a structure for 338 equations and more than 6 billion accounting relationships for allocating costs to student types and funded research activities.

Relevance Lost

Although overhead allocation systems retain utility for influencing decisions, they have been rendered obsolete by changes in organization and technology for facilitating decisions. Most overheads are transaction costs. They reflect the organization's policies, its operating and administrative procedures, and its customer relationships, including activities such as purchasing, materials handling, marketing, accounting, and asset utilization. Once upon a time, overheads could be allocated to final cost objects on the basis of direct costs without significantly biasing key operating decisions (provision, pricing, input-output mix, rate, volume, or timing), simply because overheads were relatively insignificant. In 1950, service industries played a minor role in the U.S. economy and overheads accounted for less than 15 percent of total manufacturing costs (direct labor and machine hours constituted more than 50 percent). Nowadays, even in manufacturing, overhead activities often have a greater effect on expenses than production volume. In the average U.S. manufacturing plant, for example, direct manufacturing labor accounts for only 10 to 15 percent of costs; materials and purchased components typically account for 30 to 40 percent more. This leaves roughly 50 percent for overheads. And that's the typical manufacturing plant; direct labor costs are practically irrelevant in the increasing number of high-tech firms that rely on flexible computer-aided design and manufacturing. In those organizations, 80 percent of life-cycle costs are typically incurred before a product gets to market.

The Office of Technology Assessment (1984, pp. 60–62) defines flexible manufacturing as a system "capable of producing a range of discrete products with a minimum of manual intervention. It consists of production equipment workstations (machine tools or other equipment for fabrication, assembly or treatment) linked by a materials handling system to move parts from one work station to another, and it operates as an integrated system under full programmable control." Flexible, computer-aided design and manufacturing have had the effect of making manufacturing firms much more like service organizations. Most manufacturing costs were once engineered costs. The amount of labor and the quantity of material required to make products depended entirely on the volume of output. By contrast, most service costs have always been discretionary (that is, they have depended on policy decisions).

Paradoxically, however, although flexible production has reduced the significance of exhaustible cost items, where systems are linked by modern relational or object-oriented databases, flexible production permits nonexhaustible cost items to be assigned to individual cost objects (job order costing) far more precisely than was ever before possible. In such an environment, cost analysts must still apportion expenses, but they rarely need to allocate them.

Activity-Based Costing Systems

When it became increasingly evident that traditional cost measurement systems no longer provided the information that managers needed, many tried something new (Shank and Govindarajan, 1988a, 1988b). Of particular interest here is *activity accounting* (Anderson, 1993; Brimson and Antos, 1994; Brinker, 1995; Cooper and Kaplan, 1991, 1992; Crane and Meyer, 1993; De Bruine and Sopariwala, 1994; Kaplan, 1992). Activity accounting is oriented to overheads. Indeed, as far as direct costs are concerned there is little or no difference between *activity-based costing* (ABC) and *job-order costing*. What is new about ABC is that it reflects the premise that all organizational activities, including overheads, are undertaken to produce goods and services for customers and that they are the proximate cause of all costs. This means that all costs, including overheads, are ultimately product and service costs (Harr and Godfrey, 1991, p. 24). The problem is figuring out how.

Like traditional cost measurement, ABC starts by apportioning an organization's expenses to a set of cost pools. Unlike traditional practice, which ignores activities that do not vary with output volume, mix, or production rate, ABC compiles cost information on all the activities performed in the organization. Analysts use a variety of statistical methods to figure out which transactions cause these pools to vary in size. These are called *activity drivers, resource drivers,* or *cost drivers.*

Cost analysts typically use one of five methods to establish a relationship between cost drivers and cost pools: (1) high-low method, (2) scatter diagram method, (3) regression method, (4) incremental method, and (5) element analysis. The last method is used when there are no historical data points available. The cost analyst must therefore estimate separately each cost category (such as salaries and wages) and decompose it into its various cost elements: fixed, step-function, variable, and semivariable. Once this is done, simplifying assumptions can be made concerning step function and semivariable costs, and the totals for each cost element can be summed to produce a total-cost equation. (These methods are described in greater detail by Anthony and Young, 1995.) Moreover, economists and management scientists have developed an array of analytic models that can be used in cost finding. One of the most popular is *data envelopment analysis* (DEA), a linear programming-based technique for measuring organizational performance in the presence of multiple inputs, outputs, and constraints. In December 1996, I did a quick computer search that identified 106 articles published since 1990 that explain, use, or criticize DEA. There is even a recent book on the subject focusing on public sector applications (see Ganley and Cubbin, 1992).

Examples of cost drivers in manufacturing (such as the Air Force's depot maintenance operations) include the number of inspections, work receipts, components in inventory, machine setups, or change orders. Examples of cost drivers in a service environment (such as the Air Force's supply operations) include orders processed, number of unique items held in inventory, type of items issued, physical volume and weight processed, distance shipped, and supporting facilities and equipment acquired, operated, and maintained. More general examples include time, space, transaction, service, or commodity type, distance, and weight, as well as the old standbys—output volume, mix, and rate (Harr, 1990, 1992).

In many organizations, ABC is a by-product of quality management, the basic elements of which are process value analysis (PVA), statistical process control, customer feedback, participative management, and supplier cooperation (Hyde, 1997). PVA involves five steps (Harr and Godfrey, 1991, pp. 25–26):

- Chart the entire flow of activities needed to design, create, and deliver a service.

- For each activity and step within the activity, determine its associated cost and the cause of that cost, or cost driver.

- Determine whether or not the step adds value for the customer and, if it is nonvalue adding, identify ways to eliminate it and its associated cost.

- Determine the cycle time of each activity and calculate its cycle efficiency (value-added time and total time).

- Seek ways to improve cycle efficiency and reduce associated costs due to delays, excesses, and unevenness in activities.

This approach has proved itself in a variety of settings, identifying activities and outcomes that do not add value and that arise out of defects in the service delivery process. A PVA of the Treasury's check-writing operation, for example, showed that it spent about 8 cents out of every dollar writing checks, 21 cents on administration, and 70 cents correcting errors (Keohoe, Dodson, Reeve, and Plato, 1995).

Moreover, insofar as quality management pushes significant operating decisions down to the lowest levels of the organization, cost measures and cost estimates are also needed at the lowest levels, as are measures of rework, activity cycle time, customer satisfaction, and so on. Operators especially need cost-performance standards for each value-adding activity they perform. Such standards can be based on the best the organization has achieved over time (baselining), the best practice currently being achieved somewhere (benchmarking), or an engineering standard in target costing.

A study conducted by Software Productivity Research of Burlington, Massachusetts, shows how ABC works ("Software Engineering: Made to Measure," 1993). It used a method called *function point analysis* to estimate the productivity and cost effectiveness of three kinds of software projects: small management information systems, large scale systems, and military systems. Based on a sample of thousands of software projects selected from around the world, Software Productivity Research found that U.S. military software productivity lags behind that of France, Israel, Korea, the United Kingdom, Germany, Sweden, and even Italy. The same study showed that the United States is in first place in the production of management information systems and runs a strong second to Japan in large-scale systems software projects.

Differences in cost per function point are due primarily to the amount of paperwork required per point. Preparation of this paperwork takes a lot of engineering time but contributes no value (function points) to the finished product. U.S. military projects require five times as much paper and cost twelve times as much per point as management information systems projects. They are six times as costly per function point as big systems software projects, which are arguably comparable to military software projects. This comparison is particularly telling because it suggests is that for activities like software engineering, federal procurement regulations may account for more than half their cost.

Studies like this one also confirm the weakness of traditional cost measurement systems. Focusing on direct labor costs and assigning overheads accordingly may have made sense thirty years ago when direct labor was the key to productivity, but it is unrealistic today and has probably always had the effect of diverting attention from transaction costs that arise out of the administrative process.

Field studies also show that ABC provides more accurate information for product costing than traditional cost measurement systems, which tend to understate costs for low-volume specialty-type services and overstate costs for high-volume standard services. It should probably be noted here that ABC's recent popularity is due in no small measure to improvements in computing power and systems architecture.

Modern information technology has dramatically lowered the cost of establishing, maintaining, and using cost systems, but increasing the number of cost drivers and their associated cost pools still increases information costs. This is especially true where activity data must be manually collected and where it is often more cost effective to rely on sampling procedures than universal measurement. Consequently, users should carefully weigh the costs of greater measurement precision against its benefits. The organizations that are most likely to benefit from ABC are those with high overhead costs and widely diverse operating activities and service lines. Most government agencies have these characteristics.

USING MEASURED COSTS TO INFLUENCE BEHAVIOR

One area in which traditional cost measurement continues to play a significant role is management control (that is, decision influencing). Management control is the process by which people, especially subordinate managers, are motivated to serve the policies and purposes of the organizations to which they belong. It is also secondarily a process for detecting and correcting unintentional performance errors and intentional irregularities, such as theft or misuse of resources. In many organizations the primary instrument of management control is *responsibility budgeting*, which embraces both the formulation of budgets and their execution. In responsibility budget formulation, an organization's policies are converted into financial targets that correspond to the domains of administrative units and their managers (Anthony and Young, 1994, p. 19). In responsibility budget execution, operations are monitored and subordinate managers are evaluated and rewarded.

Responsibility budgeting is as much organizational engineering as it is cost measurement. Like large organizations themselves, it is a product of the bureaucratic revolution. Large complex organizations are justified by economies of scale and scope. *Economies of scale* are produced by spreading fixed expenses over higher volumes of output, thereby reducing unit costs. *Economies of scope* are produced by exploiting the division of labor—sequentially combining highly specialized functional units in multifarious ways to produce a variety of products. Large organizations are made possible by hierarchy and bureaucracy. Bureaucracy breaks tasks down into their simplest component parts and recombines them to produce complex goods and services, allocates scarce resources to administrative units, and formulates organizational strategies (Chandler, 1962; Rosenberg and Birdsall, 1986).

Under responsibility budgeting, work is arranged into administrative units according to mission, function, region, or some combination of these. An organization's administrative units and their relationships to one another—the structure depicted in organization charts—constitute its *administrative structure*. Responsibility budgeting requires authority and responsibility to be allocated to individuals within the organization. This constitutes an organizations *responsibility structure*. Finally, responsibility budgeting requires a system of measuring and evaluating performance information on inputs, costs, activities, and outputs. This is the organization's *account* or *control structure*. Under a fully developed responsibility budgeting and accounting system, administrative units and responsibility centers are coterminous and fully aligned with the organization's account structure, because the information it provides can be used to coordinate unit activities as well as to influence the decisions of responsibility center managers.

Under responsibility budgeting, two basic rules govern organizational design. First, organizational strategy should determine structure. Strategy means the pattern of purposes and policies that defines the organization and its missions and that positions it relative to its environment. Single-mission organizations are supposed to be organized along functional lines; multimission organizations are supposed to be organized along mission lines; and multimission, multifunction organizations are supposed to be organized along matrix lines. Where a matrix organization is large enough to justify an extensive division of labor, responsibility centers are supposed to be designated as either mission or support centers, with the latter linked to the former by a system of internal markets and prices (transfer pricing).

Second, the organization should be as decentralized as possible. Most students of management believe that the effectiveness of large, complex organizations improves when authority and responsibility are delegated down into the organization. Of course authority should not be delegated arbitrarily or capriciously. Decentralization requires prior clarification of the purpose or function of each administrative unit and responsibility center, procedures for setting objectives and for monitoring and rewarding performance, and an account structure that links each responsibility center to the goals of the organization as a whole.

As Thompson and Jones (1986) explained some time ago, the biggest difference between government budgets and responsibility budgets is that government budgets tend to be highly detailed spending or resource acquisition plans which must be scrupulously executed just as they were approved; in contrast, operating budgets in the private sector are usually sparing of detail, often consisting of no more than a handful of financial targets. Indeed, the originator of what we now call responsibility budgeting, Alfred P. Sloan of General Motors, believed that it was inappropriate and unnecessary for top managers at the corporate level to know much about the details of responsibility center operations (Womack, Jones, and Roos, 1990, pp. 40–41). If the numbers on sales, market share, inventories, and profit showed that performance was poor, it was time to change the responsibility center manager. Responsibility center managers showing consistently good numbers got promoted, ultimately to headquarters.

The notion that responsibility centers should be managed objectively by the numbers from a small corporate headquarters reflects the effort to delegate authority and responsibility down into the organization. As the Organization for Economic Cooperation and Development report *Budgeting for Results: Perspectives on Public Expenditure Management* (1995) explains, delegation of authority means giving agency managers the maximum feasible authority needed to make their units productive—or alternatively, subjecting them to a minimum of constraints. Hence, delegation of authority requires operating budgets to be stripped to the minimum needed to motivate and inspire subordinates. Under responsibility budgeting, the ideal operating budget would contain a single number or performance target (such as a production quota, a unit cost standard, and a profit or return on investment target) for each administrative unit or responsibility center.

Types of Responsibility Centers

Responsibility centers are usually classified according to two dimensions: the integration dimension (the relationship between the responsibility center's objectives and the overall purposes and policies of the organization) and the decentralization dimension (the amount of authority delegated to responsibility managers, measured in terms of their discretion to acquire and use assets).

In the *integration dimension,* a responsibility center can be either a *mission center* or a *support center.* The output of a mission center contributes directly to an organization's objectives or purpose. The output of a support center is an input to another responsibility center in the organization, either another support center or a mission center.

In the decentralization dimension, accountants distinguish among four types of responsibility centers based on the authority delegated to responsibility managers to acquire and use assets. *Discretionary expense centers,* the governmental norm, are found at one extreme, and *profit centers* and *investment centers* are found at the other. A support center may be either an expense center or a profit center. If the latter, its profit is the difference between its costs and its revenue from "selling" its services to other responsibility centers. *Selling* is in quotation marks here because the organization as a whole has not sold anything to an outside party. Rather, the responsibility center providing the service records revenue in its accounts and the center receiving the service records an expense. Both revenue and expense cancel out when the organization consolidates its books. Money rarely changes hands in interdivisional transfer pricing, and responsibility centers don't get to keep their profits. Only the organization as a whole earns a profit, and selling to and buying from outsiders are the only activities that can generate real profits or losses for the organization.

Both profit and investment centers are usually free to borrow, and investment centers are also free to make decisions about plant and equipment, new products, and other issues that are significant to the long-run performance of the organization. Most government agencies are discretionary expense centers. The key difference between discretionary expense centers and other kinds of responsibility centers is that their managers have no independent authority to acquire assets. Each acquisition must be authorized by the manager's superiors. In the U.S. system, asset acquisitions must be authorized by Congress and signed into law by the president. In some cases, managers of discretionary expense centers are evaluated in terms of the number and type of activities performed by their center. For example, expense centers that earn revenue or are assigned notational revenue (transfer price) for the activities they perform are referred to as *revenue centers.* University development offices, for example, are frequently revenue centers. In contrast to standard practice in government, managerial accountants generally believe that a unit should be set up as a discretionary expense center only where there is no satisfactory way to match its expenses to final cost objects, as in an accounting department.

In a cost center, the manager is held responsible for producing a stated quantity, quality, or both of output at the lowest feasible cost. Someone else within the organization determines the output of a cost center, usually including various quality attributes, especially delivery schedules. Cost center managers are usually free to acquire short-term assets (those that are wholly consumed within a performance measurement cycle), to hire temporary or contract personnel, and to manage inventories. In a *standard cost center,* output levels are determined by requests from other responsibility centers, and the managers budget for each performance measurement cycle is determined by multiplying actual output by standard cost per unit. Performance is measured against this figure—the difference between actual costs and the standard. In a *quasi-profit center,* performance is measured by the difference between the notational revenue earned by the center and its cost.

Transfer Pricing

Under responsibility budgeting, support centers provide services or intermediate goods to other responsibility centers in return for a notational transfer price. There are two common approaches to transfer pricing: *laissez-faire transfer pricing,* in which buying and selling responsibility centers are completely free to negotiate prices, to deal, or not to deal; and *marginal* or *incremental cost pricing,* in which the responsibility center selling the service is required to charge the buying responsibility center whatever is less of market or incremental cost. The circumstances that justify large complex organizations—economies of scale and scope—render these simple transfer pricing mechanisms problematical, however. Scale economies result from large, lumpy investments in specialized plant or equipment, which gives rise to bilateral monopoly and provides an ideal environment for opportunistic behavior.

Economists once argued that this problem could be solved within a single organization by relying on incremental cost pricing. It turns out, however, that this approach eliminates incentives to performance improvement. Organizations can, therefore, promote short-run performance by using incremental cost pricing, or they can promote long-term performance by using laissez-faire pricing, but they cannot do both simultaneously.

Many economists nowadays allege that bilateral monopoly can be governed satisfactorily via an array of complex pricing arrangements, including unbalanced transfer prices, multipart transfer prices, and quasi-vertical integration. Under *unbalanced transfer prices,* the responsibility center selling the service is credited with the full cost of the transacted item (often standard cost), plus an agreed-upon markup; the buying center is charged its incremental cost; and the controller adjusts the organization's accounts to reflect the difference between the two. Under *multipart transfer prices,* the responsibility center selling the service charges the buyer a separate price for each component of the service (often a part that reflects short-run production costs and varies with service volume, a part based on plant and equipment costs, and a part based on delivering the service to a specific location). Under *quasi-vertical integration,* the buyer owns the specialized plant and the equipment needed to deliver the service and loans, and leases or rents them to the responsibility center supplying the service. These governance arrangements require sophisticated users and superior cost measurement, but they work, especially where they are reinforced by plain old-fashioned trust and shared access to cost information (Milgrom and Roberts, 1992; "Guide to Better Buying," 1986).

Responsibility Budgeting in Government

The origins of responsibility budgeting and accounting in government can be traced to the Planning, Programming, Budgeting System (PPBS) era in the U.S. Department of Defense (1961–1967). Responsibility budgeting and accounting was the centerpiece of Project Prime, perhaps the most promising of the organizational design and development efforts initiated under Secretary of Defense Robert McNamara. Project Prime was the brain child of Robert N. Anthony (Juola, 1993, pp. 43–44), who succeeded Charles Hitch as defense controller in September 1965. Anthony saw the need for clarification of the purpose of each of the administrative units that comprised the Department of Defense, their boundaries, and their relationships to one another, and for an account structure that would tie the entire organization together. Anthony (1962) proposed that the Department of Defense should

- Classify all administrative units as either mission or support centers.
- Charge all costs accrued by support centers, including charges for the use of capital assets and inventory depletion to the mission centers they serve.
- Fund mission centers to cover expected expenses, including support center charges.
- Establish a working capital fund to provide short-term financing for support units.
- Establish a capital asset fund to provide long-term financing of capital assets and to encourage efficient management of their acquisition, use, and disposition.

The principal formal device by which a measure of intraorganizational decentralization was and is accomplished within the Department of Defense is the *revolving fund*. Modern-day revolving funds date to the 1947 National Security Act, which authorized the defense secretary to use them to manage support activities within the Department of Defense. Two kinds of funds have been established under this authority: stock funds and industrial funds. *Stock funds* are used to purchase supplies in bulk from commercial sources and hold them in inventory until they are supplied to the customer—usually a military unit or facility. *Industrial funds* are used to purchase industrial or commercial services (such as depot maintenance, transportation, and so on) from production units within the Department of Defense. Both kinds of funds are supposed to be financed by reimbursements from customers' appropriations (Juola, 1993, p. 43).

Anthony's proposal would have expanded the scope of this device and enhanced its effectiveness by establishing rules for setting transfer prices prospectively rather than retrospectively and by making support center managers responsible for meeting explicit financial targets. Internal buyer-seller arrangements encourage efficient choice on the part of support centers, as well as the units that use their services, only when prices are set ahead of time; and when support centers charge all of their costs against revenues earned delivering services, their managers are authorized to incur expenses to deliver services, and they are held responsible for meeting an appropriate financial target (Bailey, 1967, p. 343).

Project Prime failed. One reason for its failure is that the federal government accounts for purchases, outlays, and obligations, but it still does not account for consumption. Full value from the application of responsibility budgeting can be obtained only where government adopts a meaningful form of consumption or accrual accounting (measuring the cost of the assets actually consumed producing goods or services). Because the U.S. government does not account for resource consumption, all of its cost figures are necessarily statistical (that is, none are tied to its basic debit and credit bookkeeping and accounting records, nor can they be). Without the discipline that debit and credit provides, these figures are likely to be useful only for illustrative purposes or when a decision maker must make a specific decision and a cost model has been tailored to the decision maker's needs.

Another reason for the demise of Project Prime is that the U.S. appropriations process fails to perform the capital budgeting function satisfactorily, a problem that PPBS did not really address and certainly did not fix. Besides, the existing process Procrusteanizes every operating cycle to fit the fiscal year.

New Zealand

In contrast, New Zealand's public management reforms have successfully introduced responsibility budgeting and accounting in government (the following discussion is based on Scott, Bushnell, and Sallee, 1990; see also Lapsley, 1994; Pollitt, 1993; Reschenthaler and Thompson, 1996). Building on its adoption of accrual accounting and performance reporting, New Zealand has published a full set of accounts, including a balance sheet of assets and liabilities and an accrual-based operating statement of income and expenses, for each of its agencies. It has also privatized everything that was not part of the core public sector, and it changed the way it appropriates funds for use by the remaining government agencies, linking appropriations directly to performance.

Currently, agencies that supply traditional, noncontestable governmental services are treated like cost or quasi-profit centers. These include the central control agencies, the State Services Commission, most regulatory and police functions, and some justice services. These are all policy agencies or activities that include an element of compulsion for the buyer. Under this system, Parliament appropriates funds retrospectively to reimburse agencies for expenses incurred in producing outputs during the period covered by contract, whether for the government or third parties. Costs are measured on an accrual basis; they include depreciation, but exclude taxes and capital charges. Changes in an agency's net asset holdings are also explicitly appropriated.

All other agencies are treated like investment centers. Appropriations pay for the outputs produced by the agency and for any changes in the agency's net assets. These agencies are required to pay interest, taxes, and dividends and must establish a capital structure. They are set up in a competitively neutral manner so that their financial performance can be assessed by comparison with firms in the private sector. The prices paid for the outputs supplied by these agencies are supposed to approximate fair market prices. In general, this means that investment center agencies must show that they are receiving no more than the next best alternative supplier would receive for providing the outputs.

Each month investment center agencies report on their financial positions, cash flows, resource usage, and revenues by output. Variances are calculated and explanations provided. In both kinds of agencies, managers are free to make some decisions about investments in plant and equipment. Indeed, the only constraints that investment center agencies face are prohibitions against direct borrowing and starting new businesses. Elected officials rely on the link between financial performance and managerial rewards to ensure that agency managers make sound decisions about asset acquisition.

United States

Responsibility budgeting and accounting have had little or no practical effect in the United States (Thompson and Jones, 1994). One reason is that many students of the expenditure process reject the notion that responsibility budgeting and accounting can be reconciled with the U.S. legislative budgetary process. Some people even assert that they can be practiced only by responsible unitary governments on the Westminster model, although that claim seems to be belied by the Swiss and Swedish examples (Schedler, 1995; Arwidi and Samuelson, 1993). Of course, it would not be easy to reconcile responsibility budgeting and the U.S. legislative process, but I do not believe that they are necessarily incompatible either (see Thompson, 1994; Harr, 1989; Harr and Godfrey, 1991, 1992). The United States also has a large number of government accountants, auditors, budgeters, program analysts, and teachers who understand the status quo and who mistrust unfamiliar alternatives. Anyone inclined to doubt the significance of this explanation should look carefully at the controversies surrounding the FASAB.

What Goes Around, Comes Around

It is somewhat ironical that governments are beginning to embrace responsibility budgeting at the same time that many well-managed businesses are abandoning it (Bruggeman, 1995; Otley, 1994; Bunce, Fraser, and Woodcock, 1995).

They are doing so because it no longer reflects the way they are organized. These organizational changes are, I believe, primarily due to the information revolution, which is breaking down giant organizations built on functional specialization and minute divisions of labor. Indeed, Michael Hammer (1990, pp. 108–112) argues that the use of modern databases, expert systems, and telecommunications networks provides many, if not all, of the benefits that once made attractive administrative centralization and specialization of administrative functions such as reporting, accounting, personnel, purchasing, or quality assurance without sacrificing any of the benefits of decentralization. Hammer asserts that jobs should be designed around an objective or outcome instead of a single function; that functional specialization and sequential execution are inherently inimical to expeditious processing; that those who use the output of activity should perform the activity and the people who produce information should process it, because they have the greatest need for information and the greatest interest in its accuracy; that information should be captured once and at the source; that parallel activities should be coordinated during their performance, not after they are completed; and that the people who do the work should be responsible for decision making, and control should be built into job designs.

This approach has led to smaller, flatter organizations. Some single-mission organizations are now organized as virtual networks, and some multimission organizations are organized as alliances of networks. Philip Evans and Thomas Wurster (1997, p. 75) refer to both of these kinds of organizational arrangements as *hyperarchies*, after the hyperlinks of the World Wide Web. They assert that these kinds of organizations, like the Internet itself, the architectures of object-oriented software programming, and packet switching in telecommunications, have eliminated the need to channel information, thereby eliminating the trade-off between information bandwidth (richness) and connectivity (reach). They describe virtual networks (structures designed around fluid, team-based collaboration within the organization) as deconstructed value chains and alliances of networks (the pattern of amorphous and permeable corporate boundaries characteristic of companies in the Silicon Valley), and as deconstructed supply chains, in which everyone communicates richly with everyone else on the basis of shared standards.

The system used by IBM at its plant in Dallas, Texas, is an example of an existing virtual network. It has been designed to mimic a marketlike, self-organizing system. Everyone in the organization plays the part of customer or provider, depending on the transaction, and the entire plant has been transformed into a network of dyads and exchanges. Each exchange is a closed loop involving four distinct steps: request from a customer and offer from a provider, negotiation of the task to be performed and the definition of success, performance, and customer acceptance. Until this last step is completed, the task remains unfinished. Each closed loop of workflow is further broken down into subloops. Under this system, even simple tasks give rise to dozens of loops and interconnecting lines; more complex tasks, such as modifying a major product, lead to hundreds; and managing the entire Austin plant leads to thousands of such connections. IBM uses powerful computers to keep track of all of these loops and lines, to chart all activities and operational flows within the plant, to keep track of progress being made at each stage of each transaction, and to prod tardy participants into action.

The effect of this system has been to break down departmental boundaries, eliminate bottlenecks, and empower employees to coordinate themselves. As a by-product, the computer systems that keep track of all these loops and lines also identify all the resources going into a particular job, almost entirely eliminating the need for cost allocation. Moreover, this information is available both prospectively and retrospectively to anyone in the organization.

Some well-managed multimission organizations such as Johnson & Johnson, 3M, and Rubbermaid have already organized themselves into loose alliances of networks, sharing only their top management, a set of core competencies, and a common culture (Quinn, 1992). The control systems used by these organizations are like those of centralized bureaucracies in that they collect a lot of real-time information on every aspect of operations, including nonfinancial information; but unlike the control systems of centralized bureaucracies, which were erected on the premise that the exercise of judgment should be passed up the managerial ranks, this information is used to push the exercise of judgment down into the organization, to wherever it is needed, at the point of sale, at delivery, or in production (Simons, 1995). From top management's perspective, the primary purpose of this information is to provide them with insight into the integrity, competence, and morale of their network managers and employees so that they can allocate their best people to the most important jobs.

How far hyperarchy will go is an open question. Evans and Wurster (1997) claim that it challenges all hierarchies, whether of logic or of power, with the possibility (or the threat) of random access and information symmetry.

On a more mundane plane, recent changes in the way work is organized have already affected cost measurement. Everyone knows that the information revolution has greatly reduced information costs, including the cost of measuring costs. But the implications of the information revolution for management control are only beginning to be understood. Control once focused on flows per period—on products produced, functions performed, expenses incurred, profits, or earnings. Capital budgeting has always been project oriented, with each project having an identifiable beginning and an end. Nevertheless, controllers viewed projects (megaprojects aside) primarily in terms of their consequences for period flows. In turn, this perspective reflected the fact that organizations used sequential processes, repetitive activities, and standardized components to produce like products.

In contrast, under flexible production jobs are tailored to the preferences of specific customer segments and treated as discrete projects. Consequently, control necessarily focuses on projects. This means that cost analysts have had to shift their attentions to projects and job cycles (Schwarzbach, 1985; Rotch, 1990; Kreuze and Newell, 1994; Thompson, 1995). Consequently, in networked, flexible production organizations, the distinction between capital and operating budgets has blurred, as has the distinction between cost estimation and cost measurement (Tani, 1995; Otley, Broadbent, and Berry, 1995).

These changes have also provided a new perspective on responsibility budgeting. It is now apparent, as it really was not before, that responsibility budgeting systems restrict the upward flow of operating information within the organization, making decentralization a necessity as well as an ideal. In networks and alliances, people work in information-rich environments. For the most part, access to information is symmetrical (equally available to all). Decentralization works in such an environment only because top management attends to top management functions such as strategic planning, organizing, staffing, and the intellectual and cultural development of the organization and refrains from meddling in the conduct of operations. This takes practice and self-restraint. For this reason, it may make sense for governments to experiment with responsibility budgeting rather than going directly to newer modes of organization and control. Few politicians or managers have had much experience with decentralization and almost none with self-restraint. As is often the case, it is necessary to learn to walk before learning to run (see Johansen, Jones, and Thompson, 1997).

GLOSSARY

These terms are defined as in the *Chief Financial Officers Managerial Cost Accounting Guide.*

Activity. The actual task or step performed in producing and delivering products and services. An aggregation of actions performed within an organization that is useful for purposes of activity-based costing.

Activity analysis. The identification and description of activities in an organization. Involves determining what activities are done within a department, how many people perform them, how much time is spent performing them, what resources are required to perform them, what operational data best reflect the performance of the activities, and what customer value the activities have for the organization. Accomplished with interviews, questionnaires, observation, and review of physical records of work. The foundation for agency PVA, which is key to overall review of program delivery.

Activity driver. A measure of the frequency and intensity of the demands placed on activities by cost objects. Used to assign costs to cost objects. Represents a line item on the bill of activities for a product or customer. An example is the number of part numbers, which is used to measure the consumption of material-related activities by each product, material type, or component. The number of customer orders measures the consumption of order-entry activities by each customer. Sometimes an activity driver is used as an indicator of the output of an activity, such as the number of purchase orders prepared by the purchasing activity.

Activity-based costing. A cost accounting method that measures the cost and performance of process-related activities and cost objects. Assigns direct and indirect costs to cost objects, such as products or customers, based on their use of activities. Recognizes the causal relationship of cost drivers to activities.

Activity-based management. A discipline that focuses on the management of activities as the route to improving the value received by the customer and the profit achieved by providing this value. Includes cost driver analysis, activity analysis, and performance measurement. Draws on activity-based costing as its major source of information.

Capacity costs. Fixed costs incurred to provide facilities that increase a firm's ability to produce, such as those related to space, equipment, and buildings, including rents, depreciation, property taxes, and insurance.

Conventional cost system. A cost system that uses only unit-based (or volume-based) cost drivers to apply overhead costs to products and services.

Cost-accounting standards. A set of rules issued by any of several authorized organizations or agencies, such as the FASAB, the Governmental Accounting Standards Board, the Cost Accounting Standards Board, the American Institute of Certified Public Accountants, or the Association of Chartered Accountants, that deal with the determination of costs to be allocated, inventoried, or expensed.

Cost accumulation. Collection of costs in an organized fashion by means of a cost-accounting system. The two primary approaches are job order and process costing. Under a job order system, the three basic elements of costs—direct materials, direct labor, and overhead—are accumulated according to assigned job numbers. Under a process cost system, costs are accumulated according to processing department or cost center.

Cost allocation. A method of assigning costs to activities, outputs, or other cost objects. The allocation base used to assign a cost to objects is not necessarily the cause of the cost. For example, assigning the cost of power to machine activities by machine hours is an allocation because machine hours are an indirect measure of power consumption.

Cost assignment. A process that identifies costs with activities, outputs, or other cost objects. In a broad sense, costs can be assigned to processes, activities, organizational divisions, products, and services. Three methods are directly tracing costs wherever economically feasible, cause-and-effect, and allocating costs on a reasonable and consistent basis.

Cost driver. Any factor that causes a change in the cost of an activity or output. For example, the quality of parts received by an activity, or the degree of complexity of tax returns reviewed by the Internal Revenue Service.

Cost element. An amount paid for a resource consumed by an activity and included in an activity cost pool. For example, power cost, engineering cost, and depreciation may be cost elements in the activity cost pool for a machine activity.

Cost estimation. Measurement of past costs for the purpose of predicting future costs or for decision-making purposes. For example, a cost volume formula (such as $y = \$300 = \$5x$) can be used to estimate a cost item y for any given value of volume x.

Cost-finding techniques. Produce cost data by analytical or sampling methods. Are appropriate for certain kinds of costs, such as indirect costs, items with costs below set thresholds within programs, or some programs in their entirety. Support the overall managerial cost-accounting process and can represent nonrecurring analysis of specific costs.

Cost object. An activity, output, or item whose cost is to be measured. In a broad sense, can be an organizational division, a function, a task, a product, a service, a customer, or a cost objective.

Cost objective. An activity, operation, or completion of a unit of work to complete a specific job for which management decides to identify, measure, and accumulate costs. Must be discrete enough and described in writing to such a level of detail as to form a basis to establish cost centers and output products.

Cost pool. Grouping of individual costs. Subsequent allocations are made of cost pools rather than of individual costs. Costs are often pooled by departments, by jobs, or by behavior pattern. For example, overhead costs in a factory are accumulated by service departments and then allocated to production departments before multiple departmental overhead rates are developed for product-costing purposes.

Cost-volume formula. A cost-accounting formula used for cost prediction and flexible budgeting purposes. A cost function in the form of $y = a + bx$ where y = the semivariable (or mixed) costs to be broken up, x = any given measure of activity such as volume and labor-hours, a = the fixed cost component, and b = the variable rate per unit of x. For example, the cost-volume formula for overhead is $y = \$200 + \$10x$ where y = estimated overhead and x = direct labor hours (that is, the overhead is estimated to be $200 fixed, plus $10 per hour of direct labor).

Direct cost. The cost of resources directly consumed by an activity. Assigned to activities by direct tracing of units of resources consumed by individual activities. A cost that is specifically identified with a single cost object.

Discretionary cost. Cost changed by management decision such as advertising, repairs and maintenance, and research and development.

Entity. A unit within the federal government, such as a department, agency, bureau, or program, for which a set of financial statements would be prepared. Also encompasses a group of related or unrelated commercial functions, revolving funds, trust funds, or other accounts for which financial statements will be prepared in accordance with annual guidance from the Office of Management and Budget on form and content of financial statements.

Fixed assets. A category of property consisting of those items used in the production of other assets or services that have a useful life of two years or more.

Fixed cost. A cost that does not vary in the short term with the volume of activity. Useful for cost savings by adjusting existing capacity or by eliminating idle facilities. Also called a nonvariable or constant cost.

Fixed overhead. Portion of total overhead that remains constant over a given period without regard to changes in the volume of activity. Examples are depreciation, rent, property taxes, insurance, and salaries of supervisors.

Full cost. The sum of all costs required by a cost object including the costs of activities performed by other entities regardless of funding sources. More specifically, the full cost of an output produced by a responsibility segment is the sum of the costs of resources consumed by the responsibility segment and that directly or indirectly contribute to the output, and the costs of identifiable supporting services provided by other reasonability segments within the reporting entity and by other reporting entities.

Historical cost. The amount of cash (or its equivalent) initially paid to acquire an asset.

Homogeneous cost pool. A group of overhead costs associated with activities that can use the same cost driver.

Incremental cost. The increase or decrease in total costs that would result from a decision to increase or decrease output level, to add a service or task, or to change any portion of operations. Helps in making decisions such as whether to contract work out, undertake a project, or increase, decrease, modify, or eliminate an activity or product.

Indirect cost. A cost that cannot be identified specifically with or traced to a given cost object in an economically feasible way.

Job (order) cost sheet. Subsidiary record for work-in-process inventory under a job order cost-accounting system. A separate cost sheet is kept for each identifiable job, accumulating the direct materials, direct labor, and overhead assigned to that job as it moves through production. The form varies according to the needs of the organization.

Job order cost-accounting system. A cost-accounting system designed to determine the cost of producing each job or job lot and that accumulates costs by job.

Job order costing. A method of cost accounting that accumulates costs for individual jobs or lots. A job may be a service or a manufactured item, such as the repair of equipment or the treatment of a patient in a hospital.

Joint cost. A single cost incurred in producing or purchasing two or more essentially different products.

Joint products. Items that have a relatively significant sales value when two or more types are produced simultaneously from the same input by a joint process. For example, gasoline, fuel oil, kerosene, and paraffin are the joint products produced from crude oil.

Opportunity cost. The value of the alternatives foregone by adopting a particular strategy or employing resources in a specific manner. Also called alternative cost or economic cost.

Outcome. The results of a program activity compared to its intended purposes. May be evaluated in terms of service or product quantity and quality, customer satisfaction, and effectiveness.

Outputs. Any product or service generated from the consumption of resources. Can include information or paperwork generated by the completion of the tasks of an activity.

Overhead. Costs that are incurred but not clearly associated with specific units of a product or service; includes all costs other than direct material and direct labor, as well as indirect materials and indirect labor, depreciation, fringe benefits, payroll taxes, and insurance.

Performance measurement. A means of evaluating efficiency, effectiveness, and results. A balanced performance measurement scorecard includes financial and nonfinancial measures focusing on quality, cycle time, and cost. Should include program accomplishments in terms of outputs (quantity of products or services provided, such as the number of items efficiently produced) and outcomes (results of providing outputs, such as whether outputs are effectively meeting intended agency mission objectives).

Performance measures. Indicators of the work performed and the results achieved in an activity, process, or organizational unit. May be financial or nonfinancial. An example of a performance measure of an activity is the number of defective parts per million. An example of a performance measure of an organizational unit is return on sales.

Period costs. Costs that are charged to expense because their benefits appear to expire as the costs are incurred.

Process. The organized method of converting inputs (people, equipment, methods, materials, and environment) to outputs (products and services). The natural aggregation of work activities and tasks performed for program delivery.

Process costing. A method of cost accounting that first collects costs by processes and then allocates the total costs of each process equally to each unit of output flowing through it during an accounting period.

Responsibility accounting. Collection, summarization, and reporting of financial information about various decision centers (responsibility centers) throughout an organization; also called *activity accounting* or *profitability accounting.* Traces costs, revenues, or profits to the individual managers primarily responsible for making decisions about the costs, revenues, or profits in question and taking appropriate actions. Is appropriate where top management has delegated authority to make decisions. The idea is that each manager's performance should be judged by how well he or she manages the items under his or her control.

Responsibility center. An organizational unit headed by a manager or group of managers who are responsible for its activities. Can be measured as revenue centers (accountable for revenue and sales only), cost centers (accountable for costs and expenses only), profit centers (accountable for revenues and costs), or investment centers (accountable for investments, revenues, and costs).

Responsibility segment. A significant organizational, operational, functional, or process component that has the following characteristics: its manager reports to the entity's top management; it is responsible for carrying out a mission, performing a line of activities or services, or producing one or more products; and its resources and results of operations can be clearly distinguished, physically and operationally, from those of other segments of the entity for financial reporting and cost management purposes.

Revenue. Increase in the assets of an organization or decrease in liabilities during an accounting period, primarily from the organizations operating activities. May include sales of products (sales), rendering of services (revenues), and earnings from interest, dividends, lease income, and royalties.

Revenue center. Unit within an organization that is responsible for generating revenues. Is a profit center because for all practical purposes it does not incur some costs during the course of generating revenues. A favorable variance occurs when actual revenue exceeds expected revenue.

Standard cost. Production or operating cost that is carefully predetermined. A target cost that should be attained. Is compared with the actual cost in order to measure the performance of a given costing department or operation. *Variances,* which are the differences between actual costs and standard costs, may indicate inefficiencies that have to be investigated. Corrective action may have to be taken.

Standard costing. A costing method that attaches costs to cost objects based on reasonable estimates or cost studies and by means of budgeted rates rather than according to actual costs incurred. The anticipated cost of producing a unit of output. A predetermined cost to be assigned to products produced. Implies a norm, or what costs should be. May be based on either absorption or direct costing principles, and may apply to all or some cost elements.

Surrogate activity driver. An activity driver that is not descriptive of an activity but is closely correlated to the performance of the activity. Should reduce measurement costs without significantly increasing the costing bias. The number of production runs, for example, is not descriptive of the material disbursing activity, but the number of production runs may be used as an activity driver if material disbursements coincide with production runs.

Target cost. A cost calculated by subtracting a desired profit margin from an estimated (or market-based) price to arrive at a desired production, engineering, or marketing cost. May not be the initial production cost, but rather the cost that is expected to be achieved during the mature production stage.

Target costing. A method used in the analysis of product and process design that involves estimating a target cost and designing the product to meet that cost.

Unit cost. The cost of a selected unit of a good or service, such as dollar cost per ton, machine hour, labor hour, or department hour.

Value-added activity. An activity that is judged to contribute to customer value or to satisfy an organizational need. The attribute "value-added" reflects a belief that the activity cannot be eliminated without reducing the quantity, responsiveness, or quality of output required by a customer or organization. Should physically change the product or service in a manner that meets customer expectations.

Variable cost. A cost that varies with changes in the level of an activity, when other factors are held constant. The cost of material handling to an activity, for example, varies according to the number of material deliveries and pickups to and from that activity.

References

Anderson, B. M. "Using Activity-Based Costing for Efficiency and Quality." *Government Finance Review,* June 1993, pp. 7–9.

Anthony, R. N. "New Frontiers in Defense Financial Management." *Federal Accountant,* 1962, *11,* 13–32.

Anthony, R. N., and Young, D. W. *Management Control in Nonprofit Organizations.* (5th ed.) Homewood, Ill.: Irwin, 1994.

Arwidi, O., and Samuelson, L. A. "The Development of Budgetary Control in Sweden: A Research Note." *Management Accounting Research,* 1993, 4(2), 93–107.

Bailey, M. J. "Defense Decentralization Through Internal Prices." In S. Enke (ed.), *Defense Management.* Upper Saddle River, N.J.: Prentice Hall, 1967.

Brimson, J. A., and Antos, J. *Activity-Based Management.* New York: Wiley, 1994.

Brinker, B. J. (ed.). *Emerging Practices in Cost Management.* Boston: Warren, Gorham, and Lamont, 1992.

Bruggeman, W. "The Impact of Technological Change on Management Accounting." *Management Accounting Research,* 1995, 6(3), 241–252.

Buchanan, J. M. *Cost and Choice: An Inquiry in Economic Theory.* Chicago: Markham, 1969.

Bunce, P., Fraser, R., and Woodcock, L. "Advanced Budgeting: A Journey to Advanced Management Systems." *Management Accounting Research,* 1995, 6(3), 253–265.

Chief Financial Officers Managerial Cost Accounting Guide. http://www.va.gov/cfo/pubs/costguide.

Chandler, A. *Strategy and Structure: Chapters in the History of Industrial Enterprise.* Cambridge, Mass.: MIT Press, 1962.

Cooper, R., and Kaplan, R. S. *The Design of Cost Management Systems.* Upper Saddle River, N.J.: Prentice Hall, 1991.

Cooper, R., and Kaplan, R. S. "Activity-Based Systems: Measuring the Costs of Resource Usage." *Accounting Horizons,* Sept. 1992, pp. 1–13.

Cost Accounting Standards Board. "Statement of Objectives, Policies, and Concepts." *Cost Accounting Standards Guide.* Washington, D.C.: Government Printing Office, 1992.

Crane, M., and Meyer, J. "Focusing on True Costs in a Service Organization." *Management Accounting,* 1993, *74*(8), 41–45.

De Bruine, M., and Sopariwala, P. R. "The Use of Practical Capacity for Better Management Decisions." *Journal of Cost Management,* Spring 1994, pp. 25–31.

Demski, J., and Feltham, G. *Cost Determination.* Ames: Iowa State University Press, 1976.

Evans, P. B., and Wurster, T. S. "Strategy and the New Economics of Information." *Harvard Business Review,* Sept.–Oct. 1997, pp. 71–82.

Fisher, G. H. *Cost Considerations in Systems Analysis.* New York: Elsevier, 1971.

Ganley, J. A., and Cubbin, J. S. *Public Sector Efficiency Measurement: Applications of Data Envelopment Analysis.* New York: Elsevier, 1992.

"Guide to Better Buying." *Economist,* Oct. 18, 1986, p. 71.

Hammer, M. "Reengineering Work: Don't Automate, Obliterate." *Harvard Business Review,* July–Aug. 1990, pp. 104–112.

Harr, D. J. "Productive Unit Resourcing: A Business Perspective on Government Financial Management." *Government Accountants Journal,* Summer 1989, pp. 51–57.

Harr, D. J. "How Activity Accounting Works in Government." *Management Accounting,* 1990, *72*, 36–40.

Harr, D. J. "How Activity Accounting Works in Government." *Government Accountants,* Winter 1992, pp. 15–24.

Harr, D. J., and Godfrey, J. T. *Private Sector Financial Performance Measures and Their Applicability to Government Operations.* Montvale, N.J.: National Association of Accountants, 1991.

Harr, D. J., and Godfrey, J. T. "The Total Unit Cost Approach to Government Financial Management." *Government Accountants,* Winter 1992, pp. 15–24.

Horngren, C. T., and Foster, G. *Cost Accounting: A Managerial Emphasis.* (7th ed.) Upper Saddle River, N.J.: Prentice Hall, 1991.

Hyde, A. "Cornerstones of Quality." *Government Executive,* 1997, *29*(7), 1997, 47–68.

Johansen, C., Jones, L. R., and Thompson, F. "Management and Control of Budget Execution." In R. Golembiewski and J. Rabin (eds.), *Public Budgeting and Finance.* (4th ed.) New York: Dekker, 1997.

Juola, P. "Unit Cost Resourcing: A Conceptual Framework for Financial Management." *Navy Comptroller,* 1993, *3*(3), 42–48.

Kaplan, R. S. *Advanced Management Accounting.* Upper Saddle River, N.J.: Prentice Hall, 1982.

Kaplan, R. S. "One Cost System Isn't Enough." *Harvard Business Review,* Jan.–Feb. 1988, pp. 61–66.

Kaplan, R. S. "In Defense of Activity-Based Cost Management." *Management Accounting,* Nov. 1992, pp. 58–63.

Keohoe, J., Dodson, W., Reeve, R., and Plato, G. *Activity-Based Management in Government.* Washington, D.C.: Coopers and Lybrand, 1995.

Kreuze, J. G., and Newell, G. E. "ABC and Life-Cycle Costing for Environmental Expenditures." *Management Accounting,* 1994, *75*(8), 38–42.

Lapsley, I. "Responsibility Accounting Revived? Market Reforms and Budgetary Control." *Management Accounting Research,* 1994, *5*(3–4), 337–352.

Littrell, E., and Thompson, F. "A Note on Fixed-Assets Reporting." *Public Budgeting and Finance,* forthcoming.

Milgrom, P., and Roberts, J. *Economics, Organization, and Management.* Upper Saddle River, N.J.: Prentice Hall, 1992.

Office of Technology Assessment. *Computerized Manufacturing Automation: Employment, Education, and the Workplace.* Washington, D.C.: Government Printing Office, 1984.

Organization for Economic Cooperation and Development. *Budgeting for Results: Perspectives on Public Expenditure Management.* Paris: Organization for Economic Cooperation and Development, 1995.

Otley, D. "Management Control in Contemporary Organizations: Towards a Wider Framework." *Management Accounting Research,* 1994, *5*(3–4), 289–299.

Otley, D., Broadbent, J., and Berry, A. "Research in Management Control: An Overview of Its Development." *British Journal of Management,* 1995, *6*(Special Issue), 31–44.

Pollitt, C. *Managerialism and the Public Services: Cuts or Cultural Change in the 1990s?* (2nd ed.) Cambridge, Mass.: Blackwell, 1993.

Quinn, J. *Brain-Intelligent Enterprise: A Knowledge- and Service-Based Paradigm for Industry.* New York: Free Press, 1992.

Reschenthaler, G. B., and Thompson, F. "The Information Revolution and the New Public Management." *Journal of Public Administration Research and Theory,* 1996, *6*(1), 125–144.

Rosenberg, N., and Birdsall, L. E. *How the West Grew Rich: The Economic Transformation of the Industrial World.* New York: Basic Books, 1986.

Rotch, W. "Activity-Based Costing in Service Industries." *Cost Management,* Summer 1990, pp. 4–14.

Schedler, K. *Ansatze einer Wirkungsorientierten Verwaltungsführung: Von der Idee des New Public Managements (NPM) zum konkreten Gestaltungsmodell* [Toward a Results-Oriented Leadership: From the Idea of New Public Management (NPM) to Concrete Examples].Bern, Switzerland: Haupt, 1995.

Schwarzbach, H. R. "The Impact of Automation for Indirect Costs." *Management Accounting,* 1985, *67*(6), 45–46.

Scott, G., Bushnell, P., and Sallee, N. "Reform of the Core Public Sector: The New Zealand Experience." *Public Sector,* 1990, *13*(3), 11–24.

Shank, J. K., and Govindarajan, V. "The Perils of Cost Allocation Based on Production Volumes." *Accounting Horizons,* 1988a, *2*(4), 71–79.

Shank, J. K., and Govindarajan, V. "Transaction-Based Costing for the Complex Product Line: A Field Study." *Journal of Cost Management,* Summer 1988b, pp. 31–38.

Simons, R. *Levers of Control: How Managers Use Innovative Control Systems to Drive Strategic Renewal.* Boston: Harvard Business School Press, 1995.

"Software Engineering: Made to Measure." *Economist,* Jan. 23, 1993, p. 79.

Tani, T. "Interactive Control in Target Cost Management." *Management Accounting Research,* 1995, *6*(4), 401–414.

Thompson, F. "Mission-Driven, Results-Oriented Budgeting: Financial Administration and the New Public Management." *Public Budgeting and Finance,* 1994, *14*(3), 90–105.

Thompson, F. "Business Strategy and the Boyd Cycle." *Journal of Contingencies and Crisis Management,* 1995, *3*(2), 81–90.

Thompson, F. "Capital Budgeting," In J. M. Shafritz (ed.), *International Encyclopedia of Public Policy and Administration.* Boulder, Colo.: Westview Press, forthcoming.

Thompson, F., and Jones, L. R. "Controllership in the Public Sector." *Journal of Policy Analysis and Management,* 1986, *5*(3), 547–571.

Thompson, F., and Jones, L. R. *Reinventing the Pentagon: How the New Public Management Can Promote Institutional Renewal.* San Francisco: Jossey-Bass, 1994.

U.S. Office of Management and Budget. *Accounting for Property, Plant and Equipment.* Statement of Federal Financial Accounting Standards no. 6. Washington, D.C.: Government Printing Office, 1995.

Womack, J. P., Jones, D. T., and Roos, D. *The Machine That Changed the World.* New York: Rawson Associates, 1990.

CHAPTER SIXTEEN

Information Technology for Financial Management

Rowan Miranda

Public sector financial management poses a significant challenge for governments at all levels in the United States. Tasks such as budget preparation, budgetary control, financial reporting, performance measurement, cost of service analysis, and revenue forecasting, while appearing deceptively simple and being extensively discussed in the scholarly and professional literature, remain one of the most time-consuming activities that finance officers face. There are governments that have made significant advances in some of these areas, but most continue to struggle with such issues (Cahill, Stevens, and La Plante, 1990; Bozeman and Rahm, 1989).

Throughout the United States, governments are increasing investments in information technology (IT) for budgeting and other financial management functions. Governments at the state and local level are also rapidly moving to replace their financial management systems (FMS) to cope with general obsolescence and the "year 2000 problem" (the inability of old software to handle years beyond 1999 because it implicitly assumes that the first two digits are "19"). The wave of public sector FMS projects taking place across the country provides a rare opportunity for scholars and practitioners to redefine and solidify linkages between budgeting systems and other management information

Note: The author would like to thank Natalee Hillman for her helpful comments, advice, and suggestions.

systems (MIS), to take advantage of database integration permitted by FMS to conceptualize more effective budgeting approaches, and to organize an IT intensive finance function that utilizes electronic commerce and Web capabilities to minimize administrative costs and improve responsiveness to citizens. It is argued that to effectively seize the opportunity there must be recognition that functional and technological aspects of budgeting are intertwined; true reengineering of the finance function requires changes to existing processes and institutions as well as investments in IT.

This chapter describes and analyzes the role of IT in public financial management. Although the focus is mostly on state and local government, many of the topics discussed have implications for federal financial management as well. The first section describes the evolution of budgetary reforms, technology trends in government administration, and the shortcomings of legacy financial systems. The next section presents the concept of integrated FMS and outlines product features that governments should consider while acquiring FMS. A survey of twenty-five state and local governments is used to assess the state-of-the-art capabilities of major FMS systems. The chapter concludes by presenting the business process reengineering method as an approach to reducing the risk of FMS implementation failure.

EVOLUTION OF BUDGETING AND TECHNOLOGY IN STATE AND LOCAL GOVERNMENT

To appreciate the role of technology in advancing public budgeting capabilities it is useful to examine briefly the objectives sought long ago by budget reformers. This section also reviews technology utilization trends in state and local government and shortcomings associated with existing FMS.

Evolution of Budgeting

During the past century, innovations in budgeting evolved rather slowly. In the early 1900s, the concept of budget reform was equated with the establishment of the executive budget and the use of basic expenditure control mechanisms. The executive budget remained an innovation for only a brief period as dissatisfaction with the "control" orientation and the limited usefulness of the line-item budget format led to budgetary reform attempts.

In his classic article on budgetary reform, Allen Schick (1966, p. 49) examined the evolution of U.S. budgeting and noted that budgetary reforms emphasized either the *planning, management,* or *control* orientations. Successive stages of reform altered the planning-management-control balance. For example, some reforms to line-item budgeting emphasized the management orientation (for example, performance budgeting as advocated by the Hoover Commission in the 1950s) and others emphasized a planning orientation (such as the Planning, Programming, Budgeting System, or PPBS, in the 1960s). In the end, the reforms that did gain acceptance were short lived; state and local governments reverted back to either traditional line-item budgeting or to a hybrid of line-item and program budgeting. If nothing else, what the history of budgetary reform illustrates is the intense interest by practitioners and scholars in improving existing approaches.

Part of the reason that many reform efforts did not gain widespread acceptance is that stakeholders responsible for various phases of government decision making (such as planning, management, and control) had vastly different informational needs. As Schick (1966, p. 48) noted, "informational needs differ in terms of time spans, levels of aggregation, linkages with organizational and operating units, and input-output foci. The apparent solution is to design a system that serves the multiple needs of budgeting. Historically, however, there has been a strong tendency to homogenize informational structures and to rely on a single classification scheme to serve all budgetary purposes."

Every major budgetary reform imposed tremendous paperwork, data collection, information management, and analytic burdens on government agencies. Performance budgeting, with its management orientation, required that activities and costs be categorized by function. It also required that measurements of productivity be used to facilitate an evaluation of efficient performance. PPBS, with its planning orientation, required objectives to be defined and data to be collected that would permit cost-benefit analysis on alternatives, multiyear financial planning, and evaluations of program effectiveness. Finally, zero-based budgeting (ZBB), with its emphasis on planning and management, required an annual rejustification of budget data from "ground zero" and the ranking of priorities by designing "decision packages." As discussed in the next section of the chapter, modern FMS provide an opportunity to serve diverse informational demands and develop multiple budgetary classification schemes.

Technology Utilization in the Public Sector

Three phases of technological change have had an impact on the public sector finance organization (Mechling, 1989). Early technological improvements to the finance function, while significant, only allowed governments to process tasks faster (high-volume transaction processing); organization-wide information quality, accessibility, and analytical capability improved only marginally. This early "mainframe" wave (circa 1965 to 1980) allowed governments to automate routine accounting functions, payroll, and budgetary control mechanisms. The major goal of automation was to increase efficiency by reducing clerical costs.

A second wave of "end-user computing" (1980 to 1990) brought the personal computer to the forefront of the government finance environment. By using spreadsheet applications and data analysis software, financial managers were now able to focus more on analytical techniques to improve their personal productivity. Mechling (1989) notes that such decentralization of computing power created a "revolt of the masses" against central data processing, leaving the latter with the limited roles of establishing standards and providing enterprise-wide resources. Independent financial management applications proliferated throughout government organizations. Integrated systems were less attractive because they would require an organization-wide effort, including the maintenance of parallel systems until conversion to the new system was complete (Kraemer and King, 1982). The current wave (since 1990) enables organizational productivity to increase through networks, shared databases, and client-server technology. Such system features also enable nearly complete integration of the finance function (that is, linkage of the general ledger to other subsystems such as purchasing and payroll). In contrast to earlier waves of technological change, integration through IT provides the opportunity to achieve goals of the budgetary function that were stated long ago in reform efforts but that have remained elusive—goals such as efficiency and economy, financial control, and accessibility to information relevant for decision making. Although modern IT cannot resolve the conceptual difficulties associated with some reform approaches (such as the ranking of alternatives in ZBB being a political decision rather than an analytic one), the data collection and information management burdens posed by other reform efforts could be far easier to cope with. Advanced capabilities now possible with leading-edge technology are likely to lead to resurgence in developing new budgetary approaches (Anderson, 1993).

Common Failures of Legacy Systems

Although many local governments are rapidly replacing their FMS, most large and midsize governments continue to operate with "legacy" systems. Legacy systems are generally mainframe-based budgeting and accounting applications that significantly improved financial management when they were adopted in the 1970s and 1980s. Although they solved many problems and improved the efficiency of tasks such as payroll and accounting, they also institutionalized various technological and functional deficiencies. By contrast, the current client-server-based systems overcome many of these deficiencies. To gain insight into how to utilize modern FMS more effectively, some of the major problems with legacy systems are reviewed next.

Technological Deficiencies. Technological deficiencies of legacy systems arise from the incapacity of hardware or software to cope with various informational demands.

Limitations on capturing new information. Once databases are designed, legacy systems are difficult and expensive to modify, especially when it is later desirable to capture other information. For example, a data entry screen may permit the recording of aggregate real-estate taxes, but efforts to disaggregate that category by changing data entry forms (for example, to record commercial and residential property data) may be expensive. To cope, MIS managers may use cumbersome manual or programming routines to work around the problem. Similarly, data entry screens related to grant management programs may be difficult to modify to permit compliance with new federal regulations. The year 2000 problem alone has led organizations to undergo expensive modifications of software.

Inability to expand the system. Many legacy systems rely on software that was customized to fit specific operational processes. Early generations of software focused on single applications (such as payroll or benefits administration) that did not "speak" to one another. Even in instances where limited integration has occurred (such as in payroll and general ledger), expansion of the system to include other applications (for example, benefits or revenue administration) remains difficult in legacy systems.

Proliferation of independent "shadow" systems. Limitations on legacy system expansion led individuals to take matters into their own hands. With the introduction of personal computers, independent applications and databases proliferated throughout government organizations without planning the relationship of that software to the core financial system. Low cost but sophisticated desktop applications such as spreadsheets, relational database programs, and suite packages put computing power in the hands of individuals. Independent databases increased personal efficiency but made the reliability of and access to data more problematic. In some cases, the overall cost of computing increased because data entry redundancies and additional checks on validating and updating data associated with "shadow" systems required staff time. Coping with the fragmentation of the data-processing organization remains one of the major IT challenges facing governments today.

Difficulty in sharing, accessing, and analyzing information. Legacy systems limit accessibility of information and their designs do not recognize that the power of any database lies in the end user's ability to manipulate it. Legacy systems restrict analysis to a select group of queries available through standard report formats. When independent databases proliferated, they did so in a proprietary way: databases were "owned" by particular departments or users. If users were fortunate enough to get another department's data, it is likely that such data would have to be reentered and validated.

The difficulty of sharing, accessing, and analyzing information in the legacy system environment, can be illustrated using the example of an emergency management services database. To build the database, citizen addresses from the real-estate tax files might be a logical place to start. Yet different software applications make it difficult to maintain a single database; expensive duplication of effort is the result. If departments do not cooperate and central authorities are too weak to encourage cooperation, it is likely that an entirely separate address file will be built. There are many more examples like this in the public sector and such problems are pervasive in governments with many independently elected offices.

Untimely data. Because of batch processing, data tape transfer, or physical hard-copy transfer, data is often produced too late to have an impact on a decision. For information to be relevant for decision making it needs to be readily accessible. In legacy systems, information often has to be batch processed with jobs scheduled to run at fixed times so that the system is not overburdened. Users generally have to wait for the results of their queries to be produced. Although legacy systems can permit more interactive programming, they do not permit the flexible interaction that modern client-server technology does. A major goal of modern IT is to put information at the fingertips of users so it can be accessed when it is most likely to influence a decision—immediately.

Hardware and other limitations. Under legacy systems, the crashing of the mainframe, complex job control language, and memory and space allocation limitations are all factors that reduce the ability of the end user to access the database. Space limitations require that historical data be archived or discarded instead of being part of the existing database. Also, once batch-processing code is written, only individuals with an understanding of programming can change it for new tasks. For the common user, this means either taking cumbersome steps to work around the problem or making decisions without the information.

Organizations have attempted to cope with technological deficiencies by standardization, where only a limited number of hardware and software platforms are used, and by interoperability guidelines, which seek to ensure procurement of only technologies that work together. Nevertheless, these standards and guidelines have not resolved the many functional deficiencies of legacy systems, discussed next.

Functional Deficiencies. Functional deficiencies result from limitations of legacy systems in permitting the attainment of various financial tasks.

Fragmentation of financial tasks. Legacy financial systems generally have a narrow view of financial tasks. The core legacy system typically includes the general ledger, payroll, and in some instances budget control. Many other finance-related functions—accounts receivable, fixed-asset management and inventory, purchasing, and budget preparation—employ stand-alone applications or manual processes. Such system fragmentation of the finance function results in the following problems.

Loss of useful data. A major output of legacy financial systems is the production of financial reports that meet mandatory requirements of standard-setting bodies, state and federal laws, and local ordinances. As Kraemer and

King (1982, p. 58) note, "the design of advanced capabilities for financial management and planning" took longer and was viewed "as a luxury to be sought only after the mandated requirements" were met. In the context of system space limitations, the designers of legacy systems sought to capture only limited transactional data for minimal financial reporting needs; other useful information generated by transactions was simply discarded. Departments coped with these deficiencies by building shadow systems to capture data unavailable in the core system, or simply made decisions without it.

Payroll systems, for example, may discard data related to workload that would be useful for service costing or performance measurement comparisons. Or an accounts payable application may process an invoice by recording the vendor's identity and the amount owed. Other information about the purchase that could have been used to update fixed-asset or inventory records is simply discarded by the system. Finally, a systemwide focus on recording transactions only on the basis of budgeted spending levels can also lead to the loss of useful information.

Proliferation of conflicting information. Independent databases or shadow systems and fragmentation of financial tasks can produce conflicting information. Considerable organizational effort then goes into reconciling the diverse databases before a decision is made. For example, it is not uncommon for large to midsize county governments considering the sale of delinquent real estate receivables to have to reconcile as many as three databases that contain the same basic information (for example, data from the assessment department, the treasurer's office, and the controller's office).

Rudimentary budgetary controls. Legacy systems provide rudimentary budgetary controls such as appropriations, encumbrances, and position controls. Some systems can also provide allotment controls that enable governments to parcel out the ability to spend in increments over time. Although such controls are important to any good financial system, legacy systems generally require that these controls be imposed systemwide. There are instances where more sophisticated controls or customized control strategies (such as the application of more restrictive controls to problem agencies) may be desirable but beyond legacy system capabilities.

Inflexible budgetary formats. Legacy budgeting systems rely mainly on line-item formats for budgetary control. Rigid databases make it difficult to convert such formats into information useful for decision making. To some extent, many demands made for different budget systems are primarily calls for information other than what is provided in the traditional line-item format (such as performance data, program data, and so on). By using integrated and relational databases across applications, the informational limitations of line-item budgets can be addressed. Under modern FMS, if systems are properly designed, information can be organized and reported in many different ways and be readily available to decision makers.

Timeliness of financial reports. Legacy financial systems are often associated with considerable lag times for the production of interim and year-end financial reports. The reasons for this stem from manual mechanisms to conduct year-end closing entries and poorly designed subsystems (such as budgeting and purchasing) that take months to reconcile. For example, it is difficult to expect accurate quarterly budget-to-actual projections if the purchasing system is months behind on processing requisitions. It is also not uncommon for larger jurisdictions to issue their comprehensive annual financial report (CAFR) six to nine months after the end of the fiscal year. Automated closing entries in financial systems can enable more timely release of the CAFR but necessitate integration with other applications.

In summary, although legacy mainframe systems have significantly improved the productivity of the finance organization, major problems nevertheless remain. One challenge for government organizations today is managing the transition to hardware and software that can overcome the technological and functional limitations of legacy systems. Of all of the approaches available in using IT for financial management, trends in the industry suggest that the use of modern client-server-based FMS holds the most promise.

INTEGRATED FINANCIAL MANAGEMENT SYSTEMS

State and local governments throughout the country have chosen one of two paths toward designing an overall FMS: independent stand-alone systems and integrated systems (Wooldridge, 1982). Independent systems are oriented toward single applications (such as payroll or purchasing) and function apart from other activities in the finance organization. Independent systems have their own sources of data, databases, software programs, hardware, and information management standards. Current trends in FMS software favor integrated systems, especially as initial problems with such systems are increasingly managed with software upgrades (Sandlin, 1996).

The main advantages of independent systems are "that they are both modular and manageable and can be modified or discarded with relatively little impact on other independent systems" (Kraemer and King, 1982, p. 62). In addition, the costs of independent systems seem lower and the smaller scale of such projects generally pose less implementation risk. Arguments in favor of independent systems point out that some applications may be "best of breed"— that is, the individual application may be superior to the overall quality of any integrated system available. Finally, another argument in favor of independent systems is that the failure of one application does not imply systemwide failure. These advantages aside, independent systems are also associated with many of the functional and technological deficiencies noted in the previous section of the chapter.

Modern integrated FMS are generally modular and built around a general ledger system (see Figure 16.1). In theory, each module can be implemented on a stand-alone basis. The power of the system, however, results when the modules are tied together through common databases, reporting tools, and development tools. An integrated FMS provides organization-wide access to shared data that are consistent and readily available. For example, in an integrated system a purchasing module can share vendor information with the accounts payable module and simultaneously streamline entry of assets to the fixed-asset module. In addition to minimizing data entry and "document handoffs," integration significantly improves timely reporting. The presence of functional integration is largely driven by features of technological architecture associated with client-server FMS.

Attributes of Information Technology Architecture

In the context of FMS, *information technology architecture* is a term used to describe the hardware and software of a system. Although many larger jurisdictions continue to use mainframe computers as platforms for their FMS, the trend in the public and private sector market is a move toward client-server technology. The accounting firm Deloitte & Touche's *Financial and Accounting Systems Survey* (1997) showed that 82 percent of all new financial and accounting system implementations (cross-industry) over the next two years will be client-server based. In large governments, however, mainframes continue to operate alongside client-server applications. This section presents technological characteristics of leading-edge FMS.

Distributed Processing. As state and local governments consider the need to modernize financial and administrative applications, mainframe systems are being replaced by "distributed" systems that rely on servers—ordinarily, networked computers that provide shared services to multiple clients. Distributed processing often places control of applications in users' departments. The servers themselves, though, are centrally located in order to facilitate backup, security, and environments that protect hardware. The client-server model is the major form of distributed processing on which modern FMS rely.

Client-Server Platforms. Client-server systems are associated with network computing. In the most common mode, the client makes requests (such as for data, analysis, and queries) from the server (Renaud, 1997, pp. 13–24). The client is a desktop computer in an end user's department that can have a relationship with different servers. As Renaud notes, the "beauty of client/server relationships is that the client and the server share the workload between them. As a result, client/server relationships are often referred to as *cooperative processing*" (p. 4).

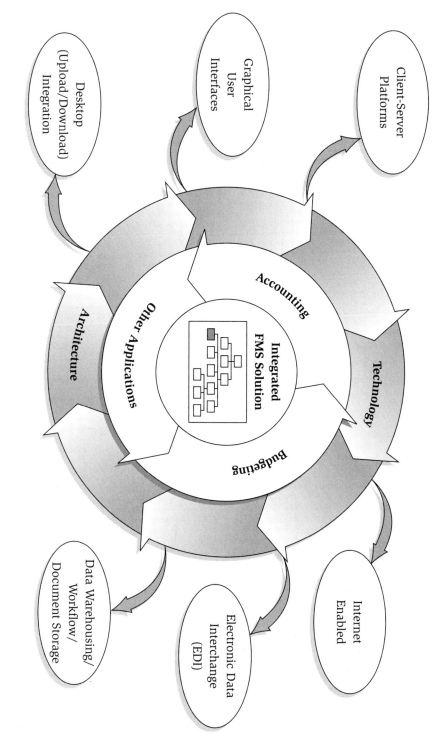

Figure 16.1. FMS Applications and Technology Architecture.

Several major FMS packages use "fat client" software. Under this arrangement, "a large part of the programming logic is in the workstation as opposed to locating it at the database server" (Stephens, 1997, p. 14). This approach significantly reduces network traffic because the "front end" of the software (screens, graphical user interfaces, and processes) is housed on the workstation of the client, with the servers maintaining institution-wide access to the databases. Client-server systems may require user departments to be responsible for data processing operations, procedures, data integrity, database security, and system maintenance. At the design stage of the client-server system it is decided what tasks will be distributed to the server or client. The main point is that the FMS is housed across clients and servers, with end users having easier access to information and data manipulation options.

Client-server systems are also associated with interoperability, adaptability, and scalability. As previously stated, *interoperability* is the ease with which different technologies can work together. In the FMS context, programming interfaces are used to get applications to do this. *Adaptability* is the ease with which important features of the system (such as data screens and storage requirements) can be changed as the organization changes. Finally, *scalability* is the ease with which the system can be expanded as the organization grows.

Relational Databases. Relational databases organize records into a series of tables. Under nonrelational structures, cumbersome but meticulous programming is required to navigate a database. In contrast, relational databases allow users to select easily files, columns, rows, and named fields using various data-access languages, such as structured query language. Data structures, storage and retrieval operations, and limitations on values define the rules of the game in relational databases. Relational databases specify "keys" that can be used to query and search a database. Finally, as their name implies, relational databases permit linkages to tables in other databases.

Graphical User Interface (GUI). Graphical user interfaces facilitate human-machine interaction by allowing point-and-click devices to choose among pull-down menus and options. GUIs are far more user friendly than previous text-based programming because they exploit window technology such as tool bars, icons, symbols, and drawings. GUI technology improves the ability of users to conduct repeated motions. It also enables help menus and on-line documentation to be readily accessible and tucked away in pull-down menus when they are not being used.

Desktop Integration. The ability to extract data from the FMS and manipulate it on the desktop is important to most end users. The power of desktop applications has increased rapidly over the past decade. Several popular suite packages consisting of word processing, spreadsheets, databases, and presentation graphics are inexpensive. Desktop integration also means that it should be easy to download from and upload to the FMS. Bringing data from the FMS to the desktop also enables the data to be used widely in the organization, including to provide decision-making support.

Data Warehousing. As costs of information storage and retrieval are rapidly declining, end users expect access to more and better information. Many legacy FMS retain limited historical data and dump the rest, because of both space constraints and the limited ability of applications to access such data. Data warehousing is a process of using tools to "mine" (query or browse) databases for decision support. The data warehouse may include the entire FMS database, or it may contain select information that is predetermined to be stored. The ultimate value of a data warehouse is closely related to the quality of information retained and the availability of query tools to access it.

Internet (Web) Enabling. Increasingly, state and local governments are demanding that FMS have Internet capabilities. Emerging Internet-related technology promises dramatic improvement in government's responsiveness to citizens and suppliers. Most major governments already have Web pages for general information; significant opportunities remain for government transactions to be conducted through the Web. Although valid security concerns in Internet commerce must still be resolved, already present are capabilities to remit taxes and fees through the Web. Web applications can also improve government's relationships to suppliers and increase the number of bidders in government procurement.

Electronic Commerce. Electronic commerce is any exchange of data that occurs electronically. There are several subcategories of electronic commerce that are especially germane to FMS. *Electronic funds transfer* (EFT) technology involves the automated transfer of funds across accounts without physical handling of currency. This technology is already being used to streamline many government processes, including payroll and tax collection. The expansion of EFT in government could significantly reduce transaction costs for citizens and thereby increase their regulatory compliance.

Another technology, electronic data interchange (EDI), seeks to provide a paperless approach to transacting business. Modules with EDI-routing capabilities are also referred to as workflow. Workflow applications focus on routing business forms both internally and externally. E-mail integration with workflow permits parallel processing of transactions—which significantly improves financial processes that require multiple levels of approval. The use of EDI and workflow in government financial management is still in its infancy. A leading professional magazine, however, noted that EDI has already changed the job of the internal auditor from focusing mainly on paper to sitting in front of the terminal and "examining different components of an electronic process, using audit utilities embedded in the various modules" (Stone, 1997, p. 28).

As the next section demonstrates, these technological attributes have significantly improved the overall functionality of FMS.

Major Components of Integrated Financial Systems

Most integrated FMS packages are a series of applications held together by common tools and standards. Integration of different applications is accomplished through software interfaces that serve as bridges from one application to another. It is easier to build interfaces with applications that employ the same technology architecture. In addition, integrated FMS have common underlying tools for programming (development tools), graphics, customized reporting (report writers), and electronic routing of documents (workflow). For example, payroll uses interfaces to interact with other modules, such as the general ledger or accounts payable. Figure 16.2 illustrates the power of integration to coordinate transactions across select applications.

In acquiring integrated FMS, governments typically begin with the implementation of core modules such as general ledger, payroll, and purchasing and then add advanced capabilities. Following is a description of each major subsystem of an integrated FMS with leading-edge features highlighted.

Budget Development. In most local governments, budget development is a time-consuming task that can take six months or more. A significant amount of effort goes into changing numbers, checking balances, and preparing documents—all tasks that can be automated with modern systems.

Budget development modules coordinate organization-wide operating and capital budget preparation, analysis, review, and approval. These modules generally rely on a database that contains historical information, comparison of year-to-date spending with appropriations, positions by department, salary and wage scales, collective bargaining contract terms, and other information. It is also important that the modules interface with the payroll, human resources, and general ledger systems.

Leading-edge features of budget development modules include coordination of department requests by the central budget office using electronic workflow capabilities. Decentralized data entry and narrative justification by departments are features that can significantly reduce the workload for budget analysts. Some modules also allow the budget office to immediately (on-line and in real time) assess the impact of their own modifications, modifications by the legislative body, and other changes to the overall budget. In addition, budget analysts have the ability to conduct "what if" or scenario analysis (for example,

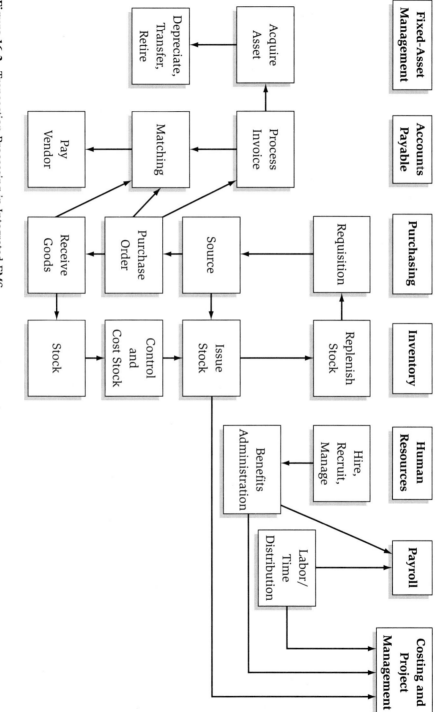

Figure 16.2. Transaction Processing in Integrated FMS.

what would be the impact of a 3 percent cut in overtime across non-public-safety departments?) to assess the impact of different budget-balancing steps. The underlying databases should also enable the budget analyst to "drill down" from summary levels (department, program, and cost categories) to lower levels (activity or cost center) and to "drill up" the other way. With expansion of the budget database over successive budget cycles, the ability to develop alternatives to the line-item format (such as program or performance budgets) is greatly enhanced. Finally, some budget development modules also have publishing capabilities that link the main database to word processing, spreadsheets, and graphics used to produce the budget document.

Many state and local governments are also considering multiyear budgeting approaches for either legal and external purposes or for internal use. It is likely that there will be demands that the budget development modules of the future address the issue of budgeting over multiple years.

General Ledger. The general ledger (GL) module is the foundation of an integrated FMS. The GL is the main accounting system for the organization. It provides basic budgetary controls (appropriations and allotments) by recording transactions and maintaining accounts and journals. It is also the main vehicle used to produce the major financial reports issued by state and local governments—the CAFR, the single audit for grant compliance, and interim financial reports. In addition, GL modules have capabilities to automate encumbrances, trial balances, account analysis, journal entries, and exception reports. Basic GL functionality includes the simultaneous posting of an accounting transaction both to the general ledger and to subsidiary ledgers.

Leading-edge capabilities of GL packages include the maintenance of multiple ledgers (to comply with different reporting requirements), flexible charts of accounts, definition of multiple periods (year, quarter, month, and week), accounting drill-down capabilities, and automated journal entries (year-end closing, reversing entries, and repeated entry of similar transactions) that accelerate the ability to produce timely reports. Many systems also have the ability to validate entries immediately (such as account combinations) and enable data to be corrected as it is being entered.

Leading-edge GL packages also enable governments to use multiple budgets as control mechanisms (such as legally approved budgets and organizational budgets in which the controlling level is different from that which is legally approved). In addition, central budget offices can designate whether a department's ability to spend is linked to the department's performance in revenue collection or receipt of grants. Pre-encumbrances allow governments to reserve appropriations at the time of issuing the requisition, prior to purchase orders and encumbrances. Finally, budget preparation is significantly enhanced if the package integrates GL and budget development modules, because year-to-date spending totals will be readily available throughout the budget-making process.

Purchasing. For government employees and suppliers alike, purchasing is one reason that government is associated with red tape. Purchasing has an impact on numerous financial management processes, such as accounts payable, fixed assets and inventory, and budgetary control. A major challenge facing governments at all levels is to improve the performance of the purchasing function. Many have focused on technology, especially methods of electronic commerce, to accomplish this. Basic functionality in purchasing includes entry and tracking of requisitions, issuance of purchase orders, receiving, and inventory management. Routine functions that can be automated include funds checking, encumbrances, requisition management, commodity coding, tabulation of bids, change-order processing, and maintenance of vendor information files.

By automating high-volume transactions, leading-edge purchasing systems focus on streamlining business processes and enabling strategic tasks such as development of procurement alternatives, contract negotiation, and the building of supplier relationships. Purchasing systems should be capable of providing an audit trail of all transactions related to a specific activity or project for a designated period. Leading-edge systems reduce paper by using EDI and workflow capabilities. Other leading-edge features include three-way-match capabilities (matching of quantities ordered, received, and inspected), use of on-line catalogs to create purchase orders, automated inventory entries, tabulation of bids, voucher-encumbrance liquidation, automated approvals (based on type of item or dollar value), and the ability to freeze transactions for budgetary control.

Purchasing is also an area in which Internet and electronic commerce capabilities significantly enhance functionality. Purchasing systems can be designed to access industrywide supply catalogs through the Web for the most up-to-date price and product information, to send and receive on-line notifications to and from suppliers, and to allow vendors to use the Web to update the government's database or obtain a status on their invoice. In addition, advanced capabilities in some systems enable the use of document imaging technology to significantly reduce paper attachments to main source documents.

Human Resources and Payroll. Human resources and payroll (HR/P) modules can provide a comprehensive solution to managing and paying employees. They can be used by managers to conduct applicant tracking (such as people who take Civil Service exams), manage employee records (such as accumulated leave, seniority, evaluations, and training), administer employee benefits, and track position information (salary and wage scales) that is useful for budget preparation. Payroll is often the most important component of these systems but it relies heavily on data produced by the other applications. Basic payroll functionality includes the processing of time sheets, personnel forms, wage deductions, payroll adjustments, and workers' compensation payments, and the production of standard payroll reports.

Leading-edge system capabilities for HR/P include analysis of automated payroll exceptions, interfaces with GL (such as automated journal entries) and accounts payable (such as accrual of vacation pay), and use of the Web to permit employment applications. In addition, automatic deposit, mass changes to employee databases (such as an across-the-board pay increase or reorganization coding), turnover analysis, tracking of accumulated benefits, adjustments for retroactive pay, wage attachments, and labor distribution capabilities (such as allocating a worker's pay across projects) are desirable features in a payroll module.

Accounts Payable. Accounts payable (A/P) modules seek to record current liabilities accurately, to utilize supplier discounts to reduce costs, and to process payment of invoices in a timely manner. A/P modules should have interfaces with the purchasing, accounting, and treasury functions. Basic A/P functionality includes maintenance of vendor master files, quick entry of recurring vouchers, duplicate invoice detection, vendor ledger maintenance, and vendor performance reporting.

Leading-edge A/P capabilities include three-way matching (reconciliation of purchase order, receiving report, and invoice), contract management capabilities, pre-encumbrancing, and recording of multiyear contracts. Many systems also have the ability to automatically record offsetting journal entries and to set tolerances for payment processing (such as 4 percent in excess of encumbrance). Electronic commerce possibilities include self-service vendor access to A/P information, workflow to reduce paper, and EFT capabilities to improve handling and management of funds.

Accounts Receivable and Billing. Governments are increasingly integrating their tax and fee collection systems with enterprise-wide FMS. The main functions of an A/R package are to produce bills, process receipts, and record payments. Basic functionality of A/R packages includes the recording of information to assess the aging of open accounts, the application of late charges and interest, and the ability to write off minimal balances.

Leading-edge capabilities in A/R include real estate billing, automated updates of GL accounts upon lockbox receipt of cash, reporting to credit agencies, administration of special payment plans, use of credit cards, and issuance of delinquency notices. The use of EFT capabilities to improve the receipt of funds is also a desirable feature of A/R packages.

Fixed-Asset and Inventory Management. Nonenterprise operations of state and local governments typically do not record fixed assets and inventories in the general fund because the measurement focus is on outflows of financial resources. Consequently, separate fixed asset and inventory management modules are used for recording, managing, and controlling government assets. This module is a repository for the acquisition and usage of land, buildings, and equipment by government agencies.

Leading-edge fixed asset and inventory management capabilities include interfaces with the accounts payable and purchasing functions, automated record keeping, standard reports (such as acquisition, depreciation, and disposition data by period), control of leased assets, and preventive maintenance records. These modules also provide automated replacement cost values and indirect cost calculations for assets used in federally sponsored programs.

Project Costing. Project-costing modules allow managers to track project costs and commitments, to maintain a detailed audit trail of project transactions, and to post to the GL. These modules focus on providing managers with information to keep projects on schedule and within budget. Especially in the areas of capital programs and grant management, managers can utilize these modules to define a project budget that is linked to a summary-level line item (such as a capital budget) or department appropriation. Basic functionality in project costing modules includes the monitoring of project activity and employee assignments, change-order control, and funds-usage tracking.

Leading-edge capabilities for project-costing modules include electronic audit support, definition of allowable cost rates (such as indirect costs), labor cost analysis, cost projection capabilities, ability to extract cost information from other applications (such as fixed asset), and drill-down capabilities to analyze expenditure detail below the budgeted category.

Geographic Information Systems. In many state and local governments, geographic information systems (GIS) are being used to improve policy analysis capabilities in areas ranging from emergency management to economic development. Yet linkages between GIS and FMS have not been well established, although there are numerous opportunities in the future to do so. GIS capabilities are sometimes used in user-fee operations such as building permits and inspections. FMS-related areas in which GIS is being examined more closely by governments include capital budget development, federal grant management and reporting (such as the need to target dollars to particular census tracts), fixed-asset management (especially in larger jurisdictions), and property assessment. Once FMS processes become more integrated, linkages with systems such as GIS will significantly enhance decision support to finance officers.

Although modern FMS systems have made substantial improvements in FMS functionality, major improvements still remain. Results of a survey of state and local government finance officers are used to assess the state of the art of various functional and technical features for FMS. The survey results should suggest, to academics and practitioners alike, functional and technical features in need of future development.

FMS: The State of the Art

In November 1997, the Government Finance Officers Association (GFOA) Research Center surveyed twenty-five state and local governments to assess their evaluation of functional and technical features of five major integrated FMS packages (five governments per vendor were contacted). Because of the paucity of fully implemented client-server FMS applications, random sampling was not used to identify respondents. Finance officers using particular software packages were asked to rate their satisfaction with the overall system, fifteen technical features, and twenty functional features. They were asked to rate each feature on scale of one to five, from unsatisfactory (1) through satisfactory, average, excellent, and finally leading edge (5). The responses of the twenty-five jurisdictions were summarized across the five software packages to obtain an average for each feature.

Figure 16.3 presents the ratings of the *technical* features of FMS. Finance officers reported that their level of satisfaction with the overall FMS system was close to excellent. Features that ranked high on the scale included inquiry and drill-down capabilities, flexibility to customize accounts, and power of the database. Features that were ranked include integration with other applications, germaneness to government, upload capability, written documentation, and reporting capabilities. The findings were supported in open-ended interviews with finance officers. Many finance officers felt that although many vendors label their products as "integrated" and "public sector" solutions, in practice most products still have integration problems and are primarily solutions designed for the private sector that have been transferred to the government environment. The unique nature of state and local government functions (such as fund accounting, purchasing, and fixed-asset account groups) makes it difficult to simply paint a public sector face on a product designed for private enterprise.

Figure 16.4 presents the ratings of *functional* features of FMS. Applications and tasks that received the highest ratings included accounts payable, human resources and payroll, contract management, and report-writing tools (for customized reporting). Applications and tasks that were rated lowest included cash and investment management, budget development, grant management, purchasing, and fixed assets. Most of the accounting-related features—encumbrance accounting, preparation of financial statements, cost accounting and allocation, and general ledger—were rated between above average and excellent.

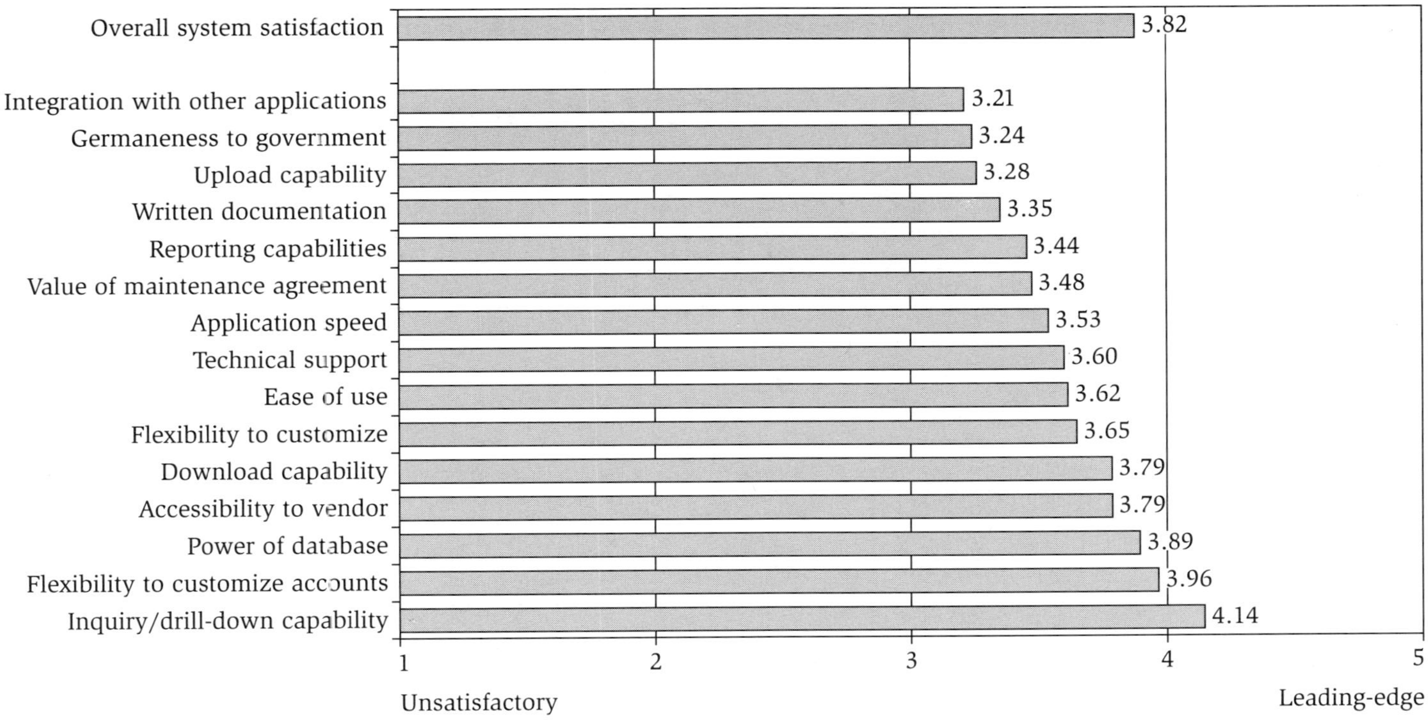

Figure 16.3. Ratings of FMS Technical Features by Twenty-Five Local Governments.

Source: Government Finance Officers Association.

The chart shows horizontal bars with the following categories and values:

Category	Rating
Overall system satisfaction	3.82
Integration with other applications	3.21
Germaneness to government	3.24
Upload capability	3.28
Written documentation	3.35
Reporting capabilities	3.44
Value of maintenance agreement	3.48
Application speed	3.53
Technical support	3.60
Ease of use	3.62
Flexibility to customize	3.65
Download capability	3.79
Accessibility to vendor	3.79
Power of database	3.89
Flexibility to customize accounts	3.96
Inquiry/drill-down capability	4.14

Scale: 1 (Unsatisfactory) to 5 (Leading-edge)

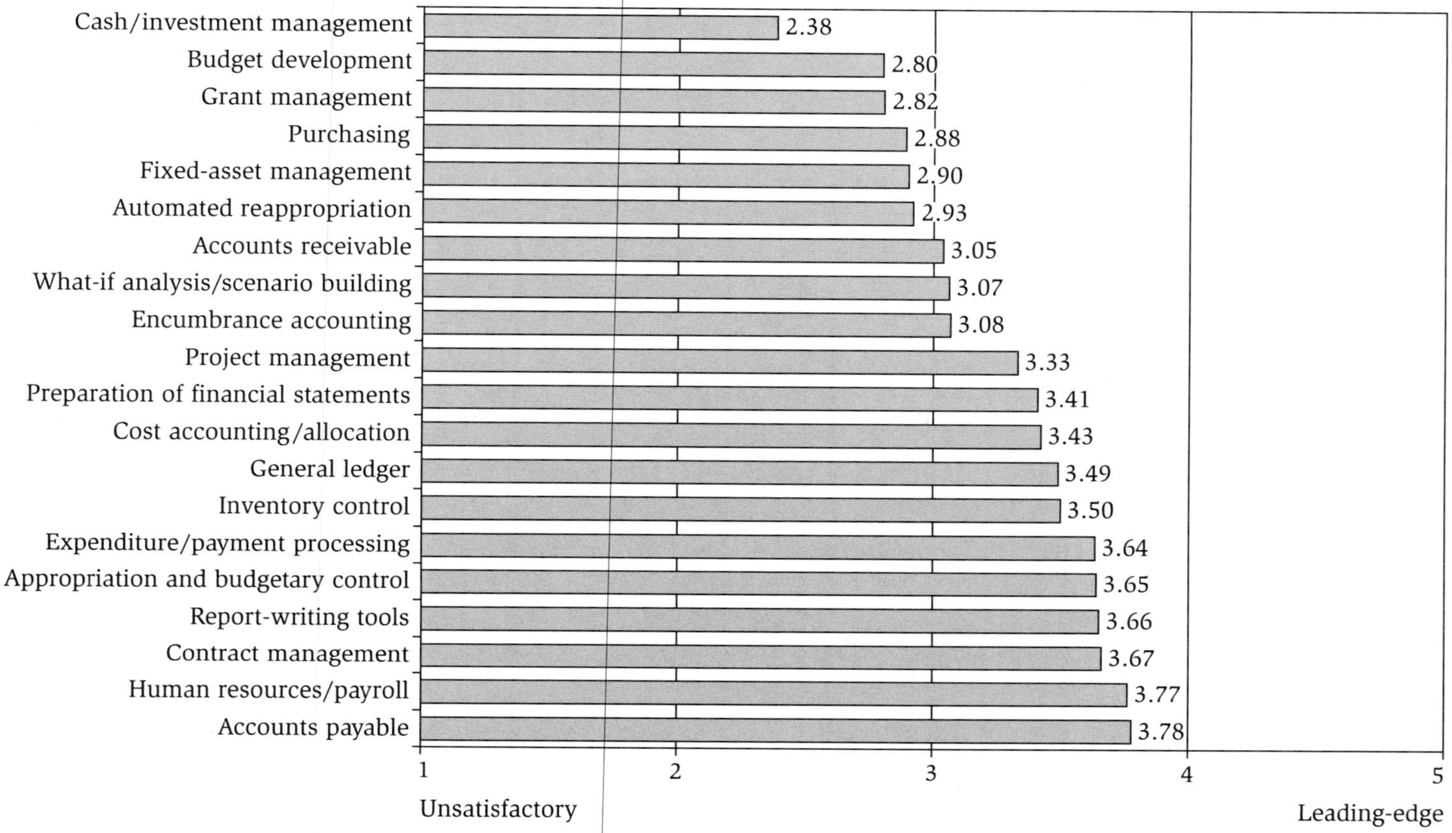

Figure 16.4. Ratings of FMS Functional Features by Twenty-Five Local Governments.

Source: Government Finance Officers Association.

Cash/investment management — 2.38
Budget development — 2.80
Grant management — 2.82
Purchasing — 2.88
Fixed-asset management — 2.90
Automated reappropriation — 2.93
Accounts receivable — 3.05
What-if analysis/scenario building — 3.07
Encumbrance accounting — 3.08
Project management — 3.33
Preparation of financial statements — 3.41
Cost accounting/allocation — 3.43
General ledger — 3.49
Inventory control — 3.50
Expenditure/payment processing — 3.64
Appropriation and budgetary control — 3.65
Report-writing tools — 3.66
Contract management — 3.67
Human resources/payroll — 3.77
Accounts payable — 3.78

1 — Unsatisfactory
2
3
4
5 — Leading-edge

In summary, these survey results show that there is a moderate to high degree of satisfaction with most major FMS packages. Nevertheless, the findings also show that there is significant opportunity to further develop these systems to meet the needs of the public sector.

FMS DESIGN AND IMPLEMENTATION CONSIDERATIONS

Although the benefits of integrated FMS are widely touted, such systems are still the exception rather than the rule in state and local governments. When government agencies do embark on modernizing their financial systems, many of them face problems during implementation (U.S. General Accounting Office, 1995, 1996). Central finance offices can also find it difficult to build internal support to procure integrated financial systems; the more common approach is every bureau for itself—for example, the budget department purchases its own budget preparation software, the controller's office gets its own GL package, and the purchasing department does the same. As Markus and Pfeffer (1983, p. 208) note, "the designing of accounting and control systems, not simply the use of them, is associated with inter-organizational power." Uncertainties over access to information, which affects the distribution of power, coupled with the short incumbency cycle of many elected officials and senior executives, provide incentives to resist investment in budgetary reform projects that may require years to complete. The trend is nevertheless clear—governments are increasingly moving toward integrated FMS; effectively harnessing the power of such technology through thoughtful system design and avoiding FMS implementation pitfalls are the main challenges to be addressed. A major implementation approach used in the public and private sector—business process reengineering (BPR)—is one method for effectively designing and implementing integrated FMS.

BPR is a change strategy that promises dramatic improvements in performance if standard operating procedures are redesigned from scratch and modern information technology is used to design new processes. BPR identifies *processes* as the fundamental units of analysis for organizational change efforts such as the implementation of FMS. BPR principles most germane to the implementation of FMS include (Linden, 1994; Miranda and Hillman, 1995):

- Substituting parallel processes for sequential processes
- Bringing downstream information upstream
- Ensuring a continuous flow of the "main sequence" (that is, removing non-value-adding steps from the process
- Capturing information once—at the source or point of entry
- Organizing around outcomes rather than functions

Table 16.1. FMS Implementation: Tips and Traps for Governments.

Stage	Tips	Traps
Project Planning	• Develop a formal charter that defines project governance • Specify an implementation plan that defines steps, strategies, resources, and time lines. • Define project costs comprehensively (e.g., internal staffing, consultants, software, hardware, training) and predict risks.	• Project should not be owned by any one agency; organization-wide participation and benefits must be emphasized. • Failure to engage political leadership early on can lead to funding problems and unrealistic expectations later.
Software Fit-Gap Analysis	• Demonstrate to user groups how software meets your detailed business requirements, and let the user groups tell you whether the requirements were interpreted correctly. • Decide whether to redesign processes or customize and modify the software.	• Failure to include appropriate stakeholders who have special requirements will lead you to repeat the fit-gap analysis process later and disrupt project schedule. • Failure to redesign chart of accounts and budgetary structures for the new FMS sacrifices the ability to undertake advanced budget analysis (such as, activity-based costing) later.
Business Process Analysis and Design	• Conduct only high-level process maps in defining system requirements (prior to software selection). • Conduct detailed process maps only after you have chosen the software. • Redesign the general ledger, payroll, and purchasing processes first to avoid project "scope creep" by less-important applications. • Develop conversion and interface strategies early.	• Failure to redesign processes at this stage leads to the automation of bad processes. • A cross-functional team of government staff should drive the process analysis and design effort because consultants will not know your processes as well as you do. • Failure to begin user training early delays implementation.

(continued)

Table 16.1. (*continued*)

Stage	Tips	Traps
Software Configuration and System Testing	• Identify unique processes, difficult data conversion areas, and custom management reports. • Prepare detailed scripts for individual applications to be used for testing (such as budget checking, liquidating encumbrances). • Use system testing to demonstrate that configuration and customized solutions function as users expected.	• Customizing software now will be expensive later because upgrades will also have to be customized. • Implementing all enterprise-wide applications concurrently increases complexity and risk of failure. Use a phase-in approach of focusing on one application at a time. • Do not ignore the need for acceptance testing before attempting to take the software "live."
Data Conversion	• Convert only data that will be used (such as vendor and commodity tables and fixed-asset information).	• Be sure to examine the volume and complexity of the data being stored because they can affect system performance.
Migration to "Live" Environment	• Terminate old system and load security tables. • Verify system start-up, initialize financial balances, and run data conversion programs.	• Failure to conduct a post-implementation review (such as, user help desk or analysis of performance statistics) can lead to system bottlenecks.

Table 16.1 describes major stages in FMS implementation and identifies tips and traps for each stage. Advocates of the BPR implementation approach recognize that a new financial system provides an opportunity to rethink budgeting, accounting, and control processes. Indeed, the most desirable processes are difficult or impossible to put into practice without a vehicle to deliver the functionality. For example, BPR principles such as organizing around outcomes rather than functions or substituting parallel processes for sequential processes are difficult to achieve without technological applications such as project costing and workflow. Although it may seem awkward for governments, BPR also emphasizes the sharing of information across the organization, the widespread use of technology, and reliance on cross-functional teams (made up of individuals

from across the departments). This approach fosters stakeholder support throughout the organization and brings the user's input into systems design decisions early on, thereby reducing implementation risk.

CONCLUSION

This chapter has described integrated FMS, its role in addressing some of the deficiencies in existing systems, and its promise as a means for significantly enhancing decision support in the public sector. The implementation of a new FMS in state and local government is a major change initiative. Like all ambitious government initiatives, the most elegant financial software solution can face implementation failure if adequate attention is not focused on managing the internal obstacles to change. Although there are numerous approaches to coping with such obstacles, this chapter proposed the use of the BPR methodology as an approach to reducing the chances of implementation failure.

References

Anderson, B. M. "Using Activity-Based Costing for Efficiency and Quality." *Government Finance Review,* 1993, *9*(3), 7–9.

Bozeman, B., and Rahm, D. "The Explosion of Technology." In J. L. Perry (ed.), *Handbook of Public Administration.* San Francisco: Jossey-Bass, 1989.

Cahill, A., Stevens, J., and La Plante, J. "The Utilization of Information Systems Technology and Its Impact on Organizational Decision Making." *Knowledge,* 1990, *12*(1), 53.

Deloitte & Touche. *Financial and Accounting Systems Survey.* Washington, D.C.: Deloitte & Touche, 1997.

Kraemer, K. L., and King, J. L. "Local Government Financial Management Systems: Independent and Integrated Design." *Government Accountants Journal,* 1982, *30*(4), 58–64.

Linden, R. M. *Seamless Government: A Practical Guide to Reengineering in the Public Sector.* San Francisco: Jossey-Bass, 1994.

Markus, M. L., and Pfeffer, J. "Power and the Design and Implementation of Accounting and Control Systems." *Accounting, Organizations and Society,* 1983, *8*(2–3), 205–218.

Mechling, J. "Computers in Local Finance." In J. E. Petersen and D. Strachota (eds.), *Local Government Finance.* Chicago: Government Finance Officers Association, 1989.

Miranda, R., and Hillman, N. "Reengineering Financial Management." *Government Finance Review,* 1995, *11,* 4.

Renaud, P. *Introduction to Client/Server Systems.* New York: Wiley, 1997.

Sandlin, R. *Manager's Guide to Purchasing an Information System.* Washington, D.C.: International City/County Management Association, 1996.

Schick, A. "The Road to PPB: The Stages of Budget Reform." *Public Administration Review,* 1966, *26*(4), 243–258.

Stephens, E. *Implementing PeopleSoft Financials.* Greenwich, Conn.: Manning, 1997.

Stone, W. "Electronic Commerce: Can Internal Auditors Help to Mitigate the Risks?" *Internal Auditor,* Dec. 1997, pp. 26–35.

U.S. General Accounting Office. *Information Technology Investment: A Government-wide Overview* (GAO/AIMD-95-208). Washington, D.C.: Government Printing Office, 1995.

U.S. General Accounting Office. *Information Technology: Best Practices Can Improve Performance and Produce Results* (GAO/T-AIMD-96-46). Washington, D.C.: Government Printing Office, 1996.

Wooldridge, B. "Towards the Development of an Integrated Financial Management System." *Government Accountants Journal,* 1982, *31*(3), 37–44.

PART FIVE

BUDGETING
BY INSTITUTIONS

CHAPTER SEVENTEEN

Preparing Agency Budgets

Jacqueline H. Rogers
Marita B. Brown

The authors' combined experience in state and local government budgeting, from the perspective of both agency director (AD) and budget director (BD), is approaching half a century. This chapter is based on practice, not on scholarly analysis. Although we have observed some changes in practice during the last several decades, many have been passing fads, and some things never really change. We have therefore placed greater emphasis on building awareness of the complex human dynamics of budgeting and less emphasis on proposing concrete processes or providing references to more technical guides to budgeting. Readers could infer from our discussion a level of cynicism that we do not intend to convey. Budgeting is fascinating: it is the nerve center of government and the place where policy is routinely made. That is precisely why issues of relationship, as described in this chapter, become paramount.

At last official count there were 85,006 units of government in the United States. If one eliminates the federal government and the fifty states from this number, 84,955 governments remain. Cities, counties, towns and townships, school districts, and a multitude of special districts cover our national landscape. These units of government have little in common. Their fundamental differences in scope, purpose, size, shape, and governance might lead one to conclude that differences are all they have in common. Not so. The budget looms large in every one of these entities.

Fortunately or unfortunately, budgeting is the least standardized of the primary governmental fiscal functions—budgeting, finance, and accounting.

Finance and accounting are constrained by law, regulation, and professional practice. Budgeting, by contrast, varies with culture, local sophistication, and the inclinations of local elected officials, as well as with the administrators who serve them. This reality of budgeting makes the discussion of budget preparation extremely difficult. Few aspects of budgeting are readily generalizable; no recipes for action can be offered.

Budget preparation also looks different depending on where an individual works within the system. Key roles include those of the elected officials, the budget office, and the agency responsible for service delivery. This discussion focuses on the perspective of the AD.

Despite these variations, insight can be developed by considering budget preparation at the agency level from three angles:

- *Context:* the budget, who plays and with what strategy
- *Process:* how an agency head prepares and defends a budget submission
- *Problems:* dilemmas that regularly confront ADs and ultimately shape the face of government

Although there is no one-size-fits-all approach to budgeting, a general treatment of context, process, and problems may help individuals who participate in the budgetary process perform more effectively. Continued downsizing, inflexible control systems, the challenges of devolution, technological change, and workforce-capacity mismatches all place enormous pressures on directors.

CONTEXT

Bureaucracies are organisms. Organisms fight to be well and to grow. Contraction is perceived to be a sign of ill health. Death is anathema. Budgeting determines the relative health of bureaucratic organisms. Old-fashioned as it may sound, most managers of bureaucratic organizations measure their own success by the size and growth of their organization. No natural forces exist to counter this reality.

All budgetary decision making is political—always political—whether at the program, agency, budget office, or elective level. The process is agenda against agenda, wit against wit, guile against guile, bludgeon against bludgeon. Everyone plays the budgeting game in the name of results for the people, arguing that more resources will enhance program effectiveness while fewer resources will threaten desired program outcomes. In reality, the game is more complex. It is about the personal power of the players and their constituencies, existing comfort zones, carefully constructed expectations, and rhetorical elegance. The fittest survive; the wiliest advocate who holds the best hand triumphs.

The game varies based on leadership styles, organizational size, local and governmental culture, and legal context. The game can be deciphered, even predicted in the short term, but it is fundamentally unreliable. As in team sports, last year's victorious team can lose and upstarts can surprise everyone. New victors define fresh rules.

Budgeting is usually played as a zero-sum game. Except for small amounts at the margin, the pie is both fixed and allocated at the outset of the process. The reason for this is that most governments usually rely on incremental budgeting. That is, they start with the prior year's budget as the baseline for the next year. This technique assumes that previously approved program levels should continue into the future, so they are projected into the next year along with estimated inflation, compensation adjustments, and other built-in cost increases, such as debt service and other legal mandates. One person's gain, therefore, is another's loss.

Styles of play come and go: incremental budgeting; planning, programming, budgeting, and evaluation; zero-based budgeting; performance budgeting; and program budgeting, to name but a few. Currently, activity-based costing and outcome-based budgeting are coming into vogue. Each approach touts improved accountability to the public, but few formats actually communicate effectively with taxpayers. Usually, only crisis—real or persuasively feigned— makes for accountability in the short term. Then again, sometimes crisis—a runaway murder rate, for example—is the very vehicle with which to thwart accountability. Politicians love to throw resources at publicly visible problems, regardless of the resources' potential to solve them.

It is not that the players do not care about results for the public. At the agency level in particular it is just that generic good government is not at the top of the list. It falls far below maintaining personal status, as measured by protecting and enhancing the size of the workforce under one's control and by capturing dollars to feed agency mission—that is, to enhance programs— and otherwise promote the growth of empire wherever feasible. The AD's goal is primarily to manipulate decision makers in such a way as to protect the agency's interests. The bigger picture has little concrete relevance.

The budget game is not played on a level playing field. Elected officials often speak of their budget "priorities," stating that budgetary emphasis has been placed on matters of local concern, such as education, economic development, or public safety. For example, in such an environment the parks and recreation director would need to look for nontraditional ways to garner budgetary resources. One way to do this effectively is to move as much of the agency's budget as legally and politically possible out of the general fund of the jurisdiction. Because they are funded by general tax revenues, activities supported by the general fund are the most vulnerable to reductions during the budget-approval process. Agencies that are supported primarily with special revenues are less vulnerable and therefore subject to less scrutiny than those supported by the general fund.

The Rules of the Game

Finance (getting the money) is governed by law and heavy regulation. Governmental accounting (tracking the money) lives within a professional standard; you can find the same information in the same place in almost any consolidated annual financial statement anywhere in the United States. By contrast, the few rules that exist for budgeting vary by jurisdiction and are found buried in state constitutions, local charters, and state and local laws.

Typically, formal budget rules address core issues such as frequency of decisions (annual or biennial), balancing the budget, timing of budget production, relative roles of the executive and legislative branches, budget approval requirements, and debt constraints if a capital budget has been authorized. The rules speak to how the legislature must approve the numbers through appropriations, but they are silent on what supporting information the budget document should contain or how it should be formatted. Most often, the recommended and adopted budget documents of a jurisdiction are not binding. They are descriptive support for line items of expenditure. The document with clout, the budget bill, is seldom seen or reviewed by either the AD or the public. Because of the discrepancy between the budget documents and the actual legislative act of appropriation, the documents should be viewed with healthy skepticism. Only the budget bill is binding.

Published budgets vary from a few standard pages filled with numbers to glossy multivolume editions. A jurisdiction's budget will tend to be predictable in appearance from year to year, because of production traditions in the budget office. It can become more or less informative, however, at the whim of those in charge. Turnover in either chief elected official or jurisdictional manager (commonly referred to herein as CO) or in BD can lead to a major shift in presentation format. Professional organizations such as the Government Finance Officers Association (GFOA) have sought to promote standards for budget documents. Although the GFOA has succeeded in articulating key elements of a good budget through its awards program, and many governments tout this recognition, participation is voluntary and no generally accepted standards have emerged.

The annual rules of play for the budget are normally promulgated centrally by the budget office. Typically, the AD has no discretion over these rules or how the budget is presented to the public and the legislature. The AD may be asked to contribute text on a selected basis, but this text is sure to be edited in the budget office to ensure consistency with the overall thematic thrust of the budget, which aligns in turn with political priorities.

The AD usually has limited knowledge of the rules governing the larger system. He or she may know the legislative origins of the agency's programs, the funding sources that are or may be available for agency activities, something about the official budget schedule, and a bit more about legislative behavior; but the AD places primary emphasis on persuading the budget office and the CO that additional resources are essential and will be well used. The AD will seek to develop dedicated sources of revenue, which are independent of the competitive process governing general revenues. The BD will resist these efforts, seeking to have most revenue pass through the general fund to give maximum flexibility to the elected decision makers. The AD will seek to make the case for resources in a way that maximizes personal and agency benefit while boxing the opposition. The AD will cast the budget request in terms that make it most attractive to the agency's constituencies and to the elective officials, who must approve it. Much of the budget request's success, therefore, is determined not by rules but by storytelling—what the resources will buy, or alternatively, what ills will befall the community if requested resources are not made available. Illusion takes precedence over reality in the contest for resources. Who would not want the streets cleaned, the crooks caught, the fires quenched, consumer complaints placated, and the most needy shielded from ruin or made more self-reliant? Is the CO willing to shoulder the consequences of even one lost life if the requested new ladder truck for firefighting is not provided?

Some jurisdictions are moving toward outcome-based budgeting, in which fiscal decisions are aligned with the articulated community-wide results being sought. When this occurs at the top, it serves to reduce interagency competitiveness. In theory, if the AD garners resources in service of achieving a community-wide outcome, he or she can be held accountable for getting the desired result. In practice, so many externally uncontrollable factors usually influence outcomes that accountability cannot be fixed. Nonetheless, if this approach is sustained, an agency that is not visibly achieving results will be spotlighted over time. There may be negative consequences for the agency and for the AD's credibility in future decision making.

There is another unspoken rule: all agencies are not created equal. They vary in importance according to public expectations for service, the power of their constituencies, their compatibility with the priorities of elected officials, and their ability to generate independent revenues. The BD, for example, may manage a small agency, but he or she is placed to enhance his or her personal power and to exert greater influence with the CO than an AD would.

Typically, a distinction is made between control agencies—in a better world this would be support agencies—and line agencies. Control agencies are internally focused within government, have few external constituents, and have more access to the CO. Line agencies can cultivate external constituencies but are circumscribed by the control agencies and often have limited access to the CO. A smart AD understands the agency's placement in the internal pecking order. Moreover, the AD fairly consistently seeks to improve that placement relative to other agencies in order to get a competitive advantage in the contest for resources.

The AD's Roles

The AD has many conflicting roles:

- Servant of the CO and legislature
- Peer, if the perspective is lateral to other agencies (but this is relative, as measured by personal grade in the personnel system and the size and clout of the agency)
- Protector of existing staff and programs, if the perspective is internal
- Enhancer of services, if the perspective is toward the agency's constituencies

All allegations to the contrary, the latter two roles often outweigh the AD'S loyalty to the CO or the AD's concern for collaboration with other agencies. Everyone who plays the budget game knows this, but it is a tacit rather than an explicit rule. This primary commitment to agency is the greatest inhibitor to interagency collaboration and resource sharing.

When weighing the AD's allegiance to the CO, it helps to know how he or she came to office, as well as whether the AD is a merit-system employee or an appointee. If the AD is in a merit system—not subject to immediate firing without cause from the CO—his or her allegiance will be weaker. The AD knows that it is possible to outlast the current administration. If the AD is appointed and comes to the job with a long history of political and personal relationship with the CO, the AD's perspective is likely to carry more weight than if the AD was appointed solely on personal qualifications without a strong history. If a newcomer demonstrates political savvy and can get good performance results, something close to parity can be produced for ADs who have a long history with the CO. This kind of informal status deriving from manner of appointment will influence how the AD shapes the budget request and how well the AD can compete.

Peer relationships are influenced by the same dynamics. In addition, however, the AD will weigh a few more variables. It matters who is "in" and who is "out" in deciding whether to collaborate in competition for resources or go it alone. Also, the AD will consider relative rank as measured by grade level and compensation. The decision to collaborate or not is also strongly influenced by historical working relationships among staffs. If these relationships are characterized by mistrust, it will be hard for the AD to propose sharing resources to solve common problems. In sum, a complex web of interpersonal relations usually mitigates against multiagency problem solving and fosters multiple fragmented approaches to the same problem.

Protector of existing staff and resources is a critical role. The AD's loss of either staff or resources during the budgetary process is likely to be perceived by the staff as weakness. Staff are reluctant to follow a weak leader, with the consequence that agency morale and performance suffer. The further down in an organization one is, the more limited is one's ability to perceive the big picture. Line supervisors do not know or care where the money comes from; they just want enough to deliver their programs and services well. When difficult trade-offs have to be made among competing programs within the agency in order to conform to budgetary guidance, it is a microcosm of the government-wide budgetary drama.

The agency subunit is the level where resistance to change is greatest. If activity-based costing analysis shows that a function such as in-home care or administration of day-care subsidy programs can be contracted out, thus freeing up resources to expand services, the units affected by such change are likely to fight it nonetheless. Then the AD has to decide whether to protect the people or get the best deal for the taxpayers.

ADs want to be popular with their constituencies. They will use these constituencies to garner support for their budget requests. Although some cultivation of the constituencies is overt, much is subterranean. Information about budgetary guidance is leaked. Rumors are allowed to circulate about what is vulnerable to the budget axe. The press gets wind of a story about a budget-related vulnerability. Members of official advisory boards are dispatched discreetly to lobby decision makers on behalf of agency needs.

PROCESS

Budgeting has become a year-round process for most governments. Agencies are often at work on a new fiscal year's budget request before the one for the upcoming year has been finalized. If fiscal conditions change at midyear—for example, if there is a sudden recession—the approved budget may have to be adjusted either up or down. Each department and agency has its own unique internal planning process, which often is as much a reflection of the AD's style as it is of the agency's size. Some managers are hands-on, with an orientation to detailed review. At the other end of the spectrum are managers who only want to talk about program changes while relying on staff to translate the manager's intentions into dollars and cents.

Steps in the Process

Budgets get prepared in stages. Figure 17.1 shows a typical schedule for preparing an operating budget; this example is from Montgomery County, Maryland.

During the budget preparation process, the AD of a medium to large agency follows a process similar to the one the BD follows for the government as a whole. Good agency planning and preparation at the earliest stages of the budgetary process are key to its ultimate success.

At this point in the process, overall guidance from the CO or the BD is generally transmitted to the agencies. Included would be statements of overall fiscal condition, status of any strategic plan that may be in place, and legislative and executive priorities. Agencies could also receive specific guidance as to allowable adjustments, such as inflation factors, as well as mandated inclusions or exclusions from the request.

Setting up Internal Process. One of the first decisions the BD has to make is who participates in the process. Traditionally this has been upper-level management. In a large agency this group would typically consist of division directors and their superiors. These individuals would in turn run a mini budgetary process within their units. In recent years, some governments seeking to improve productivity and morale have moved to Total Quality Management approaches. In these jurisdictions, the budget preparation process will be more bottom-up.

Initial Allocation. Whether bottom-up or top-down, the budget preparation process gives the AD an annual opportunity to define or refine the agency's mission, to develop a work plan to carry out that mission, and to begin building support for the program with outside constituencies. In the commonplace top-down system, the AD meets with key internal budget people at the outset of the process. Jointly they identify issues of concern, priorities, and opportunities for savings or enhancement. The internal budget staff is asked for independent cutback options so as to create maneuvering room for the AD to accommodate agency or CO priorities.

The AD sets priorities and decides the extent to which to ask managers for cutback options as well as program enhancement proposals. The agency's budget staff passes the AD's ground rules to the subunits, including an initial concept for responding to the CO's priorities. They also receive preparation instructions promulgated by the central BD. If necessary, a training session is conducted.

Internal Review. Managers prepare their budget requests with assistance from the internal budget staff in a manner consistent with both the BD's and AD's guidance. These requests are reviewed by the budget staff for accuracy and appropriateness. Work sessions are then scheduled with the AD. Agency work sessions are not regulated by the budget office; they are purely internal. They give the AD an opportunity to make decisions and consider how to get the resources necessary to implement the agency's programs.

Sometimes managers have their own meetings with the AD. If there are no issues, such a meeting is not held until a set of competing options for enhancement or reduction has surfaced. At this stage, managers are more competitors than collaborators. Their goal is to optimize resources for their unit of the organization.

The AD then chooses among cutback and enhancement options, either alone, in consultation with key advisers, or in consultation with all the managers, depending on the AD's preferences. Some ADs are very hands-off; others want to be engaged in every step of the process. Mostly, however, they are interested in funds only as a vehicle for achieving mission. Once core policy decisions have been decided by the AD, the agency begins the work of translating them into quantifiable and justifiable requests.

Submission to the Budget Office. The internal budget analysts then prepare the agency's submission to the budget office in a manner that conforms to central direction. In jurisdictions with a central budget office, agencies are usually required to submit their budgets for review on standardized forms or in a standard electronic format. The AD usually attaches a cover memorandum to the formal submission that highlights key elements of the request.

Typically, central budget systems are developed gradually over time. They are arcane and often aligned with computer programs that do the financial computations to generate summary information. Both the budget office and agency personnel are trained in implementing the system and filling out the forms in a certain way. The rules therefore have a life of their own and are quite hard either to understand at a managerial level or to change significantly.

It is important to note the role of the BD at this point in the process. In attempting to craft a politically and fiscally acceptable decision package, the BD may set aside funds to be utilized by the CO for "wish list" items. A wish list includes nice-to-have program enhancements of moderate priority that can fulfill political promises or please key constituencies. They are more discretionary than crucial.

External Decision Making. Budget requests that are complete, clear, well justified, and submitted on time have the best chance of success with the central budget office. Requests lacking in any of these areas are the easiest to cut, they give offense to the BD, and they have a lesser chance for reinstatement as the process continues.

Sometimes the AD and BD meet to decide what will be recommended. Sometimes both parties meet with the CO to make final decisions. Sometimes only

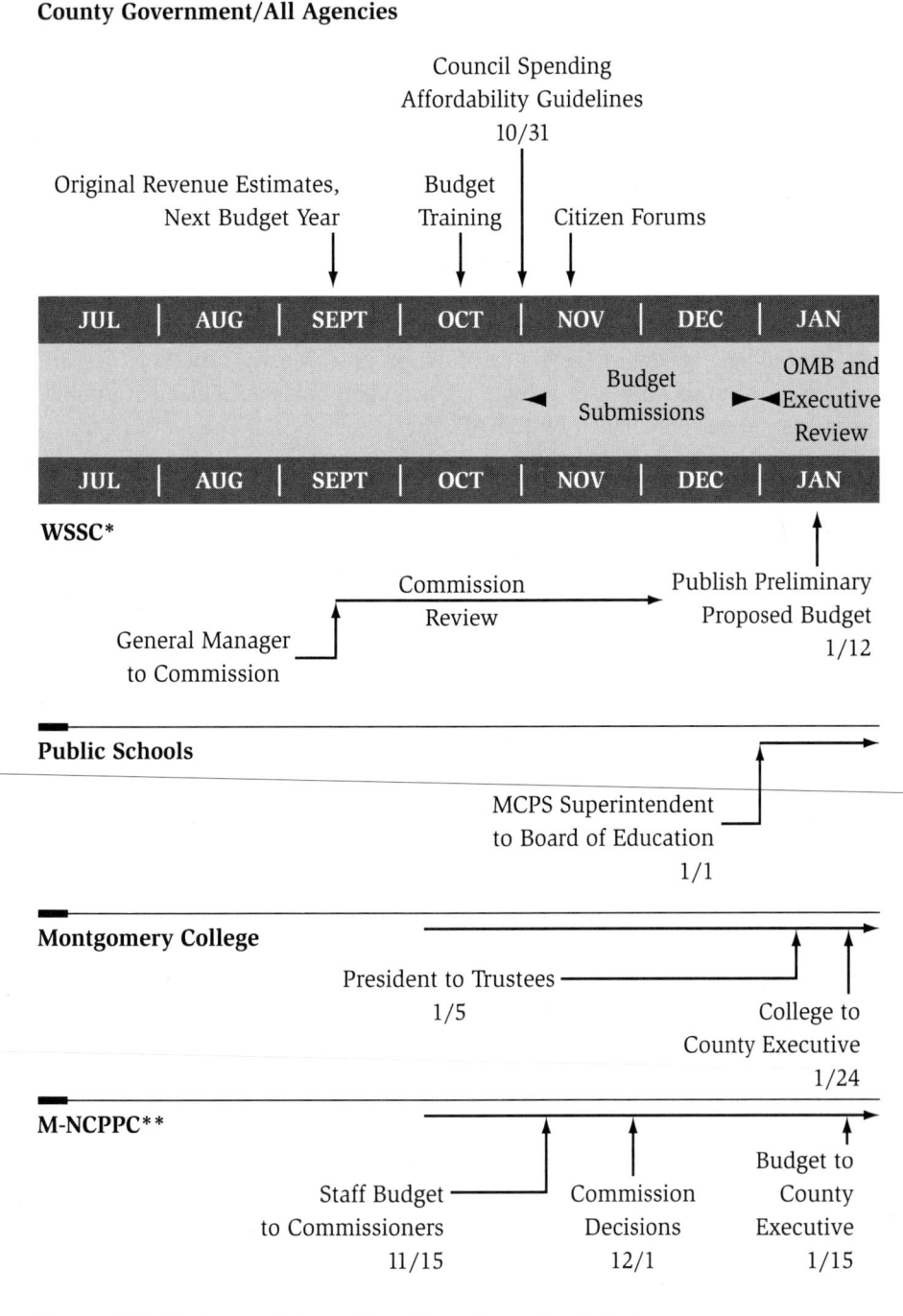

Figure 17.1. Budgetary Process Flow Chart: Operating Budget.

*WSSC: Washington Suburban Sanitary Commission

**M-NCPPC: Maryland National Capital Park and Planning Commission

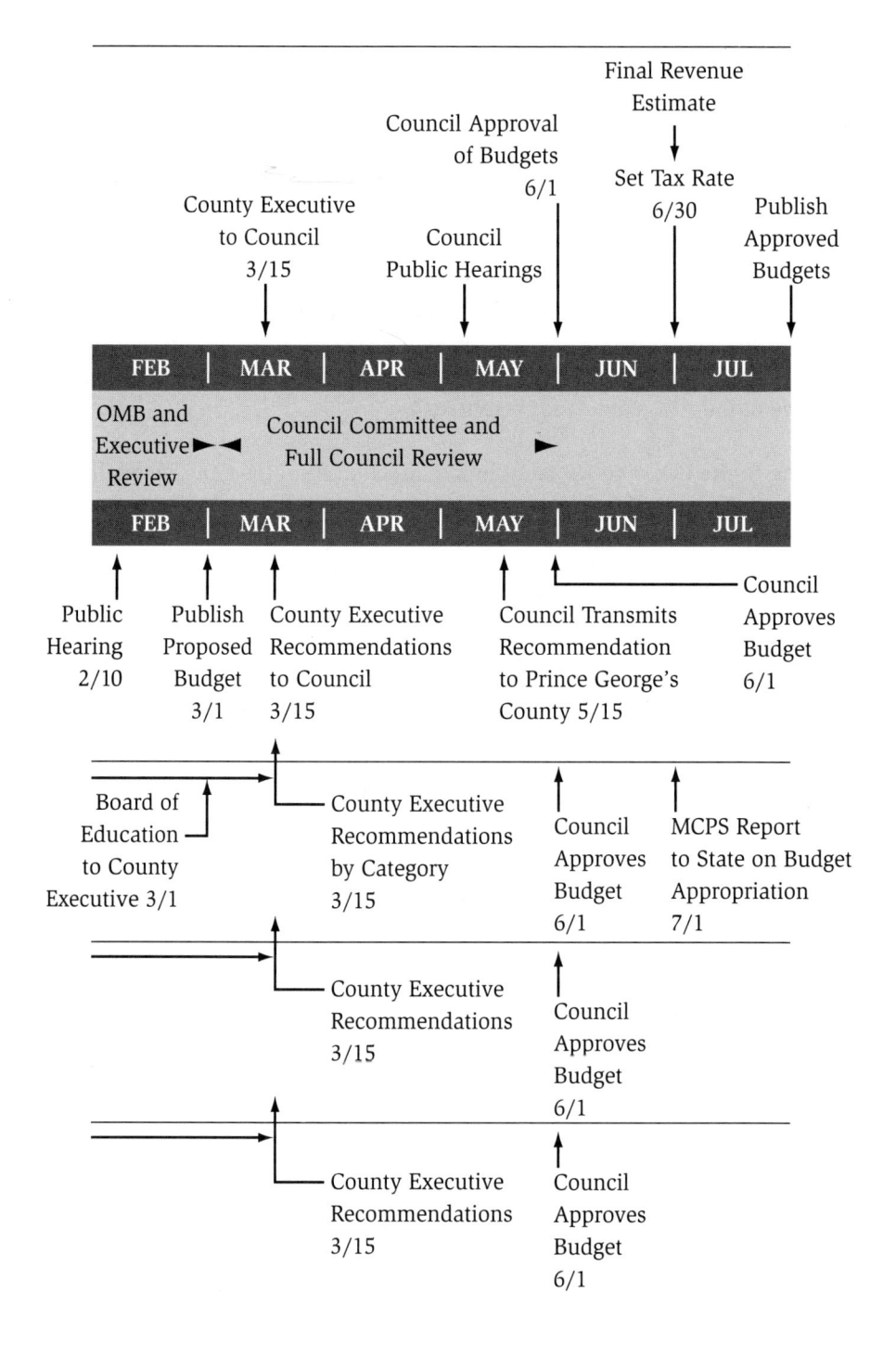

agencies with unresolved issues meet with the CO. It all depends on organizational culture and the style of the CO. The dialogue among the AD, BD, and CO is conducted at a macro level by aligning dollars with a specific enhancement or reduction. Budget staff then align the decision with the forms and the line items.

Relationships

The role of the AD changes as a budget request is evolved and negotiated. The AD must manage a complex set of relationships within the executive branch, with key legislators, within the agency, with key constituencies affected by the agency's programs, and finally with the press. All these players can affect the outcome of the AD's contest for resources.

Relating to the CO. The AD takes broad direction from the CO. The quality of the personal relationship between the AD and the CO has a significant impact on budgetary decision making. The more nonbudget "face time" the two share, the greater will be the trust that exists between them and the more likely the AD will be to prevail during the budget deliberations, particularly if the AD and the BD are not in agreement about funding levels. The greater the AD's understanding of the mind, heart, style, and priorities of the CO, the more likely it will be that the AD will be able to structure the agency's budget request so as to optimize resources.

Relating to Other Agencies. Increasingly, politicians are recognizing the interdisciplinary nature of problem solving and insisting on budget information that cuts across organizational lines. For example, they might want to know what the budget does for families, but dollars to support families might be budgeted in a half-dozen or more agencies. This diffusion has implications for lateral collaboration among ADs. Those who can coordinate efforts, pool resources, and display the big picture to COs and the public are likely to fare better in the competition for certain kinds of resources. In the last decade there has been gradual improvement in interagency collaborative budgeting to address common problems, but for the most part these alliances are fragile. They break down easily during periods of political turnover or expenditure constraint, unless they have been formalized legislatively or organizationally.

Relating to the Budget Office. The AD must also deal with the BD, and the same rules of relationship that applied to the CO apply here. If, however, the relationship is not close and is based on personal or mission conflicts, the AD will need to align even more closely with the CO. The BD's relationship to the CO is also crucial. If the BD's relationship with the CO is positive and the trust level is high, when the BD and AD are in conflict the CO is likely to align with the

BD rather than with the AD. In the budget office a seasoned fiscal conservative is usually in command. This individual is skilled at deciphering agency ruses.

The budget analysts take it as a given that the agency can do more with less. Analysts typically have never managed anything; they have a staff mentality rather than a line mentality. Their goal is to achieve an approximation of fiscal balance without sacrificing key priorities of the CO or other elected officials. They care little about the human consequences of an agency's proposals for cutbacks, but they are sensitive to the political ramifications of such cutbacks. Consequently, agencies often perceive budget analysts as arrogant, ignorant, and lacking in concern for legitimate agency needs.

An agency will both court and contend with an analyst, aiming to align the analyst's perspective with that of the agency. The agency brow beats, pulls rank, provides data selectively, and seeks to snow the analyst. If bullying and obfuscation fail, an often-employed strategy is to co-opt the analyst through education and persuasion. The BD will be alert to the relationship between analyst and agency. If it starts to seem too cozy, the BD will realign agency assignments to keep an analyst's edge.

Relating Internally to Staff. The AD is the bridge between the CO, the BD, and the agency's staff. A primary role of the AD is to translate political priorities and fiscal constraints into terms that workers can understand. To be credible and thereby secure the support of the rank and file, the AD must get as large a share of the resource pie for agency programs as is feasible. If the AD is perceived to be a weak player in the budget game, staff will feel vulnerable, and disinclined to follow the AD's lead in other matters. Agency performance will suffer. It is particularly important to secure fiscal wins if the AD is charged with changing how the bureaucracy implements its mandate.

There is a major underlying tension between the needs and perceptions of staff and those of the CO and BD. Many ADs, most of the AD's managers, and even more line workers measure ability to deliver programs effectively in terms of numbers of people available to do the task. Politically, COs may want to shrink the number of government workers while enhancing the quality of program delivery. BDs know that employees are the most costly element of the budget and they are constantly alert to alternative ways of getting the job done—hence the BD's interest in privatization, outsourcing, and other similar initiatives.

The AD is caught in the middle. To afford program resources, staff may have to be let go. If staff are let go, the rank and file will be threatened, resistant to necessary changes, and less inclined to perform effectively. When some managers keep staff and other managers lose them, the AD must be able to explain convincingly why one unit does better than another. Otherwise, resentments will arise, which again will impede agency effectiveness. An effective AD must be an adroit storyteller, able to persuade agency personnel that their programs will win more resources if they are aligned with the CO's and BD's priorities, even if such alignment means change.

Relating to the Legislature

The AD is unlikely to have much contact with the legislative branch during budget preparation. After the CO completes the recommended budget, however, the AD is expected to appear before the legislature in the company of the BD or a budget analyst to defend the CO's decisions. In theory the AD should ask for no more than was recommended by the CO. In practice, the legislative forum is often used by the AD as a second chance to argue for enhancements not supported by the CO. Sometimes this is done head on; sometimes it is done by getting to key legislators informally prior to the work sessions; and sometimes it is done by having affected constituents approach the legislature. These approaches can be fraught with peril. Divide and conquer does not always work. If the CO sees through the end run, he or she may perceive it as disloyalty, with negative consequences to the AD.

Relating to Constituencies and the Press

Line ADs manage programs and operate facilities that serve the public. Program beneficiaries can be players in the budget decision process at the agency level by focusing advocacy on the AD. They can reassert themselves at the CO level if they are dissatisfied with the decisions made at the AD level. In fact, the AD may actively encourage beneficiaries to make independent demands on the CO so that the AD can be better positioned to garner resources at the CO level.

The strongest advocates are organized groups and lobbyists. Far less powerful are individual citizens who rely on generic services such as street cleaning or garbage pickup. If the service is neighborhood based, even unorganized citizens can be rallied to participate in the budget fray. This rallying works best if the service is perceived to be at risk—for example, if community library hours are to be reduced, a fire station is to be closed, or discretionary school programs such as sports are to be cut back. Managers can fire up the appropriate constituencies to exert pressure on the AD, CO, or legislative body to protect or enhance neighborhood services. The usual vehicles for such community-based budget advocacy are meetings with decision makers, letter-writing (including e-mail) campaigns, telephone campaigns, and activities designed to attract press attention to the issue.

Skilled ADs build good relationships with the press. They visit editorial boards occasionally and cultivate relationships with certain reporters. When budget issues arise, the ADs then have easy access to coverage. Generally an AD will not want his or her fingerprints on a story, so constituents will be used as shills or information will be provided by "a knowledgeable source." Pressure from the press can be very helpful at key times in the decision-making process, during both budget development and budget defense.

COMMON PROBLEMS

The preceding discussion on budget games and process presumes that the government in question is fairly large and multipurpose. Although smaller or single-purpose jurisdictions may use similar processes, it is almost impossible to make generalizations across the spectrum. There are, however, a number of problems that are common to most governments. The issues related to downsizing or rightsizing, devolution, insufficiently flexible control systems (procurement, personnel, budget, and so on), and matching the capacity of the workforce to need, as well as technology concerns, shape the fabric of government. These issues dominate the budgetary process and usually dictate the outcome of that process, even if they are not identified by name.

Downsizing

After going through several cycles of slow or no growth in discretionary program dollars, ADs are still being asked to respond affirmatively and creatively to the program creation and enhancement demands of citizens, elected officials, and bureaucrats. Many of these demands are legitimate and represent real needs; yet agencies are unlikely to obtain new general government resources to achieve these objectives. It is the old saw: be creative, do more with less. But how?

Three trends have helped downsizing agencies to avoid negative effects on program performance:

- The flattening of organizations and consequent elimination of unnecessary managerial levels

- The substitution of technology to do tasks that people used to do (for example, in an organization where each professional has a personal computer and voice mail, the need for secretarial and clerical support is significantly reduced)

- The creation of back-office functions that can be electronically centralized to provide support to a variety of operating programs without impeding immediate service delivery

Downsizing is easier when an agency has a clear mission statement and when the AD can align program activity with that mission. Such alignment provides a context for deciding what can be done less in order to accommodate funding reductions or desired program enhancements. Even in this situation, however, it is not easy to make trade-offs. Investments in future capacity are often the first things to go. For example, when engaged in a decision simulation such as the one in Table 17.1, senior managers of a major health and human services agency uniformly cut technology and education for the staff before turning to more difficult program-related reductions.

Traditional line-item budgets, with their central focus on individual items or inputs, do little to enhance intelligent resource allocation. An AD who is absorbed in line-item details will miss the opportunity to highlight the program's accomplishments and the needs of the department. A true program budget focuses on outcomes but may not provide clear accountability for use of resources. When budget format shifts from line item to a program budget, the de-

Table 17.1. Current Allocations for Family Investment Program Reinvestment Funds.

Activity	FY97 $	FY98 $	FY99 $	FY00 $	FY01 $
Emergency Assistance to Families with Children	$350,000	$ 450,000	$ 500,000		
Welfare Avoidance Grants	165,000	213,000	300,000		
Transportation Subsidy	195,000	250,000	250,000		
Increase to Day Care Subsidy Rate	0	0	150,000		
Tuition and Book Assistance for Temporary Cash Assistance Recipients	32,000	64,000			
Staff for Nonprofits to Provide Service	0	439,000			
Employment Orientation Sites at Montgomery College	122,000	200,000			
Adult Education for GED	36,000	36,000			
HHS Staff for Key Tasks	0	248,000			
Nontraditional Jobs Preparation	0	170,000			
Educational Opportunities for HHS Staff	0	50,000			
HHS Technology Investments: PCs and Internet	0	180,000			
Totals	$900,000	$2,300,000	$1,900,000	$1,700,000	$900,000

Note: Items already entered into the FY99 column cannot be tampered with; they represent political commitments of the CO. Also, the numbers in the totals row indicate the total funding available for each year; line items must be adjusted to fit within these totals.

bate shifts from how dollars will be distributed by category to consideration of what will be accomplished with the dollars allocated.

Program budgets do not guarantee results. Their value lies in keeping the debate focused on program priorities and outcomes. Performance-based budgets may provide the best hope for directly linking resources and results. They can be difficult to implement, however, and they require the full support of both the CO and the legislative body.

Program Enhancements

New initiatives and programs have great difficulty obtaining necessary funding in today's budget climate. The merits of proposals are often overlooked and the proposals may be rejected in the earliest rounds of budget deliberations unless the AD and BD have agreed on some internal trade-offs. Well-justified new programs stand a better chance for approval if they are coupled with dedicated revenues.

Traditional sources of revenue to support new or expanded programs include grants, loans, special funds, and various types of user fees. Programs not funded through the general fund are typically harder to cut and may escape rigorous review by the budget office. Cutting them does not make their dollars available for other general fund priorities. In addition, these funds often do not come under requirements for spending affordability or budget balance.

Grant dollars for starting programs are often appealing to governments because they have short-term programmatic payoff and because the long-term costs can be handed off to future leadership. The fiscal realities of the 1990s, however, have made these dollars increasingly scarce. The federal government is offering less funding, and foundations are more inclined than local governments to fund community-based groups. Creative use of user fees can generate some flexibility at the margins for program managers, but all fee increases bring political fallout and have to be carefully weighed.

Insufficiently Flexible Control Systems

Most governments use an annual budget cycle. For an AD this can mean developing a detailed work and resource allocation plan eighteen months ahead of implementation. As a result, the best of plans will need some adjustment during the budget year.

It has often been said that mangers need to be allowed to manage. They need the flexibility to respond to changing demands by realigning resources. Unfortunately, government processes and procedures do nothing to simplify this process. The functions of government that historically have been considered control functions—central budget, personnel, and procurement—have the most detrimental effects on an agency's ability to respond quickly to changes in the environment.

ADs have very real issues to contend with that were not present or considered when they originally developed their budgets. School populations, social service caseloads, and corrections needs (prisons and jails) can all change— sometimes quite dramatically in a short period. When they do, the agency must respond. Staffing patterns may have to be shifted and other budgetary resources may need to be realigned. If the agency stays within the legally adopted budget totals, the director should be able to redirect resources as necessary. Unfortunately, most shifts require multiple levels of approval, including the concurrence of the budget and personnel staffs, and sometimes even the legislative branch.

An effective AD can make the control systems work for the agency and not against it. This effort may be more a function of the AD's persuasiveness and skill in managing relationships than a function of his or her ability to influence the systems themselves. Knowing how to finesse the rules with the tacit or explicit concurrence of the control agency's leadership may either make or break effective performance during periods of unusual, shifting demands.

Personnel Management

The cost and size of a government's workforce can dominate the budget debate, and with good reason. In many governments and agencies, labor costs can be 75 percent or more of the budget. Even in state governments and at the federal level, where budgets contain significant transfer payments, labor costs and position counts are carefully scrutinized. New positions and employee pay raises or benefit increases are often the first items to be eliminated from budget requests, because they build long-term increases into the budget base. In addition, these requests are seen by the public as the most obvious examples of government expansion.

All participants in the budgetary process would agree that effective utilization of the workforce is a critical issue. Many government operations are labor intensive and even small or incremental changes in cost or composition can have a real budgetary impact. Most governments use a merit or classified personnel system for all but a handful of top management positions. In addition, many municipal employees and some state employees are represented by organized labor. Teachers and uniformed public safety employees are the two groups most likely to be represented and to engage in collective bargaining.

Hallmarks of a classified service include rigid position classification and pay structures, with all jobs assigned to a grade and class. ADs have little control over the classification of positions because that is usually done in a central personnel office. Assigning employees to tasks outside their classification is often difficult because of union agreements or the compensation liability it may create. Pay schedules, whether collectively bargained or not, are centrally set as well. The classification and pay plan is usually legislatively adopted, making it even more difficult for an AD to alter the makeup of the workforce to respond to changing program demands.

Government downsizing has had the effect of reducing the number of public sector employees across the board. Selected functions may see slight increases—teachers in areas where enrollment is climbing and uniformed public safety personnel in areas where crime is on the rise are the most notable examples—but these increases usually come at the expense of other less visible or less critical programs. The AD is faced with the challenge of responding to changing demands for services with a reduced workforce, and is further hampered by personnel systems that are often rigid and outdated, as well as by employees with seniority whose skills do not match agency needs.

During budget preparation at the agency level, the AD will typically determine the size and composition of the workforce necessary to carry out the work plan for the following year. Costing out this plan is simply a mathematical function because these positions have been or will be assigned to a grade and class by the central personnel office. If no significant changes are planned in the size, scope, or mission of the agency, this system can work. Maintaining the status quo, however, is no longer the rule.

Reorganizations, consolidations, downsizing, and reengineering are common occurrences and are often accomplished through the budgetary process. The AD may have been the architect of this change and now must restructure the workforce to meet the new mission of the agency. Standard practices of managing public sector personnel have not adapted to the changing needs of government, but there are promising signs that this is changing. State and local governments throughout the country are revamping their systems to improve the quality of the workforce and to give employees and managers the tools they need to compete in increasingly entrepreneurial environments.

Devolution

Devolution is the best of times and the worst of times for state and local governments. After the 1994 elections, the federal government transferred significant program responsibilities to the states, which are now in the process of further transferring many of these responsibilities to local governments.

The most visible and important change was in the area of welfare reform. Although many governmental units welcome the flexibility in operating programs that devolution brings, it is also accompanied by a reduction in money. Only time will tell if this trade-off was a good one. For now, service demands will increase at the local level and the resulting concerns will be twofold: fiscal stress and capacity. Both will have significant impact on the budgetary choices to be made.

For some governments, fiscal stress will mean a choice between raising taxes or reducing services. Policy choices will become more complicated as an increasing number of programs compete for limited funding. Capacity concerns abound. These concerns are related not only to work volume but also to the availability of skills necessary for successful local management.

Flexibility-Enhancing Tool Kit

Progressive governments are allowing line managers to

- Design broad job specifications for their workers
- Hire directly
- Promote without central personnel office oversight
- Compensate differentially on the basis of skill and performance

Progressive governments are systematically investing in capacity building for their workforces, to ensure that workers can

- Work across organizational lines
- Solve problems collaboratively in teams
- Utilize information technology effectively
- Negotiate with a wide array of constituencies to pool and leverage resources

Technology

Technology has done more to change the nature of the workplace than any other element in modern history. Employees at all levels have had to learn new ways of working, and more often than not this has meant acquiring some computer skills. From executive offices to maintenance shops, work processes have changed. Although some change has been incremental, some has been brought about by the reengineering of the total business process. This trend is accelerating. Just as a personal computer at every professional workstation is now the norm in many places, by 2000 all employees will expect their computers to be connected to the world via the Internet. Having these resources available changes totally how people communicate, research issues, and work together. People who have not learned how to work in the new environment will find themselves functionally obsolete. Managers saddled with such workers will find it extremely difficult to keep pace with workload demands.

Technology decisions affect an agency's budget, its personnel management programs, and the size and scope of its annual work plan. The cost of the initial hardware and software, although often significant, can be managed in a variety of ways. For example, personal computers might be acquired through the operating budget, but the fiber optic support network to connect workstations internally and link them to the Internet might be financed through the capital budget. Although technology can make it possible to get the agency's work done with fewer employees, ongoing costs will be incurred for hardware and software upgrades and employee training.

Technology has had other implications for the AD. Telecommuting and variations in work schedules are now possible for many workers. These arrangements can have budgetary ramifications. Number and type of employees needed to do the job may change. Space needs may be less. Telecommunications costs may increase.

Continuous lifelong learning needs to be a part of every public sector job. Governments that used to view training programs as easy budget cuts will have to look elsewhere if they are to achieve real savings. Technology demands an educated, trained workforce that knows that today's skills will not be tomorrow's.

CONCLUSION

Preparing the agency budget is an annual or biennial ritual through which an AD tries to anticipate workload as well as secure necessary resources and align them with demand. Every government approaches this task differently, and within each government the agencies also follow different roads in preparing their budget submissions.

Recommended and approved budget allocations are simply the translation of myriad policy decisions into dollars through which policies are implemented. Any student of the ritual will need to learn as much as possible about local conditions, about the rules that exist in law and charter, about the traditions behind current practice, about the culture of the government, and above all, about the relationships among the players. Although the process cannot be predictably described in a chapter such as this one, it can be deciphered if one studies carefully the factors discussed herein.

CHAPTER EIGHTEEN

Examining Budgets
for Chief Executives

Barry White

This chapter discusses the craft of budget examining as generally practiced in the Office of Management and Budget (OMB). Along the way it illustrates how and why budget examining has for many decades been, and remains today, so central to executive branch policymaking.

The budget that is discussed in this chapter is the plan that by law the president prepares and sends to Congress annually. It is "frozen policy": it captures the one moment in time that one actor in the budgetary process, the president, sets out for all the world to see what he would spend and why, how he would tax and why—to provide for every single activity of the federal government, large and small, as he would define it. There is no document like it in Congress. At the end of a congressional session one can look back and add up the appropriation bills, mandatory spending bills, and revenue bills Congress passed, but there is no congressional plan at the start of the process that is comparable in detail to the president's budget against which to compare the end product of Congress. Congress's distant approximation to an annual plan is its annual budget resolution, but it sets out only the most aggregated levels of semibinding policy for congressional committees.

Note: The views and opinions expressed in this chapter are the author's alone and do not in any way represent official positions of the U.S. Office of Management and Budget or any of its leadership.

Media observers and a president's political opponents occasionally call his budget "dead on arrival" when they strongly disagree with its terms. But even in the years in which Congress's actions produce a final budget miles away from where the president wanted to be, it is the president's budget that remains the most complete benchmark that everyone uses, one way or another, to gauge the results of a year's budget battles.

The OMB manages the process of developing this annual budget. According to Paul H. O'Neill (1988), chairman and CEO of ALCOA and former budget examiner and deputy director of the OMB:

> Numbers are the keys to the doors of everything. Spending for the arts, the sciences, foreign policy and defense, health and welfare, education, agriculture, the environment, everything—and revenues from every source—are all reflected, recorded, and battled over in numbers. . . . If it matters, there are numbers that define it. And if you are responsible for advising the president about numbers, you are, de facto, in the stream of every policy decision made by the federal government. . . .
>
> We are doomed to repeat the mistakes of the past if we lack a trusted cadre of experts who can span the issues of partisan politics and survive the transition between parties in power. This is the role that is the raison d'être of this office.

This vision of the OMB is realized in the first instance by OMB budget examiners (recently called program examiners). Budget examiners are career civil servants. Their work is overseen by a layer of political appointees who are the bridge between the analysis of the examiners and the political needs of the incumbent administration. The OMB inevitably becomes closely identified with the policies of the incumbent administration—increasingly so in recent decades. OMB leadership more frequently testifies in Congress and speaks out publicly in support of specific goals of administration program policy (as opposed to overall fiscal policy).

It is a remarkable fact that each new administration overcomes (with varying speed) its wariness of the career staff who served the prior administration. The new team comes to appreciate the value of the nonpartisan career staff to the team's ability to carry forward its goals, and the budget examiners adapt to the needs of new political appointees without losing their professional status as analysts. (Once in a while some cannot adapt, so they leave.) The data and judgments that examiners supply do not change; the political or ideological prism through which they are viewed constantly changes.

A CRAFT, NOT A SCIENCE

There is no budget-examining cookbook of methods and procedures whose recipes, if carefully followed, produce a predictable budget decision. There are important broad, general rules of practice and procedure that examiners follow, but the underlying continuity that budget examiners bring to examining is influenced each year by unique circumstances—new laws, new presidential policies, new budget concepts. Examiners weave the general methods and procedures along with each year's new inputs into analysis that yields the judgments they offer to decision makers.

Standard General and Technical Procedures

There are a number of general procedures in budget analysis and a host of more technical analytical approaches that may come into play in a given issue. The most prominent of these procedures and approaches are discussed later in this chapter. Budget examiners master the general and technical approaches in order to determine how to accomplish policy with the greatest efficiency and potential effectiveness. Examiners also learn that rules are the starting rather than the ending point of the policy discussion. Where policy desires conflict with the rules of budgeting, more often than not the policy desire controls the process and a way is found to adapt the budgeting rule to meet the policy desire.

Academic Preparation

There is some academic preparation that can help a budget examiner, but as with most crafts true mastery can be acquired only by learning on the job. Schooling can teach useful skills, such as quantitative analysis, facility with spreadsheets and other computer tools, and the ability to organize and present thoughts well, both orally and in writing. The most important skill for which solid groundwork can be laid in school is learning to reason—which should be the point of a general bachelor of arts degree. A graduate degree can also be useful, especially if its focus was on learning how public policy problems have been addressed in the past.

On-the-Job Learning

It is impossible to overemphasize the importance of on-the-job learning in budget examining. Most OMB managers find that it takes about three years for a new hire to become a competent examiner, regardless of the quality of that person's academic preparation or experience in other jobs. There are few areas of budget examining and, by extension, government decision making, for which there is only one right approach. Knowing which of the many ways to do the job should be applied to a particular issue comes only with exposure to a lot of different issues over time and in a variety of policy settings—this is the key reason that budget examining is endlessly challenging and satisfying for those who are able to put up with the many aggravations and master the trade. After a while the accumulated experience translates into facility with problem solving, which generates the respect of policy officers and makes the skilled budget examiner an integral part of the policy decision-making process.

The Working Environment

Much is made of the intensity of the budgetary process—the long hours, hard work, and pressure. A lot of that is true. The stakes are, after all, enormous. During this process, new ideas live or die; current programs grow, stagnate, or wither; and the lives of program beneficiaries are or are not improved. Policy assumptions must be challenged. New data may add to rather than narrow uncertainty. Policy officers must be confronted with uncomfortable facts.

The amount of time a good examiner must devote to the process can be extraordinary, especially during the annual budget preparation process and the appropriations cycle, or when the examiner handles programs in play in a reconciliation bill or a major program reauthorization. Stretches of ten- to twelve-hour days plus weekends for weeks on end are not uncommon. More stress comes from the fact that budget examiners are often active participants in meetings with the most senior presidential advisers—on very rare occasions even with the president—at which their knowledge and judgment will be on display.

Most budget examiners do not stay in the job very long (three to five years)—partly because good jobs become available to them elsewhere on the basis of their budget examiner credential, partly because they discover that they do not have the taste or talent for the work, and partly because of the intensity of the job. The life of a budget examiner is especially hard on those men and women who have young children. Coping with the ups and downs of pressures and policy shifts is like playing baseball every day through a 162-game season; the best players strive never to get too high or too low in any one situation. But the intensity is also part of the allure—the challenge of rising to the demands of a very demanding job in which one has direct influence on high policy. For those who can handle it, few career government positions rival the satisfaction of budget examining.

The best that any description of budget examining by any one practitioner can hope to offer is a flavor of the experience, a sense of the overall process and what it can accomplish. Other practitioners will disagree with some of the views expressed in this chapter, but most should find familiar the general perception of the budget-examining craft. In regard to that perception, note that the author's experience of more than twenty years of budget examining is not in every policy arena, though it does cover a broad range of federal social policies—job training, education, welfare, social security, child nutrition, food stamps, labor law enforcement, and others. The thoughts expressed in this chapter have been reviewed by individuals specializing in state-level budget analysis, federal natural resources programs, and defense activities, and their comments have been taken into account. Each of these venues has different types of issues and different analytical approaches. In general, however, the specialists in these areas have agreed that the statements made in this chapter are equally broadly applicable in their fields.

For those who desire a view of budget examining within the context of changes throughout the history of what the OMB does and how it does it, there are a variety of studies and reviews to draw on (see list of recommended readings at the end of the chapter). The author of each study describes an OMB that his or her predecessors and successors (let alone contemporary practitioners) would find in some particulars to be at odds with their experiences. These changes, or perceptions of change, throughout the OMB's history are evidence of how the institution and its staff simultaneously carry out both traditional roles and the desires of the incumbent president.

The remainder of this chapter is organized as follows: four basic guidelines for budget examining are defined, the structure of the generic analytical process is delineated, aspects of budget examining that come into play alongside the big questions are identified, and the effort to legislate attention to performance within the context of the budgetary process is considered. The chapter's conclusion provides summary thoughts.

PRINCIPLES UNDERLYING BUDGET ANALYSIS

Although budget examining is a more complicated activity than is commonly understood, it does proceed from some simple ideas.

1. *Fiscal resources are finite.* The principle that fiscal resources are finite seems obvious, but it is the essential proposition with which to begin, and one of the toughest propositions for many program agencies, policy advocates, and interest groups to accept. As noted earlier, the president's budget adds up to totals that express the proposed reach of fiscal policy. The total itself is of necessity judgmental or arbitrary, even when, as in recent years, presidents and Congress impose spending limitations on themselves through deficit reduction plans. Arbitrary or not, the discipline of having to reach decisions within a preset total is central to budget examining. It means that choices have to be made, even in the biggest-spending budget years and even in areas that are highest on a president's priority list. States and localities with constitutional or statutory balanced-budget requirements face the even more stringent constraint of matching up revenues and expenditures without the option of deficit financing.

Most policymakers would heartily agree to a general notion that resources are finite, but most would still struggle if they were pressed to show how to fit their resource desires into the finite total. They might respond that "surely" the program they espouse deserves to be funded fulsomely while "pork" or waste, fraud, and abuse or low-priority programs in another agency should be cut to make room. They would rarely identify the specific candidate in the other agency for such a cut. Budget examining lays the groundwork for the process through which an administration sorts out what does and does not fit within each year's limits.

2. *Trade-offs must be made in the absence of straightforward ways to compare the values of the effects of different spending choices.* Even those who appreciate the real limits of resources are frustrated by the nearly limitless choices that face every budget, and by the problem of comparing those choices fairly across policy arenas. In general, a given level of spending has the same fiscal effect for one program as for another. The tough problem is how to compare the benefit to be derived from spending $100 million more in, say, cancer research (a cure just around the corner?) to the benefit to be derived from spending $100 million more for a reading program (the key to future productivity?), for weapons (victory over the transgressor?), for clean air, for space exploration, for parks, for housing, and on and on. To its proponents, every program's goal is noble and deserves funding in its own right. There simply is no common conversion table that makes the value of the investment in one specific area readily and objectively comparable to the value of the investment in every other area. Herein lies the limit of budget examining.

What budget examining can do for the decision maker in this environment of noncomparable competing demands is ensure that whatever is known about the benefits of each policy is fairly presented to the decision maker in nontechnical terms that he or she can comprehend. Budget examining provides a powerful combination of the best available information and well-informed judgment. It forces out each competitor's strongest justifications for spending.

3. *The budget's base must be examined.* Budget examiners do not accept a notion of an untouchable level of base programs; that is, that the only important budget decisions are the marginal change decisions—how much more or less might be spent. In any given year, limitations of time and energy, absence of new data, or other factors can curtail investigation of the base, but such examination always occurs to some extent. Examining the base does not require the complex, paper-intensive, zero-based budgeting construct of the late 1970s, which for a time gave examining the base a bad name. Examiners routinely explore what is known about the effectiveness and efficiency of current program spending. They search for opportunities to reduce ineffective spending, or they redirect it before considering the marginal increase or a new but similar spending proposal.

The primary reason for attention to the base should be obvious (though often it is not to program advocates): every dollar, whether in the current level or proposed as an increase, adds in the same way to total spending, and again resources are finite. Taking current program spending for granted sharply limits the ability to consider new ideas, and perhaps worse, may permit an ineffective program to continue at the expense of more effective alternatives. Arguably, as the long-term commitment to reduced-spending growth takes hold across government (currently embodied in the Balanced Budget Act of 1997 and the Taxpayer Relief Act of 1997), examination of the base will take on increasing importance.

4. *Budget examining begins with unbiased analysis of the evidence.* Budget analysis includes both factual analysis and policy judgement, but the importance of beginning with factual analysis cannot be overstated. Policy advocates, certainly the best ones, often offer factual analysis in support of their proposals, but an advocate's need to press a policy point of view can lead to tailoring analysis to support the proposals. Good budget examiners begin with no such predilections, even when the issue at hand is a previously announced policy goal of the president or Congress, or a program that the president has declared he opposes. One purpose of budget analysis is to subject such preconceptions to rigorous review. Good analysis can lead to very sensitive situations when its findings conflict with an incumbent administration's policies.

For example, some years ago an examiner was challenged to find a program in his policy area for which evidence could justify more funding. He identified a program that had good evidence of positive net effects on participants. The presentation of his analysis and judgments at a director's review meeting (where examiners and OMB policy officers debate the most important issues for the budget that year) was met with some dismay by the policy officers because the incumbent president had made campaign speeches labeling the program a failure. The examiner had known that, of course, but still felt bound to present the results of his analysis. The program did not get an increase in the budget that year, but it did survive and it prospered in later years on the strength of its demonstrated effectiveness.

Good analysis can also lead to opposite policy decisions in different administrations. For example, in the search for a way to improve the employability of certain individuals, examiners and others explored the virtues of meeting this goal through a particular policy device. The analysis indicated that some net impact was possible, but only at the expense of a significant amount of funds to pay for what the private sector was already paying for (called "buying out the base"). The decision was made not to pursue the policy because the net benefit appeared to be too low. The next administration, however, reviewed the identical analysis but applied a different set of judgments and found the net impact big enough to accept the inherent amount of buying out the base. The proposal was offered and enacted.

Sometimes an administration declares a certain program to be an "inappropriate government activity" regardless of whether it works well. Examiners still analyze such programs, but they may have to file their findings for consideration the next time around. No issue is ever settled forever; as is said among budget examiners, "there is always another bite at the apple."

THE TWO BIG QUESTIONS

Budget examining seeks the best answer to the question, *Why should this program be funded?* And if there is a good answer, budget examining asks, *At what level should it be funded?* Neither question is easy to answer.

What Is the Policy Rationale for the Program or Proposal?

A program or policy proposal may be presented by its proponents within a carefully built assessment that articulates an identifiable, well-defined problem that is worthy of government intervention. The assessment may also show that the proposed form of government intervention can successfully address the problem, that it is cost-beneficial (or at least that the cost is worth the policy gain), and that in the competition for limited resources it deserves high priority relative to other interventions.

The proposal may turn on such assessments, but it often does not. Initiatives are brought forward as much by the enthusiasm of supporters as by the unassailable logic of their justification. This is not necessarily a bad thing. The state of knowledge of how to effect change through government action is not very robust in many policy arenas. Often intuition or a sense of the need to address a problem or the courage to take chances in hopes of significant progress is what advocates really have to go on to justify action on the pressing problem they see.

Intuition, however, is what a budget examiner wants to apply after the factual analysis is done, not before. Getting the sequence correct is the source of most of the friction between examiners and policy officers, especially at the start of an administration, and between examiners and agency or other program advocates. The amount and quality of analysis that is necessary to support, for example, a campaign speech, is not the same as what examiners believe is needed to support the inclusion of a proposal for the use of limited resources in the president's budget. Harping on why is what gives good budget examiners a reputation for skepticism—some call it negativism—when faced with ideas for new or expanded spending.

Note that budget examiners also do not have the luxury of offering recommendations without having their analyses challenged. Once they reach their conclusions, examiners have to argue their case to higher officials, who ask the examiner the same questions that the examiner has asked the program proposer. Experience with this end of the process usually helps temper the tone of a budget examiner's questions to program proposers.

The components of the big question include the following:

• *Is the problem defined clearly?* The identification of vague generalities as problems, such as "people are ill-educated" or "the army needs guns" or "the air is polluted," is not sufficient justification for spending. The definition of a problem should be qualified with evidence of its nature and scope. Then the examiner can consider whether the particular spending proposal might in fact help ameliorate the identified problem. Failure to specify the problem properly almost invariably means the inability to know later whether the spending on it was effective.

For example, it can be argued that increased use of technology can improve teaching and learning. Thus, a simple problem might be defined as, How can the government get more computers into schools? The answer to this formulation might be to finance the purchase of computers. Analysis would indicate, however, that by themselves computers have little benefit. Teachers need to know how to use the computer effectively in the classroom; they need to have the right software to help students reach the school's educational standards and complete its curriculum successfully; and they need good training in the use of the software. Thus the problem more carefully articulated would be, How can government help improve teaching and learning through effective use, by properly trained teachers, of educational technology that is appropriate to the needs of the students in each school? The response to this formulation would be very different. It might still include spending money on computers, but coupled with support for the necessary software and teacher training.

• *Is the problem, however well defined, suitable for government intervention?* This is perhaps the most slippery question. As noted, assumptions about the appropriate reach of government made at one time on the basis of historical precedent must yield to the policy desires of a new administration or a new Congress. Such assumptions can also fall before new information. Budget examiners need to ask this question knowing that an answer based on current practice is not necessarily controlling.

Examples of how the answer to this question can change can be found readily in two educational policies:

Federal funds in parochial schools. Until the 1960s it was virtually unheard of for federal funding to be put into parochial schools, lest the constitutionally required separation of church and state be violated. Then, searching for ways to reach disadvantaged children in these parochial schools, the government formulated the theory of funding the child rather than the institution. The mechanism is not simple but it results in the supplementation of educational resources for disadvantaged children in parochial school classrooms.

School construction. Few federal education programs permit the use of funds for elementary and secondary school construction, except when the school is federally owned, on the theory that facilities construction is a state and local responsibility. In recent years, however, the General Accounting Office and other analysts have raised doubts about the perceived ability of states and localities to meet the cost of ensuring children's safety and adapting schools to new technology. Such reports have led to a variety of school construction proposals with widespread support from both the administration and Congress. One program was enacted, funded, then eliminated when Congress changed hands. More recently, a proposal using the tax system has been enacted. Other proposals are likely to follow.

• *Assuming that a decent problem definition and good rationale for government intervention have been provided, can a program be successfully implemented?* An apparently attractive program design has to demonstrate its practical applicability. An apocryphal story illustrates this point. During World War I, a meeting of the British Admiralty was called to confront the U-boat menace. One admiral is said to have opined that the solution was simple: "Boil the ocean." Challenged as to how that might be done, he shrugged and said, "I only make policy; implementation is someone else's problem."

Policy and implementation issues are equally central for budget examiners. One proposal's effectiveness may turn out to rely on the willingness of states to finance a portion of the activity beyond what the evidence suggests they will. Another proposal may turn on having more federal staff (such as investigators or monitors) than policy on staffing may permit. Still another may turn on a particular behavioral response by business or individuals that is not likely because it is not supported by convincing evidence. Another proposal may make good sense and have a theoretically sound implementation strategy, but the skills required in the agency may not be present or attainable in time. Examiners pursue such implementation issues to assess the practicality of the proposed policy.

Once a program is in operation, a continuing role for the budget examiner is to probe the effectiveness of actual implementation. Government agencies are generally not very agile in their management. That is, they do not always respond in a timely and effective manner to indications of problems in program implementation. Problems such as slower-than-expected startup, slower than planned spending, higher unit costs and lower levels of output than intended, and unexpected responses by grantees or the public can all be indications of problems requiring close attention and program redesign. A program can fail because of slow and inadequate response to such management information when process redesign could have saved it.

For example, some years ago a very large program was launched with great expectations. It soon developed serious problems of abuse in a few places. Program managers saw the problems but hoped to be able to resolve them quietly without major program changes. Program opponents quickly seized on the much publicized problems, touted them as endemic to the whole program, and in a relatively short time brought down not only this component but the larger structure of which it was a part. The budget examiners (and some agency staff) saw the problem and what the result might be if it continued unattended, but they could not convince policy officials to take the necessary steps in time.

- *Will it be possible to tell whether the program worked?* A good design with an effective implementation strategy that leads to efficient processes that produce the desired near-term program outputs needs to run for years before it can be known whether it has fulfilled its long-term goal. Budget examiners therefore want to know whether the program has the means or design for carrying out the necessary evaluation of long-term impact.

For example, employment programs can readily place individuals in jobs. Postprogram job placements would seem to be good indicators of program success, but there is evidence that they may not be. If the individuals placed do not stay in the jobs or advance their careers afterwards, and if as a result they do not earn more then they would have earned without participating in the program, then the program has not succeeded. Congress recently passed, at the president's request, a $3 billion program to help states and cities move long-term welfare recipients off welfare and into self-sufficiency through unsubsidized employment. To ensure that we will know whether the program has worked, the administration and Congress worked together to provide $24 million to evaluate, among other things, how well the program meets its long-term goal for participants. Provision of evaluation funding at the outset of a program promises that the question of whether the program design has eventually worked will be asked.

Few programs are designed from the beginning to collect good information on a problem and the effectiveness of the program designed to address it. This is not surprising. It is hard for any program advocate to include a program assessment mechanism in his or her initiative; it can make the advocate feel as though he does not really know whether his idea will work, or worse, that the appearance of uncertainty will weaken his argument for funding. A good budget examiner always tries to build the best data collection and evaluation mechanisms into program statutes from the beginning, lest he or she find five years later that the program's future needs to be recommended and the necessary information is not available.

This recommendation is not meant to suggest that good evaluation data will be the sole determinant of the future of a program; that is not common. But without such data, the policy debate is analytically sterile, turning mainly on ideological rhetoric, intuition, and anecdote.

What Is the Appropriate Resource Level?

The next issue is setting the resource level. Here again, uncertainties often outweigh the known. Very few social policies are deliberately designed to "cure" a given problem in a finite period. Policies are usually said to address problems, not to cure them. This language is partly due to justifiable caution about over-promising results. It can also be due to the fact that the cost of total cure is either unknown or so huge as to make the proposal unacceptable if full funding were promised. Budget examiners focus on how much spending is the minimum necessary to obtain the desired policy outcome.

Some programs, such as social security and college student loans, are open-ended entitlements with no preset limits on costs. In these programs, a statute sets the eligibility and size of benefit terms. Costs are then the result of eligible persons using their spending or services entitlement. For these programs, the budget analysis turns on determining what is known about the beneficiary population and its likely desire for the service or benefit. These and other factors form the basis for a projected cost for the budget. Complete accuracy in such projections is virtually unheard of in any program, but coming as close as possible to reality is essential. An estimate that is too high will use up room in the budget that should have gone to another program or to reduced spending. An estimate that is too low can mask a claim on budgetary resources that, if known, might have led to different policies.

The resource-need analysis for the more usual, if often smaller, programs that are not open-ended is similar. The statute or new proposal sets out a program design that describes what services or benefits should be provided to whom, but in these cases it does not automatically make the funds available. Often the program authorizes a certain amount, but the real amount is set in the annual appropriation process. For these programs, then, the resource question takes the form of, How much should the program spend this year?

Social program examiners like to believe that these "How much?" questions are not as hard to answer in other policy areas where the benefit being sought, such as a road, a transit system, a ship, or a satellite is more tangible—"the grass is always greener on the other side of the fence" syndrome. Although some of the techniques of cost analysis are surely different in each area, any cursory review of the record of cost overruns or of unsatisfactory performance of systems indicates that the craft of examining resource levels in these fields has at least as many uncertainties as are found in social program analysis.

The way into narrowing the uncertainty surrounding the big questions is through a series of smaller questions that can help determine spending levels for one year or over the multiyear period for which a given budget's policies are being debated (currently five years).

• *How much benefit, and for whom?* Answering this question seems simple. A program authorizes so much in payments or services and says who can qualify for them. But the real and much harder question is what the service or payment is supposed to result in for the beneficiary. If the program is to provide food assistance, does that assistance actually improve nutrition? If it is to provide access to college, does the college experience result in higher incomes? If it is to provide child care, is the child really better off as a result?

These questions put a special premium on relating costs to ultimate benefits that would not occur in the absence of the program. The answers to the net-impact questions are often simply not available for a given budget, or they will not be available for many years. The long-term effects of interventions in children's education, for example, may take years to determine. And there is no conclusive evidence on long-term net impacts when a budget decision has to be made.

In a few policy areas, after many years of development, there are huge, complex, nationally significant computer models, such as those used to analyze issues affecting the poverty population. These models are invaluable sources of help for estimating program costs and potential benefits. More often examiners must rely on approximations, such as data from small demonstrations or nonrepresentative case studies. The examiner probes every source for information, including questioning program managers at the federal, state, and local levels; referring to his own impressions from field visits; reading the available academic or congressional studies; and participating in research conferences.

In an ideal world, the absence of evidence of net impact might forestall any spending on a program in other than a demonstration mode. As noted earlier, however, it is rare to have all the information one wants before a decision has to be made to initiate or continue a program. In the pursuit of answers to net-impact questions, budget examiners will sometimes encourage agencies to spend money on sophisticated research and longitudinal evaluations, even though these evaluations may not pay off in useful information for several years.

• *With or without net-impact information, the next question is, How much "service" or "participation" can a given amount of money purchase?* For a given increment of funding, for example, how many more people could get college work-study jobs? How many more children could enroll in Head Start? How many more tanks could be built? Examiners delve into program data on unit cost. They look not only at averages but also at the distribution of cost levels across the program, lest they miss important variations that could indicate ways to reduce overall cost. Examiners also look at how many more people could be served, or how many more items could be provided, if a program were more efficiently run.

If, because of data limitations, examiners cannot know now precisely what difference the spending makes for beneficiaries, they must still work on making the program cost as little as necessary—or as much as necessary. Examiners may have to recommend higher spending per unit if the examiner's analysis shows that the lower spending is resulting in ineffective services. Spending more on fewer persons is a problem for some program managers who are too closely focused on how many people their programs touch (rather than help); but spending more on fewer people will be the right policy when the goal is effectiveness, not head counts. (This sounds like role reversal. It is usually budget examiners who are accused of being the "bean counters." In fact, however, it is sometimes the examiner focused on results, not the policy official, who urges higher spending per person.)

- *Is the justification for the resource level strong enough to prevail in the competition for limited resources?* Whether operating under the current regime of statutory spending limitations, or under the previous practice in all administrations of keeping the president's budget within a nonstatutory spending limit, each program competes with all others for resources. This is how the budget examiner brings into play the principle of budgeting established earlier, that programs in different policy arenas may well have noncomparable values but still must be compared to one another to make a total budget.

A program for which spending can readily be justified when examined against its own goals may not survive in its own department's budget proposal when its justification is compared to that of other programs in the department in the competition for available resources. A program that survives this screening process may still fall when the department's justification competes against justifications from other agencies. Budget examiners feed the results of their analysis of all the questions examined here into this iterative sorting-out process.

Probing for the best answers to the resource questions, pushing the available data to their limits, and confronting advocates on the quality of their justifications for a given spending level are usually the most contentious aspects of budget examining. It is a rare program for which the answer to "How much?" is straightforward, analytically derivable, and universally accepted in the face of competing demands for resources. Factual analysis takes the examiner, and thus the policy officer, only so far. After that, informed judgment comes into play.

Budget examiners' ability to bring informed judgment to the decision is their highest contribution, but the limitations of their kind of judgment also have to be understood. Some budget examiners have a hard time making the leap of faith necessary to advance a new program policy. They are tied to factual analysis, which is not necessarily the best route to innovative thinking and bold ideas. Successful policy officers respect the value of leavening the enthusiasms of advocates with budget examiner analysis, but no administration ever lets its program agenda be set solely by the input from budget examiners.

OTHER FACTORS THAT INFLUENCE BUDGET EXAMINING

To this point this chapter has explored the underlying principles of budget analysis and key aspects of the big analytical questions that inform the process. It now looks at other, often less visible influences on budget analysis that examiners take into account as they develop a budget recommendation.

Program History

Every program is the product of a unique law, agency customs, and traditional practices, and of the different interpretations of these factors that successive policy officials bring to bear. Budget examiners study, learn, and make sense of the history of these laws, customs, and practices and of their interpretations as they determine how to influence a program's future.

For example, an elementary and secondary education program for the Department of Education is traditionally run as a grant to states or to local education agencies. A job-training program in the Department of Labor is traditionally run as a grant to states, local elected officials, the private sector, or community groups. In the Department of Health and Human Services, some programs are run as grants to state social services or welfare agencies; others are run as grants to community organizations. None of these traditional approaches is necessarily wrong, but there may be a more effective way than the traditional way to deliver a particular service. A service normally provided to states through a flexible grant may be more effective if provided through a performance-based competitive grant. Resources for a number of narrowly drawn programs with related goals might generate greater net impact for beneficiaries if combined with a broader-purpose grant to states.

If budget examiners hope to convince an agency of the merits of a different approach that could be a more effective way to deliver a given service or benefit, they need to learn how agency traditions arose and who in the agency, in Congress, among interest groups, and in the states has a stake in the continuation of those traditions.

Budget Concepts and Rules

There are a host of specific budgeting concepts and rules of procedure that constrain or direct budget analysis. They are mainly dry and technical to the outsider and would not make interesting reading. The OMB provides direction to agencies on many of these concepts and rules in its annually updated Circular A-11. These rules can be adjusted in the face of strong policy desires, but it is important to note that their existence gives structure to the analytical process and provides a modicum of consistency across disparate programs. These concepts and rules cover definitions of basic terms and processes, such as budget authority, outlays, obligations, offsetting collections, and trust funds. Knowledge of these terms and processes is irrelevant to the average person but essential to the budget examiner's ability to function effectively in the budgetary process.

Concepts and rules can be more than technical details. Two important rule changes show how budget examiners can face dramatically different policy issues as a result of such changes.

Credit Budgeting. The Federal Credit Reform Act of 1990 (FCRA) was the culmination of years of debate among a small group of budget experts over the correct way to reflect the budget cost of government lending. The details are too complex for full explanation here; suffice it to say that under pre-FCRA rules, it could appear in the budget to be far more costly for the government to make a loan itself than to guarantee the same loan made by a bank, even if the government's costs over the life of the loan—taking into account repayments, servicing, defaults, and so on—were the same for the two types of loans. Program policy might lead to either approach for other reasons, but in some cases the impact of the annual budget, not the real costs, determined the loan approach chosen.

The FCRA created the concept of scoring all of a loan's costs in the first year of the loan at the "net present value" (cost and repayment streams over time, which could be decades, discounted to today's dollars), regardless of the actual cash flows in any one year. A loan that cost thousands of dollars in the budget pre-FCRA might now cost a few hundred dollars when the years of repayments, servicing, and risk of default are factored in and when the loan's cash flows are discounted back to its first year.

Although it is extremely complex in execution, the theory of the FCRA makes sense and provides a true comparison of the net costs of different types of loans. For student loan budget examiners, however, the consequences of the change were profound. When the FCRA was passed, the federal government had been guaranteeing bank loans to college students for twenty-five years. Combined with the further complexities of the higher education laws, the FCRA made direct federal loans less expensive for budget scoring than guaranteed loans. Loan expansion advocates immediately seized on the FCRA rule change as the way to greatly expand lending (and thus access to college) at lower cost by converting to a direct loan system. This change would eliminate the roles, and thus the profits, of thousands of banks and dozens of unique organizations (guarantee agencies) created for the guaranteed loan program, as well as eliminate, over time, the secondary loan markets. The move to change the program structure set off a political battle between the advocates of the two loan systems that continues unabated to the time of this writing (seven years later).

Pay as You Go. Pay-as-you-go scoring, or PAYGO, is a device to enforce budget-neutral policy changes in entitlement spending (and taxes). PAYGO says that any proposal to increase spending on the mandatory side of the budget (programs such as food stamps, social security, and unemployment insurance that are not annually provided for in appropriation acts) has to be offset dollar for dollar by lowered mandatory spending. (Higher taxes can also be used to offset higher mandatory spending.) The rule does not apply to the increased spending that comes from population growth or to the effect of inflation on unit costs. It does apply to any legislated expansion of the eligible population or to any legislated increase in the basic amount of benefits.

PAYGO makes sense as a cost-control device. It also adds dramatically to the burden of justifying new mandatory spending. New program benefits not only have to be justified on their merits and political desirability, they also have to be accompanied by comparable spending cuts in other programs or by tax increases. Budget analysis has to address the impact of the offset as well as the increase. The necessity for an offset requires a kind of two-sided analysis: first, how much should be spent to get the most positive program benefit? Then, where should the offsetting spending cut be found? It is not uncommon for the size of the available offset to dictate the amount of spending that can be requested or whether there will even be a request for new or increased spending.

Budgeting for Administrative Costs

Budgeting for administrative costs, or salaries and expenses (S&E), is the process of translating policies for what government wants to accomplish into the prosaic terms of how much money should be spent to pay for the federal employees and contractors who will carry out the policy and for their space, supplies, and equipment.

Sometimes program policy is the direct equivalent of S&E spending. For example, the strategy for safety and health inspection turns on the allocation of S&E funds among inspectors and other forms of compliance. Where policy is carried out through grants and contracts—as in education grants to states—the S&E need is for federal staff to make and monitor those grants. The latter example is much more obscure to the public.

Not surprisingly, within the government, spending levels for staffing are often the most hotly contested budget issues. Agencies in all administrations have an innate yearning to grow; budget examiner negotiations over S&E dollars can become the lever for obtaining agency agreement on a range of policy decisions that are more visible to the public.

One product of S&E budgeting does attract attention: the resulting total level of federal employment. Virtually every administration at some time becomes sensitive to how many federal employees there are as a measure of whether the administration supports bigger or smaller government. The bias is usually, though not always, toward fewer staff, thus requiring budget examiners to pay special attention to how to accomplish policy goals with fewer staff. An early statement of this OMB concern may be found in Bureau of the Budget Circular 19 (issued in 1922, p. 86): "[The Director of Budget would] not view with favor any salary increases or perfunctory enlargement of clerical forces." OMB budget examiner bias is routinely toward reducing administrative costs and full-time equivalent (FTE) staffing, wherever doing so makes sense in light of program policy goals.

For example, in FY76 the Social Security Administration (SSA) provided social security benefits to 27.5 million individuals and supplemental security income (SSI) benefits to 4.3 million individuals while employing 85,000 FTE. In FY96, the SSA provided social security benefits to 43.4 million individuals and SSI benefits to 6.6 million individuals while employing 63,400 FTE. Aggressive use of technology (computerization and communications) along with continuous improvement of processes reduced FTE requirements by 20 percent while serving 50 percent more people. These results were achieved through close collaboration between the agency and its budget examiners.

The craft of S&E budgeting is no more scientific than that of budgeting for grant or benefit programs. Still, examiners know that having the people and administrative resources needed to carry out policy can be the pivotal factor in whether a program succeeds. Examiners try to establish the closest possible relationship between the specific level of administrative resources and the policy goal those resources support.

Program Management

It is not uncommon for some observers of government to define *management* primarily in terms of administrative processes, such as procurement, use of information technology, accounting, auditing, personnel management, and space management. Each of these processes is important in budget examining. Still more important to the examiner is the broader question of whether the program is being managed as efficiently and effectively as possible. Excellence in administrative process is not the sole predictor of good program management.

The OMB does maintain cadres of technical experts in some areas of administrative process (such as financial systems, auditing, procurement, and information technology) but not in personnel or space management (expertise for these processes is in the Office of Personnel Management and the General Services Administration, respectively). These staff experts develop and monitor government-wide policies in each area of administrative process. Budget examiners work with them on issues in specific agencies, often forming ad hoc teams.

Budget examiners then go on to address the broader management questions, such as, Are funds allocated in the manner most suitable to program goals? Would the program's purposes be achieved more effectively by using grants or contracts or direct benefits? Should intermediaries be used or should the government interact directly with the individual? Is there an effective structure for accountability systems, data collection design, and evaluation? The point was made earlier in this chapter that a key analytical question for budget examiners is whether the program design is suitable to the program goal. This question is the entryway through which management enters into the budget-examining process.

Dealing with management issues can be very frustrating. Agency policy officials are normally appointed for primary reasons other than their management skills or interests. Few policy officers want to hear that a management problem endangers a policy goal if addressing the management problem might endanger support for that goal.

Top-level attention to the quality of management does occur. It can be found in the appointment to the OMB of high-ranking officials who have management as their primary focus (the effective melding of that focus with the traditional budget-examining role of the OMB is still an evolving matter). Interest in management excellence is sometimes formally raised to the level of the White House, as it now is through the National Performance Review and as it was in the Reagan administration through the Grace Commission. It is possible that the bipartisan, long-term commitment to reduced growth in federal spending achieved in 1997 will translate into heightened interest in the effectiveness and efficiency of current spending. In the meantime, whether total resources are growing or declining, budget examiners continue to address the quality of program management in their analyses.

Examining Long-Term Implications

Budget examiners take into account the long-term implications of today's policy choices. Not only is predicting the future difficult, but in new policy endeavors there is often little information to inform the debate. This is another reason that, as discussed earlier, examiners can be so fixated on the necessity for good data collection and sound net-impact evaluations: if we cannot know the answers today, at least we can build into the process the ability to learn them in the future.

It can be very tough to get agencies to address this issue, even at the career level. Few agency heads will reward staff who want to set aside money and set in motion studies to determine the actual impacts of a program that were just recently authorized and funded. One cabinet head, for example, did take on this issue by conducting rigorous reviews of what worked and what did not within the department's programs and by making the results known. The effort was strongly supported by the budget examiners and by the research community. Agency staff took as the lesson from this analysis that there were significant program areas that needed improvement. The OMB and the appropriators in Congress took from the analysis that spending less or none at all on the weakest program was justified. Some in the agency now believe that they never should have undertaken the analysis because it cost them the funding of that program. Conversely, the same analytical process provided support for continued funding for other programs whose effectiveness had been in doubt.

The Ivory Tower Versus the Front Line

An early part of this chapter identified the stresses of the budget examiner's working environment. The material that followed laid out the various aspects of budget examining in orderly fashion. It is important now to remind the reader that all this analytical effort rarely, if ever, takes place in a calm atmosphere where the budget examiner addresses one issue, resolves it, then moves on to the next. Budget examining is an extremely messy process. An examiner works his or her way through a sophisticated research study on program net impact while also answering myriad questions on many other programs with tight deadlines and attempting to master some new budget concept, trying to lay out and then do a critical piece of analysis on yet another program, and so on. There is never enough time to do analysis as thoroughly as it should be done before having to present it to an impatient agency, the OMB, or White House officials. Budget examining is not a contemplative lifestyle or for the faint of heart.

Making Choices: Triage

It follows from the preceding reminder that there is never enough time for a budget examiner to do all of the analysis needed for every program and policy issue before a decision must be made. Examiners make daily choices about what to examine and to what depth. Certain choices for immediate attention are obvious: program ideas that the administration is considering whether to support or oppose, programs for which important new data have just become available, programs whose management shortcomings the examiner has identified, or programs that are being publicly criticized. Choices for low priority can also seem obvious: programs that are small cost and low visibility—the "policy inert." The key is deciding accurately where effort will pay off the most in the short and long runs—or put another way, what risks can be accepted by not looking at certain programs immediately so that the examiner can concentrate on what seems to be the biggest or most policy-sensitive program. Even the most experienced examiners are not right all the time and pay the price for deciding wrong.

Impact of the Government Performance and Results Act

The Government Performance and Results Act (GPRA) of 1993 demands of every agency a strategic plan for achieving its goals and annual performance plans and reports on how well it is doing at reaching those goals. Ideally the act should have no significant impact on the governmental process, if that process is working as designed and as well as it can. The GPRA's precepts are the same as those that have been outlined in this chapter as the essence of budget examining; they are truisms.

Sadly, these truisms of good budgeting are honored in the breach as often as not—in the agencies, in the committees of Congress, and even sometimes in the OMB. Elevating these precepts from consensus best practices to the force of law is a major change in the budget environment. The import of this change is underlined by the fact that its full implementation is occurring with Congress and the presidency in the hands of different parties, making likely a sharper partisan edge to congressional oversight of implementation of this law and the performance reports it generates than might have occurred otherwise.

Agencies that formerly resisted defining performance in measurable terms and collecting and reporting the necessary data are now moving in this direction under the added pressure of congressional expectations generated by the GPRA. It will take years to see the implementation through to the point where the GPRA's actual impact can be judged; in the meantime, the GPRA is a welcome helping hand in the fact-gathering aspects of budget examining. The policy impact is more complex.

The fly in the GPRA ointment for some programs is that they simply do not now have performance data, positive or otherwise, yet the GPRA calls for publicizing evidence of performance for every program. In addition, some programs supported by the administration and some (not necessarily the same ones) supported by Congress have only mixed evidence. How does an agency deal with the GPRA in regard to a program for which the administration requests billions of dollars if there are no good data, or worse, if what data there are conflict with the policy preferences of the incumbent administration? How will congressional appropriators or authorizers face the same issue for similar programs they have fought for decades to enlarge?

These tensions are greatly exacerbated when Congress and the presidency are held by different parties, but they will be manifest even when both are under the same party's control; no program has 100 percent support. In their hearts, OMB budget examiners may welcome this external pressure to produce needed data, and this statutory desire to make more decisions rest on the evidence. Once an administration's policies are set, however, it is the budget examiners' duty to help support and justify them. Under the GPRA, that duty will call for some careful presentation of what data there are, to make the best case for the policy at hand. Staff to program supporters in Congress and in the interest groups will wrestle with the same problem.

With luck and conscientious implementation, the GPRA should at minimum elevate the degree to which facts and unbiased analysis are taken into account in policy decision making. It cannot, however, change the reality that all resource allocation decisions, from the largest to the tiniest, are political decisions, and always will be, as long as resources are finite—and they always will be finite.

CONCLUSION

This chapter's assessment of the limits of the GPRA is a fitting lead-in to this closing observation on budget examining. In the end, every resource allocation decision is based on a unique and complex mix of factual analysis, professional judgment, policy desires, and political needs. Budget examiners offer policy-makers a consistent source for timely factual analysis and informed judgment that takes into account, but is not completely constrained by, the politics of the moment. Notwithstanding the inevitable limitations of information and time, the enduring testament to the value of budget examining is found in the fact that every administration, regardless of party or ideological differences, sooner or later in its tenure comes to rely heavily on the OMB—and thus on budget examiners—as an indispensable part of its policymaking processes.

References

Bureau of the Budget, United States Treasury, Circular 19. "Report to the President of the United States by the Director of the Bureau of the Budget." Washington, D.C.: Government Printing Office, July 1, 1922.

O'Neill, P. H. Speech to OMB staff, Sept. 6, 1988.

Recommended Readings

Berman, L. *The Office of Management and Budget and the Presidency, 1921–1979.* Princeton, N.J.: Princeton University Press, 1979.

Bromley, P., and Crecine, J. P. "Budget Development in OMB: Aggregate Influences of the Problem and Information Environment." *Journal of Politics,* 1980, *42,* 1031–1064.

Heclo, H. "OMB and the Presidency: The Problem of 'Neutral Competence.'" *Public Interest,* 1975, *38,* 80–98.

Mosher, F. C., and Stephenson, M. O., Jr. "The Office of Management and Budget in a Changing Scene." *Public Budgeting and Finance*, 1982, *2*(4), 23–41.

Nathan, R. *The Administrative Presidency.* Old Tappan, N.J.: Macmillan, 1983.

Report of the President's Committee on Administrative Management in the Government of the United States. *Report with Special Studies.* L. Brownlow, Chairman, 1937.

Schick, A. "The Budget Bureau That Was: Thoughts on the Rise, Decline and Future of a Presidential Agency." *Law and Contemporary Problems*, 1970, *35*, 519–539.

U.S. General Accounting Office. *Managing the Government: Revised Approach Could Improve OMB's Effectiveness.* Washington, D.C.: Government Printing Office, 1989.

U.S. Senate, Congressional Research Service and the Committee on Governmental Affairs. *Office of Management and Budget: Evolving Roles and Future Issues.* Senate Report 99-134. Washington, D.C.: Government Printing Office, 1986.

CHAPTER NINETEEN

Legislatures and Budgeting

Roy T. Meyers

L
ike all chapters in this book but one, this chapter discusses a budgetary topic in relation to the United States. This country-specific focus is especially justified for this chapter, because U.S. legislatures are the most important and independent in the world, and this is especially the case in budgetary matters.

The extraordinary fiscal powers of U.S. legislatures were intended from the beginning. Look at the specific authorities granted to legislatures in federal and state constitutions. The most important example is from Article I, Section 9, Clause 7 of the U.S. Constitution, which requires that "no money shall be drawn from the Treasury, but in consequence of appropriations made by law. . . ." Section 7 begins with the requirement that "all bills for raising revenue shall originate in the House of Representatives. . . ." The revolutionary justification for these authorities was that "the people" could check the potential of elite fiscal tyranny through the institution most likely to represent the people's interests—the House of Representatives.

These constitutional authorities are collectively known in popular discussion as "the power of the purse." Yet throughout U.S. history they have been constantly misinterpreted when people have argued that the legislature alone is responsible for money matters. This is simply not the case, because of the interaction of two factors—the executive can veto legislation, and the majority party rarely has enough votes and discipline to override that veto. Legislative proposals are just that—bargaining positions that are often reversed or significantly modified. In fiscal matters, as in all other matters of consequence in the United States, the separated institutions share power (Fisher, 1993). (The budgetary power of the courts is discussed in Chapter Twenty.)

Although public expectations for legislative budgetary performance have been high (and in part *because* they have been high), the budgetary performance of U.S. legislatures has often been criticized. One of the most commonly identified legislative failures is the practice of enacting budget bills long after constitutional or statutory deadlines have passed. Although this is more the routine than the exception for the U.S. Congress, state legislatures vary significantly in their tendency to delay, with those from the largest states being more prone to this problem (Meyers, 1997; Snell, 1996).

Legislatures are also blamed for being unable to pass fiscally responsible policies. They may fail to set targets for spending totals or be unable to meet them. A common explanation is that legislators so value personal electoral rewards from particularistic and distributive spending allocations (popularly known as pork barrel spending) that they are willing to risk institutional blame for lack of fiscal discipline (Shepsle and Weingast, 1981). Another major criticism of how legislatures budget is that when they do enact spending limitations they tend to micromanage agency operations inefficiently.

At times such ascribed (and often self-confessed) failures have led legislatures to delegate their budgetary powers to executives. At other times executives have asserted powers that would reduce the legislatures to effective rubber stamps. Legislatures have not always stood up to these challenges.

Although the balance in fiscal powers during the twentieth century has shifted toward the executive branch, the period since the 1960s has been one of strong legislative assertion (Sundquist, 1981; Wander, 1982). Many state legislatures professionalized both their membership (by raising salaries) and their staff (by hiring experts) and then insisted that they have more say in revenue forecasting, in the appropriation of federal funds, and in other important matters (Yondorf, 1983; Doolittle, 1984). At the federal level, Congress reacted to President Nixon's impoundments, and to embarrassment over its own inability to control spending, by passing the landmark Congressional Budget Act in 1974 (Schick, 1980; Sundquist, 1981).

The next section of this chapter describes the challenges faced by legislatures when they attempt to budget. The chapter then reviews how Congress has asserted its budgetary role in the modern period. It concludes with a discussion of how congressional budgeting could be improved.

The emphasis on Congress is somewhat unfortunate but natural. Legislative scholars in the United States are obsessed with Congress and how it budgets, and they have developed an impressive literature on the subject. Unfortunately, quality studies of state legislatures and how they budget are few and far between. (For exceptions, see Rosenthal, 1990; Clynch and Lauth, 1991; and Gosling,

1985. On inattention to state legislatures generally, see Jewell, 1982.) Nevertheless, the opportunities for research on state legislative budgeting are significant. State legislatures are undeniably important given their resurgent budgetary powers; indeed, in some states (Texas, for example) legislatures are arguably more influential than governors (Rubin, 1997). The major research dilemma is how to overcome the logistical challenge of gathering sufficiently detailed information on numerous and different legislatures.

Congressional budgeting involves many complicated activities—setting aggregate targets for spending, taxing, and borrowing; conforming the budgets of individual agencies and programs to these targets; and ensuring that the executive branch follows budgetary directives. These tasks are accomplished with different types of legislation, internal rulemaking, and oversight (hearings, letters, and audits). This chapter does not describe all the mechanics of these processes; instead it focuses on the question of legislative capacity. (For those who wish to learn more about the mechanics of congressional budgeting, the most useful source is Schick, 1995.)

THE INSTITUTIONAL DIFFICULTIES OF LEGISLATIVE BUDGETING

Budgeting is an inherently difficult activity for a legislature. This should not be surprising because the resource allocation function of budgeting challenges organizations of all types, at least when fiscal resources are not increasing rapidly. Allocating in less than munificent times means denying requests, which leaves claimants unhappy.

The main reason, however, that budgeting is especially difficult for a legislature is the legislatures' unique organizational form (Kamlet and Mowery, 1985). Consider the most basic characteristics of the typical U.S. legislature, beginning with its members. Legislators are expected to be highly responsive to their constituents. They must visit their districts often, ask for their constituents' opinions, and reflect their districts' values when they act in the legislature. They are practically required to do so by their frequent exposure to electoral removal. As Anthony King (1997) has argued, U.S. solons are required to stand for reelection more frequently than any other politicians on earth, and because of this they run scared throughout their short terms. Electoral accountability particularly complicates budgeting when constituents and legislators appraise fiscal conditions and imperatives differently. A classic case is voters' demands for fiscal free lunches—simultaneous tax cuts, spending increases, and balanced budgets—just as legislators are told by their fiscal staff that serving this menu is impossible.

Another common feature of U.S. legislatures is deliberative majority rule. Regardless of the variance in legislators' personal abilities, in the constitutional sense they are presumptive equals. Within each legislative body, all members represent the same number of constituents (U.S. senators are the sole exception) and all have one vote. When they disagree over policies, they are expected to resolve their differences by arguing about them in full public view and then by voting, using majority rule. A natural result of this process for budgeting is that legislators demand to be treated equally, which they interpret as receiving what they most want out of the large and complicated mix of government spending and taxing policies. Remember Bismarck's famous advice to avoid watching the preparation of legislation and sausage? Deliberative majority rule gives each legislator a sharp knife with which to slice the budgetary salami, and when knives start flashing. . . .

Democratic theorists have long recognized that producing simultaneously high levels of constituency responsiveness, electoral accountability, and deliberative majority rule challenges institutional capacities. This is especially true when the number of constituencies is large and when those constituencies have opposing positions on a large number of issues, which is a perfect description of the typical state of U.S. public opinion. Numerous issue cleavages foster so-called vote cycling, in which legislative coalitions that appear to be possible winners quickly fall apart as weakly attached coalition members depart in response to better offers from other coalitions vying to become winners (Arrow, 1951). Legislatures tend toward disequilibrium, and their modal decision is a nondecision—that is, to make no change because the members cannot agree on exactly how to make the change. It is no wonder that legislative budgets are late, that spending totals are allowed to climb higher than desired, and that budget plans have short lives.

When Madison, Hamilton, and Jay defended the U.S. Constitution in *The Federalist Papers,* they did not express any worries about this potential weakness of Congress. Quite the opposite. They, along with most elites of the time, feared unbridled majoritarianism and designed a constitutional structure to limit the effects of public passions. Congressional power was to be constrained by competing executive and judicial branches, the bicameral structure of the legislative branch, and a federalism that retained substantial powers for the states. In addition, senators were not to be popularly elected but instead were to be selected by their state legislatures.

The framers of both federal and state constitutions built a strong foundation that continues to limit legislative powers. For example, bicameralism, a basic feature of constitutions except in Nebraska (which has a single house), still stymies most efforts by U.S. legislators to act quickly (Longley and Oleszek, 1989). Conversely, explicit amendments to the Constitution and many other changes have made the U.S. Congress into a much more majoritarian institution. Senators are now popularly elected, and they face just as much electoral risk, adjusting for their longer terms, as do representatives. At the state level, a related promajoritarian shift was forced by 1960s Supreme Court decisions that required each legislator within a state house to represent an equal number of constituents.

The most important change threatening the capacity of legislatures, however, has been the long-term decline of party organizations and their control of candidates' campaigns. Many candidates now gain access to ballots through self-promotion in primaries, and they control candidate-centered organizations that raise campaign funds independent of party leaders. Consequently, legislators are less dependent on legislative leaders and less loyal to the party than their predecessors were. It is especially important to note, however, that this long-term trend masks significant variation across states, in some of which strong parties retain unifying powers. Some experts have also argued that in recent years parties have been strong actors within Congress (Kiewiet and McCubbins, 1991; Rohde, 1991).

Given these features, how have legislatures organized for budgeting? Though some state legislatures are important exceptions, most legislatures, and especially the U.S. Congress, use a very decentralized structure. Legislators join district-relevant committees to further their reelection chances, and they see these memberships as property rights, particularly when the seniority rule is used to select committee leaders. Numerous committees claim long-held jurisdictions over different parts of the budget, and these jurisdictions often fail to map functional areas of the budget. For example, in the U.S. House of Representatives, one committee oversees Medicaid and another controls Medicare. The resulting confusion is multiplied by the fact that the budgets of most agencies are controlled by more than one committee in each house of the legislature—that is, committees typically share jurisdictions, and do so uncomfortably as they occasionally battle over their turf (King, 1996; Fisher, 1979). For example, each year Congress passes a bill that authorizes the defense budget and a second bill that appropriates the funds for this budget. Each bill is prepared by a different committee, and each year Congress and the Department of Defense must reconcile many differences between the particulars of these two bills.

Such decentralization has a mixed effect on the nature of legislative budgeting. It enables legislative entrepreneurship and creativity, and it provides society with an arena for choosing between competing values. Conversely, the legislative expression of value conflicts can get out of hand, preventing timely enactment of the budget while failing to focus attention on the most important trade-offs. Consider how the power of floor amendment has been used on budget bills in the U.S. Congress. Over the past three decades, changes to formal rules and informal norms have led individual legislators to propose much more often that the full membership change the "carefully crafted" bills reported by committees (Smith, 1989). This *collegial* style of decision making, which is often far less friendly than the term implies, can cost Congress valuable time (some budget bills take weeks to complete) and positive image (constituents see daily squabbles on C-SPAN). Then there is the filibuster power; because of senatorial reverence for institutional tradition and reluctance to part with a potential tool of influence, Senate leaders can fail to gain unanimous consent to consider important budgetary issues (Binder and Smith, 1997; Sinclair, 1989).

An influential yet controversial line of argument within political science is that some legislatures may deal with these challenges by "inducing equilibrium" through "structures" (Shepsle, 1986). For example, vote cycling can be reduced by granting leaders, committees, or both the right to propose alternatives in a form that makes amendments unlikely to pass. In my opinion, this line of argument is not well supported at the federal level (for a better model of legislative action, see Arnold, 1990). In contrast, strong leaders and fiscal committees who are capable of forcing compromises rather than having to plead for civility do appear more frequently at the state level.

The final institutional difficulty for any U.S. legislature is the greater capacity for budgeting of its main competitor, the executive branch. To point out this difficulty is not to deny that executive branches face many of the same challenges as legislatures do. Any president or governor is expected to be responsive to constituents' wishes. The executive will either be held electorally accountable within four years or care about the prospect that the next candidate of the executive's party will bear some burden for the current executive's actions. Also, every governor and president oversees a decentralized set of agencies that commonly differ over priorities.

Nevertheless, executive branches are relatively advantaged for budgeting in a variety of important ways. Political executives have significant formal agenda-setting powers. Executive budget requests, even when legislators pronounce them dead on arrival in front of TV cameras, normally serve as the starting point to the legislative budgetary process. In strong-executive states, legislatures are even prohibited from adding amounts to the governor's operating budget; they can only reduce. Informal agenda-setting powers are just as important. Presidents and governors receive much greater media exposure than their legislative opponents. Though political executives are certainly at risk from media investigations, they also have the ability to grab the public podium and convince citizens how to interpret different budget proposals. By comparison, most legislators receive meaningful media attention readily only in their individual districts.

Although they can use media outlets, political executives are also often able to consider a wide range of alternatives with less political exposure. Nothing requires the executive branch to prepare the budget in the open, and arguments with cabinet secretaries can remain private. Presidents and governors also command the greater analytical resources of the executive branch. In addition, a political executive is a unitary decision maker who can make snap decisions, which is a tremendous advantage in negotiations (Maraniss and Weisskopf, 1996). Finally, because executives control budget execution, they can sometimes circumvent the legislature and diminish its enaction power.

Having listed the institutional difficulties that legislatures face when they budget, the next issue to consider is whether these difficulties are overwhelming. Are legislatures, and specifically the U.S. Congress, incapable of budgeting well? Or after decades of reform does Congress now have the capacity to budget adequately?

CONGRESSIONAL BUDGETING

Although Congress has significantly reformed its budgetary process over the past two and a half decades—the focus of this section—readers who are novices on Congress should not conclude that this is the only major change in its long history of budgeting. Without going into a full chronology, the following paragraphs discuss some of the most important developments in the history of congressional budgeting prior to the 1970s.

• Nineteenth-century appropriations began as line-item directives to agencies, but were converted to lump-sum form as the size of government grew and as appropriations bills became unwieldy. In lieu of statutory directives, committees now direct agency spending with the informal but still-effective recommendations of committee reports (Fisher, 1975).

• Major battles were fought over the distribution of fiscal powers between committees. The workload of the Civil War led to the establishment of the appropriations committees; they took over the spending component of the fiscal power, leaving taxes and debt to existing committees. In the late nineteenth century, the House appropriators were thought to have abused their discretion, and other committees revolted, stripping the committee of its jurisdiction for selected, especially distributive, policy areas (such as rivers and harbors) (Stewart, 1989). The decentralization of power was completed in 1910 with the revolt against Speaker Joe Cannon, a reaction to his attempts to dictate committee actions.

• In the Budget and Accounting Act of 1921, Congress granted substantial budgetary responsibilities to the executive branch. Traditional practices had agencies forwarding "estimates" to Congress with little presidential involvement. The new law brought executive budgeting to the federal level (late in comparison to its adoption in major states and cities) by creating the Bureau of the Budget in the Treasury. The act also established the General Accounting Office as the central auditor, but placed it tenuously in the legislative branch (Mosher, 1984).

• Executive budgetary power expanded further as the demands of the New Deal and World War II led Congress to delegate authority to agencies and the president. After World War II, Congress attempted to downsize and rationalize the structure of the federal government. In 1950 it attempted the same for itself, though with less effort and even less effect, by experimenting for one year with a consolidated appropriations bill (Galloway, 1953; Nelson, 1953). The failure of this reform ratified the power of the authorizing committee chairs ("old bulls") and the appropriation subcommittee chairs (the "college of cardinals"). Though on occasion they arbitrarily exercised their discretion for personal goals, more often they tended to represent the wishes of the majority, known collectively in the Senate as the "inner club" (Matthews, 1960). Speaker Sam Rayburn's pluralist aphorism—"to get along, go along"—best expressed the accepted method of building budgetary consensus, which was facilitated by the strong growth of the economy (Fenno, 1966; Huitt, 1963).

This congressional system of budgeting was disrupted by the remarkable social changes of the 1960s, most notably those caused by the civil rights movement, the expansion of Great Society programs, and the war in Indochina. First, spending related to these factors eliminated a surplus that had been feared for its potential to slow economic growth, and it created the base of a structural deficit that was later magnified by the slowdown of economic growth in the 1970s. Second, the social conflict of this period increased tension within Congress and started the long-running decline of public confidence in U.S. institutions. Adding the strong effects of this period to the natural centrifugal tendencies of congressional organization greatly stressed the institution. Schick (1980, p. 17) labeled the period from 1966 to 1973 as the "seven-year budget war" because of the near-continuous battles over budgetary totals between the spending and taxing committees. One of the most embarrassing episodes occurred in 1972, when Congress adopted a statutory limit on the public debt that was effective for only one day.

President Nixon gleefully blamed Congress for such faults and, following his landslide victory in 1972, asserted an implicit constitutional authority to impound funds. This gambit, like the contemporaneous attempted cover-up of White House improprieties, was too ambitious to be successful. Congress was willing to confess that it had been fiscally irresponsible, but it did not feel so disgraced that it had to cede its appropriations power. Instead, Congress decided to oppose presidential aggrandizement and to correct its own inadequacies by passing the Congressional Budget and Impoundment Control Act of

1974, one of the most important laws of the twentieth century. The first nine titles of the act are collectively known as the Congressional Budget Act, or CBA.

Like most laws, the CBA was a compromise, the product of involved negotiations between institutional leaders over a number of years. It did not end conflict between the warring committees by eliminating them and then starting over. Rather, it retained the existing organizational structure and traditional budgetary procedures and then added new organizations and procedures in hopes that they would improve the existing ones. New budget committees, one each for the Senate and the House, were to coordinate the process. They were not immediate power centers, particularly the House committee, whose membership was term-limited and drawn primarily from its rival committees. House Budget Committee members who wanted to stay in Congress more than six years (that is, almost all of them) were understandably reluctant to challenge the prerogatives of the other committees. In contrast, membership on the Senate Budget Committee was permanent, and this committee soon asserted its responsibilities. With the passage of time, as the committees became institutionalized and as deficit pressures increased, even the House committee became a major force for deficit reduction.

The new budget procedures created by the act were, even at the start, quite complicated; after more than two decades of experience they mushroomed almost beyond belief. But the basic approach was actually quite simple—a two-part process of goal-setting and enforcement. A concurrent budget resolution was to set goals for the aggregates (that is, totals): budget authority (in lay terms, promises to spend), outlays (payments), revenues, and deficit. The concurrent form of the resolution meant that it was a congressional rule and not a law; this assured that the president would have no formal say in the goal-setting stage.

From the aggregate targets, the resolution distributed amounts of spending to the functional areas of the budget, that is, to international affairs, national defense, energy, education, health, and so on. During preparation of the resolution in committee and during debate on the floor, members of Congress often used the amounts listed for different budget functions to argue about priorities (for example, "guns versus butter"). In fact, however, these debates were largely symbolic. Budget committee staff "crosswalked" (that is, transformed to a different categorization) the functional allocations in the resolution to committee allocations. The latter allocations were the ones that mattered because the committees could ignore the budget resolution's functional targets. The appropriations committee, for example, could transfer money that the budget resolution "intended" for defense to nondefense spending because it had jurisdiction over both areas. Although only the House Ways and Means Committee and the Senate Finance Committee had similarly broad jurisdictions, most committees controlled parts of multiple budget functions and could shift amounts between them.

The second part of the new budgetary process added enforcement procedures to the traditional methods of authorizing and appropriating funds. Now that Congress had aggregate budget targets, it could keep track of how its individual legislative actions added up and compared to these targets. This arcane but indispensable process was known as scorekeeping. It enabled enforcement, especially for so-called discretionary spending—that which was approved by the appropriations committees. After the resolution allocated spending ceilings to these committees, the committees subdivided these allocations into ceilings for each of their thirteen subcommittees. Known from the section of the CBA as 302b allocations (and later as 602b), the subcommittees could be held to these totals, and usually were, by points of order. Under this traditional legislative procedure, a single member of Congress has the ability to make a parliamentary point that a proposed bill violates a legislative rule; if the claim is found to be accurate, consideration of the bill must stop until the offending provision is removed.

The other enforcement procedure was targeted at so-called mandatory spending—that which does not need to be approved in advance by the appropriations committees because of the provisions of existing law. Points of order are ineffective for limiting mandatory spending; because no legislation needs to be passed for mandatory spending to continue, there is usually no opportunity to raise objections. This was a major problem for aggregate spending control because most mandatory spending took the form of entitlements, which are designed to grow automatically.

The CBA immediately established a major barrier to the creation of new entitlements by requiring that the appropriations committees approve these raids on their jurisdiction, which they were loath to do. Control of existing entitlements took a bit longer. 1980 saw the first use of the reconciliation provisions of the act, in which committees with jurisdiction over mandatory spending were instructed by the budget resolution to report proposed changes to mandatory spending laws. In 1981, a coalition of Republicans and conservative Democrats packaged large reductions to entitlements, as well as controversial limits on authorizations of appropriations, into an omnibus reconciliation bill. Since then, reconciliation bills have been a standard tool for controlling mandatory spending, in part because they cannot be filibustered. Yet reconciliation has had two very important limits. First, nothing absolutely requires passage of reconciliation, so in some years committees and the floor have balked at passing the savings assumed in the budget resolution. Second, because of the greater difficulty of scorekeeping for mandatory spending, some claimed savings in reconciliation bills have been, at best, "funny money."

On balance, however, the CBA has notably improved the quality of information used in legislative budgeting. The major credit must go to the Congressional Budget Office (CBO), which with strong leadership and a professional staff has provided macroeconomic projections, scorekeeping reports, and budgetary policy analyses that rival those produced by the Office of Management and Budget (Blum, 1990). Its role has occasionally been controversial because of the highly technical nature and influential impact of its work. There is no doubt that the CBO has sometimes been very wrong, has acted arbitrarily, or has been influenced by politics. Yet the CBO has protected its objectivity by explaining its methods and by appealing to both parties to respect the competitive value of objective analysis to the legislature (Meyers, 1996). (Another asset of similar value to Congress, the General Accounting Office, has suffered in recent years in part because of congressional members' discontent with some of its reports and audits—a sorry case of blaming the messenger who brings unwelcome news.)

Not long after the CBA was enacted, observers started to ask, Has it worked? Over the years the answers have varied, in part depending on the functions desired for the process. For those who have simply wanted Congress to assert its authority, the CBA has been a success—in many years Congress has set goals in the budget resolution and met them. If an additional function was to convince the public that Congress is capable of budgeting, success is more in doubt given the extremely low ratings that Congress typically receives. Conversely, the public may be unduly harsh in its judgments by interpreting the squabbles that are inevitable in budgeting as childish arguments rather than as principled disagreements. (Admittedly, the former do occur.) Finally, if the purpose was to produce a particular policy result—to limit spending, or more ambitiously, to balance the budget—given the huge deficits of the 1980s, arguably the CBA has been a success only recently. But we cannot know with certainty the counterfactual—perhaps deficits would have been larger had Congress stuck with its traditional method of budgeting rather than experimenting as it has. (See Kamlet and Mowery, 1988, for an attempt to model macrobudgetary counterfactuals.)

Perceptions of the act's inadequacy have stimulated many attempts to reform it, some in legislation and others by changing practices. The nadir of reforms was the ironically titled Balanced Budget and Emergency Deficit Control Act of 1985; its popular name was Gramm-Rudman-Hollings (GRH), after its three Senate sponsors. GRH was enacted in frustration. The Republican-controlled Senate had just adopted significant cuts to entitlement programs, only to have President Reagan agree with Democratic Speaker Tip O'Neill to oppose the cuts. GRH was an attempt to force Reagan to match his conservative rhetoric with action. It created fixed deficit targets that declined to a balanced budget in five years, and a new procedure designed to enforce the targets—"sequestration."

If Congress failed to enact laws that would cause projected deficits to fall below the targets, then spending authority would be automatically canceled (sequestered) to reach this result.

Senator Rudman justified sequestration by calling it "a bad idea whose time has come" (White and Wildavsky, 1989, p. 445). As he soon recognized, he was right about only the first part of that phrase. A major flaw with sequestration was that not all spending was subject to it—most mandatory spending was exempt. The illogic of GRH was to assume that large automatic cuts in discretionary spending were so scary that both President Reagan and liberal Democrats would cut mandatory spending to avoid them. But the cuts were not automatic, because like all laws, GRH could be changed. When faced with the choice between huge cuts in military spending and missing the deficit targets, Congress and President Reagan agreed to raise the targets, extending the date for balancing the budget by two more years.

Under congressional pressure, budget reform took a more reasonable direction starting in 1990. President Bush abandoned his "read my lips: no new taxes" campaign bluster, which broke the interbranch deadlock over making real deficit reductions. As part of the massive bill enacted in that year, the Omnibus Budget Reconciliation Act of 1990, a section known as the Budget Enforcement Act (BEA) significantly amended the CBA and GRH. The BEA replaced fixed deficit targets with ones that would be adjusted for major macroeconomic changes; this made the deficit reduction goals more realistic. The BEA also created new methods of enforcement. For discretionary spending, it set binding multiyear caps. After the first year of the five-year agreement, these caps effectively prevented appropriations from increasing above their nominal level—the so-called hard freeze. Discretionary spending then declined between FY91 and FY97 by about 13 percent in constant dollars; it had increased by about 37 percent in constant dollars from 1975 to 1991 (author's calculations from OMB data).

The BEA's enforcement innovation for mandatory spending was called "pay as you go," or PAYGO. Unlike the constraint placed on discretionary spending, PAYGO did not force real reductions in mandatory spending. Rather, it required that the deficit increases from any new entitlement or revenue legislation be completely offset by deficit reductions from other entitlements or from taxes. Like the discretionary caps, PAYGO is widely viewed as having fulfilled its intended purpose.

In 1993, the BEA's caps were extended another two years as part of a large deficit reduction package enacted by the Democrats without a vote to spare in the House and without any Republican support. This exercise in party responsibility (and the plan's heavy reliance on tax increases), however, contributed to the Democrats' loss of control of the Congress in the 1994 elections. The victorious Republicans then attempted a self-declared revolution, with proposals for a balanced budget amendment, huge cuts in spending and taxes, and a quasi line-item veto. The latter was granted to the president, but only after a delay in its effective date until 1997. The balanced budget amendment was not adopted. And although significant spending cuts were adopted, the eventual cuts were much smaller than the Republicans wanted. They made strategic miscalculations of historic dimensions by assuming that President Clinton would not use his veto on stingy appropriations bills (he did), that U.S. citizens would not be disturbed by the resulting government shutdown (they were), and that they would not blame congressional Republicans (they did) (Meyers, 1997). After these harsh lessons about legislative ambition, Congress has reverted to a more cooperative assertion of its budgetary role.

IMPROVING CONGRESSIONAL BUDGETING

Political scientists differ greatly over the general capacity of Congress (see Mezey, 1986; Cooper, 1986). These differences are mirrored in evaluations of Congress's specific capacity to budget. Some political scientists react to the history reviewed in this chapter by concluding that Congress is simply incapable of budgeting well. Others see admirable progress since enactment of the CBA.

Given that there is no consensus on the quality of congressional budgeting, it should not be surprising that there is a huge literature on a great number of proposed and actual budget reforms. There is insufficient space here to analyze these proposals in detail (see Schick, 1990; U.S. Senate Committee on Governmental Affairs, 1988; Fisher, 1985). Instead, the chapter concludes by noting a dilemma of legislative reform that affects the likelihood that congressional budgeting will be changed for the better (whatever that "better" may be).

Return to the general model of the U.S. legislative institution described earlier. Members of Congress are expected to be responsive to their constituents and are held electorally accountable on a frequent basis. They compete against an executive who normally holds bargaining advantages over them. They must make decisions by deliberative majority rule. In reaction to these constraints they have developed an incredibly complicated organizational structure with overlapping committee jurisdictions, parties that alternately cohere and fracture, and relatively weak leaders. They use elaborate procedures to make and avoid making decisions.

As members of Congress have created the institution, which they have done piece by piece over a very long time, they have been especially concerned about how it will satisfy their individual interests and, in particular, their electoral prospects. Institutional interests have concerned many of them as well, particularly to the extent that perceived institutional failures might hurt their electoral prospects. But over time most members have made a cold and accurate calculation that they could win reelection even if the institution fails to meet expectations. *Consequently, even if many members agree that characteristics of the budgetary process are institutionally dysfunctional, they will not change those characteristics if they also offer personal opportunities.*

Now there is no denying that Congress has reformed its budgetary process significantly and repeatedly since 1974. But it is worth asking whether these reforms have made truly fundamental changes to congressional budgeting, as many seem to perceive they have. Instead, it may be that the reforms have only scratched the surface and that they have failed to change the basic characteristics of legislative processes, organization, or aspirations for power that disturb congressional critics.

Briefly consider three perceived flaws of congressional budgeting and the reforms that might remedy them. One flaw is that Congress is overloaded with rules and procedures, which often prevents it from making decisions on time. A logical approach to dealing with this problem would be to eliminate those activities that appear to have relatively low payoffs for the institution. But there is no PAYGO for rules and procedures, the number and impact of which have expanded greatly since 1974. For example, one would think that these new rules might obviate the institutional need for the debt-limit process (if there ever was one, for the debt limit is the classic case of closing the barn door after the whole herd has run far away). Yet members of Congress retain the debt limit, primarily because it gives them otherwise unavailable procedural opportunities to propose changes to policy and process (Kowalcky and Le Loup, 1993).

Another fundamental critique of congressional budgeting is that power is too decentralized. A logical but radical remedy would be to collapse the appropriations and authorizations committees into functional committees, with the budget committees serving as the regulator of their demands on the public purse. Yet in 1995, when the change in party control created an unparalleled opportunity for committee rationalization, a proposal to do this in the House was considered only briefly. It was killed because of member attachment to seniority rights and to the tradition of earmarks that is enabled by committee decentralization. (The best analysis of congressional reorganization is Davidson and Oleszek, 1977. The House Republican leadership did exercise comparatively strong influence on the selection of committee chairs in 1995, but by 1997 that influence had greatly diminished.)

At the same time, the Republicans professed their ideological disdain for earmarks and showed some self-restraint in their first year of writing appropriations bills. They also gave the president a delayed quasi–item veto, or more formally, the power of "enhanced rescission" (Joyce and Reischauer, 1997). Yet when President Clinton exercised this power in 1997, making just a few reductions, Congress effectively sent the message that even that was too much. Members crave the ability to direct funds to their districts, and neither ideology nor party platforms will get in the way. Nor have they seriously considered changing the concurrent budget resolution into a joint one, which would recognize the importance of presidential influence in the process and invite participation in the goal-setting stage (Meyers, 1990).

These examples do not prove that fundamental changes in congressional budgeting are impossible, but they do suggest that they are unlikely. In the absence of such changes, members of Congress will likely waste a lot of time, often argue with each other, and act as if the president has little legitimate role in managing agency spending or setting budgetary targets. To purists, who want government to run like a machine, this is a depressing prospect. To realists, such legislative fumbling over the budget may be an unavoidable but relatively cheap (and at times even entertaining) cost of democracy, American-style.

References

Arnold, D. R. *The Logic of Congressional Action.* New Haven, Conn.: Yale University Press, 1990.

Arrow, K. *Social Choice and Individual Values.* New York: Wiley, 1951.

Binder, S. A., and Smith, S. S. *Politics of Principle? Filibustering in the U.S. Senate.* Washington, D.C.: Brookings Institution, 1997.

Blum, J. L. *A Profile of the Congressional Budget Office.* Washington, D.C.: Congressional Budget Office, 1990.

Clynch, E. J., and Lauth, T. P. *Governors, Legislatures, and Budgets.* Westport, Conn.: Greenwood Press, 1991.

Cooper, J. "Assessing Legislative Performance: A Reply to the Critics of Congress." *Congress and the Presidency,* 1986, *13,* 21–40.

Davidson, R. H., and Oleszek, W. J. *Congress Against Itself.* Bloomington: Indiana University Press, 1977.

Doolittle, F. C. (ed.). "Minisymposium: State Legislatures and Federal Grants." *Public Budgeting and Finance,* 1984, *4,* 3–72.

Fenno, R. F., Jr. *The Power of the Purse: Appropriations Politics in Congress.* New York: Little, Brown, 1966.

Fisher, L. *Presidential Spending Power.* Princeton, N.J.: Princeton University Press, 1975.

Fisher, L. "The Authorization-Appropriations Process: Formal Rules and Informal Practices." Washington, D.C.: Congressional Research Service, 1979.

Fisher, L. "Ten Years of the Budget Act: Still Searching for Controls." *Public Budgeting and Finance,* 1985, *5,* 3–28.

Fisher, L. *The Politics of Shared Power.* (3rd. ed.) Washington, D.C.: Congressional Quarterly Press, 1993.

Galloway, G. B. "Consolidated Appropriations Bill: The 1950 Experiment." Washington, D.C.: Congressional Research Service, 1953.

Gosling, J. J. "Patterns of Influence and Choice in the Wisconsin Budgetary Process." *Legislative Studies Quarterly,* 1985, *10,* 457–482.

Huitt, R. K. "Congressional Organization and Operations in the Field of Money and Credit." In Commission on Money and Credit, *Fiscal and Debt Management Policies.* Upper Saddle River, N.J.: Prentice Hall, 1963.

Jewell, M. "The Neglected World of State Politics." *Journal of Politics,* 1982, *44,* 638–657.

Joyce, P. G., and Reischauer, R. D. "The Federal Line-Item Veto: What Is It and What Will It Do?" *Public Administration Review,* 1997, *57,* 95–104.

Kamlet, M. S., and Mowery, D. C. "The First Decade of the Congressional Budget Act: Legislative Imitation and Adaptation in Budgeting." *Policy Sciences,* 1985, *18,* 313–334.

Kamlet, M. S., Mowery, D. C., and Su, T.-T. "Upsetting the National Priorities? The Reagan Administration's Budgetary Strategy." *American Political Science Review,* 1988, *82,* 1293–1307.

Kiewiet, D. R., and McCubbins, M. D. *The Logic of Delegation.* Chicago: University of Chicago Press, 1991.

King, A. "The Vulnerable American Politician." *British Journal of Political Science,* 1997, *27,* 1–22.

King, D. C. *Turf Wars.* Ann Arbor: University of Michigan Press, 1996.

Kowalcky, L. K., and Le Loup, L. T. "Congress and the Politics of Statutory Debt Limitation." *Public Administration Review,* 1993, *53,* 14–27.

Longley, L. D., and Oleszek, W. J. *Bicameral Politics.* New Haven, Conn.: Yale University Press, 1989.

Maraniss, D., and Weisskopf, M. *"Tell Newt to Shut Up!"* New York: Simon & Schuster, 1996.

Matthews, D. R. *U.S. Senators and Their World.* New York: Random House, 1960.

Meyers, R. T. "The Budget Resolution Should Be Law." *Public Budgeting and Finance,* 1990, *10,* 103–112.

Meyers, R. T. "CBO: The Agencies' Indispensable Adversary." *Public Manager,* 1996, *25,* 11–14.

Meyers, R. T. "Late Appropriations and Government Shutdowns: Frequency, Causes, Consequences, and Remedies." *Public Budgeting and Finance,* 1997, *17,* 25–38.

Mezey, M. L. "The Legislature, the Executive, and Public Policy: The Futile Quest for Congressional Power." *Congress and the Presidency,* 1986, *13,* 1–20.

Mosher, F. C. *A Tale of Two Agencies: A Comparative Analysis of the General Accounting Office and the Office of Management and Budget.* Baton Rouge: Louisiana State University Press, 1984.

Nelson, D. H. "The Omnibus Appropriations Act of 1950." *Journal of Politics,* 1953, *15,* 274–288.

Rohde, D. W. *Parties and Leadership in the Postreform House.* Chicago: University of Chicago Press, 1991.

Rosenthal, A. *Governors and Legislators: Contending Powers.* Washington, D.C.: Congressional Quarterly Press, 1990.

Rubin, I. S. *The Politics of Public Budgeting: Getting and Spending, Borrowing and Balancing.* (3rd. ed.). Chatham, N.J.: Chatham House, 1997.

Schick, A. *Congress and Money.* Washington, D.C.: Urban Institute, 1980.

Schick, A. *The Capacity to Budget.* Washington, D.C.: Urban Institute, 1990.

Schick, A. *The Federal Budget: Politics, Policy, Process.* Washington, D.C.: Brookings Institution, 1995.

Shepsle, K. A. "Institutional Equilibrium and Equilibrium Institutions." In H. Weisberg (ed.), *Political Science: The Science of Politics.* New York: Agathon, 1986.

Shepsle, K. A., and Weingast, B. R. "Political Preferences for the Pork Barrel: A Generalization." *American Journal of Political Science,* 1981, *25,* 96–111.

Sinclair, B. *The Transformation of the U.S. Senate.* Baltimore: Johns Hopkins University Press, 1989.

Smith, S. S. *Call to Order.* Washington, D.C.: Brookings Institution, 1989.

Snell, R. K. "State Provisions Addressing Late Budgets." Denver: National Conference of State Legislatures, 1996.

Stewart, C., III. *Budget Reform Politics: The Design of the Appropriations Process in the House of Representatives, 1865–1921.* New York: Cambridge University Press, 1989.

Sundquist, J. L. *The Decline and Resurgence of Congress.* Washington, D.C.: Brookings Institution, 1981.

U.S. Senate Committee on Governmental Affairs. *Proposed Budget Reforms: A Critical Analysis.* Washington, D.C.: Government Printing Office, 1988.

Wander, W. T. "Patterns of Change in the Congressional Budget Process, 1865–1974." *Congress and the Presidency,* 1982, *9,* 23–49.

White, J., and Wildavsky, A. *The Deficit and the Public Interest.* Berkeley: University of California Press, 1989.

Yondorf, B. "A Legislator's Guide to Budget Oversight: After the Appropriations Act IIas Passed." Denver: National Conference of State Legislatures, 1983.

CHAPTER TWENTY

Courts and Fiscal
Decision Making

Phillip J. Cooper

There is a sense in which discussions of public law and debates about budgeting have a good deal in common. Both budgets and law are essential to
the task of public administration. Without legal authority and budgetary resources, agencies cannot function. Indeed, without legal authority they do not
even exist, and without financial resources they exist in name only. In both law
and budgeting, public administrators generally feel that they lack sufficient support and flexibility to perform necessary tasks. In both law and budgeting, the
processes for making decisions are understood to be time-consuming and burdensome enterprises that take energy away from the primary mission of the
agency. In both law and budgeting, line managers chafe at having to respond to
outsiders, such as legislators and judges. Managers depend on the support of
these key players (or at least avoid their opposition) even though these outsiders
may know little or nothing about the line manager's obligations or technical
field. In the case of budgeting, the budgeters may or may not be conversant in
medical policies, yet their recommendations can enable or cripple substantive
initiatives that have immediate major implications for health quality. Judges
and attorneys are often viewed by line managers in the same way that dentists
are viewed by many patients, despite the fact that judges and attorneys play
similarly legitimate and indeed essential roles in public administration.

When it comes to their views of the legal system and its participants, public
administrators often begin with a lot of mental and emotional baggage—some
of which they do not even know they carry. In U.S. culture, at least, citizens are

taught from a relatively early age to fear law and legal process, and the tension we feel toward the legal system tends to increase as we age. By the time teenagers graduate from high school, they have been warned about the many ways they might "get into trouble," an expression that frequently means having an encounter with the legal system. It is no accident that young people are warned that if they step out of line, someone will "throw the book" at them— and that means a law book. The need to learn relatively complex sets of rules for the operation of public institutions, from licensing procedures to income tax filings, and similar expectations in private relationships, from employment contracts to sales agreements, all reinforce a sense that law is about burdensome and complicated constraints on behavior.

The legal profession often does not help. Like the Mandarins of old, many in the legal field have worked to maintain the myth that law is an exotic enterprise that can be understood only by the initiated, which is to say, by the members of the legal club. Moreover, the natural tendency of attorneys is to practice preventive and protective behavior, which means they are often heard saying no to every question that is asked about possible courses of action. It is true that law is in many respects a very conservative force in society and in day-to-day practice. When judges perform badly in high-visibility cases, such as the Simpson murder trial, or render badly reasoned opinions that have obviously unjust results, as in some of the Supreme Court's worst pronouncements, all of the tendencies that have been so carefully inculcated over the years are reinforced.

Then there is the training that many public managers receive that starts from the simple proposition that to achieve results managers need the maximum amount of flexibility. Law, by definition, constrains flexibility and is therefore considered to be destructive of good management practice (see Osborne and Gaebler, 1992; Gore, 1993). When fiscal constraints are added to the legal restrictions, the logic runs, a manager is operating in the worst of all possible worlds.

To add irony to injury, budgeters, whom many managers consider only slightly less dangerous than lawyers, are among the most likely to ignore legal issues in their studies of the fiscal process; and they are among the first to lash out against perceived legal interference with governance. Thus, in budgeting texts one rarely encounters careful or thorough considerations of the legal dimensions of fiscal policy or management. To the degree that such topics are addressed, the response is almost uniformly negative.

All of these arguments and forces are eminently logical and understandable. They are also wrongheaded and dangerous. Agencies would not exist if laws did not create and empower them. Budgets, and all other elements of fiscal policy and management, are also built on legal authority, beginning with the fiscal authority provided in Article I of the U.S. Constitution. To the degree that critics speak of a preference for the forces of the marketplace over legally based decisions, one must hasten to point out that those markets were in most instances created by law. Thus, it makes little sense to speak of housing or real estate markets without reference to mortgage supports, market institution development, and interest and tax subsidies, all of which were created by statute. Neither is there anything new about a role in these discussions for the courts. It is well to remember that even before the Supreme Court first declared the power of judicial review in *Marbury* v. *Madison* (1803), a circuit court had struck down the carriage tax and ruled on the veterans pension policy issued by President Washington. Even before that, the supreme courts of states had ruled on legislative fiscal and monetary decisions.

In sum, courts, budgeters, and line administrators are, and always have been, essential partners in the enterprise of governance. It is, however, a very dynamic partnership—what Louis Fisher (1988) has termed a "constitutional dialogue"—in which the nature and intensity of the interactions vary dramatically over time. This chapter seeks to add to that discussion. It proceeds by examining a small number of important public law rulings of the past few years to demonstrate the ways in which these rulings, most of which are not, on their face, concerned with budget issues, to see how and why they are important to fiscal managers. The chapter argues in favor of increased attention to public law by fiscal decision makers in the future and suggests the importance of approaching those legal issues with the same kind of analytic attitude and sophistication that public managers normally take with respect to other aspects of fiscal decision making.

CONTEMPORARY CASES: THE RELATIONSHIP BETWEEN COURTS AND BUDGETS

To avoid lengthy and potentially confusing recitations of legal doctrine, this chapter examines a small number of contemporary cases that, taken together, provide a useful picture of the ways in which courts and fiscal processes interact. Although this is a useful approach, it is helpful to remain aware of its limitations.

First, these cases went to the U.S. Supreme Court. The significance of this, on the positive side, is that these cases have national implications. Opinions expressed in lower federal or state courts are binding only within the court's particular jurisdiction. It would be inappropriate, however, to ignore the fact that these state and federal courts render many important rulings that influence the fiscal processes of government in numerous important ways (see Lauth and Cooper, 1997). In particular, it is critical to remember that state supreme courts are the highest authorities on the meaning of the states' constitutions and laws. Although federal courts, including the U.S. Supreme Court, may review state court decisions to determine whether they violate federal law, the ultimate interpreter of the meaning of a state's laws remains its own courts.

Furthermore, it is important to be aware of two types of fiscal actions that are not discussed here but that are very important factors in public management. The first and most obvious of these categories is decisions related to government contracts, especially because such contracts include a range of special constraints and obligations. The second type of fiscal action consists of agreements that are negotiated with an awareness of the presence of legal rulings or in anticipation of possible future litigation. This type of action has been referred to as negotiating under the influence of the law.

Finally, the purpose of this chapter is not to provide a definitive survey but to give an idea of the range of relatively recent rulings. Even with these limitations, however, these few recent rulings provide a surprisingly broad range of examples of the ongoing importance of courts to fiscal management.

DEFINITION AND BOUNDARIES OF FISCAL POWERS

One of the clearest ways in which courts play a critical role in budgeting is by defining, enabling, or constraining fiscal decision-making authority. Examples include cases on impoundment (see *Train v. New York*, 1975; *City of New Haven v. United States*, 1986; *National Association for Mental Health v. Califano*, 1983; *City of Los Angeles v. Coleman*, 1975; *National Council of Community Mental Health Centers v. Weinberger*, 1973; *People ex rel. Bakalis v. Weinberger*, 1973), limits on shared control of budgetary decisions (see *Bowsher v. Synar*, 1986), and use of executive orders in fiscal matters (see *Amalgamated Meat Cutters and Butcher Workmen of North America v. Connally*, 1971; *Independent Gasoline Markets Council v. Duncan*, 1980; *Dames & Moore v. Regan*, 1981). The most recent example of the latter kind of dispute was the challenge to the presidential line-item veto, *Byrd v. Raines* (1997). After more than twenty years of debate on the matter, in April 1996 Congress adopted the Line-Item Veto Act.

Setting the Stage: Adoption of and Challenge to the Line-Item Veto

The arguments about whether presidents were absolutely bound by the congressional appropriations legislation began generations ago when the founders decided to divide the fiscal powers to avoid the royal abuses of the public purse that were well known to the framers of our Constitution. Conversely, presidents since Taft have argued that they needed to have not only significant budget preparation authority but also budget execution discretion. The modern version of the debate was joined as President Nixon moved to impound appropriated funds and Congress responded with the Impoundment Control Act of 1974 to restrict impoundments. The president could recommend rescissions, but congressional action was required to implement them.

Since at least the Reagan administration there had been pressure to give the president a line-item veto. Congress did so in March 1996 with the Line-Item Veto Act. The legislation was not to become effective, however, until early 1997 because the Republican-controlled Congress hoped that Democrat Bill Clinton would go down to defeat in November.

The act authorizes the president to cancel "any dollar amount of discretionary budget authority; any item of new direct spending; or . . . any limited tax benefit" [2 U.S.C. 691(a)]. With respect to discretionary items, the president could address not only amounts provided on the face of the legislation but also material provided in "tables, charts, or explanatory text of statements or committee reports accompanying the legislation" [2 U.S.C. 691e(7)]. Direct-spending veto authority included new entitlement programs for individuals or state or local governments [92 U.S.C. 691e(8)]. The legislation defined limited tax benefits as those that would apply to one hundred or fewer beneficiaries, as well as changes that would affect ten or fewer people or firms by a change in the tax code [2 U.S.C. 691e(9)]. These limited benefits are to be identified by Congress when they are adopted.

In exercising his authority, the president is required to determine that the veto will "reduce the Federal budget deficit; not impair any essential Government functions; and not harm the national interest" [2 U.S.C. 691(a)(A)]. If the president reaches that conclusion, he is to send a special message to Congress within five days after the statute being cut is adopted. The item is canceled when the message is received, but Congress may pass a disapproval bill within thirty days, subject to a possible presidential veto. Congress would naturally be free to override the veto using conventional procedures.

Once President Clinton had the power at his disposal, it became clear that he would face opposition to this new authority not only from Republicans but also from legislators of his own party. Congressmen David Skaggs and Henry Waxman as well as Senators Robert Byrd, Daniel Patrick Moynihan, Carl Levin, and Mark Hatfield brought a challenge in the U.S. district court for the District of Columbia. They asserted that the line-item veto statute violated Article I of the Constitution in that it effectively permitted the president to nullify duly enacted provisions of law, properly enacted appropriations bills.

Notwithstanding the popularity of the statute, the challengers had considerable reason for optimism. The last major budget-reduction effort that had gone to the federal courts, the Gramm-Rudman-Hollings Act, suffered a defeat when it was challenged on the ground of separation of powers (*Bowsher* v. *Synar*, 1986). There had also been a strong rejection of the legislative veto (*Immigration and Naturalization Service* v. *Chadha,* 1983). Although the Court had upheld a number of statutes that tested the boundaries of the separation of powers (*Mistretta* v. *United States,* 1989; *Morrison* v. *Olson,* 1988), it had also served notice that there were limits (see also *Buckley* v. *Valeo,* 1976; *Northern Pipeline Construction Co.* v. *Marathon Pipe Line,* 1982; and *Commodity Futures Trading Commission* v. *Schor,* 1986).

Early Decisions

Less than three months after the statute went into effect, Judge Thomas Penfield Jackson issued a ruling for which many in Washington had been waiting. Of course it was clear that, whatever his decision, the losing side would seek to get the case to the U.S. Supreme Court as soon as possible. That is precisely what happened. Even so, it is useful to examine Jackson's decision.

Before Jackson could determine the merits of the legislators' constitutional challenge, other issues needed to be addressed. After all, the president had not yet employed his new authority to cancel appropriations. Thus the executive's argument was that there was no injury and hence no standing to bring suit. Even if there would be standing at some point, it was argued, the case was not yet ripe for adjudication because nothing had yet been done under the statute. Finally, even if the court might satisfy the technical requirements of a live case or controversy, it might use its discretion to avoid ruling on the matter at that time.

Jackson had no difficulty finding standing, because in his view the line-item veto had infringed upon the legislators' basic law-making power. The mere existence of the law forced legislators to contemplate appropriations legislation differently because they had to proceed with the recognition that the language on which they voted would not necessarily define the ultimate nature of the appropriation.

As to the ripeness claim, the argument was that any ruling made before the president had actually cancelled an appropriation would amount to an advisory opinion. The same kind of argument had been made when the Gramm-Rudman-Hollings deficit-reduction act was challenged. Jackson replied that, as in the *Bowsher* v. *Synar* (1986) Gramm-Rudman case, there was no reason to wait, because the mere existence of the law altered the legislative authority of the members, and because the issues present were issues of law and not fact-dependent. According to Jackson, there was nothing speculative about the challenge that the six legislators had brought against the line-item veto.

Jackson had little difficulty disposing of the argument that he ought to use his discretion to avoid the case. For one thing, he pointed out, this statute, like the earlier Gramm-Rudman law, encouraged legislators to bring challenges to the new provision [2 U.S.C. 692(a)(1)]. The practical reason for encouraging a challenge, regardless of how that challenge might evolve, was that there was a danger of allowing too much time and too many decisions to pass before a thorough judicial review was carried out. If the law was to be struck in whole or in part, it was better to have that happen before a range of decisions had been made under the new procedure that would be difficult to undo at a later point.

In constitutional terms, the legislators' case asked whether the statute violated the presentment clause of Article I or whether the line-item veto statute represented an abdication of the Congress' Article I responsibility. Jackson concluded that whether a president likes a piece of legislation or not is irrelevant. What matters is whether he elects to sign the statute into law or reject it by returning it to the legislature with the administration's objections. There is no provision in the Constitution for approval or disapproval of any portion of a piece of legislation. For the president to assert such an authority is to exceed the executive power and become a lawmaker outside the process prescribed by Article I that ensures that legislation will be addressed by both houses. The line-item veto permits the chief executive to modify legislation unilaterally.

Jackson also concluded that the decision by Congress to delegate that power to the president was unlawful. What Congress did, he said, was "give away the power to shape the content of a statute of the United States" (*Byrd* v. *Raines*, 1997, p. 8). This abandonment of its constitutional role "has turned the constitutional division of responsibilities for legislating on its head" (p. 9).

The Supreme Court

In an opinion by Chief Justice William Rehnquist, the Supreme Court sent the case back to the district court with orders to dismiss it on grounds that, at least as the case stood at that point, the legislators had been unable to demonstrate a real injury or show that they had been specifically and personally injured. The opinion of the chief justice suggests that it would be unlikely that the legislators would be able to meet the standing requirements even if the president had taken action under the statute. Justice David Souter, however, joined by Justice Ruth Bader Ginsburg, argued that it was wholly appropriate for the Court to wait for a presidential action when it would very likely be the case that private parties would be able to present a much better standing argument. Justices John Paul Stevens and Stephen Breyer dissented.

Clearly, the case will come back to the Court, although possibly with different plaintiffs. Whichever way the Court moves on the case, there will be significant implications for an understanding of separation of powers, the new balance in the continuing tension between the executive and the legislature in terms of primacy in fiscal policy, as well as implications for the specific budgetary processes. It matters that there is a record and a lower court decision as well as a Supreme Court response, and they will affect the course of action in the future. Just because there was no quick and definitive ruling on the merits of the case by the Supreme Court should not be misunderstood to mean that nothing important happened. The nature of the arguments to be presented are evident. The briefs are a matter of public record. The approach of the district court has been published and some of the divisions within the Supreme Court are already apparent. The point here is not to resolve the substantive arguments about the veto itself but to demonstrate that when these issues reach a court they take on a life of their own. Thus, it matters whether a court takes a case and how the issues get defined in the course of the litigation. The decision by the Supreme Court will not likely be remembered because of its importance in budgetary terms, yet the decision to deny in very broad terms the standing of legislators to bring such cases is an important one that can be expected to change the nature of legislative debate in future arguments about fiscal processes.

CONTROL OF THE COSTS OF GOVERNMENT OPERATIONS

Although the importance of the challenges to the line-item veto are obvious, many kinds of decisions are rendered by a variety of courts that affect the cost of governance apart from those that speak directly to budgetary process and control. These decisions present issues of both direct and indirect costs for government operations. One example of the former came in a 1994 ruling on limits on development in the city of Tigard, Oregon, a southwestern suburb of rapidly growing Portland. The Supreme Court's opinion in *Dolan* v. *City of Tigard* (1994) significantly shifted the burden of proof from the property owner to the local governments, both legally and in fiscal terms, in cases that challenge local government efforts to control growth.

Tigard's Plan and Florence Dolan's Ideas

In 1991, Oregon, growing rapidly like a number of other states, adopted legislation mandating comprehensive land-use planning. Under that law, Tigard was required, like all other cities and counties in the state, to present a new comprehensive land-use plan. The city created its Community Development Code (CDC).

Among the provisions in the CDC were special requirements for those who owned property in the central business district. One of the restrictions was a 15 percent open space requirement, which meant that all buildings and parking for any property could not occupy more than 85 percent of the parcel of land involved. Further, a city transportation planning study had determined that there was a serious problem in the increase in traffic and that pedestrian pathways and bicycle paths could significantly reduce the problem if residents and customers could be encouraged to use them as alternatives to automobiles. Thus the community also required that any new development proposals must provide for a dedication of land under a pedestrian and bicycle pathway plan. In addition to these basic planning requirements, the city also now had a master drainage plan, which highlighted areas of flooding, risks for future flooding, and the problems associated with new pavement and other impervious surfaces likely to exacerbate flooding from Fanno Creek. The plan called for remedial actions in flood-prone areas, and restrictions on future development in the floodplain or on developments that might further increase the likelihood of flooding.

Florence Dolan sought to expand and diversify significantly her electrical and plumbing supply business, adding a number of related businesses to her existing store. That meant building up much of what was the undeveloped portion of her property and paving over a good deal of the rest to provide parking to replace the relatively modest gravel parking area at her current store. Moreover, a portion of the property to be developed was in the one-hundred-year floodplain.

The planning commission decided in favor of her permit request provided that she dedicate 10 percent of the parcel to a greenway and to floodplain protection, and that she add a fifteen-foot-wide piece along that floodplain area for a pedestrian and bicycle pathway. The land thus used would count toward the 15 percent requirement in the existing community development plan and the city would assume responsibility for the maintenance of the green space and pathway.

The city council agreed, but Dolan challenged the provision on grounds that she should not be held to the restrictions of the plan and that to do so constituted a taking of her property without just compensation, which was prohibited by the Fifth Amendment's takings clause as applied to the state and local governments through the Fourteenth Amendment. She lost, however, at the appeals board level, in the appellate court, and in the state supreme court. It was then that Dolan joined a growing number of people who were attempting to get cases concerning the concept of regulatory takings into the U.S. Supreme Court for decisions.

Historically, the courts have distinguished between burdens placed on property owners that resulted from regulation and those that actually involved the taking of property. Regulations do present costs and burdens for property owners, but they have been considered by the courts since at least the 1920s to be the price for the maintenance of the public interest. Takings of property for public use, however, such as the use of eminent domain to acquire rights-of-way for highways, clearly fall within the just compensation requirement of the Constitution. In the regulatory case, the general principle was that as long as the impact on the property was reasonably related to a legitimate public purpose and the decision process was not arbitrary and capricious, the property owner had little recourse.

During the 1980s, efforts were made to get rulings from courts that regulatory burdens on property should be considered takings unless they met a much higher standard. Indeed, the Supreme Court struck down California's Coastal Initiative, which had limited land uses, thus providing hope for some property owners, particularly westerners who were pressing the point, that there should be prohibitions against regulatory takings (*Nollan* v. *California Coastal Commission*, 1987). Then the Court ruled, in a case on the other end of the country, that South Carolina had gone too far in attempting to impose restraints on coastal development. In the process, the Court moved a good way toward the view, advocated by property rights groups, that unless the proposed use of the property posed what was in essence a nuisance—that is, something dangerous or destructive in itself—regulatory barriers to enjoyment of the potential value of the property should be treated as takings (*Lucas* v. *South Carolina Coastal Council*, 1992).

Shifting Burdens, Adding Cost, and Creating Uncertainty

The Dolan case sought to find out how far the Court was willing to go. In his opinion for the majority, Chief Justice Rehnquist may not have given the property rights advocates everything they had hoped for, but he gave them a good deal. The ruling in *Dolan* switched the presumption in favor of regulatory policies that were nonarbitrary and based on a comprehensive plan, and it required the community to shoulder the primary weight of justifying its decision with respect to any given piece of property. The Court also increased the level of proof required to demonstrate that it was indeed engaged in necessary regulation and not in fact taking the property for public use without just compensation.

The facts in the South Carolina and California cases were a great deal more extreme than the relatively common types of development requirements at issue in the Tigard case. After all, no one contested the conclusions that had been reached about the danger of flooding, about the need to address traffic problems, or about the role of the green space requirements. Nor had anyone disagreed with the findings that the construction and paving of the Dolan property would increase the likelihood of flooding, drainage problems, and greater traffic flow. If even this limited and very standard type of regulation was to be considered a taking, what kinds of regulations would not be so designated? And if the Tigard regulations, and presumably others like them across the nation, were to be treated as takings, how much would standard community development planning cost if the local governments were required to provide compensation to all affected property owners? Given the uncertainty produced by the three major takings rulings issued by the Court, how should prudent local government officials finance necessary infrastructure improvements required by private developers?

It is obvious to anyone with experience in local government, and to their counterparts at the state and federal levels, that the Dolan case presents a number of very immediate and important fiscal issues. It may not seem all that significant but the shifting of burden of proof and a raising of the bar to avoid what amount to condemnation proceedings means adding a heavy burden. But any number of other rulings are less obvious and seemingly at least more indirect in their impact.

Parents, School Districts, and the Meaning of a Free and Appropriate Public Education

Consider one such case involving what was once called the Education for All Handicapped Children Act but is now known in its amended form as the Individuals with Disabilities Education Act. The case in question is *Florence County School District Four* v. *Carter* (1993). Following a battle to end the segregation and inadequate education of children with special health needs, Congress enacted the Education for All Handicapped Children (EAHC) Act in 1975. The argument, which parents pursued first with some success in court (see *Pennsylvania Ass. for Retarded Children* v. *Commonwealth*, 1971; and *Mills* v. *Board of Education of the District of Columbia*, 1972) but more effectively in Congress, was that the traditional segregation of students with special needs into schools for the "disabled" or "retarded" was the same thing as the kind of segregation by race that had been outlawed in *Brown* v. *Board of Education of Topeka* (1954). The EAHC Act required a "free and appropriate public education" in the "least restrictive environment." More work was needed, however. After a number of implementation difficulties and a narrow interpretation of the meaning of the phrase "free and appropriate public education" by the Supreme Court (*Hendrick Hudson District Board of Education* v. *Rowley*, 1982), the legislature reauthorized and amended the statute, which is now known as the Individuals with Disabilities Education Act (IDEA). Among other things, there was a desire to be rid of the "handicapped" label and to have a more positive reference for the law.

Although the IDEA required a free and appropriate public education for children with special health needs, the question was how to determine in any given situation just what that requirement means. After all, parents naturally understand "appropriate" to mean whatever is necessary. School districts, local governments that provide the funds to support them, and state education departments often consider the types and costs of expenditures that are involved. Just how much support is made available and how decisions about levels of support are made vary from jurisdiction to jurisdiction. To ensure that those factors and concerns are brought together, the IDEA provides for a process to develop an individualized education plan (IEP) for each child. When properly done, the process requires the involvement of parents, educators, and such other clinical advisers as are necessary. Not surprisingly, however, there are times when the parties involved are not able to reach a consensus on the adequacy of a proposed IEP. The law also provides for an appeals process, ultimately involving a judicial review, should the parents wish to avail their family of that option.

Just such a dispute emerged when local school officials of the Florence County School District Number Four in South Carolina evaluated Shannon Carter, a ninth grade student who was found to have learning disabilities. The IEP provided that Shannon would be in regular classes but would also have three periods per week of individual instruction. In addition there would be a goal of four months' progress in reading and mathematics for the year. Shannon's parents challenged the IEP, removed her from the public school, and placed her in a private academy, where she remained for three years. They also continued their appeal of the IEP. Both local school officials and a state education department hearing officer issued decisions upholding the IEP developed at the public school.

The Trident Academy was not listed as an approved private school for placement by the state. It did not prepare IEPs, and some of its faculty were not state-certified teachers. Nevertheless, the Carters were pleased with the education Shannon received there. Trident, which specialized in educating children with special needs, boasted much smaller student-teacher ratios, with evaluations every four months instead of once a year, as had been the case in the public school. Shannon made considerable progress, advancing three years in her achievement levels in the three years she was a student there.

Who Decides and Who Pays?

While Shannon remained at Trident Academy, her parents took her case to federal court, challenging the state's IEP and demanding reimbursement for the costs of sending their daughter to the private school. Relying on the advice of a court-appointed expert, the district court found that the public school's IEP was inadequate. Notwithstanding that Trident Academy was not a state-approved institution and that it did not comply with all of the requirements in the IDEA statute, the court considered that it was in "substantial compliance with" the requirements of the law and that the Carter's were entitled to be reimbursed by the school district for their costs.

The Supreme Court unanimously upheld the decisions of the lower courts, rejecting the argument by local school authorities that such a reimbursement "puts an unreasonable burden on financially strapped local education authorities" (*Florence County School District Four* v. *Carter*, 1993, p. 293). In her opinion for the Court, Justice Sandra Day O'Connor argued that if that were true it was the school officials' own doing and not the law that was responsible.

There is no doubt that Congress has imposed a significant financial burden on states and school districts that participate in IDEA. Yet public educational authorities who want to avoid reimbursing parents for the private education of a disabled child can do one of two things: give the child a free appropriate education in a public setting or place the child in an appropriate private setting of the state's choice. This is IDEA's mandate, and school officials who conform to it need not worry about reimbursement claims (*Florence County School District*

Four v. *Carter,* 1993, p. 294). Besides, wrote Justice O'Connor, parents who take their children out of public schools and place them in private schools while they fight the IEP process take a risk that they may lose if they do not succeed on appeal. They get reimbursement only if they ultimately succeed in the appeals process and the court finds that the private school placement was proper. In the end, a federal court could refuse to provide full reimbursement if it found that the level of reimbursement was unreasonable.

Incentives, Disincentives, and Capabilities

Ironically, of course, it is parents with means who are in a position to take the risk of removing their child from the public schools and supporting them until a judicial ruling is ultimately issued on the question of the IEP's adequacy and on the reimbursement itself. These well-off parents are also the ones best able to sustain the effort and expense of the litigation. There are larger questions, however.

This case presents a situation in which the Supreme Court argues that it is not imposing a direct cost on the local government. Indeed, the local government itself is the body that decides what to do. In an environment in which neither the federal government nor many states fully fund the services that may be required under IDEA, and in which some of the communities may be relatively small, the obvious stress sometimes places children with special needs squarely in the middle of serious political battles over local taxes and expenditures. Clearly, local schools have a significant incentive under this ruling to provide the most extensive IEP possible to avoid the possibility of much higher private school costs should they ultimately lose on appeal. Thus they take a chance just as the parents do. The difficulty, of course, rests with the question of whether local governments have the wherewithal under current funding support to meet the challenge. There is also the question of what may happen if there is broad reaction against the IDEA statute on grounds that it ignores all other pressures on the community's tax burden.

COURTS, SCHOOLS, AND REMEDIAL ORDERS

The Carter case presents what is one of the less visible situations in which courts affect education spending and, by implication, the budgets of states and localities. Far more attention has been given over the years to cases in which courts have issued remedial orders to address segregation in schools or other kinds of constitutional violations in other public institutions, such as prisons (see Cooper, 1988; Di Iulio, 1990; Wood, 1990). Although there was a time in the 1960s and 1970s when federal courts seemed to have an expanding tendency to issue complex remedial orders to address institutional violations, that situation has changed, with the U.S. Supreme Court sending strong signals that courts should intervene less often, issue remedies that are more carefully tailored and less expansive if an injunction is required, and terminate supervisory jurisdiction sooner than before (see, for example, *Board of Education of Oklahoma City* v. *Dowell,* 1991; *Freeman* v. *Pitts,* 1992; *Wilson* v. *Seiter,* 1991). Many states and localities are still under remedial orders of various kinds that impose significant pressures on fiscal decision making. There is a pattern, however, of case law moving in to restrict some of those impositions.

One of these important recent rulings that admonishes courts to constrain injunctive relief is the 1995 ruling in *Missouri* v. *Jenkins.* In that decision, the Supreme Court warned that a district court cannot "accomplish indirectly what it admittedly lacks the remedial authority to mandate directly: the interdistrict transfer of students" (p. 19). In the Kansas City school desegregation case, the Court found that the wide-ranging orders concerning teacher pay raises, capital expenditures, and other programs exceeded the proper scope of the Court's remedial authority. Indeed, Chief Justice Rehnquist insisted that the district court judge must remember that he had two goals: to end the violation and to restore local control of the schools to the state and the city.

The Kansas City case had been before the district court since 1977 when the Kansas City, Missouri school district and a number of parents filed suit alleging that the city's schools had never been desegregated following the *Brown* v. *Board* ruling in 1954. At that time, the state and city had operated a legally segregated school system. The school district was also made a defendant by the district court, which eventually found both the state and the district in violation of the Supreme Court's desegregation rulings.

The district court found that the schools continued to be illegally segregated and that the segregation had resulted in a substandard educational opportunity for the city's students. At the time of the initial efforts to remedy these violations, twenty-five schools in the district enrolled more than 90 percent African American students. In fact, the district as a whole was 68.3 percent African American (*Missouri* v. *Jenkins,* 1995, p. 72). Under the Supreme Court's ruling in *Milliken* v. *Bradley* (1974), the district court could not include the suburbs in the desegregation remedy.

For these reasons the district court concluded that a series of programs for quality improvements in the city's schools was necessary to remedy the injury done to students as a result of the substandard education provided by the segregated school system. The court also held that only by ensuring enhanced quality and making the schools attractive to students in the surrounding suburbs would it be possible to bring some measure of integration to the city's schools. Such programs were extremely expensive, however. The cost exceeded $200 million by 1994 (*Missouri* v. *Jenkins,* 1995, p. 72). For example, the court ordered that all high schools and middle schools as well as half of the elementary schools had to be converted into magnet schools to attract students. There was no doubt that the physical quality of the schools had improved dramatically or that their programs were much superior to what they had been when the case began. However, even in the 1990s, the schools remained predominantly single-race.

In 1993, the district court ordered the state to pay for substantial salary increases and to continue the quality programs that had been in place since the mid-1980s. The state first challenged the authority of the judge to impose the pay raise on the grounds that it was an action not directly related to the legal violation to be remedied. It went further, however, and challenged the court's continued requirement for the financial support of the quality programs. The U.S. Circuit Court of Appeals for the Eighth Circuit upheld the district court's ruling.

The Supreme Court reversed the ruling. It found that the district court had failed to heed the Supreme Court's warnings that judges should carefully tailor the scope of remedial orders to the specific nature of the violation for which the remedial orders were issued. In this case, the Court said, that meant restoring the students to the position they would have occupied had the school system been operated in a lawful fashion (*Missouri* v. *Jenkins,* 1995, p. 81). The district court was attempting to use the quality programs to attract students from suburban districts, exceeding the intracity violation that had been found in the liability stage of the case. The judge could not use fiscal orders to create indirectly an interdistrict remedy when it would not have been within its authority to impose such a remedy directly. Neither was the court justified in asserting, in the absence of a clear showing that the current substandard performance was specifically attributable to the discrimination that had been the core of the case in the first instance, that quality programs had to be funded until city students reached national average levels on standardized test scores (pp. 88–89).

The four dissenting justices, led by Justice Souter, complained that it was Chief Justice Rehnquist and the other members of the Court's majority who were guilty of issuing a ruling far more sweeping in character than had been requested by the parties or justified by the record. For present purposes, however, the lesson that emerges is that the day of the unbridled remedial order is over. The Supreme Court has heard the complaints about the costs of such orders and is well along in a relatively consistent set of rulings warning district courts to constrain themselves and see as an important part of their goal the reduction of burdens on the community and a return of public institutions to normal political and administrative control. Unfortunately, the situation is not as simple as this prescription would suggest. It is still the case that numerous school districts have never actually been desegregated, and that there are correctional facilities that virtually all educated observers know are overcrowded and under-resourced.

THE COURTS AND RISK MANAGEMENT: THE LIABILITY ISSUE

The Carter, Dolan, and Jenkins cases not only present questions of direct and indirect costs (in the general sense of those terms) that emanate from judicial rulings but also raise risk management concerns. There are a number of ways in which court decisions make public managers think about fiscal risk and exposure (see Jenkins and Kearl, 1997). Certainly that has been true for years in such matters as tort liability judgments. Two recent cases, however, demonstrate that in the contemporary environment issues of risk are often intertwined with other complex problems, particularly privatization and intergovernmental relations.

Risk Management and the Public-Private Issue

Certainly few topics have generated more heated debate in recent years than the question of privatization. In truth, of course, the discussion is usually not really about privatization if by that is meant the shedding of responsibilities by government that will presumably be picked up by the private sector. Rather, what is usually involved is the delivery of services by surrogates, private firms or not-for-profit organizations operating under contract with a government. Certainly one of the most hotly debated of these contract operations questions has been the issue of contractor-operated correctional facilities.

The key question in many contracted-out programs concerns accountability. For example, to what degree are prison guards employed by a profit-making corporation like public employees and how do they differ, if at all? A Supreme Court opinion in 1997 (*Richardson* v. *McKnight*) addressed that issue precisely.

Tennessee contracted with the Corrections Corporation of America, a for-profit corporation, to operate a number of its corrections facilities. A prisoner at one of them, Ronnie Lee McKnight, sued, charging two guards with physical abuse that violated his constitutional rights. Normally, state officials respond to such suits by claiming a qualified immunity based on the policy argument that if officials must always fear lawsuits they will never make decisions or rigorously exercise their authority out of fear that they will be forever in court. The district court and the court of appeals rejected the claim of immunity, however, and the case came to the U.S. Supreme Court for a ruling on whether an employee of a private firm doing the same job under contract as a public sector corrections officer should have the same immunity from suit as the public sector officer.

Writing for a 5–4 majority, Justice Breyer acknowledged that a prior ruling accepted that some contract employees might, under certain circumstances, be held accountable under federal civil rights law for torts they commit in the course of their duties (*Wyatt* v. *Cole*, 1992, p. 162). He did not find, however, that the same policy argument that had traditionally been applied to justify qualified immunity for public employees applied in the private sector case.

Justice Breyer began by rejecting a claim that a simply functional analysis should be applied. The mere fact that private sector corrections officers perform the same functions as their public sector counterparts is not sufficient to make the case. Rather, Justice Breyer wrote, "government employees typically act within a different system. They work within a system that is responsible through elected officials to voters who, when they vote, rarely consider the performance of individual subdepartments or civil servants specifically and in detail. And that system is often characterized by multidepartment civil service rules that, while providing employee security, may limit the incentives or the ability of individual departments or supervisors flexibly to reward, or to punish, individual employees" (*Richardson* v. *McKnight,* 1997, p. 551). Thus the mechanisms used for accountability and the nature of the incentives and disincentives used in the public and private sectors differ. In that ambiguous public context, Justice Breyer argued, public policy considerations support an immunity for public employees that is not essential for the employees of a contractor.

In fact, Justice Breyer argued, two factors differ particularly from the private sector to the public sector context. First, "competitive pressures mean not only that a firm whose guards are too aggressive will face damages that raise costs, thereby threatening its replacement, but also that a firm whose guards are too timid will face threats of replacement by other firms with records that demonstrate their ability to do both a safer and a more effective job" (*Richardson* v. *McKnight,* 1997, p. 550). Second, the Court concluded that the requirement that the firms have sufficient insurance coverage to address potential liabilities removes whatever tendencies might exist to avoid energetic performance of duties (p. 151).

Writing for the four dissenters, Justice Antonin Scalia demanded to know why the functional analysis should not be applied. He argued that the majority had failed to explain exactly what makes the public and private guards different from one another. The dissenters saw in this case the possibility that it would make privatization of prisons more expensive and that it might "cause privatization to be prohibitively expensive" (p. 559).

Notwithstanding Justice Scalia's criticism, there is no reason to assume that Justice Breyer's opinion is an intentional attack on privatization as such. It raises as many questions as it answers, however, particularly because the majority warned that its opinion should be read narrowly. Clearly, the *McKnight* case raises a variety of issues that must be addressed by governmental units operating or anticipating contract services. For one thing, the Court's use of market arguments begs the question of whether similar logic would apply if the contractor were a not-for-profit organization providing, say, services for juveniles placed under care by the state for mental health reasons. These arguments also demonstrate that when judges make economic arguments, those arguments may not be recognizable in mainstream economic thought.

One of the related concerns has to do with who will make decisions about defending the private firms or their employees. It is the case, of course, that state attorneys general or local governments and their insurers make important strategic and tactical judgments in the course of determining when and how to defend. It is clear that the cost of legal services make up an important part of the risk calculations.

Risk Management and the Federalism Issue

The discussion of risk assessment is also complex when it is related to issues of sovereign immunity. The Court's 1996 ruling in *Seminole Tribe* v. *Florida* provides a recent case in point. This case arose from a dispute between the Seminoles and the state of Florida over the Indian Gaming Regulatory Act of 1988.

The 1980s saw widespread discussion about gambling on Native American lands, fueled in part by the concerns of state governments that feared the consequences of casino gambling and wanted to block its development in their states. To this fear was added anxiety about possible diversion of money that might otherwise go to state lotteries into casino gambling. There was also political pressure from communities that were developing riverboat gambling and other competing enterprises. The statute reaffirmed the right of Indian nations to develop gaming facilities, but it also provided a process through which states and tribes could address their differences.

The statute requires the state to "negotiate with the Indian tribe in good faith" (*Seminole Tribe* v. *Florida,* 1996, p. 262) to develop a tribal-state compact that will govern the gaming activities. If a state fails to do so, the tribe is authorized under the statute to bring suit in federal court. Once the tribe proves that it offered a proposed agreement and the state failed to respond in good faith, the burden shifts to the state to justify its behavior. If the court finds in favor of the tribe, it can order the state and tribe to complete a compact within sixty days. If the court fails to reach an accord, the parties go to mediation. The mediator selects the best draft compact under the terms of the statute and the state has sixty days in which to approve it. If the state refuses, the matter is then referred to the secretary of the interior, who prescribes a set of gaming guidelines.

The Seminole tribe sued the state and its governor, but the state promptly moved to dismiss the suit on grounds of sovereign immunity. The court of appeals ruled in favor of the state, concluding that the state did enjoy sovereign immunity under the Eleventh Amendment to the Constitution notwithstanding the fact that Congress clearly intended to abrogate the state's immunity. After all, Congress is given the authority under Article I, Section 8, to "regulate Commerce with foreign Nations, and among the several States, and with the Indian tribes." Moreover, the supremacy clause of Article VI states that "this Constitution, and the Laws of the United States which shall be made in Pursuance thereof; and all Treaties made, or which shall be made, under the Authority of the United States, shall be the supreme Law of the Land; and the Judges in every State shall be bound thereby, any Thing in the Constitution or Laws of any State to the Contrary notwithstanding."

There was no question that Congress intended to use the power of its commerce clause to supersede state authority, and that it specifically intended to make states subject to suit if they violated the statute. Florida's argument was that Congress did not have the authority to abrogate the state's immunity.

This case was fought out within the Court on two very different levels. It was ostensibly a relatively focused and specialized argument over a relatively arcane field of law, the resolution of disputes between states and Native American communities over the boundaries of control of gambling. As he had in many other situations, however, Chief Justice Rehnquist saw this case as an opportunity to make sweeping assertions that constrained congressional power with respect to the states. He did precisely that, though not without strong opposition by four members of the Court whose blistering dissents highlighted the obviously ideological character of the majority opinion.

Rehnquist reached back to a very bad ruling of a century earlier, ignoring numerous rulings before and since that argued against his position. Even with that selective reading of constitutional doctrine, Rehnquist had to address at least one direct precedent that maintained that Congress could, under its commerce clause authority, abrogate state immunity claims. He tried to suggest that the portion of the commerce clause that addressed Indian tribes was somehow different from the rest of the clause, but his broad purposes required him to reach further and overrule the precedent.

In the end he argued that Congress had no such authority under the commerce power, and in fact under no other provision of the Constitution except the Fourteenth Amendment, which he said specifically empowered Congress to act more broadly with respect to control over the states. Moreover, he went beyond merely applying immunity for the state itself, but he also refused to apply clear precedent that holds that state officials are answerable for suits that call for prospective relief in cases of violation of federal law.

As Justice Stevens observed, the significance of the opinion reaches far beyond the Indian gaming question. "Rather, it prevents Congress from providing a federal forum for a broad range of actions against States, from those sounding in copyright and patent law, to those concerning bankruptcy, environmental law, and the regulation of our vast national economy" (*Seminole Tribe* v. *Florida,* 1996, p. 280). Justice Souter wrote for three dissenters in an extremely forceful demonstration of the dangers and deficiencies of Rehnquist's opinion.

He began by observing that "the Court today holds for the first time since the founding of the Republic that Congress has no authority to subject a State to the jurisdiction of a federal court at the behest of an individual asserting a federal right" (p. 294). He ended by pointing out that not only does such a ruling fly in the face of the clear intentions of the constitutional framers but it also is contrary to a string of Supreme Court rulings reaching at least as far back as the 1821 case *Cohens v. Virginia* (p. 346).

Regardless of the merits of the Court's opinion, the fact is that this case holds the potential of significantly altering the ways in which states and their officials can be sued. The true nature of its impact will take some years to determine as both the states and the federal government decide how to respond.

Federalism and Control of the Costs of Government

The Seminole opinion is only one of a host of decisions on federalism over the past decade or more that have significantly changed what was commonly assumed to be a near complete dominance by the national government in virtually all fields.

There is often a tendency to view these cases either as policy-specific questions, such as whether the federal government could relate gun controls to the operation of public school systems (*United States v. Lopez*, 1995), or as part of an ongoing conversation about federalism in broad terms. The rulings in these case often have a great deal to do with the discretion over use of resources that different levels of government possess. The widely publicized ruling in the Brady Handgun Violence Prevention Act case is one such instance (*Printz v. United States*, 1997).

Although much of the publicity associated with this case presented the argument as a question of whether the national government had the power to impose gun control, the issue on which the case was argued was quite different. Under the Brady Act as amended, state and local law enforcement officers were to conduct background checks on prospective purchasers of handguns. Sheriffs from Arizona and Montana challenged the law on grounds that the federal government could not force them to play a role in the enforcement of federal law, arguing that the law had in effect "pressed [them] into federal service" (*Printz v. United States*, 1997, p. 925). A sharply divided Supreme Court agreed by a 5–4 majority.

The Brady case was the second of two cases that have made related though somewhat different arguments in recent years. The first case was decided in 1992. The state of New York challenged the congressional policy governing the management of low-level nuclear waste, a design that had in fact been suggested by a significant number of states. The law had required that states that were unwilling to enter into interstate compacts with their neighbors for the creation of regional waste sites would have to adopt waste disposal regulation programs in their own state. The Court agreed that Congress certainly had the power to regulate the nuclear waste, but it insisted that it did not have the power to force the states to use their regulatory authority (*New York* v. *United States,* 1992). In *Printz,* the Court extended that ruling:

> We held in New York that Congress cannot compel the states to enact or enforce a federal regulatory program. Today we hold that Congress cannot circumvent that prohibition by conscripting the States' officers directly. The Federal Government may neither issue directives requiring the States to address particular problems, nor command the States' officers, or those of their political subdivisions, to ad-minister or enforce a federal regulatory program. It matters not whether policy-making is involved, and no case-by-case weighing of the burdens or benefits is necessary; such commands are fundamentally incompatible with our constitu-tional system of dual sovereignty [*Printz* v. *United States,* 1997, pp. 944–945].

The national government may still add conditions to grants and it may regulate directly, but it cannot require the states and localities to do so. For a national government accustomed to an intergovernmental pattern for policy implementation that has been used widely over the past quarter-century, this ruling presents reason for serious reflection about just how the work of government under the host of existing policy mixes will now be accomplished.

TOWARD A BETTER UNDERSTANDING OF LAW IN THE FISCAL DECISION ENVIRONMENT

What should be apparent from the discussion of this sample of opinions from recent years is some sense of the variety of ways in which judicial rulings affect the general decision environment within which fiscal officers and public managers must live and work. It is also obvious from this sample that the rulings are not uniformly positive or negative in fiscal terms, but like most other kinds of governmental actions they are complex. Some provide protections while others increase exposure. They are also like other important factors in the public sector decision environment in that they arise within and affect a complex intergovernmental reality (see the line of cases from *National League of Cities* v. *Usery,* 1976, to *Garcia* v. *San Antonio Metropolitan Transit Authority,* 1985).

It is true that some decisions, such as the line-item veto litigation, directly address the budgetary process. But even in that case, the nuances may be just as important as the issues or the merits might suggest. For example, the discussion by the majority in the Supreme Court's ruling in *Raines* v. *Byrd* makes a variety of interesting observations about the role and rights of individual legislators in the appropriations process. Further, the fact that the Court chose to duck the issue, even though it was clear that the case would be back in the future and even though a similar case in the past (*Bowsher* v. *Synar,* 1986) had been decided in very much the same posture as the line-item veto challenge, has importance consequences and provides an interesting perspective on the nature of the debate. Important enough to hear on an expedited appeal process, the Court nevertheless was willing to let a budget year move through the entire appropriation cycle without providing an interpretation. The arguments raised in the district court and in the Supreme Court also provide a kind of primer on what to expect when the issue returns to the Court.

Apart from those few cases that address the fiscal process directly, the brief set of examples provided earlier indicates that a wide range of judicial opinions affect fiscal matters. Thus the decisions about privatization, regulatory takings, liability exposure, implementation of the IDEA, and regulatory federalism seem to be about topics other than fiscal issues, but they clearly resulted in important decisions with both direct and indirect impact on the financing of government.

It should be clear from this brief study that it is important for those concerned with fiscal matters in the public sector to understand that courts are important and continuing participants in the ongoing conversation about budgetary decisions at all levels. If a fiscal decision maker is to be fully informed, he or she must integrate that fact into the decision calculus. To do that, it becomes necessary, of course, to pay greater attention to the rulings that issue from courts that affect one's jurisdiction or agency. Although such attention requires effort, it is not as difficult as it may at first appear, because there are any number of ways to use the World Wide Web to access recent rulings in summary or in full text. For example, Cornell Law School's Legal Information Institute not only operates pages that access U.S. Supreme Court information, but also provides summaries of important and newsworthy cases from the past year from around the country in an easy-to-use summary format with links to full opinions. The *Public Administration Review* recently launched a series of short articles on cases of interest to public managers. Information can also be obtained by monitoring summary pieces in journals or by following up when a trade publication makes brief mention of a recent opinion. The process would be assisted by a return by some journals to the practice of publishing annual summary articles of judicial actions that promise important impacts for fiscal officers. These outlets provide ways of smoothing out the very uneven manner in which these opinions emerge over time.

It is also important to consider the rulings coming from courts with the same kind of sensitivity to nuance that a fiscal manager would bring to any other aspect of the decision environment. It is not enough to listen to the formal pronouncements of courts or to look only to the narrow holdings in the cases. One must also pay attention to the arguments that the courts present to support their rulings, as well as to the true scope and character of their rulings. Thus, the true importance of the Seminole case and the Brady bill opinions does not rest in their conclusions about gambling or gun control but in what they say about federalism and its relationship to fiscal matters and risk.

Just as other administrators must pay attention to fiscal decision makers as important participants in the process of public management, so fiscal actors must dispose of the idea that judges are outsiders and see them instead as regular participants in the fiscal conversation. It is true that fiscal officers are pressed for time and energy, but the same is true of generalist public managers, who must make time in their busy schedules to stay informed on fiscal issues.

Cases Cited

Amalgamated Meat Cutters and Butcher Workmen of North America v. *Connally*, 337 F.Supp. 737 (D.C.C. 1971).

Board of Education of Oklahoma City v. *Dowell*, 498 U.S. 237 (1991).

Bowsher v. *Synar*, 478 U.S. 714 (1986).

Brown v. *Board of Education of Topeka*, 347 U.S. 483 (1954).

Buckley v. *Valeo*, 424 U.S. 1 (1976).

Byrd v. *Raines*, Memorandum and Order, Civil No. 97-0001 (TPJ) (D.D.C. 1997).

City of Los Angeles v. *Coleman*, 397 F.Supp. 547 (D.D.C. 1975).

City of New Haven v. *United States*, 634 F.Supp. 1449 (D.D.C. 1986); aff'd 809 F.2d 900 (D.C.Cir. 1987).

Cohens v. *Virginia*, 19 U.S. 264 (1821).

Commodity Futures Trading Commission v. *Schor*, 478 U.S. 833 (1986).

Dames & Moore v. *Regan*, 453 U.S. 654 (1981).

Dolan v. *City of Tigard*, 129 L.Ed.2d 304 (1994).

Florence County School District Four v. *Carter*, 510 U.S. 7 (1993).

Freeman v. *Pitts*, 503 U.S. 467 (1992).

Garcia v. *San Antonio Metropolitan Transit Authority*, 469 U.S. 528 (1985).

Hendrick Hudson District Board of Education v. *Rowley*, 458 U.S. 176 (1982).

Immigration and Naturalization Service v. *Chadha*, 462 U.S. 919 1983).

Independent Gasoline Markets Council v. *Duncan*, 492 F.Supp. 614 (D.D.C. 1980).

Lucas v. *South Carolina Coastal Council*, 120 L.Ed.2d 798 (1992).

Marbury v. *Madison*, 5 U.S. 137 (1803).

Milliken v. *Bradley*, 418 U.S. 717 (1974).

Mills v. *Board of Education of the District of Columbia*, 348 F.Supp. 866 (D.D.C. 1972).

Missouri v. *Jenkins*, 132 L.Ed2d 63 (1995).

Mistretta v. *United States,* 488 U.S. 361 (1989).

Morrison v. *Olson*, 487 U.S. 654 (1988).

National Association for Mental Health v. *Califano*, 717 F. 2d 1451 (D.C. Cir. 1983).

National Council of Community Mental Health Centers v. *Weinberger*, 361 F.Supp. 897 (D.D.C. 1973).

National League of Cities v. *Usery*, 426 U.S. 833 (1976).

New York v. *United States*, 505 U.S. 144 (1992).

Nollan v. *California Coastal Commission*, 483 U.S. 825 (1987).

Northern Pipeline Construction Co. v. *Marathon Pipe Line*, 458 U.S. 50 (1982).

Pennsylvania Association for Retarded Children v. *Commonwealth*, 334 F.Supp. 1257 (EDPA 1971).

People ex rel. Bakalis v. *Weinberger*, 368 F.Supp. 721 (NDIL 1973).

Printz v. *United States*, 138 L.Ed.2d 914 (1997).

Raines v. *Byrd*, 138 L.Ed.2d 849 (1997).

Richardson v. *McKnight*, 138 L.Ed.2d 540 (1997).

Seminole Tribe v. *Florida*, 134 L.Ed.2d 252 (1996).

Train v. *New York*, 420 U.S. 35 (1975).

United States v. *Lopez*, 131 L.Ed.2d 626 (1995).

Wilson v. *Seiter*, 501 U.S. 294 (1991).

Wyatt v. *Cole*, 504 U.S. 158 (1992).

References

Cooper, P. J. *Hard Judicial Choices.* New York: Oxford University Press, 1988.

DiIulio, J. *Courts, Corrections, and the Constitution: The Impact of Judicial Intervention on Prisons and Jails.* New York: Oxford University Press, 1990.

Fisher, L. *Constitutional Dialogues.* Princeton, N.J.: Princeton University Press, 1988.

Gore, A., Jr. *From Red Tape to Results: Creating a Government That Works Better and Costs Less.* Report of the National Performance Review. Washington, D.C.: Government Printing Office, 1993.

Jenkins, B., and Kearl, R. "Problems of Discretion and Responsibility." In P. J. Cooper and C. Newland, *The Handbook of Public Law and Administration.* San Francisco: Jossey-Bass, 1997.

Lauth, T. P., and Cooper, P. J. "Legal Impacts on Budgets and Finance: Anticipating Problems and Reacting to Realities." In P. J. Cooper and C. Newland, *The Handbook of Public Law and Administration.* San Francisco: Jossey-Bass, 1997.

Osborne, D., and Gaebler, T. *Reinventing Government: How the Entrepreneurial Spirit Is Transforming the Public Sector from Schoolhouse to Statehouse, City Hall to the Pentagon.* Reading, Mass.: Addison-Wesley, 1992.

Wood, R. *Remedial Law.* Amherst: University of Massachusetts Press, 1990.

PART SIX

POLITICS, MANAGEMENT, AND ANALYSIS IN BUDGETING

CHAPTER TWENTY-ONE

Cutback Budgeting

James D. Savage
Herman M. Schwartz

During the 1970s the financial plight of a number of urban areas, particularly New York and other northeastern cities, prompted the study of what have been called *fiscal stress* and *cutback budgeting*. In its simplest interpretation, cutback budgeting refers to reducing spending, increasing revenues, and changing budgetary processes to meet fiscal constraints. Moreover, it is a subset of a broader response to fiscal stress called *cutback management* (Levine, 1978). Although various analysts have elaborated on this simple definition, cutback budgeting and cutback management typically refer to real and perceived revenue constraints, and to the actions taken by politicians and agency managers to cope with these reductions in resources.

Although the terms *fiscal stress* and *cutback budgeting* were initially applied to America's cities, since that time every level of government in the United States, as well as in most countries throughout the world, has experienced fiscal constraints that have forced significant changes in budgeting practices, financial management, the administration of public services, and even in the expectations of what the proper responsibilities of government are in society.

Before examining cutback budgeting in more detail, it is worth noting that both the academic study and the practice of budgeting have confronted resource scarcity in virtually all times and places. Rarely, if ever, have politicians and managers had access to all the revenues they thought necessary to meet various demands and needs. Perhaps only during the Gilded Age of the 1880s, with its huge budget-surplus-producing tariffs, or during the 1960s, with its rapid economic growth, has the federal government truly been awash with excess funds. In most other years, governments have been significantly exercised in their attempts to balance budgets and perhaps provide for a small rainy-day surplus.

In one of the worst years of the Great Depression, for example, Clarence Ridley and Orin Nolting (1933) offered a practical guide entitled *How Cities Can Cut Costs* at a meeting of the International City Manager's Association in Chicago. The two authors were heavily influenced by the Progressive movement's emphasis on strong mayors and managers, and by the routinized search for efficiency associated with scientific management and performance budgeting. After calling for administrative centralization, they identified economies in every major governmental activity. In the case of refuse collection, for example, they urged that "costs should be studied to determine the most economical area of collection, the best route lay-out, and the most efficient combination of men and equipment" (p. 16). Despite the shift by some governments from performance to program and other reformed budgetary processes, many of Ridley and Nolting's recommendations would be echoed forty years later. Their preference for depoliticized ways to administer public programs cheaply also resonates in today's administrative environment.

Budgeting, therefore, has always been about the possibility of cutting, reallocating, rationing, and making priorities in the use of funds. Budgeting has also involved managers' creatively searching for new revenues and, as Aaron Wildavsky (1964) and more recently Jones and Euske (1991) described, employing strategies to defend their existing resources while perhaps asking for a little bit more funding. All of these elements may be found in what has come to be called cutback budgeting.

At the same time, however, cutback budgeting is qualitatively different from budgeting in other times. For one thing, *cutback* implies that agencies have become accustomed to growth in revenues and spending, and that significant adjustments in process, organization, and politics are required to address a new fiscal regime. In this sense, the era of cutback budgeting is generally compared to the mid-1960s, when a healthy economy and a relatively generous federal government aided state and local governments through revenue sharing plans. Also, cutback budgeting usually refers to conditions in which cuts are more than small marginal changes, in which fiscal stress demands deep reductions in spending and tight constraints on revenues.

DEFINITION OF FISCAL STRESS

Cutback budgeting is generally regarded as a response to fiscal stress, but what exactly is meant by fiscal stress varies among observers. In her review of cutback budgeting, Naomi Caiden (1990) expressed concern that scholars had failed to reach agreement on what truly constitutes fiscal stress, and practitioners often viewed it as little more than the need for additional revenues. Meanwhile, Allen Schick (1980) and Roy Bahl (1990) pointed out that even a balanced budget may not constitute a proper indicator of fiscal health. Indeed, despite contemporary reports of large budget surpluses at both the municipal and state levels, with an estimated $14.2 billion accumulated by state governments in 1997, many of these governments have put themselves in the black only after many painful years of deep budget cuts and program reductions.

Moreover, there are degrees of scarcity, each with its own set of problems and responses. Schick recommended looking at a government's ability and willingness to borrow, tax, and obtain other revenues, as well as its perceived need to spend. Bahl noted that some measures of government deficits and surpluses, such as the National Income Accounts, create distortions because they aggregate data. Better objective measures, he suggested, include bond and credit ratings. In a review of eight of these measures and studies of urban fiscal health conducted during the late 1970s and early 1980s, including Standard & Poor's ratings and the Department of Housing and Urban Development's fiscal analyses, Bahl found that seventeen cities were identified in at least two of the surveys. Fifteen of these cities were located in the northeast or Midwest, which suggests that during this period urban fiscal stress reflected a broader regional problem.

In addition, a more subtle form of fiscal stress arises when governments have adequate aggregate resources for programs but cannot reallocate them to cope with shifting patterns of programmatic demand. In this situation, some programs may enjoy excess resources while others are severely cramped. Naturally, politically popular programs are hard to cut, while those with low political profiles cannot attract additional resources even when the programs need those resources to function properly.

Moreover, spending that traditionally has been classified as "uncontrollable," such as interest on public debt or entitlements, may significantly limit decision makers' ability to redistribute resources. Unfortunately, public debt costs typically rise with interest rates just in advance of recessions, and recessions also lead to more retirement and morbidity. As Pierson (1994) notes, universal entitlements are often the hardest programs to cut openly. Consequently, discretionary spending is usually what gets cut during periods of fiscal stress. Yet politicians have attempted covert attacks on entitlements during the last two decades, for example, by disguising cuts as changes in eligibility, such as raising the retirement age for social security, or as changes in inflation adjustments, as occurred in Canada, where the income level at which old age pension becomes taxable is adjusted for inflation by only an annual maximum of 3 percent.

CAUSES OF FISCAL STRESS

If fiscal stress may be identified by various objective measures, as well as by the perceived needs of politicians and managers, what are its origins? Stress has both socioeconomic and political origins, which often are present simultaneously, often interact, and often exacerbate each other. Depending on the specific government and the period analyzed, one source may be more important than others.

Socioeconomic Sources

Socioeconomic decline is characterized by a host of social and economic ills befalling a government. These ills include the economic decline of industrial bases, middle-class emigration, lower-class immigration, stagnant or shrinking tax bases, and increased demand for services; all of these maladies have seriously hurt many older urban areas (Muller, 1975; Levine, Rubin, and Wolohojian, 1981; Rubin, 1982; Pammer, 1990). The parallel international phenomenon is the erosion of domestic industrial bases through flight to low-wage, newly industrializing economies and the parallel in-migration of casualized workers (Sassen, 1988).

Exacerbating broad patterns of socioeconomic decline is the gradual shift of most economies toward services, which are harder to tax than industrial activity. Taxes on services have proved very difficult to enact in places as diverse as Florida, Japan, Canada, and Australia because of political resistance from the buyers and producers of such services. Furthermore, to the extent that many personal services are carried out on a cash basis, such taxes are also hard to implement administratively.

In contrast to secular declines in revenue, the business cycle also often causes fluctuations in public revenues and expenditures (Bahl, 1990). Because Chapter Seven in this volume, by Michael Wolkoff, discusses this in great detail, we will only note here that the revenue flows of subnational governments are strongly procyclical. International bond markets place similar constraints on the smaller European and Australasian economies. Only the U.S. federal government now has an unconstrained ability to fund cyclic additions to its deficits.

The political concern, bordering on obsession, with international economic competitiveness has also become a powerful justification for constraining government expenditures and revenues. Just as the private sector has undergone downsizing in an effort to enhance productivity, efficiency, and profits, so too has the public sector. Where deficit reduction was once seen as primarily promoting domestic economic health through reductions in domestic inflation and interest rates, cutting back government is now seen as enabling countries to improve their economic standing in the world in terms of credit ratings, access to global bond markets, and inward investment flows (Kennedy, 1987; Friedman, 1989; Sinclair, 1997). The concerns for competitiveness and for attracting investment have also led to tax cuts, which of course put further pressure on spending. In the most extreme cases, such as in Ontario, Canada, 20 percent cuts in income taxes were tied to similar cuts in spending. Because this kind of pressure is politically mediated, it is worth considering more political causes of fiscal stress.

Political Sources

Political sources of fiscal stress can be divided into three categories: the demand for public goods, the supply of public goods, and ideological pressures on the public sector.

On the demand side, public officials are often vulnerable to constituent and interest group demands for services, despite limited resources or a need to reallocate resources. Employee unions are particularly cited in U.S. urban settings and in national negotiations in other developed economies with strong social democratic movements. Moreover, the structure of government and particularly the work rules for government personnel may themselves produce expenditure inefficiencies while limiting the ability of officials and managers to control costs or redeploy resources (Meltsner, 1971; Stanley, 1972; Levine, Rubin, and Wolohojian, 1981; Ladd and Yinger, 1989).

Politicians also routinely shift costs to other jurisdictions while taking credit for expanding services or transfers. During the 1960s and 1970s, growth in federal transfer payments and grant programs encouraged state and local governments to expand their services and increase their expenditures (Sundquist, 1969; Derthick, 1970, 1975). Park (1994), for example, noted that central cities are particularly sensitive to changes in federal aid, while counties and suburbs respond more to state assistance. When these programs were cut in the 1980s, a valuable source of revenue for these governments was reduced (Nathan and Doolittle, 1983). Meanwhile, entitlements and mandates impose required costs on all levels of government (Weaver, 1988; Kettl, 1992).

The supply side of providing government services has often been characterized by a great variety of bureaucratic pathologies with either malign or benign causes, depending on the theoretical orientation of the analyst. Public choice theorists, for example, regard bureaucrats as revenue and expenditure maximizers (Downs, 1967; Niskanen, 1971; Meyer and Quigley, 1977). In this view, the inability to redeploy resources flows from bureaucrats who seek to expand their status and power by expanding their administrative authority and turf, and who actively resist redeployment.

Whereas rational choice theorists and their bureaucratic expansion models view public actors as self-interested and maximizing in their pursuits, the incompetent manager model sees politicians and public managers as often inept and unable to administer complex organizations. In some cases, as in Washington, D.C., a public agency such as the city school district may receive more than adequate resources, but incompetent management may drive the agency into the red (Stanley, 1976; Martin, 1982; Rubin, 1987; Curry, 1990; Powell, 1997).

Finally, the ideological transitions that occurred in developed countries during the 1970s greatly affected the policies and programs of the public sector. Conservative attacks on activist government have largely focused on public spending and taxing. Populist "tax rebellions," such as Denmark's 1973 "earthquake" election or California's Proposition 13, have restrained revenue growth, while similar efforts have capped expenditures through spending limits and balanced budget requirements. This kind of tax and expenditure legislation has crimped fiscal policy at all levels of government (Buchanan and Wagner, 1977; Wildavsky, 1980; Kemp, 1980). A politics of controlling deficits and restraining government, which was most visible during the Reagan Revolution, has dominated federal budgeting throughout the 1980s and 1990s (Savage, 1988; White and Wildavsky, 1989; Pierson, 1994). The core of this ideological transformation is a profound distrust of politicians and the political system, which is why these rebellions have proceeded through citizen referenda and have culminated in tax and expenditure legislation.

RESPONDING TO FISCAL STRESS: THE PRACTICE OF CUTBACK BUDGETING

Politicians and managers at every level of government have employed a variety of budgetary strategies and techniques in response to fiscal stress. These techniques are generally labeled *cutback budgeting*, which in its simplest interpretation refers to reducing spending, increasing revenues, and changing budgetary processes to meet fiscal constraints. Moreover, as noted earlier, cutback budgeting is a subset of a broader response to fiscal stress called cutback management (Levine, 1978).

Cutback budgeting was of course practiced before academics coined the term. In his study, for example, of how school districts manage and seek out additional revenue sources, Porter (1973) identified two strategies at work: *multipocket budgeting* and *marginal mobilizing.* When practicing multipocket budgeting, school administrators first employed those funding sources on which higher authorities had placed the greatest number of administrative restrictions or which were dedicated to specific uses. Meanwhile, funds with greater flexibility were saved for later use as unforeseen and unfunded contingencies arose. In marginal mobilizing, administrators focused their revenue raising efforts on the most likely sources of income. Schools that suffered from fiscal stress engaged in significantly different mobilizing activities than richer districts. Thus, both multipocket budgeting and marginal mobilizing constitute creative ways in which managers confronted constrained and shrinking resources.

The literature on local governments from the early 1970s also identified how managers engaged in privatization, outsourcing, and contracting among public entities as ways of responding to fiscal stress. Bish (1971) analyzed how local governments utilized these practices, and he noted that in order for these governments to cope with restrained resources they had to overcome the boundary problems associated with decentralization. One solution was shared agreements among public agencies that essentially centralized such financial decisions as purchasing while in the process preserving the bargaining rights of smaller governmental units.

The fundamental spending and revenue choices available to governments facing fiscal stress were outlined by Wolman (1980). Governments could reduce spending by cutting budgets according to object of expenditure, function, or program area, or by transferring functions, deferring spending, or defaulting. Revenues could be raised by increasing taxes and user fees, by liquidating assets, and by seeking revenue transfers from other governments. One question raised by Wolman was, What kinds of cuts are governments most likely to make given fiscal stress? In a summary of research he found that programs that were wholly locally funded would be the first to be trimmed, especially public works, parks and recreation, and sanitation.

The rules of cutting were also explored by Meltsner (1971), who found that budget analysts in local governments established their own lists of what should be cut. After following the incremental method of examining the previous year's spending, the analysts targeted the increment and then cut in the following order: personnel, equipment, previously cut items, new facilities, and departments with "bad" reputations. Still other researchers identified attempts at rationally prioritizing cuts. *Priority scaling,* for instance, is one technique that rank orders political and managerial preferences, thereby saving valued programs from reductions while intensifying cuts in other governmental activities (Algie, Mallen, and Foster, 1983).

In addition to these studies of agency and local-level decision making, the cutback literature produced broader interpretations of how fiscal stress influences budgeting practice and theory. In a series of three seminal articles, Schick (1983, 1986, 1988) assessed the theoretical consequences of fiscal stress in the form of decremental budgeting, microbudgeting adaptations at the level of administrative units, and macrobudgeting adaptations in national budgetary systems and processes.

For Schick, the fiscal stress of the 1970s and 1980s signaled the end of incremental budgeting as postulated by Wildavsky. Whereas incrementalism depended on budgetary growth for its familiar components of fair shares and growing budget bases, fiscal stress, Schick argued, changed the nature of budgeting and rendered the incremental model obsolete. In place of incremental growth, politicians and managers faced decremental reductions. Incrementalism was distributive in that claimants received a slice of an expanding pie; it was stable in its decision-making process; and it was calming in its effect on politics. Decrementalism was redistributive in that claimants fought for what they could get from a shrinking pie; it was unstable in its decision-making process; and it contributed to political conflict. Decrementalism shifted the focus of budgeting from the increment to the base. It thus changed the nature of politics from fights about distributing gains to fights over how to calculate the appropriate baselines and inflationary adjustments for a static budget. Depending on the outcome of political fights over the appropriate baseline, cuts could be made in discretionary spending rather than in the more politically untouchable entitlements, while programmatic eliminations could be avoided even in discretionary accounts in favor of across-the-board reductions.

The end of incrementalism was also reflected in the rise of new forms of budgeting, particularly zero-based budgeting (ZBB) and program budgeting (PPBS). Both ZBB and PPBS were intended to improve the choices of decision makers, particularly in light of constrained resources, by stripping the budget down into new decision elements, whether they be programmatic functions or "decision packages." Both reforms have experienced problematic results. The essence of ZBB, for example, requires recasting the budget into decision packages, with each package spelling out the goals, purposes, and financial requirements of the program. A common problem with ZBB, however, is determining the optimal number of packages. If packages are too small in that their programmatic and budgetary elements are too discrete, the number of such packages will overwhelm the decision makers; if the packages are too large, they may create overlapping programs, thus violating one of the purposes of ZBB. The time, resources, and extra paperwork generated by these reforms may cause decision makers to revert, consciously or not, to incrementalism (Novick, 1965; Hinrichs and Taylor, 1969; Broden, 1977; Worthley and Ludwin, 1979).

Schick's observations on micro and macro budgetary adjustments were based on widespread transformations taking place in western industrial countries, largely in response to fiscal stress. At the micro level, he identified many of the cutback techniques that had long been evident in the United States, namely budget freezes, across-the-board cuts, reduced hiring, marginal reductions in entitlements and transfer payments, raised user fees, the tightening of eligibility standards for program beneficiaries, the loosening of expenditure categories to enable greater flexibility, an increase in program analysis, and the rise of spending targets, sometimes in the form of target-based budgeting (Rubin, 1991). At the macro level, a number of European nations began to adopt many of the budgetary lessons that Americans had painfully learned in the effort to control federal deficit spending through budget resolutions and reconciliation. In particular, Schick pointed to a growing centralization of budgetary processes in which fiscal norms and targets, spending ceilings, baseline budgeting with its long-term focus on inflationary and programmatic costs, and multiyear budgeting all limited bottom-up pressures to increase spending. Moreover, in the preparation of national budgets, decisions were increasingly front-loaded in that fiscal targets, baselines, and spending limits greatly strengthened the role and power of finance ministers rather than agency ministers. Schick's observations were verified by von Hagen's study of European Community nations (1992), in which budgetary processes that centralized decision making in formal institutional terms, rather than simply depending on broad norms of budgetary control, became the necessary conditions for finance ministers to succeed in their efforts in cutback budgeting. Finally, both Schick and von Hagen noted the shift from national policies that promoted Keynesian-styled stabilization programs to ones favoring deficit control.

New proposals for budgetary reform, both in the United States and in Europe, continue this emphasis on processes that promote centralized control in conjunction with more operational autonomy. Vice President Gore's National Performance Review, for example, recommends a presidential budget resolution, biennial budgets and appropriations, and restrictions on congressional earmarked funding (Gore, 1993). Meanwhile, Congress granted to the executive branch the line-item veto, a potentially powerful tool in budgetary politics and spending control.

CUTBACK BUDGETING IN COMPARATIVE PERSPECTIVE

The new methods of cutback budgeting described by Schick and others are operationalized through four interrelated changes taking place in the public sector. These four changes have in common the introduction of practices usually associated with the hard budget constraints of the private sector (Schwartz, 1994). All of these processes are intended to reduce the ability of distributional coalitions based on interest groups, public sector unions, and concentrated interests within legislatures to impede budget reductions or reallocation of budget resources (Olson, 1982). They all place greater operational stress on managers, while sometimes compensating them through increased operational authority.

Because the pace and degree of change overseas has sometimes been greater than that in the United States, an analysis of these changes will encompass selected non-U.S. examples. In U.S. political parlance, cutting the budget generally means slowing the rate of growth of total expenditures. Elsewhere, cutback budgeting has often involved deep cuts in spending. In the most extreme case in Canada, the provincial budget of Alberta has been cut 20 percent in nominal terms from FY93–94 through FY96–97, and thus substantially more in real terms. The rapid migration of ideas such as public choice economics and of reinvention idea merchants such as Ted Osborne and David Gaebler across borders means that policy change in the United States is no longer isolated from broader world currents; Schick, for example, conducted a detailed survey of changes in New Zealand's budgeting practices in the mid-1990s that Washington think tanks rapidly incorporated into their solutions for controlling spending (Schwartz, 1994; O'Quinn, 1996).

Hard Budget Constraints

Hard budget constraints have been used at virtually all levels of government to slow the rate of growth of expenditure or to cut expenditures in response to revenue declines. These constraints—combinations of legislative and institutional changes—all limit the ability of politicians, cabinet or portfolio ministers, agency heads, and subagency management to exceed predetermined spending limits.

Constraints on Politicians

Eighteen U.S. states and four Canadian provinces have some form of legislative limit on the imposition of taxes, and more frequently on the growth of expenditures. In ten of the U.S. states these limits are constitutional; in the remaining states and in the Canadian provinces they are merely statutory. These laws generally limit spending to a defined fraction of per capita personal income in the state. These laws hinder the ability of politicians to fund agencies' budget overruns, even when this is politically desirable. They differ from balanced budget requirements in that they explicitly limit spending rather than simply mandating balance.

Many states and provinces have also adopted informal, cabinet-level practices that also constrain ministers' ability to expand their department's funding. These practices generally involve the creation of formal or informal cabinet subcommittees that have the final say on all spending and that act to redistribute resources across programs. These "inner" cabinets parallel the older, well-established use of nominally apolitical control boards or the city manager system at the municipal level. At the national or provincial level, for example, Australia, New Zealand, Alberta, British Columbia, and Ontario all have standing cabinet committees with central power over spending decisions. Of these, Alberta has the most interesting and elaborate system for disciplining politicians, and because this system has held up through four years of cutting at levels unheard of in the United States, it is worth examining briefly.

After election of a government committed to budget cuts in 1992, all ministries were told to prepare plans for two different levels of cuts, either 20 percent over four years or 40 percent over four years (Schwartz, 1997). All ministries were targeted for cutting, making it difficult for any one ministry or client group to claim that it was being unfairly targeted. A small priorities subcommittee within the cabinet then shuffled funds among programs on the basis of the programs' political and substantive importance. Education received the smallest cuts, followed by health, but everything else took deep cuts. The 40 percent scenarios prepared by other departments allowed their budgets to be deeply cut, but because cuts rarely approached the full 40 percent level, there was also some relief.

This budget exercise was linked to changes in the way ministries receive funds. The sixteen ministries are grouped by function under four standing policy committees (SPCs). SPCs are chaired by backbenchers (members not in leadership positions), membership is open to any backbencher, and majority vote prevails. Because many backbenchers were elected on promises of spending cuts and no tax increases, they have had an incentive to scrutinize department budgets and force cuts in order to be able to claim to voters that they have delivered on their campaign promises. The SPC structure allows backbenchers to gang up against specific ministers to force them to stick to their original budget targets by cutting what appear to be either politically or substantively marginal or unnecessary programs. The SPC system isolates ministers as spenders while converting the much larger number of backbenchers from individuals all seeking a share of the budgetary pie into a group with a common interest in disciplining spenders. Ministers meanwhile act as watchdogs of other ministers through their participation in the SPCs that do not monitor their own particular department.

Tax and expenditure legislation and fiscal centralization are statistically associated with slower rates of per capita spending and lower interest costs for general obligation bonds. U.S. states with above average growth in spending have grown at below-average levels after tax and expenditure legislation has been passed, although the direction of causality is somewhat unclear (Poterba, 1994). The purpose of tax and expenditure legislation in cutback budgeting is to depoliticize the reallocation of budget shares allocation and to move the politics of relocation into the hands of a much smaller, strategically oriented group of politicians. Like the nominally apolitical control boards of U.S. cities, legislatures and inner cabinets have their own clients.

Recent research suggests that successful cutbacks are more likely to occur under conservative rather than liberal governments (Alesina and Perotti, 1995). Unsurprisingly, right-wing governments are more likely to cut spending to bring budgets into balance, while leftist governments are more likely to tax. Successful episodes of budget cutting in New Zealand, Denmark, Australia, Sweden, and elsewhere in Canada were all accompanied by the centralization of authority for the distribution of budget shares as was done in Alberta. In contrast, in the United States, where power over the budget lies in the legislature rather than in the cabinet, different institutional arrangements have been required to effect budgetary discipline. The Gramm-Rudman-Hollings legislation, for example, set upper limits on the spending of appropriations subcommittees by way of the 602a and 602b allocation process, thereby forcing zero-sum trade-offs on spending. These rules have promoted the centralization of budgeting, as has occurred in other countries (Savage, 1991).

Constraints on Agencies

The centralization of allocational authority over budgets into inner cabinets has been paralleled by a decentralization of operational authority to agencies. Basically, the trade-off here involves giving agencies hard, fixed budgets but shifting from strict control over inputs to a focus on agency outputs through performance-based budgeting. The British Financial Management Initiative of 1982 is the first modern incarnation of this system.

This form of budgetary control goes under various names, such as *mission driven, envelope, block,* or *global budgets* (Osborne and Gaebler, 1992). The idea, however, is simple. Agencies are given a block budget, or sometimes a block budget with subblocks for broad categories of expenditure such as "personnel-related" or "non-personnel-related" expenses, for the year. They may spend from this budget freely—input controls having been relaxed—but they may not come back to the central government for more money if they run out before the end of the fiscal year. This method shifts the risks of cost overruns from the central budget to local managers.

The more subtle forms of block budgeting give agencies significant freedom to run themselves internally. Generally this involves decentralizing to agencies collective bargaining when it exists, as well as pay scales, job titles, and other personnel decisions such as hiring and firing. Many governments, however, retain control over hiring in order to prevent an expansion of public sector employees. Finally, agencies can sometimes carry over budget surpluses from year to year, which may smooth spending, encourage agencies to look for efficiencies, and reveal "slack" to central decision makers.

Block budgeting is sometimes associated with formal contracts between service providers and the relevant ministry or department. Budget resources are tied to the outputs specified in the contract. This kind of budgeting allows the center to substitute contracted out or privatized versions of service provision more easily, because it has already freed itself from any need to monitor anything more than contract performance and payment. Monitoring contracts involves costs and difficulties, of course. In New Zealand and other polities that have used contracting extensively, auditors general have seen their power and departments expand (Boston, 1995). At the same time, contracting out sometimes destroys an agency's ability to monitor contracts by eliminating personnel who have the specialized knowledge needed to monitor performance.

Block budgets also make it possible to use across-the-board cuts more effectively. In the past, making these cuts in the context of line-item budgets produced all manner of problems, as agencies found it impossible to shift money from one area to another, which produced a smaller-scale version of the reallocation problems the center faced. Furthermore, the pay freezes associated with across-the-board cuts demoralized the workforce. In contrast, block budgets make it difficult for agency managers to excuse their failures with reference to the center's overly burdensome regulation, supervision, or ignorance of the realities of personnel management. Instead, managers must allocate increasingly scarce resources between pay and other necessities. In turn, the center is able to excuse its budget cuts by saying that managers freed from tight input controls should be able to make their units operate more efficiently. In Australia in the 1980s, for example, uniform, preannounced annual budget cuts were labeled "efficiency dividends." The practice is widespread, albeit under different and less opaque names.

Block budgeting slides seamlessly into contracting out. This widespread phenomenon, practiced most extensively at the municipal level by Indianapolis, Philadelphia, and Phoenix, is only gradually spreading to other countries. If we compare countries that operate at a scale equivalent to these U.S. municipalities, however, contracting out sometimes rivals or exceeds these paradigmatic cases. For example, New Zealand and Victoria, Australia, both of which in population and economic terms are roughly the size of metropolitan Philadelphia, have extensively replaced internal public production with contracted or privatized services. When there are enough firms to support competitive tendering, competition tends to push down the real cost of services as wages, particularly for unskilled and semiskilled workers, are reduced and as permanent jobs are turned into part-time and other forms of contingent employment.

Constraints on Personnel

In many U.S. municipalities, as well as in the highly unionized national or provincial public services of many other industrialized countries, union work rules, centralized collective bargaining, and rigid pay scales have been accused of obstructing efficient use of government personnel or of making it difficult to hire high-quality skilled workers of all sorts from the private sector. In varying degrees, existing tenure, seniority, job classification, and uniform pay systems in the public sector have given way and managers have gained the power to hire and fire, to set fairly individual pay scales—including incentive pay—to set flexible work hours, and to determine individual job responsibilities. This change has extended to senior civil servants as well. These changes are paradoxically more prominent, however, in polities with relatively stable public sector budgets, and less salient in those in which simple privatization has occurred.

Thus British Columbia, for example, has maintained relatively stable budgets and public sector aggregate employment, in part because the use of enterprise bargaining, widespread redeployment and retraining of personnel, and limited incentive pay in effect gives the center the ability to redeploy resources. In Alberta and Ontario, by contrast, the provincial government has simply fired double-digit percentages of public employees, relieving pressure to get a more flexible workforce. In the United States, cities such as New York, Philadelphia, and Washington, D.C., have seen very rigid union work rules give way in the face of budget crises.

Enterprise or agency-level bargaining and individualized pay, of course, allow market pressures to impinge upon both management and the employee. Managers can offer larger salaries to retain skilled personnel who are in strong demand in the private sector, such as computer specialists. At the same time they can reward more productive employees. Explicit benchmarking of agencies against private sector equivalents, department or ministerial norms, or other public sector providers also indicates the efficiency of agency operations. The Australian Bureau of Industry Economics now devotes itself to the constant benchmarking of an extensive array of public sector agencies against global norms; Alberta and Ontario have built quality-of-service indicators into their ministries' annual business plans; and everywhere auditors general have come into their own as the surveillance of contracted services has grown.

Competition and User Fees

Many of these changes would be meaningless if agencies did not face real competitive pressures or have to compete for consumer dollars in a marketplace. Market pressures are ultimately what make it possible to deliver the same level of services with fewer resources. Either agencies find internal productivity gains or, by imposing user fees, generate revenues sufficient to cover the shortfall from their old budgetary levels.

User fees are now widespread and have begun to replace more general tax increases. U.S. parks now charge substantial access fees, for example. Medical care financed by quasi-insurance-like schemes such as Medicare in the United States or Canadian provincial medicare have seen premium increases, more and larger copayments, and in some cases more queuing as care is managed by third parties.

THE LESSONS OF CUTBACK BUDGETING

The overarching response of the public sector to fiscal stress in the era of cutback budgeting is the increasing centralization of the budgetary process at all levels of government throughout the industrialized world. Whether the devices are spending targets, ceilings, or reconciliation, politicians who allocate scarce resources at the macro level have centralized the process to help insulate budgetary decisions from interest groups and other claimants, both inside and outside the legislative process. These new procedures impose constraints on decision makers, managers, employees, and other vested interests, all in order to create more fiscal and political flexibility in what is essentially the global public budget.

Cumulatively, these changes have made the public sector more closely resemble private sector enterprises. Private sector enterprises routinely have to bid for scarce investment resources from central management, are refused additional resources when they overshoot their budgets and run losses, and eventually go bankrupt if they cannot generate a clientele or compete against other providers. In this sense, cutback budgeting exhibits a cultural side as well as a financial side. Particularly at the agency level, cutback budgeting is about changing the culture of the public sector from a procedural, input-control mentality into a customer service, least-cost-by-any-reasonable-means mentality. The budgetary and management changes associated with cutback budgets force managers to consider the real, long-term costs of programs and their associated spending. Conversely, only in a very few localities, New Zealand being foremost among these, have managers been asked to calculate rates of return for the capital invested in their departments. Nonetheless, the critical similarity of cutback budgeting in government to budgeting in the private sector is the introduction of competition for resources and clients, and in some instances real fear that an agency will be shut down.

These changes make it possible to consider the financial trade-offs among programs that in the past would have been subject primarily to political tests. Not surprisingly, where budgets have been cut in nominal terms, the question, Should government really be doing this? frequently arises. Private sector firms ask the same question every day. Cutback budgeting thus is simply the operational side of the general decline in both the power of the public sector and the primacy of "private" as opposed to "public" consumption that started with Proposition 13 in California in 1978.

Centralization is a two-edged sword, however. On the one hand, greater concentrations of political and administrative authority are required in the budgetary process to confront this ongoing, hostile fiscal environment. This holds true even for line managers, who should attempt to centralize the resources under their purview in order to exert the same kinds of control over their subordinates as is imposed upon them. On the other hand, these managers require administrative flexibility in order to succeed in realizing their organizational goals. Flexibility is required to administer standard agency functions, such as personnel management and purchasing, but it is also necessary to select proper budgetary strategy, to determine, for example, whether there should be across-the-board cuts, freezes, or targeted reductions. Managers also require flexibility in their programmatic accounts, so that funds may be reprioritized to true areas of need. Finally, because raising revenue is often a more difficult political task than freezing or cutting spending, managers would also benefit from greater flexibility in their opportunities to create new revenue flows, an organizational trait that is also characteristic of the private sector.

References

Alesina, A., and Perotti, R. "Fiscal Expansions and Adjustments in OECD Countries." *Economic Policy,* 1995, *21,* 205–248.

Algie, J., Mallen, G., and Foster, W. "Financial Cutback Decisions by Priority Scaling." *Journal of Management Studies,* 1983, *20*(2), 233–260.

Bahl, R. *Financing State and Local Government in the 1980s.* New York: Oxford University Press, 1990.

Bish, R. L. *The Public Economy of Metropolitan Areas.* Chicago: Markham, 1971.

Boston, J. *The State Under Contract.* Wellington, New Zealand: Bridget Williams Books, 1995.

Broden, B. C. *The IFM Simplified Guide to Zero-Based Budgeting.* Old Saybrook, Conn.: Institute for Management, 1977.

Buchanan, J., and Wagner, R. E. *Democracy in Deficit: The Political Legacy of Keynes.* Orlando, Fla.: Academic Press, 1977.

Caiden, N. "Public Budgeting in the United States: The State of the Discipline." In N. Lynn and A. Wildavsky (eds.), *Public Administration: The State of the Discipline.* Chatham, N.J.: Chatham House, 1990.

Curry, L. *The Politics of Fiscal Stress: Organizational Management of Budget Cutbacks.* Berkeley, Calif.: Institute of Governmental Studies, 1990.

Derthick, M. *The Influence of Federal Grants.* Cambridge, Mass.: Harvard University Press, 1970.

Derthick, M. *Uncontrollable Spending for Social Services Grants.* Washington, D.C.: Brookings Institution, 1975.

Downs, A. *Inside Bureaucracy.* Washington, D.C.: Brookings Institution, 1967.

Friedman, B. M. *Day of Reckoning.* New York: Vintage Books, 1989.

Gore, A., Jr. *From Red Tape to Results: Creating a Government That Works Better and Costs Less.* Report of the National Performance Review. Washington, D.C.: Government Printing Office, 1993.

Hinrichs, H. H., and Taylor, G. M. (eds.). *Program Budgeting and Benefit-Cost Analysis.* Pacific Palisades, Calif.: Goodyear, 1969.

Jones, L. R., and Euske, K. J. "Strategic Misrepresentation in Budgeting." *Journal of Public Administration Research and Theory,* 1991, *1*(4), 437–460.

Kemp, R. L. *Coping with Proposition Thirteen.* San Francisco: New Lexington Press, 1980.

Kennedy, P. *The Rise and Fall of Nations.* New York: Vintage Books, 1987.

Kettl, D. F. *Deficit Politics.* Old Tappan, N.J.: Macmillian, 1992.

Ladd, H. F., and Yinger, J. (eds.). *America's Ailing Cities: Fiscal Health and the Design of Urban Policy.* Baltimore: Johns Hopkins University Press, 1989.

Levine, C. H. "A Symposium: Organizational Decline and Cutback Management." *Public Administration Review,* 1978, *38*(4), 315–357.

Levine, C. H., Rubin, I. S., and Wolohojian, G. G. *The Politics of Retrenchment.* Thousand Oaks, Calif.: Sage, 1981.

Martin, J. K. *Urban Fiscal Stress: Why Cities Go Broke.* Westport, Conn.: Auburn House, 1982.

Meltsner, A. J. *The Politics of City Revenue.* Berkeley: University of California Press, 1971.

Meyer, J. R., and Quigley, J. M. *Local Public Finance and the Fiscal Squeeze: A Case Study.* New York: Ballinger, 1977.

Muller, T. *Growing and Declining Urban Areas.* Washington. D.C.: Urban Institute, 1975.

Nathan, R. P., and Doolittle, F. C. *The Consequences of Cuts.* Princeton, N.J.: Princeton University Press, 1983.

Niskanen, W. *Bureaucracy and Representative Government.* New York: Aldine de Gruyter, 1971.

Novick, D. (ed.). *Program Budgeting.* Cambridge, Mass.: Harvard University Press, 1965.

Olson, M. *The Rise and Decline of Nations.* New Haven, Conn.: Yale University Press, 1982.

O'Quinn, R. P. *What Americans Can Learn from New Zealand.* Washington, D.C.: Heritage Foundation, 1996.

Osborne, D., and Gaebler T. *Reinventing Government: How the Entrepreneurial Spirit Is Transforming the Public Sector from Schoolhouse to Statehouse, City Hall to the Pentagon.* Reading, Mass.: Addison-Wesley, 1992.

Pammer, W. *Managing Fiscal Strain in Major American Cities.* Westport, Conn.: Greenwood Press, 1990.

Park, K. O. "Expenditure Patterns an Interactions Among Local Governments in Metropolitan Areas." *Urban Affairs Quarterly,* 1994, *29*(4), 535–564.

Pierson, P. *Dismantling the Welfare State? Reagan, Thatcher, and the Politics of Retrenchment.* Cambridge: Cambridge University Press, 1994.

Porter, D. O. *The Politics of Budgeting Federal Aid: Resource Mobilization by Local School Districts.* Thousand Oaks, Calif.: Sage, 1973.

Poterba, J. M. "State Responses to Fiscal Crisis: The Effects of Budgetary Institutions and Politics." *Journal of Political Economy,* 1994, *102*(4), 799–821.

Powell, M. "From the Top: A City That Doesn't Work." *Washington Post,* July 20, 1997, p. 1.

Ridley, C., and Nolting, O. F. *How Cities Can Cut Costs: Practical Suggestions for Constructive Economy in Local Government.* Chicago: International City Managers Association, 1933.

Rubin, I. S. *Running in the Red.* Albany: State University of New York Press, 1982.

Rubin, I. S. "Estimated and Actual Urban Revenues: Exploring the Gap." *Public Budgeting and Finance,* 1987, *7*(4), 83–94.

Rubin, I. S. "Budgeting for Our Times: Target-Based Budgeting." *Public Budgeting and Finance,* 1991, *11*(3), 5–14.

Sassen, S. *Mobility of Labor and Capital.* Cambridge: Cambridge University Press, 1988.

Savage, J. D. *Balanced Budgets and American Politics.* Ithaca, N.Y.: Cornell University Press, 1988.

Savage, J. D. "Saints and Cardinals in Appropriations Committees and the Fight Against Distributive Politics." *Legislative Studies Quarterly,* 1991, *16*(3), 329–347.

Schick, A. "Budgetary Adaptations to Resource Scarcity." In C. H. Levine and I. S. Rubin (eds.), *Fiscal Stress and Public Policy.* Thousand Oaks, Calif.: Sage, 1980.

Schick, A. "Incremental Budgeting in a Decremental Age." *Policy Sciences,* 1983, *16,* 1–25.

Schick, A. "Macro-Budgetary Adaptations to Fiscal Stress in Industrialized Democracies." *Public Administration Review,* 1986, *46*(2), 124–134.

Schick, A. "Micro-Budgetary Adaptations to Fiscal Stress in Industrialized Democracies." *Public Administration Review,* 1988, *48*(1), 523–533.

Schwartz, H. M. "Public Choice Theory and Public Choices: Bureaucrats and State Reorganization in Australia, Denmark, New Zealand, and Sweden in the 1980s." *Administration and Society,* 1994, *26*(1), 48–77.

Schwartz, H. M. "Reinvention and Retrenchment: Lessons from the Application of the New Zealand Model to Alberta, Canada." *Journal of Policy Analysis and Management,* 1997, *16*(3), 205–232.

Sinclair, T. "Deficit Discourse: The Social Construction of Fiscal Rectitude." Coventry, England: University of Warwick, 1997.

Stanley, D. T. *Managing Local Government Under Union Pressure.* Washington, D.C.: Brookings Institution, 1972.

Stanley, D. T. *Cities in Trouble.* Columbus, Ohio: Academy for Contemporary Problems, 1976.

Sundquist, J. L. *Making Federalism Work.* Washington, D.C.: Brookings Institution, 1969.

von Hagen, J. "Budgeting Procedures and Fiscal Performance in the European Communities." *Economic Papers,* 1992, *16,* 1–79.

Weaver, R. K. *Automatic Government: The Politics of Indexation.* Washington, D.C.: Brookings Institution, 1988.

White, J., and Wildavsky, A. *The Deficit and the Public Interest: The Search for Responsible Budgeting in the 1980s.* Berkeley: University of California Press, 1989.

Wildavsky, A. *The Politics of the Budgetary Process.* New York: Little, Brown, 1964.

Wildavsky, A. *How to Limit Government Spending.* Berkeley: University of California Press, 1980.

Wolman, H. "Local Government Strategies to Cope with Fiscal Pressure." In C. H. Levine and I. S. Rubin (eds.), *Fiscal Stress and Public Policy.* Thousand Oaks, Calif.: Sage, 1980.

Worthley, J. A., and Ludwin, W. G. (eds.). *Zero-Based Budgeting in State and Local Government.* New York: Praeger, 1979.

CHAPTER TWENTY-TWO

Strategies for Spending Advocates

Roy T. Meyers

"What does it take to obtain the budget allocation I want?" Managers of government-funded programs ignore this question at their peril. This has always been the case, for even in the best of times budgeting makes programs compete for the government's limited financial resources. But with most governments now facing increasing fiscal stress and harsher macrobudgetary limits, mastering the political aspects of a very competitive budgetary process is often a practical requirement for survival. It *is* a dog-eat-dog world out there, and patiently waiting in line for a little chow will usually leave one a very hungry runt.

Yet the literature on public management features relatively little advice on how to deal with the political challenges of budgeting. This is not a recent development. Consider Gulick's classic planning, organizing, staffing, directing, coordinating, reporting, and budgeting (POSDCORB) formulation of the functions of the government executive (1937), in which budgeting was named last. The items in this list cannot have been so ordered because it made for a suggestive acronym! Rather, what mattered most to Gulick and his compatriots were the executive identification of goals and the rational alignment of organizational forms with these goals. They certainly did not ignore the potential value of budgetary reforms, nor were they ignorant of budgetary politics, but they often treated these topics as subsidiary to others.

Perhaps this emphasis was correct; after all, what is the sense of fighting for money when you do not know why or how you would spend it? The same question is implicitly asked by many modern theorists of public management. They have jettisoned the POSDCORB acronym and many of the past's principles of good administration and replaced them with consensus-driven strategic planning, a focus on customer needs, and flexibility for program line managers. But like the classical management theorists, they have either ignored the realities of budgetary politics or given them only cursory treatment. (Cohen and Eimicke, 1995, are somewhat of an exception.)

Some modern-day reformers even seem to believe that generous budgets are a barrier to improved performance. After they assume, as President Clinton has claimed, that the days of big government are over, they tell managers that shrinking budgets will give them the impetus to challenge their organizations to work better (National Performance Review, 1996). They say that the only budget increases that managers should expect are those that are self-generated—the efficiency dividends that result from inculcating an ethos of continuing improvement; the new, nongovernmental revenues that flow from program entrepreneurship; or both.

Although today's conservative political climate may make it more difficult than it used to be to win budget increases, wise managers will remember the truism, You can't do something with nothing. Politicians and citizens often seem to act as though they think otherwise. They insist that programs must solve difficult policy problems, but only on the cheap, and quickly at that; then they complain when agencies fail in such impossible circumstances (see, for example, see Derthick, 1990). When this pathology appears, managers have an obligation to say, "Either ante up or stop being so ambitious." It usually takes time *and* money to improve organizations and programs, and managers need to make this case.

Managers are also most likely to know how much new funding for staff and equipment is needed to markedly improve performance. Budget controllers, at least in recent years, have not been disposed to ask this question. Instead, they fear that managers often know more than they do about the relationship between costs and performance, and they suspect that giving managers budgetary flexibility will allow them to squirrel away extra funds or spend them on frivolous activities. To prevent such waste, controllers adopt complicated budgetary rules that are designed to say no. Unfortunately, these rules are not very discriminatory, and they frequently penalize even those managers who want to be efficient. If managers are to serve the public, they cannot meekly accept such results; instead, they must either challenge or avoid stupid budget rules.

This argument—that it is OK to fight for more—is admittedly controversial in a time when concern about deficits is well justified. Spending reductions are a necessary component of deficit reduction plans, so controllers work hard at justifying why they have selected specific programs for reduction or elimination.

They may agree with advocates that some spending is desirable, but then insist that it is unfortunately unaffordable. At other times their rhetoric is much harsher, portraying the advocates of government spending as feeding at the public trough.

Most readers can likely identify some greedy swine of this type. Conversely, as the Capitol Hill aphorism goes, one member's pork is another member's worthy project. Asking the government for money, which is protected by the First Amendment to the Constitution, is a traditional part of our political culture, and there are many defensible reasons for the government to respond, particularly to provide public goods and promote social equity.

Assuming now that the question that opened this chapter—What does it take to obtain the budget allocation I want?—is a defensible one to ask, what are its answers? The latter half of this chapter provides how-to advice for spending advocates—agency managers, program beneficiaries, and other supporters. Preceding this practical advice is a review of the development of theories about budgetary competition.

THEORIES OF BUDGETARY COMPETITION

There was a time when there was a simple and widely accepted answer to the question of how to compete for a budget. (This was also a time when asking the question would not need to be justified.) It was best expressed in one of the most influential works of American political science, Aaron Wildavsky's *Politics of the Budgetary Process* (1964). Still regarded as the classic work on budgetary politics, this book has had an extraordinary shelf life, going through four editions with its original title and two more as the largely rewritten *New Politics of the Budgetary Process* (1988). After Wildavsky's death, Naomi Caiden updated and revised the book yet again (1996).

The first edition of this work combined a theory of budgetary politics with an impressive array of insightful anecdotes. The theory was "budgetary incrementalism," which at its core was based on the more general theory of decision making popularized by Lindblom (1959). Incremental decision-making theory had no faith in the ability of humans to decide by comprehensively searching for alternatives and deftly calculating the optimal choice. Instead, it celebrated the alternative of "muddling through," in which a series of small experiments may move one toward success. Wildavsky similarly argued that a budget should be changed only slightly from the previous budget. This controversial normative argument against rational reallocations is beyond the scope of this chapter.

The book's strongest contribution was its compelling description of budgetary tactics. Wildavsky called these tactics incremental because their essence was that advocates typically asked for just a little more and then normally received some of the requested increases. (In related journal articles, Wildavsky operationalized 10 percent as the maximum for considering requests and allocations to be incremental.)

Why might incremental strategy have worked? One reason was that when claimants were careful not to ask for too much, they earned the confidence of decision makers. Those decision makers bore the difficult responsibility of allocating a limited amount of funds among many claimants. If they were pressed to award large increases to one group of claimants, they would have to fund these by taking money from the rest of the claimants, which would generate too much political discontent. Another danger was that because decision makers lacked sufficient knowledge to understand likely effects, big reallocations might eventually cause them to be blamed for the inevitable mistakes, a risk to be avoided at all costs.

This still left decision makers with the task of deciding how much they should award to each of the claimants. Wildavsky concluded that they did this by calculating each claimant's "fair share" of the total. That proportion was generally stable, arrived at after years of negotiation, and highly related to a claimant's political mobilization. The fair share of the military was always large, and that of poor kids was always small. This was not because decision makers had decided on the basis of careful analysis that undesired conditions would be improved most by this allocation. Rather, the military had a mobilized clientele (then known as the military-industrial complex), poor kids did not, and elected officials naturally responded most to those who could offer (or threaten) them the most. But Wildavsky shied away from specifying winners and losers in this way, consistent with the pluralist approach then dominant within political science.

Much of Wildavsky's remaining strategic advice flowed from this recommendation: advocates should maintain the confidence of decision makers and mobilize a program's clientele. This advice was encapsulated in short phrases like "avoid surprise," "make friends," and "they made me" and was linked to assumptions about institutional roles and aspirations. Claimants could expect that members of the House Appropriations Committee would routinely act as "guardians of the Treasury," and that senators would act as the members of the court of appeals to the miserly House. When participants played stable roles, most interactions about budgets were stylized. For example, each agency was expected, even encouraged, to pad its request. After the agency requested a bit more than it really needed, the budget bureau could then cut it down to size, showing that it knew how to do its job (on such symbolics, see Anton, 1966).

And woe to the participant who violated an unwritten rule. Wildavsky (1964, pp. 96–97) provided an interesting example, from State Department testimony before an appropriations subcommittee, of his advice that claimants should avoid extreme claims that could be tested.

REPRESENTATIVE ROONEY: I find a gentleman here, an SO-6. He got an A in Chinese and you assigned him to London.

MR. X: Yes, sir. That officer will have opportunities in London—not as many as he would have in Hong Kong, for example—

REPRESENTATIVE ROONEY: What will he do? Spend his time in Chinatown?

MR. X: No, sir. There will be opportunities in dealing with officers in the British Foreign Office who are concerned with Far Eastern affairs—

REPRESENTATIVE ROONEY: So instead of speaking English to one another, they will sit in the London office and talk Chinese?

MR. X: Yes, sir.

REPRESENTATIVE ROONEY: Is that not fantastic?

MR. X: No, sir. They are anxious to keep up their practice—

REPRESENTATIVE ROONEY: They go out to Chinese restaurants and have chop suey together?

MR. X: Yes, sir.

REPRESENTATIVE ROONEY: And that is all at the expense of the American taxpayer?

The advice here was that petitioners should talk straight to powerful people; being evasive like the diplomat would teach members of Congress not to trust him and his department. Although this advice is generally good, the situation was a bit more complex than a temporary break in an otherwise accommodating relationship between the State Department and Congress. For the decade prior to this example, China experts had been purged from the department on suspicion of being "soft" on communism. Because China would retain its geopolitical importance, the State Department took the understandable risk of stockpiling and hiding China experts. The revealed truth upset Representative Rooney, but not simply because the State Department made an unjustifiable, silly claim in testimony.

Wildavsky's book gave budgetary incrementalism widespread acceptance, and its reputation was further strengthened after Wildavsky and his colleagues published several empirical studies that apparently validated the descriptive theory. These studies were soon challenged, however, and found wanting (for a review of this literature, see Meyers, 1994, pp. 19–42).

Critics also challenged the applicability of the incrementalist model (for a review of this literature, see Meyers, 1994, pp. 6–12). It could apply, by definition, only to discretionary appropriations, because budgeting for mandatory spending does not feature annual negotiations over a permissible amount of change. As the proportion of the budget captured by discretionary appropriations declined, so did the potential purchase of incrementalism.

The critics also targeted incrementalism's mechanics. They said that some budget actors did not appear to avoid complexity; rather than relying on simple "aids to calculation," they tried to understand and debate the policy implications of spending alternatives. In addition, holders of crucial institutional positions did not always act in their supposed roles. In particular, appropriators often seemed to look the other way while their colleagues entered the Treasury Department's vault (but not before the contents were plundered by its so-called guardians).

Incrementalism also relied on economic prosperity to dampen the intensity of budgetary competition. Having new money to allocate broadly to most budget claimants invited them to acquiesce to the status quo distribution. But after 1973, economic growth fell far below its historically high rate of the post–World War II era. With no fiscal dividend, claimants learned to become more insistent.

Some empirical research has also suggested, but has not proved, that assertiveness might be a better strategy than incrementalist going-along. Agencies that ask for much more than the previous year's levels might be cut substantially from those requests, but over the long run they might gain more than meeker agencies. In other words, asking for more might be worth the risk of angering the budget office. But these studies did not adequately control for other potential causes of high budgetary growth rates. Assertive agencies might act this way because they believe conditions are favorable for big increases. For example, the defense buildup of the early 1980s may have succeeded not only because Defense Secretary Caspar Weinberger forced Office of Management and Budget director David Stockman to the wall, but also because setbacks in Iran made it possible.

Responding to these theoretical challenges, Wildavsky repeatedly modified his conceptualization of incrementalism, which led Allen Schick (1983, p. 3) to criticize the theory's validity:

> Incrementalism is an extraordinarily elastic and elusive concept. It can be made to fit just about every budgetary circumstance. When expenditure trends for particular activities and projects were shown to include budgetary decreases, the concept was reformulated into one that deals with total spending by agencies, so that incrementalism could coexist with declines in particular programs. When big dollar shifts were shown to occur in some agency budgets, incrementalism was redefined in terms of "the regularity or irregularity of the change in size, not the absolute amount of the changes themselves."
>
> . . . Incrementalism says more about what budgeting is not—and cannot be— than about what budgeting is. It asserts that budget makers cannot reexamine every item in the budget every year. They cannot pit all programs against one

another in a competition for scarce funds. They cannot canvass all the options that might merit consideration. They cannot look much beyond the next budget to gauge the effects of current decisions on future programs.

To do all these things would overload the budget process, require more data and calculations than can be handled in the time available for preparing the budget, and would open intractable conflicts over money. So rather than being "rational" and comprehensive, budget makers are incremental. But within the broad expanse of the increment, incrementalism offers little explanation as to how decisions are made. It does not deal with how the increment is divided, with "who gets what," which Wildavsky pinpointed as the all-important issue in budgeting. It does not explain why some programs grow more than others, and why shares in the budget change over time. It does not explain why spending increases are big in some years but small in others. It says very little about budget outcomes, other than that they are incremental.

With incrementalism widely viewed as an incomplete theory, and as an inadequate basis for strategic advice, Meyers (1994) proposed an alternative. In the "structural strategy" theory, spending advocates can search for advantageous budgetary structures, ones that will protect them from cuts or allow increases. Budgetary structures, defined broadly, are the characteristics of the budgetary process for individual programs. Informational structures affect how the costs and benefits of spending are perceived. Decision procedure structures determine when budgetary decisions are made and which programs will compete with each other. Policy design structures give agencies different authorities for acquiring and spending funds.

These budget structures can affect the ability of a program to obtain funds. For example, an accounting rule that allows a program to report fewer costs than the government actually bears allows the program to get something for nothing. Consider Archer Daniels Midland (ADM), an integrated agricultural products company that advertises itself as the "supermarket to the world." ADM uses the federal government as a supermarket, reaping billions in profits from tax credits for ethanol, from high tariffs on sugar imports, and from subsidies for agricultural imports (Bovard, 1995). The federal costs of these benefits are substantially underestimated in the federal budget, and this did not occur by chance. For example, many beneficiaries of tax preferences have protected their benefits by arguing that no government expenditures are involved. In reality, although beneficiaries receive no direct cash payments from the Treasury Department, preferences allow them to pay less in taxes than they otherwise would. Though the federal government does report these tax expenditures in a special analysis of the budget, the accounting visibility of these costs is far lower than that of programs funded through departmental budgets. In the case of the ethanol credit, the energy and agriculture functions in the budget highlight direct outlays made by the Energy Department and the Agriculture Department, but they ignore the Treasury Department's contribution to these functions through the gasohol credit (and other significant tax expenditures). Nor are tax expenditures reviewed annually or with the same scrutiny given to departmental budgets.

Other advocates whose programs are suffering from budget cuts may redesign their programs to take greater advantage of such weak accounting and budgetary rules. Another example of tax preferences is low-income housing tax credits. Housing advocates and financiers pushed these as a less visible replacement for the Section 8 and related construction subsidies, which were losing budget share because of their high reported costs (Stanfield, 1994; Donovan, 1994).

In response to such tactics, budgetary controllers may counter with stronger accounting rules, particularly if the tactics seem likely to diffuse widely. They respond as well to other attempts by spending advocates to structure the budgetary process to their advantage (more details are provided in the next section). The resulting budgetary process is a continuously evolving dynamic of structural innovation and control. Incrementalist strategy becomes obsolete, at least for a while, when skillful advocates become adept at manipulating structural characteristics. The outcomes are less stable than in an incremental world—some programs do very well and others are left with slim pickings. Relationships between budget process actors are also less stable. Advocates try end runs if they think they might get away with them.

Although the author of this chapter is obviously biased toward the structural strategy theory, its limitations are also obvious. As incrementalism was bound to the quiescent 1950s and early 1960s, the model of structural strategy grew out of the budgetary turmoil of the 1980s. It was also developed to provide an alternative model to incrementalism, so it did not set out a general theory of budget competition. In particular, because the structural strategy theory focused on the special characteristics of the budgetary process, it intentionally ignored institutional factors (such as the extent of centralization in Congress or the nature of congressional-presidential relations). It is hard to imagine a general theory of budgetary competition in which these factors would not play an important role. The practical advice in the next section integrates some popular theories about institutions with more budget-specific concepts.

Also needed for development of a general theory of budget competition is more quantitative research about the effects of different budgetary strategies and contexts. Some progress is already being made toward more accurately measuring the dependent variable of budgetary outcomes (see Jones, Baumgartner, and True, 1995). The related challenge is efficient sampling of independent variables. That is, to measure the marginal impact of different budget strategies, one must carefully observe how a range of strategies are used within a range of contexts (such as during both periods of fiscal stress and abundance).

HOW TO COMPETE FOR A BUDGET

This section provides practical advice on how to compete for a budget allocation. Exhibit 22.1 summarizes this advice in the form of some rules for budget advocacy.

Set Budget Allocation Goals

Strategies are plans of action designed to attain goals. Knowing how much you want is necessary for determining what it takes to obtain that much. Of course, because some ambitious goals require more influence than a program can realistically have, what it takes and how much you want must be set in tandem. Goals for budget allocations thus have to be adjustable, particularly over the long run, to prepare for the dangers and possibilities that are unknown. More generally, budgetary strategies have to be developed iteratively. Keep in mind that the rules of budget advocacy interact with one another.

Any budgetary goal has a direction and a magnitude. The direction indicates whether one is seeking an increase to the budget, can accept maintenance at its current level, or must live with a reduction. Magnitude indicates the size of the desired increase or acceptable decrease. A sample budgetary goal is a 5 percent increase the following year and 30 percent over four years.

The incremental method for goal setting—take last year's level and add a little—is certainly easy. A potentially better approach projects whether changes in short-run conditions might make the previous year's level a poor guide to the possibilities for the current year. For example, if political support for the program has substantially increased, it would be foolish to ask for a small increase; or if the level of fiscal stress has radically increased, it might be too dangerous to ask for any increase at all.

Setting a long-run budget acquisition goal should be much less affected by the current budgetary environment than a short-run goal would be. Many public organizations now announce their "visions" for their future, often grandiose ones that imply huge increases in funding. Stating the intent "to be the best in the world at . . ." has some advantages, not the least of which is justifying a long-run quantum increase in the organization's budget. If you can show that the problem you are addressing is amenable to solution, and if public concern about this problem is high, announcing your large ambitions makes sense. If these conditions are not present, however, the budgetary credibility of a greatness vision may be easily questioned by controllers and competitors. In these cases, it is generally wise to keep quiet.

Those who seek budget increases should also recognize that new money often drags strings—that is, heightened performance expectations and restrictions on operating methods—that reduce organizational autonomy and flexibility. Advocates need to consider whether these exchanges are a good deal. On occa-

Exhibit 22.1. Rules for Budget Advocacy.

Set budget allocation goals.
   Adapt them to the political environment.
   Relate them to organizational vision.

Count votes.
   Understand institutional complexity.
   Avoid well-placed blockers.
   Secure influential promoters.
   Target supporting coalitions of decision makers.

Mobilize supporters to influence decision makers.
   Identify and organize potential beneficiaries.
   Expand support by broadening spending pattern.
   Intensify support by building dependency.
   Offer support and threaten opposition for budget actions.

Develop persuasive rationales about the effects of spending.
   Use rhetoric to convert advocates' wishes into society's perceived needs.
   Predict and demonstrate efficiency and effectiveness.

Design programs to avoid budgetary process constraints.
   Seek accounting treatments that minimize reported costs.
   Gain exemptions from procedures that limit spending.
   Dedicate revenue streams.
   Require that spending match demands.

Bargain for advantages.
   Learn about different techniques and practice them.

Be curious and flexible.
   Consider how changing conditions may create opportunities for more
      funding.
   Set and meet ethical standards.

---

sion, a reduction in the budget may be preferred, if it is exchanged for abolition of an imposed, low-value performance expectation or operating restriction.

Count Votes

This rule is shorthand for "know the institutional actors and figure out how to get their support."

In the United States, the institutional context is almost always very complicated (the exception is small local governments). Multiple branches—president and Congress, governor and legislature, mayor and council—jointly enact budgets. The legislative bodies among these are often very decentralized, but many executive branches also include power centers that are somewhat independent of their chiefs. The budgetary process presents so many opportunities to affect policy and make political points that all of these actors will likely be active in budgeting, despite the attendant risk of being blamed for tax increases and spending cuts. To quote the vaudevillian Jimmy Durante, "Everybody wants to get in on the act!"

Moreover, these institutions typically use convoluted procedures. Readers may remember from their high school civics class a dense chart showing the many stages of legislation. The lesson typically drawn from such displays is that if a bill fails to pass through only one stage, it will not become law. Although the budgetary process is not that rigid (in fact, neither is the legislative process), programs do need to pass through numerous barriers throughout the budget process.

Obviously, the best strategy for dealing with this complexity is to be supported by all decision makers in all budget arenas. This is possible, as shown by the everlasting success of veterans' spending advocates, but it is not likely. There are too many claimants battling over limited funds for politicians to promise unlimited support to most groups. This means that advocates must target their efforts efficiently to gain sufficient support in the most important budget arenas.

The greatest risk that budget advocates must avoid is having a budget allocation blocked. The most influential budget blocker is the chief political executive, who normally prepares the budget and can veto proposed budget laws (especially dangerous is a line-item veto). Ranking close in influence are senators, who can filibuster against specific provisions, and committee chairs, who control the agenda for considering spending bills. Also important are professional staff—budget examiners and committee clerks—who can persuade their bosses with technical analysis (not all "votes" are formal).

Pleasing all potential blockers is not absolutely necessary, however. The institutional structure of U.S. government forces compromise. Executives who oppose spending proposals must often give in to adamant legislative supporters, and vice versa. Potential blockers can be counteracted by securing commitments from a few well-placed influentials to provide unswerving support. These influential promoters—such as committee chairs, party leaders, and legislative policy experts—must insist that programs be funded despite opposition from potential blockers.

Influential promoters need followers—supporting coalitions of at least "minimum winning size" (50 percent plus one of the total votes) in important budget arenas. A much safer tactical course is to try for supporting coalitions of somewhat larger than minimum winning size, to provide insurance against changes in support over time.

Politicians grant support in part because they believe in the goals for and supposed effects of spending. Studying the public actions and statements of politicians offers clues about their beliefs about the impacts of spending; private discussions may be even more informative. The ideologically committed usually form the core of the supporting coalition. But other politicians can be added to this group after they learn how their budgetary decisions might affect their political futures. Politicians are most afraid that their constituents will turn them out of office if they cut spending that these constituents desire. Politicians also value opportunities to claim credit for increasing constituent-favored spending or for opposing disliked cuts. An advocate who understands constituent preferences and communicates them to politicians can expand supporting coalitions to include those who are not strongly committed to the program's goals.

Mobilize Supporters to Influence Decision Makers

Each spending alternative benefits people. Spending advocates should identify and organize potential supporters. A useful categorization breaks potential supporters into the intended direct beneficiaries of spending (such as kids who are eligible for Head Start and their families), the producers of spending (such as Head Start center workers), and those who benefit either indirectly or symbolically from spending (such as local school systems and those concerned about social inequities). Some of these potential groups—particularly beneficiaries—may be difficult to organize because of physical dispersion, political apathy or inexperience, or other difficulties. Producers of services—whose material benefits from spending are most obvious (such as government employees and military contractors)—are often the most dependable group of supporters. Agencies can cultivate supporters through public relations efforts and through the allocation of funds.

Identified supporters must then be mobilized to influence budget decision makers. Influence comes from offering political support for favorable budget actions and from threatening penalties for unfavorable ones. There are too many means of influence to detail here. Suffice it to say that these methods must be chosen with care to reflect the targets' incentives and the supporters' capacities. For example, contributions for campaign finance are particularly valuable for reinforcing influential spending promoters; among providers of services, contractors with government make contributions much more easily than do government employees. In recent years, methods of budgetary influence have diversified beyond the traditional contacts of appropriators by lobbyists. Multi-million-dollar public relations campaigns have protected spending by stimulating grassroots opposition (of the so-called Astroturf strain).

One method of developing a large base of supporters is by adopting *distributive* or *universalistic* spending patterns. Distributive spending maximizes the number of geographic beneficiaries, which is of particular benefit in the legislative budgetary process. Universalistic spending broadens eligibility for benefits beyond the most deserving. Advocates can encourage legislative earmarks to districts as well as formula allocations that benefit many groups with small amounts. Though both methods reduce the efficiency of spending, they insulate programs from the political heresy of serving only a small minority.

A more targeted spending pattern can be worth this risk if it leads to intense support among beneficiaries. The downsizing of military ground forces, for example, has marked the Army as the source of almost all the military reductions; the Marines have been largely protected. One likely cause has been the work of the Marines' alumni, who though few in number have been proud and brave in the budget battles (that is, they have been well placed and active). Supporters who depend on a spending program often make heroic efforts to maintain it; encouraging such dependency may ensure that a program has a long budgetary life.

One of the most challenging aspects of budget mobilization is the shifting composition of supporting and opposing coalitions. These changes respond to the aggregation and disaggregation of budgets within "nested" arenas. For example, a transportation agency will first compete with other agencies for funds (the government-wide budget arena); it will then distribute its funds among its programs (the transportation budget arena). Groups served by this agency may join as blood brothers in the first stage to gain the largest possible allocation for the transportation agency. Then, in the second stage, like pirates dividing the spoils, they go for each others' throats—with the transportation budget fixed in amount, each advocate gains only by taking from their previous collaborators. Advocates learn that alliances are often valuable, but always temporary.

Develop Persuasive Rationales About the Effects of Spending

The simple mathematics of budgeting adds and subtracts program and agency allocations to arrive at an acceptable total. Supplementing this arithmetic is a process of argumentation about whether these allocations are worthwhile. Advocates must convince decision makers that problems should be addressed by spending, that their wishes are society's needs. Following are some common spending rationales for this purpose (Meyers, 1994):

Investments: By spending now, you will avoid larger costs in the future.

Spinoffs: Besides getting the intended benefit from spending, secondary benefits also result.

Earned right: We sacrificed before; now we are absolutely owed a benefit.

Truly needy: In the absence of spending, people in need of assistance would go wanting.

Merit goods: This spending is especially worthy; it is akin to Mom and apple pie.

Macroeconomic effects: Spending increases employment and economic growth, or reduces interest rates or inflation.

Higher-government responsibility: The higher government must spend because lower-level governments lack the fiscal capacity to deal with this problem.

Leveraging: By spending, government encourages others to spend as well.

Spending gaps: Spending is needed to cover a large shortfall in meeting needs.

Disastrous consequences: Failing to spend now guarantees terrible results sooner or later.

The level playing field: Our competitors are subsidized; it is only fair to spend a similar amount on us.

Note that spending claims using these rationales may not be supported by much evidence, but they can be convincing nevertheless. Politicians often prefer ammunition over analysis—that is, arguments that allow them to justify what they already want to do for political reasons. Successful advocates learn to supply politicians with intuitively plausible claims. Simple metaphors can often be particularly convincing. Rationales should also be varied over time to match concerns that rise high on the political agenda.

The obvious danger of this rhetorical approach is that advocates can be accused of wanting the government to throw money at problems—an especially dangerous charge in this era of renewed interest in performance measurement. Consequently, advocates should predict the effectiveness and efficiency of proposed spending using quantitative examples. These predictions are more convincing if they are based on demonstrations of similar effects from previous spending. Quality program evaluations that document success are budgetary gold.

Heightened expectations that the value of spending should be estimated can create problems for budget advocates, however. Often money has not been set aside for quality studies; advocates should notify decision makers of this information gap when they are pressed for proof of success. And even if studies have been done, reliable measures of the true impacts of spending may still be lacking. If studies have failed to control for important intervening factors, they may mistakenly report no impact. Advocates need to expose such flaws. More important, they need be involved in the identification of strategic goals and performance measures for programs.

Design Programs to Avoid Budgetary Process Constraints

Budget rules determine how often spending allocations are made, how spending is counted, and how easily programs can obtain financing and make obligations. These rules are not applied equally to all programs. In part this variance is necessary—for example, some complex financial transactions require different accounting treatments than are used for simple ones. But other exceptions to budget rules are the fruits of advocates' lobbying.

Budgetary accounting rules are often confusing but are always important. Advocates should attempt to use existing rules or suggest new ones in order to minimize the costs reported for their programs. When costs are not visible, politicians have less reason to reduce them. The most blatant way to make costs less visible in the federal government is to have a program declared off-budget (or in the state and local context, as not part of the general fund). More sophisticated accounting tactics take advantage of the difficulty of counting spending that is spread out over time or that is indefinite in amount. If programs can be designed to have these features, accounting rules may conveniently ignore spending beyond the budget year and beyond amounts that the government is certain it will spend. A common strategy that takes advantage of flawed accounting practices is to lease rather than purchase a program-critical asset.

Budget constraints can be avoided more directly by being exempted from procedures that can force cuts. For example, in 1985, the federal government adopted a *sequestration* procedure that was popularly described as a mechanism for applying across-the-board cuts to spending if deficit targets were not met. In fact, many entitlement programs gained exemption to sequestration as it was being designed, and a number of other programs gained exemption after it was put into law.

An alternative to "avoiding the knife" is "getting the combination to the safe." Programs can be designed to assure financing over time. Dedicating one or more revenue streams to a program often provides a more stable funding source than having to plead with the legislature each year for appropriations. Labeling this arrangement a "trust fund" or structuring it as an independent entity (a "public authority" or a "government-sponsored enterprise") gives additional protection. Also advantageous is the authority to spend up to demand; normally this takes the form of a legal entitlement to funds for defined beneficiaries. Agencies may continue such mandatory spending until a new law restricts it, which is the opposite of the appropriations process. Advocates of entitlements need not waste precious resources asking for assistance each year—as in many competitions, defense is easier in politics than offense.

Some of these tactics entail significant risks; they may effectively commit funds from future agency budgets or invite counterattacks by controllers. In addition, the best techniques for avoiding budget constraints vary in their specifics across governments and over time. For example, the federal government uses quite different accounting standards than do state governments; some tactics that might work in the federal government will not work in many states, and vice versa. Controllers have improved federal standards in response to successful exploitation of the past's flawed ones, requiring advocates to invent new ones. The most skillful advocates are those who know this history and who can recognize the often subtle, technical differences that can create advantages. This recognition requires a high tolerance for learning the often excruciating details of legislative procedure and government accounting practices.

Bargain for Advantages

It is understandable that much of Wildavsky's advice was about bargaining strategy; budgeting features repeated interactions with numerous players, so skill in reaching accommodations is indispensable. The thrust of Wildavsky's advice was that advocates should maintain the confidence of controllers by acting as controllers expect them to act—as generally believable but not completely honest. Advocates should be forthright, but they should also pad their requests; to do otherwise might lead controllers to suspect that something was very wrong. Perhaps the best analogy to budgetary bargaining is the U.S. ritual of auto sales, in which disingenuousness is assumed if not celebrated. (A buyer who finds a dealership that gives in to all demands should check whether all the cars on the lot are yellow.)

In some contrast, much of the current literature on bargaining emphasizes the potential in "principled bargaining" to develop win-win solutions (see, for example, Fisher and Ury, 1991). These solutions are said to be more likely when negotiators avoid being locked into positions, try to invent options for mutual gain, and use objective criteria for judging proposals. Some advocates may find this approach useful for negotiating budgetary exchanges with controllers for their mutual benefit.

Not all budgetary contexts—particularly ones with high fiscal stress—may permit such win-win resolutions, however. In more difficult situations, advocates who can employ a wider variety of positional bargaining techniques have greater prospects for success. Preparation using the rules just discussed—setting goals, counting votes, and so on—is essential. So is knowing as much relevant information as possible; ignorance about your counterpart's assertions is the supreme disadvantage. Emotional self-control is also important, such as knowing when to show and when to hide anger and which physical cues to display.

Skill with these techniques is useful in many other applications besides budgeting, but unfortunately they cannot be learned well by receiving wisdom from theorists. Whether to concede, bluff, or insist is an intuitive decision, one that is dependent on context, and particularly on the personalities of other negotiators. Experience is the best teacher of bargaining skill (few kids play poker well). Despite this proviso, helpful recommendations on bargaining strategy for budgetary advocates can be found in Bestor (1993), Jones and Euske (1991), Anthony and Young (1994), and of course Wildavsky (1964).

Be Curious and Flexible

Success in politics, particularly sustained success, usually does not come easily. As shown by the biographies of noted political leaders, success almost uniformly requires great ambition and effort. Also important, however, are a tolerance for complexity and uncertainty, the resilience to bear setbacks, and luck.

These factors surely matter as well for budgetary strategy. The budgetary process is extraordinarily complex, and the environment of budgeting changes rapidly (see Rubin, 1997, for the best analysis of factors that change budgeting from year to year). Yet sustained success is possible in budgeting for those advocates who periodically search for alternative strategies, calculate the potential consequences, and act on these opportunities. An illustration is provided in Exhibit 22.2.

Strategic opportunities in budgeting are a form of policy "window" (Kingdon, 1984); open windows are those times when conditions make it more likely that a particular proposal will be adopted. For example, the persuasiveness of rationales may change. An example mentioned earlier was the early 1980s increase in defense spending, which was advanced by "disastrous consequences" rhetoric that featured images of hostages and burned helicopters in Iran. A similar hollow military argument is now harder to make (despite a sizable procurement holiday and significant proliferation threats), because the most memorable recent image is the total dominance of the U.S. military during the Gulf War.

Advocates face major complications in perceiving and exploiting strategic opportunities. To repeat the conclusion of the theoretical section of this chapter, most assertions about which budgetary strategies work under what conditions are at best informed guesses. One reason for this is that the advantage of a tactic can naturally decline because of diffusion. Success typically breeds attention and imitation; once competing advocates learn to use your strategy, they can claim part of your budget. And once controllers learn about this dissemination, they may strike back. A tactic that once worked like a charm can lose its glitter. Maintaining an advantage may require continuous curiosity and flexibility.

A final point about flexibility is its potential moral danger, for ethical principles are inconsistent with complete flexibility. This chapter has suggested that advocates scratch backs, manipulate numbers, avoid rules, pressure officials, and create glowing impressions about results. Some managers may find these activities inherently immoral; others may consider them to be an acceptable price to pay for getting needed funds. Each budget advocate needs to decide personally how ethical it is to use these tactics.

Exhibit 22.2. Why Medicaid Spending Grew.

Since its creation in 1965, Medicaid spending has grown very rapidly, despite serving the poor, who are politically weak. This growth has continued throughout the 1980s and 1990s, as a threatening fiscal environment has placed entitlement programs under great scrutiny.

Much of this growth has been a "natural" outcome of Medicaid's mandatory spending design. Given its mandatory status, spending has grown as the number of beneficiaries, their utilization of medical services, and the prices of these services have grown. Significant drivers have been recessions and increasing poverty, a reduction in the rate of employer-provided health insurance, the aging of the population, and new medical technologies. Yet Medicaid's mandatory status has been a political as well as a policy choice, one that has defined future spending as relatively uncontrollable. Throughout most of its history, but especially at its creation, that future spending has been significantly underestimated.

During the 1980s, Medicaid's advocates (particularly Representative Henry Waxman, Democrat of California) skillfully expanded its spending. They convinced Congress to mandate that states provide coverage for poor children, and they made more beneficiaries of other poverty programs "categorically eligible" for Medicaid. Though these beneficiaries were politically weak, their interests were supported by the lobbying and campaign contributions of service providers. The expansions were packaged in reconciliation bills as partial offsets to spending cuts, taking advantage of a rare procedural opportunity to expand spending. The increases were compromises from larger (that is, padded) proposed increases. Much of the costs from the proposals were shifted beyond the five-year budget horizon; mandates typically kicked in during the sixth year. Finally, the expansions were supported by persuasive rationales—advocates shamed controllers with stories of egregious cases of low-quality medical care for the poor, backing it up with quantitative evidence about declining access to care.

Spending advocates also manipulated the rules that governed Medicaid's obligation of funds. They assured that these rules gave administrators little discretion to challenge claimed reimbursements. For example, nursing home operators convinced the courts to treat a legislative amendment that was intended to set a ceiling on reimbursements as a floor. An open-ended definition of the medical services covered by Medicaid gave states a strong incentive to reclassify costly social services as medical in nature. Exploiting a loophole in the "disproportionate share" part of Medicaid, most states also imposed phantom taxes on providers and encouraged their "contributions" (which were reimbursed) to inflate the federal match of state costs (see Morgan, 1994; U.S. General Accounting Office, 1994).

References

Anthony, R. N., and Young, D. W. *Management Control in Nonprofit Organizations.* (5th ed.) Burr Ridge, Ill.: Irwin, 1994.

Anton, T. J. *The Politics of State Expenditure in Illinois.* Urbana: University of Illinois Press, 1966.

Bestor, M. "Negotiating Skills for Budget Officers." *Government Finance Review,* Dec. 1993, pp. 15–19.

Bovard, J. *Archer Daniels Midland: A Case Study in Corporate Welfare.* Policy Analysis No. 241. Washington, D.C.: Cato Institute, Sept. 26, 1995.

Cohen, S., and Eimicke, W. *The New Effective Public Manager: Achieving Success in a Changing Government.* San Francisco: Jossey-Bass, 1995.

Derthick, M. *Agency Under Stress.* Washington, D.C.: Brookings Institution, 1990.

Donovan, S. *Learning the Low-Income Housing Tax Credit.* Cambridge, Mass.: John F. Kennedy School of Government Case Program, 1994.

Fisher, R., and Ury, W. *Getting to Yes.* (2nd ed.) New York: Penguin Books, 1991.

Gulick, L. "Notes on the Theory of Organization." In L. Gulick and L. Urwick (eds.), *Papers on the Science of Administration.* New York: Institute of Public Administration, 1937.

Jones, B. D., Baumgartner, F. R., and True, J. L. *The Shape of Change: Punctuations and Stability in U.S. Budgeting, 1946–94.* Working Paper no. 42. College Station: Texas A&M University, 1995.

Jones, L. R., and Euske, K. J. "Strategic Misrepresentation in Budgeting." *Journal of Public Administration Research and Theory, 1991, 1*(4), 437–460.

Kingdon, J. W. *Agendas, Alternatives, and Public Policies.* New York: Little, Brown, 1984.

Lindblom, C. "The Science of Muddling Through." *Public Administration Review, 1959, 19,* 79–88.

Meyers, R. T. *Strategic Budgeting.* Ann Arbor: University of Michigan Press, 1994.

Morgan, D. "How Medicaid Grew." *Washington Post,* Jan. 30–Feb. 2, 1994.

National Performance Review. *The Best Kept Secrets in Government.* Washington, D.C.: Government Printing Office, 1996.

Rubin, I. S. *The Politics of Public Budgeting: Getting and Spending, Borrowing and Balancing.* (3rd ed.) Chatham, N.J.: Chatham House, 1997.

Schick, A. "Incremental Budgeting in a Decremental Age." *Policy Sciences, 1983, 16,* 1–25.

Stanfield, R. "Big Money in Low Rents." *National Journal,* May 7, 1994, pp. 1068–1071.

U.S. General Accounting Office. *States Use Illusory Approaches to Shift Program Costs to Federal Government.* Washington, D.C.: Government Printing Office, 1994.

Wildavsky, A. *The Politics of the Budgetary Process.* New York: Little, Brown, 1964.

Wildavsky, A. *The New Politics of the Budgetary Process.* Glenview, Ill.: Scott, Foresman, 1988.

Wildavsky, A., and Caiden, N. *The New Politics of the Budgetary Process.* (3rd ed.) New York: Longman, 1996.

CHAPTER TWENTY-THREE

Budget Implementation

Rebecca Hendrick
John P. Forrester

Most people see budget implementation simply as a technical or administrative exercise in scheduling and monitoring the finances of government. By comparison, the most emotionally charged debates and visible decisions of the entire budget process, and sometimes of all government policymaking, tend to occur during budget preparation and adoption. This is true whether budgeting takes place in the halls of Congress, in state legislatures, or in the town hall. Understandably, budget implementation is viewed as somewhat perfunctory and less relevant than budget creation to the important matters of government.

Generally and traditionally, budget implementation is a means of assuring accountability and financial control and coordinating revenues with expenditures across governmental units (see Schick, 1964). Within this context, the budget provides the financial record of government decision making, giving the public benchmarks it needs to control and exercise oversight of governmental actions. The budget also is intended to be an expenditure plan that specifies how appropriations for basic items are to be divided among governmental units, thereby establishing a blueprint of fiscal responsibility for the units. During implementation, budget officers and controllers allocate appropriations, check the legality and appropriateness of expenditures before they occur, determine whether agencies have complied with the budget, and monitor expenditures and revenues to maintain a balanced budget. Accountability and financial control are checked, then, by using the budget and implementation procedures to assess, guide, monitor, and control the fiscal side of government.

Given the significance of budget implementation for accountability and coordination, relatively little is written about it (see Fisher, 1975, pp. 3–4; Draper and Pitsvada, 1981). With the exception of Jones and Thompson (1986) and Thompson and Zumeta (1981), who present the foundation of an implementation theory grounded in industrial organization and public choice theories, there has been little theoretical development and minimal empirical research on the subject. When the subject is discussed, usually in the context of input systems, emphasis is placed on methods of controlling expenditures, insuring compliance, and fixing responsibility, rather than on the broader range of programmatic needs and managerial activities (see Schick, 1966).

This chapter reviews budget implementation under traditional or input budgeting and under newer outcome or results-oriented budgeting systems. In traditional line-item budgeting, decisions focus on process, procedures, and inputs. The budget is implemented to uphold conventional views of accountability through compliance and control. In outcome budgeting (also called performance or mission-driven budgeting), decisions focus on programs, performance, and outcomes. The bounds of accountability are broadened to closely parallel the notion of accountability used by nonprofit and private sector organizations. Accountability in these sectors encompasses effectiveness, efficiency, and quality in addition to the outcome monitoring and reporting of input levels.

The next section reviews concepts and procedures of budget implementation associated with traditional budgeting processes and discusses why certain procedures are followed. An example of input budgeting at the federal level follows. Next, budget implementation under outcome budgeting is presented, followed by examples of such implementation at the federal, state, and local levels. Finally, the chapter reflects on the organizational significance of implementation under outcome budgeting.

BUDGET IMPLEMENTATION UNDER TRADITIONAL INPUT BUDGETING

Implementation procedures under input budgeting have three primary purposes: to prevent waste, fraud, and abuse; to accommodate changes in revenues or demands for expenditures that may occur throughout the fiscal year; and to ensure that public money is expended according to legislative intent (Rubin, 1997, pp. 260–283). Input systems use a variety of measures to achieve these goals, including detailed operational guidelines that specify the objects and timing for expenditures, a comprehensive system of reporting, and clear lines of authority for incurring spending obligations. The implementation process occurs in roughly three phases in most governments: the development of operating plans and schedules that communicate expenditure authority and procedures; the making of changes and adjustments to the plans and budget, instituted internally by the executive and externally by the legislative branch; and reconciliation and audit at the end of the fiscal year.

Phase 1: Developing Operating Plans and Schedules

The first implementation phase establishes expenditure authority, procedures, and the requirements for reporting expenditure activities throughout the fiscal year. These processes, in effect, operationalize the budget. They translate legislative priorities, the chief executive's agenda, and departmental missions into specific operations as the plans and schedules wind their way down to the lower levels of government. The concepts and procedures that are common to most governments in this phase are:

- *Appropriation:* The broadest specification of spending authority designated by a legislature that identifies the responsible unit and object or purpose of expenditure. Spending authority includes the ability to incur obligations and disburse funds.

- *Allocation:* A further designation of appropriations by administrative executives that delegates spending authority down the chain of command and for specific line items or categories of expenditure. This process is most commonly used in larger governments with lump-sum, aggregate appropriations.

- *Allotment:* The most common means of designating spending authority from administrative executives to subordinates that also subdivides spending authority by periods. It may also include further restrictions on types of expenditure. Allotments provide "a system of documents by which agencies (1) ensure that deficiencies will be prevented, usually referred to as administrative control of funds, and (2) allocate, distribute, and delegate spending authority down the chain of command to program and field managers, often accomplished through a financial operating plan" (Gore, 1993, pp. 34–35). The federal government also uses apportionments, prior to allotments, as an interim step in distributing spending authority from the president to major organizational units.

The period specified by allotments or apportionments can be bimonthly, monthly, or quarterly; the allotments are used to control the rate of expenditures and to coordinate spending with future events, such as receipt of grants or the opening of facilities. Additional means of financial control that are available to administrators include encumbrances, which are allocations or allotments held in reserve until an expenditure outlay is made; and preauditing procedures, such as requisitions and purchase orders, that determine the availability of uncommitted funds and whether the expenditure is consistent with legal authorization prior to the agency incurring an obligation.

As soon as agencies know their appropriation amounts, they develop their own financial operating plans. For federal agencies, the plans set "the various appropriations committee and [Office of Management and Budget (OMB)] apportionment funding limitations into the financial management control system of the agency and include allotments for the agency's organizational elements and programs, projects, and activities, as defined by congressional action." Periodic reviews of year-to-date progress also occur, usually "late in the fiscal year when management decisions are needed to ensure that spending targets are met (e.g., whether contracts can be awarded by the end of the fiscal year, whether grants will be awarded, etc.)." And to ensure that obligations are liquidated, a closeout of appropriations is usually required after the end of the fiscal year (Gore, 1993, pp. 95–96).

The reporting component of budget execution allows officials to see whether the actions of agencies have been consistent with plans and designated spending authority, and to determine whether adjustments to the budget are warranted. Although the reports usually coincide with allotment schedules, at some level governments may even require daily reports of all transactions. Monthly reports are usually cumulative daily reports, while quarterly reports show information on variances between actual and budgeted expenditures. These reports also include the financial operating plans, allotment and allocation schedules, and sometimes even the general and subsidiary ledgers that are used to record transactions.

Phase 2: Managing a Flexible Budget

During the second phase of implementation, control and compliance measures are introduced to reduce the need for changes to the budget that are contrary to the original intentions of policymakers. The diversity of the measures reflects the conflicting priorities, agendas, and missions of the legislature (its need to control the purse strings and establish policy), the executive branch (its desire to manage generally and establish policy in many cases), and the departments (their need to manage efficiently while meeting the needs of clients). The tugging gets complicated because of changing economic tides and environmental uncertainties that make revenues and expenditures hard to predict. Thus it should be no surprise that budgets will change and that budget implementation may be seen as the art of adaptation. As Rubin (1997, p. 224) argues, "A certain amount of flexibility and change during the budget year may be both necessary and desirable." Regardless of the degree of flexibility needed, the popular sentiment is that constraints must be put in place to assure that whatever changes occur do not threaten either public acceptability or accountability of the budget (see also Pitsvada, 1983).

In most cases, ensuring flexibility while also ensuring accountability during budget implementation requires elected and nonelected officials to manage a portfolio of implementation mechanisms. One of the most important is the supplemental appropriation. Supplementals generally require legislative approval and may reflect unexpected increases in demand for services or unforeseen court cases, technical or managerial needs, or even policy changes. The use of supplementals has declined somewhat at the national level, but most other governments rely heavily on the supplemental process (Rubin, 1997). State and local governments usually draw their supplemental appropriations from reserve funds residing in contingency accounts or fund balances. Contingency accounts may be created at the beginning of the fiscal year, or they may comprise funds held aside at each allotment period and placed into a separate account. General fund balances, which may be used as slack or reserve funds, are made larger for such purposes by delaying allotments, temporarily deferring expenditures or obligations, underspending in an allotment period, underestimating revenues, or overestimating expenditures (Hale, 1977; Hale and Douglass, 1977).

Another way to fund increases in budgetary expenditures, especially for managerial and technical reasons and under balanced budget restrictions, is through intrafund and interfund transfers. Intrafund transfers, which are sometimes referred to as reprogramming, are transfers between programs, objects of expenditures, or line items within the same account or governmental unit. Almost all governments have guidelines regulating the use of such transfers; but often transfers require only the approval of the chief administrator or the budget office, not that of the legislative body. As such, transfers give administrators some discretion as they execute their programs, and they are often the primary source of budgetary flexibility (Axelrod, 1988).

Interfund transfers occur between major budgetary accounts and are the least common type of budgetary change because there are other means of obtaining funds during the fiscal year. Thus they tend to be used for technical reasons, such as for short-term borrowing to manage cash flow, or as a result of overlapping commitments between two or more smaller accounts that may be part of the same program (such as for grants) (Rubin, 1997). At the federal level, both reprogrammings and appropriation transfers require congressional involvement. Transfer authority may be granted in statutory language, especially for emergencies, whereas "most reprogramming guidelines are not statutory; they are procedures mutually agreed upon between appropriations subcommittees and agencies" (Gore, 1993, p. 56).

Agencies may also rely on reapportionments and reallotments, which require the participation of only the OMB and agencies. The ability to reapportion and reallot revenues is needed because, for instance, suballotments are based on a budget prepared about two years before it is executed and thus are likely to be out of sync with current programmatic needs. The challenge for managers is to strategically chart "a course among different mechanisms for adjusting restrictions" (Gore, 1993, p. 54).

Federal and state governments also may use impoundments to reduce expenditures during the fiscal year, usually in the form of rescissions or deferrals. Rescissions are legislatively approved reductions in appropriated funds and are used at all levels of government. They can be instituted for political reasons, such as when the policy priorities of a new administration or legislature are very different from those of the prior regime, and when the new regime does not want to wait until the next fiscal year to alter the budget. Rescissions can also be used to handle unexpected declines in revenue. Deferrals are approved delays in obligations or expenditures and may be used for a variety of reasons, but they are less likely to be used to change policy. They are also very common at all levels of government (Rubin, 1997). At the federal level, the Congressional Budget and Impoundment Control Act of 1974 has significantly limited the president's authority to impound funds.

In light of the fine-tuning and other alterations to the budget during implementation, a concern under traditional input budgeting has been whether the modifications shift the balance of power between the executive and the legislative bodies. Where the chief executive has less interest in managing, Rosenthal (1990) suggests, the legislature will move in to exert control and oversight over the implementation of the budget. The extent to which this occurs, however, will undoubtedly depend on the expertise of legislative members and the extent to which they are part-time or full-time. It also depends on the reasons for the changes. Forrester and Mullins (1992) report that most changes in budgets and plans tend to occur for managerial and technical reasons. Such changes can be a way around appropriations that limit a unit's response to changes in service and supply environments or compensate for deviations of actual revenues and expenditures from estimated ones. More politically motivated changes to the budget may occur for symbolic reasons or to redress a loss of funds during the normal budgetary process.

Phase 3: Reconciliation and Audit

The last phase of budget execution, reconciliation and audit, is often a technical exercise for managers and accountants. Financial and compliance audits (done internally and externally) can determine whether expenditures have conformed with financial restrictions and legal requirements. Accounting reconciliation, which also occurs after the fiscal year ends, focuses on zeroing out appropriations and expenditures for a given fiscal year to ensure their equality and to prevent year-end deficits and surpluses in the accounts. In some cases, reconciliation is primarily a matter of transferring surpluses from some line items or service areas to others to correct for slight deviations from appropriated expenditures.

In many instances, however, administrators may incur last-minute obligations to delete anticipated year-end surpluses in their accounts. This strategy allows agencies to keep their appropriated resources and avoids having the unspent balance taken away from them and reverted back to the general fund balance, only to be redirected to another agency. Additionally, administrators often fear that surpluses will be perceived by legislators and chief executives as unneeded money, and that the next year's budget will be reduced to compensate for the unnecessary funds (Wildavsky, 1979). This "use it or lose it" mentality may result in the purchase of goods or services that are not necessarily needed, or the money may be used to fund "worthy" endeavors that were not expected to be funded at the beginning of the fiscal year.

To illustrate budget execution under traditional budgeting, we turn to the most studied and visible of all governments: the U.S. federal government.

INPUT-ORIENTED BUDGET IMPLEMENTATION IN THE FEDERAL GOVERNMENT

When a budget is implemented, so too is the president's agenda, Congress's priorities, and a department's mission. To one degree or another, these are spelled out in the budget as it winds its way through agency submission, executive preparation and proposal, and legislative adoption. The budget to be implemented is the amount appropriated by Congress and signed by the president. When spending their appropriations, agencies may feel pressure both to treat the budget as a ceiling (not spend all of the money they are budgeted) and to treat it as a target (spend all of the budget). On the basis of the Anti-Deficiency Act of 1870, agencies are instructed not to spend more than their appropriations. But paying heed to the Budget and Impoundment Control Act of 1974, managers also are cautioned "against not spending what the appropriations act intended be spent" (Gore, 1993, p. 57). Traditionally, Congress has used implementation controls to pay attention to budgetary details in the hope of getting a better grip on broader programmatic objectives (Draper and Pitsvada, 1981, pp. 24–25).

Generally, implementing the budget has been a difficult and demanding process for federal departments and agencies. To implement the budget, agencies turn to OMB's instructions of budget execution known as OMB Circular

A-34, which defines the schedule for budget execution, the types of budgetary resources, instructions for modifying the budget, and the responsibilities of agencies and the OMB. Although the instructions help agencies with this cumbersome task, agencies still struggle with their desire for flexibility (in order to deliver services effectively) and with their responsibility to be accountable to the public (see Schick, 1964; Thompson and Zumeta, 1981). Pressures for accountability emanate from Congress, the president and his staff, and even departments. Departments and agencies must determine how to be flexible within these accountability constraints.

Congress: Line Items, Annual Budgeting, and Earmarks

The most visible means Congress has employed to ensure that agencies and departments use resources in the manner that Congress intended are the line-item format and the annual budget. Although Congress writes budget laws in a lump-sum format, committees specify many line items in their reports and expect agencies to live within these limits. Accountability, in this sense, is sought over inputs, not over process or outcomes. Rarely have budget requests incorporated performance measures that go beyond resource inputs, let alone assessed the accomplishments of a program against the stated objectives of that program (Gore, 1993, pp. 23–24). Any planning that occurs has usually been independent of the budgeting process, as recommended by so much of the budgeting literature (see Wildavsky, 1979; Lauth, 1985, 1987). Congress has also exercised control over the bureaucracy and the executive by insisting that budgeting be done on an annual basis, which requires that the executive receive yearly congressional approval and minimizes the opportunity for agencies to manage their resources carelessly.

As pointed out in a recent publication by the National Performance Review (Gore, 1993), Congress also enacts "statutory requirements in appropriations, such as defining periods of availability for funds, earmarking funds for certain projects or activities, and breaking accounts down into subaccounts (activities). In addition, Congress may include detailed instructions and earmarkings in the committee reports that accompany appropriation bills" (pp. 34–35). Most earmarks are written to force agencies to distribute funds broadly across legislative districts.

Congress: Directed Apportionments and Allotments

When the Congress appropriates resources in a line-item manner and on an annual basis, these tools are usually insufficient for guaranteeing accountability on a monthly or quarterly basis. Instead these tools are intended to prevent an agency from spending more than its annual appropriation over the full fiscal year. To direct agency spending over a shorter time frame, Congress has the authority to put restrictions on executive apportionments and allotments. Congress may insert provisions that prevent spending until specified dates or events, or it may order that agencies receive their full apportionments at the beginning of the fiscal year.

The Executive: Operating Plans and FTE Ceilings

The president's budget office, the OMB, and departmental budget offices have also focused on budget inputs during budget implementation. Departments typically have operating plans that are the basis for executing budgets. But these plans must often be changed to meet external constraints. For example, since the early 1980s, the OMB has set ceilings on full-time equivalent (FTE) personnel in departments and agencies. A fixation on meeting these ceilings comes to pervade departmental budget execution. Consequently, the execution information requested at the department level is often intended to ensure that dollars are spent as budgeted, not necessarily to help management of programs.

RECENT MANAGERIAL REFORMS, OUTCOME BUDGETING, AND BUDGET IMPLEMENTATION

The need to ensure accountability and public trust through the control and monitoring of expenditures is clear and should not be undermined. Nevertheless, agencies must exercise administrative, managerial, programmatic, and fiscal discretion when necessary to accommodate rapidly changing technologies and environments. They must also try to achieve the programmatic objectives laid out by the legislature and improve the quality of services they deliver. When faced with such pressures, managers require very different types of information than what is normally provided by input budgeting systems, and they must embrace a broader set of concerns than those associated with only the values of control, compliance, and responsibility.

One proposed solution to these problems has been to base government budgeting, and other critical decisions, on outcomes rather than inputs. The origin of outcome budgeting may be traced back to private sector management reforms that grant to personnel more discretion over resources and, in exchange, hold them accountable for programmatic outcomes and performance. Understandably, such changes alter budgetary control and accountability.

Beginning in the 1980s, practitioners and students of public administration began to apply the management practices of the private sector, such as Total Quality Management and strategic planning, to public sector organizations. More recently, empowerment approaches to management have been broadened and popularized at all levels of government through the work of Osborne and Gaebler (1992) and the efforts of the NPR (Gore, 1993). These trends and ideas provide the underpinnings for recent budgeting and financial management reforms, such as the Service Efforts and Accomplishments standards being debated by the Governmental Accounting Standards Board and the performance measures required by the Government Performance and Results Act of 1993.

The arguments for outcome budgeting are based on the idea that the budget represents a contractual agreement between principals (the citizens and their elected representatives) and agents (the agencies). Within this framework, outcome budgeting establishes a very different contract between principals and agents than what exists under input budgeting systems. Under outcome budgeting, the contract, or budget, is to deliver particular services and meet performance or quality standards in exchange for funding. For input budgeting, the contract allows the agent to purchase specific items, paying no more than the specified amount. Budget implementation in both cases depends on policymakers' ability to ensure that the contractual agreement is upheld, which in turn depends on the policymakers' ability to know when the agreement has been fulfilled, and the range of choice opportunities or available contractors. Successfully controlling performance therefore requires designing the contract (and accompanying budget implementation procedures) to fit existing knowledge and opportunity states.

Jones and Thompson (1986) specify four types of contractual relationships that are appropriate to different circumstances and particularly relevant to budget implementation (see Figure 23.1). These relationships indicate that the contracts, presented as four cases, vary according to two dimensions: the ability of an agency to monitor program performance, and the degree to which programs are delivered in a competitive environment.

The first dimension designates low and high capabilities of monitoring programmatic consequences. A low capability occurs generally where agency services and outputs are unique and nonfungible or where the performance objectives are inherently complex, vague, and ambiguous. A high capability to monitor programmatic consequences exists under opposite circumstances. The second dimension of available opportunities is also divided into two states or levels: programs in which competition among service and output providers is desirable and possible, and where there is a range of providers from which to choose; and programs in which competition is undesirable or where the organization responsible for delivering programmatic services has a monopoly. Both Case 1 and Case 4 in Figure 23.1 represent conditions in which the contractual relationship is conducive to outcome budgeting. Case 3, and possibly Case 2, are closest to conditions appropriate to input budgeting.

Outputs and Outcomes

	Fungible and Measurable	Unique, Hard to Measure
Competitive	Case 1: Fixed-Price Contracts	Case 2: Flexible-Price Contracts
Monopolistic	Case 4: Variable Budgets	Case 3: Outlay Budgets

(Row label at left: **Environment**)

Figure 23.1. Budgetary Contractual Relationships.

Case 1: Fixed-Price Contracts

Where the ability to monitor performance and the range of possible providers are both high, policymakers should use fixed-price performance contracts. Here, an agreed-on level of payment for services or outputs that meet specific performance standards is made after service delivery.

Case 2: Flexible-Price Contracts

Flexible-price performance contracts (or administered contracts) are most appropriate where the ability to monitor performance is low but competition among providers exists. In this case, both service providers and policymakers have less knowledge about whether performance standards are achieved, which means that both parties have less control over whether the standards actually are achieved. These conditions require that performance standards and payment remain flexible. Flexible-price contracts are most likely to be used with internal service units whose services could easily be delivered by the private sector.

Case 3: Outlay Budgets

Lump-sum grants or outlay budgets are appropriate in circumstances where monitoring is difficult and service providers have a monopoly, such as occurs with many of the internal management functions of an organization. As with flexible-price contracts, policymakers retain the authority to monitor inputs as a means of controlling expenditures, but the organization delivering the services must also provide indicators of performance to the extent possible.

Case 4: Variable Budgets

Finally, governments may use variable budgets in instances where performance can be monitored but service providers have a monopoly. Although programmatic results may be monitored in these circumstances, the key to the success of these arrangements is a system of meaningful sanctions and rewards because there is no real option to change providers if performance standards are not met (Thompson, 1993). Many governmental agencies fit the description of a variable budget organization, and variable budgets are often utilized by nonprofit and for-profit organizations under the label of responsibility budgeting. In this system, appropriations are ceilings or guidelines rather than absolute levels of spending authority to which the agency must adhere. Additional budgetary slack and flexibility is achieved by allowing agencies to keep whatever funds are left over from a prior year, as long as the agency meets its performance objectives as set out in the budget document. The system also provides for emergencies and other major midyear budgetary changes through formal contingency allowances that are set aside from all accounts in one or more contractual (allotment) periods. Agencies that require additional funding must obtain approval from policymakers prior to transferring funds from their contingency accounts (Anthony and Young, 1995).

OUTCOME BUDGETING, INPUT BUDGETING, AND BUDGET IMPLEMENTATION

We have argued that outcome-based budgeting is conceptually rooted in contemporary management reforms and can be understood as a contractual relationship where performance can be monitored but where service providers may have a monopoly or compete for service delivery contracts. In this section we contrast outcome budgeting and input budgeting with respect to factors that are critical to budget implementation. Specifically, we consider how these systems measure success, the location of spending authority, and implementation procedures.

First, because of their different orientations toward accountability and revenue and expenditure coordination, input and outcome budgeting require different measures of success. Under traditional input budgeting, objectives are achieved through financial control via line-item budgeting and financial reporting standards. Consequently, budget implementation focuses on ensuring that resources for specific categories of tangible items, such as salaries or equipment, are expended at the levels budgeted. Under outcome budgeting, coordinating revenues and expenditures during the fiscal year is still a concern and is maintained through aggregate-level financial reporting, but accountability is redefined to emphasize control over program performance (Anthony and Young, 1995).

Unfortunately, program performance is not always easy to define or measure. Objectives associated with program effectiveness, quality, and performance may be conflicting, ambiguous, or vague. Additionally, such objectives are often difficult to standardize across agencies or environments, which may be critical to the information systems necessary to support outcome budgeting. By comparison, measures of financial control are much easier to standardize, as is evident from the multitude of regulations and definitions issued by the Governmental Accounting Standards Board.

Second, because of their different orientations toward empowerment and managerial discretion, the location of spending authority will differ under outcome and input budgeting. With input budgeting, spending authority is centralized with policymakers and upper-level administrators. Under outcome budgeting, spending authority and responsibility for other key financial management areas such as purchasing are distributed toward the lower levels of the organization through lines of managerial control. This frees policymakers from making decisions on the details of program content and spending, and encourages them to focus instead on programmatic goals. In conjunction, managers who are closer to program operations and service activities are given the opportunity to use their expertise in determining the best way to achieve results, and they are given the financial flexibility necessary to support these decisions. Thus there is a centralization of goals and a decentralization of means (Cothran, 1993).

Third, because of their differences in defining success and locating budgetary responsibilities, budget implementation procedures will not be the same under outcome and input budgeting. Implementation monitoring in input systems is usually limited to expenditures and revenues. Implementation in outcome systems focuses on monitoring objectives, standards, and targets as well as expenditures and revenues. This difference reflects fundamental differences in accountability between the two systems. Input budgeting holds administrators responsible for specific levels, types, and rates of spending. Outcome budgeting holds administrators responsible for attaining outcomes and minimizing costs within overall fiscal ceilings, which can encourage administrators to manage the bureaucracy more effectively and be less reactive to their environment (Ingraham and Kettl, 1992).

These features also reveal that budget implementation and reporting become more essential to management and programmatic decision making under outcome budgeting, and linked directly to other managerial tasks, especially strategic planning and performance monitoring. Additionally, initial budgetary agreements are less rigid in outcome budgeting, allowing administrative units more authority over day-to-day expenditure decisions, which greatly complicates the traditional resource control focus of implementation. This in turn requires changes in notions of accountability; specifically, accountability becomes broader and more focused on programmatic results than on administrative process and expenditures. All of this requires additional information and monitoring beyond what is provided by traditional financial accounting and reporting. As a result of these changes, budget implementation under outcome budgeting should become less an exercise in scheduling and monitoring expenditures and more a way to manage resources dynamically.

OTHER CONSEQUENCES OF THE OUTCOME BUDGETING FRAMEWORK

Given the fundamental differences between input and outcome budget systems, each is likely to have different implications for other budgeting and management areas that have an impact on budget implementation. Areas that are particularly affected include budget preparation and adoption, information requirements for monitoring, methods of achieving control, budget format, and organizational structure and management systems.

Budget preparation and adoption in traditional systems focus on determining the level of expenditures by estimating aggregate costs for specific categories or objects of expenditures. Both policymakers and administrators may even rely on very simplified decision procedures during these stages, such as comparing the current year's expenditures to the previous year's or making across-the-board budgetary changes. Preparation and adoption in outcome budgeting, by comparison, focus on identifying programmatic objectives, standards, and targets and examining the extent to which goals laid out in prior years have been met. For these goals and benchmarks to guide implementation effectively, however, and if they are to be the results to which managers will be held accountable, they must be well defined. Although determining goals and objectives is especially difficult in political settings, this process can be facilitated in government by establishing policy goals and organizational missions separately from the budgeting process, such as through strategic planning. In this case, the strategic plan provides a framework for the budget and helps to constrain the preparation and adoption debates (Bryson, 1995).

To support their different oversight and decision needs, the budgeting systems may also require different levels and types of information in their midyear reports as part of budget implementation. Input systems are predominately financial, while outcome systems merge financial and managerial information. It is even likely that the reports in each system may vary according to who is receiving them. Policymakers and upper-level administrators may want more information on changes in quality and effectiveness. Managers and controllers, conversely, have a greater need for information on performance, efficiency, and service coverage (Reschenthaler and Thompson, 1996). An example of their different information and reporting needs is seen in the distinction between performance auditing and financial auditing (Association of Government Accountants Task Force, 1993; Davis, 1990). Furthermore, because managers in outcome systems have greater discretion over expenditures, policymakers and controllers are likely to require them to submit reports more often.

Input and outcome budget systems also rely on different means to assure financial control during budget implementation. Input systems rely on procedural constraints and rules, such as allotments, apportionments, vouchers, and preauditing procedures, which control the means of delivering services. Outcome systems replace these traditional methods of control with monitoring and oversight of objectives that tell managers what they should be achieving. This difference suggests that the roles of controllers and others responsible for overseeing budget implementation will be different under each system. It further implies that the expertise of managers and the level of trust between them and policymakers will be an important factor for compliance in outcome systems.

Also consider that under traditional budgeting, governmental operating budgets tend to be detailed, line-item expenditure plans that must be implemented as they are approved. With outcome budgeting, however, budget authority represents an upper limit on spending, and the operating budget consists primarily of programmatic objectives, performance standards, and service-level and productivity targets. In conjunction with its methods of control, managers in outcome budgeting systems are given the maximum discretion necessary to be productive, to adapt to changing circumstances and localized conditions, to accommodate uncertainty, and to learn (see Thompson, 1994; Forrester and Adams, 1997).

Outcome systems also become more viable with a programmatic budget format and full accrual accounting, which organize performance, cost, and efficiency information in a way that is meaningful to their use in such systems. Here, all activities are grouped or aligned by program, including those that transcend organizational boundaries, and their budgets reflect all direct, indirect, and overhead costs. This ensures that all government expenditures and activities are tied to the appropriate objectives and reflect the true level of resource used in achieving those objectives. Another crucial accounting procedure in this system is using revolving funds or allowing more carryover of funds to encourage agencies to innovate and implement cost-saving measures (Thompson, 1991; Hildreth, 1993).

In contrast, expenditures in traditional budgeting systems are grouped by organizational unit and object of expenditure within units, and one program may draw resources from numerous accounts. This structure obscures programmatic objectives and true costs, and it may increase the complexity of the budget and accounting systems through the proliferation of numerous, separate funds. Additionally, year-end rescission of funds and the perspective that remaining funds are "under expenditures" may preclude agencies from becoming more efficient by discouraging programmatic savings and promoting unnecessary year-end expenditures.

The efficacy of outcome budgeting may also increase with different organizational structures and management systems. For example, a focus on objectives and standards may be easier to implement in decentralized organizations where operational authority and discretion are distributed toward the lower levels of the organization. In cases where programs cut across functional areas, a matrix organization, with its use of free-flowing teams, may provide the best means of achieving objectives. Because outcome budgeting does not rely on rules or regulations to control employee actions, management must compensate by utilizing a complete range of incentives, sanctions, and rewards to motivate employees and encourage them to improve performance (Thompson, 1991, 1994).

One fundamental problem with implementing outcome budgeting is that its focus on results and its necessary organizational structures and management methods may not be compatible with the agency's environment or tasks. For instance, it would be difficult to use competition as a means of motivating employees in situations where the organization supplying the service, either inside or outside government, is a monopoly. It would also be difficult to measure objectives and gauge performance in situations where the objectives are complex, vague, or ambiguous or where appropriate data are unavailable. Therefore, governments may not be able to implement outcome budgeting in all situations or for all programs. In these cases, agencies may have to rely on more traditional methods of budget preparation and implementation.

Other factors that can affect whether a government or agency adopts input or outcome budgeting systems are the organization's size and the philosophy of its elected officials and managers. The size of the organization can influence how many officials and subunits participate in the budgeting process (including implementation), the number of reports and documents used, and the amount and type of procedures involved. As such, larger governments may have more difficulty implementing outcome budgeting, and they may require more sophisticated and integrated management information systems to provide the appropriate information. It has even been suggested that outcome systems may work only in parliamentary governments because their planning and policy authority is concentrated rather than dispersed among different branches or elected offices (Thompson, 1994). Similarly, it may be easier for professionally managed governments, such as council-manager cities, which also have less dispersion of authority, to implement outcome budgeting as well as other private sector budgeting and management practices.

CASES IN OUTCOME BUDGETING

New Zealand has been a leader in the current reform movement, and several other nations, including Australia, Great Britain, Canada, Sweden, and Denmark, have instituted similar reforms. Studies of these countries' experiences are showing the difficulties of such reforms and their impacts on the countries' political and administrative processes (Dixon, 1996; Gray, Jenkins, Flynn, and Rutherford, 1991; Mascarenhas, 1996; Pallot, 1997; Schick, 1990). This section reviews cases of outcome budgeting in the United States.

U.S. Federal Government: National Performance Review

Recently, the U.S. federal government has begun to implement outcome budgeting, albeit on a selective basis (see Jones and McCaffery, 1992, 1993, and Chapter Three of this book). The primary force behind these changes is the National Performance Review. Headed by Vice President Albert Gore Jr., the NPR has released numerous reports since 1993 on the benefits and procedures of mission-driven, results-oriented budgeting. Its recommendations focus on enabling "policy leaders and managers to link purposes, resources, and results to make government work better and cost less" (Gore, 1993, p. 7). If the NPR's goals are to be realized, policymakers and administrators must agree on the programmatic results and measures that are based on established policy priorities. Managers must also be provided with adequate resources and have the power and flexibility to use the resources according to their discretion, and they must be given the necessary information and time to achieve results (pp. 8–9). Following are some of the NPR's specific recommendations, especially those affecting or affected by budget implementation.

Strategic Planning and Performance Measurement. Defining accountability according to results instead of inputs requires agencies to specify clearly their programmatic objectives or impacts and to have a reasonable idea of how they will accomplish these ends. The NPR recommends that agencies use comprehensive strategic planning to determine programmatic objectives, specify measures of performance, and identify plans or strategies for achieving these goals. If a performance goal cannot be expressed quantitatively, then OMB may "authorize the agency to use an alternative, descriptive form of goal" (Rivlin, 1995, p. 4). Whether quantitative or qualitative, the expectation is that the plans and goals will guide managers and staff with their fiscal and programmatic decisions throughout the year. For instance, "At the National Archives, strategic planning improved employee motivation and helped managers make more informed decisions by providing information about results" (Gore, 1993, p. 24).

Limiting Restrictions on Earmarkings, Apportionments, and Allotments.
The NPR also recommends that Congress give managers more flexibility in
using resources by removing detailed limitations on earmarkings, apportionments, and allotments. Managers note that they spend too much time complying with restrictions on small allocations of funds, and too much time
"tracking and balancing" small suballotments (Gore, 1993, pp. 34–37). To give
managers more flexibility to achieve goals, to allow them to devote more attention to accomplishing results, to increase their efficiency, and to simplify
budget execution, the NPR has made the following recommendations:

- "Revise operational plans and performance goals to reflect actual appropriations by mission and function. . . . After appropriations are enacted,
  agencies develop their financial operating plans and internal allocations"
  (p. 41).

- "Restructure appropriations accounts to reduce over-itemization and to
  align them with programs" (p. 43).

- "Agency heads should issue internal guidance to ensure that operating
  costs can be readily identified and to implement any changes necessary
  in financial management systems in the execution of the budget" (p. 42).

- "Propose revolving funds for those agencies that do not have them"
  (p. 43).

- "Reduce overly detailed restrictions and earmarks in appropriation and
  report language" (p. 44).

- "The OMB Director should immediately issue internal guidance to staff
  to use simple letter apportionments and process apportionments within
  the time frames called for in the law" (p. 44). Where OMB needs to inform agencies of changes in policy decisions, means other than apportionments should be considered.

- "Reduce the excessive administrative subdivision of funds in financial
  operating plans." This can be done if agencies "review their procedures
  for developing financial operating plans at the beginning of the operating year . . ." (p. 45).

Terminating FTE Ceilings. Supporters of the NPR assume that federal managers are required to put so much emphasis on controlling resource inputs that
they are not able to control their outputs effectively or to increase the effectiveness of services. This is true especially for FTE ceilings. Managers tend to
feel that arguments over FTE ceilings miss the more important point of how to
use employees more effectively and economically. Some of the problems cited
by the NPR in this area include the following: "Ceilings or floors requiring fewer

or more employees than needed to accomplish a mission can create mismatches with agreed upon allocations of dollars." Ceilings are too frequently arbitrary, they are often are out of sync with rules and regulations that call for more work, and "all employees count equally under FTE ceilings regardless of grade" (Gore, 1993, pp. 50–51). Given that agencies also are being pressured to privatize and contract out services, "ceilings force work to be contracted out that could be done less expensively in-house . . ." (p. 51). Consequently, the NPR recommends that budgets be prepared and managed on an operating cost basis rather than using FTE ceilings, and that Congress remove FTE floors (p. 52). Ironically, however, the request to deemphasize FTE ceilings and emphasize outcomes was undercut by the simultaneous Administration objective of cutting the size of the federal workforce by over 272,000 FTEs.

Increasing Flexibility. Although managers currently have some flexibility over the execution of their budget, the NPR recognizes that this may not be enough. For instance, the NPR argues that complications associated with various transfers provide "an incentive to spend the funds in each suballotment even though such spending may not reflect current needs and priorities" (Gore, 1993, p. 55). Also, detailed reprogramming thresholds can be very time-consuming for managers, which delays the allotment of funds (p. 56). Correcting these problems could be accomplished by fewer restrictions on transfers and by reprogramming, which encourages managers to spend money on current needs rather than on dated restrictions, and helps to ensure that customers are served in a timely manner (p. 59). Ways of further increasing flexibility include:

- Converting some appropriations to multiyear or no-year status, which removes the incentive for managers to spend all appropriated funds by the end of the fiscal year (p. 60).

- Permitting "agencies to roll over 50 percent of their unobligated year-end balances in annual operating costs to the next year," which also discourages year-end spending (p. 60).

- Expediting reprogramming of funds within agencies by sending reprogramming requests "directly from the agency head . . . to the appropriations subcommittee, after the advance notification and approval of OMB. OMB should automatically approve reprogramming unless it objects within a set period of time, such as five days" (p. 61).

- Formulating "financial operating plans and adjusting allotments and suballotments on a timely basis" to provide "timely, accurate, accessible financial and program performance information that quickly divulges trends and problems to attentive management" (p. 61).

Implementation reforms also might parallel two recommended budget preparation reforms: give agencies a chance to implement the budget with an eye toward results not just process, and allow them to manage information in a way that helps them to achieve their strategically determined results. Both reforms would change the orientation of the process from simply input management to managing a blend of input, process, output, and impacts.

Missouri Department of Revenue

At the state level, the use of performance and productivity measures is limited to revising programs, authorizing new programs, or changing funding levels during budget preparation and adoption. Although some states, such as Minnesota, Oregon, and Texas, have been cited for their reform efforts, for the most part this information is not part of the fabric of state budgetary decision making during either budget preparation or implementation. Furthermore, neither state wealth nor size is a good predictor of the use of this information (Lee, 1993). The state of Missouri's Department of Revenue (DOR) is an example of outcome-based budgeting that is very detailed and rigorous, providing both enhanced financial and programmatic control.

In 1993, the DOR, under a new director, engaged in a pilot management project and budgetary reform similar to the outcome budgeting described in this chapter. The need for reform was driven by three sets of events: personnel dilemmas, in the form of frustrated state employees who were in their third year of no salary increases; organizational dilemmas, as exemplified by an unexplained backlog of vehicle registration applications that extended for months and was reported by the press; and budgetary problems created by the DOR's budgetary requests, which reduced the credibility of the budgetary process in the eyes of the state's legislature.

It was the director's judgment that all three sets of difficulties—personnel, organizational, and budgetary—as they applied to the DOR had to be addressed for the reform to be effective. The result was a comprehensive budget and management reform, called the Detailed Base Budget Review, undertaken by the director of DOR, her division directors, and their personnel. Their new goals were to provide better service to customers (such as to shorten the time required to process automobile title applications); to encourage all DOR employees to make recommendations for improving departmental operations, especially frontline service providers; and to implement these changes without increasing budgeted resources.

In its initial stages, the reform allowed DOR employees to question and determine organizational goals and objectives effectively, and it was structured to let the DOR budget around the department's products or outcomes. Furthermore, the outcome orientation significantly affected accountability and flexibility in that the DOR gained control over its resources while, surprisingly, increasing its accountability to the public.

Flexibility. The new budgetary process gave the DOR director, midlevel management, and employees more flexibility, but in uniquely different areas. First, frontline employees were allowed more input in determining how to make programs more efficient and effective. They could recommend and implement changes in departmental operations as long as the changes did not require additional resources. As an additional incentive, it was agreed that no positions would be eliminated through the reform, except through attrition. Second, midlevel managers were given more autonomy in managing their policies. Finally, the director was given discretion to reprogram and transfer resources within the department to meet changing needs and environmental demands.

Key legislative initiatives that were necessary to implement these reforms included appropriating the DOR's budget in one lump amount instead of in separate detailed amounts for its five divisions; giving the director the authority to reprogram and transfer money to where it was needed most, even if that meant temporarily using employees from one division to help out another division or transferring money between line items; and allowing the DOR to exceed the FTE capitation in order to meet seasonal demand and to eliminate the backlog of vehicle registration applications.

Due to the reforms, several midlevel management positions were eliminated through attrition, and employee satisfaction and job retention increased. (The DOR had a problem of losing experienced auditors, for instance, to other departments, especially departments that were merit-based and where the pay was higher for comparable positions.) Also, the added flexibility allowed the director to hire temporary labor and to shift employees as needed, even if that meant exceeding the FTE ceilings. Seasonal caseload increases could now be handled in-house rather than contracted to other states. This measure saved the state several thousands of dollars in lower compensation during the first year, decreased the error rate that usually accompanied such outsourcing, increased employee satisfaction (because their jobs were no longer being shipped out of state), and increased the state's domestic product and therefore its tax revenue. Overall, the reforms produced significant benefits in the form of lowering the department's overall budget while collecting more revenue for the state's treasury.

Accountability. For the budget and management reforms to be successful, the DOR could not sacrifice accountability to the public. If anything, the reforms would have to increase accountability. Fortunately, this occurred in at least two ways. First, the DOR initiated strategic planning to guide its operations and budget and to provide it with a set of goals and strategies for achieving them. The resultant plans have provided a set of objectives for which the department is accountable. The planning process has allowed the department to learn about itself, to evaluate its successes and failures, and to determine what changes should be made to become more successful.

Second, the annually revised strategic plans have been used to frame discussions about the budget. By linking goals, programs, and resources, both the governor and the legislature are now able to assess more competently the DOR's productivity and effectiveness, making DOR line employees and managers more accountable for their actions even though they have been given more autonomy in their jobs.

Third, and most visibly, a House budget subcommittee agreed to grant the DOR increased flexibility as long as the director would in turn provide accountability for the resources appropriated. The director has accommodated the request by providing these committees with monthly summaries of the department's activities, and the results have been very positive. Legislators have embraced the increases in departmental effectiveness because of the obvious benefits to them when citizens are able to obtain services (such as licenses) faster and with fewer complications. Through the reforms, the DOR has decreased the size of its budget requests and, along with the simultaneous organizational changes, has increased state revenue collections, without an increase in taxes.

Outcome Budget Execution: The City of Milwaukee

In comparison to state governments, local governments seem to have made significant progress toward incorporating results-oriented reforms into standard budget preparation and implementation procedures. In a recent survey of 510 jurisdictions, 88 percent report workload measures in their budget requests, 83 percent report efficiency measures, and 88 percent report effectiveness measures (O'Toole, Marshall, and Grewe, 1996). Thirty-three percent of the jurisdictions monitor whether agencies meet their goals or objectives as a part of budget implementation, while 31 percent monitor operational efficiency. These factors were also considered highly influential by the jurisdictions that used them. Examining the jurisdictions' budget formats, however, suggests that local governments have not completed the transition. Fifty-one percent still rely on line-item budgeting alone, and 35 percent use a hybrid budget format (line item and program). Additionally, larger jurisdictions are more inclined than smaller jurisdictions to use budget reform tools. (See Thurmaier, 1995, for an in-depth analysis of reforms in budget execution and their impact in Kansas City–area local governments.)

The city of Milwaukee has adopted many components of outcome budgeting as part of comprehensive reforms in budgeting and management that began around 1990 when the mayor and the budgeting director initiated strategic planning. Shortly after the city completed its strategic plan in 1991, the budget office began requiring all departments with appointed heads (cabinet departments) to implement their own strategic planning process and to structure their budget requests according to the citywide plan. The four noncabinet departments, which are headed by elected officials (comptroller, treasurer, city attorney, and the municipal judges) were strongly encouraged to adopt these measures.

Two years later, all departments were required to develop their budgets according to the objectives and activities specified in their own plans. This evolution toward outcome budgeting continued in 1995, when the city extensively revised its citywide plan and began requiring departments to update their plans prior to budget preparation. Departments must now include outcome measures in their budgets, and the city intends to implement activity-based costing in some service areas (Kinney, 1995).

The city has progressed even further with implementing its focus on results. In the early 1990s, the mayor's office formally embraced a commitment to privatize service delivery whenever possible and feasible. Corresponding with this initiative, the mayor's office launched the Internal Service Improvement Project, which requires internal service units such as information systems, equipment, and some areas of personnel to compete with the private sector for internal contracts with other city departments. Initially some of these service units lost their contracts with departments, but they gradually won them back through their ability to deliver a better product at a lower cost (Enos, 1996). Most recently, the budget office has instituted a form of expenditure budgeting in which it sets agencies' expenditure limits according to a formula based on inflation and other factors prior to the agencies submitting their budget requests (Cothran, 1993).

Although these changes have increased departments' budgetary and managerial flexibility to some extent, legal requirements and political pressures still preclude a move to lump-sum budgeting and some aspects of outcome-based budget implementation. Not surprisingly, the council has been somewhat reluctant to appropriate a single amount for some departments or units, especially departments such as sanitation, which is also responsible for snowplowing. Such services are very visible and important to council members' constituents. As a result, council members want to know exactly how much these types of services cost, and they tend to micromanage such units. Additionally, because Milwaukee's comptroller is elected, which divides the responsibility for budget implementation and monitoring between the comptroller and the mayor, fiscal planning and authority are fragmented in this city. Moreover, some of the comptroller's duties related to budget implementation and specific areas of accountability are mandated. This situation makes it difficult to coordinate budgetary reforms and implement some aspects of outcome budgeting.

The comptroller, who is legally responsible for coordinating revenues and expenditures and for ensuring that funds are spent according to appropriations, must determine the availability of funds in a budgetary unit before funds are encumbered. Thus budget implementation in Milwaukee must include this form of preauditing, although the process is fairly automated by the city's current financial information system. Furthermore, the comptroller can mandate midyear budgetary changes to restore balance to the budget. By comparison, the budget office, which must approve changes to budgetary authority, becomes the unit responsible for monitoring performance and establishing the budget implementation procedures associated with outcome budgeting. Although the budget office's monitoring is not yet as routine or systematic as that of the comptroller, the budget office is beginning to monitor performance and outcomes within departments as part of its midyear review of personnel changes and quarterly reporting.

Progress in moving toward outcome budgeting and fully incorporating the budget implementation procedures associated with such a system is also hampered by the state of the city's current financial information system. Because budget implementation is seen primarily as the responsibility of the comptroller, the monitoring systems for budget implementation fit the information needs of the comptroller's office. As such, the ability to account for agency performance or to relate performance and operations to costs is limited. Although agencies in the city have always maintained numerous workload and operational measures, few performance or outcome measures have been collected systematically, and there are no recognized procedures for connecting operational information with the budget or with broader performance objectives. Currently, the comptroller's office has just issued a request for proposals for a new information system that should integrate financial, operational, performance, and outcome information and accommodate the budget execution needs of the budget office.

Although it is too early to determine the impact of all outcome budgeting components in this city, the general consensus is that strategic planning has been successful and has provided a firm basis for outcome budgeting. Overall, the reforms have encouraged the city and agencies to think more clearly about how crucial parts of management—budgeting, planning, service delivery, and monitoring—fit together. This at least holds the promise of improving agencies' performance and their focus on results.

IMPLEMENTING OUTCOME BUDGET EXECUTION: THE IMPORTANCE OF LEARNING

As the twenty-first century nears, governments at all levels are rethinking how they budget, how they should implement their budgets, and consequently, why they budget. Several states, many municipalities, and even the federal government are structuring their budgets around their goals and objectives. This story seems reminiscent of the Planning, Programming, Budgeting System (PPBS) of old, and in large measure it is, but with one profound exception. PPBS was largely implemented by externally forcing it on government agencies. Such a package is in stark contrast to outcome budgeting, which is developed largely with the involvement of government agencies. In other words, the reform is a comprehensive organizational effort, not simply the application of a new technology or a new format. The government itself is changing, and this is most evident in the way it executes its budget, as this chapter has argued.

Perhaps most significantly, a comprehensive approach to budgetary reform that integrates strategic planning, results measurements, and budgetary decision making is giving students of public budgeting an opportunity to reflect on why governments budget. Three factors have clearly influenced governments to use the reforms to learn about results and to become more competent in their actions: the extensive time and effort put into the planning phase and in developing performance measures, the bottom-up approach to developing strategic plans and performance measures, and the care taken to integrate the plans, budgets, and operations (see Rist, 1994, p. 191). Under outcome budgeting, agencies are asked to move beyond the use of current operating procedures and norms to implement means for detecting and correcting problems (see Argyris, 1982; Normann, 1985; Stata, 1989) and instead structure their processes and norms to help the agency question its values and objectives (see Forrester and Adams, 1997). Such agencies are likely to be open to inquiry and self-criticism, and hence open to innovative possibilities (see Morgan, 1986, p. 105), and will likely structure their budget implementation process to produce information on the legal as well as effective use of resources.

The most recent budget reforms are giving agencies the opportunity to become more sophisticated learners through the kind of monitoring and feedback that would occur during budget implementation under an outcome system. Two changes in particular may make this possible. First and most significantly, although traditional budget offices have required agencies to allot funds to ensure that their activities remain within their budgeted limits, outcome budgeting requires that programmatic information be gathered and assessed during implementation to determine agency progress toward meeting goals and to determine the appropriateness of the goals. Such information is mandated, for example, in the new budget request procedure for Missouri agencies, beginning with requests for the FY98 budget. Second, to the extent that the outcome budget focus is reflected in a strategic defragmenting of the organizational structure and a commensurate defragmenting of the budget structure, it will be easier to assess policies and programs that cut across funds or cost centers during and after budgetary implementation (the easiest way to defragment the budget is by cross-walking funds or items and programs). How much the agencies and departments change their management information systems and their budget decision structures depends on the organization's desire and ability to manage in a results-oriented manner, and on the openness of the organization's culture (Forrester and Adams, 1997).

References

Anthony, R. N., and Young, D. W. *Management Control in Nonprofit Organizations.* (5th ed.) Burr Ridge, Ill: Irwin, 1995.

Association of Government Accountants Task Force. "Report on Performance Monitoring." *Association of Government Accountants Journal,* 1993, *42*(2), 11–25.

Argyris, C. *Reasoning, Learning, and Action: Individual and Organizational.* San Francisco: Jossey-Bass, 1982.

Axelrod, D. *Budgeting for Modern Government.* New York: St. Martin's Press, 1988.

Bryson, J. *Strategic Planning for Public and Nonprofit Organizations: A Guide for Strengthening and Sustaining Organizational Achievement.* (rev. ed.) San Francisco: Jossey-Bass, 1995.

Cothran, D. A. "Entrepreneurial Budgeting: An Emerging Reform?" *Public Administration Review,* 1993, *53*(5), 445–454.

Davis, D. F. "Do You Want a Performance Audit or a Program Evaluation?" *Public Administration Review,* 1990, *50*(1), 35–41.

Dixon, J. "Reinventing Government: The Gore Vision and the Australian Reality." *Public Productivity and Management Review,* 1996, *19*(3), 338–362.

Draper, F. D., and Pitsvada, B. T. "Limitations in Federal Budget Execution." *Association of Government Accountants Journal,* 1981, *30*(3), 15–25.

Enos, G. "Four Words That Can Wake Up a Sleeping Bureaucracy: We May Go Private." *Governing,* 1996, *10*(2), 40–41.

Fisher, L. *Presidential Spending Power.* Princeton, N.J.: Princeton University Press, 1975.

Forrester, J. P., and Adams, G. B. "Budgetary Reform Through Organizational Learning: Toward an Organizational Theory of Budgeting." *Administration and Society,* 1997, *28*(4), 466–488.

Forrester, J. P., and Mullins, D. R. "Rebudgeting: The Serial Nature of Municipal Budgetary Processes." *Public Administration Review,* 1992, *52*(5), 467–473.

Gore, A., Jr. *From Red Tape to Results: Creating a Government That Works Better and Costs Less.* Report of the National Performance Review. Washington, D.C.: Government Printing Office, 1993.

Gray, A., Jenkins, B., Flynn, A., and Rutherford, B. "Management of Change in Whitehall: The Experience of the FMI." *Public Administration,* 1991, *69*(1), 41–59.

Hale, G. E. "State Budget Execution: The Legislature's Role." *National Civic Review,* 1977, *66*(6), 284–290.

Hale, G. E., and Douglass, S. R. "The Politics of Budget Execution: Financial Manipulation in State and Local Government." *Administration and Society,* 1977, *9*(3), 367–378.

Hildreth, W. B. "Federal Financial Management Control Systems." *Public Budgeting and Finance,* 1993, *13*(1), 77–86.

Ingraham, P. W., and Kettl, D. F. *Agenda for Excellence: Public Services in America.* Chatham, N.J.: Chatham House, 1992.

Jones, L. R., and McCaffery, J. "Symposium: Federal Financial Management Reform, Part I." *Public Budgeting and Finance,* 1992, *12*(4), 70–106.

Jones, L. R., and McCaffery, J. "Symposium: Federal Financial Management Reform, Part II." *Public Budgeting and Finance,* 1993, *13*(1), 75–86.

Jones, L. R., and Thompson, F. "Reform of Budget Execution Control." *Public Budgeting and Finance,* 1986, *6*(1), 33–49.

Kinney, A. S. "Mission, Management, and Service Delivery: Integrating Strategic Planning and Budgeting in Milwaukee." *Government Finance Review,* 1995, *11*(5), 7–11.

Lauth, T. P. "Performance Evaluation in Georgia Budgetary Process." *Public Budgeting and Finance,* 1985, *5*(1), 67–82.

Lauth, T. P. "Budgeting and Productivity in State Government: Not Integrated but Friendly." *Public Productivity Review,* 1987, *11*(3), 21–32.

Lee, R. D., Jr. "Use of Program Information and Analysis in State Budgeting: Trends of Two Decades." In T. Lynch and L. Martin (eds.), *Handbook of Comparative Public Budgeting and Financial Management.* New York: Dekker, 1993.

Mascarenhas, R. C. "Searching for Efficiency in the Public Sector: Interim Evaluation of Performance Budgeting in New Zealand." *Public Budgeting and Finance,* 1996, *16*(3), 13–27.

Morgan, G. *Images of Organizations.* Thousand Oaks, Calif.: Sage, 1986.

National Performance Review. *Mission-Driven, Results-Oriented Budgeting.* Washington, D.C.: Government Printing Office, 1993.

Normann, R. "Developing Capabilities for Organizational Learning." In J. M. Pennings and Associates, *Organizational Strategy and Change.* San Francisco: Jossey-Bass, 1985.

Osborne, D., and Gaebler, T. *Reinventing Government: How the Entrepreneurial Spirit Is Transforming the Public Sector from Schoolhouse to Statehouse, City Hall to the Pentagon.* Reading, Mass.: Addison-Wesley, 1992.

O'Toole, D. E., Marshall, J., and Grewe, T. "Current Local Government Budgeting Practices." *Governmental Finance Review,* 1996, *12*(6), 25–29.

Pallot, J. Presentation on Financial Management and Budget Innovations in New Zealand. Ninth Annual Conference on Public Budgeting and Finance, Washington, D.C., Nov. 1997.

Pitsvada, B. T. "Flexibility in Federal Budget Execution." *Public Budgeting and Finance,* 1983, *3*(2), 83–101.

Reschenthaler, G. B., and Thompson, F. "The Information Revolution and the New Public Management." *Journal of Public Administration Research and Theory,* 1996, *6*(1), 125–144.

Rhodes, R.A.W. (ed.). "The New Public Management." *Public Administration,* 1991, *69*(1), entire issue.

Rist, R. C. "The Preconditions for Learning: Lessons from the Public Sector." In F. L. Leeuw, R. C. Rist, and R. C. Sonnichsen (eds.), *Can Government Learn? Comparative Perspectives on Evaluation and Organizational Learning.* New Brunswick, N.J.: Transaction, 1994.

Rivlin, A. M. "Memo to Heads of Performance Measurement Pilot Projects" (M-95-05). Washington, D.C.: Office of Management and Budget, Mar. 8, 1995.

Rosenthal, A. *Governors and Legislators: Contending Powers.* Washington, D.C.: Congressional Quarterly Press, 1990.

Rubin, I. S. *The Politics of Public Budgeting: Getting and Spending, Borrowing and Balancing.* (3rd ed.) Chatham, N.J.: Chatham House, 1997.

Schick, A. "Control Patterns in State Budget Execution." *Public Administration Review,* 1964, *24*(3), 97–106.

Schick, A. "The Road to PPB: The Stages of Budget Reform." *Public Administration Review,* 1966, *26*(4), 243–258.

Schick, A. "Budgeting for Results: Recent Developments in Five Industrialized Countries." *Public Administration Review,* 1990, *50*(1), 26–34.

Stata, R. "Organizational Learning: The Key to Management Innovation." *Sloan Management Review,* 1989, *30*(3), 63–74.

Thompson, F. "Management Control and the Pentagon: Organizational Strategy-Structure Mismatch." *Public Administration Review,* 1991, *51*(1), 52–66.

Thompson, F. "Matching Responsibilities with Tactics: Administrative Controls and Modern Government." *Public Administration Review,* 1993, *53*(4), 303–314.

Thompson, F. "Mission-Driven, Results-Oriented Budgeting: Financial Administration and the New Public Management." *Public Budgeting and Finance,* 1994, *14*(3), 90–105.

Thompson, F. "New Public Management." *Journal of Public Policy Analysis and Management,* 1997, *16*(1), 165–176.

Thompson, F., and Zumeta, W. "Control and Controls: A Reexamination of Control Patterns in Budget Execution." *Policy Sciences,* 1981, *13*(1), 25–50.

Thurmaier, K. "Execution Phase Budgeting in Local Governments: It's Not Just for Control Anymore." *State and Local Government Review,* 1995, *27*(2), 102–117.

Wildavsky, A. *The Politics of the Budgetary Process.* (3rd ed.) New York: Little, Brown, 1979.

CHAPTER TWENTY-FOUR

Performance-Based Budgeting

Philip G. Joyce

The 1990s are witnessing a resurgence of efforts to introduce more performance information into government management. Although perhaps most clearly identified with the "reinventing government" movement (after the best-selling book of the same title; see Osborne and Gaebler, 1992), the efforts, at all levels of government, are much more pervasive than this trend. For example, the federal government is currently engaged in an ambitious effort, occasioned by the Government Performance and Results Act (GPRA) of 1993, to increase the use of performance information for both budgeting and management (Joyce, 1993). For many people, given that the budget is the key statement of government priorities, the efforts toward results-oriented management can ultimately be judged successful only when the allocation and management of resources are changed in significant ways.

It is in this context that *performance-based budgeting* can be considered. This chapter first discusses the elements of performance measurement systems and the different ways that performance measures can affect the budgeting process. Evidence is presented about current practice, and the chapter outlines the prospects for more widespread use of performance information in government budgeting processes.

WHAT IS PERFORMANCE-BASED BUDGETING?

There is no standard definition of performance-based budgeting. The confusion stems in part from the fact that there are a great many potential applications of performance measures in budgeting. Although it is not necessary to define budgeting for this chapter's audience, the concept of performance is a bit more slippery.

This chapter focuses primarily on the measurement of performance. Government performance measurement involves a complex web of relationships from inputs to outputs (the effects within the government or organization) to outcomes (the broader external effects associated with government policies or programs). The ultimate goal of reforming the government performance measurement system is to refocus attention from the former internal measures to the latter external ones. But measures of government performance have historically stressed inputs and outputs instead of outcomes. (Exhibit 24.1 defines the concepts typically used to describe the government performance measurement process.)

Now to connect the two. Performance-based budgeting assumes that outcomes are considered in the process of allocating and managing government resources. As such, it is sometimes termed "connecting resources to results." Proponents make the perfectly defensible assumption that it is desirable to focus on the accomplishment of agencies' programs relative to their uses of scarce resources. Although no one disagrees with the desirability of this goal, it is not as easy to achieve as it might seem.

Exhibit 24.1. The Performance Measurement Process: Concepts.

One of the key challenges inherent in the development of a performance measurement system has to do with terminology. Although no single precise set of definitions exists, the following discussion represents the definitions of the key performance measurement concepts used in this chapter.

Inputs. These are the resources consumed by the operation of a government program; they are ultimately used to hire personnel, build facilities, contract for services, and so on. Inputs are easily measured, usually in terms of dollars. For example, input measures for elementary and secondary education programs might focus on the number of teachers or schools required, or on the cost of paying teachers or building schools. Inputs are obviously necessary for the achievement of objectives, but the question of how many inputs are required to achieve a given level of performance usually goes unanswered. In addition, input measurement is not always straightforward or easy; for example, it is difficult for many

Exhibit 24.1. (*continued*)

agencies to estimate the full costs of delivering particular programs, given the challenges of allocating indirect costs.

Activities. These are the works performed by a given agency. They represent the observable work performed by agency staff in carrying out the agency's programs. For an environmental protection agency, for example, activities might include inspections performed to determine the extent of compliance with environmental regulations. A highway department's activities might include filling potholes. An important characteristic of activities is that they are within the control of the agency.

Outputs. These are measures of the results of an agency's immediate activities. Although outputs may not be sufficient for the agency to achieve its objectives, they are often necessary for the agency to do so. These gauges are sometimes also referred to as activity or process measures. To return to the example of education, the number of days of instruction (a measure that multiplies the number of students by the total number of days in which a given school offers classes) could be considered a measure of educational outputs.

Outcomes. These are the broader goals of an agency. Outcome measurement should assess the extent to which the activities (outputs) of the agency have the intended effect. That is, they should focus not only on the work performed but also on the results of that work. In education one might measure the performance of students on standardized tests (by estimating the change in average test scores from year to year, for example) as a barometer of the success of education programs. This moves the discussion away from the activities of the schools as ends in themselves and instead relates them to the schools' success in educating students. Outcomes, of course, are only partially under the control of the public agency or program (the home environment, for example, also affects educational outcomes in significant ways.) Outcomes often may also be referred to as impacts, which may measure progress toward the broader societal objectives that are influenced by an agency or program. Part of the goal of public education, for example, is to produce a more informed citizenry or a better-trained workforce. For our purposes, outcomes and impacts are considered synonymous, in the sense that both are measures of ultimate objectives of an agency or program, and that agency managers do not completely control them.

Ultimately, a sophisticated performance measurement system would be able to link up these four types of measures to gain a true picture of the effectiveness of a particular program or policy. What level of resources (inputs) would lead to a given level of output? How are those outputs connected to outcomes? And what is the significance of the achievement of those outcomes to the attainment of broader societal objectives (impacts)?

HOW CAN PERFORMANCE MEASUREMENT AFFECT THE BUDGETARY PROCESS?

Having established what is meant by performance-based budgeting, what are the major ways that performance measurement is thought to be able to improve the budgetary process? There are, I would argue, at least three main ways. First, agencies may replace traditional line-item budgets with a system that grants program managers greater flexibility in managing their resources but holds them accountable for achieving program results. Second, even if government-wide decisions on resource allocation are not affected, agencies may find measures that are valuable for improving their management of a given level of resources, regardless of whether the use of those measures results in a significant shift of resources from one program or agency to another. Third, the government or particular agencies may use performance measures as a part of reports on their accomplishments.

Allocation of Resources

Legislative bodies and elected chief executives may want to use performance information to make decisions on how to allocate scarce resources among competing priorities. Performance measures are most useful to these people if the measures help to determine how much money should be spent on the various purposes of government: police, transportation, health care, national defense, environmental regulation, and so on. Ideally, these choices would be aided by a better expectation of what a dollar for national defense would buy compared with spending the same dollar on some other activity, such as transportation, health, or education.

Using outcome measures to allocate resources is a substantial deviation from the way most observers describe the current budget allocation process. At present, policymakers are focused on inputs (usually represented by agency line items) and on making marginal changes in those inputs from year to year. They obviously must consider benefits as well, but assessments of benefits are less formal and comprehensive than assessments of costs. The two methods of budgeting imply substantially different emphases; line-item budgeting focuses almost exclusively on how much money is being spent, and performance-based budgeting concentrates on varying levels of program results that might accompany varying levels of performance.

Agency Management of Internal Resources

Performance measurement can do more than just inform government-wide resource allocation. Agencies may find performance measures valuable for improving the use of a given level of resources, even if they do not result in a significant shift of resources from one program to another or from one agency to another. For example, an agency that is organized geographically could use performance measures to target resources toward those regions where the workload is greatest or where the problems are most acute. Agency subunits may improve performance if workers become more highly motivated when their efforts are being scored and assessed by management. Moreover, ties may be developed between the measurement of organizational and individual performance, as proponents of so-called pay-for-performance schemes have suggested.

Financial Reporting

Performance measures can also be used to report the results of government activities to elected officials and decision makers. At the state and local levels, the Governmental Accounting Standards Board (GASB) has called for service efforts and accomplishments (SEA) reporting (Hatry and Fountain, 1990). The SEA initiative encourages state and local governments to include statements of service results in their annual financial reports. At the federal level, both the Chief Financial Officers (CFO) Act of 1990 and the Federal Accounting Standards Advisory Board (FASAB) are expected to focus on the use of performance measures for financial reporting. The CFO Act, for example, requires agencies' financial officers to develop "systematic measures of performance" for programs in their agencies. Although the FASAB is charged primarily with developing common standards for financial reporting, the need for performance measures has also been discussed in some of their deliberations (Bramlett, 1991).

PERFORMANCE-BASED BUDGETING IN HISTORICAL PERSPECTIVE

The current efforts to incorporate more performance information into the budgetary process is not the first such effort. In fact, more than thirty years ago, in the classic "The Road to PPB: The Stages of Budget Reform," Allen Schick (1966) discussed how the emphasis of budgeting changed over time from control (the executive budget movement in the early part of the twentieth century) to management (the late 1930s through the 1950s, as typified by the recommendations of the Brownlow Committee and the Hoover Commissions) to planning (the program budgeting movement of the 1960s, embodied in the federal government by the Planning, Programming, Budgeting System, or PPBS, discussed in Exhibit 24.2). Efforts to "rationalize" the budgetary process continued through the 1970s, with the emphasis on reforms such as management by objectives (MBO) and zero-based budgeting (ZBB). The 1980s saw very little government management reform, perhaps as a result of the general antipathy toward government—the emphasis was on what to do, not on how to do it.

Exhibit 24.2. The Planning, Programming, Budgeting System.

Perhaps the most frequently cited historical antecedent to current performance budget efforts is the attempt by President Lyndon Johnson to put into effect a planning, programming, budgeting system (PPBS). The president ordered the PPBS system, pioneered in the Defense Department by Secretary Robert McNamara, to be employed throughout the federal government in 1965. By 1971, however, requirements that civilian agencies include the PPBS system data were suspended. PPBS ceased to exist, at least explicitly, except in the Defense Department.

Reports and evaluations indicate that the PPBS was much less successful in civilian agencies than in the Defense Department, in part because the agencies lacked administrative commitment to integrating the system fully into their management systems. Although Secretary McNamara was clearly committed to putting PPBS into effect in the Defense Department, in most other cases the system was treated as an annual reporting requirement rather than as a management or budgeting opportunity. Several other arguments have been made for the failure of PPBS to catch on (Schick, 1973):

- It was introduced across the board without much preparation.
- It flew in the face of existing budgetary traditions and relationships; in particular, many people strongly objected to the suggestion that the budgetary process, which is inherently political, could be made "rational."
- It was not given adequate resources, and top managers were not entirely committed to it.
- Good analysts and data were in short supply, and they were necessary to produce the kind of information crucial to the success of PPBS.
- Because PPBS was intended to require a review of all activities in each year, the reform caused so much conflict that the political system was not able to handle it.
- PPBS clearly assumed that efficiency was the primary value to be considered in evaluating the usefulness of programs, which was not generally agreed to and is a difficult assumption to make in the case of a public program.
- PPBS was an executive budget system, and largely ignored the role of Congress in the budgetary process. The result was that Congress ignored the system in favor of its established procedures.

PPBS was unable to fulfill its promise as a budgetary reform. In particular, it did not change the budgetary process from one that focused primarily on making small incremental changes to one that could make comprehensive alterations. Federal budget decisions were still made largely at the margin. Like performance

Exhibit 24.2. *(continued)*

---

budgeting, however, PPBS increased the role of analysis in budgeting and led to better-informed budgetary decisions. This increase has continued long after PPBS faded from view.

Source: Summarized from Congressional Budget Office, 1993, pp. 23–24.

Although a full evaluation of these past reforms is beyond the scope of this chapter, it is worth summarizing the key themes of postmortems (Harkin, 1982; Congressional Budget Office, 1993). First, these budgeting systems typically had a difficult time overcoming opposition from those who had a vested interest in maintaining the status quo. For example, there was some fear among appropriations committees in the states and in the national government that these reforms might interfere with the flow of funds toward key electoral constituencies. Second, in each case there were disagreements among subordinates and superiors about the goals and objectives of programs; these disagreements compromised the ability to develop measures of progress toward these goals and objectives. Finally, each of the systems had an almost overwhelming need for data. This became problematic when it became clear that the target audience was not using the data for the purposes intended for that data. The lessons of these reforms should inform our effort to determine whether and under what conditions the current iteration of performance-based budgeting will succeed.

THE RETURN OF PERFORMANCE MEASUREMENT AND BUDGETING

Even though none of these past reforms prevailed on a widespread basis, the vestiges of prior budgetary reforms—particularly program budgeting—remained in many state and local governments and in parts of the federal government. For example, the demand for analysis implicit in these reforms had the effect of increasing the pool of policy analysts at all levels of government. The early 1990s saw the return of widespread efforts to integrate more performance information into state and local budgetary processes. Two particular forces fueled this movement. First, the GASB's SEA initiative encouraged the development of more performance information for financial reporting (Hatry and Fountain, 1990). Second, the reporting of many individual success stories by Osborne and Gaebler (1992) created pressure for states and localities to "reinvent" themselves.

Actual experience thus far has been spotty. In local government, the highest profile success story has been Sunnyvale, California. Sunnyvale, nestled in the heart of the Silicon Valley, has used an elaborate performance-based system since the late 1970s. The system, according to participants, seems to promote attention to results rather than inputs, and it seems to be used by both agency managers and policymakers. The government also engages in long-term planning, setting overall goals and objectives as many as twenty years in advance. The success of the system in Sunnyvale seems to be promoted by the lack of significant resource constraints, as well as a stable vision of long-term goals for the jurisdiction. There is some question, therefore, about the replicability of the Sunnyvale system in other venues. (See Exhibit 24.3 for a brief discussion of the Sunnyvale system.)

Exhibit 24.3. Performance-Based Budgeting in Sunnyvale.

The city of Sunnyvale, California, began to develop a budgeting and accounting system in the early 1970s in response to an effort spearheaded by the General Accounting Office (GAO) to assist state and local governments in developing such systems. The city developed a more elaborate system in the late 1970s. It combines strategic planning, performance-based budgeting, and pay-for-performance for management employees.

In 1991, a joint delegation from the Office of Management and Budget and the GAO visited Sunnyvale and reported that the city's budgeting system integrates performance measures, agency management, resource allocation decisions, and long-range planning. Several factors seem to contribute to the success of the Sunnyvale system:

- The city operates on a full cost-accounting basis, which allows officials to identify with some precision how much it costs to provide different levels of service.

- The budgetary process focuses on the outputs that will be produced rather than on spending. In fact, the city council does not even vote on the budget, in a traditional line-item sense. Rather, the council approves goals for city programs, and the level of resources necessary to meet these goals is implicit.

- A detailed set of objectives and performance measurements governs all municipal functions. Many of these measures are oriented toward outcomes.

- Early-warning and long-range planning are stressed. The city sets overall goals and objectives twenty years in advance, and projects the revenues and expenditures necessary to achieve these objectives for ten years in the future.

- Under a detailed pay-for-performance system, there are explicit ties between individual and organizational performance.

A 1993 Congressional Budget Office (CBO) study reported on the use of performance measures in the budget processes in Sunnyvale and in four additional local governments: Dayton, Ohio; Charlotte, North Carolina; St. Petersburg, Florida; and Portland, Oregon. According to the study, although all of these local governments were using performance measures, these measures were much more likely to be measures of output rather than of outcome. Further, little evidence was found of the use of performance information for allocating resources, although it was clear that particular local agencies were making use of such information in managing the resources they received.

More recently, the expansion of performance measurement concepts has been encouraged by the International City/County Management Association (ICMA). The ICMA, in conjunction with the Urban Institute, is engaged in an ambitious project to develop consensus performance measures in several program areas common to local government. As this chapter is being written, more than forty different local governments are participating in the project. This effort focuses on the development of the measures themselves, however, not on their uses for budgeting. The very reasonable assumption is that good measures must be developed before they can be used as part of important management processes.

Evidence on state efforts with performance-based budgeting comes from a number of sources. First, the aforementioned CBO study and a similar report by the U.S. General Accounting Office (GAO) both focused on the experience of several states with performance measurement and its ties to the budget. The GAO study focused on five states—Connecticut, Hawaii, Iowa, Louisiana, and North Carolina—chosen because surveys and other reports had listed them as among the national leaders in developing performance measures (U.S. General Accounting Office, 1993). The GAO researchers reported that

> despite long-standing efforts in states regarded as leaders in performance budgeting, performance measures have not attained sufficient credibility to influence resource allocation decisions. Instead, according to most of the state legislative and executive branch officials interviewed, resource allocation decisions continue to be driven, for the most part, by traditional budgeting practices. . . . Outside the budget process, state officials say that performance measures have aided managers in (1) establishing program priorities, (2) strengthening management improvement efforts, (3) dealing with the results of budgetary reductions, and (4) gaining more flexibility in allocating appropriated funds.

The CBO study also analyzed performance-based budgeting in two state governments—Florida and Oregon—that are currently using performance measurement (Congressional Budget Office, 1993). The results of this analysis closely mirrored the GAO findings and the CBO results concerning local governments—that is, there have been some impressive strides in managing resources in the budget execution phase, but there have been no significant changes in the decision rules for allocating resources in the first place.

More recently, Broom and McGuire (1995) evaluated performance measurement efforts in five states: Texas, Oregon, Minnesota, Virginia, and Florida. The results reported in this review were largely consistent with the GAO and CBO results listed earlier. That is, the review identified impressive efforts to develop better performance information that in some cases (particularly Oregon) were linked to the achievement of broader societal goals. (See Exhibit 24.4 for a discussion of the Oregon performance measurement system.) The study also found some cases in which performance measures were specifically linked to a reform of the budgetary process (especially in Texas but also in Virginia), but interviews with agency staff and policymakers revealed little evidence that performance information is actually used in the process of making budgetary decisions, at least on a government-wide basis (see also Carter, 1994).

As noted earlier, the GASB's SEA initiative is an important development in state and local governments that merits mention. The SEA initiative encourages state and local governments to include statements of service results in their annual financial reports. This is a significant step for an organization like GASB, which has historically devoted itself to issues of accounting and financial reporting. The initiative foreshadows a time when financial reports will include not only statements of how resources were expended, but also what was gained from the expenditure of the funds. The clear assumption is that the requirement that SEA information be reported will carry with it increased attention to performance in policymaking. The SEA initiative has already generated substantial activity among states and local governments, but it has also been criticized in some circles, particularly by state and local finance officers (Harris, 1995), as unworkable or even foolhardy.

The bottom line is this: state and local government reform cannot generally, in practice, be called performance-based budgeting in the sense that budget allocation decisions are tied to performance measures. It is unquestionably true, however, that selected jurisdictions are making much greater use of performance measures in the budgetary process, particularly for the management of resources and the reporting of information on performance. Because there are no comprehensive evaluations, it is hard to assess the extent of the use of performance information in state and local budgetary processes.

PERFORMANCE-BASED BUDGETING IN THE FEDERAL GOVERNMENT

For the federal government, the current wave of interest in tying performance measures to the budget first manifested itself (perhaps curiously) through a se-

Exhibit 24.4. Performance Measurement and Budgeting in Oregon.

Over the past decade, several events occurred that improved the environment for performance measurement in Oregon. First, in the late 1980s, a long-range planning process (called Oregon Benchmarks) was developed in advance of the performance measurement effort. The benchmarking effort brought together representatives of different parts of Oregon society, including citizens, businesses leaders, and government officials, to develop long-term targets for the state into the next century (Oregon Progress Board, 1994). The authors of this plan hoped that by establishing these broader societal goals the state could better coordinate its policies at all levels of government, and between government and the business community.

Concurrently (but somewhat separately) Oregon engaged in an ambitious effort to increase the use of performance measures in the budgetary process. This effort was spurred in part by the 1990 passage of a local property tax limitation (called Ballot Measure 5). Because this ballot measure required that lost local school revenues be made up by the state, state budgeters estimated that the initiative would ultimately create a state budget shortfall of more than 15 percent. The state has focused on training agencies to use performance measures, and on educating Oregon's citizens about the services provided by state government, an effort that is related to the development of better performance measures. Oregon has attempted to expand the reporting of performance measures in the budget, and to link performance measures and the benchmarks in the budgetary process. For example, the state has used a modified zero-based budgeting process in which agencies are required to forecast the impact of reducing their budgets by 10 to 20 percent from the previous year's level. Agencies are then given opportunities to recover a portion of these lost funds, in part by adding programs that are explicitly related to the Oregon benchmarks.

A recent analysis by Broom and McGuire (1995) suggests that the benchmarks are continuing to inform resource allocation decisions. Further, performance measures have increasingly been used by agencies in Oregon—particularly the transportation, adult and family services, and employment departments.

Although there has clearly been progress in Oregon, the picture is not all positive. First, because agencies have agreed to use the measurement process primarily as a tool for selling their programs, there are no incentives for reporting negative performance. Second, the use of the system varies widely from agency to agency; the most important single variable seems to be the commitment of the agency's head. Third, although the legislature seems supportive, it remains to be seen whether performance measures can be used to affect government-wide resource allocation in any comprehensive way.

ries of reforms of federal accounting systems. These accounting reforms had their genesis in several high-profile financial scandals in the federal government in the 1980s (the most famous of which was at the Department of Housing and Urban Development). In 1990, Congress and the Bush administration responded by passing the CFO Act, which at its base focused on the appointment of personnel and the establishment of procedures to improve federal accounting, as well as requiring that financial statements created under the act include "systematic measures of performance." (This language was not central to the CFO effort but was an attempt by the Senate Governmental Affairs Committee to pave the way for future performance measurement legislation.)

From the perspective of performance-based budgeting, perhaps the most important financial management development is the emphasis on cost accounting. In the past, efforts to move toward a greater performance orientation often focused on developing measures of results without paying adequate attention to the input side of the equation. In the current environment, not only has the FASAB developed guidance on cost accounting, but the CFO Council, driven by the Office of Management and Budget (OMB), is developing guidance for government-wide implementation of this standard (U.S. Office of Management and Budget, 1996).

The further development of an environment conducive to improved performance measurement got a major boost in 1993 with the passage of the Government Performance and Results Act (GPRA), which requires each agency to develop a strategic plan, including a comprehensive mission statement and a set of general goals or objectives for the programs, by September 30, 1997. Plans would cover at least a five-year period. Further, beginning with FY99, the budget for the U.S. government would, under this legislation, include a performance plan. These plans would include performance goals and indicators (quantitative, where possible) enabling Congress and the public to gauge whether agencies have complied with the goals. Each agency would be required to submit a specific performance plan, on a schedule to be determined by the OMB, that would cover the major activities for which it is responsible. In addition to reporting this information in the budget, beginning in FY99 each agency would be required to submit program performance reports to Congress. The first of these reports would be submitted no later than March 31, 2000. They would include information comparing actual with planned performance, a discussion of the success in meeting goals, and remedial action taken if the goals were not met.

In an effort to field test its proposed requirements, the legislation required several sets of pilot projects. The first of these projects was a pilot test for developing performance goals. Although the legislation required only ten such tests, interest was so great among the agencies that more than seventy tests were ultimately approved by the OMB. A second set of pilot projects would test the concept of managerial flexibility, operating for two years beginning in FY95.

This test was considered relevant because of the precedent (particularly in other reform-minded countries such as Australia and New Zealand) to connect accountability for outcomes to increased flexibility for the use of inputs. Third, the legislation mandated pilot projects for performance budgeting. Performance budgets would present varying levels of performance resulting from different budgeted levels. At least five agencies would be required to participate in these pilot projects, which would run for FY98 and FY99. The director of the OMB would report on the results of the performance budgeting pilots no later than March 31, 2001.

By most accounts, the GPRA has generated a great deal of interest and has been embraced enthusiastically by the central budget office. In fact, the OMB under the leadership of directors Leon Panetta and Alice Rivlin, along with deputy director John Koskinen, accelerated the process envisioned under the GPRA by taking two significant actions. First, the OMB began to require agencies to include more performance information in budget submissions as early as for the FY96 budgetary process (U.S. Office of Management and Budget, 1995). Second, the capacity for review and attention to these measures was enhanced by an internal reorganization (called OMB 2000), which combined many of the traditional management and budgetary functions and personnel into newly created resource management offices (RMOs). The RMOs, as envisioned, would go beyond traditional budgetary analysis to conduct more evaluations of performance as well. The OMB believed that agencies would be more inclined to improve management and performance if these changes were tied to the budgetary function (U.S. General Accounting Office, 1995a, 1995b).

Other results under the GPRA have so far been spotty. A November 1994 review of the pilots by the National Academy of Public Administration (NAPA) reiterated the federal government's strong interest in performance measurement, but it uncovered some weaknesses as well. Early reviews of the pilot projects suggested several problems with the measures in many agencies. First, the measures used were often not tied to legislative purpose or agency mission. Second, the measures were often limited in scope, emphasizing workload or activity data over measures of results. Third, agencies avoided using measures over which they felt they had limited control (National Academy of Public Administration, 1994). Findings of a recent analysis by the GAO largely mirrored those of the NAPA study, and the GAO flatly predicted that implementation of the GPRA would be uneven across the federal government. In addition, the other two sets of pilots required by the GPRA—focusing on managerial flexibility and performance-based budgeting—have yet to lead to any formal implementation efforts.

The CFO Act and the GPRA are by no means the only federal efforts that have focused on the performance of federal agencies. The highest-profile initiative in this area is Vice President Al Gore's National Performance Review (NPR).

The NPR advocates a reduction of hierarchical controls over administrative processes in favor of empowering managers and holding them accountable for results (Kamensky, 1996). As a part of this overall strategy, the NPR has advocated a conversion from a budgeting system focused on inputs to a system that focuses on results (Gore, 1993; National Performance Review, 1993).

Early evaluations of non-GPRA efforts suggest something of a change in culture among federal agencies, albeit a somewhat slow and uneven one. For example, the NPR spawned a number of "reinvention laboratories" in federal agencies, which were instructed to develop innovative ways to pursue the accomplishment of agencies' missions (Thompson and Ingraham, 1996). According to Kettl, "No part of [the NPR] activity has been more remarkable than the creativity that thousands of government employees across the country have shown in the reinvention labs" (1995, p. 73).

Nonetheless, the culture of performance does seem to be infiltrating federal agencies. At least three different major initiatives are focused on performance—the CFO Act, the GPRA, and the NPR. The interest seems to be both broad and deep, evidenced by the broad interest among federal agencies in becoming GPRA pilots. In addition, significant movement has occurred on the part of some federal agencies toward developing more (and better) measures of results. Although it is by no means alone, the U.S. Coast Guard has been engaged in a particularly impressive effort in this area in its development of a much clearer sense of mission and measures to evaluate performance as part of a GPRA pilot effort (see Exhibit 24.5). Further, the creation of performance-based organizations (PBOs), driven by the NPR, is designed to give service-delivery organizations in the federal government more managerial flexibility in exchange for tougher accountability for results. These organizations are patterned after Britain's "Next Steps" agencies. The Patent and Trademark Office, a part of the Commerce Department, was named the first PBO in the federal government. One estimate is that two-thirds of federal employees work in agencies that could become PBOs (Roberts, 1996). Finally, financial management reports are now required to demonstrate consistency with the GPRA. A 1996 OMB report on the status of federal financial management devoted five pages explicitly to implementation of the GPRA, focusing in large part on standards and goals promulgated by the CFO Council (U.S. Office of Management and Budget, 1996).

CHALLENGES TO PERFORMANCE-BASED BUDGETING

The road to tying performance measures to the budget is studded with obstacles. To understand the reason for this difficulty, consider successful performance-based budgeting as resting on three sequential steps. First, agreement

Exhibit 24.5. Outcome Measurement in the U.S. Coast Guard.

In early 1992, the U.S. Coast Guard (USCG) began an organizational assessment, designed in large part to determine whether the nationwide performance standards that had guided the scope and frequency of USCG activities were appropriate to allow field units the flexibility to manage toward desired outcomes. In late 1993, the USCG became a pilot project under the GPRA. The goal of the GPRA pilot was the development of performance indicators for the agency's programs.

At the outset of this process, the USCG developed a one-sentence mission statement that was to guide further goal setting: "Our mission is to protect the public, the environment, and U.S. economic interests, by preventing and mitigating marine accidents." This mission statement served to drive the development of more specific goals and encouraged the development of measures to gauge progress toward those goals. It necessitated a reorientation from measures of output to measures of outcome.

This was an evolutionary process. As an illustration, consider that the USCG originally proposed to measure passenger vessel safety by monitoring the number of accidents with more than six fatalities. This measure proved to be of limited use, because only four such accidents had occurred in the past fifteen years. A more indirect measure of risk—the rate of precursor accidents that have the potential for resulting in major losses of life—was instituted. In this case, the agency found the trends to be moving in the wrong direction—the accident rate per vessel had been rising. The USCG redirected its resources in an effort to reduce this risk.

According to the USCG, performance measures are now used to inform various management and decision-making processes. The budgetary linkage is becoming more clear. The agency uses the measures in developing its multiyear budget strategy; in fact, six program activities were slated for scaleback or termination because they made limited contributions toward achieving the USCG's goals. In addition, managers have been given more flexibility to direct resources toward the achievement of established goals. Further, the agency has used performance information as a way of justifying programs in the appropriations process, apparently with some success. The FY95 appropriation was increased by $5 million and 100 full-time equivalents above the requested level, with a Senate report citing the importance of program goals and the soundness of the planning process as the rationale.

Source: Summarized from Kowaleski, 1996.

must be reached on what agencies or programs are supposed to accomplish. Second, it must be possible to reach relevant measures of both costs and service outcomes. Third, some way must be found to tie these measurements to the allocation of resources. Each of these steps, while desirable, is ultimately very difficult to carry out. For this reason, a considerable distance remains between the ideal of performance-based budgeting and its current practice.

Agreeing on Objectives or Targets

One of the key challenges facing management for results, at all levels of government, is that legislation that creates agencies or programs tends to be ambiguous. This ambiguity is in part intentional, because this lack of clarity can promote the development of supporting coalitions. This problem is particularly acute in the federal government, where there is much more interbranch policy disagreement than there is in many state and local governments. Accordingly, it is not surprising that the greatest evidence of success in government performance measurement is in council-manager forms of local government in the United States (Sunnyvale) or in parliamentary systems internationally (especially Australia and New Zealand). In these systems, policy uncertainty is less prevalent than it is in systems where authority is more divided (particularly between the legislative and executive branches). In most state governments in the United States and in the U.S. federal government, managers must operate in an environment in which they are usually asked to respond to many actors, including legislative bodies, elected executives, and the general public. This environment promotes the development of multiple and conflicting objectives for programs, which in turn impedes the development of performance measurement systems.

Managing Costs and Results

Much of the recent debate about performance-based budgeting has concentrated on outcome measurement, without recognizing that major strides are also necessary in the measurement of inputs if the reform is ever going to reach its full potential. Without some way to approximate full-cost accounting, analysts find it difficult to relate costs to performance. This emphasis on cost accounting, as noted earlier, has been occurring in state and local governments for some time and is now occurring in the federal government. Its success is critical to the efficacy of performance-based budgeting as a reform. If the ultimate goal of performance-based budgeting is to enable comparisons to be made of alternative uses of government funds, then we must know how much it costs to produce a given incremental level of outcome. To this end, having appropriate measures of outcomes without appropriate measures of inputs provides only half the answer.

As difficult as it is to develop measures of input, it is usually even harder to develop appropriate measures of results, even in cases where objectives can be agreed on (Newcomer, 1995). As noted earlier, there is evidence of slow progress in the development of outcome measures in government, both in the state and local sector and at the national level. Much work remains to be done, however. Many agencies concentrate on measures of workload or activity, not because they are not aware that these measures are imperfect, but because it is hard to find acceptable measures of the achievement of a policy's objectives that are also under the control of program managers. It is much easier for the Internal Revenue Service to measure assistance to taxpayers according to how many phone calls were answered than by the quality of the assistance given. It is much easier for the Environmental Protection Agency to measure its success according to the number of violations than according to air and water quality. It is much easier to measure educational quality in terms of the number of days of instruction rather than by evaluating whether learning occurred. Developing measures of results is a complex business, and the ease with which they can be developed differs substantially from program to program.

Using Performance Information for Budgeting

Even if performance measures exist, this does not mean that it is easy to figure out how to use them to allocate resources, at least at a government-wide level. First, it is almost impossible to establish common denominators of performance among the activities of government. For example, the measures of success in the health area are different from those in the defense area. Using performance measures for resource allocation implies knowledge of how to compare the measures for those two activities in a way that would inform trade-offs between the two. But trade-offs between government activities are almost exclusively a function of the perceived need and priority for government action. Performance measures can aid these decisions by establishing the correct level of need, but they cannot tell decision makers how much to provide to one activity at the expense of another. Politics—in the best sense of the word—plays an important and legitimate role in budgetary decisions, even where measures of outcomes exist.

Second, the relationship between performance and the budget is not straightforward. Poor results may be caused by the difficulty of the problem being addressed rather than by inadequacies in the design or management of a program. In fact, inadequate funding of a program may cause poor performance, which would lead to the conclusion that poorly performing programs ought to get more resources, and that no increases should be given to agencies that meet their objectives. In short, performance measures may identify trends and developments that warrant attention, but it takes a more thorough program evaluation to tell whether the cause of poor performance (or good performance, for that matter) has anything to do with funding. This suggests that the goal here is not to find some magic algorithm for the allocation of resources, but to make those resource allocation decisions using more information. For this reason, a more realistic and fruitful goal may be to increase the use of performance information in the budgetary process rather than to strive for the more ambitious-sounding performance-based budgeting.

If this is true, then what of the other challenge? That is, how does one get policymakers to pay more attention to performance information? In the past there was no widespread increase in the use of performance information by top policymakers. Thus far the current effort is no different in this regard. The implication of a system that has less control over inputs and more over outcomes is that the legislative branch—and budget controllers in the executive branch as well—should also be less control oriented and should permit agencies greater flexibility. Conversely, it may be too early to blame budget controllers for not using more performance information to make decisions, because the development of such data is very much a work in progress.

The limitations and cautions are not intended to imply that there is no role for performance information in budgeting. On the contrary, the reader may ask at this point if there are any ways that performance measures can be expected to change the budgetary process. The answer is likely to be in the affirmative. Three examples can serve to illustrate the role that performance measures may play in the budgetary process.

First, performance measures may contribute to changing the culture of budgeting to be more performance oriented. As more valid performance information becomes widely available, it will become more difficult for policymakers to make clearly bad investments. The key here is transparency. The provision of performance data will itself lead to decisions that are marginally more informed by performance considerations. Perhaps an analog to this is the recently enacted Unfunded Mandate Reform Act (Conlan and others, 1995). Far from prohibiting unfunded federal mandates, this legislation requires that information be made available on the cost of these mandates, in the hope that the information will itself discourage the most egregious ones. Similarly, the provision of more performance information may lead to decisions that are more focused on results.

Second, the budgetary process itself can be structured to provide greater incentives for performance-based decisions. The chapter has already discussed the system put in place in the state of Oregon to encourage state agencies to compete for funds based on the contribution that programs make to achieving the targets implicit in the Oregon Benchmarks. This suggests a role for creating a demand among both agencies and funding bodies to pursue funding strategies that are aligned with current policy priorities.

Finally, it is important to recognize that not all resource allocation decisions are made by elected officials. In many cases, elected officials may provide agencies with discretion in allocating resources. For example, a local recreation department may have substantial autonomy in terms of how funds are allocated to various parks or facilities under its control. A federal agency may have flexibility in allocating funds among regional offices. To the extent that this discretion exists (and legislatures are often unable or unwilling to fill in all of the details of allocation), performance information can permit a given agency to make microlevel resource decisions that are consistent with performance data.

OTHER TIES BETWEEN THE BUDGET AND IMPROVED PERFORMANCE

Thus far, the chapter has focused on the following question: How can performance information have positive effects on the budgetary process? This question can be turned on its head, however, by asking the following question: What can the budgetary process do to improve performance? Given this question, we should consider at least two other issues before leaving this discussion of the budget and performance. First, there are ways in which the budgeting system itself may prove to be an impediment to a well-performing public sector. Second, changes in the budgeting system may be applied as part of an incentive package to encourage public sector managers to permit themselves to be held more broadly accountable for achieving results.

The Budgetary Process as a Barrier to Performance

Budgeting systems are often criticized for their rigid, control orientation. This calcification normally manifests itself in two ways, each of which can have negative implications for performance. The first way is that programs managers and other recipients of government money often cannot predict with any certainty when funds will be available. The second is that program managers often lack flexibility in the use of funds.

Unpredictability. Agencies often face great uncertainty when confronted with apparently arbitrary budget cuts in the fiscal year to accommodate the need to maintain adherence to fiscal discipline. In addition, there is also great uncertainty surrounding funding for current policy from one year to the next. Uncertainty is exacerbated by inaccurate budget estimates or short-term thinking, without adequate attention to the long-term effects of policies. Further, money is often not made available for spending in a timely fashion.

Failure to Link Appropriate Authority and Accountability. Managers are often given very little flexibility in the use of resources. If detailed controls prevent managers from managing—that is, from using resources in a way that could maximize results—this obviously gets in the way of a performance orientation. Changing this situation, of course, implies a need to develop better mechanisms to promote both authority and accountability.

Part of the issue here is one of capacity-building or the reform of basic budget structures and decision-making processes. For example, improved performance will be encouraged by greater predictability of financial flows, thus necessitating fewer midcourse disruptions of funding for programs. This is in turn tied to the quality of budget estimates. Of course, budget estimation is by no means a purely technical exercise. It is important to keep in mind the incentives that exist for budget preparers to be optimistic in making projections so they can avoid meeting resistance from beneficiaries and satisfy external constituencies.

The provision of greater flexibility requires that the relationship between central government officials and line agencies needs to be clearly thought out. In many cases, central officials (budget offices, for example) see the primary goal of budget implementation as control, both as the budget relates to line agencies and as it relates to regional subunits or subnational governments. These controls are frequently detailed (at the level of line items, for example) and ex ante. Such a control orientation is understandable given historical accountability problems experienced in many governments. But detailed ex ante control can also be stifling. In an environment with more flexibility, ex post control is exercised over the aggregates (accountability is maintained for results) as a substitute for detailed ex ante control over inputs (over spending by line item, without regard for the results achieved).

The Role of the Budgetary Process in Providing Incentives for Broader Reform

Most performance-based reforms (for example, the reforms undertaken in Australia, New Zealand, and Great Britain) have embraced a comprehensive strategy. The concern for improving performance has not been confined to the budget. It has involved the development of a comprehensive performance focus. It is also possible, however, to follow a more incremental model, one which relies on establishing incentives that promote an environment that is more conducive to performance. In short, this means providing something that line agencies value in exchange for a promise on the part of managers to be held accountable for the use of inputs to meet performance objectives, rather than only for the use of budget inputs.

What kinds of things might managers value? Though there may be other types of items in the basket of benefits, it has typically included the following:

- Increased agency flexibility within the budget year to use administrative resources within a single year or between fiscal years

- Greater emphasis on user charges coupled with formal agreements allowing agencies to retain a portion of revenue received to plow back into improved service

- Mechanisms to allow agencies and ministries to retain a share of efficiency gains

- Development of a more performance-oriented personnel management system, allowing agencies more flexibility in hiring and greater ability to provide financial and other awards for good performance

Increased flexibility or other benefits must be accompanied by enhanced accountability for the use of aggregate inputs to achieve results. This in turn has to mean greater transparency; both the center and the public must have the capacity to know what the objectives of the agency or program are as well as how to determine whether these objectives are being met.

Underlying all of the preceding discussion is the importance of ownership. Top-down systems (such as the PPB or ZBB systems in the United States) have been shown time and again to degenerate into paper exercises. This is why incentives are so important. Government officials—at the center and at the periphery—must clearly understand what the benefits are for them in converting to a performance orientation. If they do not, the chances for lasting reform are minimal.

CONCLUSION

As long as public budgeting involves making trade-offs among competing priorities for scarce dollars (in other words, as long as we have budgeting), efforts to make budgetary decisions more informed by considerations of performance are likely to continue. Currently these efforts fall under the rubrics of *common-sense government* (Howard, 1995), *reinventing government* (Osborne and Gaebler, 1992), and *entrepreneurial government* (Lynch, 1996), to name three.

Despite the bumper-sticker appeal of these prescriptions, however, the connection between performance and the budget in practice is elusive. Although we have to acknowledge the impressive strides that have been made by particular agencies or particular jurisdictions, we are far short of any general prescription for performance-based budgeting. We do know, however, some of the prerequisites for such a system to be successful, including some ability to reach a conclusion on what agencies or programs are to accomplish, a valid way of measuring costs and results of those agencies or programs, and a means of getting decision makers to use this information, whether government-wide or at the agency or program level.

In short, successful performance-based budgeting is hard, both in concept and in practice. The difficulty of the reform suggests that one of the biggest challenges faced by performance-based budgeting is oversimplification. If we believe that the task is straightforward and easy, we run the risk of burying promising efforts under a mound of inflated expectations.

The bottom line, then, is that if performance measures are to be used to influence the allocation of resources, the change is not likely to happen suddenly. It is much more likely to be a part of a deliberate change in culture that starts with the development of better, valid performance information at the agency level and with the reporting of that information for nonbudgetary purposes. Further, even if the increased performance measures affect management at the agency level only by changing the way mangers think about the way they use their discretion to allocate resources at the agency level, this could still have very positive effects. In short, it is not at all alarming that greater strides have not been made in performance-based budgeting. Indeed, it should be expected that the process of using performance information to allocate resources at a macro level, if it is to occur at all, will take some time.

References

Bramlett, R. W. "The Federal Accounting Standards Advisory Board: An Introduction for Non-Accountants." *Public Budgeting and Finance,* 1991, *11*(4), 11–19.

Broom, C., and McGuire, L. "Performance-Based Government Models: Building a Track Record." *Public Budgeting and Finance,* 1995, *15*(4), 3–17.

Carter, K. *The Performance Budget Revisited: A Report on State Budget Reform.* Denver: National Conference of State Legislatures, 1994.

Congressional Budget Office. *Using Performance Measures in the Federal Budget Process.* Washington, D.C.: Government Printing Office, 1993.

Conlan, T. J., and others. "Deregulating Federalism? The Politics of Mandate Reform in the 104th Congress." *Publius,* 1995, *25*(3), 23–40.

Gore, A., Jr. *From Red Tape to Results: Creating a Government That Works Better and Costs Less.* Report of the National Performance Review. Washington, D.C.: Government Printing Office, 1993.

Harkin, J. M. "Effectiveness Budgeting: The Limits of Budget Reform." *Policy Studies Review,* 1982, *2*(3), 112–126.

Harris, J. "Service Efforts and Accomplishments Standards: Fundamental Questions of an Emerging Concept." *Public Budgeting and Finance,* 1995, *15*(4), 18–37.

Hatry, H., and Fountain, J. *Service Efforts and Accomplishments Reporting—Its Time Has Come: An Overview.* Norwalk, Conn.: Governmental Accounting Standards Board, 1990.

Joyce, P. G. "Using Performance Measures in the Federal Budget Process: Proposals and Prospects." *Public Budgeting and Finance,* 1993, *13*(4), 3–17.

Kamensky, J. "Role of the Reinventing Government Movement in Federal Management Reform." *Public Administration Review,* 1996, *56*(3), 247–255.

Kettl, D. F. "Building Lasting Reform." In D. F. Kettl and J. J. Di Iulio Jr. (eds.), *Inside the Reinvention Machine*. Washington, D.C.: Brookings Institution, 1995.

Kowaleski, R. *Using Outcome Information to Redirect Programs: A Case Study of the Coast Guard's Pilot Project Under the Government Performance and Results Act*. Washington, D.C.: American Society for Public Administration, 1996.

National Academy of Public Administration. *Toward Useful Performance Measurement: Lessons Learned from Initial Pilot Performance Plans Under the Government Performance and Results Act*. Washington, D.C.: National Academy of Public Administration, 1994.

National Performance Review. *Mission-Driven, Results-Oriented Budgeting*. Washington, D.C.: Government Printing Office, 1993.

Newcomer, K. E. "Performance Measurement in the Federal Budgetary Process: Will It Stick This Time?" Paper presented at the Fifty-Sixth Annual Conference of the American Society for Public Administration, San Antonio, Texas, July 1995.

Oregon Progress Board. *Oregon Benchmarks: Standards for Measuring Statewide Progress and Institutional Performance*. Portland: Oregon Progress Board, 1994.

Osborne, D., and Gaebler, T. *Reinventing Government: How the Entrepreneurial Spirit Is Transforming the Public Sector from Schoolhouse to Statehouse, City Hall to the Pentagon*. Reading, Mass.: Addison-Wesley, 1992.

Roberts, A. "Command Performance." *Government Executive*, Aug. 1996.

Schick, A. "The Road to PPB: The Stages of Budget Reform." *Public Administration Review*, 1966, *26*(4), 243–258.

Schick, A. "A Death in the Bureaucracy: The Demise of Federal PPB." *Public Administration Review*, 1973, *33*(2), 146–156.

Thompson, J. R., and Ingraham, P. W. "The Reinvention Game." *Public Administration Review*, 1996, *56*(3), 291–298.

U.S. General Accounting Office. *Performance Budgeting: State Experiences and Implications for the Federal Government*. Washington, D.C.: Government Printing Office, 1993.

U.S. General Accounting Office. *Budget Account Structure: A Descriptive Overview*. Washington, D.C.: Government Printing Office, 1995a.

U.S. General Accounting Office. *Office of Management and Budget: Changes Resulting from the OMB 2000 Reorganization*. Washington, D.C.: Government Printing Office, 1995b.

U.S. Office of Management and Budget. *Budget of the United States Government, Fiscal Year 1996: Analytical Perspectives*. Washington, D.C.: Government Printing Office, 1995.

U.S. Office of Management and Budget. *Federal Financial Management Status Report and Five-Year Plan*. Washington, D.C.: Government Printing Office, 1996.

CHAPTER TWENTY-FIVE

Analytical Techniques for Budgeting

Marvin B. Mandell

T he desire for focusing increased attention on the results (outputs and outcomes) of budget allocation decisions, rather than on inputs by themselves, dates back at least to the early sixties and the days of the Planning,
Programming, Budgeting System (PPBS). More recently this desire has been
emphasized in the guise of performance budgeting. As Philip Joyce notes in
Chapter Twenty-Four, however, "Proponents make the perfectly defensible assumption that it is desirable to focus on the accomplishment of agencies' programs relative to their uses of scarce resources. Although no one disagrees
with the desirability of this goal, it is not as easy to achieve as it might seem."

A variety of advanced analytical techniques have considerable potential for
facilitating improved budget allocation decisions. To be sure, the potential of
such techniques has been oversold in the past. PPBS is perhaps the most note-
worthy illustration of this overselling. To disregard advanced analytical techniques because of their failure to live up to previous expectations, however,
would be proverbially throwing out the baby with the bath water.

In categorizing advanced analytical techniques, a fundamental distinction
can be drawn between those techniques that focus on specific budgetary decisions and those that focus on organizational units, such as library branches
or schools. Techniques in the former category, which is the traditional focus
of advanced analytical techniques, address such questions as Should a new
highway be built? and What, if any, new crime control program should be
implemented?

620

The potential contributions of such techniques stem from the recognition that most, if not all, budgetary decisions involve trade-offs among different consequences. A given expenditure that results in improved performance of some system usually also increases costs. Moreover, in many cases the effectiveness or cost may have several components. For example, a crime control program is likely to affect several types of crimes. A new highway may have impacts not only on costs and travel time but also on safety and environmental quality.

Advanced analytical techniques can provide several types of information to aid decision makers faced with these kinds of decisions. This chapter focuses on two types of such information. The first is *the outputs that will be obtained if certain expenditures are made.* For example, what will be the change in the rates at which various crimes are committed if five additional police officers are hired? To what extent will a needle exchange program reduce the incidence of HIV infection? A variety of advanced analytical techniques are available for helping to determine what outputs will be obtained if certain expenditures are made. Among these techniques are mathematical models of various forms, such as queuing theory and microsimulation, as well as program and policy evaluation.

Information about what outputs will be obtained if certain expenditures are made provides insight into *the trade-offs that are actually faced.* In many cases, simply identifying these trade-offs is sufficient. In other cases, however, decision makers can benefit from a second type of information, namely information that provides guidance on how to resolve conflicts among different objectives. That is, if an investment in a program produces x units of output, is it worth undertaking? Suppose there are two crime control programs, say A and B, of equal cost, and program A reduces homicides more than program B does, but program B has the larger impact in terms of reduction in the number of rapes. If only one program can be selected (perhaps due to budget constraints), which one should be selected? The second set of advanced analytical techniques presented in this chapter is aimed at providing assistance with such issues. Of particular note here are cost-benefit analysis, cost-effectiveness analysis, and decision analysis.

Advanced analytical techniques can also be used to assess the efficiency of organizational units. Unlike the techniques just mentioned, which are generally applied in a prospective mode, tools for measuring efficiency are used for retrospective assessment. The goal of such techniques is to characterize various organizational units as being more or less efficient, as well as to identify directions for improvement.

The remainder of this chapter describes several advanced analytical techniques and the ways in which they might be applied to budget allocation decisions. In addition to sketching out the main features of these techniques, I show how several of them can be applied to two illustrative budgetary decisions. The first of these decisions must be made by a municipal police force that is considering several different possible crime-reduction programs, such as increasing the number of police crackdowns, increasing foot patrol, and emphasizing "problem-solving policing." In this example, I assume that due to budget constraints or limits on managerial capacity, only one of the programs can be selected. In selecting from this set of alternatives, the relevant criteria are costs and the impact of the alternative on the number of homicides, rapes, aggravated assaults, and robberies. The second decision used to illustrate the techniques to be presented is a state's motor vehicle administration (MVA) that is concerned with reducing the amount of time customers must wait in line when renewing automobile registrations.

The description of the advanced analytical techniques and the illustrative applications of them are intended to provide the reader with the basic flavor of the techniques involved. For purposes of presentation, the illustrations are necessarily somewhat oversimplified, and many details and thorny issues associated with the various advanced analytical techniques are glossed over.

ESTIMATING CONSEQUENCES OF EXPENDITURES

To focus on the results of budget allocation decisions, it is necessary to link inputs to outputs, that is, to determine what will occur as a result of a particular allocation of resources. Several types of advanced analytical methods are available for linking resource allocation decisions with outputs.

Mathematical Models

One set of tools that is particularly useful for this purpose is mathematical models. Citro and Hanushek (1991, p. 76) define a model as "a replicable, objective sequence of computations used for generating estimates of quantities of interest." They, as well as others (such as MacRae and Whittington, 1997, p. 59; Stokey and Zeckhauser, 1978, p. 8), point out that models are simplified representations of the systems they are intended to portray. The specific simplifications that are appropriate depend on the purpose for which the model is to be used.

A wide variety of types of models can be applied to budgetary decisions. Microsimulation models, for example, are computerized models that have been applied frequently in such policy areas as health care and income maintenance and transfers (see Citro and Hanushek, 1991). Models of the spread of epidemics that are based on difference equations are another example of relevant models (MacRae and Whittington, 1997; Salzberg, Dolins, and Salzberg, 1991; Kaplan and Brandeau, 1994). Another type that also is frequently applied is queuing models; the rest of this section considers such models.

A large number of public agencies can be viewed as having service delivery as an important part of their mission. The effectiveness of service delivery is often directly related to, if not defined by, whether or how long customers must wait for service. In the case of police, fire, and emergency medical services, for example, the length of time it takes to respond to calls for service is intuitively a key determinant of the probability of loss of life as well as the extent of injury and property damage from a variety of incidents (see Swersey, 1994). In the case of renewal of automobile registrations, the amount of time spent waiting in line is often the primary measure by which citizens judge the performance of the state's MVA. Moreover, waiting time is not necessarily limited to actually standing on a line or waiting for an ambulance. In a public housing project, for example, applicants are put on a waiting list for a suitable apartment (Kaplan, 1987). As a final example, customer satisfaction with a public library may be related to how long one must wait before a copy of a desired book is available (Gleeson, 1994).

One means by which service-delivery agencies can influence waiting time for service is by changing the delivery capacity, that is, the number of "servers" that are available. A server is a unit that provides service. For a state MVA, a server might be an individual who administers driving tests to applicants, or a desk clerk. In other cases a server is a bundle of equipment and personnel. For example, in emergency medical services a server consists of a vehicle and a crew that generally, though not always, consists of two individuals. In drug treatment programs, a server is a program slot. In a public housing project, a server is an apartment (Kaplan, 1986). In still other cases, a server is a facility, such as a tennis court at a public recreational facility or a parking space at a municipal parking facility (Larson and Odoni, 1981, p. 270). In public libraries, the librarians available to help with reference requests or to check out books are servers. Less obviously, perhaps, a copy of a book is a server. Increasing the number of copies reduces the time a patron must wait to have access to the book.

Changing the number of available servers has important cost implications. To make an informed decision regarding whether or not to change delivery capacity, a reliable estimate of the effect of such a change on waiting time is often crucial. Queuing theory models can often be used to produce such estimates. Such models have found applications in a variety of public sector decisions.

To develop a queuing theory model, the following basic characteristics must be specified:

- The arrival pattern of customers
- The service pattern of servers
- The number of servers available

- The system's capacity, that is, whether there are limits on the number of customers who can be waiting for service at any given time
- The "queue discipline," that is, the manner in which customers are selected for service when a queue has formed (such as "first come, first served" and various priority schemes)

On the basis of these specifications, various measures of system performance can be computed. Commonly used measures of system performance in queuing models include the mean waiting time, the probability that at least one server will be available at the time a call is received (that is, the probability of no queuing delay), and the mean queue length.

Simply estimating the performance of a given queuing system is, of course, of little value in budgetary (or any other type of) decision making. Rather, the value of queuing theory lies in asking "what if" questions. For example, Exhibit 25.1 shows how an MVA might use queuing theory models to estimate the impact of various changes on the mean waiting time for drivers' license renewals. In the case of emergency service systems, a budget analyst might be more concerned with how varying the number of units in service at any particular time influences the probability that a server can be dispatched immediately upon receipt of a request for service.

These "what if" questions need not be limited to changes in the number of servers. For example, several local jurisdictions are considering means of diverting 911 calls so as to decrease the number of nonemergency calls to which emergency units must respond. The impact of such a policy can be represented in a queuing model as a decrease in the arrival rate of calls for service.

Traditional queuing models are *aspatial,* that is, they assume that all servers are in the same geographical location and that they are *indistinguishable* in the sense that it makes no difference to the customer which server is assigned to provide the service in question. For many applications, such a model is quite adequate. For example, when an applicant for a driver's license is to be examined, it makes little difference which examiner administers the examination. In other cases, however, it is essential that the spatial dimension be taken into account. Emergency service systems are a classic example of such an application. In such systems, different servers (as well as demand) are geographically dispersed over a particular region. Moreover, the servers are interdependent in the sense that if the most preferred (typically the closest) server is busy, another server (preferably one that is located relatively near the call location) can be assigned to the call. The different servers are distinguishable, however, rather than completely interchangeable. That is, it is relevant which server responds to a given call for service. Other things being equal, the closer the provider is to the source of the call for service, the more preferable it is that the provider respond to the call for service. In such cases, Larson's *hypercube queuing model*

Exhibit 25.1. Using Queuing Theory to Compare Alternatives
for Reducing Waiting Time for Drivers' License Renewals.

The amount of time customers spend waiting in line is often a primary measure
by which citizens judge the performance of their state MVA. An MVA can respond
to long lines in several ways. The most obvious way is to increase the number of
servers (clerks) providing service. A somewhat more innovative approach is to
open self-service terminals (SSTs; ATM-like machines at which customers can re-
new their vehicle registration and perform other functions) in supermarkets,
shopping malls, and the like. Opening such terminals has several effects. The effect of concern here is the impact on waiting time. Because some of the demand is
satisfied at these terminals, the demand at the MVA office is reduced, thereby reducing the average waiting time at that office. Depending on several parameters,
the average waiting time for those who use SSTs may be more or less than the
current average waiting time at the MVA office.

Consider a busy branch of a state MVA at which three stations for vehicle registration renewal are currently staffed. It is forecast that in the coming year, this
branch will processes an average of 12,500 vehicle registrations per month. MVA
managers fear that the wait for registrations will be excessive. They are considering several options, including adding one more station for vehicle registration renewals, opening SSTs at two satellite locations, and opening SSTs at three satellite
locations.

An analyst assigned the task of predicting the effect of each of these options
on waiting time might very well turn to queuing theory. It is relatively straightforward to apply queuing theory to the current (do nothing) configuration, which
is simply a three-server queuing system. Adding another station for registration
renewals can similarly be analyzed as a four-server queuing system. To proceed
further, we must characterize the arrival pattern of customers at the MVA office,
along with the service pattern.

It is commonly assumed that both the arrival of customers and the service pattern are governed by a Poisson process (see Gross and Harris, 1998, for a description of the properties and mathematical form of a Poisson process; in practice
these assumptions should of course be verified empirically). Given this assumption, it would be necessary to determine both the mean call volume and the mean
service rate, that is, the mean number of customers that can be served per unit
time by one server. As noted earlier, the mean call volume is expected to be
12,500 customers per month, or 74.4 customers per hour (assuming that the facility is open eight hours per day and twenty-one days per month). Suppose it has
also been determined that the mean service rate is thirty customers per hour; that
is, on average it takes two minutes to serve a customer. An analyst would be
justified to assume in this case that the system capacity is infinite (that is, that

(*continued*)

Exhibit 25.1. (*continued*)

there are no limits on how many patrons can be waiting in line at any one time) and that the queue discipline is first come, first served.

Given these assumptions, it can be shown (Gross and Harris, 1998, p. 98) that the mean waiting time at the MVA office is

$$W_{MVA} = \frac{\left[\dfrac{(\lambda_{MVA}\,\mu_{MVA})^c\,\mu_{MVA}}{(c-1)!(c\mu_{MVA}-\lambda_{MVA})^2}\right]}{\left[\displaystyle\sum_{n=0}^{c-1}\frac{1}{n!}\left(\frac{\lambda_{MVA}}{\mu_{MVA}}\right)^n + \frac{1}{c!}\left(\frac{\lambda_{MVA}}{\mu_{MVA}}\right)^c\left(\frac{c\mu_{MVA}}{c\mu_{MVA}-\lambda_{MVA}}\right)\right]} \qquad [1.1]$$

where c = the number of servers, that is, stations for vehicle registration renewal that are staffed;

λ_{MVA} = the mean arrival rate of customers at the MVA office; and

μ_{MVA} = the mean service rate for customers at the MVA office.

Substituting the appropriate parameters into Equation 1, we find that the mean waiting time will be 2.66 minutes if the current configuration (three stations) is retained but only 0.41 minutes if one more station is added.

Analyzing the effects of opening SSTs is somewhat more complex. To do so, separate models must be developed for the MVA office as well for each SST. The former is again a three-server queuing system, while each SST is a separate, single-server queuing system. To proceed further, estimates of the fraction of customers who will actually use SSTs, if they are available, are needed. In terms of queuing models, these estimates are exogenous. Table 25.1 shows (hypothetical) estimates of these fractions. Given these estimates, the mean rate at which customers arrive at the MVA office and at each SST can be calculated directly by multiplying the overall demand (12,500 customers per month) by the appropriate fraction in Table 25.1. In addition, the arrival pattern of customers at the MVA office as well as at the SSTs must be characterized. Previously we assumed that customers arrive at the MVA office according to a Poisson distribution. There seems little reason to change that assumption here. It also seems reasonable to assume that the arrivals at each SST follow a Poisson distribution. Similarly, it seems reasonable to retain the assumption that the service process at the MVA office follows a Poisson distribution with a mean service rate of thirty customers per hour and also to assume that the service process at each SST follows a Poisson process. Suppose that through testing it is estimated that the mean service rate at each SST is twenty customers per hour; that is, on average it takes three minutes to serve a customer. Finally, like the MVA office, the system capacity at each SST is assumed to be infinite (that is, there are no limits to how many patrons can be waiting on line at any one time), and the queue discipline at each SST is assumed to be first-come, first-served.

(*continued*)

Exhibit 25.1. (*continued*)

To find the mean waiting time at the MVA office if SSTs are opened, Equation 1 can again be applied. Note, however, that the mean arrival rate at the MVA office drops from to 9,812 registrations per month (58.4 per hour) if two SSTs are opened, and to 8,687 registrations per month (51.7 per hour) if three SSTs are opened. Given the assumptions we have made, the mean waiting time at the kth SST is given by

$$W_k = \frac{\lambda_k}{\mu_S(\mu_S - \lambda_k)} \qquad [1.2]$$

where λ_k = the mean arrival rate of customers at the kth SST, and
$\quad \mu_S$ = the mean service rate for customers at an SST.

Columns 2 through 5 of Table 25.2 summarize the results of applying Equations 1 and 2 to the various alternatives. The overall system mean waiting time for each alternative, which is shown in the last column of Table 25.2, was obtained by taking a weighted average of the mean waiting time at each site, with the weights being the proportion of customers expected to use each site. Several types of sensitivity analysis are relevant here. One type, shown in Figure 25.1, is how the overall system mean waiting times for the various alternatives are affected by changes in the overall demand. In addition, one might examine the sensitivity of the results to the mean service rate at both the MVA office and at SSTs, as well as to the estimates of the fraction of customers who will use the SSTs.

Table 25.1. Estimated Fraction of Customers Using SSTs.

	Fraction of Customers Using			
Alternative	MVA Office	Kiosk #1	Kiosk #2	Kiosk #3
Do nothing	100%	N/A	N/A	N/A
Add one more station at				
MVA office	100%	N/A	N/A	N/A
Open 2 SSTs	78.5%	11.1%	10.4%	N/A
Open 3 SSTs	69.5%	13.3%	1.6%	15.6%

Table 25.2. Mean Waiting Time Under Various Alternatives.

| | Mean Waiting Time (in minutes) at | | | | |
Alternative	MVA Office	Kiosk #1	Kiosk #2	Kiosk #3	Overall Mean Waiting Time
Do nothing	2.66	N/A	N/A	N/A	2.66
Add one more station at MVA office	0.41	N/A	N/A	N/A	0.41
Open 2 SSTs	0.80	2.10	1.91	N/A	1.06
Open 3 SSTs	0.51	2.93	0.19	4.14	1.39

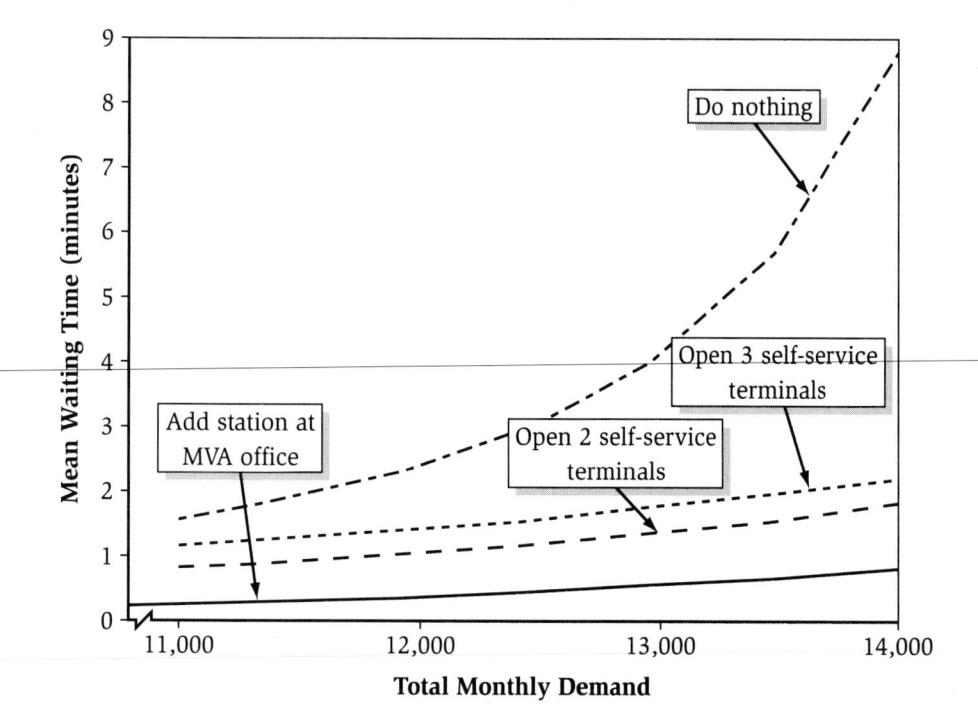

Figure 25.1. Effect of Overall Demand on Mean Waiting Times.

(1974) and extensions of it are helpful. Rather than considering simply whether *any* service provider in the region is available at the time a call is received, or considering the queuing delay until at least one service provider is available, the hypercube queuing model predicts the probability that the closest (or more generally, the most preferred) server is available to respond to a given call for service, the probability that the second closest server is available, and so on. These predictions, in turn, are used to compute such system performance measures as the mean total delay (queuing delay plus travel time).

Evaluation

Although mathematical models are often useful in predicting the impacts of resource allocation decisions, in many cases it is not possible to represent the system of concern adequately in mathematical terms. An alternative means of predicting the impacts of resource allocation decisions is program and policy evaluation.

Evaluation is traditionally viewed by those involved in the budgeting process as largely an auditing and monitoring function. In terms of performance budgeting, however, the value of evaluation lies in its ability to shed light on the question of what impacts will occur if the program being evaluated is replicated at another location or time. This is accomplished by first determining what the impacts of the program were. Next, it must be determined whether the program will result in similar impacts when replicated at the time and place of concern in the budgeting process.

The key issue in estimating the impacts of a previously implemented program revolves around comparing "what did happen . . . [with] what would have happened had the program not been implemented" (Mohr, 1988, pp. 2–3). The latter, which is generally the more problematic element, is termed a *counterfactual.* The counterfactual is problematic because it is, by definition, unobservable. Hence the comparison between what did happen and what would have happened had the program not been implemented can only be approximated. In particular, the actual level of outcomes of interest is generally compared with the level of outcomes of interest either in different populations or at different point in times.

It is widely argued (see, for example, Burtless, 1995) that the most reliable means of estimating the counterfactual level of relevant variables and thereby estimating the impact of the program or policy of concern is through a *true experiment.* The defining element of a true experiment is the random assignment of units of observation (typically but not always individuals) to two or more different groups that differ in terms of the services provided or the rules that apply. In the simplest case, two such groups—termed the *treatment* group and the *control* group—are formed. As discussed later in greater detail, experiments frequently involve more than two groups. A critical advantage of random assignment is that it guarantees that the groups that are formed are (on average) identical in terms of both measured and, more importantly, unmeasured characteristics. Consequently, any resulting differences in outcomes cannot be attributed to preexisting characteristics of the members of the groups that are compared. Greenberg and Shroder (1997) have identified 145 social experiments that were conducted between 1968 (which they identify as the initiation of the first social experiment) and 1996. (The number of experiments that are of potential interest to those involved in budgeting is potentially underestimated because the researchers focused primarily on experiments that involved economic incentives or outcomes or both. Consequently, numerous experiments in such areas as policing, public health, and education are not included in their digest.)

True experiments are not without potential drawbacks and limitations. The most commonly encountered source of opposition to experiments are ethical objections to the random assignment of individuals to treatment and control groups. Although such objections are frequently valid, this is not always the case. For one, as Greenberg and Shroder (1997), among others, argue, benefits or services often cannot be provided to the entire target population due to limited program capacity. In such cases random assignment is no more objectionable than, say, a first-come, first-served approach. Moreover, if the effects of the program or policy on the target population are indeed unknown (which is the primary justification for conducting an evaluation), withholding services or benefits from one group or another does not necessarily make them worse off than they otherwise would be. Finally, under some circumstances, those who are at risk of becoming worse off by virtue of being assigned to one group or another can be compensated for the risks they face. For example, participants in the RAND Health Insurance Experiment were provided with side payments, called Participation Incentive Payments, which ensured that no one would become financially worse off as a result of participating in the experiment (Newhouse and the Insurance Experiment Group, 1993).

Ethical objections to random assignment can also be avoided, at least in some cases, by using variants of true experiments. For one, the comparison need not be between treatment and no treatment (control). Rather, it might be between two different treatments. For example, an experiment aimed at increasing the earnings of welfare recipients might randomly assign some participants to a program that focuses on job search skills and work experience, and others to a program that focuses on skills training and basic education. Although such an experiment would not yield any information for comparing either program with providing no services, it would yield information about the effects of each approach relative to the other.

Another important, and arguably underused, variant of a true experiment is to use random assignment to determine when, rather than whether, an individual participates in a particular program. A related variant is a *switching replica-*

tions design (also called a *crossover design*). Such a design is perhaps most appropriate when the unit of analysis is a geographical area and when effects are not permanent. Sherman (1990), for example, has advocated the use of such a design for estimating the effects of police crackdowns. Specifically, he proposes that crackdowns be conducted in area targets, such as drug markets, in randomly selected periods, such as months. Thus a crackdown might be conducted at site A in months 2, 7, and 13, at site B in months 1, 9, and 15, and so on.

Nonetheless, there are indeed situations when true experiments are not desirable or possible. In some cases, ethical objections cannot be overcome. Moreover, ethical objections are not the only potential drawback of social experiments. Another common drawback is the cost of such experiments in terms of both real resources and time needed to complete the experiments (see Levitan, 1992). In addition, although true experiments generally provide impact estimates that have the greatest degree possible of internal validity, they do not necessarily eliminate all barriers to drawing valid inferences. For example, experiments may have substantial limitations in external validity, that is, the ability to generalize from the results of the evaluation. In addition, experiments have only limited ability to respond to certain types of issues, such as entry effects. (For a discussion of the limitations of social experiments, see Heckman and Smith, 1995.)

In situations where social experiments are not appropriate means for estimating the impact of a program or policy innovation, various alternative approaches to evaluation may be employed. Particularly prominent among these approaches are nonequivalent control group designs and interrupted time series (Marcantonio and Cook, 1994).

ECONOMIC EVALUATION

Insights into the impacts of budget allocation decisions, while important, are only part of the puzzle. Such insights highlight the trade-offs that are faced in budgetary decisions. Another task faced in budget allocation decisions is choosing which trade-offs are appropriate. Consider choosing among the options considered in Exhibit 25.1. As shown in that exhibit, adding one more station at the MVA office was predicted to have the largest effect on overall mean waiting time. The different options, however, are likely to differ also in terms of costs to the MVA and in terms of the distance that customers must travel. Table 25.3 shows estimates of the impacts of each alternative on customer travel distance and on costs to the MVA, along with the impacts on overall aggregate waiting time. Although adding another station at the MVA office was predicted to have the greatest impact on aggregate waiting time, it was also predicted to cost the most and to have no effect on customer travel distance. Opening three SSTs was

Table 25.3. Estimated Costs, Aggregate Travel Distance, and
Aggregate Waiting Time Under Various Alternatives.

Alternative	Annual Cost (thousands)	Aggregate Annual Travel Distance (thousands of miles)	Aggregate Annual Waiting Time (thousands of hours)
Do nothing	0	494.2	6.6
Add one more station at MVA office	100	494.2	1.0
Open 2 SSTs	30	403.9	2.6
Open 3 SSTs	40	328.7	3.5

predicted to cost more and to have a smaller effect on waiting time than opening two SSTs, but it had a larger effect on aggregate customer travel distance. Table 25.3 is useful in identifying the trade-offs that exist in choosing from among the alternatives, but it does not provide guidance regarding which trade-offs are worthwhile and which are not.

To take another example, suppose only one of the crime control programs shown in Table 25.5 can be selected. Which one should it be? Enhanced community policing costs the least and has the greatest impact on the number of robberies; expanded foot patrols have the greatest impact on the number of rapes and the number of assaults; and adopting a zero-tolerance policy, although most costly, has the greatest impact on the number of homicides. Methods of economic analysis, notably cost-benefit analysis and cost-effectiveness analysis, provide some assistance in coping with such trade-offs.

Cost-Benefit Analysis

Cost-benefit analysis combines all outcomes of interest into a single denominator, namely dollars. The first step in cost-benefit analysis is to estimate the impact of each alternative on each consequence of concern. Mathematical models and evaluation are commonly used to produce such estimates, though they are not the only means of doing so. For example, the third column of Table 25.3 is based on the results of the queuing analysis conducted in Exhibit 25.1. Estimates of the impacts of alternative crime control programs, such as those shown in Table 25.5, would typically be obtained from evaluation studies.

Next, and perhaps most difficult, a monetary equivalent must be assigned to each impact. Note that cost-benefit analysis, at least if properly conducted, does not ignore nonmonetary impacts. Rather, it converts such impacts into dollar terms. In the case of impacts for which efficient markets exist, market prices can be used to assign monetary equivalents. Assigning monetary equivalents to

Table 25.4. Cost-Benefit Analysis for the MVA Decision.

Alternative	Annual Cost ($ thousands)	Reduction in Aggregate Annual Travel Distance (thousands of miles)	Reduction in Aggregate Annual Waiting Time (thousands of hours)	Total Annual Benefits ($ thousands)	Net Annual Benefits ($ thousands)
Do nothing	0	0	0	0	0
Add one more station at MVA office	100	0	5.6	56.2	−43.8
Open 2 SSTs	30	90.3	4.0	96.7	66.7
Open 3 SSTs	40	165.6	3.2	135.5	95.5

Table 25.5. Cost-Benefit Analysis for Crime-Reduction Alternatives.

Alternative	Annual Cost ($ millions)	Expected Annual Decrease in Homicides	Rapes	Robberies	Assaults	Total Annual Benefits ($ millions)	Net Annual Benefits ($ millions)
Enhanced community policing	6.7	2	12	117	94	10.77	4.07
Expanded foot patrols	7.8	2	17	71	144	10.89	3.09
Zero tolerance	9.1	3	14	93	108	13.43	4.33

impacts for which markets either do not exist or are inefficient, such as injuries, deaths, and crime, poses a far more challenging task. In these cases, *shadow prices* for the impact of concern must be estimated (see Boardman, Greenberg, Vining, and Weimer, 1996, pp. 292–394).

The impacts of many budgetary decisions occur at different points in time. For example, new facilities typically require large up-front expenditures but are expected to yield benefits as well as incur maintenance costs well into the future. For this reason, benefits and costs arising at different points in time must be aggregated. This is done by discounting future costs and benefits into present value terms. Although the mechanics of computing present values are relatively straightforward, the appropriate discount rate to use is controversial (see Boardman, Greenberg, Vining, and Weimer, 1996, pp. 119–186).

Finally, for each alternative the total benefits are computed by adding up all benefits, and the total costs are computed by adding up all costs. Recommendations for choice are based on the *net benefits,* that is, on the difference between the total benefits and the total costs. In particular, when a choice is to be made from among several alternatives that are mutually exclusive, the project with the highest net benefits is most desirable. Of course, extensive sensitivity analysis is required.

In recent years, increasing attention has been given to presenting net benefits from a variety of perspectives. For example, many cost-benefit analyses of welfare-to-work demonstrations now commonly separate the present net benefits from the view of participants from the present net benefits of the program from the perspective of other members of society. In other cases, cost-benefit analyses may present the net benefits of the program for various geographical jurisdictions (such as legislative districts).

Exhibits 25.2 and 25.3 illustrate how cost-benefit analysis might be applied to the two cases just described.

Exhibit 25.2. Applying Cost-Benefit Analysis to the MVA Decision.

As noted in the text, the first step in applying cost-benefit analysis is to estimate the impact of each alternative on each consequence of concern. Table 25.3 contains estimates of the costs, aggregate travel distance, and aggregate waiting time for the four alternatives considered in Exhibit 25.1. Columns 2 through 4 of Table 25.4 show these estimates *relative to maintaining the status quo.*

The next step is to assign monetary values to aggregate travel distance and aggregate waiting time. Two components must be reflected in the monetary value assigned to aggregate travel distance. The first is the actual out-of-pocket costs of travel. Assuming that all MVA customers travel by automobile, this component would reflect gasoline, vehicle wear and tear, and the like. One source of the out-of-pocket costs of automobile travel is the American Automobile Association, which currently estimates the full cost of owning and operating an automobile to be $0.46 per mile.

The second component of the monetary equivalent of travel distance is the value of the travel time involved. To arrive at this component of the estimate, it is necessary both to translate travel distance into travel time and to assign a dollar value to travel time. A crude but frequently applied rule of thumb is to assume an average travel speed of thirty miles per hour. There is a large literature on the value of travel-time savings (for a summary of this literature, see Waters, 1993). In this literature the value of travel-time savings is generally expressed in terms of a percentage of the after-tax hourly wage rate. A typical estimate of the value of travel-time savings is roughly 50 percent of the after-tax hourly wage rate. Assuming an average after-tax hourly wage rate of $10, this implies that the value of a

(continued)

Exhibit 25.2. (*continued*)

reduction in travel time of one hour is $5. Combining these estimates of out-of-pocket costs of travel, average travel speed, and monetary value of travel time results in an estimate of $62.70 per hundred miles.

Like the value of travel time, the monetary value of waiting time is also generally expressed in terms of a fraction of the after-tax hourly wage rate. People generally place a higher value on reductions in waiting time, however, than they do on travel time (Mohring, Schroeter, and Wiboonchutikula, 1987). Thus an analyst might estimate the value of waiting-time savings to be approximately equal to the after-tax hourly wage rate.

Based on the foregoing estimates, the total benefits of each alternative can be computed. For example, the total annual benefits of opening two SSTs are

$$(90,300 \times \$0.627) + (4,010 \times \$10) = \$96,718$$

The total annual benefits of this and the other alternatives are shown in the fifth column of Table 25.4.

Finally, the net annual benefits of each alternative are computed by taking the difference between the total annual benefits and the annual costs. The results of this are shown in the sixth column of Table 25.4. On the basis of the estimated net benefits, opening three SSTs appears to be the best alternative.

A variety of sensitivity analyses are potentially important here. Figure 25.2 illustrates one piece of sensitivity analysis. The figure examines the effect of the monetary value assigned to waiting time reduction on the net annual benefits of each alternative. An analyst would conclude from this figure that because the effect of varying this monetary equivalent has approximately the same effect on each of the three alternatives, the choice does not depend on this parameter.

Exhibit 25.3. Applying Cost-Benefit Analysis to Crime-Reduction Programs.

This illustration involves a municipal police force that is considering three crime reduction programs. For purposes of this illustration, we will assume that only one of these programs can be selected. This might be due, for example, to fiscal constraints or limitations on managerial capacity. Estimates of the impacts of these types of programs would typically be obtained from evaluations of similar programs that had been implemented in other cities or at earlier times in the city in question. Table 25.5 contains (hypothetical) estimates of the costs of each program, along with the impact of each on the number of homicides, rapes, aggravated assaults, and robberies.

Assigning monetary equivalents to the crime reduction impacts shown in Table 25.5 presents a major challenge. One source of estimates for doing so,

(*continued*)

Exhibit 25.3. (*continued*)

however, is work by Miller, Cohen, and Rossman (1993), who have estimated the tangible and intangible costs of various types of crime. Specifically, they estimate that the victim costs (in 1994 dollars) of a homicide are approximately $2.85 million; of a rape, approximately $57,000; of a robbery, nearly $23,000; and of an assault, nearly $18,000. For existing estimates of the monetary value of a variety of other impacts, including life, injuries, time, and recreation benefits, see Boardman, Greenberg, Vining, and Weimer, 1997.) Applying these dollar equivalents to the data in Table 25.5 would allow an analyst to compute the total benefits of each crime control alternative. For example, the total benefits (in millions of dollars) of implementing an enhanced community policing program is equal to

$$(2.85 \times 2) + (0.057 \times 12) + (0.023 \times 117) + (0.018 \times 94) = 10.77$$

The total benefits of this and the other alternatives are shown in the seventh column of Table 25.5. Finally, the net benefits of each alternative are computed by taking the difference between the total benefits and the costs. The results of this are shown in the final column of Table 25.5. Based on this calculation, adopting a zero-tolerance policy appears to be the best alternative.

Figures 25.3 and 25.4 show examples of sensitivity analysis that would be relevant in this case. In particular, Figure 25.3 shows how varying the estimated victim costs of a homicide affects the net benefits of the various programs considered, while Figure 25.4 shows how varying the estimated victim costs of a rape affects the net benefits of these programs. Figure 25.3 demonstrates that the best program is quite sensitive to the estimated victim costs of a homicide. If these costs are relatively low (that is, below approximately $2.6 million), enhanced community policing is expected to produce the highest net benefits. Conversely, if these costs are relatively high (that is, above approximately $2.6 million), adopting a zero-tolerance policy is expected to produce the highest net benefits. Yet regardless of the estimated victim costs of a homicide (at least within the range considered), expanded foot patrols will not produce the highest net benefits. In contrast to Figure 25.3, Figure 25.4 suggests that, at least within the range of values considered, the best program (that is, the program that will produce the highest net benefits) is not sensitive to the estimated victim costs of rape. (For additional means of presenting sensitivity analyses of this type, see Eschenbach, 1992.)

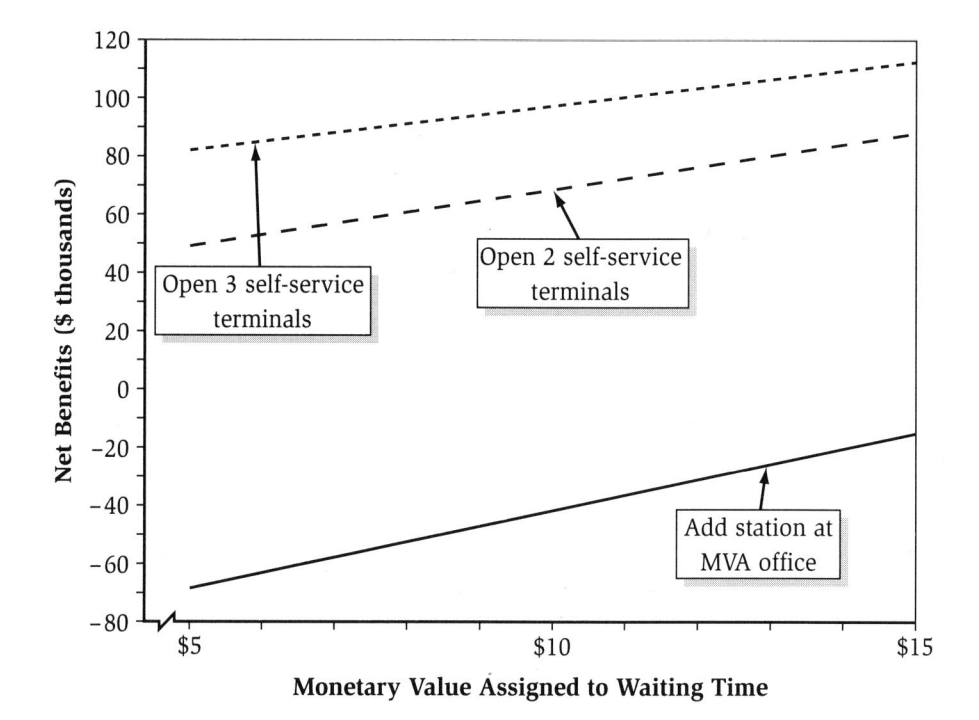

Figure 25.2. Effect of Monetary Value Assigned to Waiting-Time Reduction on Net Benefits.

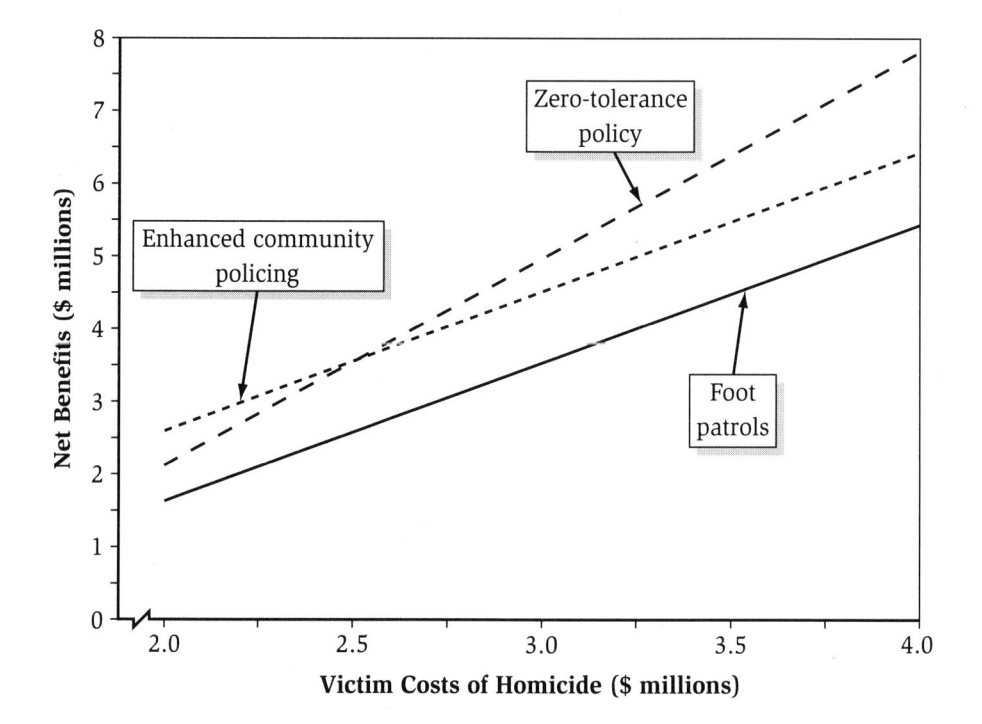

Figure 25.3. Effect of Varying Estimated Victim Costs of Homicide on Net Benefits.

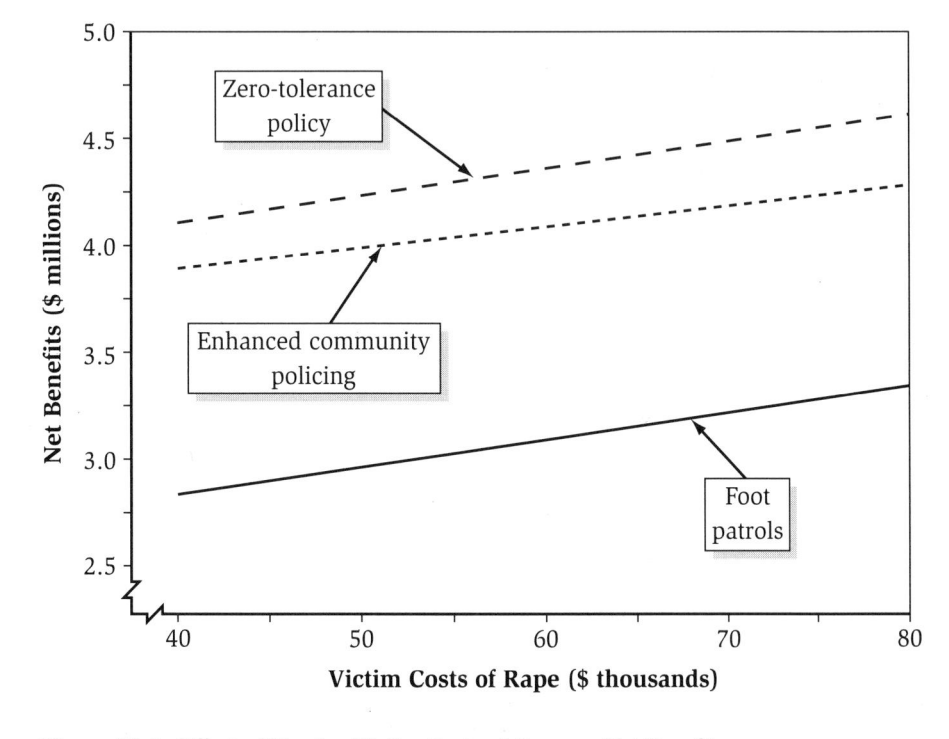

Figure 25.4. Effect of Varying Victim Costs of Rape on Net Benefits.

Cost-Effectiveness Analysis

In some cases, analysts may be unable or unwilling to place a monetary equivalent on at least some impacts. For example, it may be difficult to determine accurately the value of reducing waiting time, or it may be difficult to place a monetary value on various types of crime. In such instances, cost-effectiveness analysis may be a more viable analytic approach. Though it is widely used, there are considerable variations in how cost-effectiveness analysis (CEA) has been applied. The goal of this discussion is to identify the common elements and common variations in CEA.

The general principle of CEA is to divide impacts into two categories. The first category includes those impacts that are either already in monetary costs (such as budgetary costs) or that the analyst believes can be relatively easily and reliably converted into monetary equivalents, such as volunteer labor or reduced property damage. (In practice, some analysts ignore monetizable costs.) The second category includes all other impacts, which are then combined into a single index that is generically labeled "effectiveness." For example, in many health analyses, impacts on mortality and morbidity are combined into an index that is labeled "quality-adjusted life years" (see Drummond, Stoddard, and Torrance, 1987). Or the incidence of different types of crime might be aggregated into a quantity labeled "overall crime" (see Wolfgang, Figlio, Tracy, and Singer, 1985). (Again, this practice is not universal. In addition, some people call the approach described here "cost-utility analysis." One variation on the approach described here is to retain only the "most important" nonmonetary impact. For example, in comparing different cocaine-control programs, Caulkins, Rydell, Schwabe, and Chiesa, 1997, use reduction in cocaine consumption as their only measure of effectiveness. They proceed to examine whether their results change as they use different measures of effectiveness, such as user expenditures on cocaine, the number of cocaine-user years and the number of heavy-cocaine-user years.)

Another important variation in the application of CEA is in the step that follows the calculation of costs and effectiveness. Traditionally, one of two ratios, either the ratio of costs to effectiveness or the ratio of effectiveness to costs, is calculated. The "best" program is then thought to be the alternative with the smallest ratio of costs to effectiveness or the largest ratio of effectiveness to costs. The use of such ratios, however, contains several important but unstated assumptions that are often inappropriate, including constant returns to scale. A less commonly employed but in my view more appropriate step to employ following calculation of costs and effectiveness is to plot the location of the alternatives on a two-dimensional graph.

Exhibits 25.4 and 25.5 illustrate how CEA might be applied to the two cases we have been considering.

Exhibit 25.4. Applying Cost-Effectiveness Analysis to the MVA Decision.

One of the more controversial elements of the benefit-cost analysis presented in Exhibit 25.2 is the value placed on time savings, in both travel and waiting. One means of coping with this issue is through sensitivity analysis. Another is to avoid placing a specific monetary value on time savings by employing cost-effectiveness analysis (CEA) rather than cost-benefit analysis.

In applying CEA to this example, an analyst would again assign a monetary value to the reductions in aggregate travel distance. However, unlike the application of benefit-cost analysis, here this monetary value would reflect only the actual out-of-pocket costs of travel, which were estimated as $0.46 per mile in Exhibit 25.2. The analyst would also need to compute the hours of travel time saved by each alternative, as well as the number of hours of waiting time saved by each alternative. These estimates are available from the calculations in Exhibit 25.2. The number of hours of travel time saved and the number of hours of waiting time saved are two potential measures of effectiveness. As noted in the text, one means of dealing with these measures would be to select one or the other as the measure of effectiveness. Alternatively, and arguably more appropriately, these two nonmonetary impacts should be combined. The simplest way to do so is to take a weighted average (linear

(continued)

Exhibit 25.4. (*continued*)

combination) of them. For example, we will assume that a one-hour reduction in waiting time is as valuable as a two-hour reduction in travel time; that is, one-half hour of waiting time is as distasteful as one hour of travel time. The principle here is that it is easier, though far from trivial, to establish values of the two waiting times *relative to each other* than it is to assign monetary values to each of them. By doing so, the reduction in waiting time can be converted into an equivalent travel-time reduction (or vice versa), as shown in column 7 of Table 25.6, and a total equivalent travel-time reduction can be computed, as shown in column 8 of Table 25.6.

Figure 25.5 graphically compares the alternatives in terms of costs and effectiveness, which in this case is total equivalent travel time reduction. As can be seen from Figure 25.5, opening three SSTs will result in both lower annual net costs and greater equivalent waiting-time savings than opening two SSTs, opening an additional station at the MVA office, or doing nothing. Thus, given the assumed trade-offs between waiting time and travel time, regardless of the monetary value placed on time, the best alternative is to open three SSTs. As Figure 25.6 shows, however, this conclusion is sensitive to the value of waiting time relative to that of travel time. If waiting time is particularly onerous (that is, if 0.45 hour or less of waiting time is equal to one hour of travel time), adding a station at the MVA office becomes more effective, although still considerably more costly, than opening three SSTs.

Cost-effectiveness does not, of course, eliminate the need for sensitivity analysis. Figure 25.6, for example, shows how the effectiveness of the three alternatives being considered varies with the weight assigned to travel-time reductions relative to waiting-time reductions. This figure makes it clear that opening three SSTs will result in both lower annual net costs *and* greater equivalent waiting-time savings only if the weight assigned to travel-time reductions is greater than 0.43. If the weight assigned to travel-time reductions is less than this value, adding a station at the MVA office is a more effective though still more costly alternative than opening three SSTs.

Table 25.6. Cost-Effectiveness Analysis of the MVA Decision.

Alternative	Annual Costs ($ thousands)	Annual Out-of-Pocket Savings Due to Reduction in Aggregate Travel Distance ($ thousands)	Annual Net Costs ($ thousands)	Annual Savings Due to Reduction in Aggregate Travel Distances ($ thousands)	Annual Time Savings Due to Reduction in Aggregate Travel Distance (thousands of hours)	Annual Reduction in Waiting Time (thousands of hours)	Equivalent Annual Reduction in Travel Time (thousands of hours)	Total Equivalent Annual Reduction in Travel Time (thousands of hours)
Do nothing	0	0	0	0	0	0	0	0
Add one more station at								
MVA office	100	0	100	0	0	5.6	11.2	11.2
Open 2 SSTs	30	41.5	−11.5		3.0	4.0	8.0	11.0
Open 3 SSTs	40	76.2	−36.2		5.5	3.2	6.3	11.9

Note: Numbers are rounded to the nearest tenth.

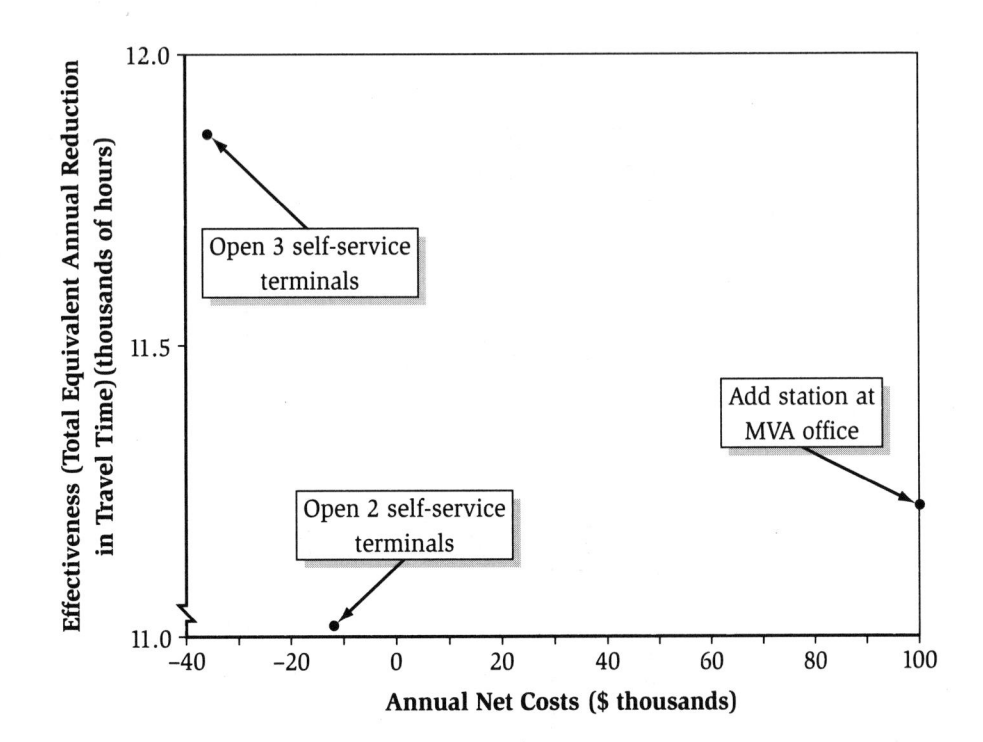

Figure 25.5. Cost-Effectiveness of MVA Alternatives.

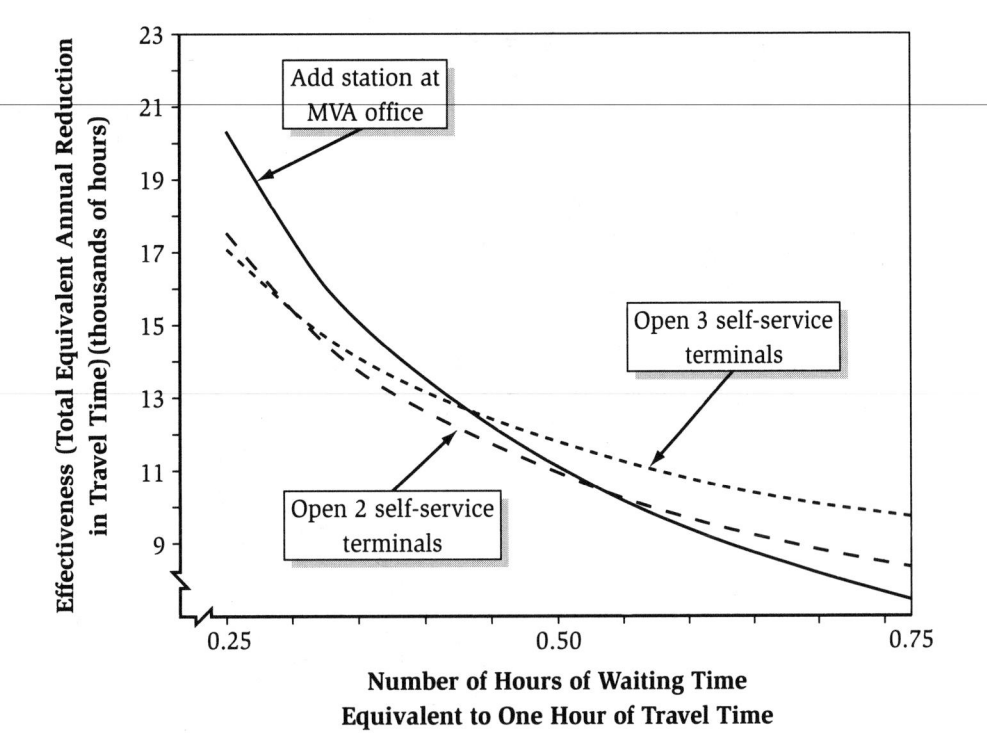

Figure 25.6. Effect on Effectiveness of Varying Travel-Time Weight.

Exhibit 25.5. Applying Cost-Effectiveness Analysis to Crime-Reduction Programs.

Assigning monetary values to the crime reduction impacts shown in Table 25.5 is likely to be even more problematic than assigning monetary values to travel-time and waiting-time savings. Hence CEA might again be an attractive means of analyzing the choice faced by a municipal police force that is considering the three crime-reduction programs considered in Exhibit 25.3. Although it would not be necessary to assign a monetary value to reducing particular types of crimes, applying CEA in this case would require that the analyst express the value of reducing one type of crime (say, robberies) relative to reducing some other type of crime (say, homicides). For example, it might be determined that preventing one homicide is as valuable as preventing 50 rapes or 124 robberies or 158 assaults. (Note that these relative values are consistent with the monetary values used in Exhibit 25.3. Another source of these types of relative values is Wolfgang, Figlio, Tracy, and Singer, 1985.)

Given these relative values, preventing 12 rapes is equivalent to preventing $12/50 = 0.24$ homicides; preventing 117 robberies is equivalent to preventing $117/124 = 0.94$ homicides; and preventing 94 assaults is equivalent to preventing $94/158 = 0.59$ homicides. Hence, given the estimates of the expected annual decrease in the various types of crimes shown in Table 25.5, implementing enhanced community policing produces reductions in crime that are as valuable as preventing 3.77 $(2 + 0.24 + 0.94 + 0.59)$ homicides per year. Similar calculations for the other two alternatives yields Table 25.7.

Figure 25.7 graphically compares the three crime-reduction alternatives in terms of total annual cost and annual equivalent reduction in homicides. Unlike the MVA case, CEA in this case does not yield an unambiguous "winner." It does show that relative to enhanced community policing, foot patrols yield very little (the equivalent of 0.05 fewer homicides) for a relatively large amount of money ($1.1 million per year). The trade-off between a zero-tolerance policy and either of the other two alternatives is not as simple. As compared to enhanced community policing, for example, a zero-tolerance policy reduces crime by an amount equivalent to nearly 1 homicide (more precisely, 0.94 homicides) at an incremental cost of $2.4 million. Thus CEA produces an insight exactly the same as we saw in Exhibit 25.3: if the value of preventing a homicide is relatively small (below approximately $2.6 million), enhanced community policing is preferred to adopting a zero-tolerance policy. Conversely, if the value of doing so is relatively high (above approximately $2.6 million), adopting a zero-tolerance policy is preferable.

Important sensitivity analyses to be conducted here include the effect of varying the values of reducing the number of rapes, robberies, and assaults relative to reducing the number of homicides. Figure 25.8 shows an illustration of this. Regardless of the value of preventing a robbery relative to preventing a homicide, adopting a zero-tolerance policy is the most effective alternative. (Note that

(continued)

Exhibit 25.5. (*continued*)

although a zero-tolerance policy is unambiguously, the most effective alternative, whether it is the best alternative or not, still depends on the trade-offs a decision maker is willing to make.) However, if the number of robberies equivalent to one homicide is less than around 110, enhanced community policing has not only lower costs than foot patrols but also higher effectiveness.

Table 25.7. Cost-Effectiveness Analysis of Crime-Control Programs.

Alternative	Annual Costs ($ millions)	Annual Equivalent Reduction in Homicides
Enhanced community policing	6.7	3.77
Expanded Foot Patrols	7.8	3.82
Zero tolerance	9.1	4.71

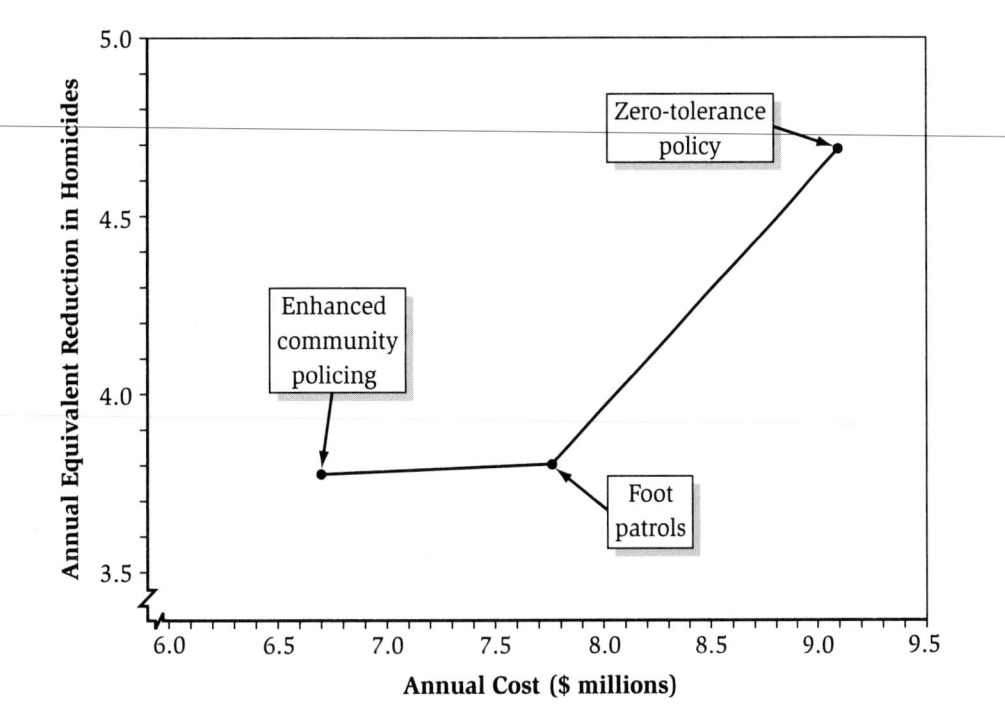

Figure 25.7. Cost-Effectiveness of Crime-Control Programs.

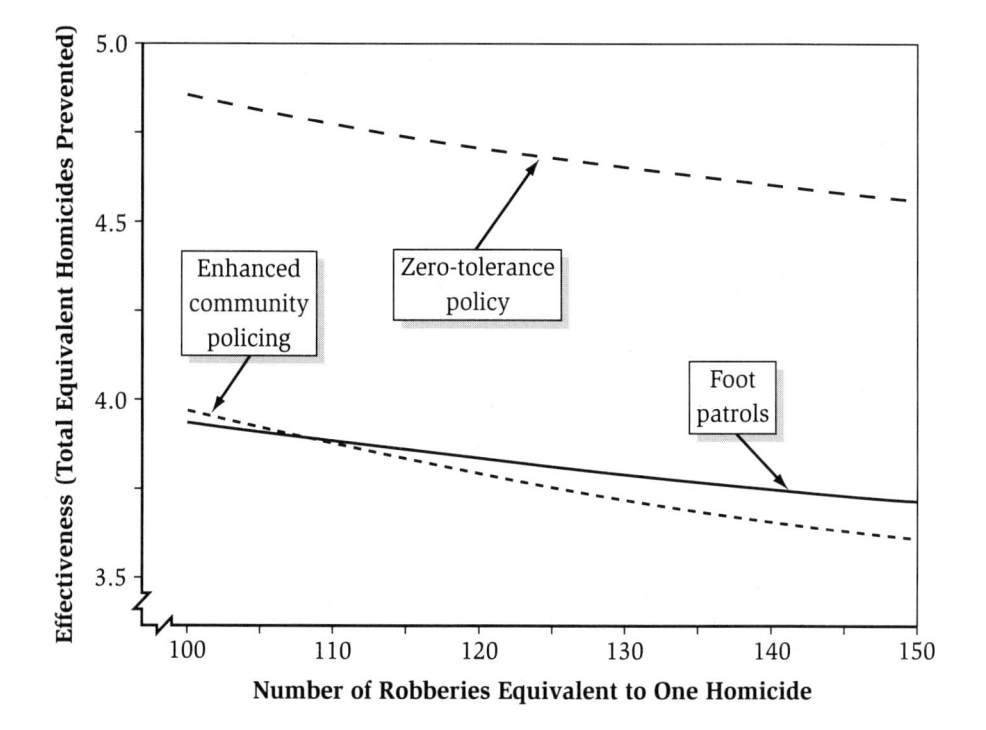

Figure 25.8. Effect on Effectiveness of Varying Relative Value of Preventing Robberies.

Decision Analysis

In many instances, the impacts of resource allocations depend on events and factors that are beyond the predictive capability of analysts. For example, the impacts of self-service terminals are highly sensitive to the fraction of all customers that actually choose to use them. The analysis in Exhibits 25.1, 25.2, and 25.4 assumed that reliable estimates of these fractions are available. Realistically, such estimates are almost sure to be highly uncertain. A particularly helpful tool in cases where considerable levels of uncertainty are present is decision analysis. Decision analysis provides both a way of structuring such problems and assistance in finding the best course of action. (For further discussion of decision analysis, see Clemen, 1996.)

MEASURING EFFICIENCY

Measuring the efficiency of organizational units such as schools or police departments has long been a goal of budget analysts. Efficiency measurement in any but the simplest of organizations, however, is an extremely challenging task. A key reason for this is that public sector organizations typically use multiple inputs and produce multiple outputs. In addition, these inputs and outputs are typically measured in incommensurable units, and efficient markets for many of these inputs and outputs do not exist.

Recent years have seen considerable developments in an approach to efficiency measurement known as data envelopment analysis (DEA). The DEA approach to efficiency measurement involves solving a series of linear programming problems. (Although standard linear programming software packages can, in principle, be used for DEA, doing so is extremely tedious. Numerous specialized software packages for DEA are available; see Charnes, Cooper, Lewin, and Seiford, 1994). One of the main advantages of this approach is that it is *nonparametric*, that is, it makes no prior assumption regarding the functional form of the production function, nor does it require prior specification of weights or prices for inputs or outputs. Perhaps the most severe weakness of the DEA approach is that it does not include an error term. Hence it fails to distinguish between random noise and "true" inefficiency.

DEA yields, for each organizational unit ("decision-making unit" in DEA), a relative efficiency score. A score of 1.0 indicates that the decision-making unit is "efficient." The extent to which a decision-making unit's efficiency score differs from 1.0 indicates the extent to which that unit is inefficient. DEA also yields, for each inefficient unit, estimates of either the extent to which that unit could reduce the level of each input used without reducing outputs, if it were fully efficient, or the extent to which that unit could increase the level of each output without using additional inputs, if it were fully efficient. (Which of the two sets of information is produced depends on whether the analyst formulates the model as input- or output-oriented; see Charnes, Cooper, Lewin, and Seiford, 1994.)

In applying DEA, an analyst specifies the *input* measures, *output* measures, and set of units to be compared. Two types of input measures can be used in DEA. The first is discretionary (controllable) inputs. For example, in applying DEA to school districts in New York State, Ruggiero, Duncombe, and Miner (1995) consider as discretionary inputs two measures of labor quantity—teacher aides per 100 pupils and teacher assistants per 100 pupils (these researchers do not include teachers per 100 pupils in their analysis because New York State regulations ensure that this ratio is nearly constant across school districts. If this were not the case, it would be appropriate to include this ratio as an additional measure of labor quantity); two measures of teacher quality—the proportion of third-grade teachers with at least a bachelor's degree plus thirty hours of graduate education and the proportion of sixth-grade teachers with at least a bachelor's degree plus thirty hours of graduate education; and two measures of labor resources—computers per 100 pupils and classrooms per 100 pupils.

The second type of input measure used in DEA is nondiscretionary (fixed) inputs. These represent factors affecting outputs over which decision makers do not exert control. Ruggiero, Duncombe, and Miner (1995), for example, argue that factors such as parental background and student characteristics affect the ability of school districts to produce educational outcomes. They specifically include a "nonpoverty rate" (the percent of children five to seventeen years old in the school district not in poverty) as an input measure in addition to the discretionary inputs. Output measures represent the goals of the decision-making units. In applying DEA to schools, measures of student achievement are typically used as output measures. Ruggiero and colleagues included average scores of sixth-grade students on Pupil Evaluation Program tests in reading, mathematics, and social studies.

While judicious selection of variables is, of course, important in any form of analysis, it is particularly important in DEA. A major reason for this is that, for a given number of decision-making units, the more inputs and outputs that are used, the less the ability of DEA to distinguish efficient from inefficient decision-making units. One rule of thumb that has been proposed (see Charnes, Cooper, Lewin, and Seiford, 1994, p. 435) is that the total number of inputs and outputs should be less than one-third the number of decision-making units included in the analysis.

CONCLUSIONS

Advanced analytical techniques have considerable potential for facilitating improved budget allocation decisions. It is important, however, that the potential contributions of advanced analytical techniques to sound budgeting decisions be kept in perspective. The sophistication of these techniques gives them a veneer of accuracy and objectivity. As a result of this veneer, the numbers produced by various analytical techniques have a tendency to take on a life of their own. To the extent that this occurs, the potential contribution of advanced analytical techniques will be lost. The numbers produced by advanced analytical techniques are, in fact, partial and imperfect estimates that are dependent on a host of both explicit and implicit assumptions, approximations, and so on. To paraphrase R. W. Hamming (1973; see also Geoffrion, 1976), the purpose of employing advanced analytical techniques should be insight, not numbers. Rather than replacing judgment and other inputs into budget decisions, the potential benefits of advanced analytical techniques will be most fully realized if they are viewed as means of aiding rather than replacing judgment. In particular, the main benefit of advanced analytical techniques is likely to be focusing the attention of decision makers on the key issues and parameters on which the choice depends.

Conducting extensive sensitivity analyses is a very useful approach for attaining this benefit. Sensitivity analysis entails considering how changes in various assumptions and input parameters affect the conclusions of the analysis.

References

Boardman, A. E., Greenberg, D. H., Vining, A. R., and Weimer, D. L. *Cost-Benefit Analysis: Concepts and Practice.* Upper Saddle River, N.J.: Prentice Hall, 1996.

Boardman, A. E., Greenberg, D. H., Vining, A. R., and Weimer, D.L. "'Plug-in' Shadow Price Estimates for Policy Analysis." *Annals of Regional Science,* 1997, *31,* 299–324.

Burtless, G. "The Case for Randomized Field Trials in Economic and Policy Research." *Journal of Economic Perspectives,* 1995, *9,* 63–84.

Caulkins, J. P., Rydell, C. P., Schwabe, W. L., and Chiesa, J. *Mandatory Minimum Drug Sentences: Throwing Away the Key or the Taxpayer's Money?* Santa Monica, Calif.: RAND, 1997.

Charnes, A., Cooper, W., Lewin, A. Y., and Seiford, L. M. (eds.). *Data Envelopment Analysis: Theory, Methodology and Applications.* Norwell, Mass.: Kluwer, 1994.

Citro, C. F., and Hanushek, E. A.. *Improving Information for Social Policy Decisions: The Uses of Microsimulation Modeling.* Washington, D.C.: National Academy Press, 1991.

Clemen, R. T. *Making Hard Decisions: An Introduction to Decision Analysis.* (2nd ed.) Boston: PWS-Kent, 1996.

Drummond, M., Stoddard, G., and Torrance, G. *Methods of Economic Evaluation of Health Care Programmes.* Oxford: Oxford University Press, 1987.

Eschenbach, T. G." Spiderplots Versus Tornado Diagrams for Sensitivity Analysis." *Interfaces,* 1992, *22*(6), 40–46.

Geoffrion, A. M. "The Purpose of Mathematical Programming Is Insight, Not Numbers." *Interfaces,* 1976, *7*(1), 81–92.

Gleeson, M. E. "Evaluating the 'Hold' Process for a Public Library System Using Queueing Models." Paper presented at the ORSA/TIMS Joint National Meeting, Detroit, 1994.

Greenberg, D., and Shroder, M. *The Digest of Social Experiments.* (2nd ed.) Washington, D.C.: Urban Institute Press, 1997.

Gross, D., and Harris, C. M. *Fundamentals of Queuing Theory.* (3rd ed.) New York: Wiley, 1998.

Hamming, R. W. *Numerical Methods for Scientists and Engineers.* (2nd ed.) New York: McGraw-Hill, 1973.

Heckman, J. J., and Smith, J. A. "Assessing the Case for Social Experiments." *Journal of Economic Perspectives,* 1995, *9,* 85–110.

Kaplan, E. H. "Analyzing Tenant Assignment Policies." *Management Science,* 1987, *33,* 395–408.

Kaplan, E. H., and Brandeau, M. L. (eds.). *Modeling the AIDS Epidemic: Planning, Policy, and Prediction.* New York: Raven Press, 1994.

Larson, R. C. "A Hypercube Queuing Model for Facility Location and Redistricting in Urban Emergency Services." *Journal of Computers and Operations Research,* 1974, *1,* 845–868.

Larson, R. C., and Odoni, A. R. *Urban Operations Research.* Upper Saddle River, N.J.: Prentice Hall, 1981.

Levitan, S. *Evaluation of Federal Social Programs: An Uncertain Impact.* Washington, D.C.: Center for Social Policy Studies, George Washington University, 1992.

MacRae, D., Jr., and Whittington, D. *Expert Advice for Policy Choice.* Washington, D.C.: Georgetown University Press, 1997.

Marcantonio, R. J., and Cook, T. D. "Convincing Quasi-Experiments: The Interrupted Time Series and Regression-Discontinuity Designs." In J. S. Wholey, H. P. Hatry, and K. E. Newcomer (eds.), *Handbook of Practical Program Evaluation.* San Francisco: Jossey-Bass, 1994.

Miller, T. R., Cohen, M. A., and Rossman, S. "Victim Costs of Violent Crime and Resulting Injuries." *Health Affairs,* 1993, *12,* 171–185.

Mohr, L. B. *Impact Analysis for Program Evaluation.* Florence, Ky.: Dorsey Press, 1988.

Mohring, H., Schroeter, J., and Wiboonchutikula, P. "The Values of Waiting Time, Travel Time, and a Seat on the Bus." *Rand Journal of Economics,* 1987, *18,* 40–56.

Newhouse, J. P., and the Insurance Experiment Group. *Free for All? Lessons from the RAND Health Insurance Experiment.* Cambridge, Mass.: Harvard University Press, 1993.

Salzberg, A. M., Dolins, S. L., and Salzberg, C. "A Multiperiod Compartmental Model of the HIV Pandemic in the USA." *Socio-Economic Planning Sciences,* 1991, *25,* 167–178.

Sherman, L. W. "Police Crackdowns: Initial and Residual Deterrence." In M. Tonry and N. Morris (eds.), *Crime and Justice: A Review of Research,* Vol. 12. Chicago: University of Chicago Press, 1990.

Stokey, E., and Zeckhauser, R. *A Primer for Policy Analysis.* New York: Norton, 1978.

Swersey, A. "The Deployment of Police, Fire, and Emergency Medical Units." In S. M. Pollock, M. H. Rothkopf, and A. Barnett (eds.), *Operations Research and the Public Sector.* Amsterdam: Elsevier North-Holland, 1994.

Waters, W. G., II. "Variations in the Value of Travel Time Savings: Empirical Studies and the Values for Road Project Evaluation," mimeo, 1993.

Wolfgang, M. E., Figlio, R. M., Tracy, P. E., and Singer, S. I. *The National Survey of Crime Severity.* Washington, D.C.: U.S. Department of Justice, Bureau of Justice Statistics, 1985.

PART SEVEN

BUDGETING OVER TIME
FOR LARGE AMOUNTS

CHAPTER TWENTY-SIX

Budgeting for Capital Improvements

Robert L. Bland
Wes Clarke

No discussion of government budgeting is complete without addressing the special case of budgeting for infrastructure. Broadly defined, capital expenditures are for fixed assets that produce benefits beyond the current year, while operating expenditures are for assets that produce benefits only in the current year (Vogt, 1996, pp. 128–129).

How governments distinguish capital from operating expenditures is a critical policy decision that depends on past practices and management philosophy. For example, some governments choose not to distinguish between capital and operating expenditures—all expenditures are consolidated into one unified budget. This is the approach used by the federal government since 1968 (Schick, 1995, pp. 14–15). The main reason for adoption of this unified approach at the national level was to understand the impact of federal spending on the economy.

By contrast, state and local governments generally adopt separate capital and operating budgets. Considerable variety exists, however, in how governments present capital spending proposals. According to a recent study, forty states use some systematic method for prioritizing major capital projects, ranging from simple lists of approved projects to more complex systems designed to monitor and manage investment in capital (Hush and Peroff, 1988; Thomassen, 1990). Cope (1995, pp. 42–52) reports that of 1,396 cities she surveyed, ranging in population from 2,500 to more than one million, 1,343 (96.2 percent) use some form of capital budget, and 40 percent of these report that preparation and adoption of the capital budget is separate from the operating budget process.

THE CONTEXT OF CAPITAL BUDGETING

A decision to budget capital acquisitions separately from operations raises a number of issues that must be resolved. For example, what capital items should be included in the capital budget, and what ones should be included in the operating budget? Should budgets reflect the cost of using up capital assets? What effect, if any, do capital investments have on economic growth? The following discussion sets the political context of capital budgeting by addressing these key policy questions.

Distinguishing Capital and Operating Expenditures

Not all capital expenditures are reported in the capital budget, especially for less expensive items such as office equipment. Operating budgets also include a line item for capital outlay. Typically, the budget office, with the approval of the legislature, may set a minimum dollar value for items to include in the capital budget, such as $10,000. Acquisitions costing less than this amount are requested through the operating budget. The minimum value will vary depending on the size of the budget and the policy preferences of each government.

Unlike the operating budget, with its emphasis on spending categories, the capital budget presents information by project, sources of funding, and a projection of expenditures to complete the project. Capital budgets are also funded differently than operating budgets. Governments rely on debt in part to fund the cost of capital improvements, with the debt repaid over the life of the fixed asset. In the case of general obligation debt, governments must first gain voter approval through a bond referendum before selling the bonds. In some cases, governments may choose not to issue debt but to establish capital reserve funds to accumulate sufficient resources to construct, remodel, or replace a capital improvement when the need arises. More typically, governments use a mix of current revenues and bond proceeds to fund larger capital projects, such as street improvements.

Whereas transactions emanating from the operating budget will be accounted for largely in the general fund, spending authorized by the capital budget will be accounted for in capital project funds. A separate fund is established for each major project—for example, a storm drainage project, or construction of a new university building. Revenue flowing into the fund may come from bond proceeds, current revenues, or grant income. Outflows from the fund are for expenditures associated with the project's payments to contractors, materials, land acquisition, and other costs. Once a project is completed, its capital project fund is closed out; any remaining balances are transferred to another fund.

Capital Expenditure and Capital Consumption

Another important distinction is between capital expenditure and capital consumption. Expenditures occur as governments buy or build something. Consumption occurs over the asset's useful life. For example, the purchase of a fire truck constitutes a capital expenditure, say $500,000. If the truck is expected to provide useful service for the next fifteen years, the city consumes $33,333 in capital each year. In the first year, the city adds $500,000 to its fixed assets and at year's end has consumed one-fifteenth of the asset's value.

Some writers have commented on the lack of consideration given to capital consumption (Pagano, 1984; Thomassen, 1990). This issue is usually illustrated by arguing that the lack of maintenance reduces the useful life of an asset (or the life is not extended), resulting in capital consumption at a faster rate. For example, failure to spend resources to maintain a bridge reduces its useful life, requiring replacement sooner than expected. If the city that just bought a new fire truck fails to provide proper maintenance and the useful life is reduced to twelve years, capital consumption increases to $41,666 per year.

A number of procedural changes have been suggested to alleviate the effect of decision makers' bias against or failure to consider maintenance. Some governments now establish capital reserve accounts for maintenance or replacement of fixed assets. Under these programs, the operating budget includes an allocation each year to a reserve account that is used specifically for these purposes. The city of Plano, Texas, has adopted such a mechanism with the intention that the allocation for repair and maintenance will become institutionalized. The city also maintains a reserve account for fleet vehicle replacement.

Kachelmeier and Granof (1993) found that decision makers who have data on previous capital spending levels and depreciation costs are more likely to allocate more resources to maintenance in order to extend the useful life of fixed assets. In the authors' simulation, persons with such information invested more heavily in capital and were more likely to maintain existing stock.

Poterba (1995) concluded in his study of the effect of capital budgets on state spending for capital improvements that those states with separate capital budgets, and especially those that use debt rather than financing on a pay-as-you-go basis, have significantly higher levels of capital investment. Thus the presence of a capital budget process has an effect on the willingness of governments to invest in public improvements.

Capital Spending and Economic Growth

Few would dispute the assertion that public capital investment is essential for economic growth (National Council on Public Works Improvement, 1988, p. 35). Commerce would be difficult or impossible without a system of roads, airports, and harbors. Mass transit systems reduce commute times and traffic congestion and may improve air quality. Roads and airports facilitate the movement of goods and persons. Citizens want high-quality schools, recreation facilities, and parks. These basic systems support our quality of life.

Although the amount of capital spending by state and local governments depends on the cost of debt and general economic growth, they have generally increased the amount of investments in capital over the past three decades. One indicator of investment in new capital by state and local governments is their outstanding long-term debt. According to Figure 26.1, the amount of debt as a percent of gross domestic product (GDP) held by state, city, and other local governments steadily increased through the 1980s, although the rate of increase leveled off for city governments in the late 1980s and early 1990s. In 1980, state and local outstanding debt amounted to 10 percent of GDP. By 1992 it had increased to more than 15 percent. One effect of the 1986 Tax Reform Act is evident from Figure 26.1. As special district governments rushed to issue debt that soon would not qualify as tax-exempt, the percentage of all government debt held by these entities increased markedly.

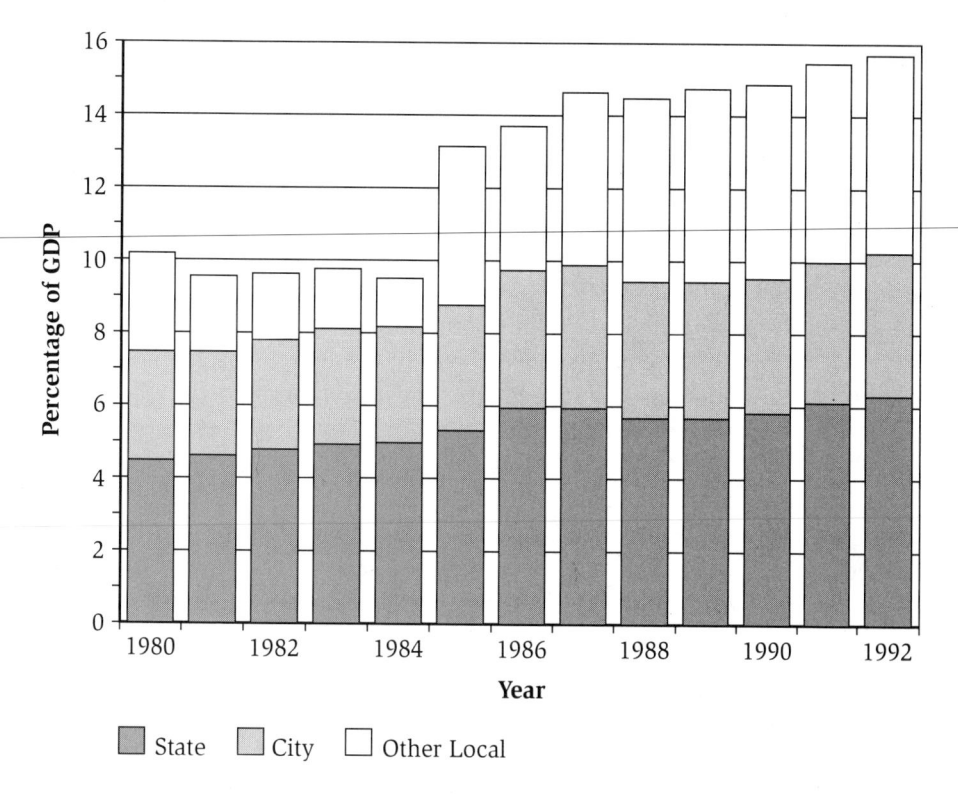

Figure 26.1. State and Local Long-Term Debt as a Percentage of GDP, 1980–1992.

Sources: U.S. Department of Commerce; *The Bond Buyer Yearbook,* various editions.

Another indicator of state and local investment in capital improvements is the Bureau of Economic Analysis's measure of gross investment expressed as a percent of GDP. Since 1972, the amount of state and local investment in capital improvements has increased threefold (see Figure 26.2), indicating a substantial commitment to upgrading public assets.

Capital investment from a macroeconomic perspective has been shown to have salutary effects on total economic output (Aschauer, 1993; Munnell, 1990), even if the effects are overestimated, as some have claimed (Lansing, 1995). Public capital investment is needed to sustain private enterprise that creates jobs and economic opportunities. Some have argued (Aschauer, 1993) that the reduction in the rate of public capital investment has adversely affected the private sector's productivity gains.

Research on the economic returns of public capital investment is mixed. Lansing (1995) reviews findings that report output elasticity of capital investment ranging from 0.04 to 0.39. On the basis of these figures he maintains that the optimal level of total public investment ranges from 4 percent to 20 percent of GNP. Such a wide range gives little guidance to policymakers who must

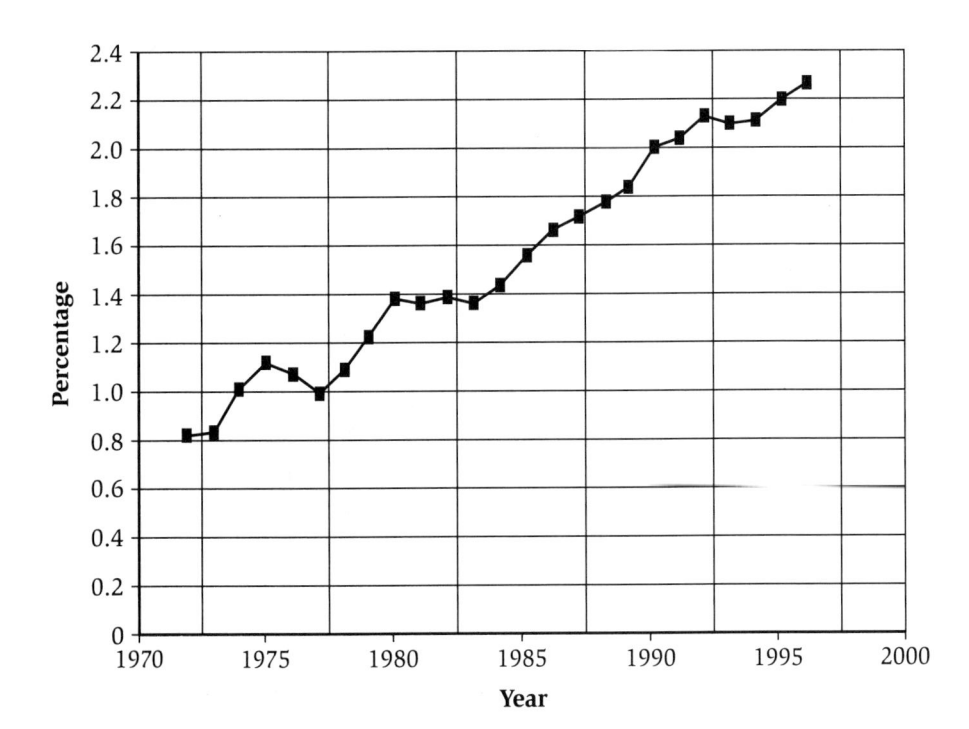

Figure 26.2. State and Local Government Investment in Structures and Equipment as a Percentage of GDP, 1972–1996.

Source: Bureau of Economic Analysis.

decide how much to invest in local infrastructure. Although investment in the private sector has the sole purpose of increasing productivity, public investment has multiple purposes, including enhancing quality of life. A new state park adds little to economic output but may greatly augment leisure opportunities for users. Comparing only the economic benefits of a public investment potentially underestimates other benefits valued by the community.

Nunn (1991b) found that public capital investment in Fort Worth, Texas, was associated with positive effects on both private capital formation and assessed property values. He found that public investment moved cyclically with private investment and property values. Nunn cautions, however, about attributing a causal relationship between public investment and changes in private investment or property value. Investment decisions based on the build-it-and-they-will-come philosophy may be shortsighted because regional and even national economic conditions play an important part in determining local growth. Investment in superior public infrastructure may distinguish a community when businesses are choosing a location, but regional economic conditions and workforce quality must also be considered. As a consequence, investment aimed at reversing depressed economic conditions may be ineffective when used alone. Capital investment should be part of a larger strategy for economic development that identifies projects for promoting business investment.

THE CAPITAL BUDGETING PROCESS

Conflict permeates the public budgeting process. While much of the literature focuses on the conflicts inherent in the operating budget (Guess, 1985), the capital budgeting cycle also possesses its own conflicts that require constant attention from the chief executive. The six sources of conflict presented in Figure 26.3 are discussed in the remainder of this chapter.

Organizing the Capital Budget Cycle

The first set of issues in organizing the capital budget is deciding what unit should have responsibility for overseeing the budget's preparation, the range of duties for that unit, and the extent to which the operating and capital budget cycles should overlap each other.

With respect to the organizational location for overseeing capital budget preparation, three possibilities exist: the finance department; the budget office, if separate from finance; and the planning department (Bland and Rubin, 1997, p. 175). The public works department may be a fourth, but unlikely, possibility given its primary focus on infrastructure, especially street improvements. The most logical locus is the budget office (especially if it is separate from the finance department), but the budget office should draw on the land use expertise of the planning office.

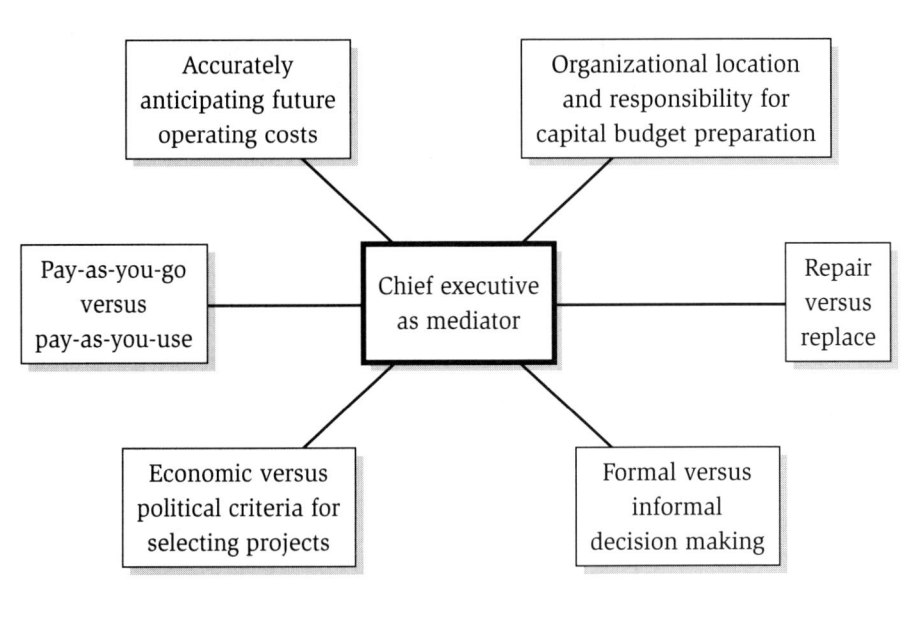

Figure 26.3. Sources of Conflict in the Capital Budgeting Process.

The second issue in organizing the capital budget function is the unit's range of duties. In principle, the unit should have responsibility for the full range of capital improvements, from planning to acquisition to inventorying and monitoring their condition. In reality, duties will depend on the chief executive's preferences and the abilities of the capital budgeting unit.

The final organizational issue involves the timing of the capital budget cycle (Bland and Rubin, 1997, pp. 176–177). Little documentation exists on the actual practice among state and local governments. Preparing operating and capital budgets concurrently has the advantage of focusing the attention of department heads and the legislature on budget issues at one time without prolonging budget deliberations. The impact of capital spending on the operating budget (and vice versa) will be recognized more readily when the two cycles are concurrent. Conversely, preparing the capital budget countercyclical to the operating budget cycle makes better use of staff time by distributing the workload throughout the year and eases the amount of information that must be processed by lawmakers. Ultimately, the choice on timing depends on the preferences of policymakers and the size of the budget staff.

The process for allocating resources to capital improvements can be divided into three distinct stages: planning, budget adoption, and implementation (see Figure 26.4). Because of the long-lived nature of capital assets, the planning phase is the most critical because it is here that proposed projects are identified, evaluated, costed, and ranked. Unlike the operating budget cycle, the capital budgeting cycle closely links planning (the capital improvement plan, or CIP) with allocation of resources (budgeting).

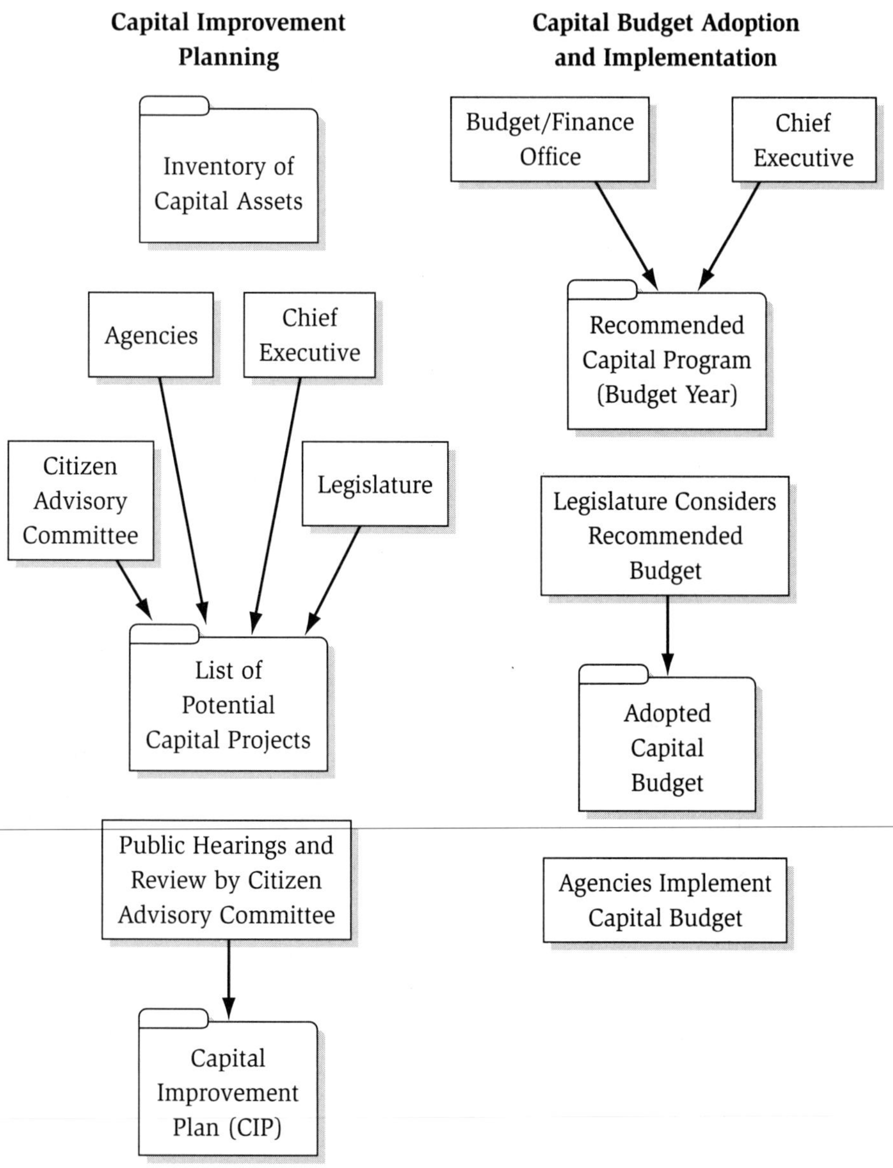

Capital Improvement Planning

Capital Budget Adoption and Implementation

Inventory of Capital Assets

Budget/Finance Office

Chief Executive

Agencies

Chief Executive

Recommended Capital Program (Budget Year)

Citizen Advisory Committee

Legislature

Legislature Considers Recommended Budget

List of Potential Capital Projects

Adopted Capital Budget

Public Hearings and Review by Citizen Advisory Committee

Agencies Implement Capital Budget

Capital Improvement Plan (CIP)

Figure 26.4. The Capital Budget Process.

Preparing the Capital Improvement Plan

An effective capital budgeting process must begin with an inventory of the government's existing stock of capital investments and an evaluation of their current condition. This provides information on whether to repair or replace an existing asset, and on the relative urgency of proposed capital acquisitions.

Inventory of Existing Assets. An inventory of existing assets begins with a description of each asset and an estimation of its replacement cost. The next step in the process is to evaluate the condition of existing capital assets. As Riordan, Oria, and Tuss (1987, p. 10) point out, the condition appraisal is the most time-consuming aspect of the capital planning phase. Yet it helps illustrate to citizens and lawmakers whether previous investment in maintenance and repair is paying off. Most importantly, an inventory and condition assessment gives legitimacy to investing in maintenance and repair, and it can be an indispensable managerial aid in building consensus on spending priorities.

Repair or Replace? Public administrators know firsthand the difficulty of obtaining funding for maintenance and repair. Politically, new construction possesses much greater appeal than renovation or repair, and consequently it receives priority in the funding process. One of the conflicts illustrated in Figure 26.3 was between outlays for repair and outlays for new construction. Yet investing in maintenance may provide returns that greatly exceed comparable investment in new acquisitions. As Pagano (1984, p. 33) has noted, it is far easier for decision makers to eliminate funding for maintenance and repair than to eliminate funding for acquisitions, especially during economic downturns, because maintenance and repair are less visible and less politically sensitive, and because there are no immediate repercussions on service delivery compared to other budget reductions. Conversely, new construction usually costs more than renovation, and in a tight budget environment, it may be less attractive.

The inventory assessment and replacement analysis gives priority to projects that need immediate attention, that will fail sooner rather than later, and whose serviceability can be extended with some investment in maintenance.

Rating schemes can also aid decision makers in making the choice between repair and replacement. In the case of a street needing repair, its score might be poor, fair, good, or excellent, which would translate into a predetermined course of action such as reconstruction, resurfacing, patching, or doing nothing. Benefit-cost analyses of each option can be useful in making comparisons. Any rating scheme should be reviewed periodically and adjusted when technology changes. For instance, a new street-patching material may provide better results than those previously available, making patching an effective alternative to resurfacing in more cases. Too often the old rules of thumb that guide decisions are based on outdated technology or information.

The Capital Improvement Plan. Planning for capital improvements then requires the preparation of a capital improvement plan. This document usually spans a five-to-seven-year period and schedules the multitude of projects that a government wishes to undertake. Figure 26.5 provides an example of a project sheet from the CIP for the city of Plano, Texas.

For multiyear projects such as a major road construction, the CIP identifies the year in which the project begins, the expected cost for each year of the project, and the expected completion date. The plan for the first year of the CIP becomes the *capital budget,* which when adopted becomes the legislative appropriation for the forthcoming year. Each year the CIP is updated, revenue and expenditure estimates for the outlying years are revised, and another year of projects is added, thereby maintaining a rolling five-year time frame. Annual review of the CIP forces administrators and legislators to reevaluate projects more than once and to judge the urgency of new capital requests against those already in the CIP. As the CIP is updated, new projects may be added and others dropped or delayed to a later date.

In a few cases, requests may require immediate approval for funding because of their urgency. If this happens repeatedly, however, the CIP loses much of its value as a planning device. The primary benefit of the CIP is that it forces decision makers to examine and rank the full range of potential projects. The CIP also forces the finance office to identify revenue sources and, if debt is used, to schedule the issuance of bonds.

Selecting Proposals for Inclusion in the CIP. Whoever participates in the capital planning process greatly influences the outcome. A citizens' advisory group, such as the Bedford 2000 Committee described in the adjoining sidebar, can provide valuable input in selecting projects for inclusion in the CIP, and if needed, follow-up support for a bond referendum. One frequently used approach is the creation of a capital allocation committee to review and rank proposals for inclusion in the CIP and capital budget. In its survey of state budget officials, the National Association of State Budget Officers (1992, p. 16) found that at least twenty states rely on an interorganizational board to review and recommend projects for inclusion in the governor's budget.

Bedford 2000

Bedford, Texas, a city of 46,000 in the Dallas–Fort Worth metroplex, was in a difficult situation in the early 1990s. Infrastructure needs were great and increasing yearly due to phenomenal growth. A lack of planning had led to inefficient use of bond proceeds approved in the 1984 referendum. So many citizens were opposed to additional debt that city officials had refrained from calling a bond election. Bedford officials decided that the only way to overcome this opposition was to involve as many citizens and civic organizations as possible in reviewing

Proposition:	1995 Fire Facilities (Proposition #2)
Project Title:	Fire Station #9
Project No:	28-P04
Description:	Fire Station #9 will be located near Parker Road and Marsh Lane in far west Plano. The site was acquired in conjunction with a park site. This station will serve an area of the City east of the western city limits, north of Park Blvd., south of Spring Creek Parkway, and west of the Tollway.

Map

Projected Fire Stations and Districts

Schedule	Start	Complete
Land	Mar-91	Jul-95
Design	Jan-96	Jun-96
Construction	Sep-96	Jul-97
Equipment	Jun-96	Jun-97

Construction Budget (000's)	
Land	50
Design	100
Construction	1,135
Equipment	400
Miscellaneous	
TOTAL	1,685

Construction-Funding Schedule (000's)

Funding Source	Prior Yrs	Re-Est 95-96	1996-97	1997-98	1998-99	1999-00	2000-01	Future Yrs	Total
City		50	335	1,300	0	0	0	0	1,685
Total	0	50	335	1,300	0	0	0	0	1,685

Estimated Operating Budget Expenditures (000's)

Expenditure Type	1996-97	1997-98	1998-99	1999-00	2000-01	Future	Operating Notes
Personnel	202	450					3 Captains, 3 Fire Apparatus Operators, and 9 Firefighters plus associated O&M and related capital outlay. 2 months impact in 96-97, remainder necessary for full year impact in 97-98
O&M	34	108					
Capital	106						
Total	342	558					

Figure 26.5. City of Plano, Texas, Capital Improvement Program.

Source: City of Plano, Texas, Proposed Capital Improvement Plan, 1996–1997, p. 48.

the city's capital needs. Newly appointed city manager Linda Barton and public information officer Beth Davis decided to organize a major initiative that would not only generate citizen involvement but also ensure that expenditures followed an approved plan. The project, called Bedford 2000, was managed by Davis.

About 125 people were recruited for inclusion in the citizen committee to study Bedford's capital needs, to prioritize projects, and to make recommendations to the mayor and the city council. These volunteers represented business interests, neighborhoods, school PTAs, and all civic organizations that officials could identify. About seventy-five volunteers remained actively involved in the committee. The group was organized into five subcommittees and, with city staff assistance, inspected, inventoried, and assessed the condition of all city assets, including civic buildings, streets, water and sewer systems, parks and recreation facilities, and drainage systems.

Between May and September 1995, the subcommittees did their work, compiling from firsthand inspections a list of more than 150 needed projects, ranging from water and sewer upgrades to new buildings for the fire and police departments. The process included meetings with council to get their sense of the city's needs, a survey of citizens, meetings to draft recommendations, a community forum, and preparation of a full committee report.

In early September the committee members canvassed neighborhoods and their own civic groups to generate support for the election held on September 12, 1995. Barton credits the members with success in passing all eight ballot propositions. In her words, "Their 'ownership' of the plan was the key to its success."

As noted in Figure 26.3, another source of conflict that requires the chief executive's attention is the ongoing struggle over what criteria to use in project selection. While casual observation may suggest that preparing the CIP proceeds rather mechanically, it is a highly political process. Nunn (1991a) has identified two competing policy procedures in capital decision making: formal policymaking, which selects proposals on the basis of formal organizational procedures such as the CIP; and informal policymaking, which occurs as a result of ad hoc deals between a government and developers or among elected officials. The interaction between these two policymaking procedures determines the final choice of capital investment projects included in the CIP.

Governments use multiple criteria—political, economic, or administrative—to evaluate the projects being considered for funding. Ideally the criteria used to select projects should be clearly specified in a capital planning policy statement. In reality, project selection is more often the result of a blend of politics (distributing benefits to all regions or districts) and formal procedures (selecting projects that maximize benefits).

Operationalization of these factors requires that specific indicators be developed. Some local governments use a project rating sheet to score each project (Bland and Rubin, 1997, pp. 184–186). Each member of the capital allocation committee assigns a rating for each project; the scores are totaled and the projects are then ranked by their total score. On completion of its deliberations, the committee submits its list of recommended projects to the chief executive for inclusion in the CIP.

Theoretically, projects move from the out-years of the CIP to the first, or budget, year. The most intensive scrutiny is given to those projects that survive to the first year of the CIP—that is, those that will be funded in the capital budget. Projects not funded are reconsidered the following year or are dropped from the CIP. Some projects, however, never seem to find their way to the capital budget due to more pressing needs or politics.

Economic Criteria. One of the most noticeable and fundamental differences between government and business procedures for evaluating projects is the private sector's much greater reliance on economic criteria, such as net present value (NPV) and internal rate of return computations, in making capital investment choices. Public administrators have shown less interest in using these criteria in their funding choices (Sharp, 1986).

In the case of infrastructure and the general fixed assets of government, the utility of economic measures has a lower priority. The costs of such projects, and especially the value of their benefits, elude easy quantification because most of the benefits are intangible and can only be crudely estimated.

Such techniques may have greater merit, however, in evaluating income-producing projects such as those associated with public utilities or other enterprises. Here, determining a clear net income stream for the life of the project and thus estimating the NPV is relatively straightforward. For example, in the case of a golf course, a city may confront a decision to build or not build a new facility, renovate an existing course, or build a nine-hole instead of an eighteen-hole facility. Each alternative has identifiable costs and an expected stream of revenue for the life of the course. This scenario lends itself to a benefit-cost analysis to choose the alternative that maximizes the present value of benefits relative to costs.

The analysis begins by estimating the stream of revenues (benefits) and expenses for each alternative. These streams are then discounted for the time value of money using a discount rate that reasonably approximates the opportunity costs of capital and risks associated with the project. A ratio of the present value of benefits to costs is then computed, and the alternative with the highest ratio is the preferred choice, other things held constant.

A blanket call for the use of such techniques in evaluating all projects is inappropriate, however. A manager needs to know when to request more formal analysis using the economic criteria of NPV and when to balance the conflicting political and social criteria.

Political Criteria. When several knowledgeable government officials were asked what determines whether a project is included in the CIP, William Lucy, a former city administrator, found that the answer was always politics (Lucy, 1988, pp. 135–138). A lot is at stake when it comes to funding a project. The location of major intersections on a new highway project can mean a windfall in increased values to nearby property owners. Politically active, or connected, property owners can use their influence to ensure that development provides positive gains for the value and marketability of their land. Conversely if development (such as a landfill or airport expansion) is likely to have an adverse impact on property values, property owners may be successful in opposing the project.

The broad priorities in capital allocation must initially be established by the chief executive in consultation with the legislature. Every government has its own political traditions for selecting capital projects. The leadership in one community may specify several service areas that will receive priority in capital funding, while another may rely on broad guidelines for capital funding. The important point is that the task of a government's political leadership is to specify the general capital-spending priorities that will guide project selection.

Corwin and Getzels (1981) maintain that regardless of the form of government, the method for electing council members (at large versus by district) appears to have significant implications for capital allocation decisions. At-large council members are more inclined to support improvements for the good of the whole community, while district representatives are more preoccupied with the equitable distribution of improvements among regions of the city, giving rise to "logrolling" and "pork barrel" politics. One common practice, especially when a jurisdiction has single-member districts, is to fund capital projects on a revolving basis across those districts. This may or may not provide the distribution of capital spending that is most beneficial overall. A district that needs a major street improvement may have to wait if it received a new park the previous year. The capital investment implications of different legislative arrangements is an area in which additional research is needed.

Bland and Rubin (1997) recommend that the CIP be submitted to the legislature for review and approval. Because the CIP is a planning document, legislative approval does not authorize money for any of the projects in the plan. It does, however, add credibility to the planning process and legitimizes the work of the capital allocation committee, budget office, and chief executive.

Adopting the Capital Budget

While the CIP provides a five-year schedule of proposed projects that a government wishes to undertake, and the proposed sources of financing, the capital budget provides detailed information on the design, cost, and financing of improvements recommended for the forthcoming year. The appropriation adopting the capital budget gives the executive branch the same type of authorization for capital improvements that the operating budget gives for recurring expenditures.

The estimates for project costs used in the CIP have most likely been based on departmental projections, prepared in consultation with the budget office, or preliminary engineering studies. As proposals become more firm candidates for funding, officials need detailed cost estimates, often produced by private contractors or engineering firms. The engineering firm prepares specifications for the project and an estimate of the cost. In the case of income-producing projects, such as utility improvements or a parking garage, it is at this point that the government must determine the economic viability of the project. One widely used technique is the payback period—that is, the number of years required before the project pays back in net earnings the cost of the initial capital investment. The longer the payback period is, the less economically viable the project will be. Other, more sophisticated techniques may also be used by the consulting engineer. For non-income-producing projects, such as street improvements or renovations to city buildings, project evaluation is confined to a detailed estimate of the costs.

Also during the budget preparation phase, the budget office must make detailed estimates of available funding for the capital budget. The budget office most likely has been making revenue estimates all along and has a reasonably good idea of the amount of money available from current revenues (taxes, fund balances, grants, special assessments, and service charges). Accurate revenue estimates increase in importance because capital budgets at the state and local levels, like operating budgets, are revenue driven. State and local governments usually rely on a mix of revenue sources to fund a project, including current revenues, bond proceeds, and grant revenue. Capital budgets are constrained by both revenue availability and the ability to issue new debt. In the case of improvements to the utility system or public housing, accurate estimates of consumer demand also are essential to gauge accurately the revenue available for servicing future debt obligations.

The final step in the capital budgeting cycle is a public hearing on the proposed spending plan. This hearing most often is combined with the hearing on the CIP so that citizens have an opportunity to comment not only on the projects being proposed for the budget year but also on those being considered for future years.

As with the operating budget, an appropriation by the legislature is required by law before implementation of the capital budget. In their survey of state capital budgeting practices, Hush and Peroff (1988, p. 71) found that thirty-four of the forty-two states with capital budgets enacted a separate appropriation bill for capital spending. Some states enact several capital appropriations; for instance, Maryland one year had twenty-four separate bills. For smaller projects, Hush and Peroff note, appropriations are usually for the entire project. For larger improvements, appropriations are often made in three phases: planning and design, construction, and project completion.

Financing the Capital Budget

Decisions on financing methods are another source of conflict in the process, as noted in Figure 26.2. State and local governments can finance capital acquisitions either by expending current revenues (pay as you go) or by issuing debt (pay as you use) that is paid back over the useful life of the asset. Both methods have certain opportunity costs in that the amount appropriated for capital acquisition is unavailable for other uses. The immediate opportunity costs are much lower, however, for the expenditure needed to service a bond issue over ten or twenty years than to pay for a large project out of current revenues.

Population-sensitive investment tends to occur unevenly over time. To illustrate, as a city reaches certain population thresholds, it may need a new school, fire station, and park and water system expansion within a short period. Once completed, these facilities will likely meet the city's needs for a number of years, until the next threshold is reached. The use of debt financing has a number of advantages that alleviate this problem. Debt financing allows a government to acquire capital as needed yet devote a relatively stable amount of current revenue each year for debt service. Debt financing also removes capital acquisition decisions from the operating budget process, which is often completed under a tight time constraint. The decisions that must be made during the operating budget process are determining what portion of capital spending to fund with current revenues, and how much is available for debt service. Removal from the operating budget environment allows officials to give more thought to decisions that will affect the jurisdiction's long-term well-being.

The role of the CIP as discussed earlier facilitates the use of debt to finance capital acquisition. Because projects are approved via a planning process that is separate from budget deliberations, they are considered on their merits and relative benefits. Once approved, projects are queued and funded in accordance with their priority as appropriations for debt service are available. Revenue to fund debt service is made available either through retirement of old debt or by committing additional new amounts.

Hackbart and Ramsey (1993; Ramsey and Hackbart, 1996) have shown that capital projects are completed at a rate determined by the amount of revenue allocated to debt service. According to these authors, fiscal pressure resulting from growing demands for government services, spending for economic development, and the loss of federal revenue to finance infrastructure has led governments to pay more attention to their debt capacity.

Both debt capacity and the amount of debt acquired by a jurisdiction are affected by bond ratings and by the political process. The cost of debt is indicated largely by the bond rating that reflects underlying economic conditions. If the rating agencies become concerned about the amount of debt taken on by a government, usually measured as a percentage of the operating budget and community wealth, they may downgrade the bond rating, thereby increasing the cost of debt. The rating agencies also consider economic factors that indicate the amount of revenue that a jurisdiction may be able to raise at acceptable tax rates.

The political process produces a balance between spending for debt service and other current operating purposes (Hackbart and Ramsey, 1993). As bond ratings fall below a certain level, debt may become prohibitively costly, making it a less politically viable option for financing capital improvements. In the 1970s and 1980s, voters in a number of states approved tax limitations and other procedures that require officials to publicize their intent to raise tax rates or increase the amount of a tax levy. These types of limitations may affect bond ratings and thus the ability of a government to issue debt. Even if economic indicators indicate untapped capacity for additional debt, rating agencies may be wary if a government needs voter approval to gain access to those resources. Most local governments hold bond referenda infrequently, and bundle projects from the CIP for voter approval in order not to bring such issues before the voters too often.

Once a bond referendum is held, a jurisdiction will bring bond issues to market until it has exhausted the amount of debt approved by voters. Officials may choose to issue only enough debt at one time to cover the current year's capital budget needs, especially if market interest rates are declining.

Creative Financing Techniques

The increased reliance on own-source funding, and either the presence or the specter of tax increase limitations, have forced local governments to devise new ways of funding capital projects. Two techniques—tax-increment financing and impact development fees—associated with capital improvements have become more common as methods of financing the capital budget.

Tax increment financing (TIF) is a technique for concentrating development effort in an area that has suffered decline. Initially, the area targeted for redevelopment is designated a tax increment district. The land may be cleared or otherwise readied for redevelopment. The value of the property at this point is determined and becomes the baseline for determining the increment added by redevelopment. Under the typical TIF agreement, revenue from property (or sales) taxes levied on the baseline value continues to flow to the taxing jurisdictions (city, county, school district, and any special districts with property-taxing powers). Revenue from property taxes levied on the increases in property values from the baseline flows to a restricted tax increment fund that is used to repay the costs of the public improvements in the tax increment district. Usually bonds are sold by the TIF authority to provide up-front financing for infrastructure improvements. Repayment of the bonds is then made from the TIF fund. Once the debt is retired, the district is dissolved and all property tax revenues revert to the overlapping taxing jurisdictions.

Tax increment financing places the burden of development costs on the overlapping governments that ultimately benefit from the increased tax base (Paetsch and Dahlstrom, 1990). Resistance to TIFs may come from school and special districts if the redevelopment results in a population increase that places demands on their budgets while they subsidize infrastructure other than their own. Opposition to a TIF may also result if the technique is used in an area where development probably would have occurred without the TIF district.

By contrast, impact fees place part of the cost for infrastructure on developers who either directly pay a portion of those costs or contribute land for streets or parks. In the case of residential development, fees are usually collected either when the subdivision is platted or when lots are sold. Fees vary by city and may even vary within a jurisdiction because they are often negotiated for individual projects (Snyder and Stegman, 1987, p. 74). State laws and court decisions require that land exactions and revenue from development fees be linked to capital improvements designed to serve the development. (For a discussion, see Smith, 1987; Snyder and Stegman, 1987. For a good treatment of the history of fee usage and structure, see Altshuler and Gómez-Ibáñez, 1993.)

Project Implementation

The final phase in the capital spending cycle is implementation by executive agencies, which undertake the projects funded by the capital budget. Once the appropriation is adopted, executive agencies can award contracts for the various projects. As with the operating budget, however, spending must be carefully coordinated with available revenues. Here again the central budget office, working in conjunction with the finance department, monitors incoming revenues to make certain they are consistent with budget projections.

The central budget office also has an important role in reviewing contracts before they are signed to make certain they are consistent with the appropriation. The planning office similarly reviews contracts for their adherence to the CIP. The engineering office may review them for their technical content, making certain that they meet construction needs.

ISSUES IN CAPITAL BUDGETING

A number of policy issues in capital investment resurface periodically as economic and political conditions change. Methods for financing capital improvements is a persistent issue, especially when interest rates are rising and the economy is slowing. In recent years, concern has resurfaced about the seriously deteriorated state of the nation's infrastructure. Two other issues that pique the interest of public finance scholars have been the impact of capital spending on operating budgets and the advisability of using a separate capital spending plan at the federal level. The following sections examine these latter two issues.

The Link Between Operating and Capital Budgets

A final issue in preparing the capital budget concerns its impact on the operating budget. Every capital acquisition, whether new or the renovation or maintenance of an existing asset, affects the operating side. Managers must carefully assess that effect as part of the evaluation of the capital improvement. Will it increase operating costs and, if so, by how much? Will the operating budget be able to absorb the additional costs?

Managers know that capital investment decisions made today may have favorable future impacts, such as reducing labor costs. Conversely, capital spending may increase future operating costs, such as the completion of a new fire station that will require staffing and utilities. Similarly, deferring capital improvements may increase operating costs through higher maintenance outlays, as in the case of a deteriorated road surface.

In their article on the linkage between capital and operating spending, Bland and Nunn (1992) examine several complications that arise. First, capital spending's effect likely varies depending on whether the service is labor- or capital-intensive, and depending on the relative prices of these factors. To the extent that a capital purchase replaces labor or older facilities, it reduces future operating costs. Conversely, labor-intensive services, such as police protection, will be more sensitive to capital expenditures that expand capacity. Thus some capital spending is made in the expectation that operating costs will decline, while other expenditures are made in the expectation that operating costs will increase.

Second, the length of time it takes capital spending to have an impact on operating expenditures will likely vary by the type of service. For example, labor-intensive services will likely be more sensitive to capital investment because labor must be employed immediately after a new facility is constructed.

Should the Federal Government Adopt a Capital Budget?

Investment spending by the national government is quite different from that of state and local governments. Although subnational governments fund education and job-training programs, both of which are investments, spending for these items is predominantly an operating budget item. Capital spending by the national government, conversely, is about equally divided (49 percent versus 51 percent in 1995) between intangible investments (scientific research, education, training, and grants for these purposes) and fixed assets, primarily defense hardware. Those fixed assets are very difficult to value and can depreciate rather quickly in the event of armed conflict. Further devaluation occurs as technology changes; the missile system that provided adequate defense capabilities five or ten years ago may now be obsolete.

Many projects undertaken by the federal government require more than one year for completion. Since there is no distinction between capital and operating expenditures, Congress authorizes budget authority sufficient to cover the expected costs of the project, often referred to as full funding. The Office of Management and Budget (OMB) has sought to apply the full-funding rule more uniformly, but Congress often provides funding for discrete stages of acquisition, especially for large defense purchases. Other types of multiyear projects are dams and transportation infrastructure.

A capital budget at the national level similar to those used by state and local governments would include only about half of all federal spending for investment. More problematic is the treatment of intangible investments, such as research and training. In addition, separating research and development costs from construction poses further difficulties. For instance, would research and development costs for a weapons system like the B-1 bomber be treated differently than the cost of production of the aircraft? Using the rationale of state and local governments, research and development would be funded from current resources, while the production would be funded through the capital budget.

A number of recommendations have been made concerning a capital budget for the national government. The President's Commission on Budget Concepts (1967) recommended the unified budget concept over a separate capital budget in order to avoid favoring fixed assets at the expense of other types of investment, commonly labeled a "bricks and mortar bias." Fixed assets often provide legislators with greater political currency than intangibles do.

Another reason for the commission's recommendation was to support a comprehensive view on the demands government places on economic resources (Goldman, 1987). In a symposium on the subject, Robert W. Kilpatrick echoed the philosophy that separating investment spending from operating accounts would make analyzing the impact of government spending on the economy more difficult (Goldman, 1987). As noted earlier, one reason for separating capital and operating budgets at the local level is to even out the workload for budget staff. It would be hard to make this argument for the national government where staff and resources are more plentiful and the time frame for budget development is much longer.

In 1987, Harry Havens, assistant comptroller general at the General Accounting Office (GAO), commented at the same symposium that the GAO favored a capital budget because investment spending and operating spending were distinctly different (Goldman, 1987). Havens also argued that the failure to distinguish between the two forms of spending distorted decisions by overpricing capital, which is costed in the year of acquisition, and underpricing labor. In 1993, however, the GAO supported incorporating an investment section within the unified budget to focus attention on capital spending as one component of the total national budget (U.S. General Accounting Office, 1993).

The GAO again expressed this opinion in 1996 when it concluded that the benefits of the unified budget in helping understand the economic impacts of capital spending outweighed the problems associated with full up-front funding of major acquisitions (U.S. General Accounting Office, 1996). The complaint from agencies that up-front funding makes acquisitions seems prohibitively expensive and creates difficulties with their operating budgets can be resolved without resorting to a separate capital budget. The GAO report suggest mechanisms including "budgeting for stand-alone stages of capital acquisitions" and "using a revolving fund or an investment component in a working capital fund." Similar devices are used by many states to fund capital acquisitions by local governments. (As further evidence that the issue of capital budgeting at the national level survives is the President's Commission to Study Capital Budgeting, created in 1997. The committee is charged with studying the capital budget processes of state and local governments and making recommendations to President Clinton.)

Labeling an expenditure as an investment does not guarantee that it is a good one. Some roads meant to provide useful services for a long time turn out to be roads to nowhere. Conversely, some operating expenditures can have long-term benefits; immunization is a good example. The tendency among politicians is to hang the investment label on anything they like. Budget analysts and bond markets respond to the effects of this practice and have settled on one of two obviously flawed controls: at the state and local level, bond only for certain tangibles; at the federal level, expense everything.

One argument offered for the adoption of a capital budget at the national level is that such a system would alleviate the need to balance the budget under the current system. The operating budget would be funded with current revenues and the capital budget would be funded with debt, as is done by state and local governments. This argument is weakened, however, by the fact that bond ratings limit state use of debt (Jacobson, 1995); no such constraint limits spending by the national government. If anything, as noted earlier in this chapter, a capital budget might increase acquisition of tangibles, not only at the expense of intangible investment but also at the expense of operating expenditures. Once such spending is removed from its current competition with operating expenditures (which might include intangible investment) and financed with debt that needs no bond rating, investment in tangibles might increase dramatically. The unified budget as it now exists not only helps analysts identify the impact of overall spending on the economy, but it may also produce a salutary balance between operating and investment expenditures.

A number of recent pieces of legislation have changed the process by which agencies in the national government acquire physical capital (buildings and equipment). The Government Performance and Results Act (1993) requires development of a linkage between strategic plans and the acquisition of capital. The Acquisition Reform Act of 1996 and the Information Technology Management Reform Act of 1996 (together known as the Clinger-Cohen Act) address the process requirements for acquiring information technology equipment (computers and systems). One of the major changes to asset procurement is the move toward obtaining pieces of systems using existing technology, rather than contracting for complete systems. For instance, rather than procuring a completely new air traffic control system, the new guidelines dictate acquisition of modules as the technology becomes available. This requires the use of open computer architecture that can be expanded in future years. A second change has been a move away from the one-for-one mentality of acquisition. For example, the Coast Guard recently replaced thirty-seven ships that clean buoys in coastal water channels with thirty higher-capacity ships. The Coast Guard realized significant savings in personnel costs with the elimination of seven ships, yet it is more efficient in getting buoys scrubbed. Rear Admiral Thad W. Allen of the Coast Guard refers to this approach as thinking about a "system of systems." A decade ago, the capital planning mentality of the Coast Guard was to replace old ships one-for-one with new ones (Allen, 1997).

In accordance with these changes and requirements, the OMB has developed "three pesky questions" that it requires agencies to apply to all acquisition requests (U.S. Office of Management and Budget, 1997, p. 8):

- Does the investment in a major capital asset support core or priority mission functions that need to be performed by the federal government?
- Does the investment need to be undertaken by the requesting agency because no alternative private sector or governmental source can better support the function?
- Does the investment support work processes that have been simplified or otherwise redesigned to reduce costs, improve effectiveness, and make maximum use of commercial off-the-shelf technology?

If any answer is negative, the agency must reconsider the capital acquisition. If all answers are affirmative, the agency is required to consider alternatives to acquisition, including meeting the need through regulation, user fees, and human capital rather than physical assets. These changes have redefined the process of capital acquisition and addressed the roles of the national government that demand capital investment.

In summary, the purposes of capital budgeting at the state and local levels are not fully applicable to the national government. Investment by the national government is fundamentally different because of the large component of intangibles and the need to assess how federal government spending affects the economy. Also, the requirement that state and local governments must balance their operating budgets forces them to finance major acquisitions while at the same time protecting their bond ratings through due prudence. The lack of a balanced budget requirement and bond rating mechanism to control debt-financed spending suggests that a separate capital budget would be of little benefit. It would be difficult to determine what gets capitalized and what must remain an operating expense; those decisions might be used to balance the operating budget rather than made according to some logical definition of capital. Nor is there a reason to suppose that a process to make decisions about investment spending removed from the operating budget would result in better decisions because the limitations that make the process advantageous at the local level do not hinder the national government.

References

Allen, T. W., Rear Admiral, Director of Resources, U.S. Coast Guard. Presentation to the Association for Budgeting and Financial Management Annual Conference, Washington, D.C., Nov. 6–8, 1997.

Altshuler, A. A., and Gómez-Ibáñez, J. A. *Regulation for Revenue: The Political Economy of Land Use Exactions.* Washington, D.C.: Brookings Institution, 1993.

Aschauer, D. A. "Genuine Economic Returns to Infrastructure Investment." *Policy Studies Journal,* 1993, *21*(2), 380–390.

Bland, R. L., and Nunn, S. "The Impact of Capital Spending on Municipal Operating Budgets." *Public Budgeting and Finance,* 1992, *12*(2), 32–47.

Bland, R. L., and Rubin, I. S. *Budgeting: A Guide for Local Governments.* Washington, D.C.: International City/County Management Association, 1997.

Cope, G. H. "Budgeting for Performance in Local Government." In *The Municipal Yearbook, 1995.* Washington, D.C.: International City/County Management Association, 1995.

Corwin, M., and Getzels, J. "Capital Expenditures: Causes and Controls." In R. Burchell and D. Litoskin (eds.), *Cities Under Stress.* Piscataway, N.J.: Center for Urban Policy Research, Rutgers University, 1981.

Goldman, G. M. "Role Conflict in Capital Project Implementation: The Case of Dade County Metrorail." *Public Administration Review,* 1985, *45*(5), 576–585.

Goldman, S. "Symposium: Capital Budgets—Expanded Use in the Federal Sector." *Public Budgeting and Finance,* 1987, *7*(3), 4–13.

Hackbart, M., and Ramsey, J. R. "Debt Management and Debt Capacity." In R. Lamb, J. Leigland, and S. Rappaport (eds.), *The Handbook of Municipal Bonds and Public Finance.* New York: New York Institute of Finance, 1993.

Hush, L. W., and Peroff, K. "The Variety of State Capital Budgets." *Public Budgeting and Finance,* 1988, *8*(2), 67–79.

Jacobson, L. "A Capital Idea, or a Fiscal Sand Trap?" *National Journal,* Apr. 1, 1995, pp. 816–817.

Kachelmeier, S. J., and Granof, M. H. "Depreciation and Capital Investment Decisions: Experimental Evidence in a Governmental Setting." *Journal of Accounting and Public Policy,* 1993, *12*(4), 291–323.

Lansing, K. J. "Is Public Capital Productive? A Review of the Evidence." *Economic Commentary,* Mar. 1, 1995, pp. 1–5.

Lucy, W. *Close to Power, Setting Priorities with Elected Officials.* Washington, D.C.: American Planning Association, 1988.

Munnell, A. H. "Why Has Productivity Growth Declined? Productivity and Public Investment." *New England Economic Review,* 1990, 3–22.

National Association of State Budget Officers. *Capital Budgeting in the States: Paths to Success.* Washington, D.C.: National Association of State Budget Officers, 1992.

National Council on Public Works Improvement. *Fragile Foundations: A Report on America's Public Works.* Washington, D.C.: Government Printing Office, 1988.

Nunn, S. "Formal and Informal Processes in Infrastructure Policy-Making." *Journal of the American Planning Association,* 1991a, *57*(3), 273–287.

Nunn, S. "Public Capital Investment and Economic Growth in Fort Worth: The Implications for Public Budgeting and Infrastructure Management." *Public Budgeting and Finance,* 1991b, *11*(2), 62–94.

Paetsch, J. R., and Dahlstrom, R. K. "Tax Increment Financing: What It Is and How It Works." In R. D. Bingham and E. W. Hill (eds.), *Financing for Economic Development: An Institutional Response.* Thousand Oaks, Calif.: Sage, 1990.

Pagano, M. "Notes on Capital Budgeting." *Public Budgeting and Finance,* 1984, *4*(3), 31–40.

Poterba, J. "Capital Budgets, Borrowing Rules, and State Capital Spending." *Journal of Public Economics,* 1995, *56*(2), 165–187.

President's Commission on Budget Concepts. *Report of the President's Commission on Budget Concepts.* Washington, D.C.: Government Printing Office, 1967.

Ramsey, J. R., and Hackbart, M. "Municipal Bond Sales in Foreign Markets: Experience and Results." *Public Budgeting and Finance,* 1996, *16*(3), 3–12.

Riordan, T., Oria, M., and Tuss, J. "The Bridge from Dreams to Realities: Dayton's Capital Allocation Process." *Government Finance Review,* 1987, *3*(2), 7–13.

Schick, A. *The Federal Budget: Politics, Policy, Process.* Washington, D.C.: Brookings Institution, 1995.

Sharp, F. "Factors Affecting Asset Acquisition Decisions of Municipalities." *Government Accountants Journal,* 1986, *35*(2), 30–37.

Smith, R. M. "From Subdivision Improvement Requirements to Community Benefit Assessments and Linkage Payments: A Brief History of Land Exactions." *Law and Contemporary Problems,* 1987, *50*(1), 5–30.

Snyder, T. P., and Stegman, M. A. *Paying for Growth.* Chapel Hill, N.C.: Urban Land Institute, 1987.

Thomassen, H. "Capital Budgeting for a State." *Public Budgeting and Finance,* 1990, *10*(4), 72–86.

U.S. General Accounting Office. *Incorporating an Investment Component in the Federal Budget.* Washington, D.C.: Government Printing Office, 1993.

U.S. General Accounting Office. *Budget Issues: Budgeting for Capital.* Washington, D.C.: Government Printing Office, 1996.

U.S. Office of Management and Budget. *Capital Programming Guide,* version 1.0. Washington, D.C.: Government Printing Office, 1997.

Vogt, A. J. "Budgeting Capital Outlays and Improvements." In J. Rabin, W. B. Hildreth, and G. J. Miller (eds.), *Budgeting: Formulation and Execution.* Athens: University of Georgia, 1996.

CHAPTER TWENTY-SEVEN

Budgeting for Entitlements

Joseph White

The subject of this chapter, budgeting for entitlements, suggests fundamental questions about both the means and the ends, or functions and form, of government budgeting.

These questions are especially, but hardly exclusively, relevant to U.S. federal budgeting. *Entitlement* is a term with precise meaning within the federal policy and budgeting framework that may not have exact parallels in other contexts. The concept of entitlement presumes that courts can enforce the right to benefits against the sovereign (monarch or parliament), but that may not in fact be the case. The U.S. form of entitlement is not necessary to produce the distinction between traditional budgeting and the form of entitlement budgeting described in this chapter. Programs that make specific promises unmediated through a bureau will provide much the same challenges in any system.

This chapter focuses, therefore, on the U.S. federal budget. Yet the basic problem posed by entitlements relative to traditional budgeting occurs in other contexts as well, such as in the U.S. states and in other national governments of the Organization for Economic Cooperation and Development, even if it may be defined or discussed differently.

In the continual debate about the federal budget, entitlements have been blamed for the deficits of the 1980s and 1990s, and they are widely viewed as threatening massive deficits in the future (Bipartisan Commission on Entitlement and Tax Reform, 1995). It has become conventional wisdom to talk about "the middle-class entitlement monsters that will consume the budget if left unchecked" (Pooley, 1997), about the "ticking time bomb" (Calmes, 1997) of future growth in entitlement spending that threatens "fiscal calamity" (Broder, 1996). One would think, therefore, that budgeting institutions should be designed, above all, to control entitlement spending.

Yet the traditional means of budgeting—annual estimates and requests funded through annual appropriations legislation—are virtually useless for controlling entitlement spending. As a result, federal lawmakers in the past quarter-century have invented new institutions for entitlement budgeting. Integrating these institutions with the traditional budgetary process has proved difficult. Complaints that entitlements are "out of control" have only intensified (Schick, 1990; Peterson, 1996).

This chapter argues that the federal government's difficulties in budgeting for entitlements can best be understood by recognizing how the basic tasks of budgeting for entitlements differ from traditional budgeting. Entitlements have somewhat different purposes and significantly different designs than other policies and programs. Fundamental concepts of traditional budgeting, such as the meaning of control and the usefulness of an annual decision-making process, are therefore put into question when governments try to budget for entitlements.

DISTINGUISHING ENTITLEMENT FROM BUREAU BUDGETING

As used here, the term *entitlement* developed out of the "new property" movement of legal thought that began in the 1960s and was brought into budgeting through its use by the Supreme Court. In *Goldberg* v. *Kelly* (397 U.S. 254, 1969), Justice William Brennan wrote that benefits in the Aid to Families with Dependent Children (AFDC) program were "a matter of statutory entitlement for persons qualified to receive them." The General Accounting Office (GAO) came to define the term as "legislation that requires the payment of benefits . . . to any person or unit of government that meets the eligibility requirements established by such law." The key is that "eligible recipients have legal recourse if the obligation is not fulfilled" (Weaver, 1985, pp. 308–309). In principle, an entitlement need not be created by legislation alone; in particular, U.S. states might create entitlements within their constitutions.

In federal budgeting, the term *entitlement* is almost synonymous with a series of other terms: uncontrollable spending, mandatory spending, and direct spending. All of these terms refer to spending that is not controlled by the traditional annual appropriations process. The term *uncontrollable spending* was more common in the 1980s and has in essence been succeeded by *direct spending. Mandatory spending* is another term for direct spending, used especially in presentations of budget data by the Office of Management and Budget (OMB) and the Congressional Budget Office (CBO) and in the distinctions made for points of order under the Congressional Budget Act (as amended). *Direct spending* is "budget authority and ensuing outlays provided in laws other than appropriations acts, including annually appropriated entitlements." *Entitlement authority* is "a provision of law that requires payments to eligible persons or governments" (Schick, 1995, p. 210). The difference between entitlement authority and direct spending involves some spending provided in authorizations that are not entitlements, and the food stamp program.

For our purposes here, especially for generalization about how entitlement budgeting differs from traditional budgeting in general rather than only in the U.S. federal government, what matters is the structure and promises of an entitlement program rather than the differences among these terms. (Thus, contrary to the CBO, I will treat food stamps as an entitlement.) The legislation that creates an entitlement program also validates its budgetary claims. If such a separate process is the main form of budgeting, then entitlements can seem, by definition, an end run around budgetary controls.

Yet creation of an entitlement is not simply (or necessarily) a budgeting maneuver. It is a choice about program design, and the basic conundrum of entitlement budgeting is that different program designs seem to require different budgetary processes.

Traditional budgeting is designed to finance bureaus that provide a service to the public or, more generally, that perform some government function. It may be policing or fire fighting or defense of the seas or medical research or medical care for veterans or primary and secondary education or collecting taxes or space exploration, or any of thousands of other activities. In spite of their different social purposes, all of these programs share a fundamental structure: the government establishes a set of goals and then provides a bureaucracy to pursue those ends. Each of the functions just listed is performed by a specific bureaucracy, such as the Navy or the Internal Revenue Service or the National Aeronautics and Space Administration. Government has not committed itself legally to a precise level of services. Rather, it has promised to provide a bureaucracy that it hopes will provide an acceptable level of service. The objectives may be defined and sold in personal terms, but whether they occur depends on the performance of the bureaucracy in question. Budgeting may then be described, in W. F. Willougby's classic phrase, as the creation of a "general financial and work plan" for agencies (Mosher, 1984, p. 21). Thus, the federal government establishes a bureau, such as the Department of Veterans Affairs, from which medical services may be claimed; but what veterans receive depends on two factors: a separate decision about the bureau's funding, and a decision about how the bureau is to perform its tasks. Budgeting is a process of deciding amounts to provide to each bureau. This can be called *bureau budgeting.*

In an entitlement program, the recipients—whether persons, legal persons (firms), or governments—are entitled by law to quantifiable benefits. The benefits are either directly delivered to the beneficiary or they are payments on behalf of the beneficiary for services purchased in a cash transaction from a third party.

The quantifiable nature of the benefits means that they can ultimately be estimated in terms of cash outlays (basically, the value of individual benefits times their volume). In the legal sense, an entitlement need not be quantifiable: for example, many constitutions provide some form of entitlement to education. Such provisions make cost control more difficult. One method of cost control, explicitly refusing services, is foreclosed. In Germany, the entitlement to education makes restricting the number of medical students (and thus physicians) difficult. But the cost of medical education may still be manipulated by squeezing the budgets of medical schools. So a quantifiable entitlement is a more severe budgetary problem than an entitlement that is vaguely defined. Thus, entitlement budgeting involves estimating and attempting to influence the sum of separate payments determined by entitlement law. The recipient is actually entitled to an amount of budget. In bureau budgeting, some recipients may make claims on a share of the bureau's funds, on the basis of a distribution formula in law, but the amount of bureau funding is not itself determined by the sum of individual claims. Individuals who qualify for entitlement benefits also may not receive them because they may not be aware of their eligibility, because the application process is discouraging, or for some other reason. Entitlement budgeting therefore often involves estimates of the "take up" of eligible benefits. Yet entitlement budgeting, unlike bureau budgeting, does not involve a concrete choice about how much to fund an existing law each year.

In bureau budgeting, the object of attention is the bureau itself. How much does the bureau really need to fulfill its legal obligations? How much (and which) inputs will produce how much (and which) outputs? Or because outputs are difficult to measure, the question may be more practically put as, How good an argument can be made that more (or fewer) inputs will lead to more (or not much less) output? Could the bureau operate more efficiently if it operated differently?

In this context, the primal meaning of the term *budgetary control* is control of how the bureau spends its appropriation (Schick, 1966). A political authority's first problem is to ensure that the bureau does not waste the money outright, spend more than it has, spend corruptly, or spend contrary to the wishes of the political authority (albeit perhaps in accordance with the wishes of another political authority). One practical example of these issues is the level of detail in line items, which involves a choice between efficiency (if one believes that efficiency is encouraged by managerial flexibility through broader accounts) and accountability to the legislature (which is best enforced through detailed accounts or a surrogate, such as virtually binding report language). Another example of traditional budgeting controls is the federal Anti-Deficiency Act of 1870 and the related processes of apportionment, all designed to ensure that agencies do not overspend their allocations.

In entitlement budgeting, the main object of attention is the specific promise to recipients. There must be an administering bureau (the Social Security Administration for pensions, or the Health Care Financing Administration for Medicare and Medicaid), but relatively little budgetary attention is paid to its personnel and performance. The conflict and work of devising spending reductions mainly focuses not on limiting the bureau's funds and relying on its management to stretch resources, but on altering the terms of eligibility or benefit.

The traditional control questions about the level of specificity of line items and "coercive deficiencies" (likely overspending that is important enough to be funded) have little relevance to entitlements. It is meaningless to talk of choice between more or less specific line items for entitlements: the program rules are the practical specifications for the budget. Nor does entitlement spending involve a gray area comparable to those in coercive deficiencies. Spending either does or does not conform to program rules; if it conforms and yet exceeds a budget target, the agency should not be blamed.

Management may still influence entitlement spending. Savings might be achieved in Medicare, for example, by spending more on administration so as to reduce fraudulent payments to medical providers. Yet such interactions between bureau funding and entitlement costs are definitely a secondary theme in entitlement budgeting (indeed, public focus on potential savings from such measures is reported by experts as evidence of insufficient education) (Blendon and others, 1997). Moreover, during development of entitlement savings proposals, their administrative implications may be an afterthought. That is certainly widely suggested by observers of both the Clinton administration's development of its FY98 Medicare savings proposals and then of the package passed by Congress in the Balanced Budget Act of 1997.

In bureau budgeting, the relationship of inputs to outputs is a basic concern. Inputs—money for salaries, buildings, and travel, for example—are the resources of agencies. Much of the subject of budgeting is how many inputs are needed to produce a particular level of output (medical care, arrests, or whatever). Reformers continually want bureau budgeting to pay more attention to outputs, or programs. Traditional budgeting disappoints reformers by emphasizing inputs, for two main reasons: inputs are what politicians actually provide to bureaus, and control of inputs is a way to (try to) control behavior (Wildavsky, 1978).

In entitlement budgeting, however, inputs and outputs are virtually identical. The objects of expenditure are the actual outputs. One can argue about whether the program achieves its social goal efficiently: in essence, whether the outcome of social security or Medicare is worth the money. Yet there is little disjunction between inputs and outputs: the money comes in, and it goes out. In essence, entitlement budgets are automatically program budgets.

To a certain extent, the difference between entitlement programs and bureau programs follows from the goals of the programs. An entitlement ought to be quantifiable. Protection from crime cannot be quantified because recipients do not know from how much crime they have been protected. States or localities could be entitled to a given amount of money for crime fighting, or to funding for a certain amount of new police officers. But this is a step removed from citizens' concerns; there could be no comparable entitlement to safety for citizens at the local level. A pension, however, is quite precise.

At the same time, the goals of some policies may be pursued more effectively by establishing specific promises to individuals. That is true of any policy in which a government seeks to encourage or reward specific behaviors, such as interest paid in return for lending the government money, or veterans' benefits distributed in return for serving in the armed services, or pensions for current workers in the future in return for their paying for the pensions of current retirees now. In this sense, entitlements involve a form of contracting behavior between a government and members of the public in which the terms of the offer have to be sufficiently concrete to be credible.

In other cases, whether to pursue a social goal through creating a service-delivering bureau or an enforceable entitlement is more clearly a political and social choice. A government may respond to the health care needs of its citizens, for example, by promising to reimburse their expenses for care purchased in the private market—an entitlement. Instead, a government may provide services directly, through public hospitals, clinics, or direct contracts between the government and individual providers—a service organization. The U.S. federal government provides health care for the elderly as an entitlement (Medicare), and health care for veterans as a bureau (the Veterans Affairs medical system). Individual nations rely to a greater or lesser extent on these options of a guaranteed health service (such as the National Health Service in the United Kingdom) or guaranteed health care payments (such as the provincial systems in Canada). In practice, most systems are mixtures of the two approaches: the organizational sponsorship of health insurance may not be directly through government, and administrators of health care systems that rely more on entitlement continually search for ways to make them operate more like bureaus (White, 1993b, 1995b).

In such cases, the choice, however, is hardly random. It depends on powerful political factors, such as the ability of health care providers and conservatives to resist "socialized medicine" (and instead limit the guarantee to social insurance). Thus, even in this case the decision for an entitlement structure is not a budgetary evasion but a fundamental policy choice. Yet the entitlement form does make constraining spending a different challenge from the task in bureau budgeting.

ENTITLEMENTS AND THE ANNUAL BUDGET

Because the object of attention is not the behavior of bureaus, and because the logic of the programs is that promises made to recipients should not expire after a year, entitlement programs fit poorly into the traditional annual appropriations cycle.

Indeed, the Bipartisan Commission on Entitlement and Tax Reform of 1993 reported that "the first and most important of our recommendations" was to make "major spending and tax decisions" in a thirty–year time frame. "When discretionary spending was the largest share of our budget," the Commission explained, "short-term planning may have been appropriate," but it could not be appropriate for budgeting the massive social-insurance programs that are the major entitlements (Bipartisan Commission on Entitlement and Tax Reform, 1994, p. 2).

The misfit between program design and budgeting schedule can be exacerbated by institutional design within the legislature. Specialized appropriations committees, which are expected to recognize a distinction between appropriating and authorization, are especially unable to deal with entitlements. This distinction is probably greatest within the U.S. Congress, where the conflict between appropriators and authorizers is a basic tension (White, 1993a; Fisher, 1979).

In U.S. state legislatures, the budget or finance or appropriations committees may be more powerful, while in parliamentary systems the treasury or the ministry of finance normally has jurisdiction over all budgetary matters and the legislature is relatively undifferentiated. In some cases, such as France, there may be a separate social security budget, but that still tends to be strongly influenced by the ministry of finance or whoever the main budgetary actor in the system may be.

In the U.S. federal government, most entitlement spending is not under the jurisdiction of the appropriations committees. The giant Old Age, Survivors, Disability and Health Insurance (OASDHI) system is financed by a dedicated tax. These revenues flow into trust funds, and the law provides a permanent appropriation: any money in the trust fund is available for spending without annual appropriations laws. The programs—more commonly called social security and Medicare part A—are under the jurisdiction of the revenue committees, the House Ways and Means Committee, and the Senate Finance Committee.

Many other programs that are structurally entitlements, however, do not have dedicated revenues and therefore require annual appropriations. Food stamps, Medicaid, and commodity price supports are just a few examples. In the 1970s and early 1980s, this arrangement proved especially anomalous. If appropriations committees reported, and Congress passed, legislation that did not fund the commitments created by underlying law, it was presumed that the courts could order Congress to make good those commitments. Whether appropriators could report legislation that in fact changed the underlying promises was technically ambiguous but practically rather clear (majorities of the rest of Congress would object to such a raid on their jurisdiction). It is perhaps conceivable that such legislation on appropriations bills could be approved with a liberal interpretation of the Holman Rule point of order in the House, which prohibits "legislation" in appropriations bills. The point of order could be waived by a special rule when the appropriations bill is considered in the House, or waived on the Senate floor. In 1996, for example, a freeze on inflation adjustments to food stamp benefits was passed in the Agriculture Appropriations Act. Nevertheless, such legislation is decidedly not the norm. Therefore, when Congress did not appropriate adequate funding, the administration requested supplemental appropriations as the funding began to run out, and Congress always responded (though not without some close calls).

After a few years of this experience, Congress decided to recognize its own practice, and its budget rules established the concept of *mandatory appropriations.* While the House and Senate Appropriations Committees write the legislation that provides funding for Medicaid and other entitlements, the committees basically plug the most recent estimate into the previous year's language. Otherwise, they pretty much ignore the mandatory programs, save for some public and private grousing about how entitlements, whether annually appropriated or not, put pressure on the "discretionary" appropriations that are the committees' main concern.

Properly understood, then, entitlement budgeting occurs for all "mandatory" spending. In 1995, as Table 27.1 shows, mandatory spending (including interest, which differs from other entitlements only in that there is actually a discrete contract with each individual guaranteeing payment) was by far the largest part of the federal budget.

The mandatory share was expected only to continue to grow. On the one hand, both an aging population and the expectation that medical care costs per capita would grow more quickly than the economy would led to predictions that the costs of social security, Medicare, and Medicaid would explode over the long term. Then the deficits predicted from failing to control or pay for that growth were expected to compound themselves, leading to massive interest expenses. As a result, the CBO in 1997 was projecting massive deficits and an

Table 27.1. Mandatory Spending as a Share of the Federal Budget.

Outlays	1965	1975	1985	1995	2002 (esti-mated)
Total (in billions of FY92 dollars)	$530.7	$847.7	$1,015.5	$1,410.7	$1,461.3
Discretionary	65.8%	47.5%	43.9%	36.0%	30.2%
Mandatory and Net Interest	39.2%	56.6%	59.5%	66.9%	73.4%
Mandatory	31.9%	49.6%	45.8%	51.6%	60.7%
Net Interest	7.3%	7.0%	13.7%	15.3%	12.7%
Social Security (OASDI)	14.5%	19.1%	19.7%	22.0%	24.5%
Medicare	—	3.7%	6.8%	10.4%	13.9%
Medicaid	—	2.0%	2.4%	5.9%	7.1%
Federal Employees	0.5%	4.0%	4.1%	4.3%	4.6%

Note: The total is less than the sum of the individual components because it includes undistributed off-setting receipts; spending for Medicare and Medicaid in 1965 was less than 0.5 percent; and outlays for federal employees constitute retirement and disability benefits.

Source: Calculated using Office of Management and Budget figures.

economic meltdown within thirty or forty years (Congressional Budget Office, 1997b). On the other hand, even in the relatively short term, and even assuming that some action was taken to reduce entitlement costs, their share of the budget was expected to rise. Thus Table 27.1, based on the president's budget proposal for FY98, shows a substantial expansion in the entitlement share of the federal budget, not from accelerated growth of entitlements but because he proposed to control discretionary spending more strictly. That he could propose stricter controls on discretionary spending, however, only shows the difference between entitlement and bureau budgeting from a different angle.

As the table shows, the term *entitlement* can make the budgetary difficulties seem more a matter of procedure and less a matter of preferences and program than they really are. By 2002, according to the OMB's estimates in 1995, four entitlement programs were to take up 54.7 percent of the federal budget. The budgetary problem is not entitlements per se but these four programs, and especially the first three (social security, Medicare, and federal employee retirement and disability) which involve long-term specific promises. The fourth program, Medicaid, also provides specific benefits; it was designed that way in part because financing of direct public health services for the poor, elderly, and disabled in the states was less popular. All of these programs are politically strong and therefore difficult to cut no matter what their form. (Medicaid might seem weak as a "welfare" program, but the fact that about two-thirds of its money goes to the elderly and disabled makes it, as congressional Republicans discovered in the 104th Congress, more popular than its means-tested design might make one expect.)

Budgeting for this spending occurs in what might be called a quasi-annual process that has two parts. First, as part of fiscal policy, the president proposes, and Congress accepts or rejects, formally or informally, a goal for policy change to alter the deficit that would otherwise occur. Second, the president and Congress decide how much and how to change entitlement law so as to facilitate meeting this fiscal target. Annually appropriated spending could then be (and often is) forced to conform to these targets, because individual appropriations bills might be ruled out of order (under congressional budget rules since 1985) or vetoed (if the president has the strength) or simply voted down for failing to do their part for deficit control. But entitlement law (like revenue law) is permanent; no approval is necessary for spending to continue.

Before 1980, therefore, entitlement spending would be brought into conformance with broader deficit policy only if authorization legislation happened to be passed for that purpose. We can say "happened to be passed" because there was no formal process to encourage, never mind require, its passage.

In 1980, Congress invented the use of *reconciliation* to encourage passage of entitlement legislation that would reconcile entitlement spending (and revenue) totals to the deficit goals set in the congressional budget resolution. Thus, in theory Congress would set a deficit reduction goal; it would provide *reconciliation instructions* to specify the amount of entitlement spending reduction required from each committee in order to meet that goal; committees would report *reconciliation legislation* (or risk having substitute legislation sponsored by the budget committees); the legislation would benefit from special procedures (especially tightly limited debate on the Senate floor); and as a result entitlement spending would be assimilated into an annual budgetary process. In theory this process could be used to stimulate the economy through higher deficits as well as to contract it through lower ones (Schick, 1995; Gilmour, 1990; White and Wildavsky, 1989). In practice, it generally has been used to lower projected deficits, though the legislation sometimes has included expansions in some programs (such as Medicaid) as part of coalition building to pass larger cuts (such as in Medicare).

Whether reconciliation is an annual budgetary process is a matter of perspective. Significant reconciliation legislation does not pass on anything resembling an annual basis. As the process was invented, bills were passed in 1980, 1981, and 1982. Since then, however, only the laws passed in 1984, 1987, 1990, 1993, and 1997 could reasonably be termed major—and in some years (such as 1983 and 1995, for very different reasons), instructions from the budget resolution failed to result in the planned legislation.

One can argue that the absence of reconciliation legislation for entitlements is in fact a budget choice, comparable to appropriating to bureaus an amount adequate to maintain current services. But it differs at least in that there is not a routine annual review at the programmatic level by the committees of jurisdiction. They may have hearings on individual issues, but they will consider overall budgets only when the alignment of the political planets provides the necessary gravitational pull, and not otherwise. As the record suggests, the reconciliation process is not action forcing in the same way as annual appropriations. If annual appropriations do not occur, the government shuts down. If reconciliation does not occur, the deficit is higher than desired. The latter is not as severe a consequence.

This difference in the consequence of inaction reveals an underlying point about the purposes of budgeting. Meeting a target deficit is only one of its functions. Ensuring that the government is financed is even more important than the balance sheet that results from that financing. To the extent that entitlements have permanent appropriations, they need not be part of an annual budgetary process for this financing purpose.

That does not mean that entitlements are truly uncontrollable. They are less subject to budgetary constraint on average than bureau programs, for two reasons. First, entitlements tend to be especially popular. Popularity tends to be a factor in winning approval of the entitlement form, and most of the entitlement money is in the hugely popular OASDHI system. The second reason is more basic: entitlements are relatively uncontrollable in the sense that they are not automatically subject to annual budget review, and they do not need annual reapproval. The legislature must take extra steps to change entitlement law, and the advantages of playing defense accrue to opponents of those reductions. Moreover, any expansion, once achieved, is normally achieved for the foreseeable future, rather than just for one year. Indeed, an expansion might be phased in over time, or scheduled to occur at some future date. Program proponents may win a benefit without increasing immediate deficits, the focus of control in an annual budgetary process.

Some entitlements nevertheless grow relatively slowly or even shrink. They may, like Title XX social services grants to states, or to AFDC, serve unpopular constituencies, so they grow more slowly than a bureau program with a popular constituency (such as the National Institutes of Health or veterans' medical care). The claimants for AFDC were so weak and the program was eventually so widely criticized on various grounds that it was replaced in 1996.

Moreover, even very powerful claimants may not, for technical reasons, be claiming an increasing share of the budget. The share of the budget spent on veterans' entitlements has fallen as veterans' share of the population has declined, even though they remain an extremely powerful interest group. Thus outlays on veterans' entitlements fell from 2.37 percent of total outlays in FY75 to 1.25 percent in FY95. Even social security, which grew very quickly relative to the economy and budget, for both demographic and programmatic reasons, during the 1970s, grew much more slowly relative to the economy, due to demographic trends, in the 1990s. Thus, after peaking at 4.7 percent of gross domestic product in 1981, social security spending stabilized and was at only 4.9 percent in 1996. As a share of the total budget, it grew during this period from 20.3 percent to 21.9 percent.

For purposes of spending control, therefore, considering entitlements as a single class is useful only to a certain point. Beyond that, one must look to the dynamics of political support and actual program need that explain the strength of any particular entitlement's claim on the total budget. Yet the common misfit between entitlement design and the logics of traditional budgeting, as well as the size and growth rates of the more popular entitlement programs, have helped cause substantial changes in the federal budgetary process. The most basic change is that reconciliations evolved from being scored over one year (in 1980) to being scored over three years (1981), five years (1990, 1993), and seven years (the vetoed legislation of 1995). Entitlements are not the only source of this change. Revenues involve the same basic dynamics. Further, the very size of the deficit required that anyone who wished to pursue a balanced budget had to adopt a longer time horizon (as in 1995). Yet it is clear that entitlements alone are sufficient reason to make budgeting, if still an annual exercise, not solely an exercise in annual control. In the 1990s, the development of longer budget horizons began to impact the process of budgeting for traditional bureau programs.

STRATEGIES AND TACTICS OF ENTITLEMENT BUDGETING

The differences between entitlement and bureau programs mean that the strategies and tactics of budgetary control, as well as the institutions, can differ. Yet some of the logic of budgetary restraint remains the same.

Governments budget for entitlements in the most basic sense of the term: they forecast expenses under various scenarios, estimate whether revenues will be available to meet those expenses, and then consider what to do about the result. Budgeting is about forecasting and planning to reconcile preferences about details to preferences about totals. A government may alter its preferences on either side of the equation: to more borrowing on the one hand, to higher taxes or lower spending on the other. Each year there is some process by which government decision makers evaluate the trends and their desirability, and on the basis of the results, propose alternatives.

The estimation and alternative generation for major entitlements is, in fact, extensive. One aspect is simply a part of the overall budgetary process. Thus the CBO estimates the trends of all programs and publishes alternatives for deficit reduction in its annual *Reducing the Deficit: Spending and Revenue Options* volume. The 1996 edition included 148 pages of analysis and options as to entitlements, including a chapter on Medicare and Medicaid restructuring, a chapter on the impact of an aging population on the long-term federal deficit, and fifty-one entitlement options outside Medicare and Medicaid (Congressional Budget Office, 1996, pp. 325–472). The president's budget also includes estimates and suggested reforms to entitlement programs.

In addition, there are separate estimation processes for some programs, particularly those that have been designed as trust funds. Each year, for example, the trustees of the OASDHI (social security) and Federal Hospital Insurance (HI; Medicare part A) trust funds issue reports about trends in costs, revenues, and thus actuarial balance over the coming seventy-five-year period (Board of Trustees of Old-Age, Survivors, Disability and Health Insurance Trust Fund, 1996; Board of Trustees of the Federal Hospital Insurance Trust Fund, 1996). The trustees include a mix of government officials and outside members; thus the OASDHI trustees include the secretaries of the Treasury, Labor, and Health and Human Services. The reports are prepared largely by the actuarial staffs of the programs, and are generally regarded as authoritative sources on program financing. These reports can become occasions for advocates of budget control to publicize their fears; thus, projections that the HI trust fund would go broke provided the occasion for Republican claims that they had to cut Medicare in order to save it (Rosenbaum, 1996; Rich, 1996).

The extensive development of processes for estimation and option generation, however, do not provide those who would control entitlements with the same levers that they can exercise on bureau budgets. These controllers cannot threaten to eliminate the program by stalling action. Nor can they usually claim, as they can with bureaus, that spending can be reduced by giving less money to managers and challenging them to manage more efficiently.

Entitlement spending may thus be more subject to manipulation if some aspect of design makes it more similar to bureau spending. In any entitlement that does not simply mail checks, there may be private operators with a stake in the program, such as grocery stores for food stamps or banks for guaranteed student loans. If these operators can be identified, it is normally easier to cut spending by reducing payments to operators than by changing the promise of benefits for recipients. Normally, significant savings cannot be realized from these operators. Medical care entitlements, however, are a major exception. Especially in Medicare, cost control has proceeded mainly by altering payments to physicians, hospitals, and other health care providers, rather than by explicitly changing the promises to patients.

In both forms of budgeting, the availability of this tactic depends on the power of the operators. Operators may be powerful either because of their own resources or because of their allies (and weak if they have many enemies). In entitlement budgeting, then, one condition that makes taking from the operators easier is if, politically, the impression can be given that the beneficiaries would otherwise pay the bill. This tactic may not help when the beneficiary is relatively weak (such as food stamp recipients) in comparison to operators (such as grocers). But it is especially relevant to Medicare, where the beneficiary, the elderly, may be the strongest group in the country. Proposals to increase costs to beneficiaries have regularly been scaled back and replaced by fee reductions for hospitals, physicians, or other providers. The politics has played out in a way that has made cutting the providers a way to limit blame from the elderly (White, 1995b).

Entitlements are also subject to the general rule that it is easier to cut grants to a lower level of government than to cut a program that is solely the responsibility of one's own level. Cuts in intergovernmental grants can be justified by claiming that the lower level has the money to do the job itself, or that it should have the flexibility to maximize utility for its own citizens by making its own priorities, or that it is "closer to the people," or even that it could operate more efficiently. All these arguments could be made, for example, to justify Medicaid or AFDC reductions, but not cuts in Medicare or food stamps.

The easiest way to reduce an entitlement, as with bureau spending, is to allow inflation to make stable or increasing nominal spending hide a real decline in a program's purchasing power and share of the economy. In some cases, such as Title XX social services grants, inflation has eroded benefits. Unfortunately for budgeters, however, entitlements lend themselves especially easily to indexation of benefits, that is, to automatic inflation adjustments included in the underlying law (Weaver, 1988). So they are less subject to control by erosion.

When budget controllers cannot take advantage of resemblances between an entitlement and bureau programs, they may instead try to reform the entitlement to make it operate more like a bureau program. That tactic is especially prominent in current health care budgeting debates. The most common proposal for a long-term "fix" of Medicare is to replace the current entitlement to benefits with an entitlement to a voucher that would be used to buy insurance coverage. The services a person actually received would then depend, as with a bureau program, on an organization's performance—except that it would be a private organization, the managed care organization or insurer. Advocates of such proposals may or may not argue correctly that market competition would provide an incentive for productivity that government bureaus do not enjoy. But even if this difference were real, the logic of budgetary control remains the same whether the bureau is public or private. Rather than pay per service, the government pays a fixed sum to an organization (Cutler, 1997; Aaron and Reischauer, 1995; Butler and Moffitt, 1995).

Another approach is to provide incentives for spending control that are specific to the individual program. The best example is creation of a trust fund with dedicated revenues. Then the threat that the trust fund will run out of money becomes an action-forcing device similar to the expiration of an annual appropriation. Thus periodic crises of the social security trust fund have indeed forced action, and projected shortfalls in the Medicare part A fund provide a powerful argument for action about that program (Light, 1985). It is more powerful, of course, if the threatened default is due sooner rather than later, and if the policies suggested are plausibly related to the trust fund deficit. Thus the argument worked better as an incentive for legislation to "save" Social Security in 1983 than as an incentive to "save" HI in 1995. HI's shortfall was due in 2002 rather than within the year, and some of the cuts proposed by the congressional Republicans would not have affected HI.

Although the trust fund device provides an impetus for action, it is not necessarily an impetus for spending restraint. It may equally encourage revenue increases. Thus if *budget control* is defined as "deficit control," then trust funds are a more desirable measure than if the person calling for budget control really wants to limit the total budget. And if a trust fund is in balance, it should be harder to sell program cuts as part of a general campaign of deficit reduction.

BUDGETARY ROLES

To the extent that different members of a legislature have jurisdiction over entitlement spending rather than over annual appropriations, budgetary roles for the former differ from the latter.

Within the confines of some traditional budget theory, the question would be who takes the role of "guardian of the purse" for entitlements, a role supposedly once taken by the appropriations committees for bureau budgets (Fenno, 1966; Wildavsky, 1964). The notion that members of the congressional appropriations committees were once more disposed than other legislators to guard the purse should be qualified rather heavily. Yet it is fair to say that committees whose members and staff spend most of their time in budgeting mode, asking questions about inputs and outputs and what can be quantified, should have different perspectives than committees whose normal activity is to try to design programs in response to supposed problems (White, 1989, forthcoming). In the U.S. Congress, reconciliation legislation must be written by authorizing committees, so one has to wonder how the traditional claimants could simultaneously be the guardians. The institutional answer might seem to be that the budget committees are the new guardians, forcing the authorizers to control the programs. Yet the power of the budget committees is quite limited. At best they are surrogates for the majority party leadership.

That leadership does have some incentive and power to focus on budget control and thus try to bring budget details in line with some preference about budget totals. Yet party leaders have limited knowledge with which to draft and enact legislative changes; ultimately they depend on the experts in the authorizing committees, who know more about both the technical and political sides of their programs. Thus, in 1983 the authorizers in the revenue committees ignored reconciliation instructions, finally producing legislation only in 1984, when they had determined a way to meet a somewhat smaller target. Similarly, in 1990 the deal brokered by party leaders collapsed on the floor of the House of Representatives, to be replaced by a package largely created within the Ways and Means and Finance committees.

The answer to the question, Who are the guardians? therefore cannot be limited to party leaders. In fact, the nature of entitlements means that guardianship itself requires different skills than for bureau budgets.

To guard against increases in bureau budgets, one has to say no to requests. It is nice to be able to think of a rationale for no, but technical knowledge is less important than political strength. Budgeting expertise is a matter of resource planning, and budget controllers have the option of telling an agency to work out its own plan within a lower total.

Compared to bureau budgeting, technical knowledge is more important for guarding against entitlement spending increases, or for designing cuts. In entitlement budgeting the question is rarely put as, Can we have an increase of the following specific size? Instead, a change in eligibility or some other regulation is suggested, accompanied by some estimate of the financial effects of that change. Without technical knowledge, guardians may not even know that the claimants are requesting increases. Entitlement budgeting therefore requires expertise in forecasting, or "scorekeeping."

In this context the roles of guardian and claimant can be transposed to estimators—whoever prepares the forecasts of budgetary effects. Some estimators (for example, in agencies, or in the OMB if a president seeks a programmatic expansion) may be disposed to overestimate spending. In personal conversations with CBO and GAO staff, and with other health care policy participants, I encountered a consensus that the Clinton administration's OMB has tended to estimate generously the baseline spending in state Medicaid programs so as to encourage coverage expansions through the Section 1115 waiver process (Robert Wood Johnson Foundation, 1995). A system then needs some estimators who are biased somewhat in a conservative direction.

At some times, that might be the role of the OMB vis-à-vis agencies and Congress. As part of its efforts to achieve greater control of entitlement spending, however, Congress created its own set of conservative estimators, the CBO, and processes to ensure that those estimates have a place in Congress's budget decisions. The CBO must "score" proposed entitlement legislation: that is, it must issue reports of the legislation's estimated budgetary effects. When the proposal is supposed to cut spending, the CBO's estimate influences how much political credit the proponents may claim for reducing the deficit. If the proposal is for an increase, the CBO estimate activates the pay-as-you-go (PAYGO) procedures that require cuts in other areas to pay for increases in entitlement programs.

There are two types of federal PAYGO rules. One type consists of points of order against legislation that increases entitlement spending without some form of offset. This procedural constraint has some moral force, but more important, it cannot be waived without a supermajority of sixty votes out of a hundred in the Senate. Application of the point of order then depends on CBO estimates. The second level requires that certain entitlements be subjected to automatic reductions (sequesters) if, at the end of a fiscal year, Congress's actions on entitlements have summed to a net increase in spending, as estimated by the OMB (Schick, 1995).

Entitlements therefore create a new class of guardians, the guardian estimators. But the PAYGO device represents a further attempt to create guardianship. In essence, it means that any member of Congress who has more interest in the programs that might be cut than in the programs that might be expanded has an incentive to become a guardian vis-à-vis the planned expansion. In this sense, guardianship is not a role but a situational position.

PAYGO rules are not foolproof, and certainly not proof against all manipulation by very clever people. Sometimes a savings must be scored by the CBO but may be unlikely to occur in practice. Or knowing that savings will occur for some unrelated reason, making the sequester unnecessary, Congress might use them to finance an unrelated program expansion.

The ability to limit spending on any given entitlement is related to the overall pressure for budgetary restraint. PAYGO in essence provides a cap on total entitlement spending: it should not exceed the level provided in law as of the start of a legislative session. This overall cap does encourage specific restraint.

Restraint of entitlements is easier if the goals are relatively unambitious. It is easier to guard against increases than to force decreases. This naturally is true of bureau budgets as well. The so-called guardian House Appropriations Committee of the 1950s was only a guardian in comparison to executive requests; relative to the spending baseline, it was more generous than the supposedly less guardianlike House Appropriators of the 1980s (White, 1995a). Yet the relative ease of preventing increases is especially evident in the enforcement of PAYGO as opposed to the attempts to force entitlement reductions through the 1985 Gramm-Rudman-Hollings legislation. Gramm-Rudman-Hollings's attempt to force cuts clearly failed; PAYGO's restraint of increases pretty much has succeeded (Reischauer, 1997; White and Wildavsky, 1989).

Entitlement spending has not been immune to congressional reductions since the deficit became the dominant issue in national politics in 1980. Medicare especially has been subject to major reforms that for many years reduced its trend in spending growth per capita significantly below the trend for private insurance, to the detriment of those who benefit from the program (such as hospitals and physicians). Guardians and their tactics have had some success. But spending has continued to rise because the claims have been especially strong.

Strong claims are not limited to entitlement programs. Military spending during a war is bureau budgeting, yet it represents the politically strongest possible claim. In recent years, however, the major entitlements—especially social security, Medicare, and Medicaid—have happened to be especially strong claimants.

CONCLUSION: ENTITLEMENTS AND THE FUTURE OF GOVERNMENT BUDGETING

The good news about entitlement budgeting is that it does not involve many of the issues that traditionally have bedeviled bureau budgeting. Thus concerns like the level of detail in line items, coercive deficiencies, and the difficulty of creating program budgets shrink when programs are organized as entitlements.

The bad news is that not only is entitlement spending particularly difficult to constrain, but budgeting for both entitlements and bureaus within the same process poses serious problems.

Entitlements fit poorly within annual budgeting. To change entitlements each year violates both the technical and political logics of such programs. That is why, in spite of the creation of processes to create annual budgeting of entitlements, such as annual budget resolutions and reconciliation, reconciliations do not pass every year.

Yet the effort to create multiyear budgeting of entitlements threatens ironic and, I believe, negative effects on bureau budgeting. One such effect is the devaluing of the original purposes of annual budgets for bureaus: review of operations and legislative control of the executive. The other effect is encouragement of the colonization of bureau budgeting by a multiyear perspective.

Multiyear budgeting is one cause of the adoption of long-term caps on appropriations. Without multiyear reconciliations, it is hard to imagine how the long-term caps of 1990, 1993, and 1997 could have been adopted. Precisely because the legislature and executive do not have to specify the policy changes to enforce those caps, it is easier to project savings this way than through legislating entitlement changes. Thus both congressional Republicans and President Clinton relied more and more, as the budget battles of 1995–96 continued, on reductions in discretionary spending targets to attain their budgetary goals (Reischauer, 1997).

The attempt to control entitlements thus leads to the creation of targets for bureau budgets at a different time than the decision about how to meet those targets. This alteration of the federal budgetary process to respond to entitlements threatens to create a disjunction between the processes of considering details and considering totals, and adjusting the two to each other, which is at the heart of most budgetary processes. Rather than being an iterative process of mutual adjustment, bureau budgeting, if the current trend continues, will become a process of target setting and a later scramble to meet the targets. That should make the traditional questions of control—how much is needed to achieve certain ends efficiently—in essence irrelevant, supplanted by How on earth can we meet this target?

If the only goal of budgeting were to restrain budgets, this would not be a problem. Even limited advances in controlling entitlement spending could justify abandoning other functions of bureau budgeting—especially because the result would probably be lower bureau budgets as well.

Yet if budgetary processes have purposes beyond spending restraint, then how to improve entitlement budgeting without damaging bureau budgeting must be one of the most important challenges to budget theorists.

References

Aaron, H. J., and Reischauer, R. D. "The Medicare Reform Debate: What Is the Next Step?" *Health Affairs*, 1995, *14*(4), 8–30.

Bipartisan Commission on Entitlement and Tax Reform. *Interim Report to the President.* Washington, D.C.: Government Printing Office, 1994.

Bipartisan Commission on Entitlement and Tax Reform. *Final Report to the President.* Washington, D.C.: Government Printing Office, 1995.

Blendon, R. J., and others. "Trends: What Do Americans Know About Entitlements?" *Health Affairs*, 1997, *16*(5), 113–15.

Board of Trustees of the Federal Hospital Insurance Trust Fund. *The 1996 Annual Report of the Board of Trustees of the Federal Hospital Insurance Trust Fund.* Washington, D.C.: Government Printing Office, 1996.

Board of Trustees of Old-Age, Survivors, Disability and Health Insurance Trust Fund. *The 1996 Annual Report of the Board of Trustees of the Federal Old-Age, Survivors, Disability and Health Insurance Trust Fund.* House Document 104–228. Washington, D.C.: Government Printing Office, 1996.

Broder, D. "The Party's Over." *Washington Post*, Aug. 11, 1996, p. C1.

Butler, S. M., and Moffitt, R. E. "The FEHBP as a Model for a New Medicare Program." *Health Affairs*, 1995, *14*(4), 47–61.

Calmes, J. "Fiscal Fitness: Washington Wants Discipline in Budgets to Carry Beyond 2002." *Wall Street Journal*, Feb. 3, 1997, p. A1.

Congressional Budget Office. *Reducing the Deficit: Spending and Revenue Options.* Washington, D.C.: Government Printing Office, 1996.

Congressional Budget Office. *The Economic and Budget Outlook, Fiscal Years 1998–2007.* Washington, D.C.: Government Printing Office, 1997a.

Congressional Budget Office. *Long-Term Budgetary Pressures and Policy Options.* Washington, D.C.: Government Printing Office, 1997b.

Cutler, D. M. "Restructuring Medicare for the Future." In R. D. Reischauer (ed.), *Setting National Priorities: Budget Choices for the Next Century.* Washington, D.C.: Brookings Institution, 1997.

Fenno, R. F., Jr. *The Power of the Purse: Appropriations Politics in Congress.* New York: Little, Brown, 1966.

Fisher, L. "The Authorization-Appropriations Politics in Congress: Formal Rules and Informal Practices." *Catholic University Law Review,* 1979, *29,* 51–105.

Gilmour, J. B. *Reconcilable Differences? Congress, the Budget Process, and the Deficit.* Berkeley: University of California Press, 1990.

Light, P. *Artful Work: The Politics of Social Security Reform.* New York: Random House, 1985.

Mosher, F. C. *A Tale of Two Agencies: A Comparative Analysis of the General Accounting Office and the Office of Management and Budget.* Baton Rouge: Louisiana State University Press, 1984.

Peterson, P. G. *Will America Grow Up Before It Grows Old?* New York: Random House, 1996.

Pooley, E. "No Guts, No Glory." *Time,* Jan. 20, 1997, pp. 23–26.

Reischauer, R. D. "The Budget: Crucible for the Policy Agenda." In R. D. Reischauer (ed.), *Setting National Priorities: Budget Choices for the Next Century.* Washington: Brookings Institution, 1997.

Rich, S. "Report Sets Clock Ahead on Medicare Insolvency." *Washington Post,* June 6, 1996, p. A12.

Robert Wood Johnson Foundation. *State Initiatives in Health Care Reform,* July-Aug. 1995, pp. 7–9, 12.

Rosenbaum, D. E. "Gloomy Forecast Touches Off Feud on Medicare Fund." *New York Times,* June 6, 1996, p. A1.

Schick, A. "The Road to PPB: The Stages of Budget Reform." *Public Administration Review,* 1966, *26*(4), 243–258.

Schick, A. *The Capacity to Budget.* Washington, D.C.: Urban Institute, 1990.

Schick, A. *The Federal Budget: Politics, Policy, Process.* Washington, D.C.: Brookings Institution, 1995.

Weaver, R. K. "Controlling Entitlements." In J. E. Chubb and P. E. Peterson (eds.), *The New Direction in American Politics.* Washington, D.C.: Brookings Institution, 1985.

Weaver, R. K. *Automatic Government: The Politics of Indexation.* Washington, D.C.: Brookings Institution, 1988.

White, J. "The Functions and Power of the House Appropriations Committee." Ph.D. dissertation, Department of Political Science, University of California, Berkeley, 1989.

White, J. "Decision Making in the Appropriations Subcommittees on Defense and Foreign Operations." In R. B. Ripley and J. M. Lindsay (eds.), *Congress Resurgent: Foreign and Defense Policy on Capital Hill.* Ann Arbor: University of Michigan Press, 1993a.

White, J. "Markets, Budgets, and Health Care Cost Control." *Health Affairs,* 1993b, *12*(3), 44–57.

White, J. "(Almost) Nothing New Under the Sun: Why the Work of Budgeting Remains Incremental." In N. Caiden and J. White (eds.), *Budgeting, Policy, Politics: An Appreciation of Aaron Wildavsky.* New Brunswick, N.J.: Transaction Books, 1995a.

White, J. "Budgeting and Health Policymaking." In T. E. Mann and N. J. Ornstein (eds.), *Intensive Care: How Congress Shapes Health Care Policy.* Washington, D.C.: Brookings Institution, 1995b.

White, J. *Competing Solutions: American Health Care Proposals and International Experience.* Washington, D.C.: Brookings Institution, 1995c.

White, J. *Treasured Authority.* Washington, D.C.: Brookings Institution, forthcoming.

White, J., and Wildavsky, A. *The Deficit and the Public Interest: The Search for Responsible Budgeting in the 1980s.* Berkeley: University of California Press, 1989.

Wildavsky, A. *The Politics of the Budgetary Process.* New York: Little, Brown, 1964.

Wildavsky, A. "A Budget for All Seasons? Why the Traditional Budget Lasts." *Public Administration Review,* 1978, *38*(6), 501–509.

CHAPTER TWENTY-EIGHT

Budgeting for
Contingent Losses

Marvin Phaup
David F. Torregrosa

With rare exception, governments do not budget for the losses expected from providing insurance to individuals, firms, and other jurisdictions. This is not a benign oversight: it harms individuals and society at large by increasing losses from hazards, by reducing the ability of society to absorb catastrophes, and by increasing the political risk of default by government on long-standing commitments. Recognizing expected losses in the budget at the point when government accepts the contingent obligation could remedy this damaging gap in budget coverage, although it would not be easy to do so.

Contingent losses are future sacrifices of resources that are foreseeable under current policy but whose size and timing are uncertain. Public insurance programs that spread individual economic risks over a large population are the dominant source of contingent losses for governments. Budgeting for contingencies therefore means recognizing in the present the resources that will be required in the future to compensate those who will suffer covered losses under existing government insurance.

The largest and most important public insurance programs are those that promise compensation for losses from natural disasters, insolvencies of banks

Note: The views expressed in this chapter are those of the authors alone and should not be attributed to the Congressional Budget Office. We are deeply indebted to Robert W. Harman, Arlene Holen, and Robin Seiler for numerous helpful suggestions and to David Rafferty for research assistance. We, however, are responsible for any errors that remain.

and other insured borrowers, and failed private pension plans, and in some tabulations, for "social insurance" against privation from having grown old without adequate savings. The federal government acknowledges total contingencies of almost $5.5 trillion (U.S. Department of the Treasury, 1997). By comparison, annual U.S. gross domestic product is about $8 trillion and federal budget outlays total $1.6 trillion. The largest of the contingencies reported by the Treasury Department are

- Federal deposit insurance commitments to repay up to $3.5 trillion of depositors' funds, in the event that insured banks, thrifts, and credit unions are unable to do so.

- Federal guarantees of more than $650 billion in loans to students, home buyers, farmers, and other assisted borrowers. If the borrower defaults, the lender has a claim for repayment on the federal government for the guaranteed portion of the loan.

Including additional federal contingencies, which were omitted from the Treasury's statement, would increase the total to $9 trillion and include

- About $2 trillion in securities issued by government-sponsored enterprises, such as Fannie Mae and Freddie Mac, which bear the implicit rather than the explicit guarantee of the federal government.

- Federal pension insurance, which protects the retirement income of more than 42 million employees of private firms against default by their pension plans. As of the end of 1996, the federal government's Pension Benefit Guaranty Corporation insured more than $1 trillion in defined pension benefits.

- Under the federal government's crop and flood insurance programs, promises to indemnify owners when they suffer covered losses. Insurance in force amounted to almost $400 billion at the end of 1996.

It is important to distinguish total risk exposure, the number reported here, from the much smaller expected payout under the insurance programs. The budget provides little information about these expected values because the U.S. government does not budget for contingencies, except as noted in Exhibit 28.1. Rather, federal contingent claims arising under current law and policy, including disaster, deposit, pension, and disability insurance, are all treated in the budget on a cash basis.

Cash-basis accounting for insurance recognizes the revenue from the transaction before it recognizes the corresponding cost. When the government collects fees, premiums, or earmarked taxes under these insurance programs, it records them immediately as budget receipts that reduce the current-period budget deficit. But outlays for contingent payments are not recorded until

---

Exhibit 28.1. Budgeting for Contingent Losses.

A notable exception to the rule that the U.S. government does not budget for contingencies is the policy of recognizing expected losses on federal direct loans and guarantees. Under the Credit Reform Act of 1990, the federal budget records the discounted present value of net expected losses on direct and guaranteed loans when the loans are disbursed, rather than at default (Phaup, 1996). For example, a direct or guaranteed loan of $1 million on which the government expects to lose $100,000—net of all fees and recoveries—is recorded as an increase in budget outlays, and as a deficit of $100,000 in the fiscal year in which the loan is advanced to the borrower. This cost is recognized in lieu of the cash disbursement (for a direct loan) because the government expects to recover the rest of the economic value of the loan from the borrower. The $100,000 cost is also recognized instead of the cash inflows from fees and premiums collected from the borrower (for a guarantee). Prior to credit reform, disbursements for direct loans and fees collected for loan guarantees were recorded when paid or received, but no corresponding costs were recognized for expected default losses.

---

benefits are paid, often years after the premiums are received. Consequently, under current accounting, earmarked collections to pay for future contingencies reduce the deficit in the year received and thus are regarded as a signal of an improvement in the financial condition of government.

The federal budget recognizes contingencies only to the extent that cash collections in excess of current period insurance disbursements are—in some cases—credited to an on-budget revolving or trust fund. These fund accounts are used to ensure that earmarked amounts are spent for the authorized purpose. Any excess of collections over expenditures, however, is invested in government securities. This investment gives the trust fund an asset that is a liability to the Treasury Department. For example, the Bank Insurance Fund currently reports a positive accumulated and earmarked balance invested in Treasury IOUs. The parent Federal Deposit Insurance Corporation's asset balance with the Treasury is a liability of the Treasury. Together the two items net to zero from a government-wide, unified budget perspective. Further, these credits on the government's books consist only of the cumulative excess of cash receipts over cash outlays. They do not reflect expected future payments to those whose remittances are the source of the credits.

State governments in the United States often reserve funds against the contingency of an economic slowdown and the attendant shortfall in planned government revenues (National Association of State Budget Officers, 1995). These "rainy day" funds, however, are usually motivated by requirements for a balanced budget or are intended to secure a favorable rating for the government's bond issues. They do not represent an estimate of expected payments for insured losses. In some cases, state governments have established state guarantee funds aimed at specific environmental risks (Freeman and Kunreuther, 1997).

To be sure, there are a number of justifications for a cash-basis treatment of government insurance programs: future disbursements for losses may not be required; estimates of future payments are difficult to produce and highly volatile; and for government, it may be easier to finance losses after the insured event than before. (See Exhibit 28.2 for an illustrative debate that uses some of these arguments.) First, there is some probability that no insurance outlays will be required, owing either to good luck, effective regulation, or exercise of the legislative prerogative to change the terms of the insurance before payments are made. For instance, it is possible that for some commitments (such as guarantees of obligations of government-sponsored enterprises) no further outlays will be required. This happy result might occur either because government regulators succeed in preventing insolvency among those institutions or because of the fortuitous absence of financial shocks to these enterprises. For insurance programs in which payments are virtually certain to occur under current policy—pension guarantees, for example—the government might exercise its right to curtail benefits before expected payments are made. Given the conditional nature of payments, budgeting for contingencies runs the risk of allocating resources to purposes for which they would never be spent.

A second reason for deferring the recognition of insurance costs until paid is that these payments are difficult to estimate in advance. Projecting the cost of private pension insurance, for example, requires forecasts of the financial condition of numerous plan sponsors and the performance of various risky investments. These forecasts are subject to substantial uncertainty and error. A small change in the underlying assumptions could swing the expected cost of this insurance by billions of dollars. Recognizing expected costs in the budget requires that changes in expected cost must also appear as either a gain or loss of fiscal resources. Thus, budgeting for expected insurance costs might introduce potentially large fluctuations into budget outlays and the deficit.

A third reason for deferring recognition of insurance costs is the view that it is easier—and perhaps more equitable—for government to collect the funds to pay off losses after the event rather than before. The idea is that government's ability to tax to pay for losses after they have occurred makes advance funding of contingencies unnecessary, and taxing now to pay for losses that have not yet occurred may shift the burden from richer, later generations to poorer, current ones.

Despite these justifications for current policy, this chapter argues for reconsidering the budgetary treatment of contingencies because doing so would

- Reduce actual losses from hazardous events
- Lower the political risk of default by government insurers
- Increase national saving and the capacity to absorb losses without a reduction in living standards

Exhibit 28.2. A Fable of Hard Choices: Can This One Be Avoided?

Conflict has erupted over a proposal by the Department of Transportation to begin budgeting now for the expected cost of rebuilding highways and roadbeds that will be damaged or destroyed by the next severe hurricane. The plan is opposed by an education association and others due to concern that most of the funds to be set aside for disaster recovery would be taken from the postsecondary education budget.

The transportation secretary has argued that hurricanes have dealt major losses to the highway system three times within the last thirty years. Experts have warned that another hurricane of equal or greater force is almost certain to occur. The cost and value of roadways at risk has increased sharply since the last storm, because of the commercial development of the coasts. The secretary maintains that the department needs the flexibility to respond quickly in case of emergency and that it must have assured funding to do so. An association of governmental financial managers has joined in support of the proposal, arguing that budgeting for expected losses is good management and is required by professional standards of conduct. "To neglect this looming claim on public resources in the budget," an official of the association has said, "materially overstates the availability of resources and misleads policymakers and citizens."

The education association has responded: "For years we have shortchanged the education of our youth. In doing so, we have placed their hopes and lifetime prospects at extreme risk. To do so yet again to satisfy a bookkeeping provision for repair of roads that we have paid for once, in case of a possibility that has not occurred and may never occur, would be unconscionable." The educators have noted that none of the hurricane experts cited by the transportation department is able to say when such a storm will occur, nor even that it will happen in the next decade. Rather than trying to recognize all the adverse events that might happen sometime in the future, they argue, the government should address the clear and present needs of today. Experience also demonstrates, according to the education association, that other levels of government will pay for at least 75 percent of any loss of public infrastructure. As for the remainder, popular support for recovery will be far stronger after the event than before. With strong public backing, rebuilding can be financed with debt that will be repaid gradually by road users without sacrificing essential public services today.

The case for this change rests on some key principles of private insurance, on basic differences between private and government insurance, and on the importance of measured cost in the budget for policy decisions. We consider each of these principles in turn.

THE BENEFITS AND DANGERS OF INSURANCE

Insurance can improve the quality of life, but because of the way insurance changes expectations and behavior, the failure of an insurance system can leave the insured further from realizing their plans than if they had remained uninsured.

Insurance offers people in a risky world the opportunity to pay a small annual premium or fee to avoid the possibility of a calamitous economic loss. At its best, insurance can dispel uncertainty and allow plans to be fully realized. Insurance achieves these results by enabling people to do something collectively that they cannot do alone: accumulate savings sufficient to replace losses that would be catastrophic for an individual.

The downside of insurance is that it is subject to the risk of system failure—the possibility that the insurer will not be able to honor its commitments to compensate the insured when losses occur. For private insurance, the risk of failure is primarily financial. If premiums are set too low to cover actual losses, or if the premiums are misused or imprudently invested, the insurance pool may not be able to indemnify the insured. Required disclosures by private insurers are primarily intended to permit outsiders to monitor the financial condition of the insurer.

The gains from and threats to private insurance can be illustrated with the familiar case of fire insurance. If the annual probability that any particular house will be destroyed by fire is one in ten thousand, or 0.01 percent, and if the value of the average house is $100,000, then the average annual expected loss to a home owner is $10. Although this value is small, loss of a house would destroy such a large share of the average owner's wealth as to constitute economic ruin. Acting alone, the average home owner might save and invest that $10 per year. But even after thirty years of saving, his contingency reserve would fall far short of the resources he would need to maintain his living standard following the destruction of his house. By contrast, if all homeowners join together and pool the value of their annually expected losses, the proceeds will be sufficient to indemnify all those who actually suffer losses. Insurance thus adds to well-being by creating an opportunity for the property owner to purchase freedom from disastrous misfortune.

The first requirement for a sound insurance system is to establish premiums sufficient to fund losses, plus an allowance for administrative costs. Historical data can be used to estimate both the annual probability that any randomly selected house will catch fire and the expected loss from such an event. Not all houses, however, are equally likely to catch fire or to be destroyed if fire should strike. Risk of loss varies with many factors, including the presence of functioning smoke detectors and fire alarms, the use of open fireplaces, the quality and composition of electrical wiring and other construction materials, the house's distance from a fire hydrant or fire station, and the number of smokers living in the house.

If these risk differences are ignored and premiums are set to cover losses from the average risk, then low-risk owners will pay premiums that are too high in relation to the risks they pose, while high-risk owners will pay too little. Average risk pricing, therefore, will give low-risk owners an incentive to drop out of the pool. The exodus of some low-risk properties will mean that a disproportionate number of high-risk properties are in the insurance pool. Insured losses, therefore, will be proportionately higher than for the universe of all properties and higher than the level of premium income based on losses for the entire population. In this case, the insurance system will be suffering from an "adverse selection" of risks. If the insurer attempts to correct this imbalance of risks by simply raising all premiums, adverse selection will worsen because owners of low-risk properties still in the pool would then have a stronger incentive to drop the insurance. Adverse selection can destroy the ability of insurance to provide economic benefits that derive from spreading risk over a large number of participants.

One solution to adverse selection is for the insurance system to acquire and process the information needed to distinguish various categories of risk and to adjust premiums for differences in expected losses. The necessity of adjusting insurance premiums to match variations in risk is not a static, one-time requirement, however. Because of the ongoing effects of insurance on the incentives of the insured to avoid risks, properties become more risky with insurance than without. Often referred to as the "moral hazard" of insurance, freedom from the risk of catastrophic loss changes the behavior of the insured in ways that are likely to increase losses from insured events. For example, with diminished incentives for avoiding losses, property owners are likely to take less care to avoid losses with insurance than without. The more general point is that casualty losses are not simply fixed by nature; they are significantly affected by human behavior, which in turn depends on the incentives facing those in a position to affect the probabilities of loss (Bipartisan Task Force on Disasters, 1994; Federal Emergency Management Agency, 1997; and Zeckhauser, 1996).

One technique that has proved effective in dampening the rise in losses due to moral hazard has been to impose loss deductibles, or coinsurance requirements, on policyholders so that the insured must share in every loss. Another technique is to adjust premiums for risk-reduction measures adopted by property owners. If coinsurance and risk-adjusted premiums are not effective in controlling moral hazard, insured losses can spiral upward and destroy the ability of the pool to pay losses from premiums.

The interaction between nature and humans that determines the loss makes insurance into a double-edged sword. On the one hand, insurance creates an opportunity to pay a small fee to avoid the risk of an economic calamity. It enables people to collectively accumulate savings out of current income that is sufficient to absorb the shocks of individual catastrophes. On the other hand, private insurance systems are subject to the risk of financial failure from adverse selection and moral hazard. An insurance system that fails has the potential to leave the insured worse off than they would have been without insurance. Why? Because it leaves those suffering loss without the promised indemnity and without the protections they would have put in place in the absence of insurance.

GOVERNMENT AS INSURER

Private insurance is not available against all risks. Where substantial ambiguity exists about the probability and magnitude of loss, such as from earthquakes and leaking underground storage tanks, insurers will not be able to determine the losses likely to be incurred, or the appropriate premiums (Freeman and Kunreuther, 1997). Private insurers are also unable to provide coverage where the cost of addressing moral hazard and adverse selection is prohibitive (such as hard-to-diagnose or self-inflicted sources of personal disability), where individual risks are not independent and therefore not diversifiable (such as banking system failures), and where losses have already occurred (such as environmental hazards created by past actions or indemnities to those who are already aged and poor). Even under these circumstances, however, government, with its unique power to compel payment of taxes by the entire population, may be able to provide the services of spreading individual risks across a large population and of compelling those who have not suffered losses to compensate those who have (Stiglitz, 1993).

Government's power to tax, which frees federal insurance from the razor's-edge necessity of maintaining balance between premiums and expected losses, constitutes the defining difference between private and government insurance. This authority gives government license to set insurance premiums below expected cost and thereby provide subsidies to the insured. Government's preference for deferring the taxes to cover a subsidy until after losses have occurred results in subsidy transfers that are not only interpersonal but also often intertemporal, from future taxpayers to current beneficiaries. But the practice of deferring tax collections to pay the subsidies is the major source of risk to the insured: that future voters will not consent to pay the requisite taxes to honor prior commitments. Thus, while the power to tax frees government insurance from the restrictions of financial balance before the loss, the conditional nature of that power—requiring the consent of future voters—exposes beneficiaries to the threat that consent and expected benefits will be withheld after the loss.

POLITICAL RISK AND BUDGETING

Political risk increases with the magnitude of the burden on future taxpayers, especially when the burden is in excess of the amount that future taxpayers expect to pay. A measure of political risk therefore consists of losses in excess of expected losses recognized, expressed as a percentage of national income. Political risk is thus negatively related to the share of future losses paid by up-front premiums and current period taxes, positively related to realized losses, and negatively related to national income.

Current cash-basis budgetary accounting for government insurance increases political risk. It does so by increasing the amount of loss from the insured event, by raising the share of insurance losses to be paid by future taxpayers, and by reducing national saving and national income. By treating current period claims as the appropriate measure of cost for current policy decisions, the budget promotes a fatalism about insured losses that discourages the management and control of losses. It emphasizes a measure of costs incurred in the current period that cannot be controlled, only paid or defaulted on.

Government insurance serves to increase losses when government relieves those at risk of the need to avoid and mitigate losses, without simultaneously taking steps to offset the increase in moral hazard (Kane, 1996; Kunreuther, 1996). Private insurance pools protect themselves against moral hazard by recreating incentives for the insured to avoid loss through requirements for coinsurance, deductibles, risk-based premiums, and the credible threat of withdrawal of coverage. Federal insurance programs rarely contain such provisions and appear designed for a world in which moral hazard does not exist.

Cash accounting, which provides no budgetary signal of the need for or incentives to adopt loss-control measures, bears significant responsibility for the absence of federal efforts to align the self-interest of the insured with the need to control losses. The institutionalized fatalism of federal policy means that losses with government insurance will inevitably be higher than they would have been with no insurance, because owners would have acted to reduce losses, or with private insurance, because the insurer would have countered moral hazard. (For a vivid example involving federal flood insurance, see Stossel, 1995.) Absence of control means rising losses under government insurance programs raise the political risk of insurance system failure.

The cash-basis treatment of government insurance programs combined with unaddressed moral hazard also increases the share of losses paid by future taxpayers. By recognizing budget-year premiums and budget-year payments for losses, the budget defines financial balance for insurance programs in terms of today's premiums and today's losses. Thus, financial balance appears to exist, even though moral hazard is likely to increase losses. When these higher losses are recognized as paid, it is too late to charge those who benefited from the insurance. Increased losses have to be borne by future taxpayers.

The absence of information on future expected losses also means that the cash-basis budget treatment fails to alert policy makers to the need for government to save in the current period to avoid a reduction in consumption later when the losses occur. The grant of insurance coverage reduces precautionary saving by those at risk. With private insurance, premium payments equal to expected losses absorb disposable income and increase savings sufficient to cover expected losses. With government insurance, some of the saving—the portion to be paid by taxpayers—is deferred until after the loss. Thus, with government insurance, pre-loss saving and capital accumulation will be lower than with private or no insurance. Consequently, income will be lower at the time of loss. Lower income combined with the higher losses of government insurance means that the proportion of national income required to compensate for losses under government insurance will be higher than the income required under private or no insurance alternatives. This increase in the tax burden required to pay losses raises the political risk that promised benefits will not be paid. If expected future losses were recognized in the budget as increasing the current period's budget deficit and government's draw on the economy's saving, then policymakers would be alerted to the need to offset the induced fall in private saving. To do so, the government could impose higher premiums or higher taxes in the current period.

The argument for recognizing the expected costs of federal insurance as a means of reducing political risk is that doing so will provide appropriate policy incentives for Congress so that losses from moral hazard are reduced, taxes shifted to the future are lightened, and national savings and income are increased.

Exhibit 28.3. Is Social Security Government Insurance?

Despite its official name—Old Age, Survivors', and Disability and Health Insurance—many observers are hesitant to classify social security as government insurance, preferring instead to categorize it separately as "social insurance," or simply a benefit program. Social security has attributes that make it unique among government programs. Most notable among these is its size: social security is far and away the largest single program in the federal budget. Every month, 43 million Americans receive a benefit check from social security. Consuming $22 of every $100 dollars of federal spending, social security outlays are larger than spending for defense. The principal reason for excluding social security from the category of insurance, however, is that benefits are not contingent upon the occurrence of an uncertain loss. Surviving to the age of eligibility, which does not constitute an economic loss or hardship, triggers the payment of benefits. If social security benefits were paid only to those with low incomes, the case for its inclusion in government insurance would be stronger.

Yet social security has many features in common with federal insurance programs. Social security is a pooling of the risks to individuals of economic hardship resulting from outliving one's retirement savings, losing a family breadwinner, or suffering disability. It is financed by payments from the insured that are referred to as social insurance premiums or earmarked taxes. A trust fund is used to monitor and report on the financial condition of the program, but budgetary reporting is on a cash-flow basis: current period collections and current period outlays. Adverse selection is avoided by near-universal, compulsory participation. Social security is subject to moral hazard, however, as the promise of contingent benefits reduces personal saving and raises dependency on the promised benefits. Like virtually all federal insurance programs, social security was underpriced to the early generations of beneficiaries, with the consequence that the burden is now being shifted to future generations. In fact, current U.S. social insurance programs cannot be sustained at current levels of benefits and taxes. Projected benefits cannot be paid from current levels of taxation without explosive growth in the public debt. Young people whose long-term plans for economic security assume the continuation of current social insurance benefits and taxes are unlikely to see those plans realized. By ignoring the sacrifices required to pay contingent claims while recognizing the receipt of premium payments, government is inviting citizens to anticipate having more income than the economy is likely to be able to produce. The revelation of this error and the frustration of failed expectations will leave many worse off than they had planned. The sooner the imbalance between planned and available resources is corrected, the smaller will be the harm that will result from unrealizable expectations. So, whether or not social security is regarded as government insurance, it has many of the attributes and consequences of these programs.

Exhibit 28.4. Budget Recognition and Cost Mitigation: Some Evidence.

A recent budget innovation, the Credit Reform Act of 1990, has demonstrated the power that a noncash basis of accounting has in effecting cost-control measures in federal insurance programs. The act required the federal government to estimate and budget systematically for the expected losses on federal direct loans and guarantees (U.S. Office of Management and Budget, 1996). Prior to the act, credit transactions were recorded in the budget on a fiscal year cash-flow basis. The budgetary cost of a federal loan guarantee therefore consisted of its net cash outlays for each budget period. Before this legislation, "credit cost control" efforts were focused on reducing net cash outlays from credit transactions in the relevant budget period. Thus budgetary resources could be freed for use elsewhere by generating short-term cash inflows. In the case of guarantees, this could be accomplished by increasing the volume of loans guaranteed by the federal government for which the government collected a fee—even if the fee was less than the expected cost of the guarantee to the issuer. Virtually no budgetary incentive existed to adopt measures that would reduce the government's long-term cost of insured credit. Accordingly, few such measures were proposed; even fewer were adopted.

By providing analysts and policymakers with the information and incentives to focus on those features of credit programs that affect their costs, credit reform has produced a sea change in policies aimed at controlling the cost of federal direct loans and loan guarantees. Single-year cash flows are now seen as irrelevant, while cash flows over the life of the credit contract are properly regarded as the key component of cost (Bent, 1994). For example, as shown in Table 28.1, the vast majority of proposed changes in existing federal credit programs in the president's budget since the introduction of credit reform have been to reduce the long-run cost to the government. Corresponding data are unavailable for the prereform years because those costs were not pertinent to budget decisions and hence were not measured. The effect of proposals to reduce subsidies is also beginning to show up in the aggregate subsidy data shown in Table 28.2. The cost per dollar of new credit, especially direct loans, is being whittled down by the ongoing effort to reduce the deficit and balance the budget. An increase in the share of new credit made up of direct loans is also evident in Table 28.2. This shift is at least partly the result of credit reform's effect on increasing the budget cost of new guarantees in relation to the cost of new direct loans.

Table 28.1. Proposed Credit Subsidy Changes and Proposed Subsidy Reductions
in the President's Budget, 1992–1998.

| Year | Subsidy Changes Proposed | | | Reductions Proposed | | | Reductions as a Percentage of Total Proposed Changes |
	Total	Direct	Guarantees	Total	Direct	Guarantees	
1992	39	21	18	32	20	12	82
1993	36	23	13	31	19	12	86
1994	31	19	12	28	18	10	90
1995	20	9	11	13	6	7	65
1996	27	11	16	14	4	10	52
1997	15	6	9	13	6	7	87
1998	11	4	7	7	1	6	64

Note: 1994 budget was the first Clinton budget.

Source: Calculated using Office of Management and Budget data.

Table 28.2. Assisted Credit and Subsidies, 1992–1998 (in Billions of Dollars).

	1992	1993	1994	1995	1996	1997	1998
Direct Loans							
Obligations	16.4	22.1	22.7	30.9	23.4	36.8	37.4
Subsidy BA	2.0	2.1	2.8	2.6	1.8	2.2	2.0
Subsidy per $100 of direct loans	12.2	9.5	12.3	8.4	7.7	6.0	5.4
Guarantees							
Commitments	130.2	169.9	204.1	138.5	175.4	208.1	196.2
Subsidy BA	3.2	4.1	2.4	4.6	4.0	2.3	1.9
Subsidy per $100 of loan guarantees	2.5	2.4	1.2	3.3	2.3	1.1	1.0

Note: 1997 and 1998 are estimates.

THE MECHANICS OF BUDGETING FOR CONTINGENCIES

Three elements are required to budget effectively for insurance contingencies: a procedure for estimating expected losses under current policy, an appropriations and expenditure account structure to incorporate expected losses into the budget, and a means of accommodating both reestimates of expected losses under current policy and the effects of policy changes on expected losses.

Loss Estimates

The first requirement is the ability to produce estimates of expected losses based on existing information about the nature of the hazard and the exposure to loss. Although perfect accuracy of estimates is impossible, perfection is not necessary to improve on a policy of ignoring expected losses or of implicitly assuming that they will be equal to future premium income. Responsibility for producing estimates of expected losses should be assigned to an entity with access to expert knowledge and insulated from political influence. One model is that of the trustees of a pension plan, who draw on expert and independent advice in discharging their responsibilities to plan beneficiaries. Another model is provided by the Office of Management and Budget and the Congressional Budget Office, which routinely estimate the future costs of complex programs such as Medicare, crop insurance, and student loans. The analytical task of estimating the expected cost of contingencies is comparable in scope and difficulty to work already being performed at a useful level of accuracy.

Account Structure

A workable account structure for contingent losses can be developed from those structures used in reformed federal credit budgeting (Congressional Budget Office, 1989; Phaup, 1996). Closely related to state and local fund accounting, this approach makes use of two separate accounts: an on-budget expense account and a revolving insurance fund account that is outside the budget (see Figure 28.1). For each recognized contingency, the expense account records the government's annual appropriations and payment from the general fund for the current period cost of the contingency. The associated insurance fund receives this annual payment from the expense account and disburses funds when contingent losses are realized. The insurance revolving fund should have authority to borrow—from the Treasury—to make payments in excess of current balances, as may occur if a large insured loss occurs soon after such a budgeting plan is adopted or when two or more adverse events occur close together.

The insurance revolving fund needs to be outside the budget in order to recognize the expected cost of insurance in budget outlays and in the deficit when provision is made for losses, rather than after the disaster has occurred and as-

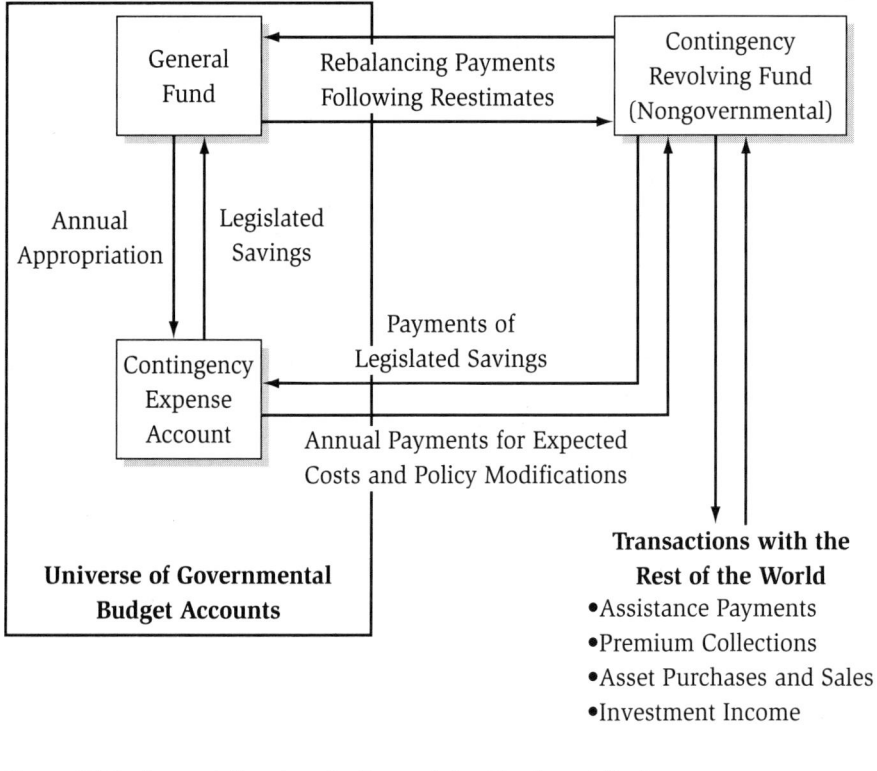

Figure 28.1. Account Structure for Recognizing Contingent Costs.

sistance payments are made. The revolving fund can be given nonbudget status either by law or by placing it under private management. The effect of the off-budget status of the revolving fund on the timing of costs is illustrated in Figure 28.1. Budget outlays from the expense account to the revolving fund are included in the budget when paid. And no costs are recorded in the government's budget when monies are disbursed by the insurance revolving fund.

Collections of insurance premiums by the government can be accounted for in either of two ways. First, the premiums may be credited directly to the revolving fund. Under that alternative, the collections would not show up directly in the federal budget; their only effect would be to reduce the size of the general fund payment required to pay for expected future claims. Second, premiums can be reported as governmental receipts credited to the expense account and then paid to the revolving fund. The effect of this alternative is to "gross up" federal receipts and outlays, without affecting the reported deficit. This latter option permits total budget receipts and outlays to more completely depict the size of government where the payment of premiums or earmarked taxes is compulsory rather than voluntary.

Classifying the contingency or insurance fund as nongovernmental can also insulate these public funds somewhat from the temptation to use them for financing other federal spending. With the insurance fund inside the budget universe, public saving for contingencies would require the government to operate with a budget surplus. Treating the insurance fund as nongovernmental scores federal contributions to the insurance fund as outlays and avoids the misleading implication that budgetary resources required for future payments are in excess of current commitments.

The temptation to consolidate expense and insurance funds across hazards should be resisted. Although maintaining an account for each insurance program may increase the number of accounts, monitoring and managing a government insurance system is extraordinarily difficult under the best of circumstances (Burby and others, 1991; McCool, 1994; Priest, 1996). To attempt to do so without information on financial performance by each program is impossible. Separating insurance programs in the budget is also highly useful for providing appropriate incentives to legislators and the executive to reduce costs through specific modifications to particular programs.

Benign Reestimates and Scorable Policy Modifications

As projections of uncertain future events, all budget estimates contain errors. These errors need not be a major source of concern, however. If the estimates take into account all the information available when the budget is formulated, errors may be unbiased and offsetting across all programs. Similarly, it may be desirable to hold decision makers harmless from the subsequent discovery of technical errors if those errors were unavoidable, given the information available when the decision to extend assistance was made.

Cost reestimates and their treatment in the budget are to be sharply distinguished from changes in the costs of contingencies attributable to modifications of law and policy. If budgetary incentives are to be compatible with the social objective of minimizing the overall cost of contingencies, those responsible for increasing or decreasing costs must be held accountable for added costs and rewarded for achieving savings. Thus, legislation or executive action that changes expected cost of contingencies should be scored with those budgetary effects. In the case of budgetary savings realized from imposing risk-based insurance premiums on beneficiaries, for example, the saving in governmental resources ought to be attributed to the enabling legislation. This credited saving could provide the motive for congressional committees to seek out such measures.

Reestimates not only affect current period cost estimates, they also necessitate adjustments in the insurance fund balance. In credit reform, this need was addressed by providing permanent and indefinite budget authority for automatic rebalancing of the revolving funds. This means that fund deficits and surpluses are periodically corrected by adjusting payments from either the Treasury or the financing accounts to the other. Balancing payments are fully reflected in budget outlays and the deficit, but are not charged or credited to any budgetary player or limitation. They therefore do not force cutbacks or finance increases in other spending. In terms of Figure 28.1, payments to rebalance the fund would flow between the contingency fund and the general fund of the Treasury.

DISADVANTAGES AND DRAWBACKS

A number of factors argue against the practice of budgeting for contingencies. Almost all of these factors arise from the uncertainty of the estimates of expected losses from contingencies. If governments could accurately anticipate contingent cost, few supportable objections could be raised against the practice. Although the capacity for making the necessary estimates is continually improving, the potential benefits of budgeting for contingencies must be weighed against the potential for weakening fiscal discipline, burdening the budget process with excessive analytical demands, and diluting the informational content of the budget by adding another source of error.

Threat of Gimmickry

The existence of a large pool of funds, ostensibly earmarked for anticipated but uncertain insurance losses, creates opportunities for political entrepreneurs. The fear is that after a contingency or insurance fund accumulates substantial balances, political authorities will find irresistible the desire to spend those funds on other purposes. The insurance fund could be raided by such means as obtaining a favorable cost reestimate or making a strategic policy modification. In the first case, policymakers presumably would bring sufficient pressure to bear on the technical budget staff to elicit a determination that expected losses from contingencies have been overestimated. This finding would trigger a payment from the insurance fund to the general fund, reduce the deficit, and provide financing for other government activities. The second method gives a similar result but requires the legislative body to enact a policy modification that would be scored with spendable budget savings but which the legislature would intend to overturn before the savings could be realized. A crude example of this would be enactment of legislation that reduced the share of private losses covered by government insurance but that was expected to be repealed or overridden with an occurrence of loss.

This objection to budgeting for contingencies is especially worrisome if a limiting constraint on governmental spending is the availability of devices for disguising and understating the fiscal character of a transaction. Yet it is also quite possible that a political authority capable of extracting a favorable technical reestimate from a budget office or so determined to spend as to enact phantom savings would never face a shortage of such vehicles, even without the convenience of a contingency fund.

Increased Demands on Budgetary Process

Budgeting for contingencies increases the complexity of the budgetary process. It increases the number of accounts, requires the provision of and accounting for reserves, draws on technical knowledge and data to form estimates, and increases the size of budget reestimates. In general, budget complexity is undesirable because it raises the cost of getting information from the budget for policymakers and citizens. The more complex the budget, the less likely it is to be consulted and used.

Added Budget Errors

As noted earlier, budgeting for contingencies is almost certain to add to the discrepancy between budgeted and actual figures. Periodic reestimates will introduce large changes in budget outlays and deficits. These budget errors may contribute to a loss of legitimacy, and hence to the ability of the budget to discipline fiscal decisions.

CURRENT POLICY AND RECENT PROPOSALS FOR CHANGE

The lack of budgeting for contingencies in the federal government is especially troubling given the significant share of the contingent losses that has been shifted to the central government. Currently, federal budgetary practice largely reflects those policies adopted in the Budget Enforcement Act of 1990 (BEA), which amended the Congressional Budget Act. Although the 1990 act took a major step toward budgeting for expected future losses of direct loans and guarantees, it explicitly excluded deposit and pension insurance from a forward-looking accrual cost treatment (Congressional Budget Office, 1991, 1993). Further, under the PAYGO rules adopted in the BEA, statutory increases in deposit or pension insurance premiums may be used to pay for increased spending in other programs or for tax cuts. PAYGO credit for such actions reduces the chances that these premiums and fees will increase federal or national saving in anticipation of losses. In addition, by authorizing declarations of "emergencies" under which the budgetary restraints on discretionary spending are relaxed, the act further reduces incentives for policymakers to anticipate future threats to economic well-being. The president's proposed budget for 1998 took a small step in the direction of budgeting for natural disasters (U.S. Office of Management and Budget, 1997a, 1997b). It requested a contingent appropriation of $5.8 billion for the Federal Emergency Management Agency, wildland firefighting, flood control, emergency highway reconstruction, and Small Business Administration disaster loans. That proposal, however, left the BEA treatment of designated emergencies unchanged. At a March 6, 1997, hearing, the deputy chief financial officer of the Small Business Administration told the House Small Business Committee that it was "not the administration's position to request funds for catastrophic events that may or may not happen" ("Alvarez Questioned," 1997).

A direct attack on the privileged position of emergency spending has been offered by Representative Michael Castle (Republican from Delaware) in H.R. 457. This bill would repeal the BEA provision for emergency appropriations and require appropriations in advance of disasters. Unless Congress agreed to waive its rules, emergency appropriations would be subject to the ceiling on discretionary spending. Closely related bills (H.R. 2599 and H.R. 4285) were introduced in the 104th Congress by Representatives Joe Barton and Christopher Cox (Suttle, 1997).

The practice of effective budgeting for specific contingencies also falls short at the state and local levels (Burby and others, 1991; Sullivan, 1992). Although many states make use of rainy day general fiscal reserve funds and small contingency reserves (California, for example, has a $4.5 million reserve for emergencies), the practice of recognizing expected future (and controllable) losses for specific insured risks is rare. In light of the expanded federal responsibility for state losses, perhaps a policy of budgetary neglect at the state and local levels should be expected.

SUMMARY AND CONCLUSION

Public budgeting for contingent losses is a means of strengthening incentives for government to take appropriate care to avoid losses that must be borne by taxpayers and of reducing political risks to the beneficiaries of government insurance. To the extent that government succeeds in doing so, it reduces society's losses from contingencies, raises income, and improves the ability of citizens to make and realize lifetime consumption plans. To the extent that government fails to control its own losses, its policies may leave citizens worse off.

The biggest barrier to budgeting for contingencies is the technical difficulty of estimating expected losses accurately. The ability of analysts to project these costs is improving. But it remains a matter of judgment as to whether the gains from budgeting for contingencies are worth the disadvantages of doing so.

References

"Alvarez Questioned on Business Disaster Funds and User Fees." *CQ Monitor,* Mar. 7, 1997.

Bent, R. "Remarks." Fall Symposium, American Association for Budget and Program Analysis, Nov. 22, 1994, Washington, D.C.

Bipartisan Task Force on Disasters, House of Representatives, U.S. Congress. *Report*. Washington, D.C.: Government Printing Office, 1994.

Burby, R. J., and others. *Sharing Environmental Risks: How to Control Governments' Losses in Natural Disasters*. Boulder, Colo.: Westview Press, 1991.

Congressional Budget Office. *Credit Reform: Comparable Budget Costs for Cash and Credit*. Washington, D.C.: Government Printing Office, 1989.

Congressional Budget Office. *Budgetary Treatment of Deposit Insurance: A Framework for Reform*. Washington, D.C.: Government Printing Office, 1991.

Congressional Budget Office. *Controlling Losses of the Pension Benefit Guaranty Corporation*. Washington, D.C.: Government Printing Office, 1993.

Federal Emergency Management Agency. *Report on Costs and Benefits of Natural Hazard Mitigation*. Washington, D.C.: Government Printing Office, 1997.

Freeman, P. K., and Kunreuther, H. *Managing Environmental Risk Through Insurance*. Norwell, Mass.: Kluwer, 1997.

Kane, E. "Difficulties in Making Implicit Government Risk-Bearing Partnerships Explicit." *Journal of Risk and Uncertainty*, 1996, *12*(2–3), 189–199.

Kunreuther, H. "Mitigating Disaster Losses Through Insurance." *Journal of Risk and Uncertainty*, 1996, *12*(2–3), 171–187.

McCool, T. J. Testimony Before the Committee on Commerce, Science, and Transportation, U.S. Senate, May 26, 1994 (GAO/T-GGD-94-153). Washington, D.C.: U.S. General Accounting Office, 1994.

National Association of State Budget Officers. *Budget Processes in the States*. Washington, D.C.: National Association of State Budget Officers, 1995.

Phaup, M. "Credit Reform, Negative Subsidies, and FHA." *Public Budgeting and Finance*, 1996, *16*(1), 23–36.

Priest, G. L. "The Government, the Market, and the Problem of Catastrophic Loss." *Journal of Risk and Uncertainty*, 1996, 12(2–3), 219–237.

Stiglitz, J. E. "The Role of the State in Financial Markets." *Proceedings of the World Bank Annual Conference on Development Economics, 1993*. Washington, D.C.: World Bank, 1994.

Stossel, J. "Swept Away by Welfare for the Wealthy." *Wall Street Journal*, Aug. 16, 1995, p. A-26

Sullivan, J. F. "Jersey Looks for Money to Restore the Shore." *New York Times*, Apr. 19, 1992, p. E-12.

Suttle, J. *Selected Budget Process Reforms: Actions in the 104th Congress and Issues for the 105th Congress*. CRS Report for Congress 97-161 GOV. Washington, D.C.: Congressional Research Service, Library of Congress, 1997.

U.S. Department of the Treasury, Financial Management Service. *Consolidated Financial Statements of the U.S. Government, 1996* (Prototype). Washington, D.C.: Government Printing Office, 1997.

U.S. Office of Management and Budget. *Analytical Perspectives: Budget of the United States Government, Fiscal Year 1997.* Washington, D.C.: Government Printing Office, 1996.

U.S. Office of Management and Budget. "Appendix." *Budget of the United States Government, Fiscal Year 1998.* Washington, D.C.: Government Printing Office, 1997a.

U.S. Office of Management and Budget. "Underwriting Federal Credit and Insurance." *Analytical Perspectives: Budget of the United States Government, Fiscal Year 1998.* Washington, D.C.: Government Printing Office, 1997b.

Zeckhauser, R. "The Economics of Catastrophes." *Journal of Risk and Uncertainty,* 1996, *12*(2–3), 113–114.

CONCLUSION

CHAPTER TWENTY-NINE

The Future of Government Budgeting

Roy T. Meyers

Each year, budgets are wrong about the future. The magnitude of these errors can be huge. So if there is any governmental process for which projections of the future should be judged carefully, it is budgeting.

One reason that forecasts can be dangerous is that some humans long for what they lack. When these optimists peer into opaque crystal balls, they see the future with remarkable clarity, and it looks much better than the poverty of today. For example, some advocates of performance budgeting argue that because it is so desirable, its adoption is inevitable. They forget all the reasons why traditional budgeting has lasted so long (Wildavsky, 1992).

Pessimists can also err when they forecast the future of budgeting, but in two very different ways. Cynics mistakenly believe that the world never changes for the better. This is off the mark for budgeting—consider how computers have markedly improved the timeliness, accuracy, and accessibility of budgetary data. The other style of pessimism is to deny the possibility of projecting the future with tolerable certainty. But although social, economic, and political systems are indeed substantially chaotic, some budgetary trends are so obvious that anticipating specific outcomes is the only reasonable course of action. Who can deny that in the future those who budget must confront the fiscal challenges presented by retiring baby boomers?

This chapter does not attempt to predict specifically the future of budgeting. Rather, it discusses three aspects of the budgetary future that are at least partially amenable to control. Covered first is the priority that society places on budgeting. Might the process of budgeting be losing the prominence it has enjoyed recently, and is this desirable or not? The second section of the chapter discusses how practitioners and academics can learn about budgeting. How can descriptive knowledge about government budgeting best be acquired and created? The final section discusses how budgetary experts should go about reforming the process. How might government budgeting practices best be improved?

THE END OF BUDGETING?

"Life goes on." "Wait until next year!" "Every day is a new day." As in life, disappointments in budgeting are often soothed by the prospect of doing better next year. Future success is plausible because budgeting is so routine. Even though the process changes a bit from year to year, its basic elements are the same—conflict over numbers, a focus on the bottom line, and so on. And the most important constant of budgeting is that come hell or high water there will be a budget next year.

Yet sometimes in life our expectations of stability are shattered, and we recognize turning points. Francis Fukuyama (1989) captured well the potential of such shocks with the title of his controversial article "The End of History?" written as the collapse of the European communist regimes was eliminating the axis of geopolitical competition during the second half of the twentieth century. His argument was not that historically significant events would no longer occur, but that all the "big questions" of social structure might have been resolved by the victory of the West.

Let us borrow the style of Fukuyama's title to ask, Are we observing the end of budgeting's importance? And if so, should this disturb us?

The twentieth century was bracketed by two periods in which budgeting was extraordinarily important. The first was when the Progressives pushed the executive budget as a central method of reforming state and local governments. Designed to reduce the fraud and waste generated by corrupt party politics, it forced agencies to gain permission to spend funds and to report how they actually did spend. By making explicit the executive's responsibility to oversee budget preparation and execution, in a constitutional system where the legislature is to write the spending laws, the executive budget helped clarify how the separate branches could jointly promote fiscal accountability. When executive budgeting finally reached the federal government in 1921 with passage of the Budget and Accounting Act, budgeting had arrived for good (Rubin, 1994; Kahn, 1997).

The second period of extraordinary importance for budgeting began in 1981. Much of the credit (or blame) is due to President Reagan and those in Congress who supported his 1981 proposals. They were confronted with a growing structural deficit, the product of increasing entitlement spending and a stagnating economy. Yet they responded with a large boost in defense spending and a huge tax cut. They only partially offset the resulting deficit increases with reductions in domestic discretionary spending, just as the Federal Reserve was jacking up interest rates. Add the effects of a recession, and the resulting deficits were astoundingly large for peacetime. Ever since, U.S. politics has been fixated on the challenge of reducing these deficits (White and Wildavsky, 1989).

Yet as this chapter is completed, in mid-1998, federal deficits have apparently evaporated as quickly as puddles in the summer Arizona sun. The shock is especially radiant to those who budgeted from 1981 to the near present; that period felt like the gray, unending drizzle of a Northwest winter.

These fiscal "glory days" have not delighted everyone. Some of the strongest advocates of reducing deficits now bemoan the "deficit deficit." Impending surpluses weaken the desire of most Americans to make more "hard choices"—that is, cutting the size of administrative government, reducing the reach of the welfare state, or increasing revenues to save for the fiscal challenge of baby-boomer retirement. Budget gurus risk declining values for their intellectual capital, and employees of budget agencies worry about losing power. The millennium approaches, and in the nightmares of those who dream about reducing deficits, the prophet's placard proclaims "the end of budgeting is at hand."

Like most would-be prophets, this one is false, for as in the Bruce Springsteen song, glory days are usually short and wistfully memorable. Current surpluses are based on a peak in the business cycle and conveniently ignore many challenges that lie ahead. Revenue projections underestimate the likely losses from the recent infatuation with tax expenditures, and spending projections assume cuts in nondefense discretionary accounts that are highly unlikely (Reischauer, 1997).

Moreover, system-level forces guarantee the future importance of budgeting. Even if the recent record of impressive macroeconomic management continues, states and localities will still face unrelenting intergovernmental competition over tax sources, and bear the scrutiny of the bond market. Their fiscal positions will be continually threatened by demands from constituents to spend more money for an almost countless number of purposes. If state and local governments do not budget to constrain such pressures, they will risk capital flight and fiscal disaster (for example, see Brecher, Horton, and Mead, 1994).

Budgeting is also imperative for the federal government, though for a different mix of reasons. The federal government is less sensitive to economic downturns than are state and local governments, due to its stabilization responsibilities and to the greater size and diversification of the U.S. economy. But this fiscal potential is typically challenged by the greater magnitude of spending claims made against the federal government. Despite the huge deficit reductions of the last decade, long-run projections still show such a large excess of spending over revenues that the economy tailspins into a deep dive (U.S. General Accounting Office, 1997).

Many citizens recognize that their collective demands might cause the government to tax them excessively. Americans have feared taxes ever since the fight for independence, which in the popular imagination was fought to prevent coercive taxation by a predatory state. Its legacy is a strong antitax political culture, which has kept tax rates far below those imposed by governments in other developed countries. It has also made budgeting indispensable for politicians who want to keep power. And because budgets are also a tool for wielding power, the institutions that control budgets strongly defend the importance of budgeting.

To paraphrase Samuel Clemens, reports of the death of budgeting are therefore greatly exaggerated. But that does not mean that government budgeting is in the greatest of health. For beyond the descriptive issue of whether the demise of budgeting is near, there is an normative debate about the "ends" of budgeting (Lowi, 1969). Which functions *should* government budgeting perform? And can governments meet these expectations?

Some conservatives and more liberals have argued that the recent obsession with federal deficits has been a terrible distraction, one that has prevented governments from dealing with more important problems. Pick your poison—a failing educational system, racial conflict, a decline in moral values, proliferation of weapons of mass destruction, global warming, widespread drug abuse, international famine—and ask if reducing the deficit is significantly more important that dealing with these challenges. And ponder whether concerns about the deficit have absolutely barred application of sufficient fiscal resources to these problems (see Eisner, 1994; Reich, 1997; Shaviro, 1997).

The fixation on deficit reduction has also had a procedural opportunity cost, because neither the mass public nor political elites can wrestle with a large number of major problems at a time. Many claim that deficit obsession has also biased political debate, though of course the perceptions of liberals and conservatives about the direction of bias vary greatly. But even the more disinterested policy analysts could legitimately complain that policymaking has been overly fiscalized. For example, debates over child support enforcement focus on opportunities to reduce government spending by collecting more from "deadbeat dads," and they minimize attention to critical issues of family structure and employment opportunities. Similarly, many aspects of current budgetary practices have been antithetical to good management, to the extent that a leading budget scholar has proposed that budget reformers adopt a Hippocratic oath: "first, do no harm to management" (Rubin, 1997a).

Such discontent about current budgetary practices means that many will seek to change them. The prospect of change brings to mind a third use of *end,* from recent political debate—"the end of welfare as we know it." That was a slick phrase, as all it promised was the change that almost everyone desired without specifying which controversial changes should occur. Many welfare policy experts, and particularly the more liberal ones, were frustrated by the final welfare reform legislation, believing that the imperative of change aided adoption of mistaken policies.

As with welfare, reforms to budgeting will likely be adopted primarily because of their political attractiveness. Yet some role will be played by budgetary experts. And even if all you know about government budgeting comes from reading this book, you now qualify as an expert, relative to most Americans. So welcome to the club! To complete the induction ceremony, read the remainder of this chapter. It first discusses how experts might want to learn more about budgeting, and then analyzes how experts might go about making budgeting better.

ACQUIRING AND CREATING BUDGETARY KNOWLEDGE

A careful reader of the full contents of this book, having started with no knowledge of government budgeting, should have learned a great deal. One of the most important things that a reader should have learned is that there is much to learn about government budgeting that is not covered in this book. In part this lack is due to the space constraints for the book, long as it is. Another reason is that budgeting is a multidisciplinary field, and all of its associated disciplines make distinctive assumptions and require extensive training to become full members. No single book can teach all that one might want to know.

Assuming that the reader wants to learn more about budgeting, here are some suggestions. First, seek personal experience. For the reader who has not had a course in budgeting, take one that uses case discussions, role-playing, and quantitative exercises to illustrate the complexities of the material covered in this book.

For the reader who works in budgeting, set out a short-to-medium-term career plan that will rotate you into different responsibilities. There really is no substitute for what you can learn on the job. But what you learn there will be enhanced if you take occasional educational breaks—courses for graduate credit in the disciplines that contribute theory and method to budgeting, professional conferences, career development programs—to refine what you have learned and to place your experiences in perspective.

There are numerous written sources where you can learn more about budgeting. The best available texts, each of which have different strengths, are by Mikesell (1995), Rubin (1997b), Axelrod (1995), and Wildavsky and Caiden (1997). Each of these texts includes a useful bibliography.

Several professional journals concentrate on government budgeting and finance. The best are *Public Budgeting and Finance* (cosponsored by the Association for Budgeting and Financial Management and the American Association for Budget and Program Analysis) and *Government Finance Review* (published by the Government Finance Officers Association). All three organizations run annual conferences with informative panels on important topics. Members of these organizations enjoy journal subscriptions and discounts for conference attendance, and can network with other budgeting professionals. Exhibit 29.1 displays membership addresses and Web page URLs for the three groups.

There are many other serials that present interesting materials on government budgeting. Readers with specific interests might begin by consulting the following:

- *Public Administration Review* for scholarly articles that relate budgeting to government management
- *National Tax Journal* for articles on revenue topics
- *Management Accounting* for a mix of articles and reporting on numbers and management
- *The Bond Buyer* for the journal of record on the municipal bond market
- *National Journal* and especially *Congressional Quarterly Weekly Report* for updates on federal budgeting

A final valuable source, one that is sure to grow in importance, is the Internet. The central site for government budgeting and related topics is FinanceNet, which can be reached at http://financenet.gov/. From this location, links will take you to almost all relevant Web pages.

Readers may note that I have neglected to include in this short list some highly respected journals from the disciplinary mainstreams. In my own discipline of political science, these are refereed journals such as *American Political Science Review, Journal of Politics,* and *American Journal of Political Science.* Unfortunately, the few articles on budgeting that can be found in discipline-focused journals are of little use to practitioners. These journals tend to over-respect facilities in abstract logic and quantitative analysis, and mistakenly assume away some important complexities. Were more academics to make better connections with the real world, their analytical skills and rigor could help reduce knowledge gaps. To be evenhanded, others who specialize on budgeting have sometimes overvalued the wisdom contained in practitioner folklore. In a review of public management literature, Lynn (1996) faults scholars who avoid opportunities to collect data and test hypotheses; this critique arguably applies to budgetary studies as well.

Another barrier to creating knowledge about budgeting is personal over-attachment to a discipline's favorite assumptions and methods. Because almost

Exhibit 29.1. Major Professional Organizations for Government Budgeting.

Association for Budgeting and Financial Management
A subsection of the American Society for Public Administration, ABFM holds an annual conference in the fall. Its membership is a mix of academics and practitioners who focus on federal and state governments and have interests across all fields of government budgeting and finance.

For membership information, contact:
American Society for Public Administration
1120 G Street NW, Suite 700
Washington, DC 20005
(202) 393-7878
http://www.pubadm.fsu.edu/abfm/

American Association for Budget and Program Analysis
An organization whose membership is primarily federal government employees and contractors who work with federal agencies, AABPA holds semiannual conferences and monthly meetings in Washington, D.C.

For membership information, contact:
American Association for Budget and Program Analysis
P.O. Box 1157
Falls Church, VA 22041
(703) 941–4300
http://www.wizard.net. ~ hatter/aabpa/index.html

Government Finance Officers Association
The largest professional organization for government finance in the country, its membership is primarily those working in state and local finance. It is especially active on government accounting issues. GFOA holds an annual conference and runs an active professional education program.

For membership information, contact:
Government Finance Officers Association
180 North Michigan Avenue, Suite 800
Chicago, IL 60601
(312) 997-9700
http://www.gfoa.org/index.htm

---

all academics come to budgeting with training in one discipline, they tend to think about budgeting using only that perspective. Public finance economists tend to be interested more in taxes and debt than in spending, and those with backgrounds in accounting, political science, management, and other disciplines or areas of expertise concentrate on other issues. Few pay much attention to the research done in other disciplines, much like the parallel play of three-year-old children who sit next to each other, jabbering away but rarely speaking to each other. It would be great if budget experts from different disciplines could grow up to interact like older kids. More cross-training in relevant disciplines is one way to stimulate this behavior; participation in multidisciplinary conferences is another.

IMPROVING THE PRACTICE OF GOVERNMENT BUDGETING

Reform is so integral to U.S. political culture that some observers diagnose it as equivalent to malpractice on the body politic, with too little time devoted to seeing if the last effort succeeded before trying a new one (Light, 1997). Reform also has a long tradition in budgeting, with a similar pattern of underinformed experimentation. Consider the major rationalist reforms of the past century—the executive budget movement bracketing the turn of the century, the managerial budgeting advocated by the Hoover Commissions, the attempts to budget systematically during the 1960s, and today's emphasis on performance measurement and financial management. In their attempts to sell each new rationalist reform, advocates made little reference to the related experiments of the past. For some advocates, this was tactical—why acknowledge what they believed were the minor flaws of a reform that could bring major improvements? But one has to suspect that other reformers had little knowledge of the challenges faced by their predecessors—a sure way of encouraging failure (Joyce, 1993).

My message is not that it is impossible to change government budgeting for the better. Rather, the best advice I can offer is that budget reform can be worth the effort, but only if reform is guided by analytical and political expertise.

Consider two approaches to budgetary reform that are currently in vogue. Both are consistent with the tradition of administrative reform in the United States to look for the "one best way." The first approach is to establish credentials for those who budget. The second is to develop lists of recommended practices for budgeting.

Credentials

The movement to establish budgetary credentials is seen most strongly among accountants, who are already familiar with certification processes. The Government Finance Officers Association, which represents those working for state and local governments, is now offering the title of Certified Public Finance Officer. Bart Hildreth has proposed that budget units within organizations be similarly certified (1997). At the federal level, the Association of Government Accountants, in cooperation with Sylvan Technology Centers, offers a process that when completed entitles one to self-advertise as a Certified Government Financial Manager. Required are twenty-four credits in relevant college courses, two years of government experience in a financial management role, and passage of three examinations. These requirements are typical for credentialing organizations; they ask three questions: "Where have you been?" "What have you done?" and "What do you know?"

Credentials are one way to stimulate the education called for in the preceding section. Credentials are perhaps most appropriate for the more specialized roles associated with budgeting, such as financial auditing. But valid credentials would be very difficult to establish for budgetary roles that are more multifunctional. Budget examiners, says Barry White in Chapter Eighteen, need to be able not only to count but also to write, to negotiate, and especially to think. It is questionable whether tests can certify possession of these skills but still be targeted on the special responsibilities of budget examiners. Moreover, there may be little practical need for such tests—examiner jobs tend to be so intense that it is not difficult to see if someone is incapable of performing.

Credentialing in other professions is not without critics. In education, credentialing is blamed for enforcing labor cartels, for giving too much influence to standard-setting organizations, and for reducing teacher responsiveness to so-called nonspecialists (including parents). If these are the effects of educational credentialing—there are legitimate arguments on each side of the issue—it seems likely that these effects are largely unintentional. Similarly, budgetary credentialing appears to be stimulated primarily by desires to increase the professionalism of personnel and to justify sufficient funding for budget organizations. Whether credentialing is the best way to attain these worthy goals deserves more discussion among budgetary experts.

Recommended Practices

The recommended-practices approach deserves a more extended analysis. The National Advisory Council on State and Local Budgeting, a coalition of state and local government organizations, has recently offered a long list of recommended practices for budgeting (1997; see also Strachota, 1994). The Pew Charitable Trust is sponsoring a large project that is rating state governments, selected large local governments, and the largest federal agencies on the quality of their management practices, including their financial management (Ingraham, Joyce, and Kneedler, 1997). Perhaps the most influential set of recommended budgetary practices are those enforced by the International Monetary Fund and the World Bank.

The typical form of practice recommendations is a long list of statements that use the form, "A government should do *X* to address goal *A*." Exhibit 29.2 provides an example from the draft practices of the National Advisory Council.

As with the efforts to establish budgetary credentials, there are benefits from identifying recommended budgetary practices. Lists that identify goals for each practice can foster debates about the purposes of budgeting. And good practices can diffuse faster when they are listed and publicized.

Yet there is a serious problem with the recommended-practices approach that some advocates have ignored. When a list of recommended practices is taken as the final word on the topic, governments can be exposed to undeserved blame if the list asks governments to do the impossible. This can happen in three ways. First, the longer the list of recommended practices, the more likely it is that different goals will conflict with one another and that they cannot be maximized simultaneously. Second, recommended-practice lists can

---

Exhibit 29.2. An Example of a Recommended Budgetary Practice.

Principle: Establish broad goals to guide government decision making.

Practice: A government should identify and assess the programs and services that it provides, their intended purpose, and factors that could affect their provision in the future.

Rationale: Changes in community conditions or other factors may result in a program or service no longer addressing the needs it was intended to serve. Also, changes in the operating environment may affect the cost or effectiveness of service delivery in the future. These changes must be understood before an assessment can be made of whether existing programs should be continued or adjustments should be made.

Outputs: A government should have a process for inventorying and evaluating programs and services to determine the relationship of these programs to the needs and priorities of the community. The review should include an assessment of the programs' purposes, beneficiaries and needs served, and issues, challenges, and opportunities affecting their provision in the future. The inventory of programs and services should identify the organization responsible for service delivery if it is not the government itself. An evaluation of factors affecting service delivery also should be undertaken, such as funding issues; changes in technology; economic, demographic, or other factors that may affect demand; and legal or regulatory changes. These reviews will typically utilize a variety of information sources. Stakeholder involvement in these reviews should be encouraged.

Source: National Advisory Council, 1997.

implicitly assume away instrumental uncertainty—the possibility that doing *A* will *not* produce *X*—when there are often grounds for doubt about the actual effects of practices. Third, recommended practice lists often fail to acknowledge that doing *A* through *N* might be near impossible because a government has failed to do even *A* for many years.

Begin with the challenge of instrumental uncertainty. Some economists argue that budgeting can fulfill three goals: aggregate fiscal discipline, prioritization (for allocative efficiency and equity), and technical efficiency (Campos and Pradhan, 1997). But instrumental uncertainty greatly complicates attainment of these goals through budgeting. Is the goal of aggregate fiscal discipline met merely by avoiding insolvency, or must a government also use fiscal policy to minimize the amount of social savings demanded by the government? Regarding prioritization, what is the most efficient mix of alternative projects, programs, and policies, and the proper distribution of benefits and burdens across generations and classes? And what levels of operational results (for example, unit costs) are sufficient to say that an agency has met the requirements for technical efficiency? Economists have strong and contradictory views about how to answer these questions.

But assume for the sake of argument that economists know exactly how to reach these goals. In the United States, these economic goals will be balanced with the political goals held by elected officials. A very important political goal is regime dominance—the desire of those in power to retain it. In the short run, which is the only time horizon for some elected officials, fostering regime dominance may hinder attainment of the economic goals. For example, it is well known that mobilizing the supporters of deficit reduction is more difficult than mobilizing the supporters of existing, narrowly targeted benefits. If regimes want to protect their political base, they will allocate some budgetary resources to the latter group, even if doing so reduces aggregate fiscal discipline, devotes resources to less-than-beneficial uses, and is technically inefficient.

How might recommended practices deal with this goal conflict? The *depoliticization* approach would be to empower budgetary technicians, who through rules and analysis could prevent "bad" decisions by politicians. The *accountability* approach would be to push all budgetary decisions into the sunshine, hoping that an educated public would learn about its long-term interests and punish politicians who acted against them. Both approaches make sense, but neither are foolproof. The depoliticization approach assumes that politicians are stupid and incapable of controlling subordinates. The accountability approach assumes that the public is highly interested in minute budgetary details. But in the real world of government, politicians are intelligent, and the informed and active public is a relatively small group. Recommended practices are at constant risk of being changed to enable the exercise of power.

There is an alternative method to the one-best-way approach of expecting government to adopt all recommended budgetary practices (Meyers, 1996). That method relies on instrumental search—an inductive, iterative, and incremental method of designing effective and politically feasible reforms. The approach is consistent with the modern style of policy analysis that emphasizes the importance of recognizing tradeoffs (MacRae and Whittington, 1997).

The approach begins by postulating a list of design standards for good budgeting—that is, some desirable characteristics of a budget process. Exhibit 29.3 lists ten of these characteristics, selected because of my impression that they are frequently used in debates over budgetary issues. Because my impressions may be wrong, the list is meant to be illustrative of the approach, and not the last word.

Linked to each design standard are good practices—those elements of budgeting systems (organizations, procedures, and documents) that are thought to maximize attainment of specific design standards. Exhibit 29.4 shows good practices for two of the design standards. Again, these lists are meant to be illustrative, not definitive.

My approach differs from the one-best-way method of developing recommended practices because it is more cautious. One can begin with an ambitious list of recommended practices to survey the practices a government is not using; this would generate a list of practices the government might consider adopting. But then one must do three additional things. First, consider the amount of uncertainty associated with the proposed budgetary practice. If it seems possible that it would not have the desired effect, one should think about how its implementation could be evaluated, and also about alternative means

---

Exhibit 29.3. Design Standards for Good Budgeting.

Constrained: limits the amount of money that needs to be acquired by the government

Honest: based on unbiased projections

Comprehensive: includes all uses of the government's financial resources

Perceptive: considers the long term as well as the near term

Judgmental: seeks ways of obtaining the most effects for the least costs

Cooperative: does not dominate other important decision processes

Timely: completes regular tasks when expected

Legitimate: reserves important decisions for legally appropriate authorities

Transparent: is understandable without intensive effort

Responsive: adopts policies that match public preferences

Exhibit 29.4. Good Practices for Perceptive and Transparent Design Standards.

Perceptive

  Use budget horizons of greater than one or two years.

  Prepare program estimates that appropriately adjust for inflation and demographic changes.

  Recognize long-lived expenses and income through accrual accounting methods.

  Allocate funds for long-lived assets using discounting and by taking life-cycle operating costs into account.

Transparent

  Require open debate on the budget.

  Distribute a popular budget.

  Schedule opportunities for popular comment and deliberation on budget plans.

  Empower nongovernmental organizations to serve as budget watchdogs.

---

of creating the desired effect. Second, consider whether adoption of the practice, in order to improve attainment of one design standard, might also decrease attainment of another design standard. If such a trade-off exists, one might rank the two standards for priority. Last, but certainly not least, consider whether the good practice is likely to be adopted and continued over time. If it is controversial, one might consider whether it is worth the expenditure of political capital.

The method can be illustrated by considering a proposal to show in the current budget a charge for future spending on social security benefits for current workers. A justification for adopting this practice is that it might increase the perceptiveness of the budget. If elected officials are shown possible costs, they might think harder about intergenerational equity, and reduce the chance that future generations will bear unnecessary fiscal burdens.

The instrumental uncertainties associated with this practice are well-known. Future social security spending depends on a number of cost drivers (retirement age, lifetime earnings, longevity, and so on) that cannot be predicted with certainty. Best estimates of spending are therefore bounded by fairly wide ranges. Because budgets require point estimates, selecting a place within the wide range would be highly controversial. Assume that the Office of Management and Budget (OMB) chose one point estimate and placed it in the budget. For those who made different assumptions about cost drivers, the preferred point estimate might imply that the OMB was changing the implicit government commitment to provide the current level of retirement benefits. Then there is the additional question of how government decision makers, particularly elected officials, would interpret the cost charge for future social security spending. Those who lacked an understanding of the technical details might make substantial errors of interpretation (as has been the case with generational accounting).

This difficulty in interpretation might also affect the transparency of the budget to citizens. Would a cost charge educate or confuse citizens? It might do the latter, as developing public understanding of a complicated issue usually takes much more than governments simply telling citizens what to think (Yankelovich, 1991). Conceivably, a charge for future spending might be interpreted as a signal that government was strengthening its commitment to pay the current level of benefits, and induce a decline in the personal savings rate.

The third hurdle for a recommended practice is that of political feasibility. The metaphor of social security being the third rail of American politics is overdone, but for good reason. A cost charge for social security will be adopted only if politicians are convinced it will not significantly hurt their electoral interests. Might there be other ways of improving the budgetary process that would require less political risk?

CONCLUSION

One of the few predictable things about the future of government budgeting is that it will continue to be a vital part of the political process. Much else is difficult to predict because it depends on how those who budget choose to act. If the future of government budgeting is to be brighter, we need to stimulate the creation and acquisition of budgetary knowledge, and promote careful deliberation about proposed budget reforms.

References

Axelrod, D. *Budgeting for Modern Government.* (2nd ed.) New York: St. Martin's Press, 1995.

Brecher, C., Horton, R. D., and Mead, D. M. "Budget Balancing in Difficult Times: The Case of the Two New Yorks." *Public Budgeting and Finance,* 1994, *14,* 79–102.

Campos, J. E., and Pradhan, S. "Evaluating Public Expenditure Management Systems: An Experimental Methodology with an Application to the Australia and New Zealand Reforms." *Journal of Policy Analysis and Management,* 1997, *16,* 423–445.

Eisner, R. *The Misunderstood Economy.* Boston: Harvard Business School Press, 1994.

Fukuyama, F. "The End of History?" *National Interest,* 1989, *16,* 3–18.

Hildreth, W. B. "A Proposal for Accreditation of Finance and Budget Offices." Presented to the Association for Budgeting and Financial Management, Washington, D.C., Nov. 7, 1997.

Ingraham, P. W., Joyce, P. G., and Kneedler, A. E. "Dissecting the Black Box: Toward a Model of Government Management Performance." Working paper. Alan K. Campbell Public Affairs Institute, Syracuse University, Oct. 1997.

Joyce, P. G. "The Reiterative Nature of Budget Reform: Is There Anything New in Federal Budgeting?" *Public Budgeting and Finance,* 1993, 13, 36–48.

Kahn, J. *Budgeting Democracy.* Ithaca, N.Y.: Cornell University Press, 1997.

Light, P. C. *The Tides of Reform.* New Haven, Conn.: Yale University Press, 1997.

Lowi, T. *The End of Liberalism.* New York: Norton, 1969.

Lynn, L. E., Jr. *Public Management as Art, Science, and Profession.* Chatham, N.J.: Chatham House, 1996.

MacRae, D., Jr., and Whittington, D. *Expert Advice for Policy Choice.* Washington, D.C.: Georgetown University Press, 1997.

Meyers, R. T. "Is There a Key to the Normative Budgeting Lock?" *Policy Sciences,* 1996, 29(3), 171–188.

Mikesell, J. L. *Fiscal Administration.* (4th ed.) Belmont, Calif.: Wadsworth, 1995.

National Advisory Council on State and Local Budgeting. *A Framework for Improved State and Local Government Budgeting and Recommended Budget Practices.* Chicago: National Advisory Council on State and Local Budgeting, 1997.

Reich, R. B. *Locked in the Cabinet.* New York: Knopf, 1997.

Reischauer, R. D. "The Unfulfillable Promise: Cutting Nondefense Discretionary Spending." In R. D. Reischauer (ed.), *Setting National Priorities: Budget Choices for the Next Century.* Washington, D.C.: Brookings Institution, 1997.

Rubin, I. S. "Early Budget Reformers: Democracy, Efficiency, and Budget Reforms." *American Review of Public Administration,* 1994, 24, 229–251.

Rubin, I. S. "Budgeting's Hippocratic Oath: Do No Harm to Management." Paper prepared for the annual conference of the Association for Budgeting and Financial Management, Washington, D.C., Nov. 6, 1997a.

Rubin, I. S. *The Politics of Public Budgeting: Getting and Spending, Borrowing and Balancing.* (3rd ed.) Chatham, N.J.: Chatham House, 1997b.

Shaviro, D. *Do Deficits Matter?* Chicago: University of Chicago Press, 1997.

Strachota, D. *The Best of Government Budgeting: A Guide to Preparing Budget Documents.* Chicago: Government Finance Officers Association, 1994.

U.S. General Accounting Office. *Budget Issues: Analysis of Long-Term Fiscal Outlook.* Washington, D.C.: Government Printing Office, 1997.

White, J., and Wildavsky, A. *The Deficit and the Public Interest: The Search for Responsible Budgeting in the 1980s.* Berkeley: University of California Press, 1989.

Wildavsky, A. "Political Implications of Budget Reform: A Retrospective" *Public Administration Review,* 1992, 21, 183–190.

Wildavsky, A., and Caiden, N. *The New Politics of the Budgetary Process.* (3rd ed.) New York: Longman, 1996.

Yankelovich, D. *Coming to Public Judgment.* Syracuse, N.Y.: Syracuse University Press, 1991.

NAME INDEX

SUBJECT INDEX

A

Account groups, in balance sheet, 124, 145–147

Accountability: and authority, 615–616; and budgetary management, 88, 90, 91, 100, 108–109, 111; implementation for, 568–596; and recommended practices, 733; reports, 76

Accounting: accrual basis models for, 121–122, 131, 142, 147–148; for budgetary and GAAP reporting, 149–150; equation for, 360–361; managerial, 381–411; and outcome budgets, 582–583; and reconciliation and audit, 573–574; uses of, 153–155; visibility in, 554–555, 562

Accounting bases: analysis of, 357–380; background on, 357–358; and budgeting, 359–360, 374–379; case illustrations for, 365–368, 375–376; conclusions on, 378–379; and degrees of accrual, 358–365; and federal standards, 371–374; measurement focus for, 361–363; for state and local governments, 368–371; and stewardship requirements, 372

Accounting recognition, 362

Accounting rules, and tax expenditure, 289

Accounting systems, and financial management reform, 62–63, 65–66, 68–71

Accounts payable and receivable, information technology for, 428

Accrual, degree of, 363

Accrual accounting: and balanced budgets, 238; prospective, 378; standards for, 373–374; for state and local governments, 368–370

Acquisition Reform Act of 1996, 674

Activities, 401, 599

Activity analysis, 401–402

Activity-based costing (ABC) systems, in cost measurement, 388–391, 402

Activity-based management, 402

Activity driver, 402

Administrative control systems, 25–26

Administrative costs, budget examining for, 478–479

Adverse selection, and contingency losses, 705, 709

Africa, budgetary management in, 86, 87

Agencies: assertive, 553; and budgetary management, 101, 102–103, 104–105, 110–111; in budgetary process, 6–9, 19–20, 24–26; in conflict with budget office, 35–37; constraints on, 540–541, 543; and financial management reform, 57, 62–63, 65, 68–71, 74–76, 78; and outcome budgets, 583–584; and performance measurement, 600–601; queuing models for, 623–629

Agency budgeting: aspects of, 441–461;